Human Dignity:
Lodestar for Equality in South Africa

Human Dignity:
Lodestar for Equality in South Africa

Laurie Ackermann
BA LLB LLD hc (Stellenbosch) MA (Oxon)
Hon Fellow Worcester College, Oxford.
Retired Justice of the South African Constitutional Court

JUTA

Human Dignity: Lodestar for Equality in South Africa

© Juta & Co, Ltd
First floor, Sunclare Building,
21 Dreyer Street, Claremont, 7708,
Cape Town, South Africa
www.juta.co.za

ISBN 978 0 7021 9901 1

Typeset in 10.5 pt on 13 pt Sabon LT Std

Typesetter: ANdtp Services, Cape Town
Cover design: Drag and Drop

Printed and bound by

For Denise

ABOUT THE AUTHOR

Laurie Ackermann is a retired Justice of the first South African Constitutional Court. After completing his legal studies at Stellenbosch and — as a Rhodes Scholar — at Oxford, he practised at the Bar in Pretoria until his permanent appointment as a judge of the erstwhile Transvaal Supreme Court in 1980. In 1987 he resigned from the Bench to inaugurate the Harry Oppenheimer Chair in Human Rights Law at Stellenbosch University, a position which he held until 1992. During this period he also served as a judge on the Lesotho Court of Appeal and the post-independence Namibian Supreme Court. He was reappointed to the South African Bench in 1993 and served on the South African Constitutional Court from 1994 to 2004. He is an Honorary Research Associate at the University of Cape Town's Department of Public Law, a Professor Extraordinarius at Stellenbosch University's Faculty of Law, holds an honorary LLD from Stellenbosch University, and is an Honorary Fellow of Worcester College, Oxford.

ACKNOWLEDGMENTS

When I started writing this book in 2005, a year after my retirement from active service on the South African Constitutional Court, I felt myself to be in *terra incognito*, rather older but like Dante when–

'Midway this way of life we're bound upon,
I woke to find myself in a dark wood,
Where the right road was wholly lost and gone.'[1]

I was of course also venturing into the fields of philosophy and theology in which I have no formal training, but this was not the sole cause of my disquiet. During my forensic life I had written numerous opinions, heads of argument and judgments, but these had not — I found — prepared me properly for writing a book. I am not sure why. It may be that forensic writing involves an intellectual movement from the outside inwards in the process of solving discrete legal problems presented to one for solution, whereas the writing of a book is the other way round; a process of forming hypotheses and critically reflecting on them, which involves an intellectual movement from the inside outwards, or so it seemed to me.

Be that as it may, the result of all this was that I had to seek the advice, guidance and assistance of many people during the course of writing. I would like to recognise and thank all who helped so generously in this regard, whether as advisers, discussants, critics or simply encouragers.

I am greatly indebted to many institutions. A writing fellowship from the Rockefeller Institute spent at their Villa Serbelloni in Bellagio, Italy, during 2005 started it all, and my enjoyment of such largesse also firmly shut the gate on any thought of retreating from the book. On my retirement, the University of Cape Town's Department of Public Law kindly appointed me an honorary research associate which gave me full access to the law library, and its helpful staff. For Mrs Sheryl Luthuli, the Director of the Constitutional Court Library, no request for assistance was too onerous; she truly delights in helping others. A special word of thanks must go to the Max Planck Institute for Comparative Public Law and International Law in Heidelberg, Germany, who on several occasions during the past number of years has granted me generous research fellowships.

[1] Dante (1949: Canto I, 1–3).

The Institute's library must rank as one of the most comprehensive public law libraries in the world, operated by a staff that seemed to find their greatest delight in solving the most difficult queries. The kindness and collegiality of the Institute's directors went far beyond the call of duty. I must make special mention here of Prof. Jochen Frowein who first invited me to the Institute and has been a supportive colleague and friend for many years. I am also beholden to many of the Institute's senior researchers whose office doors were always open for even the silliest of my queries and who were happy at all times to debate my misconceptions of German public law.

The list of individuals who assisted me in many different ways is a long one. I should like, at the very outset, to acknowledge the two legal giants who have exerted the greatest personal influence on my jurisprudential development. The first is Prof. 'JC' de Wet (1912–1990) whom I first encountered in 1952 during my second year at Stellenbosch University's Law Faculty, and the second Prof. Louis Henkin (1917–2010), of the Columbia University Law School, whom I first met some 31 years later. To have had one truly great teaching master in one's life is the height of good fortune, to have had two is stretching things. My debt to them is enormous; one I can neither adequately quantify nor properly articulate. I also owe a significant intellectual debt to Dr Hendrik Verloren van Themaat who first introduced me to Immanuel Kant's ethical and jurisprudential thoughts in 1954 and much more recently to Prof Allen W Wood and his writings on Kant's ethical thought.

I must thank Prof. Michael Sachs of Cologne University, who gave so generously of his time and knowledge on a number of occasions, trying to steer me onto and keep me on the right path. He kindly made available to me several of his unpublished papers written in English.

There are a number of other people whom I must thank for their assistance in different ways: Profs Drusilla Cornell, Thaddeus Metz, and Theunis Roux, Dr Sebastian Seedorf, Dr Anja Seibert-Fohr for reading parts of earlier drafts; Dr Matthias Hartwig who responded kindly on innumerable occasions to questions on German dignity and equality law, my son Lourens for critical input, Prof. Henk Botha for many illuminating discussions on human dignity, Mr Justice Davis for his help on Jewish theology, Prof Ebrahim Moosa for his comments on Islamic Theology, and Profs Michael Welker and Dirkie Smit for their assistance on Christian Theology.

Two persons demand special mention: my friend and colleague Justice Edwin Cameron for reading and commenting on parts of several earlier drafts and Justice Kate O'Regan for her great kindness as a colleague and a friend in reading and commenting on several earlier drafts of the entire book. Because of all the generous assistance that I have received it becomes all the more necessary to stress that I alone take full responsibility for the ultimate content of this book.

On a more technical level I should like to commend Stephen Allcock of Juta and Co Ltd for his aplomb and good humour in guiding the book through the printing and publishing process and for patiently answering many inane questions from the author.

Lastly I should like to thank my wife Denise for her patience, forbearance, support and encouragement during the researching and writing of this book. Without her it would not have happened, as with so many of the good things in my life. The book is dedicated to her.

FOREWORD

South Africa's history of colonialism and apartheid has resulted in deep social inequality. Indeed, on most assessments, South Africa has one of the highest rates of inequality in the word. The new constitutional democracy, born on 27 April 1994, must address this difficult legacy.

The Preamble to the Constitution bravely proclaims that it is adopted '... to heal the divisions of the past and establish a society based on democratic values, social justice and fundamental human rights, lay the foundations for a democratic and open society in which government is based on the will of the people and every citizen is equally protected by law; ... [and] improve the quality of life of all citizens and free the potential of each person'.

The concepts of human dignity and equality are central to this constitutional project. Indeed, the first section of the Constitution asserts that the new order will be founded on the values of 'Human dignity, the achievement of equality and the advancement of human rights and freedoms ...'. Moreover, the equality clause is the first substantive provision of the Bill of Rights, and the clause protecting human dignity, the second.

From early on, the Constitutional Court asserted that human dignity was key to the interpretation of the equality clause. This approach has been criticised in some quarters, and supported in others.

This book is a sustained argument for the proposition that the concept of human dignity is integral to the interpretation of the equality clause, as the Court has asserted.

Justice Ackermann analyses the concept of equality and argues that one cannot give meaning to the equality clause without answering the question 'equality of what?' He then argues that the answer to this question is 'equality of worth' or dignity.

But the book goes much further. It provides a helpful analysis of the German and Canadian approaches to equality and human dignity as well as an account of the South African jurisprudence so far. It includes an interesting contribution to the lively debate on the horizontal application of rights as well as a principled consideration of the question of restitutionary equality, or what is commonly referred to as affirmative action.

Bringing a Constitution to life is difficult. It is made possible by the fact that it is a collective project, pursued by citizens, activists, politicians, lawyers, judges and legal and political commentators. The project is enhanced by thorough and thoughtful public engagement on key constitutional issues.

This book is a model of conscientious and painstaking engagement and it will greatly enrich our constitutional debate. It contains a candid explanation of

Justice Ackermann's jurisprudential credo and will illuminate any study of his jurisprudence and the work of the Constitutional Court generally.

Kate O'Regan
Cape Town
September 2012
Judge of the Constitutional Court 1994–2009

CONTENTS

BIBLIOGRAPHY

Achterberg, N, Krawietz, W & Wyduckel, D (eds)(1983) *Recht und Staat im sozialen Wandel: Festschrift für Hans Ulrich Scupin* (Berlin, Duncker & Humblot)

Ackermann, LWH (2000) 'Equality and the South African Constitution: The role of dignity' in vol 60 Nr 3–4 (2000) *Zeitschrift für ausländisches öffentliches Recht und Völkerrecht* (*Heidelberg Journal of International Law*) 537–556

Ackermann, LWH (2003) 'Equality under the 1996 South African Constitution' in Rüdiger Wolfrum (ed) *Gleichheit und Nichtdiskriminierung im nationalen und internationalen Menschenrechtsschutz* Vol 165 in the series *Beiträge zum ausländischen öffentlichen Recht und Völkerrecht* (Berlin, Springer Verlag) 105–117

Ackermann, LWH (2004) 'The legal nature of the South African constitutional revolution' 2004 *NZLR* 633–679

Ackermann, LWH (2005) 'Constitutional comparativism in South Africa: A response to the article "The judge as comparativist" by Sir Basil Markesinis and Dr Jörg Fedtke' (2005) 80(1) *Tulane LR* 169

Ackermann, LWH (2006) 'Equality and non-discrimination: Some analytical thoughts' (2006) 22 *SAJHR* 597

Addis, A (1997) 'On human diversity and the limits of toleration' in Shapiro & Kymlica (eds) *Nomos XXXIX: Ethnicity and Group Rights* (New York, New York Press 1997) 112

Agarwal, RK & Agarwal, RP (2009) 2 *J Parliament & Pol L* 335

Albertyn, C & Goldblatt, B (1998) 'Facing the challenge of transformation: Difficulties in the development of an indigenous jurisprudence of equality' in (1998) 14 *SAJHR* 248

Albertyn, C & Kentridge, J (1994) 'Introducing the right to equality in the Interim Constitution' (1994) 10 *SAJHR* 149

Alexy, R (2002) *A Theory of Constitutional Rights* (trans J Rivers) (Oxford, OUP)

Alexy, R (2003) 'Constitutional rights, balancing, and rationality' in (2003) 16 *Ratio Juris* 130

An-Na'im, AA (1987) 'Religious minorities under Islamic law and the limits of cultural relativism' (1987) 9 *HRQ* 1

Arieli, Y (2002) 'On the necessary and sufficient conditions for the emergence of the doctrine of the dignity of man and his rights' in D Kretzmer &

E Klein (eds) *The Concept of Human Dignity in Human Rights Discourse* (The Hague, Kluwer International) 1

Aristotle (1893) *The Nichomachean Ethics* Book V, Chapter 3, in J Gillies, *Aristotle's Ethics Comprising his Practical Philosophy* (London, Routledge)

Aristotle (1946) *The Politics* Book III, Chapter XII, in *The Politics of Aristotle* (trans Ernest Barker) (Oxford, Clarendon Press)

Aristotle (1976) *The Nichomachean Ethics* Book V, Chapter 3, in *The Ethics of Aristotle: The Nicomachean Ethics* (trans JAK Thomas, rev H Tredennick, intro and bibl J Barnes) (London, Penguin)

Aristotle (1998) *The Nichomachean Ethics* Book V, Chapter 3, in *The Nichomachean Ethics* (trans and ed D Ross, rev JL Ackrill and JO Urmson) (Oxford, OUP)

Azizah al-Hibri (1997) 'Redefining Muslim women's rights' in (1997) 12 *Am U J Int Law* 1

Baderin, MA (2005) *International Human Rights and Islamic Law* (Oxford, OUP)

Badura, P & Dreier, H (eds) (2001) *Festschrift 50 Jahres Bundesverfassungsgericht* Band II (Tübingen, Mohr Siebeck)

Baer, JA (ed) (1990) *Politics and the Constitution: The Nature and Extent of Interpretation* (Washington DC, National Legal Center for the Public Interest: American Studies Center)

Baer, S (1995) *Würde oder Gleichheit* (Baden-Baden, Nomos Verlag)

Baer, S (2009) 'Dignity, liberty, equality: A fundamental triangle of constitutionalism' (2009) 59 *U Toronto LJ*, 417

Baker, JB (1985) 'Fighting city hall with the equality rights provision of the Charter' (1985) 43 *Adv (Van)* 69

Barak, A (2001) 'Constitutional human rights and private law' in D Friedmann & E Barak-Erez (eds) *Human Rights in Private Law* (Oxford, Hart) 13

Barak, A (2012) *Proportionality: Constitutional Rights and Limitations* (Cambridge, CUP)

Barker, E (1946) *The Politics of Aristotle* (Oxford, Clarendon Press)

Beatson, J & Grosz, S (2000) 'Horizontality: A footnote' (2000) 116 *LQR* 385

Bedau, HA (1967) 'Egalitarianism and the idea of equality' in JR Pennock & JW Chapman (eds) *Equality* (being *Nomos IX, Yearbook of the American Society for Political and Legal Philosophy*) (New York, Atherton Press)

Benater, D (2008) 'Justice, diversity and racial preference: A critique of affirmative action' (2008) 125 *SALJ* 274

Benn, SI (1967) 'Egalitarianism and equal consideration of interests' in JR Pennock & JW Chapman (eds) *Equality* (being *Nomos IX, Yearbook of the American Society for Political and Legal Philosophy*) (NewYork, Atherton Press) 61

Berger, R (1992) 'Justice Brennan, "human dignity", and constitutional interpretation' in MJ Meyer & WA Parent (eds) *The Constitution of Rights: Human Dignity and American Values* (Ithaca and London, Cornell UP) 130 n 2

Bergson, H (1935) *The Two Sources of Morality and Religion* (trans RA Audra & C Brereton) (New York, Doubleday)

Berlin, I (1969) *Four Essays on Liberty* (Oxford, OUP)

Berlin, I (1990) *The Crooked Timber of Humanity* (ed H Hardy) (London, Fontana)

Birds, J, Clark, B et al (2007) *Boyle and Birds' Company Law* 6 ed (Bristol, Jordans)

Böckenförde, E-W (2006) *Recht, Staat, Freiheit* expanded ed (Frankfurt am Main, Suhrkamp)

Botha, H (2009) 'Human dignity in comparative perspective' (2009) 2 *Stell LR* 171

Botman, HR (2006) 'Covenental anthropology: Integrating three contemporary discourses of human dignity' in KR Soulen & L Woodhead (eds) *God and Human Dignity* (Grand Rapids, Michigan, William B Eerdmans) 72–84

Brandeis, L & Warren, S (1890–1) 'The right to privacy' (1890–1) 4 *Harvard LR* 193

Brinktrine, R (2001) 'The horizontal effect of human rights in German constitutional law: The British debate on horizontality and the possible role model of the German doctrine of "mittelbare Drittwirkung der Grundrechte"' in (2001) 4 *EHRLR* 421

Brown, DM (2003) 'Reconciling equality and other rights: Paradigm lost?' in (2003) 15 *Nat J Con Law* 1

Brugger, W (2000) 'Vom unbedingten Verbot der Folter zum bedingten Recht auf Folter' 2000 *JZ* 165

Brugger, W (2005) 'Das andere Auge. Folter als zweitschlechteste Lösung' in P Nitschke (ed) *Rechtsfolter im modernen Rechtsstaat?* (Bochum, Kamp)

Burchell, JM (1996) 'The protection of personality rights' in R Zimmermann & D Visser (eds) *Under the Southern Cross: Civil Law and Common Law in South Africa* (Cape Town, Juta) 639

Burchell, JM (1998) *Personality Rights and Freedom of Expression: The Modern Actio Injuriarum* (Cape Town, Juta)

Buxton, R (2000) 'The Human Rights Act and private law' (2000) 116 *LQR* 48

Cambridge Edition of the Works of Immanuel Kant (gen eds P Guyer and AW Wood) (1992) (Cambridge, CUP)

Carstens, K & Peters, H (eds) (1964) *Festschrift Hermann Jahrreiss* (Berlin, Carl Heymanns)

Cheadle, H & Davis, D (1997) 'The application of the 1996 Constitution in the private sphere' in (1997) 1 *SAJHR* 44

Cockrell, A (1998) 'Private law and the Bill of Rights: A threshold issue of horizontality' in Y Mokgoro & P Tlakula (consult eds) *Bill of Rights Compendium* (Durban, LexisNexis)
Classen, CD (1997) *Drittwirkung der Grundrechte in der Rechtsprechung des BVerfG* in (1997) 122 *AöR 65*
Coetzee, PH & Roux, APJ (eds) (2003) *The African Philosophy Reader* 2 ed (London, Routledge and Cape Town, OUP)
Coing, H (1997) *Die obersten Grundsätze des Rechts* (Heidelberg, Schneider)
Coons, JE & Brennan, PM (1999) *By Nature Equal: The Anatomy of a Western Insight* (Princeton, Princeton UP)
Corbett, MM (1967) 'Aspects of the role of policy in the evolution of the common law' (1967) 104 *SALJ* 52
Cornell, D (1995) *The Imaginary Domain: Abortion, Pornography & Sexual Harassment* (New York and London, Routledge)
Cornell, D (2011) Memorandum of 22 August 2011 on file with the author
Cowen, S (2001) 'Can "dignity" guide South Africa's equality jurisprudence?' (2001) 17 *SAJHR* 34
Currie, DP (1994) *The Constitutional Jurisprudence of the Federal Republic of Germany* (Chicago and London, University of Chicago Press)
Currie, I & De Waal, J (2005) *The Bill of Rights Handbook* 5 ed (Cape Town, Juta)
Dagan, H (2004) *The Law and Ethics of Restitution* (Cambridge, CUP)
Danieli, Y et al (eds) (1999) *The Universal Declaration of Human Rights: Fifty Years and Beyond* (New York, Baywood)
Dante (1949) *The Divine Comedy* (trans Dorothy L Sayers) (London, Penguin)
Davis, DM (1999) 'Equality: The majesty of legoland jurisprudence' (1999) 116 *SALJ* 398
Deng, FM (2004) 'Human rights in the African context' in K Wiredu (ed) *A Companion to African Theology* (Malden, Mass, Blackwell) 499
Denniger, E (ed) (2001) *Alternativ Kommentar GG* (Neuwied and Kniftel, Luchterhand)
De Waal, J (1995) 'A comparative analysis of the provisions of German origin in the interim Bill of Rights' in (1995) 11 *SAJHR* 1
De Waal, MJ (1998) 'The Law of Succession and the Bill of Rights' in Y Mokgoro & P Tlakula (consult eds) *Bill of Rights Compendium* (Durban, LexisNexis)
Domanski, A (1986) 'Piercing the corporate veil' (1986) 103 *SALJ* 224
Dorsen, N (1967) 'A lawyer's look at egalitarianism and equality' in JR Pennock & JW Chapman (eds) *Equality* (being *Nomos IX, Yearbook of the American Society for Political and Legal Philosophy*) (New York, Atherton Press) 28
Douglas, JD et al (eds) (1962) *The New Bible Dictionary* (London, Intervarsity Press)
Dreier, H (ed) (2004) *Grundgesetz Kommentar* (Tübingen, Mohr Siebeck)

Drumbl, MA & Craig, JDR (1997) 'Affirmative action in question: A coherent theory for section 15(2)' (1997) 4 *Rev Const Studies* 80

Du Plessis, J (2005) 'Towards a rational structure of liability for unjustified enrichment: Thoughts from two mixed systems' (2005) 122 *SALJ* 142

Dupper, O (2006) 'Affirmative action in South Africa: (M)any lessons for europe?' (2006) 39 *Verfassung und Recht in Übersee: Law and Politics in Africa, Asia and Latin America* 138

Dupper, O (2008) 'Affirmative action: Who, how and how long?' (2008) 24 *SAJHR* 425

Dupré, C (2003) *Importing the Law in Post-Communist Transitions: The Hungarian Constitution and the Right to Human Dignity* (Oxford, Portland, Hart)

Dürig, G (1956) 'Der Grundrechtssatz von der Menschenwürde' (1956) 81 *AöR* 117

Dürig, G (1956a) 'Grundrechte und Zivilrechtsprechung' in T Maunz (ed) (1956) *Vom Bonner Grundgesetz zur gesamtdeutschen Verfassung.* Festschrift zum 75. Geburtstag von Hans Nawiasky (München, Isar Verlag) 157

Dürig, G (1958) *Commentary on Art 1(1) GG* in Maunz, Dürig, et al (eds) *Kommentar zum Grundgesetz* (looseleaf ed) (Munich, CH Beck)

Dürig, G (1958a) *Commentary on Art 2(1) GG* in Maunz, Dürig, et al (eds) *Kommentar zum Grundgesetz* (looseleaf ed) (Munich, CH Beck)

Dürig, G (1973) *Commentary on Art 3(1) GG* in Maunz, Dürig, et al (eds) *Kommentar zum Grundgesetz* (looseleaf ed) (Munich, CH Beck)

Dürig, G (1973a) *Commentary on Art 3(3) GG* in Maunz, Dürig, et al (eds) *Kommentar zum Grundgesetz* (looseleaf ed) (Munich, CH Beck)

Dürig, G (1984) 'Das Eigentum als Menschenrecht' in Glaeser & Häberle (eds) *Günter Dürig: Gesammelte Schriften, Schriften zum Öffentlichen Recht*, Band 463 (Berlin, Duncker & Humblot) 47f

Du Toit, F (1999) 'The impact of social and economic factors on freedom of testation in Roman and Roman-Dutch law' 1999 *Stell LR* 232

Du Toit, F (2000) 'The limits imposed upon freedom of testation by the *boni mores*: Lessons from common law and civil law (continental legal systems)' in 2000 *Stell LR* 358

Du Toit, F (2000a) 'Testeervreiheid in die Suid-Afrikaanse reg in die lig van 'n handves van regte' (Unpublished thesis for the Doctorate in Law degree at the University of Stellenbosch)

Du Toit, F (2001) 'The constitutionally bound dead hand? The impact of constitutional rights and principles on freedom of testation' in 2001 *Stell LR* 222

Dworkin, R (1993) *Life's Dominion: An Argument about Abortion and Euthanasia* (London, Harper Collins)

Dworkin, R (1997) *Taking Rights Seriously* (London, Duckworth)

Dzobo, NK (1992) 'Values in a changing society: Man, ancestors and God' (http://www.crvp.org/book/Series02/II-1/chapterxihtm) 1–10. Originally published in Wiredu & Gyekye (eds) *Person and Community, Ghanaian Philosophical Studies* vol 1 (Washington, DC, CRVP) 223–240

Easterbrook, FH (1990) 'Approaches to judicial review' in JA Baer (ed) *Politics and the Constitution: The Nature and Extent of Interpretation* (Washington DC, National Legal Center for the Public Interest, American Studies Center) 29

Eberle, EJ (2002) *Dignity and Liberty: Constitutional Visions in Germany and the United States* (Westport, Connecticut, Praeger)

Eccles, J (1970) *Facing Reality* (New York, Springer-Verlag)

Eckert, J (2002) 'Legal Roots of Human Dignity in the German Law' in D Kretzmer & E Klein (eds) *The Concept of Human Dignity in Human Rights Discourse* (The Hague, Kluwer International) 41

Egli, P (2002) *Drittwirkung von Grundrechten: Zugleich ein Beitrag zur Dogmatik der grundrechtlichen Schutzpflichten im Schweizer Recht* (Zurich, Schulthess)

Einstein, A (1950) *Out of My Later Years* as quoted in B Swainson (ed) *Encarta Book of Quotations* (London, Bloomsbury) 305, item 30

Einstein, A (2000) as attributed to him in Swainson (ed) *Encarta Book of Quotations* (London, Bloomsbury) 306, item 57

Ellington, J (trans) (1983) 'The metaphysical principles of virtue' in *Immanuel Kant: Ethical Philosophy* (Indianapolis, Hackett)

Ely, JH (1974) 'The constitutionality of reverse discrimination' (1974) 41 *U Chicago L Rev* 23

Enders, C (1997) *Die Menschenwürde in der Verfassungsordnung* Jus Publicum Band 27 (Tübingen, Mohr Siebeck)

Enders, C (2009) Art 1 GG in KH Friauf & W Höfling (eds) *Berliner Kommentar zum Grundgesetz* (Berlin, Schmidt Verlag)

Epiney, A (1995) *Umgekehrte Diskriminierungen: Zulässigkeit und Grenzen der Discrimination à rebours nach europäischem Gemeinschaftsrecht und nationalem Verfassungsrecht* (Köln/Berlin/Bonn/München, Carl Heymanns)

Evans, JF & Ward, LR (eds) (1956) *The Social and Political Philosophy of Jacques Maritain* (London, Geoffrey Bles)

Fagan, A (1998) 'Dignity and unfair discrimination: A value misplaced and a right misunderstood' (1998) 14 *SAJR* 220

Farlam, P (2007) 'Freedom of religion, belief and opinion' in Woolman, Roux & Bishop (eds) *Constitutional Law of South Africa* 2 ed (looseleaf) (Cape Town, Juta) ch 36

Feenstra, R (1995) 'Grotius' doctrine of unjust enrichment as a source of obligation: Its origin and its influence in Roman-Dutch law' in EJH Scharge (ed) *Unjust Enrichment: The Comparative Legal History of the Law of Restitution* vol

15, *Comparative Studies in Continental and Anglo-American Legal History* series (Berlin, Duncker & Humblot) 197
Finkelstein, N (1985–86) 'Sections 1 and 15 of the Charter and the relevance of US experience' (1985–86) 6 *Adv Q* 188
Fletcher, GP (1999) 'In God's image: The religious imperative of equality under the law' (1999) 99 *Columbia LR* 1608
Foot, P (ed) (1967) *Theories of Ethics* (Oxford, OUP)
Foot, P (2001) *Natural Goodness* (Oxford, Clarendon Press)
Forrester, DB (2001) *On Human Worth: A Christian Vindication of Equality* (London, SCM)
Forst, R (1992) 'How (not) to speak about identity: The concept of the person in a theory of justice' (1992) 18 *Philosophy and Social Criticism* 293
Frowein, JA (1998) 'Die Überwindung von Diskriminierung als Staatsauftrag in Art 3 Abs 3 GG' in F Ruland (ed) *Verfassung, Theorie und Praxis des Sozialstaats: Festschrift für Hans F Zacher zum 70. Geburtstag* (Heidelberg, CF Müller)
Friauf, KH & Höfling, W (eds) (2009) *Berliner Kommentar zum Grundgesetz* (Berlin, Schmidt Verlag)
Friedmann, D & Barak-Erez, D (eds) (2001) *Human Rights in Private Law* (Oxford, Hart)
Gadamer, H-G (1989) *Truth and Method* 2 rev Eng ed (New York, Continuum)
Geach, PT (1967) 'Good and evil' in P Foot (ed) *Theories of Ethics* (Oxford, OUP) 64
Geach, PT (1977) *The Virtues* (Cambridge, CUP)
Geddis, A (2004) 'The horizontal effects of the New Zealand Bill of Rights Act, as applied in *Hosking v Runting*' 2004 *NZ Law Review* 681–705
Gibson, D (1990) *The Law of the Charter: Equality Rights* (Toronto, Carswell)
Glaeser, WS (1997) 'In memoriam Günter Dürig' (1997) 122 *AöR* 134
Glaeser, WS & Häberle, Peter (eds) (1984) *Günter Dürig: Gesammelte Schriften, Schriften zum öffentlichen Recht*, Band 463 (Berlin, Duncker & Humblot)
Glendon, MA (1991) *Rights Talk: The Impoverishment of Political Discourse* (New York, Free Press)
Goldstein, W (2006) *Defending the Human Spirit: Jewish Law's Vision for a Moral Society* (Jerusalem, Feldheim Publishers)
Goren, SL (1994) *The German Civil Code* (Littleton, Colorado, Fred B. Rothman)
Greenawalt, K (1978) 'The enduring significance of neutral principles' (1978) 78 *Columbia LR* 982
Greenawalt, K (1983) 'How empty is the idea of equality?' (1983) 83 *Columbia LR* 1167
Greenberg, M (1960) 'Some postulates of biblical criminal law' in M Haran (ed) *Yehezkel Kaufmann Jubilee Volume* (Jerusalem, Magnes Press) 5
Gregor, MJ (ed) (1996) *Immanuel Kant: Practical Philosophy* (Cambridge, CUP)

Greschner, D (2001–2002) 'Does law advance the cause of equality' in (2001–2002) 27 *Queen's LJ* 299
Grundgesetz für die Bundesrepublik Deutschland 8 ed (Munich, CH Beck)
Gubelt, M (1992) 'Art 3 Gleichheit' in I von Münch & P Kunig (eds) *Grundgesetz-Kommentar* 4 ed vol 1 (Munich, CH Beck)
Guyer, P (ed) (1992) *The Cambridge Companion to Kant* (Cambridge, CUP)
Guyer, P (ed) (2005) *Immanuel Kant: Notes and Fragments* (Cambridge, CUP)
Häberle, P (1997) 'Günter Dürig' (1997) 5 *NJW* 306
Häberle, P (2004) 'Die Menschenwürde als Grundlage der staatlichen Gemeinschaft' in J Isensee & P Kirchhof (eds) *Handbuch des Staatsrechts der Bundesrepublik Deutschland* vols I–VI (Heidelberg, CF Müller) 317–367
Häberle, P (2008) *Das Menschenbild im Verfassungsstaat* (Berlin, Duncker & Humblot)
Haferkamp, H-P, Szöllösi-Janze, M & Ulmann, HP (eds) (2006) *Justiz im Nationalsocializmus* (Hamburg, Lit Verlag)
Haran, M (ed) (1960) *Yehezkel Kaufmann Jubilee Volume* (Jerusalem, Magnes Press)
Harakas, SS (1982) 'Human rights: An Eastern Orthodox perspective' in A Swidler (ed) *Human Rights in Religious Traditions* (New York, The Pilgrim Press) 13
Hassan, R (1982) 'On human rights and the Qur'anic perspective' in Swidler, Arlene (ed) *Human Rights in Religious Traditions* (New York, The Pilgrim Press) 51
Henkel, H (1977) *Einführung in die Rechtsphilosophie* (Munich, CH Beck)
Henkin, L (1961) 'Some reflections on current constitutional controversy' (1961) 109 *Univ Pa LR* 637
Henkin, L (1962) 'Shelley v Kraemer: Notes for a revised opinion' (1962) 110 *Univ Pa LR* 473
Henkin, L (1978) 'Infallibility under law: Constitutional balancing' (1978) 78 *Columbia LR* 1022
Henkin, L (1992) 'Human dignity and constitutional rights' in MJ Meyer & WA Parent (eds) *The Constitution of Rights: Human Dignity and American Values* (Ithaca and London, Cornell University Press)
Henkin, L (1995) *Human Dignity and Human Rights* (Jerusalem, The Israeli Academy of Sciences and Humanities)
Henkin, L et al (2009) *Human Rights* 2 ed (New York, Foundation Press)
Herdegen, Matthias (2005) in Maunz, Dürig, et al (eds) second commentary (2005) on Art1(1) Rn 43
Herzog, R (1996) 'Der allgemeine Gleichheitssatz (Art 3 Abs 1 GG) in der Rechtsprechung des Bundesverfassungsgerichts' in 'Anh. Art 3' in Maunz, Dürig, et al (eds) *Kommentar zum Grundgesetz* (Munich, CH Beck)
Hesse, K (1951) 'Der Gleichheitsgrundsatz im Staatsrecht' in (1951) 77 *AöR* 167

Heun, W (2004) 'Artikel 3 Gleichheit' in H Dreier (ed) *Grundgesetz Kommentar* (Tübingen, Mohr Siebeck) 398
Hill, TE Jr (1992) *Dignity and Practical Reason in Kant's Moral Theory* (Ithaca and London, Cornell University Press)
Höfling, W (2007) Art 1 in M Sachs (2007(a)) *Grundgesetz Kommentar* 4 ed (Munich, CH Beck)
Höfling, W (2009) Art 1 in M Sachs (2009) *Grundgesetz Kommentar* 5 ed (Munich, CH Beck)
Hofmann, H (1993) 'Die versprochene Menschenwürde' in (1993) 118 *AöR* 353
Hogg, PW (1992) *Constitutional Law of Canada* 3 ed (Scarborough, Ontario, Carswell)
Hogg, PW (2005) 'What is equality? The winding course of judicial interpretation' (2005) 29 *SCLR* (2nd) 39–62
Hogg, PW (2007) *Constitutional Law of Canada* 5th (loose-leaf) ed (Toronto, Thompson, Carswell) Although 2007 is furnished as the publication date, citations are to the dates of the replacement pages.
Honderich, T (ed) (1995) *The Oxford Companion to Philosophy* (Oxford, OUP)
Honoré, T (1999) *Responsibility and Fault* (Oxford, Hart)
Honoré, T (2002) *Ulpian: Pioneer of Human Rights* 2 ed (Oxford, OUP)
Hook, S (ed) (1970) *Law and Philosophy* 2 ed (New York, New York UP)
Huber, ER (1939) *Verfassung des Großdeutschen Reiches* 2 ed (Hamburg, Hanseatische Verlag)
Huber, W (1996) *Violence: The Unrelenting Assault on Human Dignity* trans RCL Gritsch (Minneapolis, Fortress Press)
Huber, W (1996a) *Gerechtigheit und Recht* (Gütersloh, Gütersloher Verlagshaus)
Huber, W (2010) 'The dignity of the different: Towards a Christian ethic for pluralistic societies' unpublished paper delivered 4 March 2010, Stellenbosch Institute for Advanced Study. A copy is on file with the author.
Hunt, M (1998) 'The "Horizontal Effect" of the Human Rights Act' (1998) *Public Law* 423
Isensee, J (2006) 'Menschenwürde: Die säkulare Gesellschaft auf der Suche nach dem Absoluten' (2006) 131 *AöR* 173
Isensee, J & Kirchhof, P (eds) (2003–8) *Handbuch des Staatsrechts der Bundesrepublik Deutschland* vols I–VI (Heidelberg, CF Müller)
Jarass, HD (2006) *Commentary on Art 3 GG* in Jarass & Pieroth (2006) *Grundgesetz für die Bundesrepublik Deutschland* 8 ed (Munich, CH Beck)
Joubert, WA (1953) *Grondslae van die Persoonlikheidsreg* (Cape Town, AA Balkema)
Joubert, WA (1958) 'Die realitiet van die subjektiewe reg en die betekenis van 'n realistiese begrip daarvan vir die privaatreg' 1958 *THRHR* 12
Kamali, MH (2002) *The Dignity of Man: An Islamic Perspective* (Cambridge, Islamic Texts Society)

Khāmeneī, H-ISM (1989) 'Human rights for women in Islam and in other Laws' (1989) *Naquavi* 257

Kirchhof, P (2000) 'Der allgemeine Gleichheitssatz' §124 in J Isensee & P Kirchhof (eds) (2003–8) *Handbuch des Staatsrechts der Bundesrepublik Deutschland* vols I–VI (Heidelberg, CF Müller)

Klein, Eckardt (2002) 'Human Dignity in German Law' in D Kretzmer & E Klein (eds) *The Concept of Human Dignity in Human Rights Discourse* (The Hague, Kluwer International) 145

Kommers, DP (1989) *The Constitutional Jurisprudence of the Federal Republic of Germany* (Durham and London, Duke UP)

Kommers, DP (1997) *The Constitutional Jurisprudence of the Federal Republic of Germany* 2 ed (Durham and London, Duke UP)

Kommers, DP (1998) 'Can German constitutionalism serve as a model for the United States?' (1998) 58 *ZaöRV* (*Heidelberg Journal of International Law*) 787

Korsgaard, CM (1996) *Creating the Kingdom of Ends* (Cambridge, CUP)

Krebs, W (1992) *Commentary on Art 18 GG* in I von Münch & P Kunig (eds) *Grundgesetz-Kommentar* 4 ed vol 1 (Munich, CH Beck)

Kretzmer, D & Klein, E (eds) (2002) *The Concept of Human Dignity in Human Rights Discourse* (The Hague, Kluwer International)

Krüger, H (1949) 'Die Verfassung in der Zivilrechtsprechung' 1949 *NJW* 163

Laslett, P & Runciman, WG (eds) (1967) *Philosophy, Politics and Society* (2nd Series) (Oxford, Basil Blackwell)

Leibholz, G (1925) *Die Gleichheit vor dem Gesetz* (Berlin, Liebmann)

Leibholz, G (1959) *Die Gleichheit vor dem Gesetz* 2 ed (Munich/Berlin, CH Beck)

Leigh, I (1999) 'Horizontal rights, the Human Rights Act and privacy: Lessons from the Commonwealth' (1999) 48 *Int and Comp LQ* 57

Lester, A & Pannick, D (2000) 'The impact of the Human Rights Act on private law: The knight's move' (2000) 116 *LQR* 380

Liebenberg, S (2010) *Socio-Economic Rights: Adjudication under a transformative constitution* (Cape Town, Juta)

Lin, TE (1999) 'Social norms and judicial decisionmaking: Examining the role of narrative in same-sex adoption cases' (1999) 99 *Columbia LR* 739

Lloyd, D (1972) *Introduction to Jurisprudence* 3 ed (London, Stephens)

Locke, J (1988) *Two Treatises of Government* ed P Laslett (Cambridge, CUP)

Lorberbaum, Y (2002) 'Blood and the image of God: On the sacrifice of life in biblical and early rabbinical law, myth and ritual' in D Kretzmer & E Klein (eds) *The Concept of Human Dignity in Human Rights Discourse* (The Hague, Kluwer International) 55

Lorz, RA (1993) *Modernes Grund- und Menschenrechtsverständnis und die Philosophie der Freiheit Kants* (Stuttgart/Marburg, Boorberg)

Lücke, J & Sachs, M (2007) *Art 79* in M Sachs (2007(a)) *Grundgesetz Kommentar* 4 ed (Munich, CH Beck)

Magee, B (1985) *Popper* (London, Fontana) 85

Markesinis, BS (1997) *The German Law of Obligations* 3 ed (Oxford, Clarendon Press)

Markesinis, BS (1999) 'Privacy, freedom of expression and the horizontal effect of the Human Rights Bill: Lessons from Germany' in (1999) 115 *LQR* 47

Markesinis, BS & Fedke, J (2005) 'Constitutional comparativism' in (2005) 80 *Tulane LR* 11

Markesinis, BS & Unberath, H (2002) *The German Law of Torts: A Comparative Treatise* 4 ed (Oxford, Hart)

Maunz, T (ed) (1956) *Vom Bonner Grundgesetz zur gesamtdeutschen Verfassung. Festschrift zum 75. Geburtstag von Hans Nawiasky* (München, Isar Verlag)

Maunz et al (eds) *Kommentar zum Grundgesetz* looseleaf ed (Munich, CH Beck)

Maurer, H (ed) (1990) *Das akzeptierte Grundgesetz: Festschrift für Günther Dürig zum 70. Geburtstag* (Munich, CH Beck).

Mayer, AE (1991) *Islam and Human Rights: Traditions and Politics* (Boulder, Colorado, Westview Press)

Mays, LM (2006) 'The self in the Psalms and the image of God' in KR Soulen & L Woodhead (eds) *God and Human Dignity* (Grand Rapids, Michigan, William B Eerdmans) 27–43

McAllister, DM (2003) 'Section 15: The unpredictability of the *Law* test' (2003) 15 *Nat J Const Law* 35

McAllister, DM (2009) 'Overview: Supreme Court of Canada Charter decisions' in (2009) 25 *Nat J Const Law* 1

McCrudden, C (2008) 'Human dignity and judicial interpretation of human rights' (2008) 19 *European J Int Law* 655–724

Meeks, MD (1984) 'Introduction' in J Moltmann (1984) *On Human Dignity* (Philadelphia, Fortress Press)

Merten, D & Papier, H-J (eds) (2006) *Handbuch der Grundrechte in Deutschland und Europa* vol II (Heidelberg, CF Müller)

Metz, T (2010) 'Human dignity, capital punishment, and an African moral theory: Towards a new philosophy of human rights' (2010) 9 *J Human Rights* 81

Metz, T & Gaie, JBR (2010) 'The African ethics of *ubuntu/botho*: Implications for research on morality' (2010) 39(3) *J Moral Education* 273

Metzger, BM & Coogan, MD, (eds) (1993) *The Oxford Companion to the Bible* (Oxford, OUP)

Meyer, MJ & Parent, WA (eds) (1992) *The Constitution of Rights: Human Dignity and American Values* (Ithaca and London, Cornell UP)

Miller, D (ed) (1983) *A Pocket Popper* (London, Fontana)

Mokgoro, Y & Tlakula, P (1998) (consult eds) *Bill of Rights Compendium* (Durban, LexisNexis)
Moltmann, J (1984) *On Human Dignity* trans D Meeks (Philadelphia, Fortress Press)
Moosa, E (2000–2001) 'The dilemma of Islamic rights schemes' in (2000-2001) 15 *Journal of Law and Religion* 185
Moreau, S (2008–2009) 'R v Kapp: New directions for section 15' (2008–2009) 40 *Ottawa LR* 283
Moussalli, AS (2001) *The Islamic Quest for Democracy, Pluralism, and Human Rights* (Gainesville, Florida, University Press of Florida)
Müller, G (1989) 'Der Gleichheitssatz' in R Zippelius & G Müller (eds) 'Der Gleichheitssatz' 47 *Veröffentlichungen der Vereinigung der deutschen Staatsrechtslehrer* 37
Naquavi, SKH (ed) (1989) *Human Rights in Islam: Papers presented at 5th Islamic Thought Conference Teheran, 29–31 January 1987* (Tehran, Islamic Propagation Organization)
Neethling, J (1976) *Die Reg op Privaatheid* (LLD dissertation: University of South Africa)
Neethling, J et al (1994) *Law of Delict* 2 ed (Durban, Butterworths)
Neethling, J et al (2005) *Neethling's Law of Personality* 2 ed (Durban, LexisNexis Butterworths)
Nitschke, P (ed) (2005) *Rechtsfolter im modernen Rechtsstaat?* (Bochum, Kamp)
Nussbaum, MC (2007) *Frontiers of Justice* (Cambridge, Massachusetts, The Belknap Press of Harvard UP)
Osterloh, L (2007) *Commentary on Art 3 GG* in M Sachs (2007(a)) *Grundgesetz Kommentar* 4 ed (Munich, CH Beck)
Pagenkopf, M (2007) *Commentary on Art 18 GG* in M Sachs (2007(a)) *Grundgesetz Kommentar* 4 ed (Munich, CH Beck)
Peltason, JW (1994) *Corwin and Peltason's Understanding the Constitution* 13 ed (New York, Harcourt Brace)
Pennock, JR & Chapman, JW (eds) (1967) *Equality* (being *Nomos IX, Yearbook of the American Society for Political and Legal Philosophy*) (NewYork, Atherton Press)
Pieterse, M (2007) 'Indirect horizontal operation of the right to have access to health care' (2007) 23 *SAJHR* 157
Pieterse, M (2009) 'Relational socio-economic rights' (2009) 25 *SAJHR* 198
Plamnatz, J (1967) 'Diversity of Rights and Kinds of Equality' in JR Pennock & JW Chapman (eds) (1967) *Equality* (being *Nomos IX, Yearbook of the American Society for Political and Legal Philosophy*) (New York, Atherton Press) 79
Podlech, A (1971) *Gehalt und Funktionen des allgemeinen verfassungsrechtlichen Gleichheitssatzes* (Heidelberg, Duncker & Humblot)

Podlech, A (2001) *Commentary on Art 1(1) GG* in E Denniger (ed) *Alternativ Kommentar GG* (Neuwied and Kniftel, Luchterhand)

Pojman, L (1997) 'On equal human worth: A critique of contemporary egalitarianism' in L Pojman & R Westmorland (eds) *Equality: Selected Readings* (Oxford, OUP)

Polish, DF (1982) 'Judaism and human rights' in A Swidler (ed) *Human Rights in Religious Traditions* (New York, Pilgrim Press) 40

Polkinghorne, J (2006) *Anthropology in an Evolutionary Context* in KR Soulen & L Woodhead (eds) *God and Human Dignity* (Grand Rapids, Michigan, William B Eerdmans) 89–103

Popper, K (1966) *The Open Society and its Enemies* 5 rev ed (Princeton, New Jersey, Princeton UP)

Popper, K (1983) *Conjectures and Refutations* as quoted in David Miller (ed) *A Pocket Popper* (London, Fontana)

Popper, K (1999) *All Life is Problem Solving* (London, Routledge)

Pound, R (1914) 'The Right to Privacy' in (1914-1915) 28 *Harvard LR* 343, 445

Pretorius, JL, Klinck, ME & Ngwena, CG (eds) (2001) *Employment Equity Law* (Durban, Butterworths)

Rabe, J (2001) *Equality, Affirmative Action and Fairness* (Norderstedt, Germany, Books on Demand)

Rackman, E (1967) 'Judaism and equality' in JR Pennock & JW Chapman (eds) (1967) *Equality* (being *Nomos IX, Yearbook of the American Society for Political and Legal Philosophy*) (New York, Atherton Press) 154

Rae, D (1981) *Equalities* (Cambridge, MA, Harvard UP)

Ramose, MB (2003) 'The philosophy of *ubuntu* and the *ubuntu* of philosophy' in PH Coetzee & APJ Roux (eds) (2003)

Ramose, MB (2003a) 'The ethics of *ubuntu*' in PH Coetzee & APJ Roux (eds) (2003)

Rautenbach, I et al (1998) *Bill of Rights Compendium* (Durban, Butterworths) and looseleaf replacement issues

Rawls, J (1973) *A Theory of Justice* (Oxford, OUP)

Rawls, J (1993) *Political Liberalism* (New York, Columbia UP)

Réaume, DG (2003) 'Discrimination and dignity' (2003) 63 *Louisiana LR* 645

Ruland, F (ed) (1998) *Verfassung, Theorie und Praxis des Sozialstaats: Festschrift für Hans F Zacher zum 70. Geburtstag* (Heidelberg, CF Müller)

Ruston, R (2004) *Human Rights and the Image of God* (London, SCM Press)

Rwelamira, MR & Werle, G (eds) (1996) *Confronting Past Injustices: Approaches to Amnesty, Punishment, Reparation and Restitution* (Durban, Butterworths)

Sachs, M (1987) *Grenzen des Diskriminierungsverbots* (Munich, Franz Fahlen)

Sachs, M (1997) 'Human dignity and German public law'. Lecture given in Düsseldorf on 6 June 1997. English manuscript on file with the author.

Sachs, M (1998a) 'The Equality rule before the German Federal Constitutional Court' in 1998 *Saint Louis-Warsaw Transatlantic LJ* 139
Sachs, M (1998b) 'The transplantation law of 1997 and the basic right to life'. Lecture delivered at the Israeli-German symposium on 'Law at the End of Life' held at Radzyner School of Law on 6 November 1998. Manuscript on file with the author.
Sachs, M (2000) 'Besondere Gleichheitsgarantien' in J Isensee & P Kirchhof (eds) (2003–8) *Handbuch des Staatsrechts der Bundesrepublik Deutschland* vols I–VI (Heidelberg, CF Müller)
Sachs, M (2003a) *Verfassungsrecht II. Grundrechte* 2 ed (Berlin, Springer)
Sachs, M (2004) 'Equality questions in German constitutional law'. Seminar lecture delivered at Stellenbosch University on 11 August 2004. English manuscript on file with the author.
Sachs, M (2005) 'Equality'. Workshop presentation at Stellenbosch University on 9 September 2005. English manuscript on file with the author.
Sachs, M (2007(a)) *Grundgesetz Kommentar* 4 ed (Munich, CH Beck)
Sachs, M (2007(b)) *Vor Art 1 GG* in M Sachs (2007(a))
Sachs, M (2007(c)) 'Human dignity as a constitutional concept in Germany'. Paper presented in Jerusalem on 4 January 2007. English manuscript on file with the author.
Sachs, M (2009) *Grundgesetz Kommentar* 5 ed (Munich, CH Beck)
Sachs, M & Biskup, U (2003) 'Equality rights'. English manuscript on file with the author.[1]
Sacks, J (2002) *The Dignity of Difference* (London, Continuum)
Salzwedel, J (1964) in K Carstens & H Peters (eds) *Festschrift Hermann Jahrreiss* (Berlin, Carl Heymanns) 339
Scharge, EJH (ed) (1995) *Unjust Enrichment: The Comparative Legal History of the Law of Restitution* vol 15 in the *Comparative Studies in Continental and Anglo-American Legal History* series (Berlin, Duncker & Humblot)
Schlaich, K (1994) *Das Bundesverfassungsgericht* 3 ed (Munich, CH Beck)
Sen, A (1992) *Inequality Reexamined* (New York, Russell Sage Foundation and Oxford, Clarendon Press)
Sen, A (1999) *Development as Freedom* (Oxford, OUP)
Schneewind, JB (1992) 'Autonomy, obligation, and virtue: An overview of Kant's moral philosophy' in P Guyer (ed) *The Cambridge Companion to Kant* (Cambridge, CUP) 309
Schwöbel, C (2006) *Recovering Human Dignity* in KR Soulen & L Woodhead (eds) *God and Human Dignity* (Grand Rapids, Michigan, William B Eerdmans) 44

[1] The author has been informed by Prof Sachs that the article was published in *Fundamental Rights in Europe and North America: Germany* (Leiden/Boston: Martinus Nijhoff, 2008). Neither Prof Sachs nor the present author has been able to access a copy of this book.

Shapiro, I & Kymlicka, W (eds) (1997) *Nomos XXXIX: Ethnicity and Group Rights* (New York, New York University Press)

Shutte, A (2001) *Ubuntu: An ethic for a New South Africa* (Pietermaritzburg, Cluster Publications)

Singer, P (1977) *Animal Liberation* (New York, Avon Books)

Smith, L (2001) 'Restitution: The heart of corrective justice' (2001) 79 *Texas LR* 2115

Sólyom, L & Brunner, G (2000) *Constitutional Judiciary in a New Democracy: The Hungarian Constitutional Court* (Ann Arbor, Michigan, University of Michigan Press)

Soulen, KR. & Woodhead, L (eds) (2006) *God and Human Dignity* (Grand Rapids, Michigan, William B Eerdmans)

Starck, C (1985) *Commentary on Art 3 GG* in H Von Mangoldt, F Klein & C Starck (eds) *Das Bonner Grundgesetz* 3 ed (Munich, Frank Fahlen) vol 1

Starck, C (2005) *Commentary on Art 3 GG* in H Von Mangoldt, F Klein & C Starck (eds) *Kommentar zum Grundgesetz* 5 ed (Munich, Frank Fahlen) vol 1

Starck, C (2005a) *Commentary on Art 1 GG* in H Von Mangoldt, F Klein & C Starck (eds) *Kommentar zum Grundgesetz* 5 ed (Munich, Frank Fahlen) vol 1

Stern, F (2006) *Five Germanys I Have Known* (New York, Farrar, Strauss & Giroux)

Stern, K (1983) *Menschenwürde als Wurzel der Menschen- und Grundrechte* in N Achterberg, W Krawietz & D Wyduckel (eds) *Recht und Staat im sozialen Wandel: Festschrift für Hans Ulrich Scupin* (Berlin, Duncker & Humblot) 627

Stern, K (1988) *Das Staatsrecht der Bundesrepublik Deutschland* Band III/I (Munich, CH Beck)

Stern, K (1990) *Das Gebot zur Ungleichbehandlung* in H Maurer (ed) *Das akzeptierte Grundgesetz: Festschrift für Günther Dürig zum 70. Geburtstag* (Munich, CH Beck) 207

Stern, K (2001) 'Die Grundrechte und ihre Schranken' in P Badura & H Dreier (eds) (2001) *Festschrift 50 Jahre Bundesverfassungsgericht* Band II (Tübingen, Mohr Siebeck)

Stern, K (2002) 'Basic questions of constitutional law en route to German unity' in PJ Tettinger & M Sachs (eds) *Klaus Stern: Im Dienste von Recht, Staat und Wissenschaft* (Cologne, Berlin, Bonn, Munich, Carl Heymanns)

Stern, K (2006) *Das Staatsrecht der Bundesrepublik Deutschland* vol 4.1 (Munich, CH Beck)

Strydom, HA (1995) 'The private domain and the Bill of Rights' in (1995) 11 *SA Publiekreg* 52

Swainson, B (ed) (2000) *Encarta Book of Quotations* (London, Bloomsbury)

Swidler, A (ed) (1982) *Human Rights in Religious Traditions* (New York, Pilgrim Press)

Tawney, RH (1964) *Equality* (London, Unwin)

Tettinger, PJ. & Sachs, M (eds) (2002) *Klaus Stern: Im Dienste von Recht, Staat und Wissenschaft* (Cologne, Berlin, Bonn, Munich, Carl Heymanns)

The Kairos Document (1987) *The Kairos Document: Challenge to the Church* 2 ed (Braamfontein, South Africa, Skotaville)

Tiedemann, P (2006) *Was ist Menschenwürde?* (Regensburg, Martin Veicht)

Tribe, LH (1988) *American Constitutional Law* 2 ed (Mineola, New York, Foundation Press)

Van der Merwe, NJ & Rowland CJ (1987) *Die Suid-Afrikaanse Erfreg* 5 ed (Pretoria, Van der Walt)

Venter, Francois (2000) *Constitutional Comparison: Japan, Germany, Canada and South Africa as Constitutional States* (Cape Town, Juta/Dordrecht, Kluwer Law International)

Visser, D (2008) *Unjustified Enrichment* (Cape Town, Juta)

Visser, D & Roux, T (1996) 'Giving back the country: South Africa's Restitution of Land Rights Act, 1994, in context' in MR Rwelamira & G Werle (eds) (1996) *Confronting Past Injustices: Approaches to Amnesty, Punishment, Reparation and Restitution* (Durban, Butterworths) 89

Von Bernstorff, J (2008) 'Pflichtenkollision und Messchenwürdegarantie: Zum Vorrang staatlicher Achtungspflichten im Normbereich von Art 1 GG' (2008) 47 *Der Staat* 21

Von Mangoldt, H, Klein, F & Starck, C (eds) (1985) *Das Bonner Grundgesetz* 3 ed (Munich, Frank Fahlen)

Von Mangoldt, H, Klein, F & Starck, C (eds) (2005) *Kommentar zum Grundgesetz* 5 ed (Munich, Frank Fahlen)

Von Münch, I (1992) *Vorb Art 1–19 GG* in I Von Münch & P Kunig (eds) (1992)

Von Münch, I & Kunig, P (eds) (1992) *Grundgesetz-Kommentar* 4 ed, vol 1 (Munich, CH Beck)

Wade, HWR (1988) *Adminstrative Law* 6 ed (Oxford, Clarendon Press)

Waldron, J (1993) 'Religious contributions in public deliberation' (1993) 30 *San Diego LR* 817

Waldron, J (2002) *God, Locke and Equality: Christian Foundations in Locke's Political Thought* (Cambridge, CUP)

Wechsler, H (1959) 'Towards neutral principles of constitutional law' (1959) 73 *Harvard LR* 1

Wechsler, H (1970) 'The nature of judicial reasoning' in S Hook (ed) *Law and Philosophy* 2 ed (New York, New York UP) 290

Weinrib, LE & Weinrib, EJ (2001) 'Constitutional values and private law in Canada' in D Friedmann & D Barak-Erez (eds) *Human Rights in Private Law* (Oxford, Hart) 43

Werneke, KG *Bonner Kommentar zum Grundgesetz* Art 1 Abs 1 Rn 2,3
Westen, P (1982) 'The empty idea of equality' (1982) 95 *Harvard LR* 537
Westen, P (1990) *Speaking of Equality: An Analysis of the Rhetorical Force of 'Equality' in Moral and Legal Discourse* (New Jersey, Princeton UP)
Will, R (2004) 'Christus oder Kant: Der Glaubenskrieg um die Menschenrechte' 2004 *Blätter für deutsche und internationale Politik* 1228
Williams, B (1967) 'The idea of equality' in P Laslett & WG Runciman (eds) *Philosophy, Politics and Society* Second Series (Oxford, Basil Blackwell)
Williams, B (1981) 'Moral luck' in B Williams *Moral Luck: Philosophical Papers 1973–1980* (Cambridge, CUP)
Wintrich, JM (1957) *Zur Problematik der Grundrechte* Heft 71, Arbeitsgemeinschaft für Forschung des Landes Nordrhein-Westfalen (Cologne & Opladen, Westdeutscher Verlag)
Wiredu, K (1996) *Cultural Universals and Particulars* (Bloomington, Indiana, Indiana UP)
Wiredu, K (ed) (2004) *A Companion to African Theology* (Malden, Massachusetts, Blackwell)
Wiredu, K & Gyekye, K (eds) (1992) *Person and Community, Ghanaian Philosophical Studies* vol 1 (Washington, DC, CRVP)
Wolff, M (1938) 'On the nature of legal persons' (1938) 54 *LQR* 496
Wood, AW (1990) *Hegel's Ethical Thought* (New York, Cambridge UP)
Wood, AW (ed) (1991) *Hegel: Elements of the Philosophy of Right* (Cambridge, CUP)
Wood, AW (1996) 'Introduction' in MJ Gregor *Immanuel Kant: Practical Philosophy* (Cambridge, CUP)
Wood, AW (1999) *Kant's Ethical Thought* (Cambridge, CUP)
Wood, AW (ed and trans) (2002a) *Groundwork for the Metaphysics of Morals: Immanuel Kant* (New Haven and London, Yale UP)
Wood, AW (2002b) 'A note on the translation' in Wood (ed and trans) (2002a) xiii-xv
Woolman, S (2007) 'Dignity' in Woolman, Roux & Bishop (eds) Constitutional Law of South Africa 2 ed (2007) Chapter 36
Woolman, Roux & Bishop (eds) (2007) *Constitutional Law of South Africa* 2 ed (looseleaf) (Cape Town Juta)
Zimmermann, R & Visser, D (eds) (1996) *Under the Southern Cross: Civil Law and Common Law in South Africa* (Cape Town, Juta)
Zippelius, R & Müller, G (eds) (1989) 'Der Gleichheitssatz' (1989) 47 *Veröffentlichungen der Vereinigung der deutschen Staatsrechtslehrer* 7

TABLE OF CASES

SOUTH AFRICA

AUSTRALIA

CANADA

GERMANY

NEW ZEALAND

TANZANIA

UNITED KINGDOM

UNITED STATES

TABLE OF STATUTES

Section of Act — *Page number*

SOUTH AFRICA

Constitution of the Republic of South Africa, 1996

Constitution of the Republic of South Africa Act 200 of 1993

German Civil Code (Bürgerliches Gesetzbuch)

UNITED STATES

CHAPTER ONE

INTRODUCTION

I emphasise at the outset that this book is no more — and does not pretend to be anything other — than an *introduction* to the topics discussed. The first should be clear to anyone reading the book; for the themes of equality and dignity, as discussed in Chapters 2 to 4, are vast and complex, and have confronted the finest philosophical and legal minds for centuries. The issues of horizontal and restitutionary equality dealt with in Chapters 5 and 6, are no less complex, and relate to significant challenges in modern constitutionalism; challenges that the South African Constitution has faced with boldness and foresight. This introductory disclaimer is to protect both myself and the reader. I should not like anyone to think that I myself believe the topics to have been comprehensively covered.

In a sense I feel compelled to write this book. This imperative arises from my conviction that the rights, values and other constitutional provisions discussed, if properly interpreted and applied, offer South Africa the opportunity for rescuing itself more fully from its apartheid past. They are analytically important because they enable one properly to understand the impact of apartheid on human dignity. They are also important for the future, helping us not to commit similar transgressions again and to guide the implementation of restitution. They are not the only significant rights and values but, from the perspective of the South African Bill of Rights, some of the most important. They are also the ones with which my work has been mostly preoccupied for the past twenty years and more. Constitutional lawyers (academic, forensic and others), legal philosophers, political scientists, economists and so forth have an opportunity, historically given to very few, to help shape the proper growth of the Constitution. By growth I mean giving shape to its development and putting flesh, muscle and nerves to its bones. It is also an opportunity for lawyers and others to provide significant leadership to the constitutional enterprise throughout the world. As the German Basic Law became paradigmatic for post-Second World War constitutional development, so our own Constitution might modestly play a similar role in the 21st century. Given my background, I feel that any serious attempt to make a contribution to the solution of highly complex and interrelated constitutional problems, or even to correctly identify the true problems and questions, would be a worthwhile endeavour. I trust the book will provide some guidance to all those toiling in the vineyard of equality and dignity, in whatever capacity.

The use of the word 'lodestar' in the title is intended to be descriptive, purposive and inspirational, for as the dictionary indicates it is a star 'that serves as a guide for navigation ... a ... thing on which one's attention or hopes are fixed; a guiding principle ... an object of pursuit'.

I was delighted to discover subsequently that German constitutional law scholar Professor Josef Isensee (2006: 217) uses a similar metaphor in concluding an article on human worth:

> 'The metaphor of a fixed star is an apt one for human worth. One cannot live from the star. But its distant light points the way at night, and it helps one to endure the inevitable uncertainty.' (My translation.)[1]

This book is in part an attempt by a lawyer — predominantly a forensic one — to delve more deeply than is customary, at least for the forensic lawyer, into the *values* of other ethical disciplines. This is done as an aid to the proper understanding of certain constitutional rights and values that are not self-defining[2] and to solving constitutional problems. For the same reason I also look to Canadian and German jurisprudence for comparative insights.[3]

Being more than a little apprehensive about judicial forays into philosophy, I have found support in the comments by Tony Honoré (2002: 78–80) that, as far back as AD 200 and in relation to the law, 'intellectuals were becoming dissatisfied with the view that whatever is traditional or customary in a society is automatically right' and 'were looking in both politics and religion for something more universal, rational, and philosophical'. He points out that law is, in a broad sense, a philosophical discipline but that '[i]t is a mistake to attribute to a lawyer a system of philosophy rather than a set of values'. My own concern, I repeat, is not with systems but with values and sets of values.

An important shift has been taking place in the concept of constitutional law and its sources since the Second World War; a shift from the predominantly historical to the predominantly normative. Whereas the United States, where the paradigm shift first took place, has for more than two centuries had a written Constitution against which the validity of all federal law can be tested, this was not true of the Anglo-Saxon countries and other members of the Commonwealth until after 1945. Their constitutions did not constitute a superior entrenched norm against

[1] Quite independently, my former colleague, Justice Kate O'Regan, also used the concept 'dignity' as a 'lodestar' in *MEC for Education: KwaZulu-Natal and Others v Pillay and Others* 2008 (1) SA 474 (CC)(2008 (2) BCLR 99) para 156.

[2] As Isensee (2006: 180) so pithily puts it in relation to the meaning of human worth: 'No legal provision interprets itself. Its fate depends on the interpreter' ('Kein Rechtssatz legt sich selbst aus. Sein Schicksal hängt ab von den Interpreten').

[3] As to the great value I attach to the comparative constitutional approach, see LWH Ackermann (2005).

which the validity of statute or common law could be tested. The 'common law'[4] involved either a search for judicial precedent — in civilian systems, a search for the law in the Pandects or later authoritative legal writings or, in mixed systems, a search for both. This was primarily what I would call an historical exercise. The same was true, generally speaking, in Europe, despite extensive codification, because these codes themselves were, for the most part, not subject to a higher constitutional norm. That was also true of Germany until the adoption of the GBL in 1949.[5] Much earlier Immanuel Kant famously remarked that 'a purely empirical theory of law is ... a head, that might be beautiful, but alas! one that has no brain'.[6]

This shift has been caused, in the main, by the development of international human rights, the international human rights conventions, and the movement of many countries to or towards becoming constitutional states, the main feature of which is a Bill of Rights in an entrenched written constitution that functions as the supreme law of the land, and against which the validity of all law and all government conduct can be reviewed by an independent judiciary. It has been a development even more significant than that described by Tony Honoré (2002: 78–79), and to which I have already referred.

This is not to suggest that the extent of this shift has been the same in all cases. Certainly, in the case of South Africa, the shift has brought about a substantive legal revolution.[7] But developments of greatly varying compass have taken place in, for example, Germany, India, Canada and New Zealand. The United Kingdom's membership of the European Union and the coming into force in 2000 of its Human Rights Act has also, albeit indirectly, caused a significant change, the extent of which I do not consider in this book. Of course the paradigmatic shift

---

[4] Unless otherwise indicated I use 'common law' throughout in its wider meaning as connoting non-statutory uncodified law as opposed to 'the common law' in its narrower sense as indicating the common law of the Anglo-Saxon legal systems, including that of North America. I will also, throughout, use the expression 'constitutional state' as an equivalent of the German 'Rechtsstaat' rather than the more customary English expression 'state based on the rule of law'.

[5] Professor Dieter Grimm (1994: 267–296) — at the time a justice of the German Federal Constitutional Court (BVerfG) — explains that the Revolution of 1848 brought forth a constitution, but this was never adopted and the catalogue of liberal rights that had been passed earlier was abolished in 1851. The Weimar Constitution of 1919 embodied civil, political and certain social rights, and provided for a constitutional court (*Staatsgerichtshof*) but its powers were limited to settling controversies between the Reich and its member states, and to election cases. A younger generation of scholars contended that human rights were constitutional rights and binding on the legislature, and this gave rise to a lively debate that was still unsettled when the Weimar Republic failed. The inconclusive nature of the debate was poignantly expressed at the time in English by Carl Friedrich (1928: 200): 'Will the bulk of the German people be inclined to uphold this charter with the same almost religious veneration with which the American people look upon the Constitution of the United States?'

[6] 'Eine bloß empirische Rechtslehre ist ... ein Kopf, der schön sein mag, nur schade! daß er kein Gehirn hat.' (*Metaphysik der Sitten* AK 6: 230) as quoted in Huber (1996a: 21). See also Gregor (1996: 387).

[7] A revolution in substance, but not procedurally. See LWH.Ackermann (2004: 633–679), in particular at 646.

took place in the United States more than two centuries ago, but for the moment I am considering the changes that have occurred since the Second World War.

In the same way that Ulpian and his fellow jurists around AD 200 became 'dissatisfied with the view that whatsoever is traditional or customary in society is automatically right' and were looking 'in both politics and religion for something more universal, rational, and political' (Honore 2002: 78), so too lawyers, in the wake of the Second World War, have been looking for something more universal and indefeasible. Much attention has been focused on the concept of human dignity (worth). This is hardly surprising, given the centrality of this idea in the Universal Declaration of Human Rights.

At the outset I wish to emphasise that, throughout this book, I use 'dignity' as being the equivalent of the German 'Menschenwürde' (as used in Art 1 of the German Basic Law) and its obvious Afrikaans derivative 'menswaardigheid' (being the Afrikaans equivalent of 'dignity' as used in s 10 of the Afrikaans text of the Constitution), and as conveying the idea of *inherent human worth.* I do so because the English word 'dignity' is sometimes understood more narrowly, for example in the South African law of delict, or as connoting an adjunct of high social status or as in the phrase 'standing on one's dignity'. It must further be emphasised that I use *worth* in contradistinction to *price*, in the Kantian sense as is so clearly illustrated by the quotations from Immanuel Kant in the following chapters. According to Kant things have a *price*, which can be replaced by some*thing* else, human beings have a *worth* that is infinite and cannot be replaced by a *thing.* Whenever I use the word 'dignity' I use it in the Kantian sense of infinite human worth. To remind my readers of this, I will often use the expression 'human worth' literally in place of or as an adjunct to the word 'dignity'.

Yehoshua Arieli, Emeritus Professor of American History and Modern History at the Hebrew University of Jerusalem, when writing on the expressions 'dignity of man' and the 'inherent dignity of man' as used in the 1948 Universal Declaration of Human Rights (Arieli 2002: 1) states that their meaning cannot be adequately understood unless they are seen 'in their historical context, in the perspective of the colossal events of the 20th century, and beyond that in the wider perspective of the last two centuries going back to the age of the enlightenment'. He stresses that they should be seen as the 'essence of the lesson which the initiators of the Universal Declaration drew from their past experience, and in particular from the terrifying events of [the 20th century]'. The Declaration could only have been called into being by 'the catastrophe of two World Wars and the Holocaust' and 'the threat of a world dominated and enslaved by a ruthless power which rejected the fundamental principles and norms of the spiritual and moral heritage of the West.'

This wide, contextual understanding is particularly important for grasping the meaning of human dignity (ie human worth) and equality (and unfair discrimination) under the South African Constitution. Despite the appeals made in the Universal Declaration, the denial of these rights and values became even harsher and more systemic in South Africa after 1948. What springs to mind in this regard are the words of West German President von Weizsäcker in his address to a joint sitting of the West German Parliament on 8 May 1985, the fortieth anniversary of Germany's unconditional surrender, as quoted in Haferkamp, Szöllösi-Janze and Ulmann (2006: vii):

> 'All of us, whether guilty or not, whether old or young, must accept the past. Those who shut their eyes for the past, become blind to the present. Those who do not want to remember the inhumanity of the past will be vulnerable again to new dangers of infection.'[8]

Professor Fritz Stern (2006: 432) observes that Von Weizsäcker, 'invoking Jewish tradition, ... insisted that remembrance was the only path to reconciliation'. This, I believe, is also true for reconciliation in South Africa; but not remembrance in the shallow sense of a brusque apology by those unjustly advantaged by apartheid, merely in order to get matters behind one and to pursue 'business as usual', nor — conversely — in the sometimes manipulative sense of blaming all current ills on apartheid. I use remembrance in the sense of a continuous attempt to grasp, firmly and comprehensively, what apartheid did to the human worth of those disadvantaged by apartheid. Yet even this form of remembrance must be coupled with the appreciation that it can never place the advantaged fully in the emotional, psychological or spiritual shoes of the disadvantaged; at best it will lead to a deeper and fuller understanding, for the future, of what human worth means. It is unfortunately a failing of humanity in general that often we fully comprehend the concept of human dignity only by reflecting on actual indignities suffered.

The concept, value, and right of 'dignity' (in the sense of human worth) play so pre-eminent a role, in many different ways, in the Constitution of the Republic of South Africa of 1996 (the '1996 Constitution' or simply 'the Constitution') and its progenitor, the Constitution of the Republic of South Africa Act 200 of 1993 (the 'Interim Constitution'), that ongoing reflection on the meaning, influence and importance of human worth is fully warranted.[9] The interim and 1996 Constitutions brought about a 'substantive constitutional revolution' in South Africa.[10] The Constitution is a transforming constitution, aimed at — among other things — setting right the injustices and distortions caused by apartheid in

[8] My translation. See also Prof Fritz Stern (2006: 432).

[9] See ss 1*(a)*, 10, 36(1), 37(5)*(c)*, read with the associated Table of Non-Derogable Rights, and s 39(1)*(a)* and (2). For readers not familiar with the dramatic history of the birth of the 1996 Constitution, see LWH Ackermann (2004: 633–642) for a brief overview.

[10] As to the nature of this revolution, and the distinction between a 'substantive' and a 'procedural' constitutional revolution, see LWH Ackermann (2004). Although the South African constitutional revolution constituted a substantive revolution, it was not one procedurally (LWH Ackermann 2004: 646).

so many spheres. This task cannot be fulfilled without a proper understanding of human worth (dignity) and equality, and their full implications for a transforming endeavour like this.

The Constitution's equality provisions in s 9 of the Bill of Rights rank amongst the most extensive in existing national constitutions.[11] Not only are equality before the law and equal protection and benefit of the law guaranteed[12] but unconstitutional discrimination (called 'unfair' discrimination) is widely defined in s 9(3) with reference to seventeen enumerated grounds on which discrimination is forbidden.[13] These enumerated grounds do not, it must be emphasised, constitute an exclusive or closed category, because unfair discrimination on grounds analogous to those enumerated is also outlawed. The concept of dignity (human worth) plays a crucial role in equality and non-discrimination jurisprudence as developed by the courts under the Constitution,[14] because in determining whether differentiating legislation, for example, constitutes 'unfair discrimination' in violation of s 9(3) of the Constitution, it is essential to have regard to whether or not the discrimination in question has a negative impact on the human dignity of the person(s) against whom the differentiation operates. The importance of dignity in this context is also borne out by the comparable Canadian and German jurisprudence.

The framers of the Constitution were alive to the fact that pre-constitutional discrimination would, even post-constitutionally, have ongoing negative consequences for the victims of prior discrimination. These negative consequences would neither speedily eradicate themselves of their own accord post-constitutionally, nor be eradicated by merely prohibiting future unfair discrimination in the Constitution. The framers saw that, in the South African context, equality had to include the concept of *restitutionary equality*.[15] To this end s 9(2) of the Constitution, in its relevant part provides:

> 'To promote the achievement of equality, legislative and other measures designed to protect or advance persons, or categories of persons, disadvantaged by unfair discrimination may be taken.'

Human worth is destined to play an important role in determining what the nature, extent, limitations, and duration of restitutionary equality are, as I will endeavour to show in due course.

---

[11] See Appendix 'A' for the full text of the Bill of Rights.

[12] In s 9(1).

[13] Section 9(3) provides as follows:

> 'The state may not unfairly discriminate directly or indirectly against anyone on one or more grounds, including race, gender, sex, pregnancy, marital status, ethnic or social origin, colour, sexual orientation, age, disability, religion, conscience, belief, culture, language and birth.'

[14] See Chapters 4, 5 and 6.

[15] So termed by the Constitutional Court. See further Chapters 4 and 6.

The South African Bill of Rights has gone further than most, if not all, other constitutions with regard to the application of its Bill of Rights provisions to the legal relationships between persons *inter se*. Many national constitutions limit, either in whole or in part, the application of their respective Bills of Rights to the legal relationships between subject and state and are said to operate 'vertically', thus affording protection for the individual only against the state. The South African Bill of Rights, in addition to operating vertically, also operates 'horizontally' in the sense that its provisions also apply to the legal relationships between subjects themselves. Thus, in relation to the prohibition of unfair discrimination — for example, s 9(4) in its relevant part provides:

> 'No person may unfairly discriminate directly or indirectly against anyone on one or more grounds in terms of subsection (3)....'

Horizontal operation is not, however, limited to equality and unfair discrimination. Section 8(2) provides, in wide terms, that a provision — potentially any provision therefore — of the Bill of Rights

> 'binds a natural or a juristic person if, and to the extent that, it is applicable, taking into account the nature of the right and the nature of any duty imposed by the right'.

The horizontal application of the rights embodied in a Bill of Rights gives rise to the possibility of tensions and clashes between the respective rights of the subjects whose legal relationship is placed under the scrutiny of the Bill of Rights. The most obvious examples are clashes between the constitutional rights of equality and non-discrimination of one subject, and those of the freedom, privacy and property rights of another. This can arise, for example, when a white seller of immoveable property seeks in the deed of sale to prohibit the seller from in turn re-selling the property to a black purchaser. The framers, aware of these potential tensions and clashes, made quite elaborate provision for their resolution in s 8(3).[16] Without detailing here precisely how this resolution is to take place,[17] I am convinced that it cannot be done in a manner that is consistent with the Constitution unless human worth (dignity) is used as a guiding principle in the resolution of such conflicts and tensions.

In conformity with, to the best of my knowledge, all democratic constitutions, the South African Constitution does not regard all constitutional rights as being absolute, but recognises that in appropriate circumstances and for legitimate

---

[16] Section 8(3) provides as follows:
'(3) When applying a provision of the Bill of Rights to a natural or juristic person in terms of subsection (2), a court —
(a) in order to give effect to a right in the Bill, must apply, or develop, the common law to the extent that legislation does not give effect to that right; and
(b) may develop rules of the common law to limit the right, provided that the limitation is in accordance with section 36(1).'

[17] See Chapter 5, where the matter is dealt with comprehensively.

and sufficiently persuasive governmental or societal objectives, individual rights may be appropriately limited by legislation. In certain countries, for example the United States and Germany, the principles on which rights may properly be limited have been developed by the courts. In others, such as Canada and New Zealand, general 'limitation clauses' have been enacted in their respective constitutional instruments. The South African Bill of Rights also incorporates a general limitation clause, s 36(1),[18] which — although considerably more detailed — follows in broad terms a similar provision in the Canadian Charter. Without detailing its provisions here, it is important for my purpose to point out that, apart from other requirements, the limitation of a right will not pass constitutional muster unless it is 'reasonable and justifiable in an open and democratic society based on human dignity, equality and freedom'. Without a proper understanding of human dignity and its demands, the jurisprudence in relation to the permissible limitation of rights cannot be soundly developed.

Of particular significance in evaluating the nature of the change brought about by the new constitutional dispensation in South Africa, and the important role that human dignity is to play in this transforming Constitution, is the fact that the Constitution is not merely a formal constitutional document limited to protecting individuals against the unconstitutional exercise of public power, even though its Bill of Rights has the most extensive and detailed provisions of any constitution of which I am aware. Courts must, in addition, when interpreting legislation, and when developing the common law or customary law, 'promote the spirit, purport and objects of the Bill of Rights'.[19] This is over and above the obligation that s 39(1)*(a)* places on courts, when interpreting the Bill of Rights, to 'promote the values that underlie an open and democratic society based on human dignity, equality and freedom'. But the Constitution goes even further. It also establishes an objective normative value system which, as an underlying constitutional value for all areas of the law, acts as a guiding principle and stimulus for the legislature, as well as for the executive and the judiciary.[20]

Viewed in a broader international context, it is essential to do everything in one's power to support the proclamation in the preamble to the 1948 Universal Declaration to the effect that the 'inherent dignity' and the equality of 'all

[18] In this respect s 36(1) provides as follows:

'The rights in the Bill of Rights may be limited only in terms of law of general application to the extent that the limitation is reasonable and justifiable in an open and democratic society based on human dignity, equality and freedom, taking into account all relevant facts including —

(a) the nature of the right;
(b) the importance of the purpose of the limitation;
(c) the nature and extent of the limitation;
(d) the relation between the limitation and its purpose; and
(e) less restrictive means to achieve the purpose.'

[19] Section 39(2).

[20] *Carmichele v The Minister of Safety and Security and the Minster of Justice and Constitutional Development* 2001 (4) SA 938 (CC) (2001 (10) BCLR 995) para 54.

members of the human family' belong to those values and human rights that constitute 'the foundation of freedom, justice and peace in the world'; and whose contemptuous disregard has 'resulted in barbarous acts which have outraged the conscience of mankind'. It is obligatory to respond to the Declaration's appeal for the mandatory protection of these rights by the rule of law — which in my view includes the concept of the constitutional state (*Rechtsstaat*), if human beings are not 'to be compelled to have recourse, as a last resort, to rebellion against tyranny and oppression'. Human societies throughout the world have, in the more than 60 years since the Universal Declaration, failed lamentably to turn this appeal into a reality. Any attempt to present human worth and equality in terms that may lead to greater global understanding and acceptance of these core concepts and values, and that may thereby contribute to eliminating 'barbarous acts which ... outrag[e] the conscience of mankind' is worthwhile. Greater global understanding will, one hopes, also counteract the negative influence of culture when it serves in any community to undermine human dignity.

On a more personal level, I consider it important that the legal concept of human dignity in relation to equality be extensively investigated. I do not wish to trivialise the ills of apartheid by attempting a passing summary of them. However, it seems to me that what lay at the heart of apartheid pathology, quite apart from the murder, torture and other physical brutality that it eventually led to, was the extensive and sustained attempt to deny to the majority of the South African population the right of self-identification and self-determination. The fact that the apartheid laws did not ultimately achieve their ends and that the greater majority of black South Africans claimed their freedom and exerted their moral agency does not detract from the human indignity and trauma inflicted. The apartheid state not only denied to black South Africans all meaningful participation in the political process, but tried generally to legislate the lives of its people on the sole criterion of race or ethnic origin. Who you were, where you could live, what schools and universities you could attend, what you could do and aspire to, and with whom you could form intimate personal relationships was determined for you by the state, or at least the state directed all its power towards achieving this end. In certain cases apartheid legislation, by its very nature, also denied identity determination to whites. However, because the overall effect of apartheid was to benefit whites, the impact of this denial was different, although it could nevertheless still be damaging. As Archbishop Emeritus Desmond Tutu has expressed it: 'Apartheid claimed that what imbued anyone with worth was actually a biological irrelevance — the colour of one's skin....'[21]

The state did its best to deny to black South Africans that which is definitional to being human, namely the ability to understand or at least define oneself through one's own powers and to act freely as a moral agent pursuant to this

[21] In Danieli et al, eds (1999: xiii).

understanding or self-definition. Black people were treated as means to an end and hardly ever as an end in themselves; an almost complete reversal of the categorically imperative concept of priceless inner worth and dignity.

This denial by the apartheid state of innate dignity, understood as absolute worth, inevitably (because of the very nature of human worth, as I shall attempt to demonstrate) led to a similarly fundamental denial of freedom and also a most egregious denial of equality. The awareness of gender discrimination was, I think, obscured in part by the all-pervading racism, but when analysed in terms of a denial of inner worth and dignity it eventually became clear to me that there was, in principle, no difference between the two forms of discrimination. For the same reason, and because of personal friendships with people following gay and lesbian lifestyles, I subsequently reached the same conclusion with regard to sexual orientation.[22]

Constitutions are often reactive, in the sense that they are a response to and an attempt to deal with and heal tragic and traumatic ills of the past. Thus art 1 of the German Basic Law (GBL), which places human dignity (*Menschenwürde*) at the centre of and determinative for the GBL and its protection of fundamental rights, constitutes a direct reaction to and an outright rejection of the totalitarianism and inhumanity of the preceding Nazi period encapsulated by the phrase 'You are nothing; your 'volk' is everything' (*Du bist nichts, dein Volk ist alles*).[23] The same can be said of the South African Constitution, which treats fundamental human dignity (worth) and — flowing therefrom — freedom and equality as its cornerstones. For South Africa it constitutes an uncompromising rejection, not only of the idea that 'you are nothing; your 'volk' is everything' but also of the idea that 'you are nothing, your skin colour, gender and sexual orientation are everything'. Not only constitutions but also human beings at times react to traumatic ills of the past, for which they must bear responsibility. It should therefore not come as a surprise that I consider the investigation of dignity (human worth) and equality in the context of the Constitution to be of great importance. It was my own personal realisation and full acceptance, *inter alia*, of Kant's concept of human worth as the absolute and hence equal worth of all human beings, that led me to the total rejection of apartheid in all its transmogrifications, and eventually (under personal circumstances not wholly untrying) to resign from the Transvaal High Court in 1987, and to accept appointment to the newly established Harry Oppenheimer Chair in Human Rights Law at Stellenbosch University, which I held until the beginning of 1993. As Bernard Williams (1967: 116), has so correctly pointed out:

> 'The ground of the respect owed to each man thus emerges in the Kantian theory as a kind of secular analogue of the Christian conception of the respect owed to all men as equally

[22] See the pre-constitutional judgment in *S v H* 1995 (1) SA 120 (C).
[23] See, for example, Werneke (art 1.1 Rn 2–3), and von Münch/Kunig (1992: art 1 Rn6).

children of God. Though secular, it is equally metaphysical: in neither case is it anything empirical *about* men that constitutes the ground of equal respect.'[24]

I also share the more general disquiet, applicable also to our society, so eloquently expressed in 1999 by the distinguished contemporary Kantian scholar, Prof Allen Wood (1999: xiv–xv) regarding his own country, the United States of America:

'In the past twenty years, my interest has been drawn back to Kant's ethical thoughts also by my experience of the present age. Our time (the twentieth century, and especially its last two decades) has been, and still is, a disillusioning time in which to live. The social, political and intellectual climate of my own country (and therefore the globe over which it tyrannizes) has grown blinder, nastier, more irrational. The always dominant economic and political structures have become increasingly wealthy, powerful, arrogant, ambitious, greedy, and short-sighted. As life becomes harder and more hopeless for those excluded from these structures, large numbers of people turn back to old enthusiasms and superstitions, which are usually the pretext for outgrown passions and old hatreds. Ancient and parochial forms of community reassert themselves because the only order presenting itself as new and rational is devoid of any genuine community, since it holds people together only by entangling them in a confused nexus of unbridled power and self-interest. Progressive social movements, whose vocation has been to build a free community grounded on the rational dignity of all human beings, must now use their full strength and courage merely to survive in a world grown hostile to them. The job of intellectuals is to oppose unreason, speak truth to power, and think the way toward a genuine community. Some, as always, choose instead to apologize for the rationally indefensible; but too many others in our age are caught up in the fashionable mood of irony, absurdity, and self-destruction because they have lost confidence in the mind's authority over human life and its power to find better ways for people to live.

At such a time it is not difficult to see some truth in Kant's sombre account of the evil in human nature. It even becomes easier to sympathize with his stern, moralistic insistence that people must subject their ways of thinking to rational criticism and reform their ways of acting through a fundamental change of heart. Still more than that, however, the age needs Kant's sober, principled hope for a more rational, cosmopolitan future. In other words, we need to recapture an authentically Enlightenment conception of the human condition, especially an interpretation of that conception that makes clear the Enlightenment's still unrealized radical potential.'

As to enlightenment, Immanuel Kant himself describes it thus:

'*Enlightenment is the human being's emergence from his self-incurred minority* [*Unmündigkeit*]. *Minority* is inability to make use of one's own understanding without direction from another. This minority is *self-incurred* when its cause lies not in lack of understanding but in lack of resolution and courage to use it without direction from

[24] The concept of fundamental human worth, as espoused by the Christian and other Abrahamic religions, is more generally based on the belief that that all human beings are created in the image of God and hence equally so created. See Chapter 2.

another. *Sapere aude!* [Literally "dare to be wise"] Have courage to make use of your *own* understanding! is thus the motto of enlightenment.'[25] (Emphasis in the original.)

It is also necessary to indicate at the outset what this book is *not* about, in an attempt to forestall criticism for omissions that are in fact deliberate. I have previously (LWH Ackermann 2004: 678–679) emphasised the following:

'As a transforming constitution, [the South African Constitution] has extended established ideas regarding enforceable fundamental rights to socio-economic and environmental spheres. Without entrenching socio-economic and environmental rights, the Constitution may very well have little or no credibility for the dispossessed, the poor, and the socially marginalised. By entrenching them, the Constitution has highlighted the greatest challenge facing South African society at large in the decades to come....

The framers [of the Constitution] are to be applauded for taking the best from the world's existing constitutions and contextualising them for the particular needs of South Africa. The most sophisticated tools have been fashioned for the courts to enforce, promote, and protect the Constitution and its values. But the ultimate fate of the Constitution, a bridge with a very long span, will not be decided by the jurisprudence of its courts alone, however devoted and inspired that might prove to be. A transforming constitution such as ours will only succeed if everyone, in government as well as in civil society at all levels, embraces and lives out its values and its demands. It will only succeed if restitutionary equality becomes a reality and basic material needs are met, because it borders on the obscene to preach human dignity to the homeless and the starving. This must, however, be achieved in a manner consonant with the human dignity of all. We are, after 10 years, only at the end of the beginning.'[26]

The compass of my present inquiry into dignity as an essential component of constitutional equality and non-discrimination is a narrower one. I shall not be dealing expressly with socio-economic rights,[27] or with the government/civil society commitment and partnership essential for the ultimate success of our Constitution and its aspirations. This is not because I underestimate the value of socio-economic rights, or the crucial importance of the material upliftment so urgently required by so many, but because my investigation is a more modest one, which has to be confined within manageable limits. For the same reason I do not give attention independently to the right and value of freedom, other than

[25] 'An answer to the question: What is enlightenment?' [AK 8: 35] in *Practical Philosophy*, Gregor (ed) (1996: 17). Unless otherwise stated, the English translation of Kant's work will throughout be from *The Cambridge Edition of the Works of Immanuel Kant*. The numerals in square brackets refer to the Berlin Academy Edition (AK) of Kant's writings by volume: page number. This is followed by the English title in the Cambridge edition (which in this particular case is *Practical Philosophy*) and thereafter by the name of the editor of the particular English title and (in parentheses) by the date of publication of the title and the page reference.

[26] LWH Ackermann (2004: 678–679).

[27] As to which I would refer to the leading work of Liebenberg (2010).

as an element of human dignity, despite the equal importance I attach to it.[28] I trust, therefore, that the above self-limitation will be constantly borne in mind by those who read this book.

I have chosen Germany and Canada for comparative perspectives.[29] Germany, for a variety of reasons: It is the paradigmatic post-World War II reactive Constitution; its response to its Nazi past has lessons for our reaction to the apartheid times; many of the fundamental ideas of the German Constitution have found their way into our Constitution;[30] our law still has Roman-Dutch roots in Europe;[31] and Germany has probably the richest and most deeply philosophically grounded scholarship and jurisprudence on human worth and equality in the world.[32]

Professor Donald Kommers, a distinguished Anglo-American scholar on German constitutional jurisprudence, emphasises (1998: 786–787) the rising influence throughout the world since 1945 of the German Basic Law (GBL) and the corresponding decline of the Constitution of the United States of America.

> 'In the nineteenth and for the most part of this century, constitution-makers around the world, particularly in Latin America and Europe, looked to the United States Constitution for guidance in designing their systems of constitutional governance. In recent decades, however, Germany's Basic Law has replaced the American Constitution as the world's leading model of democratic constitutionalism. The Basic Law's influence is clearly discernable in dozens of democratic constitutions drafted in the last decade, paradigmatic examples of which are several recent Latin American constitutions, the post-1990 constitutions of Eastern Europe, and the 1996 Constitution of South Africa.'

---

[28] I refer a doubting Thomas on this score to *Ferreira v Levine NO and Others; Vreyenhoek and Others v Powell NO and Others* 1996 (1) SA 984 (CC) (1996 (1) BCLR 1) paras 47–69 and in particular to para 49 where the following is stated:

> 'Human dignity cannot be fully valued or respected unless individuals are able to develop their humanity, their "humanness" to the full extent of its potential. Each human being is uniquely talented. Part of the dignity of every human being is the fact and awareness of this uniqueness. An individual's human dignity cannot be fully respected or valued unless the individual is permitted to develop his or her unique talents optimally. Human dignity has little value without freedom; for without freedom personal development and fulfilment are not possible. Without freedom, human dignity is little more than an abstraction. Freedom and dignity are inseparably linked. To deny people their freedom is to deny them their dignity. Although freedom is indispensable for the protection of dignity, it has an intrinsic constitutional value of its own. It is likewise the foundation of many of the other rights that are specifically entrenched. Viewed from this perspective, the starting point must be that an individual's right to freedom must be defined as widely as possible, consonant with a similar breadth of freedom for others.' (Footnotes omitted.)

[29] For the value of 'Constitutional comparativism' see, for example, Markesinis and Fedke (2005) and LWH Ackermann (2005).

[30] See the illuminating article by De Waal (1995), 'A Comparative Analysis of the Provisions of German Origin in the Interim Bill of Rights.'

[31] See Ackermann (2005: 171–175).

[32] For further material in English on the GBL and the BVerfG's jurisprudence, readers are referred to the important and pioneering work of Kommers (1997) (the 3rd edition of which is expected to be published shortly) as well as the books by Currie (1994) and Eberle (2002).

Kommers (1998: 786 n 2) has the impression that 'American scholars tend to attribute far greater influence to the United States than the evidence warrants'. This is particularly true, he says, with regard to the GBL. With regard to the Herrenchiemsee Conference and the Parliamentary Council that drafted the GBL in 1949, he remarks that he could find fewer than a dozen references to the United States in their proceedings.

I also refer to certain features of Canadian constitutionalism because of its own modern, post-Second World War Charter of Rights, because Canada's equality jurisprudence is also grounded in dignity, and because s 15(2) of its Charter contains provisions, similar to those in the South African Constitution, providing for what I term 'restitutionary' equality. As Weinrib and Weinrib (2001: 72) so aptly point out with regard to, inter alia, the relationship between constitutional and private law:

> 'Other jurisdictions have extensive experience in applying constitutional norms to private law. *In this respect, as in others, one should be mindful of the new cosmopolitanism of constitutional law.* Canada's Constitution, while distinctive in its own way, is nonetheless one member in a family of constitutions that set up similar legal frameworks and present similar challenges. By looking into past experiences of others we can perhaps glimpse our own future, or at least learn both from the good and the bad examples.' (Emphasis supplied, footnote omitted.)

Moreover, from the point of view of forensic epistemology, constitutional comparison is important, if not essential, for the falsification of hypotheses, for ensuring that the right questions are being identified and answered, and from preventing hypotheses or arguments proceeding unchallenged down narrow, windowless corridors of the mind.[33]

There is a further aspirational purpose to the book. I would feel fully rewarded if it induced even one or two scholars, isolated in the conventional Anglo-Saxon constitutional law bubble, to investigate fully the treasures to be found in German constitutional law. While there are random translations, in various formats, of the judgments of the German Constitutional Court (for which one is only too grateful) there is, as yet, no systematic process of translating into English all its reported judgments. Likewise there has not, to the best of my knowledge, been any translation to date of any one of the great German constitutional law commentaries or comprehensive textbooks into English. I do hope that this will be remedied by the next generation of lawyers in Germany and the Anglo-Saxon countries.[34]

I have elsewhere (Ackermann 2004: 646) expressed the view that the adoption of the Interim and 1996 Constitutions constituted a *substantive constitutional*

---

[33] See LWH Ackermann (2005: 183–186).

[34] Materials in English on German constitutional law are appearing with increasing regularity. The Library of the South African Constitutional Court holds, with the kind permission of Prof Donald Kommers, a manuscript index produced by him of these materials.

revolution (but not a constitutional revolution *procedurally* — because of the procedures followed in the adoption of these constitutions). This is particularly the case in relation to the rights of equality, equal treatment and non-discrimination. Others, in court judgments and elsewhere, have referred to a 'transformative Constitution', 'transformative constitutionalism' and similar expressions. I do not imply any difference between my concept of a substantive constitutional revolution and these other expressions, although I would like to think that mine is more accurate. But whatever expression is used, a number of things need to be emphasised. The substantive constitutional revolution (or transformation) is not yet complete. This is particularly the case with regard to achieving equality, and especially restitutionary equality, and also regarding human dignity (worth). The 1996 Constitution is transcendental in the sense that, given the imperfections (to put it no higher) of human beings and human society, the vision it incorporates may never be fully realised. But this is no reason for not holding this vision constantly before us, and to pursue it with all diligence. Finally, in this regard, it needs to be emphasised that, whether one calls it a revolution or a transformation, the process must take place strictly within the confines and constraints of the Constitution itself, which is after all the constitutional 'grundnorm' (basic/fundamental constitutional norm) chosen by the people themselves.

I greatly admire the South African Constitution, particularly for its superbly articulated and integrated Bill of Rights. This I am able to do dispassionately, and I trust without chauvinism, because I had no hand, directly or indirectly in any of the discussions or negotiations after 1989, nor advised any of the negotiators. The Constitution represents, among other things, a set of values and commitments that all South Africans have accepted, and thus represents the first step to integrated nationhood. It represents the best from Europe and North America and from Africa. Having worked with it intimately since 1994, I believe that the Bill of Rights might well become paradigmatic for the 21st century, and I hope that any serious attempt to examine its fundamental values and rights might have some worth for interested persons in other jurisdictions.

As far as translation from the German is concerned, all translations — unless otherwise indicated — are my own. Where a German author has written in English, I shall indicate this. The bibliography will indicate what material has been composed in German. I have, particularly with regard to works in German, quoted more extensively than would normally be the case, in order to convey some feeling of the original. In these cases I have very seldom quoted — in addition — the original German, since this would have increased unduly the length of the present book. If my exposition of the German materials encourages even a single English reader to investigate German constitutional law more closely and in the original, I would consider myself amply rewarded. I have myself tried to use gender-inclusive language, but quotations are in the original.

The rest of the book is structured as follows. Chapter 2 provides some theoretical background to human dignity, equality and non-discrimination as constitutional legal concepts, drawing on the development of related values in the Abrahamic religions and secular philosophy. It is, in my view, essential to do so before dealing with the meaning attached to these rights and values in South Africa, Germany and Canada, because the critique of this jurisprudence cannot be properly understood without theoretical background of this nature. This background discussion involves, in part, the crucial contention that a lack of proper linguistic and logical analysis on the part of lawyers has rendered the legal discussion of equality and non-discrimination confused (and confusing), unnecessarily sceptical and needlessly complex. In Chapter 3 I deal with the meaning of human dignity (worth) under the Constitution and in the countries referred to above, but only to the extent necessary for my argument regarding equality and non-discrimination and in Chapter 4 with equality and non-discrimination in the same countries. In Chapter 5 the role of dignity, in relation to the so-called 'horizontal' application of the Bill of Rights in South Africa, is considered, with reference also to Germany and Canada, but limited to a consideration of the horizontal operation of the right to equality and non-discrimination. In conclusion, Chapter 6 addresses the issue of restitutionary equality in South Africa.

CHAPTER TWO

THEORETICAL BACKGROUND TO HUMAN DIGNITY, EQUALITY AND NON-DISCRIMINATION AS CONSTITUTIONAL LEGAL CONCEPTS

2.1 INTRODUCTION

The purpose of this chapter is fourfold. In the first place it seeks to clarify, in a principled manner, the confusion that is caused by arguing that all people are born equal, or are equal in rights, notwithstanding the self-evident empirical fact that all human beings differ extensively as far as their physical, mental, intellectual, emotional, artistic and creative abilities, and their economic, social, cultural circumstances in life, are concerned. The main contention in this regard is that, in a special logico-grammatical sense — which I shall try to explain more fully in the next section — the noun *equality* and the adjective *equal* cannot be used substantively but only in an attributive sense. Put more simply, intelligible meaning can only be given to equality, as applied to human beings, if the antecedent question 'Equality of *what*?' is first asked, or, more expansively, 'In respect of what are all human beings equal and in respect of what may no one be discriminated against?' The 'what' and the 'in respect of what' will for the sake of brevity be referred to as the *criterion of attribution* or the *criterion of reference*. It will be argued that, without first answering these questions, without first postulating a *criterion of attribution or reference*, debates about equality will necessarily be unproductive. This underlying problem will similarly be referred to as the *logico-grammatical problem*. Some European scholars refer, in the context of equality, to this criterion of reference or attribution as the *tertium comparationis*. As this latter expression falls somewhat heavily on certain ears, one is told, it might be preferable to use the expression *criterion of reference* or *criterion of attribution* without suggesting any substantive difference between the two expressions.

Secondly, the chapter argues that, for legal puposes, the answer to the question 'equality of what?' (or the *criterion of attribution*) is/should be human worth (dignity).

Thirdly, it is argued that, contrary to the views of some sceptics, meaningful content can in principle be given to the concept and value of human dignity that is not dependent on the mere whim of the interpreter. I shall be suggesting a particular (Kantian) account of what it is that gives us dignity, or by virtue of what we have innate dignity.

Lastly, the chapter explores crucial aspects of the theological and secular philosophic background, and indeed grounding, of the legal concepts of human worth and equality and seeks to justify this theological and philosophical use in the process of giving meaning to these concepts in constitutional law. Apart from the importance of the history of ideas generally, the use of this theological and secular philosophic background is justified in the attempt to establish, with regard to the meaning of dignity — particularly in its relationship to equality — and of equality itself, a broad 'overlapping consensus' in the sense that the political philosopher John Rawls has developed this concept, as more fully explained in section 2.4 below.

Before dealing with the nature and scope of the relevant constitutional provisions dealing with dignity and equality, whether in the South African, German or Canadian constitutional instruments,[1] the mind of the interpreter needs first to be preconditioned before seeking to attach any firm meaning to these Constitutional provisions. We need to remind ourselves again, in the present context, of Prof Isensee's warning (2006: 180)[2] that these provisions 'do not interpret themselves, their fate depends on the interpreter'. This preconditioning relates to antecedent historical, philosophical, theological and other social ideas and knowledge. In isolation the relevant constitutional provisions dealing with dignity and equality tell us little of the outcomes they seek to achieve when they are applied to the diversities of human beings and human life. In applying, for example, s 9 of the South African Constitution dealing with equality and non-discrimination, what must we make of the fact that a special status is conferred on the values of human dignity, equality and freedom by s 1?[3] Moreover, neither s 9 nor s 10[4] can be construed in isolation.

The historical circumstances in which the 1996 Constitution came into being must be taken into account, and these are not limited to the events immediately preceding its coming into force, or the coming into force of the Interim

[1] For South Africa the Interim and 1996 Constitutions; for Germany the Basic Law for the Federal Republic of Germany (*Grundgesetz für die Bundesrepublik Deutschland*), hereinafter referred to as the 'German Basic Law' or simply the 'GBL'; and for Canada the Canadian Charter of Rights and Freedoms, hereinafter 'the Charter'.

[2] See Chapter 1 n 2.

[3] Which provides, inter alia, that '[h]uman dignity, the achievement of equality and the advancement of human rights and freedoms' are certain of the 'values' on which the state of the Republic of South Africa is 'founded'. Moreover s 74(1) entrenches s 1 more deeply against amendment than any other section of the Constitution, requiring inter alia the supporting vote of at least 75 per cent of the members of the National Assembly.

[4] Section 10 deals with the postulation of and guarantees relating to dignity.

Constitution. The 1996 Constitution was not born into an ethical, religious or historical vacuum. Its provisions, particularly those in the Founding Provisions and the Bill of Rights,[5] reflect the shared values of all those represented when its provisions came into force. If this is not empirically strictly correct, then at least its provisions were chosen on behalf of those represented as the public values on which the new democracy was founded and would be developed.[6] In order for its provisions to stand shoulder to shoulder with those of other 'open and democratic societ[ies] based on human dignity, equality and freedom'[7] we need, like the Roman jurists described by Tony Honoré and referred to in Chapter 1, to search for values that are 'more universal'.

Some explanation is also due for not, at the very outset, addressing in detail the South African Constitution's provisions on equality, non-discrimination and dignity, and the related jurisprudence, but instead leaving this discussion to later chapters. In the first place it is essential, in my view, to resolve the abovementioned logico-grammatical problems inherent in working with concepts such as human dignity, equality and non-discrimination. Only when these difficulties have been resolved, or placed in a proper perspective, does it make sense to investigate the equality provisions of the Constitution and the resulting jurisprudence in any detail. My contention throughout is that human beings, regardless of their many other differences, are equal in law with regard to their human dignity (worth) and may not be discriminated against in a manner that negatively affects their human dignity. Differently stated, human dignity (worth) is the *criterion of reference*, or the *criterion of attribution* in seeking to answer (as one must), the question (which one cannot avoid asking): 'In respect of what are all human beings equal and in respect of what may no one be discriminated against?' If this criterion of reference proposition is correct, then this close linkage between equality and

[5] Chapter 1 (ss 1–6) and Chapter 2 (ss 7–39) respectively of the 1996 Constitution.

[6] For some background to the constitution-making process which ultimately led to the 1996 South African Constitution coming into force and effect, and the 'certification' role played in this regard by the South African Constitutional Court, readers are referred to its judgment in *Chairperson of the Constitutional Assembly, Ex parte: In re Certification of the Constitution of the Republic of South Africa, 1996* 1996 (4) SA 744 (CC) (1996 (10) BCLR 1253) paras 1–31 (hereinafter called the 'First Certification Judgment') and to its judgment in *Chairperson of the National Assembly, Ex parte: In re Certification of the Amended Text of the Constitution of the Republic of South Africa, 1996* 1997 (2) SA 97 (CC) (1997 (10) BCLR 1653) (the 'Second Certification Judgment'). The work of the Constitutional Assembly ('CA') was throughout widely publicised and not only all political parties but also the general public invited to participate in the drafting of the 1996 Constitution. The CA and all political parties represented in the CA were invited by the Constitutional Court to lodge written argument, including objections to the certification of the Constitution, and in addition (by means of published notices in all official languages) any other body or person wishing to object to the certification was invited to submit a written objection. In the result written representations and oral argument were submitted on behalf of five political parties. In addition objections were lodged on behalf of 84 private parties. The CA and the political parties were afforded a right of audience before the Court, as were 27 of the other bodies or persons.

[7] The limitation of rights provision in s 36 of the Constitution.

dignity makes it implausible to discuss equality without some reference to dignity and vice versa.

Before dealing more fully with the two aspects of what I have termed the logico-grammatical equality problem,[8] and indeed for purposes of this book as a whole, brief reference should be made to the general methodological approach favoured in this book. According to Popper (1983: 103) and others, Hume's 'problem with induction' arose from his discovery that it is impossible to justify a law by observation or experiment, and 'that there simply is no such logical entity as an inductive inference'; or, differently put, 'that all so-called inductive inferences are logically invalid'. Popper's well-known solution to Hume's problem points to a logical asymmetry between verification and falsification. While accepting the validity of Hume's problem, as far as it goes, Popper (1983: 102,110) contends that 'we *are* justified in reasoning [deductively] from a counter-instance to the falsity of the corresponding universal law (that is, of any law of which it is a counter-instance)'. Popper's famous explanatory example is rendered thus by Magee (1985: 22):

> '[A]lthough no number of observation statements reporting observations of white swans allows us logically to derive the universal statement 'All swans are white', one single observation statement, reporting one single observation of a black swan, allows us logically to derive the statement 'not all swans are white'.

Popper (1999: 14) presents his four-stage model as follows:

> '1. *the old problem*;
> 2. *formation of tentative theories*;
> 3. *attempts at elimination* through critical discussion, including experimental testing;
> 4. *the new problems* that arise from the critical discussion of our theories.'

According to Miller (1983: 31–32) Einstein's approach is similar. Einstein (2000) is said to have observed that 'No amount of experimentation can prove me right; a single experiment can prove me wrong'.[9] Einstein (1950) applied this approach to ethical reasoning as well: 'Ethical axioms are found and tested not very differently from the axioms of science. Truth is what stands the test of experience.'

No good reason exists why the same or a similar approach should not be applied to legal reasoning. The distinguished German constitutional law scholar Prof Peter Häberle (2008: 35) considers the critical rationalism of Popper's 'open society' to be the 'appropriate (tolerant) philosophical foundation for the lawyer'.

At some stage in this reasoning process, which contains inductive as well as deductive elements, a preliminary conclusion (hypothesis) is reached as to what

[8] The first is whether it is correct that in regard to equality a grammatico-logical problem exists which necessitates an enquiry into a criterion of attribution or reference. The second is whether human dignity is the appropriate/correct criterion of reference or attribution.

[9] As attributed to him in Swainson (2000: 306, item 57).

the result should be and why. The best way of testing this preliminary conclusion is by means of rigorous attempts to falsify it. The intellectually liberating effect of this methodology is described as follows by the scientist and Nobel prize-winner Sir John Eccles (1970: 107):

> 'The erroneous belief that science eventually leads to the certainty of a definitive explanation carries with it the implication that it is a grave scientific misdemeanour to have published some hypothesis that eventually is falsified. As a consequence scientists have often been loath to admit the falsification of such an hypothesis, and their lives may be wasted in defending the no longer defensible. Whereas according to Popper, falsification in whole or in part is the anticipated fate of all hypotheses, and we should even rejoice in the falsification of an hypothesis that we have cherished as our brain-child.'

Popper's falsification approach provides strong justification for the comparative approach in constitutional law. By applying the comparative methodology, the suppositions, rules and principles of one's own system can be subjected to the critique of another system. Even though a comparative approach might not result in the amendment of a principle of one's own system, it may greatly assist in strengthening the defence of the principle. In the chapters that follow I look at the relevant principles in German and Canadian law with a purpose like this in mind. The following comment of Thomas Mann[10] is to the point:

> 'For only by making comparisons can we distinguish ourselves from others and discover who we are, in order to become all that we are meant to be.'

2.2 EQUALITY, NON-DISCRIMINATION AND DIGNITY: THE ANTECEDENT LOGICO-GRAMMATICAL PROBLEM[11]

Differently stated: Why is it necessary to ask the question 'Equality of what?' A lack of linguistic and logical analysis has made the debate on equality and non-discrimination in the law needlessly complex and confusing. A basic argument made in this book is that in law (as in ethics) the words 'equality', 'equal', or 'unequal', in order to be meaningful, can only be used as *attributive* parts of speech and not as *predicative* nouns or adjectives. The terms 'attributive' and 'predicative' are, however, not used in this exposition in a strictly grammatical sense, but in a special logical sense that requires identification of the object referred to (human dignity, for example), in order that the appropriateness of the attributive term (equal or equality) can be judged. The vital question, so consistently ignored in legal equality analysis, is: 'With regard to what are all human beings equal?' It is precisely in order to address the second leg of the logico-grammatical problem that the proposition is advanced that human worth (dignity) is the *criterion of reference*, or *criterion of attribution* that must be

[10] As translated by Currie (1994: v).
[11] See further LWH Ackermann (2006).

used in seeking to answer the obligatory question, namely 'in respect of what are all human beings equal and in respect of what may no one be discriminated against?'

At the root of the concerned and troubled thinking on equality and discrimination (in law and ethics) that will be referred to later is the mistaken analytical assumption I have referred to. The error is to regard, in the logico-grammatical sense, the word 'equal' — in such phrases as 'equality before the law', 'equal treatment by the law', 'non-equal treatment', and even when used as a noun in an expression such as 'equality before the law', — as a *predicative* adjective or a *predicative* noun, instead of as an *attributive* adjective or noun.

As far as I am aware the most illuminating work on this logico-grammatical problem has been that done by the philosophers Peter Geach and Philippa Foot.[12] Although their work relates to the concept of 'good' as opposed to 'bad', no good reason suggests itself why their mode of reasoning and conclusions should not also apply to such concepts as 'equality', 'inequality', 'non-discrimination', etc.

Geach (1967: 64–65) uses the terms '*predicative* adjective' and '*attributive* adjective' in a special logical sense. In this sense he points out, by way of example:

> '"big" and "small" are attributive; "x is a big flea" does not split up into "x is a flea" and "x is big", nor "x is a small elephant" into "x is an elephant" and "x is small"; for if these analyses were legitimate, a simple argument would show that a big flea is a big animal and a small elephant a small animal.'

On the other hand:

> '[I]n the phrase "a red book" "red" is a predicative adjective in my sense although not grammatically so, for "is a red book" logically splits up into "is a book" and "is red."'

Geach concludes that 'good' and 'bad' are always attributive, not predicative adjectives and invites us to consider the contrast in such phrases as 'red car' and 'good car'. Person A, with poor eyesight, can see at a distance that an object is red and B, a colour-blind friend with keener eyesight, can merely see that it is a car. By pooling information it can be established that the object is a red car. But, says Geach,

> 'there is no such possibility of ascertaining that a thing is a good car by pooling information that it is good and that it is a car. This sort of example shows that "good" like "bad" is essentially an attributive adjective. Even when "good" or "bad" stands by itself as a predicate, and is thus grammatically predicative, some substantive has to be understood; there is no such thing as being just good or bad, there is only being a good or bad so-and-so.'

Foot (2001: 2–3), affirms the foregoing with the following examples:

---

[12] In saying this, the invaluable work of Prof Amartya Sen (1992) on equality (dealt with in section 2.9*(f)* below) is not overlooked. Although implicitly recognising the logico-grammatical problem inherent in using the expressions *equal*, *equality* and so forth, and the solution thereto, Prof Sen does not analyse these issues in the detail that Geach and Foot do.

> 'Peter Geach puts "good" in the class of attributive adjectives, to which, for example, "large" and "small" belong, contrasting such adjectives with "predicative" adjectives such as "red". Such a colour word operates in independence of any noun to which it is attached, but whether a particular F is a good F depends radically on what we substitute for "F". As "large" must change to "small" when we find that what we thought was a mouse was a rat, so "bad" may change to "good" when we consider a certain book of philosophy first as a book on philosophy and then as a soporific.'

The same can be said of 'equality' or 'equal' when applied to human beings and the application to them of the law. They are also words which, in the Geach and Foot sense, are attributive expressions. The expression that person A 'is equal' to person B is on its own meaningless. Something has to be added to 'equal' to give it meaning. It must be 'equal' *with respect to* something else. The argument throughout is that this *something else* is 'dignity' as meaning 'human worth' ('*Menschenwürde*' in German, 'menswaardigheid' in Afrikaans). Thus human dignity is the *criterion of reference or attribution* for equality (and non-equality) in the law.

If my contention is correct, namely that 'equal', 'equality' and similar expressions are attributive words or expressions in the Geach and Foot sense, then the real debate should centre upon the question '*in what respects* are all human beings equal', 'in *what respect*s should all human beings be treated equally' and '*in what respects* may human beings not be treated unequally'. Those who would reject 'human worth' as the 'attribute' of human equality, ought at least to come up with an alternative attribute.

Inasmuch as I contend that human worth (dignity) constitutes the criterion of attribution in relation to matters of equality and non-discrimination, and before dealing with the jurisprudence on the topic, it is incumbent on me to give some indication of what I understand by human dignity (worth). While s 10 of the Constitution powerfully proclaims that everyone 'has inherent dignity' and has 'the right to have their dignity respected and protected', nothing further is said as to what 'inherent dignity' or 'dignity' means. Human dignity (worth) constitutes a crucial criterion of reference and attribution in the particular understanding of equality and non-discrimination that I seek to defend in this book. It is dealt with extensively later, so I shall indicate here, briefly and without further elaboration, the understanding of dignity (human worth) that I seek to defend and employ.

I suggest that *the human worth (dignity) of each and every person is the capacity for and the right to respect as a human being. This arises from all those aspects of the human personality that flow from human intellectual and moral capacity; which in turn separate humans from the impersonality of nature, enables them to exercise their own judgment, to have self-awareness and a sense of self-worth, to exercise self-determination, to shape themselves and nature, to develop their personalities and to strive for self-fulfilment in their lives. It also arises from the capacity of human beings to enter into meaningful relationships with others and thereby achieve self-fulfilment at least in part.*

With certain additions of my own, this description has been modelled very closely on the widely accepted German formulation by the distinguished constitutional law scholar Professor Günther Dürig (1956: 125):[13]

> 'Each and every human being is a human being by virtue of his or her intellect ["*kraft seines Geistes*"] which serves to separate them from the impersonality of nature and enables them to exercise their own judgment, to have self-awareness, to exercise self-determination and to shape themselves and nature.'[14] (My translation.)[15]

Böckenförde (2006: 382) rightly stresses that Dürig was inspired by the human image and ethos — for 'how', as Böckenförde rhetorically enquires, 'can human dignity be concretized without an image of the human being?' and then quotes with implicit approval (381) Dürig's above formulation.

I have somewhat broadened Dürig's description by introducing the *desire for self-fulfilment*, and by adding the individual's *own sense of self-worth*, as components of human personality and dignity. The second of these further components arises from the fact that when a person is dealt with in a demeaning way, by someone in the exercise of power — whether public or private — the observer can actually experience the impairment of the victim's sense of self-worth.[16] Criticism of another provides a

---

[13] Often cited as the classic description of human dignity (worth). See the tributes on Dürig's death, in 1996, by Prof Peter Häberle (1997) and Prof Walter Glaeser (1997).

[14] '*Jeder Mensch ist Mensch kraft seines Geistes, der ihn abhebt von der unpersönlichen Natur und ihn aus eigener Entscheidung dazu befähigt, seiner selbst bewußt zu werden, sich selbst zu bestimmen und sich und die Umwelt zu gestalten.*'

For a discussion of Dürig's formulation see Böckenförde (2006: 381–382); Enders (1997: 10–13), Häberle (2004: §22, Rn 38–43) and Isensee (2006: 185–187).

Dürig (1956: 125) introduces this formulation by pointing out that the normative constitutional stipulation in Art 1(1) of the German Basic Law, that human dignity (worth) is untouchable, contains a value statement that is based upon an assessment of a particular practical reality, one that 'is' (exists) independently from space and time and 'shall be' brought to reality by the law. This practical reality is the nature of human beings as set out in the above quotation.

[15] Unless otherwise stated, all German sources that are quoted in English will be translations by myself from the German. To have reproduced in parallel the German text of each quotation would have added unduly to the volume of this book.

[16] For this perspective I am indebted to my son, Lourens W Ackermann, who expressed it in a note to me as follows:

> 'You know my own views on the use of reason as the basis for moral imperatives so I won't repeat them. My notion of dignity, as of rights, is one of 'negative capability'. This accords also with the historical process by which the concept became currency. What I mean by this is that the moral imagination though capable of appreciating dignity as splendid, say for example in the words of the Bard 'what a piece of work is man, how noble in reason, how infinite in faculties, in form and movement how express, in appreciation how like an angel' ... it was not this positive affirmation that gave rise to rights talk. It was the moral imagination engaged in empathy for suffering. I find it therefore more useful, and perhaps more accurate to refer to human dignity as that which triggers our conscience when we look into the eyes of a person whose dignity is being abused.'

See also Wood (1999) 74:

subtle example. No matter how objectively justified the content of criticism might be, if it is delivered in an insulting or demeaning way, it could still unlawfully impair the victim's legitimate *sense* and *experience* of self-worth as a human being. It is also implicit in the description of human dignity (worth) here proffered that human beings are also able, in a unique way and for a variety of unique reasons, to enter into relationships with other human beings. One might call this the 'relationality' aspect of human dignity. Thus the human being is capable of entering into the most intimate of personal relationships and, radiating out from these, relationships in ever-expanding contexts, from the small family group to the circle of friends, to cultural association (in a variety of forms), to civic association, and even further. Relationality assists, and in some cases enables, human beings to develop a sense of self-worth, to shape themselves, to develop their personalities and to strive for self-fulfilment. The rights relating to relationality are recognised in the South African Constitution[17] and have been referred to by the Constitutional Court in the *Second Certification* case[18] as the 'associational individual rights' of the Constitution,[19] the Court characterising rights of this nature as 'those rights which cannot be fully or properly exercised by individuals otherwise than in association with others of like disposition'.[20] While I would, for the sake of descriptive convenience, limit the concept of 'relationality' to human beings, human beings also — in a certain sense — have a 'relationship' with the environment, which in a variety of ways is essential for human dignity. In the most immediate sense it is essential for basic sustenance, without which human dignity is impossible, but also in many more subtle ways for the shaping and development of human personality.[21]

For human dignity to flourish certain basic physical needs have to be met.[22] While falling outside the purview of the present work it will be interesting to see

> 'The desire to be rational can arise only in consequence of the practically effective recognition of reasons that are already there.
>
> The ground of these reasons consists in a rational being's conception of its *self-worth*.'

Wolfgang Huber (1996) 10, the former Lutheran Bishop of Berlin, expresses a similar idea:

> 'Yet those whose dignity has been disregarded or even trampled on know full well what human dignity means. Its meaning is established by the denial of it. Human dignity attains an indisputable obviousness from the massive government attacks on the life, liberty and integrity of innumerable human beings.'

I remember, many years ago in Pretoria, watching two young white louts — in an act of racism — all but physically shove a black father and his son, who was about twelve years of age, from the pavement into the street. The black father did not protest. Apart from the obvious immediate assault on his dignity, I wondered to myself how the father's sense of self-worth would be further (and perhaps even more harshly) impugned, if the young son were to ask his father how two young men could treat him in this way. Our sense of ourselves is an indispensable part of our humanity, of 'being' a 'human being'.

17 For example in ss 15(2), 17, 18, 19, 23, 29(3), 30, 31.

18 Above, n 6.

19 Id paras 22–27.

20 Id para 24.

21 Rights to the environment are guaranteed by s 24 of the 1996 Constitution.

22 Accordingly certain rights to housing, health care, food, water and social security are formulated and guaranteed by ss 26 and 27 of the 1996 Constitution.

whether, and to what extent, horizontal operation is given to the environmental and socio-economic rights in the Constitution. While it has been assumed by some that these rights only have vertical operation, scholars are beginning seriously to question this.[23]

In seeking to describe human dignity — here as well as in other chapters — I deliberately refrain from using the word *definition*, since this conveys the idea of having neatly and comprehensively captured all the essential components of a concept. As German jurisprudence makes plain, the meaning or content of human worth cannot be fully captured at one given moment. Our understanding of human dignity will be extended as our knowledge of the human being increases, and as we view the human being in the context of the development of the modern natural sciences. The developments so rapidly taking place in the genetic, embryo, stem-cell and similar branches of the biological sciences will constantly challenge us to reflect on our understanding of the human being and her protection. In what follows an attempt will be made to explain, develop and justify this view. In this process it will be seen that aspects of human dignity sometimes manifest themselves negatively, ie by their denial, a phenomenon commented on by German scholars.[24]

There is, in my view, a proper appreciation, albeit mostly implicitly, of this so-called logico-grammatical problem with regard to equality in the Abrahamic religious writings and in secular philosophy, and just as importantly there is the explicit recognition that human worth (dignity) — or something closely resembling it — is the necessary criterion of attribution when considering issues of equality. Not only do these religious and secular philosophical views, as part of the general history of ideas, inform the legal meaning of equality and human worth, but they quite independently form part of an 'overlapping consensus' in the sense that the political philosopher John Rawls uses this concept, as more fully explained in section 2.4 below. An overlapping consensus of this nature can be constituted although different premises are used by different people to reach the same conclusion, in our case the same legal conclusion regarding dignity and equality.

2.3 THE LEGAL RELEVANCE OF THE THEOLOGICAL AND PHILOSOPHICAL ROOTS OF HUMAN LEGAL EQUALITY AND DIGNITY, FOR CONSTITUTIONAL INTERPRETATION

The investigation of certain theological and secular philosophical roots of dignity, equality before the law and non-discrimination may be criticised on the basis that they constitute no more than an irrelevant history of certain ideas. I have indeed

[23] See, for example, Liebenberg (2010: 317ff), and Pieterse (2007) and (2009).

[24] Huber (1996:10) and Böckenförde (2006: 382).

deliberately tried to follow the historical development of certain ideas, however briefly and selectively. To this part of the charge I therefore happily plead guilty.

I deny, however, the allegation of irrelevance. It is for the courts, and ultimately the Constitutional Court, to say what the provisions of the Constitution mean. I would imagine that many judges, at some time or other, secretly covet the wish that the judicial interpretation of constitutional provisions could take place with no interpretative tool other than the express provisions of the Constitution in question. This is, of course, impossible, but the desire is not necessarily an ignoble one. Properly modest and prudent judges are rightly anxious not to trespass outside their proper constitutional role of *interpreting* 'the' Constitution and 'its' provisions. It is after all not the subjective ideas and beliefs of judges that should guide the meaning of the Constitution. The properly modest and prudent judge has the understandable desire, though one impossible to fulfil, of finding something objective 'out there' that will reliably guide the interpretative exercise. This, I repeat, is not necessarily a foolish wish. The judge ought to see her role as the servant of the Constitution, and not its ruler. She is anxious not to obtrude her subjective ideas and prejudices on the Constitution. She is acutely aware that we are living in a constitutional age when no one, not even a monarch, can claim that 'the law is me' (*'le loi c'est moi'*[25]). The judge may not rule by *ipse dixit*, she may not simply declare that her word, by utterance alone, constitutes the law. What she says must *reflect* the law. In reality it is, of course, impossible to seek constitutional truth in so disembodied a way. It is always a human individual carrying on a dialogue with the constitutional text. As Gadamer (1989: 387) puts it: '[O]ne partner in the hermeneutical conversation, the text, speaks only through the interpreter. Only through him are the written marks changed back into meaning.' The text always speaks to an individual human being whose mind is not a clean slate when 'hearing' and responding to the text. The judge's slate contains the history of her own ideas through which the constitutional text filters. The influence of a filter like this cannot be avoided. At best the interpreter can remain aware at all times of her own history of ideas when seeking to apply 'objectively' the conventional interpretative tools. One of the most important of these tools is of course the purpose of the particular constitutional provision, determined in the context of the Constitution as a whole and *its* overall purpose.

It should be self-evident that in order to determine this purpose, history cannot be excluded. On the contrary, without considering history it would be impossible to ascertain this purpose with any pretence of objectivity or certainty. It is impossible, I argue, to determine properly the purpose of s 9 of the Constitution without delving further back and determining the history of concepts and ideas such as equality, equality before the law, and non-discrimination. This history must include not only the secular history and development, but also the theological

[25] Attributed to Louis XIV.

— in the context of the so-called Abrahamic religions — because theological ideas have had their influence on philosophical and even constitutional concepts. I stress that, in considering theological views, I do not, for purposes of this book, claim for them any higher or greater authority than for secular philosophical views. The aim is to pursue as broad an 'overlapping consensus'[26] as possible.

An important part of the history alluded to is the way ideas and concepts such as these have been used and developed in other 'open and democratic societ[ies] based on human dignity, equality and freedom,'[27] particularly when this use and development has been in relation to constitutional provisions clearly used as models for similar provisions in our own Constitution.[28]

While there are other important justifications — alluded to below — for applying a comparative constitutional methodology, the historical approach I have just referred to is another reason why comparative law can be so useful in attempting to understand our own Constitution.

At the risk of tedious repetition it needs to be stressed (again) that the pursuit of certain theological and philosophical ideas is not an attempt to *be* a theologian or a philosopher, or to be *doing* theology or philosophy, or to be constructing a theological or philosophical *system*. It is no more than an attempt to find normative guidance on certain issues from related disciplines, as judges have been doing — consciously or unconsciously, expressly or implicitly — for centuries. Whether one likes it or not, our Constitution, among other things, embodies an objective normative value system, quite apart from the rights it enshrines. As was held in the *Carmichele* case:[29]

> '*Our Constitution* is not merely a formal document regulating public power. It also *embodies*, like the German Constitution, *an objective, normative value system*. As was stated by the German Federal Constitutional Court:
>
> > "The jurisprudence of the Federal Constitutional Court is consistently to the effect that the basic right norms contain not only defensive subjective rights for the individual but embody at the same time an objective value system which, as a fundamental constitutional value for all areas of the law, acts as a guiding principle and stimulus for the legislature, executive and judiciary."
>
> The same is true of our Constitution.' (Emphasis supplied, internal footnotes omitted.)

Yet the Constitution is not a detailed and comprehensive code, spelling out elaborately and minutely the full content of these rights and values. The Constitution does not itself interpret these rights and values. This is left to the

[26] See the work of John Rawls referred to below.

[27] See n 7 above.

[28] For the substantial influence that the German Basic Law has had on the constitutional provisions in our own constitutions, see for example Johan de Waal (1995) in his article 'A comparative analysis of the provisions of German origin in the Interim Bill of Rights'.

[29] *Carmichele v The Minister of Safety and Security and the Minister of Justice and Constitutional Development* 2001 (4) SA 938 (CC) (2001 (10) BCLR 995) para 54.

judicial interpreter. The interpreter is not the Constitution speaking, but a human being seeking to give meaning to a non-comprehensive text. Part of this task is to determine the purpose of the text. Aspects of this purpose emerge (though never fully) from the text itself and from the historical setting preceding the particular text in question. But it goes further than this. Particularly since the Second World War there has been a steady move, by means of international, regional and domestic instruments to better protect human beings from the excesses of public power and even, in certain cases, from the excesses of their fellow citizens. These instruments have not, it is true, always met with the success envisaged. Yet few would wish to denigrate the validity of the aspirations pursued. Our Constitution forms part of this international enterprise. This is, in my view, clear from the nature of the rights protected therein and the way the rights have been formulated. Nowhere is this purpose more evident than the fact that courts, in seeking to establish the limits of rights, are obliged by s 36 to have regard to rights dispensations in other 'open and democratic societ[ies] based on human dignity, equality and freedom'. It is accordingly both important and necessary, when considering the nature and extent of rights and values under our own Constitution, to have regard to the way these rights and values have developed historically, not merely as a direct background to our own Constitution, but also in a broader international sense. In referring to theology and secular philosophy one seeks to paint a broader picture; one attempts to show how certain theological and secular philosophical *values* have influenced constitutional rights and values, and may still influence them. The purpose is not to construct a system, whether theological or philosophical, but to find values that might be widely shared, albeit for different reasons. In this regard the Kantian scholar Professor Christine M Korsgaard[30] (1996: 335) observes that

> '[i]n recent years philosophers have welcomed the development of a widespread interest in philosophical ethics. In their concern about the bewildering ethical questions generated by medical technology, legal practice, and the power and responsibility of the modern corporation, members of the professions and of the public have turned to philosophy, traditional repository of rigorous moral thought. This concern has provided philosophers with an opportunity to show that our subject is important and useful, and that we have knowledge on which others might draw.'

This book attempts to draw on this knowledge. Korsgaard further observes that the gap between traditional ethical philosophy and the solution of ethical problems might also be due to the fact that 'we have not thought enough yet about what sort of activity "applying" an ethical theory is'.

[30] The Arthur Kingsley Porter Professor of Philosophy in Harvard University.

2.4 THE USE OF RELIGIOUS VALUES AND VIEWS

At the outset it is necessary to acknowledge the difficulty of trying to separate neatly the treatment of human worth (dignity) from that of equality. In certain theological writings (as in certain philosophical writings) these concepts are intertwined, and often human dignity is used to explain or define equality. This is hardly surprising if one of the fundamental contentions in this book is correct, namely that 'equality', in concepts such as 'equal protection and benefit of the law' and, as correlative, unlawful 'unequal treatment' (unfair discrimination) relate directly and inextricably to whether treatment by the law does, or does not, impact negatively on the human dignity of persons. Differently stated, this intertwining in fact demonstrates that human dignity is the *criterion of reference* or the *criterion of attribution* essential to the understanding of equality.

My motive for dealing with certain theological views in the so-called Abrahamic religions[31] is in order to show how these ideas have influenced the development of closely related secular concepts concerning human dignity and have given meaning to the legal development of equality and other fundamental rights. It is also part of traditional African religion to accord human beings a dignity and I shall allude briefly thereto in s 2.9(l) below when discussing the sub-Saharan indigenous concept of *ubuntu*.

The Dutch jurist (and theologian) Hugo de Groot (Grotius), contended that fundamental principles of law and morality would have binding force — *etsi Deus non daretur* — as if (even if) God did not exist. In his powerful and challenging work *On Human Worth: A Christian Vindication of Equality*, theologian Duncan Forrester (2001: 51) points out, with regard to these views of De Groot, that they do not constitute atheism or even what has been called 'methodological atheism', but rather

> 'the simple recognition that a common morality is necessary for people to flourish together in community, and this cannot rest any longer on the foundation of Christian theology because of the bitter religious fragmentation in Europe.... But natural law continued, according to Grotius, to rest on the existence of an objective cosmic moral order.'

Theology cannot simply be ignored in tracing the history of secular ideas. It has both hindered — as in the case of apartheid theology — and helped the recognition of human dignity. In referring to theological views in this book they are considered as sociological and historical phenomena in the course of the human race's intellectual and ethical development. They are referred to, at the very least, as ethical values that have featured in human self-reflection for many

---

[31] According to Douglas et al (1962: 7), Judaism, Christianity and Islam all perceive Abraham as playing a unique roll as a great prophet and recipient of the divine covenant. Metzger and Coogan (1993: 5) believe that 'Abraham is to be looked to as a source of unity and harmony rather than dissent among Jews, Christians and Muslims'.

ages and are open to rational enquiry. Professor Isensee (2006: 218) concludes the English summary of his article[32] in similar vein:

> 'Christendom has prepared the ground for the modern constitutional state. The latter does not embrace the religious rationale for the Christian doctrine of dignity, but only its secular-ethical conclusions. From these the concepts of human dignity, attributed to every human's personality and a precondition to all positive law, derives substance and contour: each person's status of liberty and responsibility, equality, universal claim to respect and his obligation to show solidarity. In that, Christian tradition forms the source of a constitutional theory that is in accordance with the secular concept of human dignity as embraced by the German basic law.'

The political philosopher John Rawls (1973: 387) developed a concept of 'overlapping consensus' which, although expressed in the context of civil disobedience, is of general import and relevant to the use of theological ethics. His assumption is that in a nearly just society there is a public acceptance of the same principles of justice and although there can be considerable difference in citizens' conception of justice this does not matter, provided that these conceptions lead to similar political judgments. All this is possible, Rawls says, since 'different premises can yield the same conclusion. In this case there exists what we may refer to as overlapping rather than strict consensus.'

This idea is discussed more fully in Rawls (1993: 133–172) where the following is stated (1993: 147) regarding this overlapping consensus:

> 'All those who affirm the political conception start from within their own comprehensive view and draw on the religious, philosophical, and moral grounds it provides. The fact that people affirm the same political conception on these grounds does not make their affirming it less religious, philosophical, or moral, as the case may be, since the grounds sincerely held determine the nature of their affirmation.'

In the present context these views are understood to mean that in order to build a universal consensus on the nature of human worth and the understanding of equality as meaning equality of human worth (human worth being beyond price), it is legitimate to refer to religious views despite the fact that some would not accept their relevance or persuasiveness, but would reach the same conclusion via a line of secular reasoning. It is for this reason also that theological perspectives are relevant in a discussion of constitutional values and rights in a constitutional state. In our Constitution the right to and the value of human dignity are not further elaborated in the text; neither is this the case regarding the right and concept of equality, despite the listed examples of unfair discrimination in s 9(3). Full content must be given them by judicial interpretation of the Constitution. The best and most legitimate way of doing so is by appealing to values that

---

[32] The German title of which can be translated into English as 'Human dignity: Secular society in search of the absolute'.

command universal respect whether derived from religious or secular ethics or cultural norms.

In this regard the following passage from the last pages of John Locke's *The Reasonableness of Christianity*, as quoted by Roger Ruston (2004: 287), is particularly apt:

> 'He that travels the roads now, applauds his own strength and legs that have carried him so far in such a scantling of time, and ascribes all to his own vigour, little considering how much he owes to their pains, who cleared the woods, drained the bogs, built the bridges, and made the ways passable; without which he might have toiled much with little progress. A great many things which we have been bred up in the belief of, from our cradles ... we take for unquestionable truths, obvious truths, and easily demonstrable; without considering how long we might have been in doubt or ignorance of them, had revelation been silent.... *It is no diminishing to revelation that reason gives its suffrage too to the truths revelation has discovered.* But it is our mistake to think that because reason confirms them to us, we had the first certain knowledge of them from thence; and in that clear evidence we now possess them.'

Forrester (2001: 249–250) points out that modern secular discussions of equality 'rarely relate seriously to the history or roots of the conviction — dare one say "faith"? — that *human beings are of equal worth* ...'. In this context American philosopher Louis Pojman (1997: 296)[33] pithily adds:

> 'The question is whether the kind of democratic ideals that egalitarianism espouses can do without a religious tradition. If it cannot, then egalitarians may be living off the borrowed interest of a religious metaphysic, which (in their eyes) has gone bankrupt. The question is: Where is the capital?'

Referring to the British economic historian RH Tawney (1964), Forrester (2001: 46) observes that for Tawney the ultimate ground for human equality, which is sometimes concealed and sometimes secularised so that all specific theological reference is removed, goes something like this:

> 'God affirms the infinite worth of each person, independently of the individual's qualities and achievements, and God wills and establishes fellowship which expresses and bears witness to God's equal love for all.'

Forrester (2001: 47) argues that for all the problems of allowing religion a voice in the public forum in a pluralistic modern society, religion does offer a way of relating the values and principles of the social order to an objective moral order. Moreover, Forrester believes that 'something of this sort is surely necessary if we are able to stand at the gates of Auschwitz, or in Rwanda, or in Pol Pot's Kampuchea and say in a totally unqualified way: "What happened here was radically evil."'

[33] As quoted by Forrester (2001: 250).

Forrester (2001: 48) maintains that theology is, in a sense, a theory, that operates beyond a particular tradition of faith. The boundaries between theology and secular theory are not always clear, and even when they appear to be well demarcated, the frontiers are porous and '[l]ike some more secular theories, theology can, and sometimes does, light up what is really happening, and issues an insistent call to action'. He does recognise, of course, that much theology justifies oppression.

In its preamble, the American Declaration of Independence of 1776 unselfconsciously proclaims that certain truths are held to be self-evident, namely 'that all men are created equal, and that they are endowed by their Creator with certain inalienable rights, that among these are Life, Liberty and the Pursuit of Happiness'.

As Forrester (2001: 56) points out, the Declaration at this point is 'saturated with theological language' and suggests that the 'ultimate and only ground for equality ... lies in the will of the creator God'.

Although there might be many conceptions of equality that influence American thinking, George P Fletcher (1999: 1613–1614), a professor of jurisprudence, maintains that Americans 'also have a distinctive theological foundation for our commitment to equality'. He therefore finds it a strange feature of American political theory that 'committed egalitarians totally ignore the theological foundations of American thinking about equality and write as though the religious views of the world were totally irrelevant to their egalitarian projects'. Fletcher is not overly concerned with this disregard because 'if there is indeed a strong conceptual connection between Western religious thought and the principle of human equality, that connection can persist as a background philosophical assumption, even though we no longer refer to the arguments that lead us to regard the assumption as self-evident'. Fletcher (1999: 1611–1612), further contends that at the very least a clear subsidiary meaning of the 1776 Declaration of Independence was that 'all individuals are equal in the sight of God' did emerge. This is confirmed by Abraham Lincoln's Gettysburg Address of 1863 and, nearly a century later, by Martin Luther King's classic speech.[34]

Legal philosopher Jeremy Waldron (1993: 846–847) argues that in a number of ways the Christian conception out of which modern liberalism originated remains richer and deeper than their secular offspring and that '[w]e might reasonably expect to find further clues to a rich and adequate conception of

[34] 'I still have a dream ... that one day this nation will rise up and live out the true meaning of its creed — *we hold these truths to be self-evident, that all men are created equal.* I have a dream that one day on the red hills of Georgia, sons of former slaves and sons of former slave-owners will be able to sit down together at the table of brotherhood.'

persons, equality, justice, and rights in what is currently made of the Christian-centred tradition by those who remain centered in Christ'.[35]

German constitutional law scholars are not reluctant to acknowledge the theological origins of the legal concept of equality, and refer in this regard to the *imago Dei* concept, namely that all human beings are created in the image of God and must thereof reflect this image equally.[36] Professor Peter Häberle (2008: 17ff) unashamedly adopts an interdisciplinary approach (including the theological) in his work on the human image in the constitutional state.

The Abrahamic religions tend to understand human equality and human worth (dignity) as being rooted in the fact that every human being is an image and reflection of the Divine Being, and accordingly has priceless and incomparable dignity. For this reason every human being is in essence equal to every other human being in *image* and *humanity*, hence in dignity. Certainly in Christianity, and possibly also in the other Abrahamic religions, there is a further but closely related grounding of human dignity in the creation account. This further ground is the single origin of human beings as created by God; hence all human beings constitute one family and are brothers/sisters under God (the creator) and before each other. The idea of all human beings being neighbours is but another version of being siblings. The so-called Golden Rule may also be an expression of this idea of common/equal worth and dignity.[37] This rule is formulated positively as the injunction to 'do unto others as you would have them do unto you' (Matthew 7:12) or negatively by the prohibition 'not to do unto others what you would not wish them to do unto you'. There are connections and similarities with regard to it in Hellenistic ethics, Judaism and Confucianism.[38]

I turn to deal next with the understanding of human worth (dignity) and equality in the Abrahamic religions, from the historically oldest to the youngest (Judaism, Christianity and Islam). There is a common thread linking them, namely the relationship of the individual with the creator God and the unique status conferred on the individual through this Godly creation. It is hoped that this theological investigation will contribute to establishing a solid 'overlapping consensus' with regard to the understanding of dignity and equality.

It also needs to be emphasised that religious institutions have not always, in practice, lived out what they have taught or professed. Thus, speaking for the moment only of the Christian religion, we have the example of the Crusades

---

[35] See also Waldron (2002) for an in-depth treatment of the Christian foundations in John Locke's political thought.

[36] For example, German legal scholar Paul Kirchhof (2000: Rn 49) makes no bones about asserting:

> 'The fundamental idea of equality, according to which every person lays equal claim to inner worth and personality as being already founded in the law, finds its origin in Christianity. Christian ethics derives its regulating principle from the conception of the original equality of all who bear the human image. Every person is "the image of God"'.

[37] See Huber (1996: 28) below in my discussion of Christianity.

[38] Ted Honderich (ed) (1995: 321).

where fundamental Christian teachings were simply jettisoned. Nearer home we have the example of apartheid theology which sought to justify the separation of human beings, even at communion, on the basis of so-called Christian theological principles. The prohibition on women from attaining clerical status in certain Christian denominations is another example. The same is true of other religions. The practitioners of religion do not cease being human beings, with all the fallibility that this implies. As Isaiah Berlin's favourite quotation from Kant [AK 8:23] goes, 'Out of timber so crooked as that from which man is made nothing entirely straight can be built'.[39] But the fallibility of humanity is not a logical reason for discarding *truths* expounded by fallible human beings.

2.5 JUDAISM

In both the Judaic and Christian defences of dignity and equality particular reliance is generally placed on the so-called 'priestly' creation narrative in Genesis 1: 26–27. Verse 27 reads:

> 'So God created humankind in his image, in the image of God he created them; male and female he created them.'

This is prefaced by verse 26 as follows:

> 'Then God said, "Let us make humankind in our image, according to our own likeness; and let them have dominium over the fish of the sea, and over the birds of the air, and over the cattle, and over all the wild animals of the earth, and over every creeping thing that creeps upon the earth."'[40]

Since all human beings are made in the image of God then their worth (dignity) must be absolute, because the image of the infinite is reflected. Furthermore, since all human beings reflect this infinite image, it must follow that all human beings individually have an image (worth) that cannot be qualitatively or quantitatively distinguished from that of any other human being, and therefore all human beings are equal with respect to their own image (worth/dignity).

Rabbi Dr Daniel Polish (1982: 41) explains that respect for the 'sanctity of the individual', which thus grows out of a proper understanding of the Genesis account, is 'fundamental to the Jewish world view'. Two cardinal principles emerge: the sovereignty of God and the sacredness of the individual. The second 'motif' is

> 'underscored by the phrase, "the image of God". Genesis teaches that human beings carry the divine stamp. Each should be treated with the dignity attendant to that station'.

---

[39] Berlin (1990: v).

[40] Genesis 1:26, 27 as rendered in the The New Revised Standard Version of the Bible.

The late Rabbi Emanuel Rackman (1997: 154–155), of Yeshiva University, explains that while Biblical Hebrew has no word for 'equality,' the idea of equality before the law, according to Judaism, is divinely ordained. He points out that, even at creation 'did He [God] will human equality as a fact' and that Judaism holds 'that God endows all humans with His image — the *Tselem Elohim*'.

Professor Emeritus Yehoshua Arieli (2002: 7–8) of the Hebrew University of Jerusalem contends that the Enlightenment's philosophy of the human being was 'clearly based on a deistic or theistic worldview, and derived ultimately from a humanistic and secularizing reinterpretation of the fundamental beliefs of Jewish-Christian monotheism'. He also correctly points out that the Universal Declaration of Human Rights, embracing all people and cultures, had of necessity to avoid theological language in justifying the fundamental values enshrined therein. This justification 'is therefore defined in the meta-language of a universal secular order, which is capable of addressing the community of nations and cultures in the neutral terms of secularity'. Arieli moreover sees in the Universal Declaration the link between 'inherent dignity' and 'equal rights':

> 'It is the concept and term of "the inherent Dignity" [in the Universal Declaration] that carries the whole burden of being the fountainhead from which the equal rights of man follow which leads one back to the deistic or theistic world-view.'

According to Arieli (2002: 9) the expression 'the inherent dignity of man' defines the ontological status of human beings which derives ultimately 'from the fundamental conception of the West created by the fusion of Jewish-Christian monotheism with those derived from classical and humanistic conceptions of man'.

Yair Lorberbaum (2002: 55) of the University of Bar-Ilan Faculty of Law also relies on the *imago Dei*. According to him the roots of *imago Dei* are to be found in Mesopotamia and perhaps even in Egypt. Describing the many interpretations of the concept of *imago Dei*, Loberbaum (2002: 56) points out that all interpretations of the concept of the *imago Dei* share the assumption that 'there is a divine "spark"' as it were, in human beings, which 'establishes man's humanity and grants him unique status among the creatures in God's creation, or in other words, his dignity'. This concept of the divine also provides, in Loberbaum's view, the basis for the equality in principle among human beings, 'for all are in the image of God'. In this view human dignity, through the *imago Dei* creation account, clearly constitutes the attributive criterion for equality. In similar vein is the writing of the Chief Rabbi of South Africa, Dr Warren Goldstein (2006: 27–34) who uses the *imago Dei* account of creation to conclude that the human being has a 'God-given soul' and that it is this soul 'that invests a person with significance and greatness'.

2.6 CHRISTIANITY

Dr M Douglas Meeks, Professor of Theology in Vanderbilt University, points out (1984: x–xi) that from the perspective of the biblical testimonies human rights are grounded in God's creation of the human being in God's image.

German theologian Jürgen Moltmann (1984: 23), also emphasising that fundamental human rights all grow out of dignity and not the other way round, explains *fundamental* human rights as meaning

> 'those rights and duties which belong essentially to what it means to be truly human, because without their being fully acknowledged and exercised human beings cannot fulfil their original destiny of having been created in the image of God'

and points out that

> '[e]conomy, society and the state have to respect this dignity and responsibility of human beings, for their role as human beings, with rights and duties, comes before any constituting of society and government ... [h]uman beings do not exist for the sake of rule; rule, rather, exists for the sake of human beings'.

He also refers (1984: 11) to the key sentence in the 1974 declaration of the Roman Synod of Bishops to the effect that '[t]he dignity of man has its roots in the fact that every human being is an image and reflection of God. As a result of this all men are equal with one another in their essence', and to the comprehensive Reformed Theological Basis, which according to Moltmann — 'saw the dignity of the human in his or her being in God's image, and unfolding this being in God's image in its important dimensions'.

Wolfgang Huber (1996: 9) the former Lutheran Bishop of Berlin,[41] states quite simply that for Christians 'the confession of the dignity and value of human beings is anchored in the insight that all human beings are created in the image of God'. He also points out that the enlightenment tradition 'renewed this concept of human dignity by considering rational human beings as those who must never be used simply as means toward an end, but rather must be acknowledged as ends in themselves'. While recognising that human dignity is a controversial concept, Huber (1996:10) makes the point that, notwithstanding any disagreements that might exist,

> 'those whose dignity has been disregarded or even trampled on know full well what human dignity means. Its meaning is established by the denial of it. Human dignity attains an indisputable obviousness from the massive government attacks on the life, liberty and integrity of innumerable human beings'.

He contends (1996: 28) that an elementary aspect of a universal ethic is

> 'the fact that I respect the dignity of the other just as much as I depend on respect from others for my own dignity.... In every exchange with an equal I am forced to grant the other

[41] And formerly Professor of Theology in the University of Heidelberg.

the freedom I myself have. Consequently I can never view others as merely means: I must acknowledge them as ends in themselves — that is precisely where the dignity of persons is found'.[42]

The idea that human beings should always be treated as ends in themselves and never merely as means is of course, as we shall see, central to the ethics of Immanuel Kant.

Stanley S Harakas (1982: 18), a Greek Orthodox priest and former professor of Orthodox ethics, expresses the Eastern Orthodox position as also being founded on the *imago Dei* creation concept. There is, he says, a 'common human dignity', a 'commonly shared human nature' and an 'essential and inalienable human equality'.

Duncan Forrester (2001) *On Human Worth: A Christian Vindication of Equality* provides a deep, insightful and consistent theological linking of human worth (dignity) with equality in its various aspects. Forrester (2001: 7) writes as a Christian practical theologian and it is implicit in his account that human dignity (arising from the *imago Dei* creation) is the criterion of attribution for equality because we are, despite our many 'temporal' differences, equal in our human dignity because we are all created in the image of the divine. He points out (2001: 30) that, at the heart of this theology

> '... lies the conviction that each person is of infinite, and hence equal, worth and should be treated as such.... To affirm human equality is both to say something important about what human beings are, and also how relationships and social institutions should be arranged, and how we should behave to one another'.

This also lies at the heart of his argument (2001: 30–31) that human beings are entitled to be treated with respect because they are 'of equal worth, independently of their ability, contribution, success, work or desert'. This is for him the bottom line and the justification and motive for 'generous and respectful treatment of people with severe disabilities, of the senile, and of the unemployable'.

Dealing with the tension between equality and freedom, Forrester (2001: 32) appreciates that a 'certain absolutist and fanatical search for an imposed equality of condition leads to the forfeiture of freedom', but urges that it has not been demonstrated that 'well-thought-through moves towards greater equality lead to [a] drastic erosion of freedom'. Most importantly he points out that it is only 'the draconian pursuit of sameness of condition to the exclusion of all regard for other social values' that involves 'the sacrifice of liberty to equality of a sort'. He points out that the case 'that equality necessarily involves an increase of freedom and capability has been powerfully argued in recent times by Amartya Sen'. Forrester (2001: 35–39) rejects equality which assumes 'a kind of extreme individualism,' but does not, however, reject individual equality in favour of

[42] Huber's concept of human dignity is of course clearly influenced by the writings of Kant, as will become clear in due course.

group or class equality. He argues that human beings cannot be fully understood except in terms of their relationships.

As far as 'equality of opportunity' is concerned, Forrester (2001: 37) distinguishes between equal opportunity as 'equal possibility of achieving the goal' and equal opportunity as 'demanding equal means for the achievement of the goal'. It is this latter form of understanding that Forrester suggests commands the widest support. He stresses (2001: 38) that '[e]ven the most talented of individuals do not "deserve" their success or the advantages of endowment or upbringing which makes that success possible'.

Forrester (2001: 45) rightly rejects the idea that equality is empirically based, for we have to 'find grounds for affirming the equality of people and of groups whose empirically observable qualities and characteristics are very different indeed'. This of course emphasises that equality of dignity is demanded.

Fletcher (1999: 1611–1612) argues that because of the *imago Dei* creation concept 'all individuals are of infinite human dignity (equal in being unbounded in value)' and therefore deserving of the same or equivalent treatment with respect to their dignity. This response, he says 'appeals to the German, liberal tradition drawing primarily on the moral philosophy of Immanuel Kant'. Fletcher recognises (1999: 1619) that the 'structure of Kant's thinking closely parallels the reasoning of Genesis' more particularly because of Kant's assertion that each human life has a dignity beyond price and because, according to Fletcher, Kant's idea of universal humanity 'functions as the secular analogue to the creation in the image of God'. The common image, for Fletcher (1999: 1618), is the equality of dignity. He contends (1999: 1619–1620) that there is 'no better case for equality than Shakespeare's art' and that the 'holistic sense of humanity' has nowhere been better captured than in Shylock's retort to Antonio's expression of contempt for him:

> 'And what's his reason? I am a Jew. Hath not a Jew eyes? hath not a Jew hands, organs, dimensions, senses, affections, passions? fed with the same food, hurt with the same weapons, subject to the same diseases, healed by the same means, warmed and cooled by the same winter and summer as a Christian is? If you prick us, do we not bleed? If you tickle us, do we not laugh? if you poison us do we not die? and if you wrong us, shall we not revenge?'[43]

Fletcher (1999: 1622) urges that this passage is effective precisely because 'it speaks in an image of a complex being.' It does not limit the quality of humanness by reducing it to a single feature that can be rejected or ignored. Rather 'it allows the humanity of the other to ease by our defences, as the wave breaks and flows past any barrier that we place in its way'. He warns us not to discard the methodology of images because we mistakenly believe it lacks precision and legal merit: 'We crave the scientific, the analytic, a litmus test for critical concepts. Nothing

[43] *The Merchant of Venice* Act III, scene 1, as quoted by Fletcher (1999).

could be further from the nature of the problem of recognizing and valuing humanity.'

The warning is a timely one. There are lawyers, referred to later, who are sceptical, and even dismissive, about the role of human worth in modern constitutional law and particularly in the shaping of equality. Human worth (dignity) cannot, it is true, be captured in a litmus test definition, precisely because of the complexity of humanity itself. Images help us to understand that — this complexity notwithstanding — our being human is holistic. The concept of human worth (dignity) is powerfully relational, for when we impugn the dignity of others we at the same time impugn our own. It is by looking into the eyes of someone suffering indignity that we are moved to identify the nature of the hurt and accept the challenge of relationality. Imagery forces us to face the other, literally to *imagine* the other, with whom we share equal humanity. In this process we better understand the content of our own humanity and the humanity of others.

In conclusion, it is necessary to sound a few cautionary remarks.[44] The implications of the monotheistic belief that human beings are created in the image of God are of course substantially wider than merely providing the source of human dignity and equality. The creation of human beings in the *imago Dei* places certain obligation on human beings, but the discharge of these obligations *does not constitute a condition precedent* to the enjoyment of the human status and the privileges flowing from being so created, nor to the exercise of the rights so accorded. Although created to subdue and have dominion over the earth and its resources, human beings have obligations. One obligation is to reproduce ourselves and to care for the resources that are the object of our rule. In this context Moltmann (1984: 23) points out that although fundamental rights grow out of dignity, duties arise out of human creation in order for human beings to fulfil 'their original destiny'. Huber (1996: 9) also refers to 'our responsibility to the dignity shared by all human beings'. Apart from being obliged to have fellowship with God, human beings are called upon to care for the weak and the needy. It is interesting to note how the German constitutional law scholar Prof Christian Starck (2005a: Rn 5), in his overview of the religious and more specifically the *imago Dei* roots of the concept of human dignity and equality, also draws attention to the obligations on all human beings flowing from their 'responsibility before God'.

Roger Ruston (2004), who worked closely on the Dominican Justice and Peace Commission, places creation in the image of God at the core of equality, inter alia between men and women, in his thoughtful and challenging work *Human Rights and the Image of God*. For him, (2004: 34–35) equality means equality

[44] I am particularly indebted to Prof Michael Welker of the University of Heidelberg for the many important insights he has given me in this regard, and indeed regarding the theological basis for human dignity and equality.

of human dignity. However, creation in the image of God brings with it duties for the individual. Ruston (2004: 186), referring approvingly to the work of Bartholomé des Las Casas, points out that doctrines of the natural inferiority of women and the natural slavery of 'barbarians', 'were subverted by the Christian doctrine of the image of God, which introduced a radical and natural equality of status into their picture of human society'. However, Ruston comments:

> 'Central to Christianity's moral message is the subordination of the self to the good of others, which is not obviously served when individuals are encouraged to put their rights first. In a world where everyone is keen to assert their rights, duties, where they are remembered at all, tend to come a poor second.'

Nevertheless it must be pointed out that the argument of subordination, as ordained principle of creation, is the one that has from the beginning been used to vindicate the secondary status of women (and servants and slaves). This secondary status has also been made possible by neglect of the Golden Rule, in both its positive and negative formulations.

There is an eschatological[45] element to equality. It is not a natural given, but something to be achieved. Morals are indispensable for the human condition and the achievement of equality in part depends on the free yet creative withdrawal of oneself for the benefit of others.

For a fairly detailed discussion, by a German constitutional law scholar, of the Christian origins of human dignity and their impact on secular thinking, readers are referred to Isensee (2006: 199–209). The translated title of his article, 'Human dignity: Secular society in search of the absolute' gives an indication of his thesis that no successful search for the absolute can be uncoupled from its religious roots. I would suggest that this thesis is only partly true. One would not, of course, go so far as to suggest that a Kantian approach to human dignity can, at its very essence, *empirically prove* the existence of human dignity, for it calls at some stage for an acceptance of the reality of freedom. At the same time the religious acceptance of human dignity is based, essentially at least, on the *imago Dei*, the acceptance of which is itself an act of faith. I would not wish, however, to lose myself in an epistemological debate of this nature. At the very least the theological and the Kantian approaches do establish a broad overlapping consensus in the John Rawls sense, to which I have alluded. What Isensee (2006: 199–209) does helpfully do is trace the history of the secular adoption of the religious bases for the understanding of human dignity, from Pico della Mirandela onwards. As he argues (2006: 209): 'The absolute, that shines forth from human dignity [as envisaged in the GBL] is a reflection of the religious.' He also (2006: 208–209) expresses concern that

[45] The note in Metzger and Coogan (1993: 192) refers to 'eschatology' as '[t]he teaching concerning last things, such as the resurrection of the dead, the Last Judgment, the end of this world and the creation of a new one'.

> '[t]he reference to the sacred origins of the human dignity concept is denounced by the spirit of the age (*Zeitgeist*) as a malaise of fundamentalist theologising that makes the legal order dependent on religious truth, a sickness which discourse has contracted. *Christophobia* is at work here'.

This seems a rather severe denunciation. While it may be true of an extreme fringe view, I would not have thought it represented, in general, the sentiments of secular humanism. It has, however, been suggested that, in the USA, with its strict separation between church and state, strict neutrality is not maintained in legal debates between the non-secular and the secular (the religious and the non-religious) and that in fact a preferential position is given to the secular. Whether this is true I am not equipped to say, but certainly in South Africa under the 1996 Constitution, a strict neutrality is maintained between these positions. [46]

The essays in Soulen and Woodhead (eds) (2006) focus on two specific challenges to human dignity in contemporary culture and society. The first is the various ways in which it is being threatened — for example by globalisation, biotechnology, representations of race and gender, death, severe handicap and political organisation. The second is the danger the concept faces because it 'has suffered a kind of inflation through undisciplined use to the point where its value is endangered'. (Soulen and Woodward (eds) (2006: 2).) This is similar to the fears expressed in the context of German constitutional law by Isensee (2006: 187–199).[47]

The guiding idea for Dr Wolfgang Huber's reflections on a Christian ethic for pluralistic societies (2010),[48] is the *dignity of the different* — not, it should be noted, the dignity of *difference*. The Christian understanding of the human person is based on the conviction that all human beings are created in the image of God, as creatures corresponding to God, as responsive and responsible selves. They are ends in themselves and not merely means to alien purposes. That is what human dignity is all about.

It is often stressed that every understanding of human dignity has to be inclusive. Huber (2010) maintains that the term 'dignity' itself is taken seriously only when it applies to all human beings equally, and that Jürgen Habermas, among others, emphasises that this egalitarian universalism is a specific contribution of Judeo-Christian thinking to modernity.

However, Huber (2010) contends, as important as this emphasis on the equal dignity of all human beings is, it must be understood as being concerned with the equal dignity of the different. Human beings have to respect and to love, to protect

[46] See Farlam (2007: Ch. 41.17), Currie and De Waal (2005: 336–338), *S v Lawrence; S v Negal; S v Solberg* 1997 (4) SA 1176 (CC) (1997 (10) BCLR 1348) paras 92–105 and compare, for example, the *First Certification judgment* above n 6 paras 203–204.

[47] Referred to more fully in Chapter 3, section 3.4 below.

[48] Huber (2010), presented in preliminary form in a paper delivered at the Stellenbosch Institute for Advanced Study on 4 March 2010.

and to promote one another in their otherness. Respect for the uniqueness of the other is at the core of respect for his or her dignity. Only under these auspices can we see human dignity as a guiding principle for a radically pluralistic, namely a multi-individual society.

In 2002 Sir Jonathan Sacks, the Chief Rabbi of the United Hebrew Congregations of the Commonwealth, published a book entitled *The Dignity of Difference.*[49] This term is also used by other theologians. Rabbi Sacks relates the term 'dignity of difference' to the difference of cultures, mainly religions. According to Huber (2010) Rabbi Sacks shares the fear that those differences can lead to a 'clash of civilisations', as Samuel Huntington predicted. But, Sacks says, every one of those cultures echoes and reaches out to God in its own way. Therefore he speaks about the *dignity of difference.*

Huber (2010) argues, however, that not every *difference* is good or acceptable, or should even be dignified. Not all diversity has its place in an 'ordered complexity', to use Sacks' phrase. The question, according to Huber, is not whether the difference of cultures has an inherent dignity, but rather whether those cultures respect the equal dignity of human beings (and also the dignity of nature). Cultures often reflect the brokenness of the human existence; they even express the selfishness of human endeavours and become instruments for the arrogance of superiority. Therefore not the dignity of difference but the dignity of *the different* should, in Huber's view, be respected as a guiding moral principle in the 21st century — a 'time of many worlds'.

It should not be thought that, because the *imago Dei* concept features so prominently in the theological literature of the Abrahamic religions as the basis for human dignity and equality, all the implications of the *imago Dei* doctrine are reflected in the *practice* of the various religious *institutions.* On the contrary and, as already pointed out, the history of the Christian church shows, for example, that there was theological support in the past for slavery and, more recently, for apartheid by certain churches in South Africa. The failure to implement the *imago Dei* concept in practice is particularly true in the case of women striving for equality, and in particular for equality in the offices of the church and other religious institutions, as it is for gays and lesbians. Despite this failure in practice, the *imago Dei* concept remains a crucial focal point in the debates around the furthering of dignity and equality in these religious institutions.

Whereas the thrust of this book is to defend a certain legal understanding of equality and dignity, one should not leave out of the reckoning the influence that theology (and even law) have had on philosophy, and the influence that philosophy has had on theology and the law. We are living in a time when medical and biological technology is posing profound challenges to theology, philosophy and the law, and when the need for inter-disciplinary debate becomes more urgent.

---

49 Sacks (2002).

In none of these areas of human endeavour has the full potential of human dignity and equality (through dignity) been achieved, but these disciplines have their own unique contributions to make in striving towards this goal.

2.7 ISLAM

The objective in this section is the modest and limited one of attempting to show how at least a certain stream of (progressive) Islamic scholarship does in effect trace equal human dignity back to God's creation of the human race.

Islam, built in a sense on the religious traditions of Judaism and Christianity, is a monotheistic religion articulated by the *Qur'ān*, which is believed by Muslims to be the word of God. Islam considers that, among others, Abraham, Moses, and Jesus were prophets, but that the final prophet was Muhammad.

American scholar Ann Elizabeth Mayer (1991: xi) rightly cautions against speaking of 'Islam' and human rights — 'as if Islam were a monolith or as if there existed one settled Islamic human rights philosophy that caused all Muslims to look at rights in a particular way'. As already pointed out, other major religions with long and complex traditions have been interpreted in ways that create conflict between religious doctrine and human rights norms.

The progressive Islamic scholar Abdullahi A An-Na'im (1987: 2–3), concerned with the fact that large-scale human-rights violations continue to occur throughout the world, is of the view that 'culturally rooted norms' have the best chance of ensuring compliance with international human rights instruments, if they can be shown to be 'the natural and legitimate evolution of the cultural tradition of the particular community'. Although cultural norms have complex origins, An-Na'im argues (1987: 9) that 'the religious factor seems to be a major formative force'. The thrust of An-Na'im's article (1987: 17) is that it is possible for *shari'a* to be reformed within the fundamental sources of Islam, namely the *Qur'ān* and *Sunnah* in a way 'that would at once be both Islamic and fully consistent with universal human rights standards'.[50] The need for this arises because he is of the view that, for example, the status of non-Muslim religious minorities under *Shari'ah* is not consistent with current universal human rights and cannot be justified under claims of Islamic cultural relativism.

Ahmad S Moussali (2001: 2–3), writing on moderate Islamism, argues that it indirectly employs the most important doctrines of the Enlightenment 'to

[50] Very broadly stated his argument (1987: 9–11) is that the *Shari'ah* is 'not the totality of the word of God'. According to Muslim belief, 'the *Qur'ān* is the literal and final word of God while *Sunnah* is the record of what the Prophet is believed to have said'. While conceding (1987: 17) that not all aspects of *Shari'ah* are open to restatement and reinterpretation, An-Na'im does contend (1987: 10) that *Shari'ah* is no more than the 'understanding of the early Muslims of the sources of Islam' influenced by their historical context and 'experience and perception of the world'. It developed under the conditions and was influenced by the problems of an Islamic state in seventh century Arabia. Since these problems have altered and the historical answers are no longer valid, An-Na'im argues (1987: 11) that 'new answers must be developed out of the *Qur'ān* and *Sunnah* ... the Islamic *Shari'ah* for today'.

reinterpret Islam' but whereas the Enlightenment grounded its doctrines in natural reason, 'Islamism ultimately grounds these doctrines in a novel interpretation of the fundamental Islamic texts'. He argues (2001: 128) that even in classical and medieval times Islam saw men and women as 'springing from the same origin and therefore as equal morally, educationally, socially, and religiously before the law'. He points out (2001: 152) that 'Islam acknowledges the unity of mankind, all being the offspring of Adam, and only piety distinguishes one individual or group from others'. In Islam, the *Qur'ān* 4:1 appears to support the Genesis 1 version of the simultaneous creation of men and women from one source: 'Men, have fear of your Lord, who created you from a single soul. From that soul he created its mate, and through them He bestrewed the earth with countless men and women.'[51]

Azizah al-Hibri (1997: 26) contends that the *Qur'ān* 'states clearly and repeatedly that we were all created from the same *nafs* (soul)'.

The Cairo Declaration on Human Rights in Islam (the Cairo Declaration) adopted by the Organization of the Islamic Conference in Cairo on 5 August 1990 states, in art 1(a):

> 'All human beings form one family whose members are united by submission to God and descent from Adam. All men are *equal in terms of basic human dignity and basic obligations and responsibilities*, without any discrimination on the grounds of race, colour, language, sex, religious belief, political affiliation, social status or other considerations. True faith is the guarantee for enhancing such dignity along the path to human perfection.' (Emphasis supplied.)

Because of the use of 'All human beings' in the first line, and 'All men' in the second, it is difficult to say whether this article's purpose is to do away only with the pre-modern *shari'a* rules in respect of discrimination against non-Muslim men, or whether its purpose is to do away with these rules against women as well. Whatever the correct answer to this question may be, the point to be noted is that human dignity is considered to be the attribute in respect whereof members of a particular class of persons are equal. Depending on one's construction of the article in question, the class chosen may well be far too narrow, but the analysis remains important because of its reliance on dignity.

Commenting on the text of *Qur'ān* 4:1, quoted above, Hujjatul-Islam Seyed Muhammad Khāmeneī (1989: 281) also implicitly recognises the attributive role of dignity in an understanding of equality, for he states that 'in the eyes of the Almighty Allah man and woman are equal and so are they as far as their human aspect and individual dignity is concerned'. Of more than passing interest is the way in which Khāmeneī (1989: 329–343) defends the difference between the rights of men and women with regard to inheritance, evidence, blood money, divorce and polygamy. To the Western ear much of it sounds like special pleading and

[51] Dawood translation (NJ, Penguin Books, 1990).

the stereotyping of women with regard to their emotions, sentiments, intelligence and nature in a way that we would find unacceptable. Yet, in Khāmeneī's defence of these differences, he does not reject or deny the equal dignity which women and men have but, instead, attempts to show (1989: 332–333) that the differences in rights that he discusses, when seen in their proper context and having regard to certain counterbalancing benefits that women enjoy in these areas, do not demean the dignity of women. My point is not that the defence raised is successful, but that the way it is raised indicates a point of departure that regards equality as being linked to dignity.

The *imago Dei* concept is recognised by Mohamad Hashim Kamali (2005: 14) in unqualified terms: 'Since man is created in God's image, he is endowed with the appropriate faculties to perfect himself and fulfil his enormous potential.' According to Kamali (2005: 5),

> '[t]he Qur'ānic vision of mankind is basically that of a single, unified entity, regardless of any difference of origin and status. Unity and equality are the necessary postulates of human dignity, as without these human dignity as a universal value will necessarily be compromised.'

Islam's perception of human dignity, according to Kamali (2005: 102) 'is predicated on the unity in origin of mankind, and its basic equality in regard to the essence of humanity, rights and obligations'. He moreover (2005: 45) clearly sees dignity as informing the meaning of equality in the context of creation.

In her sensitive and instructive work, Mayer (1991: xiii–xiv) warns that it is important to distinguish between the Islamic source documents and the interpretations of these sources by various schools of law or sects. Commentators often neglect to have regard to 'evolutions and reforms in interpretations that have taken place over time ...'.

Mayer points out (1991: 61–62) that in conservative Islamic circles the emphasis is on duty and not on rights; that the individual is obliged to obey the duly constituted authorities and the latter are in turn obliged to obey God. The assumption is that 'the government will be obedient to the dictates of the *shari'a*, so that individual will have no cause to complain of government conduct'. It should be pointed out that exclusive theocentric thinking like this is not limited to conservative followers of Islam, but occurs in Christianity as well. In South Africa in the 1980s, similar objections were raised by ultra-conservative neo-Calvinists to the idea of a bill of fundamental rights, on the basis that human beings only have duties to God, lived solely by grace, and could claim no fundamental rights against the state.

Mayer (1991: 93) states that there 'is much in the sources of Islamic law that bespeaks a fundamentally egalitarian philosophy' and that Muslims — who have generally agreed that slavery is a retrograde and unacceptable institution and have effectively discarded pre-modern *shari'a* law on slavery — 'are deeply divided on the question of whether legal distinctions based on sex and religion have become similarly superseded, so that pre-modern *shari'a* rules in this area should be discarded as well'.

The comments of Mayer (1991: 94), dealing with two different approaches by those supporting the retention of the pre-modern *shari'a* rules affecting women and non-Muslims, are instructive in this regard. She points out that one approach is to affirm that the principle of equality violates *shari'a* law: 'Conservative Muslim clerics in the past have been outspoken in their condemnation of the principle of equality on the grounds that it makes equal those who under the *shari'a* must be treated differently.' The other approach, she says, is to offer reasons why the principle of equality is not infringed by the retention of the discriminatory rules of the pre-modern *shari'a* and to justify, accordingly, the subordinate status of women and non-Muslims: 'Today it is rare for spokespersons of Islam to take the former position, and it is the second approach that one commonly encounters.'

Professor Ebrahim Moosa[52] (2000–2001: 186–187), while readily acknowledging that there have been human rights abuses in Islamic countries, points out that 'the media debates and dramatic events conceal much more complex issues of history, tradition and the contested perceptions of law and religion'. He asserts, no doubt correctly, that few Westerners are aware that the debate within Muslim societies about human rights is 'fierce in its intellectual rigour as well as its political consequences' but concedes that the content of human rights doctrine 'remains a vexed question within contemporary Muslim legal, political and ethical theory'. The success of a modern Islamic human rights theory is, in Moosa's view, dependent on the extent to which 'modern Islamic thought would be open to a revisionist or reconstructionist approach in philosophy and ethical orientation'. This is not as radical as it sounds, because early Muslim thinking allowed for the evolution of religious experience in Islam and, as Moosa states, 'from its very inception in seventh-century Arabia, the message of Islam demonstrated a preoccupation with the social, moral and spiritual conditions of human beings' and that the subject of the *Qur'ān* was 'not exclusively a self-revelation of God to humanity, but an instance where humanity became the very leitmotif of revelation'. Moosa (2000–2001: 209) stresses the importance of human dignity in Muslim theology:

> 'Most Muslim scholars would argue that the pith of the modern human rights debate is about the preservation of human dignity (*karāma*), even though some secular proponents would disagree. The Qur'ān and the teachings of the Prophet explicitly entrench human dignity as a fundamental ethical norm in human conduct. Islamic law and ethics have an established philosophy that was designed to protect human dignity.'

Moosa sees a connection between dignity and equality in Islam theology.[53] *Qur'ān* 17:70 states that 'we have honoured the children of Adam (*karramna bani adam*)'. Moosa points out that the verb for 'honoured', *karramna*, is the

[52] Formerly of the University of Cape Town, currently at Duke University.

[53] In correspondence on file with the present author.

same as for 'dignify' and that the noun *karama* is the same as for 'dignity,' and that 'all modern Muslim theologies invoke human dignity as the exemplar for equality whether it be gender or democratic polity'.

2.8 CONSTITUTIONAL OBLIGATIONS

From the above it is clear, certainly in Christian theology, that the *imago Dei* ground for dignity and equality also imposes specific obligations on human beings. The question may well be raised whether a rights-entrenching constitution, and the concept of a substantive constitutional state, do not also, albeit implicitly, place constitutional obligations on all members of the body politic. I deal in Chapter 5 with the so-called horizontal operation of the Bill of Rights in relation to equality and non-discrimination. Other than that I do not propose discussing the question of broader constitutional obligations on those who enjoy rights under a secular Constitution. I have in mind obligations that go beyond the phenomenon of horizontality; for example, duties by members of society to the state or to society at large; obligations going beyond duties that are simply the correlative of rights under the Constitution. In this context I suggest no more than that, in my view, there are such constitutional obligations, the discharge of which is essential for the achievement of democracy and the rule of law, for securing the rights promised in the Bill of Rights for all, and for the enjoyment of the benefits of the constitutional state. However, two matters must be stressed. First, I do not suggest that these obligations are necessarily legal ones (although they might very well be — or become — legal ones) and, secondly, I do not suggest that the discharge of constitutional obligations like these is a condition precedent to the enjoyment of constitutional rights. One can only be grateful for and applaud the advances made in the past sixty years in securing acceptance of the idea of universal human rights and for securing their actual enforcement. But the discourse can become one-sided. The effective securing of human rights, and the full and true constitutional state, cannot be achieved, in my view, unless all members of the political community in question discharge their own constitutional obligations. I do not pursue any further the nature and extent of these obligations. It seems to me, however, that the black African concept of *ubuntu*, which I touch on briefly in Chapter 4, does emphasise the corresponding (but *not* interdependent) duty of the individual to give the same respect, dignity, value and acceptance to each member of society.

2.9 SECULAR PHILOSOPHICAL PERSPECTIVES

(a) Introduction

I shall not repeat what I have already stressed with regard to a philosophical enquiry as a search for as broad an 'overlapping consensus' as possible. Nor that it is well-nigh impossible for lawyers properly to interpret and apply the provisions of the 1996 Constitution, and in particular its Bill of Rights provisions, without regard to philosophical values.

As is more fully explained in Chapter 5, the 1996 Constitution is not merely a formal document regulating public power. It also embodies, as already pointed out above, an objective, normative value system. The basic rights norms contain not only defensive subjective rights for the individual but embody at the same time an objective value system which, as a fundamental constitutional value for all areas of the law, acts as a guiding principle and stimulus for the legislature, executive and judiciary.[54]

If the judiciary is to be guided and stimulated by this objective value system, it must interpret this value system in the light of the rights and values recognised and protected under the Constitution. This cannot be done without reference to philosophical values and in particular ethical philosophical values.

I must also stress — what ought to be self-evident by this time — that the sections in this book referring to the views of certain philosophers do not pretend to constitute substantive philosophical reflection. They likewise do not pretend to be the elaboration of a system, but merely the presentation of certain philosophical values that are, in my view at least, relevant to the understanding of the rights and values of dignity and equality in the Constitution, and their application. My choice of philosophers does not pretend to be representative. Their views are invoked to demonstrate that there are respectable arguments supporting the main theses on equality and dignity argued for in this book. Relevant German legal scholarship is not dealt with here but later in Chapters 3, 4 and 5.

(b) From theology to secular philosophy

Jeremy Waldron's work *God, Locke and Equality: Christian Foundations in Locke's Political Thought* (2002), provides a useful modern point of transition from theological to secular views on dignity and equality. He describes the thrust of his book (2002: 15–19) as being about 'the relation in Locke's thought between basic equality and religious doctrine' and the exploration of a theory that 'equality may actually *need* theological foundations'. Waldron (2002: 1–3) distinguishes between an understanding of equality as a policy aim, of which there are many variations, and the question as to what the very concept of human equality is based on. 'Not "what are its implications?" but "what does this foundational equality amount to?" and "what is it based on?"' He bemoans the paucity of modern scholarship on the substance of this last question, which he terms 'basic equality', and remarks that even Dworkin, who identifies the underlying principle as 'the principle of equal concern and respect', has said little about the nature and grounding of the principle of equal respect.

[54] See *Carmichele* (above, n 29) para 54.

Waldron's contention (2002: 6) is that John Locke has developed a theory of basic equality as sound as there is in the canon of political philosophy. He typifies Locke's 'normative doctrine' in this regard (2002: 13) as being the 'equality of all men in virtue of their shared species-membership'. Waldron (2002: 7) rightly warns that — with regard to many of the *implications* of equality which are of modern concern — it would be anachronistic to look to John Locke for any help. Yet, he points out (2002: 9) that Locke and his contemporaries were concerned 'with the [same] duality between surface issues of equal treatment in politics and economy and a deeper idea of respecting people as equals', and indeed people who are respected as being equal *by nature*. Although the issues may not be identical, Waldron — three centuries later — is also exploring (2002: 9–10) the 'possibility that humans are *by nature* worthy of respect as one another's equals ...'. The nature of the *basic* equality that Waldron is searching for is immune to the vicissitudes of history; it has to be grounded on something that is 'discernable in different ages' and must be a commitment that is in principle 'recognizable in all sorts of contexts and circumstances', one that looks beyond the 'contexts and circumstances' that might distinguish one human individual from another, and holds constant 'an element of enduring respect for the sheer fact of their underlying humanity'.

Waldron (2002: 13) expresses doubts as to whether one '*can* shape and defend an adequate conception of basic human equality apart from some religious foundation'. I have sympathy for the doubt, but believe that Kant, and others, have provided us with an adequate secular foundation. Yet the religious foundation is a very important one, one that deeply influenced Kant and others.

Waldron (2002: 14) believes that basic equality is so fundamental to innumerable aspects of our ethical outlook that it requires a special defence that can underpin the starting point of public justification and also 'prevail in the face of the various temptations that invite us to start drawing distinctions between types or grades of human being'. He deals (2002: 22ff) with Locke's personal struggle with the fact that 'women as much as men are created in the image of God and endowed with the modicum of reason that is, for Locke, the criterion of human equality'. It is not my purpose to examine whether Locke eventually won the struggle in favour of women's human equality with men, but to highlight that his conception of equality is rooted in the *imago Dei* concept. Waldron (2002: 25) is clear on this point:

> 'Locke associates humankind in general with the Judeo-Christian idea of *imago dei*, the image of God, in a way that makes it absolutely clear that that characterisation applies to Eve (the only other member of the species around) as well as to Adam, to women as well as men.'

Waldron (2002: 45–46) doubts whether one can 'bracket out' the theology from Locke's theory of equality and still have a 'defensible theory of equality' left. He refers to this stratagem as a trick, describing it as putting 'the religious premises in parentheses — leaving them available for anyone who needs that sort of persuasion, but not presented as an integral part of the package — and still be left with something recognizably egalitarian in its content, which even an atheist could support'. The hope that this trick can be pulled off, not only with regard to Locke's theory but even in the cases of Rawls and Kant is, in Waldron's view, 'crucial for modern secular liberalism'. He doubts, however, that a 'stratagem' like this can work in the case of either Rawls or (by implication) Kant. I believe Waldron to be mistaken in this regard, certainly in the case of Kant. The *imago Dei* concept is a convincing theological foundation for a theory of equality that is based on equality of human worth (dignity), a basis that I argue for throughout. At the same time I am convinced that Kant, and others, provide an equally powerful foundation for a closely similar secular theory. The fact that a secular principle may not have, as Waldron (2002: 47) suggests, 'the same texture as the Lockean principle', does not detract from its force. Nor is it necessary to 'kid' oneself that it is the 'same principle'. It is analogous and sufficient if it is equally sound and persuasive.

According to Waldron (2002: 49) John Locke 'asserts as a matter of principle the fundamental equality of *all members of the human species*' and (2002: 49) that he more closely defines this specification as including those who have 'the capacity for abstraction' and 'can reason to the existence of God' and 'can relate the idea of God to there being a law that applies to [them] both in [their] conduct in this world and as to [their] prospects in the next'. Waldron explains (2002: 83) that human beings are one another's equals, in Locke's eyes, by virtue of 'their possession of a rather modest intellectual capacity — the capacity to form and manipulate abstract ideas, which enables a person to reason to the existence of God and to the necessity of finding out what if anything God requires of him'.

He further points out (2002: 113) that Locke's approach is 'to draw the range of normal human reason more narrowly, but then to define a *special* relation of the human infant to that range'. Locke argues that although infants are not in infancy within the range of normal human reason, they have the capacity and are destined to grow up into the adult range. Children, in Locke's 'felicitous phrasing' as quoted by Waldron (113), 'are born *to* this basic equality, even though they are not born in it'. This would also be the case in the approach, basically Kantian, that I seek to defend. The dignity accruing to any person does not depend on the fact that this person is able to exercise a particular degree of reason or *any reason at all.* All that is required is membership of the human species. In order to protect the dignity of all members of the species, it is necessary that protection be given (not necessarily absolute protection) in certain circumstances to a member even before birth and even after death. For human dignity does not have a price, but an inestimable value. This will be considered more fully when Kant's philosophy is referred to below. At this juncture, however, it needs to be stressed that in adopting an approach to dignity founded on Kantian values, which rely on the empirical fact that the human species distinguishes itself by its capacity for moral reasoning, one should not conclude that a human being only has human dignity when, or to the extent that, she/he can in actual fact exercise this reasoning. A young baby has human dignity even though it may not (yet) be able to exercise reason. I would argue this to be so even in a case where, through defect or disease, a child will never be able to exercise reason. My argument in this regard is clearly a *species* argument. Not only the individual is created in the image of God, or in secular terms has innate dignity and absolute worth, but so is and does the species of which the individual is a representative. Whatever the subjective frame of mind of the procreating partners, the act of conception is destined to produce a member of the species and accordingly that which results from conception (the '*conceptus*', to use a neutral term) partakes of the worth of the species. It is irrelevant, for this purpose, that the *conceptus* does not develop into a perfect example of the species, or even one with the barest minimum of intellect and emotion.

Such an approach would also apply to an adult who, though previously perfectly capable of reasoning, has — for whatever reason — lost that capacity entirely. I would also argue that certain aspects of human dignity pre-date birth and survive death. While the interpreter of the Constitution will have due regard to information emerging from the rapidly expanding biological and other natural sciences, it is the Constitution (and not the scientist) that must ultimately determine when the various aspects of human dignity, guaranteed by the Constitution, begin and cease. This is alluded to again when aspects of German jurisprudence are dealt with in Chapter 3 but will not, in a book of this general nature, be dealt with in any further detail. This obviously has implications for the abortion debate, which I cannot pursue in this book. One point needs clarification. I am not for a moment suggesting that the mother of the *conceptus* does not have rights which are to be weighed up against the dignity rights of the *conceptus* and which, in particular circumstances, would prevail. I simply cannot pursue this issue in any greater detail in a book of this nature.

Towards the end of his book Waldron (2002: 239–241) draws an analogy between John Locke on God and John Rawls on moral personality. He considers this analogy to be particularly striking because, in the case of Rawls 'moral personality has to be able to do by itself ... all the work for equality that is done, for Locke, by our status in the eyes of God'. Waldron points out that for Locke, the religious foundation is indispensable as a premise and as a constraint. For Rawls, 'the moral personality stuff is a similarly load-bearing part of the theoretical structure, and similarly indispensable'.

In the approach to equality that I adopt in this book, the concept of inestimable — and hence equal — human worth (dignity) is equally the load-bearing and indispensable component. Equality, as a legal concept, means equality of human worth (dignity). I would suggest that my proposed concept of human worth (dignity) at the commencement of this chapter, although stated in secular terms, has many features in common with what Waldron (2002) considers John Locke to have espoused in relation to his idea of the species created in the image of God.

(c) Aristotle

Aristotle is commonly said to have defined equality on the basis that equals ought to be treated equally and unequals treated unequally in proportion to their inequality; that proportion is the equality of ratios; and that 'just' is that which is proportional and 'unjust' that which violates proportionality.[55] Aristotle is not, for present purposes, helpful in determining the particular quality shared by persons who are said to be equal. Not because 'it is stated at too high a level of generality',[56] but because, in my view, it does not appreciate the crucial necessity of articulating a criterion of attribution for human equality. It is therefore hardly surprising that so much confusion and disagreement exists amongst certain schools of lawyers as to what 'equal' means in the concept of equal protection (and benefit) of the law, or what the circumstances are that render differentiation (used in this context as a neutral term) constitutionally objectionable. Aristotle

---

[55] Aristotle *The Nicomachean Ethics* Book V, ch 3. There is some inconsistency in the translations. In Aristotle (1998) 112–114, renders the relevant passage as follows:

> 'The just, therefore, involves at least four terms; for the persons for whom it is in fact just are two, and the things in which it is manifested, the objects distributed, are two. *And the same equality will exist between the persons and between the things concerned; for as the latter — the things concerned — are related, so are the former; if they are not equal, they will not have what is equal, but this is the origin of quarrels and complaints — when either equals have and are awarded unequal shares, or unequals equal shares. Further, this is plain from the fact that awards should be "according to merit"; for all men agree that what is just in distribution must be according to merit in some sense, though they do not all specify the same sort of merit, but democrats identify it with the status of freeman, supporters of oligarchy with wealth (or with noble birth), and supporters of aristocracy with excellence.* (Emphasis supplied.) The just, then, is a species of the proportionate.... For proportionate is equality of ratios.... This, then, is what the just is — the proportional; the unjust is what violates the proportion.'

The emphasised passage is translated thus in Aristotle (1976) 177– 178:

> 'And there will be the same equality between the shares as between the persons, because the shares will be in the same ratio to one another as the persons; for if the persons are not equal, they will not have equal shares; and it is when equals have or are assigned unequal shares, or people who are not equal, equal shares, that quarrels and complaints break out.
>
> This is also clear from the principle of assignment according to merit. Everyone agrees that justice in distribution must be in accordance with merit in some sense, but they do not all mean the same kind of merit: the democratic view is that the criterion is free birth; the oligarchic that it is wealth or good family; the aristocratic that it is excellence.'

By contrast, the above emphasised passage is thus reflected in Aristotle (1893) 252:

> 'If the persons are exactly equal, so ought to be their shares; but if the persons are unequal, the shares ought also to be unequal in the same proportion: for complaints and strife always will arise, when either persons of unequal worth meet with the same treatment; or when persons of nearly equal worth are distinguished from each other by too considerably differences. This is universally acknowledged; but men's notions of worth vary with their political principles. In democracies it is measured by liberty; in oligarchies, by wealth or birth; in aristocracies, by virtue.'

I have chosen to follow the first two translations above.

[56] Hogg (1992: para 52.4) and compare similar remarks by Gibson (1990: 58).

seems to have been aware of some of the difficulties, and (without giving really helpful guidance) touches on some of them in his *Politics* (1946: paras 1–2 and 4–5). After again stating that the equality required by justice requires that 'persons who are equal should have assigned to them equal things' Aristotle raises the crucial question which, he says, must not be overlooked: 'Equals and unequals — yes; but equals and unequals *in what*?' This is a question which, in Aristotle's view 'raises difficulties, and involves us in philosophical speculation in politics'. The flute player example he then gives is not, in my view at least, particularly helpful.[57]

(d) Kant

I make no pretense to being a Kantian scholar. This, however, does not relieve me, or any other lawyer for that matter, from the duty of grappling with Immanuel Kant's ethical thought, because it has guided much legal thinking on dignity and equality in Germany (and to a certain extent also in South Africa and elsewhere) and has featured in the judgments of the German Federal Constitutional Court and even (though to a much lesser degree) in our own Constitutional Court. Before turning to Kant's express pronouncements on dignity and equality, some background to his philosophy and its impact is necessary.

Such knowledge as I have of Kant has been gained mainly from the works of Prof Allen W Wood, and in particular his book *Kant's Ethical Thought* (1999).[58] Wood (1999: xiii) tells us that the idea for this last-mentioned work was already taking shape when he was working on *Hegel's Ethical Thought* (1990) and realised that 'Hegel's criticisms of the Kantian principles of morality do not entirely succeed because, like most of Kant's readers, Hegel attended exclusively to the Formula of Universal Law, ignoring the other formulations, which are more adequate statements of the principle'. Wood (1999: xiii) also makes the important point, which will be referred to again later, that Kant's position is grounded on a 'distinctive theory of human nature and history, whose

[57] 'If you were dealing with a number of flute players who were equal in their art, you would not assign them flutes on the principle that the better born should have a greater amount. Nobody would play the better for being better born; and it is to those who are better at the job that the better tools should be given. If our point is not yet plain, it can be made so if we push it further. § 5. Let us suppose a man who is superior to others in flute-playing, but far inferior in birth and beauty. Birth and beauty may be greater goods than ability to play the flute, and those who possess them may, on balance, surpass the flute-player more in these qualities than he surpasses them in his flute-playing; but the fact remains that *he* is the man who ought to get the better supplies of flutes.'

[58] Prof Wood is, inter alia, co-General Editor of the Cambridge Edition of *The Works of Immanuel Kant*; co-translator and co-editor of Kant's *Critique of Pure Reason*; the author of the 'General Introduction' to *Immanuel Kant: Practical Philosphy*; and co-translator and co-editor of *Immanuel Kant: Religion and Rational Theology*, all in the Cambridge Edition. I was first exposed to Kant's categorical imperative and his 'Formulation of Humanity as End in Itself' in the jurisprudence lectures of Dr Hendrik Verloren van Themaat (Snr) at Stellenbosch University in the 1950s. The views of Kant so expounded made a deep impression on me and have stayed with me since, although subliminally for lengthy periods.

importance for Kant's ethics has seldom been appreciated' and that 'the neglect of Kant's empirical theory of human nature and history is responsible for most of the misunderstandings of Kant's ethical thought that prevails amongst its supporters as well as its critics'. Wood (1999: 9–10) stresses that many of these misconceptions 'are based on misinterpretations of Kant's important claim that the *fundamental moral principle* must be *a priori* and owe nothing to empirical anthropology'. (Emphases in the original.) On this basis Wood takes critics of Kant, such as Bernard Williams, Alisdair MacIntyre, Richard Rorty and Philippa Foot, to task. Wood argues that Kant 'as a self-conscious representative of the Enlightenment' does not mean to deny 'the essential place in ethics of an empirical study of human nature'. Wood (1999: 11) points out that Kant is sometimes criticised for his 'deep distrust of human nature' when, for example, he opposes 'reason and inclination and his reservation of moral esteem only to actions motivated only by duty'. These critics, says Wood, 'overlook the fact that Kant's interpretation of the *a priori* moral principle, as well as his conception of its application to the human will, depends on some quite distinctive views about human nature and history'.

Wood, when emphasising certain crucial features of Kant's ethical thought, the centrality of which, he says 'is not fully appreciated or whose very presence is often barely recognised', succinctly states (1999: xiv) that 'at the top of that list is Kant's conception of human dignity: *the absolute, hence equal, worth of all rational beings*'. (Emphasis supplied.) Wood further comments (1999: 6) that 'Kant's commitment to the equal worth of all human beings pervades his ethical thought'.

Wood argues that by no reasonable standard could Kant 'be considered conservative in relation to the issues of his day' whether in regard to politics, religion or education. Despite certain negative racialist beliefs held by him, to which Wood makes reference, Kant, according to Wood (1999:7), 'conspicuously declines' to infer from them that there is 'any difference in the human rights possessed by other peoples', and his attitude to European colonialism 'is therefore one of strong and unqualified disapproval....'

There is a false image of Kant's ethical thought as 'individualistic'. Wood (1999: 281) asserts that Kant's theory of friendship immediately gives the lie to this image:

> 'For although Kant is an uncompromising defender of the dignity of human individuals and the rights grounded on it, we can hardly regard "individualist" as an accurate classification of any moral philosopher who thinks we have an ethical duty to enter into personal relationships involving us in the mutual surrender of ourselves, the common possession of each other, and the swallowing up of our happiness in commitment to collective ends.'

Far from there being no necessary conflict between the Kantian ideals of autonomy, equality and community, Woods (1999: 335) points out that they 'can be grasped and pursued only as a unity'.

In this regard he further contends that

> 'to think that greater equality can be had only at the proportional cost in freedom is to confuse the liberties necessary for human dignity with the licence to dominate and exploit others, which is inimical to it'. (Footnote omitted.)

Furthermore, both detractors and supporters of Kant have criticised his work because of erroneous images of his work, and often from wrong conclusions drawn by Kant from his own principles. Wood (1999) does not shrink from dealing with and answering these criticisms on the basis that, even when justified in a particular case, they do not detract from Kant's main theses.[59] He explains (1999: 4) that '[t]o read historical philosophers critically is to read them with intellectual sympathy, but it is never to treat them as oracles whose pronouncements on any subjects we should accept blindly on trust'. The wisdom and virtue of philosophers 'since they are human and bound by the limitations of their age, are always far from perfect'. Wood (1999: 4) emphasises that we need to respect the 'unity of a philosopher's thought' because we can gain most from a set of doctrines by appreciating how some depend on others that are not always obvious; but respecting the unity of Kant's thought 'is not only compatible with but even requires distinguishing the teachings that are central to it from those that are peripheral, and separating the conclusions that actually follow from his principles from the conclusions he may have drawn but do not follow'.

It is not possible to separate neatly Kant's writings on human dignity from those on equality, precisely because equality is described in terms of dignity. Human dignity is the central and defining feature of Kant's categorical concept of equality. For example:

> '[A] human being regarded as a *persona*, that is, as the subject of a morally practical reason, is exalted above any price; for as a person (*homo noumenon*) he is not to be valued merely as a means to the ends of others or even to his own ends, but as an end in itself, that is, he possesses a *dignity* (an absolute inner worth) by which he exacts *respect* for himself from all other rational beings in the world. He can measure himself with every other being of this kind and value himself on a footing of equality with them.'[60]

Every human being has an absolute inner worth. Because this worth is absolute, all human beings are equal to one another with regard to this absolute worth. This absolute inner worth is human dignity.

---

[59] I do not propose entering these lists here, but merely mention some significant examples dealt with by Wood (1999). At 2 he refers to the fact that 'Kant infamously maintains that it is wrong to lie even to a would-be murderer in order to protect his intended victim' and that 'Kant's views about sex are repugnant to nearly everyone today (just as they were to many in his own time)'. At 3 he remarks that no 'enlightened person today [can] approve Kant's opinions about race and gender', nor can one support Kant's view that 'it is always unjust to rebel against the existing government or depose the head of state, no matter how unjust the rulers might themselves be', and adds that Kant was politically conservative in other ways too.

[60] *The Metaphysics of Morals* [AK 6: 434–435], Gregor (1996) 557.

This conclusion of Kant's flows almost directly from

(i) Kant's *Formula of Humanity as an End in Itself* (FH):

> 'So act that you use humanity, whether in your own person or in the person of any other, always at the same time as an end, never merely as a means.... This principle of humanity, and in general of every rational nature, *as an end in itself* (which is the supreme limiting condition of the freedom of action of every human being) is not borrowed from experience; first because of its universality, since it applies to all rational beings as such and no experience is sufficient to determine anything about them; second because in it humanity is represented not as and end of human beings (subjectively), that is, not as an object that we of ourselves actually make our end, but as an objective end that, whatever ends we may have, ought as law to constitute the supreme limiting condition of all subjective ends, so that the principle must arise from pure reason.'[61]

and

(ii) from his concept of human dignity as being beyond price:

> 'In the kingdom of ends everything has either a *price* or a *dignity* [fn *Würde*]. What has a price can be replaced by something else as its *equivalent*; what on the other hand is raised above all price and therefore admits of no equivalent has a dignity.
>
> What is related to general human inclinations and needs has a *market price;* that which, even without presupposing a need, conforms with a certain taste, that is, with a delight [fn *Wohlgefallen*] in the mere purposeless [fn *swecklosen*] play of our mental powers, has a *fancy price* [fn *Affectionspreis*]*;* but that which constitutes the condition under which alone something can be an end in itself has not merely a relative worth, that is, a price, but an inner worth, that is, *dignity*.'[62]

If dignity is beyond price and therefore infinite, then bearers of dignity must bear it equally.

Wood (1999: 132–133) points out that absolute worth is non-comparative and that Kant's thesis that every rational being is an end in itself with absolute worth has an immediate but radical corollary: 'The worth of all rational beings is *equal.* In other words, the worst rational being (in any possible respect you can name) has the same dignity or absolute worth as the best rational being in that respect (or any other).' Wood (1999: 133) explains that Kant's *Formula of Humanity as an End in Itself* (FH) (quoted above) implies that 'all the normal (comparative and competitive) measures of people's self-worth — wealth, power, honor, prestige, charm, charisma, even happy relationships with others — are expressions of an utterly false set of values'. Wood (1999: 135) states that it is a consistent position of Kant that the worth of a person never varies in comparison to others, 'since the good and the bad alike possess the dignity of humanity'.

---

[61] *Groundwork of the Metaphysics of Morals* [AK 4:429, 4:431] in Gregor (ed) (1996: 80–81).
[62] *Groundwork of the Metaphysics of Morals* [AK 4:434–435] in Gregor (ed) (1996: 84).

Another way of expressing this, says Wood (following Thomas Hill, Jr) is that 'the respect we owe others simply as rational beings is not a respect they have to *earn*'. (Emphasis in the original, footnote omitted.)

Kant also warns us not to compare our own worth with others: 'When a human being measures his worth by comparison to others, he seeks either to raise himself above the other or to diminish the worth of the other. The latter is envy (VP 9: 491).'[63] Commenting on this passage Wood (1999: 136) explains that Kant is of the view that such a comparison has a bad effect on one's character 'leading to self-deception, envy and malice'. Malice is indeed an offshoot of envy, but I would add a further ill-effect, namely that comparison to another can easily lead to a denigration of one's own worth, when the worth of the other is judged higher than one's own. Wood points out that Kant also proposes that 'we reinterpret the moral judgments we make comparing ourselves to others. Such judgments really involve a comparison of ourselves with the moral law, *not with* others at all'.

In concluding this section of his book, Wood (1999: 138–139) points out that

> '[t]he discomfort with ourselves that critics notice in Kant — his distrust of our feelings and inclinations, his intolerance of our tendencies towards moral complacency and laxity — all these are chiefly expressions of how far he thinks we still have to go on that historical path of progress towards the proper recognition of our equal human dignity'.

The work of Immanuel Kant occupies high ground in any attempt to understand the meaning of human dignity, and to defend its position at the core of fundamental human rights. It establishes a universal basis for the fundamental recognition and protection of dignity, particularly through the categorical imperatives, their different formulations and their applications. For Kant, *autonomy or freedom* is not only a pre-condition for dignity, but also a *necessary element of dignity.*[64]

Kant's famous *Formula of Humanity as End in Itself* (FH) has been quoted above. Kant reaches this 'practical imperative' by searching for a 'supreme

---

[63] *Lectures on Pedagogy* [AK 9:491] in Ca *Anthropology, History and Education.*

[64] This emerges from the following passages from his work:

> '[Because the rational being is] an end in itself and, for that very reason, as lawgiving in the kingdom of ends — [this being] is as free with respect to all laws of nature, obeying only those which he himself gives and in accordance with which his maxims can belong to a giving of universal law (to which at the same time he subjects himself). For nothing can have a worth other than that which the law determines for it. But the lawgiving itself, which determines all worth, must for that reason have a dignity, that is, an unconditional, incomparable worth; and the word *respect* alone provides a becoming expression for the estimate of it that a rational human being must give. *Autonomy* is therefore the ground of the dignity of human nature and of every rational creature.' (*Groundwork* [AK 4: 436] in Gregor and Wood 85).
>
> '*There is only one innate right: Freedom* (independence from being constrained by another's choice), insofar as it can coexist with the freedom of every other in accordance with a general law, is the only original right belonging to every man by virtue of his humanity.' (*The Metaphysics of Morals* [AK 6: 237] in Gregor (1996: 393).

practical principle', because it is an end in itself, and constitutes an 'objective principle of the will'. The ground of this principle is:

> '*[R]ational nature exists as an end in itself.* The human being necessarily represents his own existence in this way; so far it is thus a *subjective* principle of human actions. But every other rational being also represents his existence in this way consequent on just the same rational ground that also holds for me; thus it is at the same time an *objective* principle from which, as a supreme practical ground, it must be possible to derive all laws of the will.'[65]

Kant further stresses that this principle of humanity is not borrowed from experience.

In this regard Wood (1999: 133) explains that the law, as formulated in FH, tells us that 'the worth of rational nature is absolute, an end in itself'. Accordingly, says Kant, 'a human being must be judged only by what constitutes his absolute worth';[66] that is to say, by the dignity of humanity. Wood points out that Kant 'often insists that even the worst human beings have dignity' and that Kant '[a]lthough he identifies dignity with the *capacity* for morality or for having a good will, ... never makes it contingent on *acting* morally or on actual goodness of will (G 4:428, 435; MS 6:329–330, 404–405, 462–463)'.[[67]] (Emphasis in the original.)

Kant, according to Wood (1999: 139) did not see FH 'as high-sounding but too abstract to yield determinate moral principles or duties'. Neither does Wood (1999: 139–155), who asserts (139) that our impression that FH is too abstract to be easily applicable 'is rather like the Sermon on the Mount, the principles of communism, or other admirable utopian visions of human society, whose demands require such a radical departure from our customary practices and accepted attitudes towards ourselves and others that we are at first perplexed when we try to apply them'. Kant, according to Wood, 'views our ordinary moral duties as the first small steps we must take in the direction that the moral law dictates, hoping that in human history our species may eventually transform itself so that eventually "art will be strong enough to become a second nature" (MA 8:117)'.[[68]]

I do not propose following Wood in his treatment of at least eight ethical duties directly founded on FH. It must be noted, however, that — as Wood explains (1999: 140) — it is from FH that 'Kant derives our innate right to freedom in the Doctrine of Right' and that Kant glosses Ulpian's principle of natural right *honeste vive* as 'asserting one's worth as a human being in relation to others, a

[65] *Groundwork of the Metaphysics of Morals* [AK 4:429] in Gregor (1996: 79–80).
[66] Id AK 4:439.
[67] Id AK 4:428, 435; *Metaphysics of Morals* [AK 6:329–330, 404–405, 462–463] respectively.
[68] *Conjectural beginning of human history* [AK 8:117] in Ca *Anthropology, History and Education.*

duty expressed by the saying: "Do not make yourself a mere means for others but be at the same time an end for them."' (MS 6: 237).[69]

It is important to note that FH does not prohibit one from treating another person as a means, provided one *also and at the same time* treats the other person as an end. Wood (1999: 142–145) explains that '[a]s HJ Paton long ago pointed out' the FH does not forbid us to use a person (whether ourselves or another) as a means to our ends. It forbids only '*omitting* to treat a person "at the *same time* as an end."'[70]

Professor Hill[71] (1992: 38–57) discusses in some detail the meaning of 'Humanity as an end in Itself' and as part of this discussion (1992: 50–55) outlines seven implications of the thesis 'that humanity [being our rationality and capacity to set ends] in persons has an unconditional and incomparable worth'. First, that one would not do anything to damage or impair a person's rational capacities, whether the person is oneself or another. 'For example, drugs or frontal lobotomies that render a criminal non-violent at the cost of making him permanently cowlike would be forbidden.' Secondly, one would not destroy the persons themselves. Thirdly, if rational capacities have an incomparable value 'then surely one should try to develop them and improve them in oneself and others'. Fourthly, one should strive to exercise these capacities 'as far as possible'. Fifthly, since the exercise of rationality is something to be cherished, in trying to influence others 'one should try to appeal to their reason rather than try to manipulate them by non-rational techniques'. Sixthly, one should leave others 'freedom to set and pursue ends in a rational (moral and prudential) way, subject only to whatever further constraints reason imposes'. Seventhly, humanity should be honoured and respected, 'or at least not mocked, dishonoured or degraded. This is suggested by the term dignity (*Würde*), which is Kant's label for this special value.' Hill then proceeds to demonstrate how these implications are consistent with Kant's views, and certain discrepancies are explained.

I hope it will become clear, in what follows in later chapters, that most (if not all) the above implications have shaped the understanding of human dignity in its legal and constitutional development in Germany and South Africa in general, and the development of the so-called personality rights in particular.

Professor Christine Korsgaard[72] (1996: ix–x) explains that the basis of Kant's FH is that 'we *confer* value on the objects of our rational choice' and that Kant argues that the conception of ourselves as 'ends-in-ourselves' is a 'presupposition of rational choice'. To choose something is to take it to be worth pursuing; and

[69] *Metaphysics of Morals* [AK 6:237] in Ca *Practical Philosophy*.
[70] Citing 'HJ Paton *The Categorical Imperative*, p 165'.
[71] William Keenan Professor of Philosophy in the University of North Carolina at Chapel Hill.
[72] The Arthur Kingsley Porter Professor of Philosophy in Harvard University.

'when we choose things because they are important *to us* we are in effect taking *ourselves* to be important'.

Korsgaard (1996: 3) elegantly captures one of the consequences of Kant's Formula of Humanity as follows — 'Practical reason directs that every human being as a free and autonomous being must be regarded as unconditionally valuable.' She further points out that in his ethical writings 'Kant shows how this directive provides a rational foundation for morality, politics, and a religion of moral faith'. The task of morality is to bring reason into the world, which is 'the work as well as the hope of humanity'. According to Korsgaard (1996: 110) the most complete statement of Kant's notion of humanity is found thus in the *Metaphysical Principles of Virtue*:

> 'The capacity to propose an end to oneself is the characteristic of humanity (as distinguished from animality). The rational will is therefore bound up with the end of the humanity in our own person, as is also, consequently, the duty to deserve well of humanity by means of culture in general, and to acquire or promote the capacity of carrying out all sorts of ends, as far as this capacity is to be found in man.(MVP) 392'[73]

For Korsgaard (1996: 111) it is important, for a proper understanding of FH, to emphasise that 'it is the capacity for the rational determination of ends in general, not just the capacity for adopting morally obligatory ends, that the Formula of Humanity orders us to cherish'. The author further explains (115) that when Kant says that the characteristic of humanity is the power to set an end,

> 'he is not merely referring to personality, which would encompass the power to adopt an end for moral or sufficient reasons. Rather he is referring to a more general capacity for choosing, desiring, or valuing ends different from the ones that instinct lays down for us, and to which our interest is directed by the operation of reason. At the same time, of course, it is important to emphasize that this capacity is only completed and perfected when our ends are fully determined by reason, and this occurs only when we respond to moral incentives. Humanity, completed and perfected becomes personality....'

In a final section dealing with the conferring of value, Korsgaard (1996: 128) asserts, in relation to various passages in Kant's *Critique of Judgment,* that they seem to her 'to support in a very forceful way the idea that it is our power to confer objective value that Kant thinks of as having unconditional worth'. Korsgaard (1996: 130–131) concludes her discussion of the formula of humanity by asserting that it is our capacity to set ends, the ability to choose an end by means of reason, that makes every rational being an end in itself. More than this, it is only this capacity — 'that has its value completely in itself; so that this not only forms the basis of a possible categorical imperative, but also the only possible basis for a completely teleological view of creation....

[73] The translation is by Ellington (1983).

On Kant's view it is human beings, with our capacities for valuing things, that bring the world such value as it has. Even the justification of nature is up to us.'

The importance of Kant for the understanding of human dignity has been recognised by scholars from different disciplines. Thus Arieli (2002: 7), for example, writing as an historian on the 1948 Universal Declaration of Human Rights, and considering an underpinning for the principles contained in the Declaration, suggests Kant as a guide since his philosophy, 'presents a feasible link between a possible metaphysic and secularism which is the existential dimension of modernity and of modern history'. He considers that Kant's basic assumption throughout is 'man's capacity to shape his individual and collective existence according to the highest ideals implied in the concept of the dignity of man and his existential autonomy and freedom'.

Before leaving Kant (one of the most celebrated 'anti-utilitarianists') I would refer to the observation by Korsgaard (1996: 275) that to later generations, 'much of the moral philosophy of the twentieth century will look like a struggle to escape from utilitarianism' and that one has scarcely succeeded in disproving one utilitarian doctrine, 'only to find ourselves in the grip of another'. She believes this to be the case because a basic feature of the consequentialist outlook 'still evades and distorts our thinking', namely 'the view that the business of morality is to *bring something about*'. Korsgaard argues that the subject matter of morality 'is not what we should bring about, but how we should relate to one another'. If only Rawls has succeeded in escaping utilitarianism, she argues, it is because 'only Rawls has fully grasped this point. His primal scene, the original position, is one in which a group of people must make a decision together. Their task is to find the reasons they can share.'

(e) Bernard Williams

The renewal of the Abrahamic theological concept of human dignity in secular form through the Enlightenment tradition generally, and in Immanuel Kant's philosophy in particular, is pointedly commented on by Bernard Williams in his celebrated essay 'The Idea of Equality' (1967: 115–116) as follows: 'This strain of thought has found many types of religious expression; but in philosophy is to be found in its purest form in Kant.... The ground of the respect owed to each man thus emerges in the Kantian theory as a kind of secular analogue of the Christian conception of the respect owed to all men as equally children of God. Though secular, it is equally metaphysical: in neither case is it anything empirical *about* men that constitutes the ground of equal respect.' Wood (1999: 368 n 24), referring to the last sentence quoted above, somewhat wryly remarks that 'Bernard Williams gets Kant right on this point'.

Concerning the Christian conception, Williams is correct as far as he goes, but he omits to mention the further basis in the Abrahamic theologies for the innate dignity and equality of human beings — of which Kant's theory is equally a secular analogue — and that is the belief, referred to above, that all human beings are created in the image of God.

Williams (1967: 115–116) contends, however, that the 'very considerable consistency' of Kant's view 'is bought at what would generally be agreed to be a very high price.' Williams contends that this is the case because the detachment of moral worth from all contingencies is achieved by Kant 'only by making man's characteristics as a moral or rational agent a transcendental characteristic; man's capacity to will freely as a rational agent is not dependent on any empirical capacities which men may possess' and because in the Kantian view, 'the capacity to be a rational agent is not itself an empirical capacity at all'.

However, as Wood (1999: 9–10) points out, this criticism of Kant is based on a misconception. In his Introduction (xiii) Wood frankly points out that he decided to write a book on Kant's ethical thought when he realised that, with the overemphasis on the Formula of Universal Law, 'the neglect of Kant's empirical theory of human nature and history is responsible for most of the misunderstandings of Kant's ethical thought that prevails among its supporters as well as its critics'.

He goes on to point out (1999: 9–10) that '[t]he fact that Kant's empirical conception of our human nature and his philosophy of history plays a significant role in his ethical thought often comes as a surprise to those who know his ethics only through the standard images, interpretations, and caricatures'. Many of these are based on 'misinterpretations of Kant's important claim that the *fundamental moral principle* must be *a priori* and owe nothing to empirical anthropology'. This claim is taken to mean 'that Kant's ethical thought attaches no importance to the empirical nature of human beings or the social and historical situatedness of moral thinking'. Wood rejects this conclusion by pointing out that 'of course as a self-conscious representative of the Enlightenment, Kant never meant to deny the essential place in ethics of an empirical study of human nature'. On the contrary, '[w]e can see immediately that Kant's ethics is very much concerned with empirical human nature as soon as we consider the *reasons* Kant gives for stressing the very point that the supreme principle of morality must be grasped as *a priori* and independent of the empirical nature of human beings'.

In my view Bernard Williams (1967: 110), although disavowing reliance on Kant, implicitly adopts a logico-grammatical approach in relation to equality similar to the one I suggest, and is implicit in Kant's reasoning. He advances a number of considerations (1967: 111) 'that can help to save the political notion of equality from [the] extremes of absurdity and of triviality'. The absurdity, says Williams correctly, relates to the *factual* statement that human beings are equal in respect of, for example, physical, intellectual, emotional, creative gifts, and the triviality to the *political* statement that human beings '*should* be equal, as at present they are not'. Although his solution to the problem does not explicitly embody the points made by Geach and Foot, to which I have referred, his very statement of the problem and the content of his solution do affirm that the unavoidable question to be asked is '*with respect to what* are humans equal?'

One consideration that Williams alludes to is 'common humanity' (1967: 112–113) whose features include the anatomical membership of the species *homo sapiens*, the capacity to speak a language, to feel pain — both from immediate physical causes and from 'various situations represented in perception and in thought', and the capacity to feel affection for others and 'the consequences of this, connected with the frustration of this affection, loss of its objects, etc'. He correctly points out that alikeness in the possession of these characteristics is not trivial, and reminds us that there are political and social arrangements that systematically neglect these characteristics in the case of some groups while acknowledging and protecting them in others. He rightly rejects as false the suggestion that the different treatment of persons with regard to these human characteristics merely on grounds of colour rests on some special sort of moral principle. Such a view, he maintains, is 'a purely arbitrary assertion of will, like that of some Caligulan ruler who decided to execute everyone whose name contained three "R's"', a view shared by Isaiah Berlin (1969: xxxi–xxxii) who expresses himself in remarkably similar terms. For him the acceptance of some irreducible minimum of common values is not only intrinsic to human communication but grounds our conception of a normal human being. The possibility of understanding human beings at any time depends on the existence of some common values and that a person who literally cannot grasp what conceivable objection anyone can have to a rule permitting the killing of any man with blue eyes 'would be considered about as normal a specimen of the human race as one who ... thinks it probable that he is Julius Caesar'. Williams contends (1967: 113–114) that those who neglect the moral claims of certain men that arise from their human capacity to feel pain, etc, 'are *overlooking* or *disregarding* those capacities; and are not just operating with a special moral principle, conceding the capacities to such men, but denying the moral claim'.

Williams so develops his concept of common humanity that its features accord with many aspects of the notion of human dignity for which I argue. Thus he indicates (1967: 113–114) that one of the less definable categories of common humanity is 'a certain human desire to be identified with what one is doing, to be able to realise purposes of one's own, and not to be the instrument of another's will unless one has willingly accepted such role'. These features would accord with those aspects of human dignity relating to the self-awareness of dignity, the free unfolding of the human personality, freedom generally and the entitlement not to be treated as a mere means to an end.

Other respects in which, according to Williams (1967: 114–115), human beings are equal, and which also relate to human dignity are 'certain sorts of moral ability or capacity, the capacity for virtue or achievement of the highest kind of moral worth'. In this regard Williams (1967: 115) relies on Kant, in whom, he believes, this strain of thought is to be found 'in its purest form'. Not only does Kant carry 'to the limit the notion that moral worth cannot depend on contingencies', but, as Williams puts it, Kant also 'emphasizes in his Kingdom of Ends the idea of *respect* as a moral agent — and, since men are equally such agents, is owed equally to all', unlike admiration and similar attitudes, 'which are commanded unequally by men in proportion to their unequal possession of different kinds of natural excellence'. Williams here implicitly accepts human dignity as the criterion of attribution for equality.

But Williams (1967: 116) argues that this transcendental Kantian conception cannot provide any solid foundation for the notions of equality among men, or of equality of respect owed to them. Apart from the general difficulties of these transcendental conceptions, 'there is' he says, 'the obstinate fact that the concept of "moral agent", and the concepts allied to it such as responsibility, do and must have an empirical basis'. This proposition also rests on an attenuated reading of Kant. The fact that priceless inner worth (dignity) attaches to the human being must, and does, have an empirical basis (even in Kant), to the extent that it attaches to human beings and not to rocks, for the very reasons that human beings have (empirical) characteristics (the potential for reason) that rocks do not have. The priceless inner worth rests on humanity's *capacity* for, amongst other things, moral agency, not on the degree to which a particular human can exercise it. The fact, for example, that the criminal law rightly distinguishes between degrees of moral responsibility for the determination of criminal liability and for the purposes of sentence, does not detract from the equal *respect* due to all human beings because of their shared inner worth, which is beyond price, this inner worth being based, in part, on their moral *capacity,* and not on variable moral *talents*.

But Williams (1967: 117–118) sees further injunctions connected with the Kantian imperative, and with the notion of 'respect'. He points out that it is 'precisely a mark of extreme exploitation or degradation that those who suffer it do *not* see themselves differently from the way they are seen by the exploiters'. Here, he says, 'we evidently need something more than the precept that one should respect and try to understand another man's consciousness of his own activities; it is also that one may not suppress or destroy that consciousness'. This is but another aspect of human dignity. Kant expressly makes a very similar point when he states that 'the opinion of inequality also makes people unequal' and that 'only the doctrine of Mr *Rousseau* can make it the case that even the most learned philosopher with all his knowledge and without the help of religion is as upright and no better than the common man'.[74] In the context of this passage Wood (1996: xvii) comments that 'all social inequalities are ... founded on falsehood and deception' and that '[t]he reason that Kant's egalitarianism is unqualified is that the worth of every human being is a "dignity" — that is, an absolute and incomparable worth for which nothing else can be substituted as its equivalent'.

Despite his reservations about Kant, Williams (1967: 116–117) develops a concept of 'respect' owed to all persons that is more limited than, but not inconsistent with the description of human dignity advanced at the beginning of this chapter. He argues that each person is 'owed an effort of identification'. There is a distinction, he argues, between regarding a person's character and achievements from a technical point of view and from a point of view 'which is concerned primarily with what it is *for him* to live that life and do those actions in that character'. Thus, from a technological point of view, an inventor who produces no significant invention during her life is merely 'a failed inventor' regardless of the effort and commitment she devoted to her career. But this effort and commitment is not irrelevant because we are concerned with a person like this person 'not merely as a "failed engineer", but as a person "who wanted to be a successful inventor"'. There are many examples of technological titles, which say nothing of the subject as a human being. Williams (1967: 117) reverts to Kant when he asserts that the claim that people 'should be regarded from the human point of view and not merely under these sorts of titles' is part of the content 'that might be attached to Kant's celebrated injunction "treat each man as an end in himself, and never as a means only"'. However, according to Williams (1967: 118) there is more embodied in the notion of 'respect', for each man is owed an effort at identification: that he 'should not be regarded as the surface to which a certain label can be applied, but one should try to see the world (including the label) from his point of view'. These injunctions of Williams are based 'on the proposition that men are beings who are necessarily to some extent conscious of themselves and the world they live in'. Williams (1967: 115) considers it ridiculous to consider 'that the achievement of the highest kind of moral worth should depend on natural capacities, unequally and fortuitously distributed as they are; and this feeling is backed up by the observation that these capacities are not in themselves the bearer of the moral worth, since those that have them are as gifted for vice as for virtue'.

The 'effort of identification' which Williams rightly contends is owed by us to all, and which in my opinion is but another demand arising from a Kantian concept of dignity, is rightly regarded by Williams as important for an understanding and achievement of equality. Looking past the 'label' is but an attempt to escape, quite rightly, the attempts of society to objectify human beings.

[74] 'Notes on the observations on the feeling of the beautiful and sublime' [AK 20:176]; Guyer (ed) (2005: 23).

Although he views the concept of 'respect' as being both complex and unclear, Williams (1967: 116–118) considers that it 'needs, and would repay a good deal of investigation'. Human lives should not be viewed from the perspective of their 'success' in a competitive sense and according to a hierarchy of values attaching to different forms of work, to which various titles are attached, but from the perspective of the person concerned, what it *means for this person* to have lived the life in question and to have performed the work in question.

This is not the place to discuss in any detail the treatment by Williams (1967: 120ff) of 'equality in unequal circumstances' or 'equality of opportunity'. I would, however, contend that in this treatment, and particularly where he justifies remedial action to eradicate inequalities, significant reliance is placed on aspects of human dignity that I would categorise as the human being's sense of self-worth, the desire for the full unfolding of human personality, and the desire for self-fulfilment.

In dealing with *equality of opportunity* Williams (1967: 124) understands this in 'the normal political sense' of 'equality of opportunity for *everyone in society* to secure certain goods'.[75] Contending that equality of opportunity is more complex than generally supposed, Williams (1967: 125–126) is of the view that equality of opportunity requires not merely 'that there should be no exclusion from access on grounds other than those appropriate or rational for the good in question', but that the 'grounds considered appropriate for the good should themselves be such that people from all sections of society have an equal chance of satisfying them'. But this is not adequate where, for example the inability of the poor to meet 'the access requirements', although appropriate or rational in themselves, is in itself caused (albeit indirectly) by factors that could be eliminated by further reform or social action. Hence Williams (1967: 127) argues that a system of allocation will fall short of equality of opportunity 'if the allocation of goods in question in fact works out unequally or disproportionately between different sections of society,

[75] This notion arises, Williams explains, when there is a question of access to goods which are:

(a) desired by (at least) large numbers of people in all ss of society;

(b) are goods which people may be said to earn or achieve;

(c) are goods which not all the people who desire them can have because —

- (i) 'some desired goods, like position of prestige, management, etc are *by their very nature* limited'; or,
- (ii) 'are *contingently* limited [like a university education] in the sense that there are certain conditions of access to them which in fact not everyone satisfies, but there is no intrinsic limit to the numbers who may gain access'; or,
- (iii) 'are *fortuitously* limited, in the sense that although everyone or large numbers of people satisfy the conditions of access to [these goods], there is just not enough of them to go round; so some more stringent conditions or system of rationing have to be imposed, to govern access in an imperfect situation'.

if the unsuccessful sections are under a disadvantage which could be removed by further reform or social action'.[76]

Williams (1967: 127–128) contends that the above approach points to 'a connection between the idea of equality of opportunity, and the idea of equality of persons, which is stronger than might at first be suspected'. What Williams is in effect saying when he speaks in this context of the equality of 'persons' is that these persons are equal with regard to particular aspects of their human dignity which arise from their 'personhood' in the particular case. This becomes even clearer when Williams deals with equality of opportunity in the context of two persons taking educational admission examinations where one is affected by unfavourable environmental conditions and the other not. For in this context Williams says of the two persons that '[t]heir *identity*, for these purposes, does not include their curable environment, which is itself unequal and a contributor to inequality' and that '[t]his abstraction of *persons in themselves from unequal environments* is a way, if not as regarding them as equal, at least of moving recognizably in that direction; and is itself involved in equality of opportunity'. (Emphasis supplied.) In a significant passage Williams (1967: 130) warns that 'an ideal of *equality of respect* that made no contact with such things as the economic needs of society for certain skills, and *human desire for some sort of prestige*, would be condemned to a futile Utopianism, and to having no rational effect on the distribution of goods, position and power that would inevitably proceed'. (Emphasis supplied.) When referring to 'equality of respect' in this context and alluding then to 'human desire for some sort of prestige' Williams is in fact equating human equality with the equality of human beings with regard to significant aspects of what I would call human dignity.

By emphasising such concepts as 'identity', 'persons in themselves', 'equality of respect' and 'human desire for some sort of prestige' one is moving considerably closer to Kant's idea of equality of dignity. Williams comes close to (rightly) embracing self-fulfilment as an important aspect of human worth when he refers to 'a strain of philosophical thought which identifies the end of life as happiness, happiness as reflective tranquillity, and tranquillity as the product of self-sufficiency ...'.

I certainly do not suggest that Williams explicity chooses human dignity as the criterion of reference for equality. His investigation pursues a narrower course. He does, however, acknowledge, albeit implicitly, that there must be *a* criterion

---

[76] Williams (1967: 127) explains this with the following example:

> 'It is a known fact that the system of selection for grammar schools by the "11+" examination favours children in direct proportion to their social class, the children of professional homes having proportionately greater success than those from working class homes. We have every reason to suppose that these results are the product, in good part, of environmental factors; and we know that imaginative social reform, both of the primary educational system and of living conditions, would favourably affect those environmental factors. In these circumstances, this system of educational selection falls short of equality of opportunity.'

of reference, and then proceeds to investigate what it is. Many of the features that he mentions in this regard form part of the description of dignity I propose.

(f) Amartya Sen

Although concentrating in the main on economic aspects of equality, Prof Amartya Sen has, in the Anglo-Saxon world, made a significant contribution to the proper understanding of the concept of equality in human affairs. In his preface to *Inequality Reexamined*, Sen (1992: i) cuts through the logico-grammatical underbrush with one stroke and states quite simply that:

> 'The central question in the analysis and assessment of equality is, I argue here, "equality of *what?*"'

He emphasises that a common characteristic of virtually all the approaches to the ethics of social arrangements that have stood the test of time 'is to want equality of *something* — something that has an important place in the particular theory'. To see the battle as one 'between those "in favour of" and those "against" equality (as the problem is often posed in the literature) is to miss something central to the subject'. Sen also argues that this common feature of being egalitarian in some significant way relates to 'the need to have *equal concern*, at some level, for all the persons involved — the absence of which would tend to make a proposal lack social plausibility'. (Emphasis supplied.) The use of the word 'concern' in this context, which one also encounters elsewhere, and which connotes an attitude which is to be entertained with regard to all human beings, is surely closely related to human worth (dignity). What *is* it that we must be equally concerned about? Surely it must be the humanity (human worth/dignity) of all persons. This emerges, in my view — although in slightly attenuated form — in the development of Sen's argument.

The substantive importance of the question 'equality of what?' relates, according to Sen (1992: xi), to the 'empirical fact of pervasive human diversity'. Any investigation of equality, whether theoretical or practical, that assumes antecedent uniformity thus 'miss[es] out on a major aspect of the problem. Human diversity is no secondary complication (to be ignored, or to be introduced "later on"); it is a fundamental aspect of our interest in equality'. As Sen (192: 117) emphasises, the force of the question 'equality of *what*?' therefore rests to a great extent on the *empirical fact* of our *dissimilarity* 'in physical and mental abilities and disabilities, in epidemiological vulnerability, in age, in gender, and of course, in the social and economic bases of our well-being and freedom'.

Sen's approach to answering the question 'equality of what?' concentrates, as he puts it, 'on our capability to achieve valuable functionings that make up our lives, and more generally, our freedom to promote objectives we have reason to value'. In this connection Sen remarks that at one stage his book was called *Equality and Freedom*. I am indebted to Sen for making this point because

I contend throughout that the value of freedom is an essential component of human worth (dignity). For obvious reasons I rely heavily on Sen's emphasis on the inescapability of posing and answering the question 'equality of what?' While I contend that Sen's 'equality of capability' is somewhat narrow for my legal purposes, it does emphasise significant aspects of human dignity, in respect of which we have a right to be equal, namely those relating to the free unfolding of the human personality and to self-fulfilment.

As Sen puts it (1992: 2), the assessment of claims of equality 'has to come to terms with the existence of pervasive human diversity' and that a failure to recognise this can lead to 'hiding the fact that equal consideration for all may demand very unequal treatment in favour of the disadvantaged'. This warning has even greater force when directed to equality of dignity.

Sen uses his own expressions to indicate the *criterion of reference*, or the *criterion of attribution* in seeking to answer the question 'In respect of what are all human beings equal and in respect of what may no one be discriminated against?' One of these (1992: 2) is 'focal variable', namely the variable 'on which the analysis focuses in comparing different people'. For this purpose he also uses the word 'space'[77] as a 'useful classificatory device ... to separate out the problem of the choice of focal variables ("the choice of space") from other issues in the assessment of inequality'. Sen (1992: 3–4) makes the important point that '[e]thical plausibility is hard to achieve unless everyone is given equal consideration in *some* space that is important in the particular theory', and that 'it is difficult to see how an ethical theory can have general social plausibility without extending equal consideration to all at *some* level'. My argument is, of course, that under our Constitution this important 'focus' or 'space' is human worth (dignity), sufficiently widely defined to include freedom, and in particular the freedom of persons to determine the development of their own personalities and to achieve their own self-fulfilment. I would therefore endorse Sen's emphasis (1992: 4) on considering not only achievement but also the freedom to achieve.

The capability perspective defended by Sen also differs (1992: 7) from various concepts of 'equality of opportunity' which do not 'amount to anything like equality of *overall* freedoms'. His position is that 'a more adequate way of considering "real" equality of opportunity must be through equality of capabilities (or through the elimination of unambiguous inequalities in capabilities, since capability comparisons are typically incomplete)'.

Sen (1992: 12–13) argues that even such philosophers as Robert Nozick and James Buchanan demand equality in some 'space', and that the equality that utilitarianism seeks 'takes the form of equal treatment of human beings in the space of *gains and losses of utilities*'.

[77] Which Sen, in his informal and self-deprecatory manner, refers to 'as language for which we economists are often — not unreasonably — teased'.

Importantly Sen (1992: 21–23) also emphasises that it is fundamentally wrong to pose a radical contrast between equality and freedom. 'The libertarian demands for liberty typically include important features of "equal liberty"'. One should not see the differences posed by equality and freedom in terms of liberty *versus* freedom.

> '[P]osing the problem in terms of this latter contrast reflects a "category" mistake. They are not alternatives. Liberty is among the possible *fields of application* of equality, and equality is among the possible *patterns* of distribution of liberty.'

Sen (1992: 23–26) rejects, inter alia, the claim that equality is an 'empty' idea. First, because, even before a specific space is chosen, 'equality in *some space that is seen to be particularly important* is not an empty demand'. It relates to the 'discipline imposed by the needs for some impartiality, some form of equal concern'. Secondly, because 'once the context is fixed, equality can be a particularly powerful and exacting demand', for example the demand for 'some ranking of patterns'. Thirdly, 'the diversity of spaces in which equality may be demanded really reflects a deeper diversity, to wit, different diagnoses of objects of values'. It is not unique to equality evaluation and 'the different demands of equality reflect divergent views as to what things are to be directly valued in that context'.

In the economic sphere Sen (1992: 28–30) reflects on the problem arising from 'concentrating on inequality of *incomes* as the primary focus of attention in the analysis of inequality'. He argues that the 'extent of real inequality of opportunities that people face cannot be readily deduced from the magnitude of inequality of *incomes*, since what we can and cannot do, can or cannot achieve, do not depend just on our incomes but also on the variety of physical and social characteristics that effect our lives and make us what we are'. By not giving sufficient attention to the actual physical and social diversity of persons 'we are made to overlook the substantive inequalities in, say, well-being and freedom that may directly result from an equal distribution of incomes (given our variable needs and disparate social circumstances). Both pragmatic shortcuts and grand rhetoric can be helpful for some purposes and altogether unhelpful and misleading for others'. While Sen's chapter 'Freedom, achievements and resources' (1992: 31–38) is substantially economic, he does — for my purposes — draw the important distinction between actual achievement (what we manage to accomplish) and the freedom to achieve (being the '*real opportunity* that we have to accomplish what we value'). He points out that the two 'need not be congruent' and they 'need not coincide'.

In his chapter on 'Functionings and capability' Sen (1992: 39ff) argues that '[l]iving may be seen as consisting of a set of interrelated "functionings", consisting of beings and doings'. Functionings can vary from the most elementary things to 'complex achievements such as being happy, having self-respect, taking part in the life of the community and so on'. Sen argues that these functionings are '*constitutive* of a person's being, and an evaluation of well-being has to take the form of an assessment of these constituent elements'. Sen contends that the *capability* to function is closely related to the notion of functionings. This arises from two distinct but interrelated considerations:

> 'First, if the achieved functionings constitute a person's well-being, then the capability to achieve functionings ... will constitute the person's freedom — the real opportunities — to have well-being.
>
> ...
>
> The second connection between well-being and capability takes the direct form of making *achieved* well-being depend on the *capability* to function. Choosing may itself be a valuable part of living, and a life of genuine choice with serious options may be seen to be — for that reason — richer. In this view, at least some types of capabilities contribute *directly* to well-being, making one's life richer with the opportunity of reflective choice.'

According to Sen (1992: 49ff) although '[c]apability is ... a reflection of the freedom to achieve valuable functionings' and 'can be read as a reflection of substantive freedom', capability 'may be relevant even for the *level of well-being achieved,* and not only for the *freedom to achieve well-being*'. I would once again point out that the way Sen links freedom, capability, achievement and well-being clearly indicates that these concepts are linked to human dignity, for their achievement or realisation are essential for the achievement of full humanity.

The following comments of Sen (1992: 69), as an economist, are significant:

> 'I have discussed the scope of the idea of freedom at some length here partly because freedom is one of the most powerful social ideas, and its relevance to the analysis of equality and justice is far-reaching and strong. When we assess inequalities across the world in being able to avoid preventable morbidity, or escapable hunger, or premature mortality, we are not merely examining differences in well-being, but also in the basic freedoms that we value and cherish.'

Sen's treatment is both methodological and substantive. Methodologically he points to the unavoidable necessity of asking the question 'Equality of what?' and in this context draws attention to the diversity of human beings — 'the fact that we differ from each other in personal characteristics as well as external circumstances' (1992: 129) — and to the plurality of spaces in which equality can be judged, spaces that can serve as the sphere of comparison. Substantively he has identified and defended the space or spaces in which equality is to be judged.

Sen (1992: 128ff) sums up his substantive approach as one that involves

> 'judging human advantage by *the freedom to achieve*, incorporating (but going beyond) the *actual functioning*. In many contexts, particularly in the assessment of individual well-being, these conditions can, I have argued, be fruitfully seen in terms of *the capability to function*, incorporating (but going beyond) the actual functionings that a person can achieve. The "capability approach" builds on a general concern with freedom to achieve (including the capability to function).'

Importantly, Sen (1992: 132) points out that it is possible for an ethical theory to include more than one type of variable in the *criterion of reference* or criterion *of attribution*:

> 'We may be concerned with liberties and with levels of well-being. We may attach intrinsic importance both to well-being and to agency. We may value freedom as well as other achievements.'

In the sphere of poverty alleviation Sen argues (1992: 151) that the

> 'orientation from an income-centered to a capability-centered view gives us a better understanding of what is involved in the challenge of poverty. It provides clearer guidance on the priorities of anti-poverty policy and also helps to understand better the genesis of poverty in apparently unlikely circumstances (eg in the rich countries of Europe and America). The wisdom of focusing on poverty as lack of freedom is consistent with a variety of foundational concerns.'

Once again the link with human dignity is, as I understand Sen, obvious.

I do not believe that there is any real inconsistency between Sen's capability and functionings approach and a legal one that posits human worth (dignity) as the attributive criterion for equality analysis and application. Sen's criterion is no doubt narrower than my conception of human dignity, but would include certain of the features of human dignity. His approach certainly enriches the freedom component of human dignity and in particular its effect on the ability of human beings to strive for self-fulfilment in their lives.

(g) Martha Nussbaum

Like Amartya Sen, Martha Nussbaum (2007) also supports a capabilities approach, which she links with human dignity and equality. Without formulating it in these terms, she clearly sees human dignity as the appropriate criterion of attribution for equality. Nussbaum (2007: 179) explains that the capabilities approach uses the notion of 'a threshold level of each of the capabilities, which is taken to be a minimum beneath which a decently dignified life for citizens is not available'. (As we shall see, German jurisprudence adopts a similar approach when it comes to the minimum material support that the social state owes its inhabitants.) Nussbaum further contends (2007: 273–274) that two of the central facts that a human being's 'moral intelligence' (which she derives from Grotius) apprehends is 'the dignity of the human being as an ethical being, a *dignity that is fully equal* no matter where humans are placed ...' and 'a common life with others organized so as to respect that *equal dignity*....' (Emphasis supplied.) Nussbaum (2007: 291–292) pleads for a capabilities approach that insists on a minimum threshold level for each important entitlement — 'people are entitled not only to a mere life, but to a life compatible with human dignity'. She points out that one of the capabilities speaks of 'being able to be treated as a dignified being whose worth is equal to that of others'. She then, in a particularly important passage for my purposes, contends as follows:

> 'We have seen that the idea of dignity is spelt out from the beginning in terms of equality; it is the *equal dignity* of all human beings that demands recognition.'

(h) Louis Henkin

For Prof Louis Henkin (1995: 210), dignity '[o]n the highest level ... is a quality of worth or excellence, and when used in the compound term "human dignity", it suggests all that for Kant is inherent in the human "personhood" of every human being'. A few years earlier Henkin (1992: 210–211) with reference to Kant's *Foundations of a Metaphysics of Morals*, wrote a little more expansively when he observed that human dignity requires that 'in every society every person counts, that he (she) be considered worthy as an individual, not merely as part of the collectivity'. Specifically, he believed that human dignity 'requires respect for every individual's physical and psychic integrity, for his (her) "personhood" before the law, for his/her autonomy and freedom'. He moreover considered that these were 'not to be lightly sacrificed, even for the welfare of the majority or for the common good'. Sometimes human dignity is seen as requiring more — 'the full development of the individual's personality, respect by society and by one's neighbours, security for one's "honour" and self-esteem'.

Although not expressly mentioning self-fulfilment, I do not see any material inconsistency between the above views and the approach I am espousing. It is significant too that Henkin sees autonomy as part of human dignity.

(i) Ronald Dworkin and John Rawls

For Prof Dworkin (1977: 181), quoting John Rawls in part, the entitlement of everybody to equal respect is '"owed to human beings as moral persons", and follows from the moral personality that distinguishes humans from animals'. Rawls (1971: 563) sees 'moral personality and not the capacity for pleasure and pain as the fundamental aspect of the self'.

(j) A wider application of respect and concern?

In his book entitled *Animal Liberation* (1977: 5) the philosopher Peter Singer correctly points to the multiplicity of respects in which human beings differ from one another. He then contends that the principle of the equality of human beings 'is not a description of alleged actual equality' among human beings, but 'a prescription of how we should treat humans'. But he also contends that equality 'is a moral idea not an assertion of fact'. It may be a matter of semantics, but why can one not assert (at least logically) that human beings, as members of the same species, have the qualities, functions and abilities making up human dignity that I have tried to sketch and that, with regard to such dignity, they are equal? At the very least they are *entitled* to be treated equally *with regard to* such dignity, to *have* equal dignity. It is not Singer's purpose, as I understand it, to deny or challenge this idea that human beings should be treated with equal respect regarding their dignity. The thrust of his argument, rather (1977: x), is that 'the basic moral principle of equal consideration of interests is not arbitrarily restricted to members of our own species'; and flowing from this his assertion (1977: 8) that 'suffering and enjoyment' is the criterion of reference for equal consideration and respect. From this he argues that 'if a being is not capable of suffering or of experiencing enjoyment or happiness, there is nothing to take into account'.

I make no bones that my conception of human dignity is, in a certain sense of the word, a 'species' argument. I trust, however, that I am not guilty of 'speciesism' in the pejorative sense that Singer (1977: 7) uses the term, namely 'a prejudice or attitude of bias towards the interests of one's own species and against those of members of other species'. I agree with Singer that, for example, a high and cumulative degree of pain is unnecessarily inflicted on what Singer terms 'factory farms' and that in numerous other areas unnecessary pain is inflicted on animals. His argument that human beings should adopt a vegetarian diet is powerful and compelling. I would also follow his argument — that the permissible infliction of pain on animals should be confined to narrow limits — a long way. It is immoral to inflict pain gratuitously on animals and greater efforts could be made to eliminate such behaviour.

Yet I disagree with Singer when he asserts (1977: 8) that '[i]f a being is not capable of suffering or of experiencing enjoyment or happiness, there is nothing to take into account'. For the sake of the species and ourselves, I am of the view that no matter how disabled, ill or injured a person is, she still has dignity which must be respected and protected. Moreover I agree with the German jurisprudence that human dignity can survive a person's death. Singer's position is nuanced and he is of the view (1977: 22) that 'if we have to choose between the life of a human being and the life of an animal we should choose to save the life of the human ...'. This is so because the greater intellectual capacity (in various respects) of the human enables it to suffer pain (in various respects) at a higher level and similarly to experience higher pleasure and enjoyment. Yet, Singer continues, 'there may be special cases where the reverse holds true, because the human being in question does not have the capacities of a normal human being'. For the reasons already stated, I must disagree.

For my purposes, however, the most important question is whether Singer's views on the respect due to non-human beings detract from my extensive description of human dignity, and the ensuing respect and protection due to it. I believe not. The proposition that, at a certain basic level, human beings and non-human beings are equal with regard to their ability to experience pain and pleasure, by no means implies that human beings do not have many other capacities and attributes (which they do not share with non-human beings) that are fully deserving of protection and respect. Exhibiting greater concern for non-human beings does not imply lesser concern for human beings. Likewise I do not believe that Singer's views in any way detract from the proposition that human beings are all equal with respect to their human dignity.

(k) The secular in search of the absolute

The title of Professor Isensee's illuminating article (2006) '*Menschenwürde: die säkulare Gesellschaft auf der Suche nach dem Absoluten*' ('Human worth: Secular society in search of the absolute') [78] captures both the pathos and the dilemma of the 21st century's search for a better world, or at least a world in which the regular slaughter (by sword or famine) of millions of innocent women and children no longer takes place. The disfavour with which religion, and in particular the theistic religions, are presently regarded in certain quarters, has resulted in secular humanists' passionate search for a secular absolute in this desire for a better world, and in the process forgetting or ignoring the fact that some of the strongest secular attempts at finding the absolute (or even the universal) rely, directly or indirectly on theological models. Isensee (2006: 173–174), writing about a constitution in which the acknowledgment and protection of human worth is of the very highest order, expresses this dilemma brilliantly in the opening paragraphs of his article:

> '"The worth of human beings is inviolable", according to the German Basic Law in the first sentence of Art 1(1): pithy, solemn, mysterious. Reality denies this: human worth is violable, and is repeatedly violated. Nonetheless the law itself accepts it. "... [I]t is inviolable." Pathos rules defiantly here. What is expressed in the indicative is in fact imperative. The apparently descriptive word use expresses the categorical nature of the norm particularly clearly. The norm takes its stand against threatening reality. In the empire of the law, nobody touches the worth of human beings. In the constitutional text inviolability stands as truth. Yet it is not something empirical, but a matter of belief and a truth to be believed, and yet as an ought ("*sollen*").'

Isensee (2006: 178–179) also speaks of human worth in terms of a 'civil religion'. At times when 'everything is shattered that customarily holds society together' — Christian religion and cultural tradition, civil forms of life and national solidarity — 'society finds unity in confessing to human worth, and demands something like a state of fundamental moral certainty' and dignity's constitutional protection provision proves itself to be 'an article of faith in a civil religion'.

While Isensee vividly portrays the dilemma the modern world faces, I believe that Kant makes out a far stronger secular case for human worth as an absolute than Isensee gives him credit for. I share the views of Allen Wood (1999: xv), expressed in part of the long quotation from his work that features in Chapter 1:

[78] I am indebted to Prof Henk Botha for bringing this article to my attention.

> 'Still more than that, however, the age needs Kant's sober, principled hope for a more rational, cosmopolitan future. In other words, we need to recapture an authentically Enlightenment conception of the human condition, especially an interpretation of that conception that makes clear the Enlightenment's still unrealized radical potential.'

Our stark choice is, I believe, between the transcendental ideal of human worth on the one hand and 'law and economics' on the other.

(l) Ubuntu

The sub-Saharan indigenous concept of *ubuntu* has been proffered as an aid to the proper contextual understanding of the value of dignity under the Constitution. I shall deal with the constitutional jurisprudence invoking *ubuntu* in the next chapter, and deal here with its theological and philosophical background.

Deng (2004: 501) points out that according to Dinka tribal views, God created humankind in its totality and therefore every human being 'no matter what his race or religion, has a sanctity and moral or spiritual value that must be respected'. To wrong a human being, it is said, 'is to wrong God himself'.

The word 'Akan' refers, amongst other things, to peoples who speak one of a group of closely interrelated languages and who live mainly in Ghana and the neighbouring Côte d'Ivoire. Wiredu (1996: 157–158), writing about an Akan conception of a person, explains that one of the three elements constituting the human personality is the life principle *okra*, which comes directly from God. 'It is supposed to be an actual speck of God that he gives out of himself as a gift of life along with a specific destiny.' Because they possess an *okra*, all persons have 'an intrinsic value, the same in each, which they do not owe to any earthly circumstance'. Flowing from this value is 'a concept of human dignity, which implies that every human being is entitled in an equal measure to a certain basic respect'. Wiredu points to the fact that, flowing from the doctrine of *okra*, every person has the right 'as the recipient of a destiny, to pursue that unique destiny assigned to him by God'. This, I would suggest, is akin to the concepts of self-fulfilment and the free unfolding of the human personality in the Western understanding of human dignity. Wiredu further points out that the Akans have 'an acute sense of the dependency of the human being' on other human beings.

Dzobo (1992: 3)[79] suggests that there are three salient features of the African humanistic orientation: the value of life, the value of the human being and the value of communal social organisation. The human being counts for more than material and economic values (Dzobo 1992: 4) and 'embodies the dynamic creative power'. It also has 'creative power' and a 'creative personality or creative

[79] Citations will be from the internet site referred to in the bibliography.

humanity which is the supreme goal of life'.[80] In a formulation that harmonises significantly with Kant, Dzobo (1992: 4) asserts that

> '[i]n the humanistic orientation persons are treated as ends and not as tools because they have a creative purpose to fulfil in life; this is one's ultimate destiny ...'.

He concludes as follows on this aspect:

> 'A person therefore is good not because he is good for something, but primarily because he has a creative humanity and so is the creator of the good.'

Dzobo (1992: 5) points out that in a humanistically orientated society 'the individual always has a stake in the welfare of the community and vice versa, but room is also made for individual initiative, drive and enterprise'.

I turn now to deal more specifically with *ubuntu*.

Shutte (2001: 10–11) regards *ubuntu* as 'the idea of community, that persons depend on other persons to be persons'. He contends that *ubuntu* is an ethical concept and that 'the understanding and vision of humanity embodied in *ubuntu* is of vital importance to the contemporary world, not just to contemporary South Africa but to all the rest of the nations as well, developed or undeveloped'.

Ubuntu has been referred to, somewhat cursorily, in a number of Constitutional Court judgments but with very sparse reference to any literature on its meaning.[81] From my limited hearsay knowledge of *ubuntu* it would appear to play a significant ongoing role in black culture, custom and ethics.

The literature available to me has not always been particularly illuminating on *ubuntu* in the constitutional context. According to Ramose (2003: 230–231),

> '*ubu-ntu* is the fundamental ontological and epistemological category in the African thought of the Bantu-speaking people.... *Ubu-* as the generalized understanding of be-ing may be said to be distinctly ontological. Whereas *-ntu* as the nodal point at which be-ing assumes concrete form or a mode of being in the process of continual unfolding may be said to be distinctly epistemological.
>
> The word *umu-* shares an identical ontological feature with the word *ubu-*. Whereas the range of *ubu-* is the widest generality, *umu-* tends towards the more specific. Joined together with *-ntu* then, *umu-* becomes *umuntu*. *Umuntu* means the emergence of homo-loquens who is simultaneously a *homo sapiens*.'

[80] I suggest that this concept of a human being's 'dynamic creative power' corresponds broadly with human beings' exercising 'their own judgment ... [and] self-determination ... [shaping] themselves and nature ... [developing] their personalities and ... [striving] for self-fulfilment' in my description of human dignity.

[81] In *S v Makwanyane and Another* 1995 (3) SA 391 (CC) (1995 (6) BCLR 665 (CC)) paras 371–372, Sachs J observed that 'our law reports and legal textbooks contain few references to African sources as part of the general law of the country' and that appropriate source material, implicitly including material relating to *ubuntu* 'is limited and any conclusions that individual members of this Court might wish to offer would inevitably have to be tentative rather than definitive'.

After referring to the maxim or aphorism *umuntu ngumuntu nga bantu (motho ke motho ka batho)*, Ramose (2003: 231) states the following:

> 'Although the English language does not exhaust the meaning of this maxim or aphorism, it may nonetheless be construed to mean that to be a human be-ing is to affirm one's humanity by recognizing the humanity of others and, on that basis, establish humane relations with them. Ubuntu, understood as be-ing human (human-ness); a humane, respectful, and polite attitude towards others constitutes the core meaning of this aphorism.'

Professor Thaddeus Metz (2010: 83) regards *ubuntu* as a widespread aspect of sub-Saharan morality and he translates the expression as 'A person is a person through other persons' or 'I am because we are'. He (2010: 84) considers the former of these two expressions to be somewhat vague and reworks it as 'A human being lives a genuinely human way of life as she values harmony with other human beings' or 'A person becomes a real person through communal relationships'. It is a communal relationship that is key to having *ubuntu* and acting rightly. He quotes Steve Biko as asserting that 'our action is usually joint community orientated action rather than the individualism which is the hallmark of the capitalist approach'. Solidarity with one another requires, according to Metz (2010: 84), 'people to engage in mutual aid, to act in ways that are expected to benefit each other'. He sees *ubuntu* as an ethical principle that holds, for example, that an action 'is wrong insofar it fails to honour relationships in which people share a way of life and care for one another's quality of life'.[82]

Metz (2010: 84–85) contends that *ubuntu* embodies 'a communitarian perspective that differs from dominant Western moral theories, particularly in virtue of deeming relationships of a certain kind to have basic moral worth'. An approach like this is indeed commendable, but I have difficulty in accepting that it really differs from Western moral theories, particularly those that are communitarian, while at the same time postulating individual autonomy and responsibility. But Metz (2010: 83) goes further, contending that the idea of *ubuntu* expresses a moral claim indicating that being human is '*entirely constituted* by relating to others in a certain manner'. (Emphasis supplied.) I have considerable doubts whether the claim for *ubuntu* has ever gone so far as suggested in the emphasised phrase. If it does, then it certainly conflicts with important Western moral theories that prize individual identity and particularly individual responsibility too much to countenance its sacrifice to the group. To do so would be to sow the seeds of totalitarianism. As I have stressed throughout, the Kantian approach to freedom and individuality does not reject the associational aspects of the human being. I readily accept the proposition that one becomes fully human only through association, in myriad ways, with other human beings, but this does not constitute my total humanity or my total human dignity.

[82] See also, on *ubuntu* generally, Metz and Gaie (2010: 273–277).

It is important to note that Professor Drusilla Cornell, who held the National Research Foundation chair in Customary Law, Indigenous Ideals and Dignity Jurisprudence in the University of Cape Town, is engaged in a multi-disciplinary research project into the concept of *ubuntu*. The results have not yet been published, but will no doubt make a significant contribution to the understanding of the concept, also in the jurisprudential sphere. Cornell (2011) considers it important to separate the 'normative and descriptive aspects of uBuntu'. According to *ubuntu* 'human beings are intertwined in a world of ethical relations and obligations with other people from the time they are born ... [w]e come into the world obligated to others, and in turn these others are obligated to us'. This mutuality is thus not considered as one 'between separate, atomistic individuals'. Rather, 'the ethical, political and moral inscription of each one of us into a web of relations is fundamentally drawn from the fact that we are born into a community with others'. This, however, is not simply a 'social fact' but points instead to 'an ethical relationship, which is the basis of our humanness'. Cornell (2011) asserts that it is 'a profound misunderstanding of uBuntu to confuse it with simple-minded communitarianism'. Rather, it is only through 'the engagement and support of others that a person is able to realize a true individuality'. Our social relations to others are, according to Cornell, 'inseparable from how we are both embedded and supported by a community that is not outside each of us but is inscribed alongside each of us. The inscription of the other calls the other out of himself or herself back toward the ancestor and forward to the community. Thereby, this inscription brings about relations of mutual support for the safeguarding of the potential inherent within every person.'

Cornell understands the various linguistic formulations of *ubuntu* to mean that 'a person is a person by or through other people' and points to the fact that Justice Emeritus Yvonne Mokgoro renders the mutuality and reciprocity of *ubuntu* as 'I am a person because you are a person'. Accordingly, if this human reciprocity or egalitarian relationship is violated, uBuntu is violated. This 'does not imply any simple notion of communitarianism or social cohesion' for '[e]ach of us is called to become our own person and at the same time to realize and support an ethical quality of humanness in all others.... It is still up to me to realize my personal destiny and become a person.' Therefore it is humanity and not just my community that has a stake in my ethical action. If I relate to another person in a manner that lives up to *ubuntu*, then there is at least an ethical relationship between the two of us.

Cornell deals as follows with the criticism that *ubuntu* is a term that has no well-defined content and can be made to mean almost anything to anyone:

> 'This ignores the rich and very specific historical meanings of uBuntu as a concept that has developed in the broader context of modern African Humanism. The European philosopher Hegel argued famously that the project of human freedom has no African

history, and thus no African future. In Hegel's formulation, Africa lacked the institutions of mutual recognition, reciprocity and civility that could make political life into something more than the naked exercise of coercive force. This idea is of course not restricted to Hegel: it infuses modern stereotypes about the past and future of the continent. Against this backdrop, uBuntu joins a panoply of concepts — negritude, ujamaa, harambee and so forth — that focus the modern tradition of African Humanism. Whatever their flaws and their differences, all these concepts contribute to an insistence that there are indeed indigenous African forms of mutual recognition, reciprocity and civility. And that therefore there is a life to the hope for freedom on this continent. This makes uBuntu a concept with a well-defined place in the landscape of political and ethical thought. Whatever else has been done with it in the world of brands and labels, a central strand of its modern development draws together concerns with mutuality and freedom in the context of the decolonization of Africa.'

(m) Dissident voices

I do not intend surveying the confusion around equality that has been caused, mainly, by a failure to appreciate the existence and nature of the inherent logico-grammatical problem to which frequent reference has already been made. It might be useful, however, to consider a paradigmatic example of the confusing consequences of this failure. One of the best-known attempts to demonstrate that equality has no substantive content and is not an independent right is Peter Westen's article 'The empty idea of equality' (1982: 537), in which he contends (1982: 538) that in 1982 equality was becoming the 'argument of first choice' that 'threatens to swallow "rights" that once ranked far above it'. I choose Westen as an example, because his approach has been the cause of confusion in South Africa.

After adopting the Aristotelian definition of equality, Westen postulates that '[equality] ... is an idea that should be banished from moral and legal discourse as an explanatory term' on the basis of two propositions that he seeks to establish (1982: 542):

(1) that statements about equality logically entail (and necessarily collapse into) simpler statements of rights; and
(2) that the additional step of transforming simple statements of rights into statements of equality not only involves unnecessary work but also engenders profound conceptual confusion.

I do not doubt that confusion abounds, but will argue that it is for reasons differing profoundly from those that Westen asserts. Moreover, I believe that he is fundamentally mistaken when asserting that all statements about equality *logically entail and necessarily collapse into* simpler statements of rights. In developing his thesis (1982: 543–558) that the Aristotelian proposition that likes should be treated alike 'is tautological [*sic*]', Westen advances arguments that ignore the logico-grammatical problem. He raises many well-known arguments seeking to demonstrate the absurdity of trying to explain what it means to call two people alike. Dealing with 'alike' as meaning 'alike in every respect' he points out the obvious that no two people are exactly alike in every respect and (1982: 544) that 'the only things that are completely alike in every respect are immaterial symbols and forms, such as ideal numbers and geometric figures, which are not themselves the subject of morals'. The logic is unassailable, but only if Westen's undisclosed and unsubstantiated major premise is granted, namely that the only characteristics of human beings which are relevant to a comparative equality enquiry are their biological ones. If one were to postulate that a fundamental characteristic of human beings is their dignity (fundamental human worth), that all human beings are endowed with equal dignity, and that human dignity is the only criterion of attribution for human equality, Westen's conclusion simply does not follow.

Dealing with 'alike' as meaning people who are alike in some but not all respects Westen (1982: 544) asserts:

> '[W]hile the previous definition excludes every person in the world, the present definition includes every person and thing because all persons and things are alike in some respect; and one is left with the morally absurd proposition that "all people and things should be treated alike."'

It ceases to be absurd if, as I argue throughout, the proposition is changed to 'all people should be treated alike with regard to their human dignity (worth)'.

Dealing with 'alike' as referring to people who 'are *morally* alike in a certain respect' Westen (1982: 547) remarks that

> '[t]o say that people who are morally alike in a certain respect "should be treated alike" means that they should be treated in accord with the moral rule by which they are determined to be alike ... more simply, people who by a rule should be treated alike should by the rule be treated alike'

and then somewhat triumphantly concludes:

> 'So there it is: equality is entirely "[c]ircular".... Equality is an empty vessel with no substantive moral content of its own. Without moral standards, equality remains meaningless, a formula that can have nothing to say about how we should act. With such standards, equality becomes superfluous, a formula that can do nothing but repeat what we already know.'

It is not, however, my purpose here to point out the circular reasoning of this very attack. I merely want to highlight that Westen does not deal at all with how different the argument would be if 'alike' meant treating 'alike with respect to their innate human dignity' and that like treatment referred to 'like treatment with respect to this innate dignity'. Westen (1982: n 23) cites, with apparent approval, the following:

'The idea of equality or non-discrimination is essentially a value judgment which cannot be derived from any assertions or speculations regarding the nature of man.'[83]

Apart from asking why it cannot be so derived, one must point out that the proposition dismisses, in one fell swoop, virtually the entire body of Kant's work on ethics.

At the heart of Westen's criticism of equality as a moral or legal norm or right is his repeated assertion (1982: 557–559) that equality is 'an entirely formal concept', a 'form' of discourse with no substantive content of its own. He moreover contends (1982: 579–580) that equality as a form of analysis 'confuses far more that it clarifies' for at least four reasons: (1) it 'masquerad[es]' as an independent norm, while concealing the real nature of the substantive rights it incorporates by reference; (2) it frames a person's entitlements in terms of his equivalence to others, and misleadingly suggests that one person's right vis-à-vis another's are identical in all contexts; (3) it encourages the use of 'monolithic levels of judicial scrutiny' undifferentiated by the importance of the underlying fundamental right, and erroneously suggests that 'all questions of equality are to be scrutinised under a single (or sometimes, a two-tier) standard of justification'; and (4) by emphasising that some issues of equality entail dual remedies, equality erroneously implies that it entails uniquely flexible remedies.

I refrain from commenting on the correctness of Westen's analysis and criticism, in his article, of American equality jurisprudence or on the different 'standards of review' developed in this jurisprudence. My contention is a more fundamental one. Equality and its correlative, unfair discrimination (unfair non-equal treatment) do not — properly understood — lead to the negative consequences detailed by Westen. In my view there is an understanding of equality, namely equality of dignity of all human beings, that *does not* 'camouflage [...] rights under a formula that makes no explicit reference to the substantive rights it incorporates from elsewhere.... [or] produce [...] unnecessary confusion, because it does circuitously what could be done directly',[84] and that *does not* limit itself to 'a search for equivalences' with a 'tendency to assume that what makes for equality in mathematics also makes for equality in law and morals';[85] and that *does not* 'mystify — and ... skew moral and political discourse ... [because] it is an empty form having no substantive content of its own'.[86]

Although Westen has in a subsequent book, *Speaking of Equality: An Analysis of the Rhetorical Force of 'Equality' in Moral and Legal Discourse* (1990)

[83] Lloyd (1972: 87).
[84] Compare Westen (1982: 580–581).
[85] Compare Westen (1982: 581–584).
[86] Westen (1982: 596).

modified his original views in several respects (1990: xxi)[87] he has not yet, in my view, discovered the key to unlocking the confusion. In the following passage he moves closer to the solution, but skirts past it (1990: xxi):

> 'In order to declare people identical in relevant respects, therefore, one must possess a standard of comparison that is an appropriate measure of the state of affairs one wishes to bring about. To declare people identical in *normatively* relevant respects, one must possess a standard of comparison that is a *normatively* appropriate measure of the state of affairs one wishes to bring about.... The concept of equality does not itself contain criteria for judging standards of comparison; it presupposes them. Equality is a relationship that obtains amongst persons or things by reference to *such standards of comparison as have been independently established as appropriate to the states of affairs one wishes to bring about.*' (Emphasis in the original.)

This still deprives equality of substantive content, even in the context of its use in relation to the treatment of human beings. As Westen describes it, it is not a right or an end in itself, but something dependent ultimately on a state of affairs 'one wishes to bring about'. Unless of course one postulates (which Westen does not) that the state of affairs one wishes to bring about is one where the dignity of all is equally respected and protected. With regard to Westen's assertion regarding 'the state of affairs one wishes to bring about' this would of course attract the opprobrium of Korsgaard (1996: 275), already referred to, concerning the 'struggle to escape from utilitarianism,' an approach that 'distorts our thinking' because the consequentialist outlook wrongly believes that 'the business of morality is to *bring something about*' instead of indicating 'how we should relate to one another'. Greenawalt (1983) in his article 'How empty is the idea of equality?' provides a sustained refutation of Westen's (1982) thesis, and concludes (1983: 1184) with the following observation:

> 'Professor Westen's claim that equality is empty has been shown to be based on his extraordinarily narrow conception of what equality means, a conception that excludes substantive norms of equality altogether and sharply constricts the range of the formal principle of equality as well.'

2.10 CONCLUSION

I have in this chapter, at a somewhat theoretical level, advanced two hypotheses with regard to equality. I have done so against a theological and secular philosophic background in an attempt to construct as broad and solid an 'overlapping consensus' as possible.

[87] Where he states:

> 'I now believe that equality in mathematics may differ fundamentally from equality elsewhere; that a certain class of rights may indeed be usefully viewed as "equality rights"; that the so-called presumption of equality has plausible force; and that the inherent ambiguities of equality, which I once considered solely a vice, may be a virtue in some contexts.'

The first hypothesis is that legal concepts such as equality and non-discrimination, when applied to human beings, cannot make sense unless a criterion of reference or attribution is added in order to answer the inescapable question: 'In respect of what are human beings equal and in respect of what may they not be discriminated against?' The second hypothesis, flowing from the first, is that human worth (dignity) is the criterion of reference or attribution as the answer to the above question.

I would argue that at the theoretical level there is substantial support for the first hypothesis and nothing — that I have been able to discover — that convincingly falsifies it. As far as the second hypothesis is concerned, there appears to be considerable and respectable support for human dignity (in the broad sense I contend for) as the appropriate criterion of reference or attribution for equality. I am not suggesting that in all cases the criterion so supported necessarily follows the precise contours of dignity as I have argued for it. Most, if not all, do however choose values that form at least part of my description of dignity. For Amartya Sen, for example, the relevant criterion is the capability of human beings to achieve valuable functionings that make up their lives, and more generally, their freedom to promote objectives they have reason to value. I would suggest that this criterion covers at least certain of the aspects of human dignity that I propose — for example, those that relate to the ability of human beings to exercise judgment and self-determination, to shape themselves and nature and to strive for self-fulfilment in their lives. German academic writing also firmly supports both these hypotheses, but will be dealt with in Chapters 3 and 4 below.

CHAPTER THREE

HUMAN DIGNITY (HUMAN WORTH) UNDER THE CONSTITUTION[1]

3.1 PRELIMINARY DESCRIPTION OF HUMAN DIGNITY (WORTH)

As stated in Chapter 2, section 2.1, I propose that the human dignity (worth) of each and every person be understood as both the capacity for and the right to respect as a human being. Human dignity arises from all those aspects of the human personality that flow from human intellectual and moral capacity; which in turn separate human beings from the impersonality of nature, enables them to exercise their own judgment, to have self-awareness and a sense of self-worth, to exercise self-determination, to shape themselves and nature, to develop their personalities and to strive for self-fulfilment in their lives; it also arises from the capacity of human beings to enter into meaningful relationships with others and thereby achieve self-fulfilment at least in part. I have already indicated that this *description* is closely modelled on the classic description of Professor Günther Dürig (1956: 125), with additions of my own.

This description postulates

(a) Certain *qualities* of the human being, namely:
those aspects of the human personality that flow from human intellectual and moral capacity; which in turn separate human beings from the impersonality of nature;
(b) Certain *functions* that these qualities *enable* human beings to perform, namely,
  (i) to exercise their own judgment;
  (ii) to have self-awareness;
  (iii) to have a sense of self-worth;
  (iv) to exercise self-determination;
  (v) to shape themselves and nature;
  (vi) to develop their personalities; and
  (vii) to strive for self-fulfilment in their lives.

[1] At the outset mention should be made of Professor Henk Botha's article 'Human dignity in comparative perspective' (2009). Not only is it a valuable contribution to the debate on human dignity in comparative perspective, but it also provides an insightful analysis of human dignity in German constitutional law.

It is these qualities and abilities that make up human dignity. I have not included in the above functions the ability to form meaningful relationships with other human beings. I certainly do regard this ability as a facet of human worth, hence the presence of associational individual rights in the Constitution, but consider that it forms part of self-determination, the shaping of self and personality, and the striving for self-fulfilment.

3.2 THE SOUTH AFRICAN COMMON LAW BEFORE 27 APRIL 1994[2]

It might at first blush seem strange that the common law is considered to be of assistance in analysing a provision of a constitution that constitutes the supreme law of the land. However, the South African common law relating to personality rights has developed so creatively and humanely that, liberated from the statutory apartheid cancers that it suffered from, it can in my view play a significant role in the task of concretizing the human image, so essential for the understanding of human dignity under the Constitution. As Burchell (1996: 650) correctly points out, the protection of human dignity under the *action iniuriarum* is 'undoubtedly one of the most impressive and enduring legacies of Roman law, and a feature which places the South African Law of Delict in the forefront of the protection of what is arguably the most fundamental of all human rights'.

We are fortunate in South Africa to have this rich personality right jurisprudence. Professor Eberle (2002: 261) who writes in the field of comparative (US/German) constitutional law, ascribes the significant differences in the two systems regarding the constitutional protection of the individual's personality to the fact that American private law, unlike German law, 'did not develop privacy concepts comprehensively, and thus, unlike German constitutional law, American constitutional law had no ready base to stand on'.

This conclusion is reached by Eberle with full appreciation (2002: 261 n 16) of the early pioneering work of Brandeis and Warren (1890) and Pound (1914) in this field in the United States. While this may have mirrored German law at the time 'American personality law never fully developed'.

I do not propose delving deeply into the substantive South African private law concerning the right(s) to personality, and will not deal with the nature of the available private law remedies. Instead I shall attempt to demonstrate the importance of the private law *dogmatics* in this field in order better to understand the meaning of human dignity as a value and a right under the South African Constitution. I am in full agreement with Burchell's view (1996: 650) that '[t]he further potential which lies within the *actio iniuriarum* to protect dignity in a Bill of Rights is enormous' and in particular with his further comment (1996: 653), quoted with approval by Neethling et al (2005: 17 n 181) that the '[s]ymbiotic growth of both the personality rights protected by the *actio iniuriarum* and equivalent rights under the Constitution is inevitable and highly desirable'.

---

[2] The date on which the interim Constitution came into existence.

The South African legal system is said to be 'mixed', with its roots originally exclusively in the Roman-Dutch Law of Holland, before developing side-roots into the English law since 1815. In those areas of the common law that are still principally of Roman-Dutch origin, courts have not hesitated to look to European law for comparative guidance. There is particular justification — in the task of fleshing out the meaning of dignity — for looking to the Roman jurist Ulpian and his successors for universal principles relating to dignity. Indeed Honoré (2002: 78–93) regards Ulpian as a pioneer of human rights:

> 'Ulpian's exposition of Roman Law and administration ... can be regarded as the legal corollary of the cosmopolitan and egalitarian movement that culminated in the Antonine constitution. The interpretation of the law, the adjudication of disputes and the exercise of discretion by public officials should take account of the natural freedom, equality and dignity of all. Roman law possessed a technical remedy, the action for wrongs (*actio iniuriarum*), that was designed to protect bodily integrity, reputation and human dignity. ... Ulpian cites Labeo for the proposition that the wrongs that the action seeks to remedy are either against the body, or relate to dignity or reputation. To be beaten up or defamed infringes a person's dignity. *Hence dignity, as the core of one's personality, can be taken as the overarching value that the action for wrongs seeks to protect.* It is in practice *those forms of unfreedom and inequality that infringe human dignity* that the law, then and now, takes account of and seeks, so far as is consistent with authority, to correct. ....
>
> These three principles — freedom, equality, and dignity — lie at the root of the contemporary civil rights movement. The trend towards enacting charters of rights is no more than an attempt to cast in concrete form what these principles require in modern society. Because they form the framework and underpinning of Ulpian's writing, he is properly to be regarded as the first human rights lawyer. He did not originate either the philosophical thinking or the law on the subject, but he played a major role in elaborating, disseminating and justifying it.' (Emphasis supplied.)

Although the Antonine Constitution of AD 212 did not apply to slaves, in Ulpian's work 'the personality and dignity of a slave (*persona servi*) has come to be recognized, at least to a limited extent': Honoré (2002: 86). An action could be brought in the slave's name (admittedly by the slave owner) not only for physical assaults, but also for defamation, both the action and the remedy viewing the slave as a person endowed with dignity: Honoré (2002: 86–87). As Honoré (2002: 90) contends, the action for wrongs (*actio iniuriarum*) was therefore 'the technique for vindicating human rights as far as they were recognized in Ulpian's day'.

Specifically with regard to dignity (human worth) an important line of enquiry to follow is the rich development that has taken place in the sphere of personality rights (German *Persönlichkeitsrechte*, Afrikaans *Persoonliheidsregte*), particularly in continental and in modern South African private law.[3]

---

[3] For a masterly comparative historical account and analysis of this development from a South African perspective, see the groundbreaking work of the late Professor WA Joubert (1953) and for its more recent development in South Africa, see Neethling (1976), Neethling et al (2005), and Burchell (1998).

As Joubert (1953: 9) points out, the greatest development that took place in the 19th century in the field of private law related to the protection of the products of the individual's creative personality and the recognition of the so-called intellectual property rights (German *Immaterialrechten*, French *les droits intellectuels*). This in turn gave impetus to the flowering of the personality rights. According to Joubert (1953: 10):

> '[T]he meaning of the concept of a *right of personality* is to be found in the fact that it ultimately led to the identification [analytically] of a discrete category of rights, *not in respect of goods located outside the individual like the completed work of the author, but in respect of aspects of the personality itself*: like one's body, honour, reputation, voice, image, etc — in short, the whole panoply of personality components, which make up the human personality protected by private law.'[4] (Emphasis supplied.)

Personality would include its 'physical and intellectual/spiritual integrity, on which the development of technology has made so many new forms of infringement possible': Joubert (1953: 9). According to Joubert (1953: 12) it is essential for any modern legal system that seeks to protect the human personality comprehensively 'to create the basis from which protection like this can evolve and adapt to the needs of a developing culture and technology. And if the South African common law can pride itself on the rich protection of the personality through the *actio iniuriarum*, then jurisprudential work on the *rights* that give rise to this action can no longer be deferred.'

Joubert (1953: 11–14) emphasises that although the development of the right of personality relied on the *actio iniuriarum* it drew heavily on natural law. He points to the fact that Immanuel Kant himself gave central position to the autonomous individual personality in its realm of freedom, and postulated a general right of personality; thus law and philosophy reach the same goal. In this regard Joubert is clearly relying[5] on Kant's *Metaphysics of Morals* (AK 6: 237) where the following is stated:

> '*There is only one innate right.*
>
> *Freedom* (independence from being constrained by another's choice), insofar as it can coexist with the freedom of every other in accordance with a universal law, is the only original right belonging to every man by virtue of his humanity. — This principle of innate freedom already involves the following authorizations, which are not really distinct from it (as if they were members of the division of some higher concept of a right): innate *equality*,

[4] Translation by the author from the Afrikaans. This, as well as other translations from the Afrikaans in this section are deliberately literal, with a consequent loss of elegance, in an attempt to convey the Afrikaans meaning as accurately as possible. See Wood (2002b).

[5] In the accompanying footnote, and in the bibliography, Joubert merely cites *Metaphysische Anfangsgründe der Rechtslehre, Einleitung* XLV and the year 1797 without giving a reference to the standard 'Academy' edition ('Ak'). This is clearly a reference to the section 'Introduction to the doctrine of right' in Kant's *The Metaphysics of Morals* (AK 6: 237).

> that is, independence from being bound by others to more than one can in turn bind them; hence a human being's quality of being *his own master* (*sui iuris*),
> As well as being a human being *beyond* reproach....'[6]

Joubert (1953: 16) also points out that it was only in the time of Kant that it became customary to distinguish between the poles of subject and object in a legal relationship. In concluding chapter II of his work, which comprises a comparative survey of the development of the personality right in Germany, Austria, Switzerland, France, and the USA,[7] Joubert (1953: 74) comments that this exercise has made it very clear to him that in order to systematise the field of the personality right 'it is essential, firstly, to present a clear concept of the *subjective* right, and, secondly, to analyze and determine properly the *object* of the subjective right'. (Emphasis in the original.)

Joubert (1953: 118) comes to the conclusion that for insight into the system of personality protection, for the scholarly (literally: scientific) treatment of the field, as well as for its practical application,

> 'it has become essential that one no longer remains fixated on the actions that flow from acts directed at the personality, but should enquire after the *legal relationships* that are impaired by these acts. With legal relationships I here mean the relationships between the human being as legal subject and the *legal goods* that collectively constitute the circle of his/her legally protected personality'. (Emphasis in the original.)

Joubert (1953: 146) argues that although the South African sources provide no concrete links with the right to individuality no one would deny 'that it is an impairment of human *dignity* to deprive a person of his/her distinctiveness or individuality'.

Neethling et al (2005: 10) summarise the development of the personality rights as follows:

> 'The continental doctrine of the law of personality resulted in the recognition of personality rights apart from the rights to objects existing separately from the personality and led eventually to the placing of every right which is not inseparably associated with the personality outside the law of personality.'

They further explain (12) that through 'the legal recognition of a personality interest worthy of protection, a subjective right with regard to such interest as legal object comes into existence'. It is moreover crucial to point out that 'the *nature* of the object determines the nature of the subjective right in respect of it. The rights which may be classified as personality rights therefore depend on which individual interests are accepted as objects of personality.' Personality interests are therefore 'characterised by the fact that they cannot exist independently of

[6] Gregor (ed) (1996: 393–394).

[7] For early developments in the USA see Brandeis and Warren (1890: 193f) and Pound (1914: 343f, 445f).

a person since they are closely bound up with his personality.... [T]he highly personal nature of personality interests implies their non-patrimonial nature.'[8]

Important for this common law development of the rights to personality is the construction of the subjective right theory (Joubert: 1958). Part of the reason for its development on the continent and in South Africa is that in some of the Germanic languages the same word (for example 'recht' in German and 'reg' in Afrikaans) is used both as 'right' in the subjective sense and 'law' in the objective sense. It involves a dual aspect. First, it connotes the legal relationship between legal subject (as holder of the right) and the legal object; secondly, it connotes the legal relationship between the legal subject as holder of the right and all other legal subjects in respect of the legal object in question (Joubert 1958: 110–111; 114–115); and Neethling et al (2005: 11–12).

Its first connotation, namely the legal relationship between legal subject and object, is of particular importance for my investigation, for as Neethling et al (2005: 11–12) point out 'the content of this relationship includes all the powers ("entitlements") which, according to law, a legal subject may exercise in respect of his legal object'. By the legal recognition of a personality interest worthy of protection 'a subjective right with regard to such interest as legal object comes into existence, the *nature* of the object determining the nature of the subjective right in respect of it'. Accordingly the rights 'which may be classified as personality rights therefore depend on which individual interests are accepted as objects of personality'. Hence the crucial importance, as Kant realised, of determining what the nature of the human person and human personality is.

Rights which in the sphere of private law have come to be regarded as personality rights are stated by Neethling et al (2005: 24–38) to include the right to life and bodily integrity, the right to physical liberty, to autonomy, dignity, reputation, feelings, privacy, and identity.

Of particular importance is the personality right to self-realisation, which I have included as part of my definition of dignity, in the broad sense, under the concepts of the *development of personality* and the *striving for self-fulfilment*. These latter two concepts probably go wider than self-realisation, justifiably so in my view. Joubert (1953: 127) distinguishes between, on the one hand, the personality right to freedom, where the object of the personality right is the body itself (or as he would rather have it, physical integrity) and, on the other hand, the 'right to freedom of activity (vryheid van doenigheid) ... [which] goes much further than physical freedom, since it comprises the entire scope of the exercise of one's will and the living out of oneself, one's self-determination, in society'. Yet Joubert balks at recognising this as a personality right because, according to him 'the only conceivable object of a right like this is the human will itself, and from the very nature of things the human will does not lend itself to legal

[8] See also Joubert (1953: 121).

objectification, it is not a legal object in respect whereof a competency to enjoy or dispose can exist.... [The right to freedom of activity] belongs to legal subjectivity itself, and should not be confused with one or other subjective right.' Neethling et al (2005: 35) share this view. I believe it to be erroneous, at least in so far as the development of personality rights in public law is concerned. In the first place I think it is taking too a narrow a view to insist that the only conceivable object of the right to freedom of activity is the human will. It could just as easily be said to be closely akin to, or to form part of, the right to free development of the personality, which is entrenched in art 2(1) of the German Basic Law and to which reference will in due course be made. Moreover it seems erroneous to contend that because one cannot dispose of the human will, it cannot be the object of a personality right. One cannot dispose of either freedom or privacy or honour, yet this does not prevent these from being rights of personality. Moreover, I would have thought that one can certainly enjoy the exercise of one's will and in so doing direct the free development of one's personality through one's various activities. Joubert (1953: 127) makes much play of the fact that if one were to 'persist with the untenable and see the freedom to be active as a subjective right', it would be a right falling under both the corporeal rights as well as the personality rights, and he quotes the example of someone burning down my shop. This he finds untenable, because one can form no image of a right of this nature. I have difficulty in following this argument. I can see no problem with the proposition that one act (the burning of a shop) can give rise to patrimonial loss, which can be recovered though the *actio legis Aquiliae,* and also constitute an infringement of a personality right to be active in a particular way, and actionable under the *actio iniuriarum.* This is after all something that occurs in most personal injury claims, where patrimonial and non-patrimonial loss are recovered in the same action.

The courts in South Africa were slow to develop properly the right to personality. In *R v Umfaan*[9] it was pointed out that one of the essentials of an *injuria* was the violation of 'one or other of those real rights, those rights *in rem*, related to personality, which every free man is entitled to enjoy'. There was also reference to 'various species of *injuria*', 'insults to chastity' 'forcible and wrongful intrusion into the house of another ... not because it was a trespass on the property, but because it was a violation of family sanctity — of that peace and dignity which a free man was entitled to enjoy'.[10] In the *Whittaker; Morant* case,[11] it was held that to 'interfere with those absolute natural rights relating to personality, to which every man is entitled' constituted an *injuria*. The *O'Keeffe* case[12] decided that a woman whose photograph was used for an advertisement without her

[9] 1908 TS 62, 68 per Innes CJ.
[10] Id at 67.
[11] *Whittaker v Roos and Bateman; Morant v Roos and Bateman* 1912 AD 92, 122.
[12] *O'Keeffe v Argus Printing and Publishing Co Ltd and Another* 1954 (3) SA 244 (C) 249A, D–E.

consent could contend that that she had been subjected to 'offensive, degrading or humiliating treatment' and that her dignity had been impaired. In *S v A and Another*[13] it was observed that there was no doubt '... that the right to privacy is included in the concept of *dignitas* ...'.

In *Minister of Justice v Hofmeyer*[14] Hoexter JA pointed out that '[o]ne of the individual's absolute rights of personality is his right to bodily integrity. The interest concerned is sometimes described as one in *corpus*, but it has several facets.... It comprehends also a mental element.' The learned Judge then proceeds to quote with approval the following passage from Joubert (1953: 131):

> '(1) *The right to physical integrity*
> In this instance the objectified legal property is not the body in its ordinary concrete sense, but *the whole physical-psychic aspect of personality.* Under this heading human beings have a personality right with respect to:
> - their *bodies,* protecting them against any physical impairment, whether through violent injury, or in a more indirect way like the administration of poison, the occasioning of physical shocks, etc;
> - inseparably from the foregoing, their *health* in its fullest sense, including mental health;
> - *bodily* freedom, so that they are not only protected against imprisonment but also against any interference with their freedom of movement and action.'

In the *Tommie Meyer Films* case[15] a significant contribution was made to confirming the concept of the subjective right (*subjektiewe reg*) and the doctrine of personality rights in South African jurisprudence. As Mostert J pointed out:

> 'The modern continental theories on subjective rights distinguish between rights to aspects of the human personality (the so-called personality rights) and rights to objects located outside the human personality. These other rights are property rights (*saaklike regte*) (with corporeals as their object), obligations (*vorderingsregte*) (with human performance as their object), and incorporeal property rights (with incorporeal products of the human intellect, to which a visible external form has been given, as their object).'[16]

After referring to the seminal contribution made by Joubert (1953) and (1958) to the concept of the subjective right and to the doctrine of personality rights, and to the significant development since then by various South African academics, Mostert J quotes with approval[17] Joubert's (1958: 113) fourfold classification of subjective rights with reference to their legal objects, and in particular the following description of the legal objects of personality rights:

[13] 1971 (2) SA 293 (T) 297H per Botha AJ.
[14] 1993 (3) SA 131 (A) 132C ff.
[15] *Universiteit van Pretoria v Tommie Meyer Films (Edms) Bpk* 1977 (4) SA 376 (T).
[16] Id 381F. All English quotations from this case are translations by the author from the Afrikaans.
[17] Id 382H–383C.

'(2) Objects of personality, ie components of the human personality that can be juridically objectified and consequently become objects of personality rights: bodily integrity, dignity (*eer*) and reputation (*die goeie naam*), even "privacy", etc.'

He continues by quoting with approval[18] the following conclusion of Neethling (1976: 287): 'The implication of a recognition in law of the individual interest in privacy cannot, in my view, be determined in isolation from the (doctrine of) subjective rights.'

In the *Tommie Meyer Films* case,[19] the Appellate Division upheld Mostert J's above judgment and dismissed the appeal on the facts. There is nothing in the appeal judgment to suggest any disagreement with the lower Court's judgment, and there are passages which strongly suggest implicit approval of Mostert J's legal analysis and formulations. Rabie JA, who delivered the judgment of the Appellate Division, after referring to earlier cases dealing with the right to privacy, said the following:

'With regard to these judgments the view has already been expressed that the Court was really concerned with cases of the impairment of the particular person's privacy, that privacy should be seen as a substantive legal interest (*regsgoed*) namely, a personality interest (*persoonlikheidsgoed*) (see Van der Merwe and Oliver *Die Onregmatige Daad in die Suid-Afrikaanse Reg* 3 ed at 425) and that it is unnecessary, or even unsound, to categorize the impairment of a person's privacy under an impairment of dignity. See *Van der Merwe and Olivier* (*op cit* at 424–426); De Wet and Swanepoel *Strafreg* 3 ed at 238–239; Neethling *Die Reg op Privaatheid* at 373–375. (In the last-mentioned work it is submitted that the *O'Keeffe* case and similar cases following it, should rather be viewed as instances of impairment of a person's identity. According to the author, "identity" should be understood as

"facets of a person's personality that identify him/her as a *particular person*; which are therefore characteristic of or particular to this person, and in this way *distinguish* this person from others, ie the person's life history, character, voice, handwriting, corporeal image (*gestaltebeeld*), name, etc"

(at 295)).' [20]

In *Jooste*'s case[21] the right to privacy was expressly held to be one of the rights to personality. It was also correctly held that 'the outer limits of the right to privacy are in the final instance determined by objective norms'. The comment in the judgment immediately following, namely 'which in turn relate back to the views and *mores* of society' will now, since the constitutional revolution, of course have to be read subject to the important principles enunciated by the Constitutional

[18] Id 383G–H.
[19] 1979 (1) SA 441 (A).
[20] Id 456D–F. Translation by the author from the Afrikaans.
[21] *Jooste v National Media Ltd en 'n Ander* 1994 (2) SA 634 (O) 634C 645F. Author's translation from the Afrikaans.

Court in the *Carmichele* case[22] with regard to, inter alia, the development of the common law under s 39(2) of the Constitution, and the objective normative value system established by the Constitution. Aspects of these issues are dealt with in Chapter 4, section 4.1 and Chapter 5, section 5.1.

3.3 DIGNITY UNDER THE SOUTH AFRICAN CONSTITUTION[23]

(a) Section 10

Dignity has been formulated in the following unique manner in s 10 of the Constitution:

> 'Everyone has inherent dignity and the right to have their dignity respected and protected.'

Viewed in the context of s 1*(a)* of the Constitution — which proclaims 'human dignity' as one of the values on which the South African state is founded[24] — s 10 makes it clear that human dignity, besides being a value and a right, is also a categorical imperative. The phrase '[e]veryone *has* inherent dignity' ('Elkeen *het* ingebore waardigheid', in the Afrikaans text) (emphasis supplied), is a constitutional proclamation about the essence of the natural person respected and protected by the Constitution. It is a supra-constitutional declaration — an onto-anthropological statement if you will — of what this person already *is*, what she *has*, before the invocation of any right under the Constitution. Human dignity is not acquired by the human being from the Constitution; it is already *inherent* in every human being. It is not something to be acquired at a later date; it already exists in every human being. However much the *right to dignity* may suffer infringement in an imperfect world, the inherent dignity that everyone *has* cannot be destroyed. Section 10 must be read with s 7(2), which provides that '[t]he state must respect, protect, promote and fulfil the rights in the Bill of Rights' and s 8(1), which enacts that, inter alia, the Bill of Rights 'binds the legislature, the executive, the judiciary and *all organs of state*'. (Emphasis supplied.) It thus emerges that there is a double emphasis on the state's duty to protect the human dignity of all, namely in s 10 itself and in addition in s 7(2). The following passage from the judgment of Moseneke ACJ and Cameron J in the *Glenister* case,[25] in which they emphasise the scrupulous nature of the state's obligation under s 7(2), is with even stronger reason applicable to the state's obligation under s 10 to protect human dignity:

---

[22] *Carmichele v The Minister of Safety and Security and the Minister of Justice and Constitutional Development* 2001 (4) SA 938 (CC) (2001 (10) BCLR 995).

[23] For a recent and comprehensive discussion of dignity under the 1996 Constitution see Woolman (2007: ch 36, 1–75).

[24] The relevant part of s 1 reads:

> 'The Republic of South Africa is one, sovereign, democratic state founded on the following values:
> *(a)* Human dignity, ...'

[25] *Glenister v President of the RSA and Others; Helen Suzman Foundation as Amicus Curiae* 2011 (3) SA 347 (CC) (2011 (7) BCLR 651) paras 189–191.

> '[189] ... Implicit in s 7(2) is the requirement that the steps the state takes to respect, protect, promote and fulfil constitutional rights must be *reasonable and effective.*
>
> [190] And since in terms of s 8(1), the Bill of Rights "binds the legislature, the executive, the judiciary and all organs of the state", it follows that the executive, when exercising the powers granted to it under the Constitution, including the power to prepare and initiate legislation, and in some circumstances Parliament, when enacting legislation, must give effect to the obligations s 7(2) imposes on the state.
>
> [191] ... The Court will not be prescriptive as to what measures the state takes, as long as they fall within the range of possible conduct that a reasonable decision-maker in the circumstances may adopt. A range of possible measures is therefore open to the state, all of which will accord with the duty the Constitution imposes, so long as the measures are reasonable.'

Article 1(1) of the German Basic Law provides as follows:

> 'Human dignity shall be inviolable. To respect and protect it shall be the duty of all state authority.'

Human dignity under the German Basic Law is discussed in section 3.4 below and at this stage I merely quote, without comment, the provisions of art 1(1) in order to emphasise their remarkable similarity (no mere coincidence, I suggest) with those of s 10 read with s 7(2) of the South African Constitution. This virtual identity strengthens my argument that German dignity jurisprudence is singularly important for a proper understanding of dignity under the South African Constitution.

The shift in the concept and the sources of law, already referred to, has gone much further under the South African Constitution. The Bill of Rights is as detailed and far-reaching as any in existence. Moreover, it is one of the few constitutions whose Bill of Rights provisions operate with *express*, *direct horizontality*; that is to say they also apply directly and expressly to legal relationships between natural and juristic persons.[26] Important aspects of this horizontal application with regard to equality rights are discussed in Chapter 5. Moreover, the courts, when interpreting the Bill of Rights, are obliged by s 39(1)*(a)* of the Constitution to 'promote the values that underlie an open and democratic society based on human dignity, equality and freedom', and by s 39(2), when interpreting legislation, and when developing the common law or customary law, 'to promote the spirit, purport and objects of the Bill of Rights'. The correct interrelationship between the provisions of s 39 and those dealing with the horizontal application of the Bill of Rights will be dealt with in Chapter 5 as well.

The extent of the Constitution's normative function and sweep was emphasised by the Constitutional Court in the *Carmichele* case. The Court held that

[26] Section 8(2) provides that

> '[a] provision of the Bill of Rights binds a natural or juristic person if, and to the extent that, it is applicable, taking into account the nature of the right and the nature of any duty imposed by the right'.

Section 8(4) provides that a juristic person is entitled to the rights in the Bill of Rights

> 'to the extent required by the nature of the rights and the nature of that juristic person'.

(i) the Constitution is not merely a formal document regulating public power;
(ii) the Bill of Rights contains not only defensive subjective rights for the individual;
(iii) the Bill of Rights also embodies an objective, normative value system;
(iv) this objective, normative value system, as a fundamental constitutional value for all areas of the law, acts as a guiding principle and stimulus for the legislature, executive and judiciary;
(v) the influence of the fundamental constitutional values on the common law is mandated by s 39(2) of the Constitution; and
(vi) it is within the matrix of this objective, normative value system that the common law must be developed. [27]

It is important to emphasise, for reasons that will appear more fully in Chapter 5, that *Carmichele* is a case concerning the *vertical* operation of the Bill of Rights.

The Constitution, and for present purposes s 39(1)*(a)* in particular, makes the search for the universal obligatory, specifically in the spheres of dignity, equality and freedom.

It is significant that the Constitutional Court in the *Carmichele* case[28] clearly categorised the rights that individuals had under the Bill of Rights as 'subjective rights', aligning itself with German jurisprudence in this regard. Although most of the academic literature and cases deal with personality rights in their private law manifestation, sources such as this are of importance for public law, because of their systematic analysis of the nature of these rights and what their legal objects are. This is particularly the case in South Africa, since the Constitution refers to dignity (human worth) not only as a right but also as a value. In answering the question of what precisely human dignity is under the Constitution, the private law analysis and dogmatics will be of great value. Certain of these personality rights, for example, the *rights* to physical liberty, dignity (in a narrower sense), and privacy are expressly protected in the Constitution. The *value* of dignity is, however, a broader concept and would include — at least — the values inherent in the abovementioned personality rights.

(b) Dignity as human worth and inherent human worth

Although the word 'dignity' and mostly 'human dignity' are used in the Constitution[29] to describe the right to as well as the value of dignity,[30] there can

---

[27] *Carmichele* (above, n 22) para 54.

[28] Id para 54.

[29] Whenever 'Constitution' is used without qualification it refers to the 1996 Constitution and when 'interim Constitution' is used, to the Constitution of the Republic of South Africa Act 200 of 1993.

[30] See in particular ss 1*(a)* ('the value ... [of] human dignity); 7(1) ('the democratic values of human dignity ...'); 10 ('Everyone has inherent dignity and the right to have their dignity respected and protected'); 36(1) ('... an open and democratic society based on human dignity...'); 39(1) ('... must promote the values that underlie an open and democratic society based on human dignity, equality and freedom').

be no doubt, in my view, that in the context of the Constitution 'dignity' means 'human worth' or 'inherent human worth'. This makes the expression synonymous with 'menswaardigheid' in the Afrikaans text and with '*Menschenwürde*' and '*Würde des Menschen*' in the equivalent art 1(1) of the German Basic Law. This is implicit in views expressed by the South African Constitutional Court.[31] This is not the place to consider whether the distinction between the 'right' to and the 'value' of human dignity has always been properly appreciated by scholars or the courts.[32]

(c) *Privacy as an aspect of dignity*

In *Bernstein*'s case[33] the Constitutional Court confirmed, for purposes of the application of the Bill of Rights, the concept of personality rights and the fact that '[i]n South African common law "the right to privacy is recognized as an independent personality right ..."'.[34] In the same case the Court pointed out[35] that '[t]he scope of privacy has been closely related to the concept of identity and it has been stated that "rights, like the rights to privacy, are not based on notions of the unencumbered self, but on the notion of what is necessary to have one's own autonomous identity"'.[36] O'Regan J, writing for a unanimous Court in *Khumalo v Holomisa*,[37] also links dignity under the Constitution with the

---

[31] See for example *National Coalition for Gay and Lesbian Equality and Another v Minister of Justice and Others* 1999 (1) SA 6 (CC) (1998 (12) BCLR 1517) para 28

> '... the constitutional protection of dignity requires us to acknowledge the value and worth of all individuals ...'.

[32] In *National Coalition for Gay and Lesbian Equality and Others v Minister of Home Affairs and Others* 2000 (2) SA 1 (CC) (2000 (1) BCLR 39), dealing with a case of unfair discrimination informed by the impact of the discriminatory measure on human dignity, the judgment of the Constitutional Court (written, it must be confessed, by the present author on behalf of a unanimous Court) states in para 42 that

> '[the discrimination] denies to gays and lesbians that which is foundational to our Constitution and the *concepts* of equality and dignity, *which at this point are closely intertwined*, namely that all persons have the same inherent worth and dignity as human beings, whatever their other differences may be'. (Emphasis supplied.)

With the passage of time I am concerned that the emphasised words were not further explained. In determining what unfair discrimination is, it is the *value* of dignity that informs the *right* not to be unfairly discriminated against. It is of course also the *value* of dignity that informs the *right* to equality before the law and the *right* to equal protection and benefit of the law. But this only in passing; a fuller treatment must wait for later. That dignity is a right and a value is confirmed by the Court in *Thint Holdings (Southern Africa) (Pty) Ltd and Another v National Director of Public Prosecutions; Zuma v National Director of Public Prosecutions* 2009 (1) SA 147 (CC) (2009 (3) BCLR 309) para 50. The Court also held that a person's dignity is not infringed when named as a suspect in a case of alleged corruption. I have peace with the ultimate result, but consider that it would have been sounder and more principled to have found an infringement of dignity but held the infringement to be justified under s 36(1) of the Constitution by the true factual position that the suspicion was objectively and reasonably entertained on the facts.

[33] *Bernstein and Others v Bester and Others NNO* 1996 (2) SA 751 (CC) (1996 (4) BCLR 449) para 68.

[34] Id quoting with approval from Neethling (1994: 333) and referring also to the *Tommie Meyer Films* case above n 20, 455H–456H.

[35] Id para 65.

[36] Id quoting from Forst (1992: 303).

[37] 2002 (5) SA 401 (CC) (2002 (8) BCLR 771) para 27.

concept of personality rights, and also follows *Bernstein* regarding the concept of privacy as follows:

> 'In the context of the *actio injuriarum*, our common law has separated the causes of action for claims for injuries to reputation (*fama*) and *dignitas. Dignitas* concerns the individual's own sense of self worth, but included in the concept are a variety of personal rights including, for example, privacy. In our new constitutional order, no sharp line can be drawn between these injuries to personality rights. The value of human dignity in our Constitution is not only concerned with an individual's sense of self-worth, but constitutes an affirmation of the worth of human beings in our society. It includes the intrinsic worth of human beings shared by all people as well as the individual reputation of each person built upon his or her own individual achievements.... It should also be noted that there is a close link between human dignity and privacy in our constitutional order. The right to privacy, entrenched in s 14 of the Constitution, recognises that human beings have a right to a sphere of intimacy and autonomy that should be protected from invasion. This right serves to foster human dignity.'

(d) Personality rights

In its jurisprudence the Constitutional Court has, with reference to Neethling et al (2005), adopted an expansive approach to personality rights and interests and included among them 'mental integrity, bodily freedom, reputation, privacy, feeling and identity'.[38]

(e) Dignity understood in Kantian terms

The Constitutional Court has throughout understood human dignity (worth) in unmistakable (though not always explicit) Kantian terms and has regarded the concepts of *human dignity* and *human worth* as synonymous,[39] as I do throughout this book.

In the *Dawood* case the Court also, and importantly for present purposes, distinguished between the *value* of dignity and the *right* to dignity and defined the *value* of equality broadly.[40] Writing for the Court, O'Regan J points out[41] that

[38] *Van der Merwe v Road Accident Fund and Others* 2006 (4) SA 230 (CC) (2006 (6) BCLR 682) para 40.

[39] See for example *National Coalition for Gay and Lesbian Equality and Others v Minister of Home Affairs and Others* above n 32 para 42, and *MEC for Education: KwaZulu-Natal and Others v Pillay and Others* 2008 (1) SA 474 (CC) (2008 (2) BCLR 99) para 150 per O'Regan J.

[40] *Dawood and Another; Shalabi and Another; Thomas and Another v Minister of Home Affairs and Others* 2000 (3) SA 936 (CC) (2000 (8) BCLR 837) para 35.

[41] Id paras 34–35.

it is clear from the text of the Constitution[42] that 'human dignity is a fundamental value of our Constitution'. O'Regan J goes on to emphasise the following:

> 'Human dignity therefore informs constitutional adjudication at a range of levels. It is a value that informs the interpretation of many, possibly all, other rights. The Court has already acknowledged the importance of the constitutional value of dignity in interpreting rights such as the right to equality, the right not to be punished in a cruel, inhuman or degrading way, and the right to life. Human dignity is also a constitutional value that is of central significance in the limitations analysis. Section 10, however, makes it plain that dignity is not only a *value* fundamental to our Constitution, it is a justiciable and enforceable *right* that must be respected and protected. In many cases, however, where the value of human dignity is offended, the primary constitutional breach occasioned may be of a more specific right such as the right to bodily integrity, the right to equality or the right not to be subjected to slavery, servitude or forced labour.'[43] (Emphasis in the original.)

This insightful and important analysis makes clear that in using human worth (dignity) as the criterion of attribution in our equality jurisprudence, one is using it as a value and in the broadest conception of value.

The Kantian nature of the Constitutional Court's jurisprudence appears clearly from its repeated emphasis that human worth is impaired when persons are treated, not as ends in themselves, but as mere objects. In *Makwanyane*[44] it was pointed out that the death penalty is also an inhuman and degrading punishment because 'it strips the convicted person of all dignity and *treats him or her as an object* to be eliminated by the state'. (Emphasis supplied.) It was also stated,[45] in relation to the death penalty's inevitably arbitrary nature that '[f]or one person

---

[42] O'Regan J referred to ss 1, 7(1), 36(1) and 39(1) of the Constitution, which provide as follows:

's 1*(a)*:

> The Republic of South Africa is one sovereign, democratic state founded on the following values:
>
> *(a)* human dignity, the achievement of equality, and the advancement of human rights and freedoms;

s 7(1):

> This Bill of Rights is a cornerstone of democracy in South Africa.... It enshrines the rights of all people in our country and affirms the democratic values of human dignity, equality and freedom;

s 36(1):

> The rights in the Bill of Rights may be limited only in terms of law of general application to the extent that the limitation is reasonable and justifiable in an open and democratic society based on human dignity, equality and freedom ...;

s 39(1)*(a)*:

> When interpreting the Bill of Rights, a court, tribunal or forum —
>
> *(a)* must promote the values that underlie an open and democratic society based on human dignity, equality and freedom.'

[43] *Dawood* above n 40 para 35, footnotes omitted. Quoted with approval again in *NM and Others v Smith and Others (Freedom of Expression Institute as Amicus Curiae)* 2007 (5) SA 250 (CC) (2007 (7) BCLR 751) para 50.

[44] *S v Makwanyane and Another* 1995 (3) SA 391 (CC) (1995 (6) BCLR 665) per Chaskalson P para 26. See also paras 57 and 59 and the foreign authorities there cited with approval.

[45] Id para 166 per Ackermann J.

to receive the death sentence, where a similarly placed person does not, is, in my assessment of values, cruel to the person receiving it. To allow chance, in this way, to determine the life or death of a person, is to *reduce the person to a cipher* in a sophisticated judicial lottery. This is to treat the sentenced person as inhuman.' (Emphasis supplied.) In *Makwanyane*[46] O'Regan J asserts that the

> 'importance of dignity as a founding value of the Constitution cannot be overemphasised. Recognising a right to dignity is an acknowledgment of the intrinsic worth of human beings: human beings are entitled to be treated as worthy of respect and concern'.

The learned judge, moreover, recognises that it is inconsistent with human dignity to treat human beings 'as objects to be toyed with and discarded' ie as mere objects. [47]

The Constitutional Court has affirmed that treating a human being as a mere object, in the Kantian sense of the word, is an infringement of human dignity. In *S v Dodo*[48] this was explained in the following terms:

> 'To attempt to justify any period of penal incarceration, let alone imprisonment for life as in the present case, without inquiring into the proportionality between the offence and the period of imprisonment, is to ignore, if not to deny, that which lies at the very heart of human dignity. Human beings are not commodities to which a price can be attached; they are creatures with inherent and infinite worth; they ought to be treated as ends in themselves, never merely as means to an end. Where the length of a sentence, which has been imposed because of its general deterrent effect on others, bears no relation to the gravity of the offence (in the sense defined in paragraph 37 above) the offender is being used essentially as a means to another end and the offender's dignity assailed. So too where the reformative effect of the punishment is predominant and the offender sentenced to lengthy imprisonment, principally because he cannot be reformed in a shorter period, but the length of imprisonment bears no relationship to what the committed offence merits. Even in the absence of such features, mere disproportionality between the offence and the period of imprisonment would also tend to treat the offender as a means to an end, thereby denying the offender's humanity.' (Footnote omitted.)

In *Larbi-Odam*[49] it was pointed out that under the former Bantustan policies many persons became 'statutory foreigners' in their own country who were 'treated as instruments of cheap labour to be discarded at will'. This fits closely with the Kantian imperative against objectifying persons, and how this objectifying leads to the impairment of dignity. This was used[50] by the Court as one of the grounds for finding that certain statutory regulations had the potential

[46] Id para 328.

[47] Id, quoting with approval from Brennan J's judgment in *Furman v Georgia* 408 US 238 at 272–273 (1972).

[48] *Dodo v The State* 2001 (3) SA 382 (CC) (2001 (5) BCLR 423) para 38.

[49] *Larbi-Odam and Others v MEC for Education (North-West Province) and Another* 1998 (1) SA 745 (CC) (1997 (12) BCLR 1655) para 19.

[50] Id para 20.

to harm the dignity of non-citizens hit by these regulations, since 'the overall imputation seems to be that because persons are not citizens of South Africa they are for that reason alone not worthy of filling a permanent post'. Clearly related to the dignity assessment was the holding that '[a] person's profession is an important part of his or her life. Security of tenure permits a person to plan his or her family, social and professional life.... Conversely, denial of security of tenure precludes a person from making such personal life choices.'

(f) The value of freedom as an aspect of dignity

In *Ferreira v Levin (1)*[51] the following was said with regard to the nature of human dignity and its close relationship with freedom:

> 'Human dignity cannot be fully valued or respected unless individuals are able to develop their humanity, their "humanness" to the full extent of its potential. Each human being is uniquely talented. Part of the dignity of every human being is the fact and awareness of this uniqueness. An individual's human dignity cannot be fully respected or valued unless the individual is permitted to develop his or her talents optimally. *Human dignity has little value without freedom; for without freedom personal development and fulfilment is not possible. Without freedom human dignity is little more than an abstraction. Freedom and dignity are inseparably linked. To deny people their freedom is to deny them their dignity.*'[52] (Emphasis supplied.)

The passage emphasised was expressly approved by the Court in the *Pillay* case.[53] In *Ferreira v Levin (1)*[54] express reference is made to Kant's view that freedom is an essential part of human dignity:

> 'Kant luminously conceptualizes freedom as the "only one innate right" in the following terms:
>
> > "Freedom (independence from the constraint of another's will), insofar as it is compatible with the freedom of everyone else in accordance with a universal law, is the one sole and original right that belongs to every human being by virtue of his humanity."'

In the *Robinson* case[55] Davis J refers to the 'dignity of difference' as follows:

> 'It is surely trite to claim that our constitutional society recognizes the dignity of difference. It accords respect for the existence of a domestic life partnership and those who live within this arrangement.
>
> ...

[51] *Ferreira v Levin NO and Others; Vryenhoek and Others v Powell NO and Others* 1996 (1) SA 984 (CC) (1996 (1) BCLR 1) para 49.

[52] Although the majority of the Court dissented from this judgment in regard to the nature of the right that had been infringed, and in relation to the extensive definition of freedom it proposed, there was no dissent from the quoted description of human dignity.

[53] Above n 39 para 63 per Langa CJ.

[54] Above n 51 para 52.

[55] *Robinson and Another v Volks NO and Others* 2004 (6) SA 288 (C) (2004 (6) BCLR 671) 299D–I.

> For a vast range of reasons ... domestic partnerships are a significant part of the South African family life. To ignore them and to impose a particular religious view on their world is to undermine the dignity of difference and to render the guarantee of equality somewhat illusory insofar as a significant percentage of the population is concerned.'

I leave aside entirely the question as to precisely what legal benefits of a heterosexual marriage would accrue to a heterosexual domestic partnership, and under what circumstances this would occur, to which Davis J was alive.[56] I agree fully with the conclusion that dignity requires freedom, and that freedom is accordingly a cardinal aspect of dignity. If, as I argue,[57] an important aspect of human dignity is the capacity to exercise one's own judgment, to shape oneself, to develop one's personality and to strive for self-fulfilment (in a manner compatible of course with the exercise of similar capacities of others) then freedom is essential for the exercise of these capacities, forms an integral part of these capacities, and indeed constitutes a capacity of this nature.

I do, however, have substantial reservations concerning the use, in the above judgment, of the phrase 'dignity of *difference*', despite the currency it might have gained. It ought properly to be 'dignity of the *different*'. This is no petty semantic distinction. To speak of the dignity of *difference* is potentially dangerous because it draws the focus of dignity away from the human being and concentrates it on the dignity of actions of the human being. Dignity accrues to human beings, not to abstract nouns. Dignity accrues to different *people*. We must respect the equal dignity of *all* human beings, no matter how 'different' to us they may be, no matter how wholly 'other'. It is the equal dignity of *different* human beings, thus the dignity of *the different*. I refer back in this regard to the supporting views of Huber (2010) discussed in Chapter 2, section 2.6 above.[58]

The Supreme Court of Appeal has pointed out that contractual autonomy is part of freedom and also informs human dignity. In *Brisley v Drotsky*[59] Cameron JA summarised the position as follows:

---

[56] Id 299D.

[57] In section 2.1 of Chapter 2.

[58] As there pointed out:

> 'Huber (2010) argues, however, that not every *difference* is good ... or acceptable or should even be dignified. Not all diversity has its place in an "ordered complexity", to use Sacks' phrase. The question, according to Huber, is not whether the difference of cultures has an inherent dignity, but rather whether those cultures respect the equal dignity of human beings (and also the dignity of nature). Cultures often reflect the brokenness of the human existence, they even express the selfishness of human endeavours and become instruments for the arrogance of superiority. Therefore not the dignity of difference but the dignity of *the different* should in Huber's view be respected as a guiding moral principle in the 21st century — a "time of many worlds".'

[59] 2002 (4) SA 1 (SCA) (2002 (12) BCLR 1229) para 94, footnotes omitted. See also *Afrox Healthcare Bpk v Strydom* 2002 (6) SA 21 (SCA) paras 22–23, and *Price Waterhouse Coopers Inc and Others v National Potato Co-operative Ltd* 2004 (9) 930 (SCA) (2004 (9) BCLR 930) para 44, where the quoted passage was cited with approval.

'[T]he Constitution's values of dignity and equality and freedom require that the courts approach their task of striking down contracts or declining to enforce them with perceptive restraint ... contractual autonomy is part of freedom. Shorn of its obscene excesses, contractual autonomy informs also the constitutional value of dignity.

...

The Constitution requires that its values be employed to achieve a careful balance between the unacceptable excesses of contractual "freedom", and securing a framework within which the ability to contract enhances rather than diminishes our self-respect and dignity.'

The *Zealand* case[60] illustrates the close link between freedom and dignity, and indeed how freedom is a component of dignity, broadly defined. The applicant in the case, despite being an un-sentenced prisoner, had been detained in the maximum security section of a prison instead of in the medium security awaiting trial section of the prison, to which he was entitled and which would have afforded him more amenities than the maximum security section. The Court held[61] that the applicant, by being denied his legal entitlement to these greater amenities,

'... was detained in accordance with a legal status that is characterized by a lesser set of legal rights and liberties (which included the right to be presumed innocent) than to which he was rightly entitled. That deprivation of legal rights and liberties must amount to a deprivation of freedom [under s 12(1)*(a)* of the Constitution[62]].'

In the course of its judgment[63] the Court pointed to the 'great significance' of the differences between the prison section for persons awaiting the conclusions of their trials and the section for those convicted and sentenced, and how this can impact on the dignity of a person wrongly detained in the maximum security section, rather than in the medium security section:

'Respect for fundamental human dignity, which is entrenched in our Constitution, demands that this fundamental difference in status be always recognised, and that it be reflected in prisons wherever possible.'

Individual moral agency forms part of the concept of human worth. As Honoré (1999: 125) points out:

'At the same time it [asserting the possibility of moral agency] makes possible a sense of personal character and identity that is valuable for its own sake.'

---

[60] *Zealand v Minister of Constitutional Development and Another* 2008 (4) SA 458 (CC) (2008 (6) BCLR 601).

[61] Id para 32.

[62] Which provides:

'Everyone has the right to freedom and security of the person, which includes the right —

(a) not to be deprived of freedom arbitrarily or without just cause.'

[63] The *Zealand* case (above, n 60) para 30.

This passage was quoted with approval in *S v Manamela*[64] where the following was also said:

> 'The conduct of each individual can and will contribute to a climate in which the rights of others are respected. Our society asserts individual moral agency and it does not flinch from recognizing the responsibilities that flow from it. It is upon this principle that democracy and respect for human rights are built.'[65]

In *NM v Smith*[66] these passages from Honoré and *Manamela* were quoted with approval and the following view expressed:

> 'The first reason for asserting the value of privacy therefore lies in our constitutional understanding of what it means to be a human being. An implicit part of this aspect of privacy is the right to choose what personal information of ours is released.... That decision should not be made by others....'

Sachs J in the *Van Heerden* case[67] underscores the inseverable bond between human dignity and freedom when he eloquently states that 'human dignity ... by its very nature prospers least when caged'. He describes human dignity as 'a quality'.[68] In my view, as I have argued above, human dignity is better described as the 'capacity for and the right to respect as a human being that arise from' various singular aspects of the human personality.

The close link between freedom and self-esteem is emphasised by Isaiah Berlin (1969: xliii): 'I wish to determine myself, and not be directed by others, no matter how wise and benevolent; *my conduct derives an irreplaceable value from the sole fact that it is my own*, and not imposed upon me.' (Emphasis supplied.)

The concepts of talent and personal development are very closely related, if not identical, to the right to the free unfolding of the personality, a right guaranteed under art 2 of the GBL, and closely related in German constitutional law to the concept of dignity, as will be seen in section 3.4 below. These concepts, as well as the human being's awareness of his/her uniqueness, and the idea of self-fulfilment, are important components of my suggested description of human dignity at the beginning of section 3.1 above.

---

[64] *S v Manamela* 2000 (3) SA 1 (CC) (2000 (5) BCLR 491) para 100 per O'Regan J and Cameron AJ. Although in a minority judgment, this aspect of the judgment was not at odds with the views of the majority.

[65] Id.

[66] Above n 43 at para 132 per O'Regan J. Although this was in a minority judgment, it was not on this aspect at odds with the views of the majority.

[67] *Minister of Finance and Another v Van Heerden* 2004 (6) SA 121 (CC) (2004 (11) BCLR 1125) para 146.

[68] Id.

(g) *Human dignity, self-esteem and self-identification*

In the *Gay and Lesbian (Minister of Justice)* case[69] the concept of dignity was considered to include also the notions of identity formation, the free development of the personality and self-fulfilment; and the judgment also indicates that the objectification of persons is an infringement of their dignity. Importantly, *self-esteem* was also regarded as forming part of dignity; this is but another way of formulating the idea of *self-awareness and a sense of self-worth*. The discriminatory prohibitions on sex between men, even when not enforced, reduces gay men to 'unapprehended felons' and entrenches the stigma imposed on gays,[70] the effect of which, in my view, is to objectify them as human beings, in breach of the Kantian imperative. By 'reinforcing the misapprehension ... of the public'[71] gay men are hampered in their identity formation, and 'fear of discrimination' leads to 'concealment of true identity', which is 'harmful to ... self-esteem'[72] as well as to self-identification and self-fulfilment[73] and, I would add, to the free development of their personalities. There are aspects of privacy that fall within the wider concept of dignity as a value. Privacy recognises that we all have a right to a sphere of private intimacy and autonomy which 'allows us to establish and nurture human relationships' without interference from the outside community.[74]

It is implicit in the *Gay and Lesbian (Minister of Home Affairs)* case[75] that a component of human worth (dignity) is the ability to form human relationships, to find personal meaning in these relationships and to determine personal identity in and through these relationships:

> 'The sting of past and continuing discrimination against both gays and lesbians is the clear message that it conveys, namely, that they, whether as individuals or in their same-sex relationships, do not have the inherent dignity of and are not worthy of the human respect possessed by and accorded to heterosexuals and their relationships. This discrimination occurs at a deeply intimate level of human existence and relationality.'

The Court also held that at the heart of the harmful and hurtful stereotypes of gays and lesbians lie misconceptions based on the fact that

> 'the sexual orientation of lesbians and gays is such that they have an erotic and emotional affinity for persons of the same sex and may give physical expression thereto with same-sex partners'[76]

---

[69] *Gay and Lesbian (Minister of Justice)* case (above, n 31) para 23.
[70] Id.
[71] Id.
[72] Id.
[73] Id para 36.
[74] Id para 32.
[75] *Gay and Lesbian (Minister of Home Affairs)* case (above, n 32) para 42.
[76] Id para 49.

and that

> '[t]he classification of lesbians and gays as "exclusively sexual beings" stands in stark contrast to the perception of heterosexual parents as "people who, along with very many other activities in their lives, occasionally indulge in sex". Through this narrative, lesbians and gays are reduced to one-dimensional creatures, defined by their sex and sexuality.'[77]

The aspects of dignity here violated are the capacities of human beings to 'exercise self-determination, to shape themselves ..., to develop their personalities and to strive for self-fulfilment in their lives'.[78]

In this same context the Court made plain that 'procreative potential' is not 'a defining characteristic of conjugal relationships' and, if it were, would be 'deeply demeaning' of couples (whether married or not) who embarked on a relationship when they were, for whatever reason, incapable of procreating or who voluntarily decided not to have children or sexual relations with one another.[79]

In the *Dawood* case[80] O'Regan J emphasised that both *self-identification* and *self-fulfilment* are important aspects of dignity:

> 'The decision to enter into a marriage relationship and to sustain such a relationship is a matter of defining significance for many if not most people and to prohibit the establishment of such a relationship impairs the ability of the individual to achieve personal fulfilment in an aspect of life that is of central significance. In my view, such legislation would clearly constitute an infringement of the right to dignity.'

On my reading of the judgment, the Court also saw *self-determination* as an element of dignity:

> '[A]ny legislation that significantly impairs the ability of spouses to honour their obligations to one another would also limit that right.'[81]

In an important recent judgment by Cameron and Froneman JJ in the *Le Roux* case it was again emphasised (in the context of a heterosexual man being portrayed as gay) that one's own sense of self-worth constitutes an aspect of human dignity as one of the personality rights:[82]

> 'Our common law recognises that people have different *claims for injuries* to their reputation (*fama*) and *to their own sense of self-worth* (*dignitas*). *Both are affronts to the rights of personality*, and although the Bill of Rights does not always draw sharp lines between the two, the distinction is important to our new constitutional order. It illuminates the tolerance and respect for other people's dignity expected of us by the Constitution in our public and private encounters with one another. We may be deeply hurt and insulted

[77] Id, quoting with approval from Lin (1999: 741–742).

[78] From my working definition of human dignity (worth) in section 3.1 above.

[79] The *Gay and Lesbian (Minister of Home Affairs)* case (above, n 32) para 56.

[80] The *Dawood* case (above, n 40) para 37.

[81] Id.

[82] *Le Roux and Others v Dey; Freedom of Expression Institute and Another as Amici Curiae* 2011 (3) SA 274 (CC) (2011 (6) BCLR 577) para 154.

by the actions of others, in calling or portraying us as what we have chosen, freely, not to be, or to keep private, even though we are not defamed. It may be that the personal insult or injury may not be considered, in the public eye, as something that harmed our reputation. But within limits our common law, and the Constitution, *still value and protect our subjective feelings about our dignity.* It is this difference between public and private esteem that explains, in our view, why Dr Dey cannot succeed in his defamation claim, but must do so in his dignity claim.' (Emphasis supplied, internal footnotes omitted.)

(h) Human self-fulfilment

The Constitutional Court has recognised the importance of work for the human personality and, although not always stated in express terms, for human self-fulfilment. In commenting on s 22 of the Constitution, which guarantees to citizens 'the right to choose their trade, occupation or profession freely', Ngcobo J stated the following in the *Affordable Medicines Trust* case:[83]

> 'What is at stake is more than one's right to earn a living, important though that is. Freedom to choose a vocation is intrinsic to the nature of a society based on human dignity as contemplated by the Constitution. One's work is part of one's identity and is constitutive of one's dignity. Every individual has a right to take up any activity which he or she believes himself or herself prepared to undertake as a profession and to make that very activity the very basis of his or her life. And there is a relationship between work and the human personality as a whole. "It is a relationship that shapes and completes the individual over a lifetime of devoted activity; it is the foundation of a person's existence."'[84]

In *August*'s case[85] Sachs J described the right to vote of each and every citizen as a 'badge of dignity and personhood. Quite literally it says that everybody counts.' True and striking as this aphorism might be, it justifies a little unpacking in order to enhance our understanding of dignity.[86] The right to vote is of course an indication of true enlightenment and, in the context of dignity, signifies certain of its most important aspects. It is a recognition of our intellectual and moral capacity and our ability to exercise our own judgment, to strive for self-fulfilment and to shape collectively our worlds (and in so doing ourselves and our personalities). See also paragraph *(g)* above.

---

[83] *Affordable Medicines Trust and Others v Minister of Health of RSA and Another* 2006 (3) SA 247 (CC) (2005 (6) BCLR 529) para 59.

[84] The quotation is from the German *Pharmacy* case (BverfGE 7, 377) as translated by Kommers (1997: 274).

[85] *August and Another v Electoral Commission and Others* 1999 (3) SA 1 (CC) (1999 (4) BCLR 363) para 17.

[86] The right to vote, and its exercise, has of course other significant aspects, as O'Regan J pointed out in *Richter v Minister of Home Affairs and Others* 2009 (3) SA 61 (CC) (2009 (1) BCLR 448) paras 52–58, but here I highlight its significance for dignity.

(i) The individual is not seen as an isolated or unencumbered being

The Constitution does not consider dignity in a narrow light, or the individual, the bearer of dignity, as an isolated and unencumbered being. In *Bernstein*'s case[87] the Constitutional Court, in holding that the right to privacy is an independent personality right, and hence part of the concept of human dignity (worth), quoted the following proposition of Forst (1992: 303) with approval:

> '[R]ights, like the rights to privacy, are not based on notions of the unencumbered self, but on the notion of what is necessary to have one's own autonomous identity.'

Forst formulated this proposition in rejecting Michael J Sandel's communitarian critique of the 'liberal self': liberalism is said, first, to rely on the concept of the atomistic self, individualised prior to communal relations and constitutive goods and, secondly, to subsume this individual under universalist and individualistic notions of 'right' that, despite their intention, destroy the real individuality of a communal being, rendering the 'unencumbered self' to become the disempowered citizen of the modern state.

Moreover the Constitutional Court in the *Second Certification* case[88] accorded full recognition under the Constitution to the communal nature of human beings (and hence of human dignity) and its protection by means of, inter alia, the 'associational individual rights' of the Constitution.[89] The 'associational individual rights' to which the Court was referring included those guaranteed by s 31 as follows:

> '31. Cultural, religious and linguistic communities
> (1) Persons belonging to a cultural, religious or linguistic community may not be denied the right, with other members of that community–
> *(a)* to enjoy their culture, practise their religion and use their language; and
> *(b)* to form, join and maintain cultural, religious and linguistic associations and other organs of civil society.
> (2) The rights in subsection (1) may not be exercised in a manner inconsistent with any provision of the Bill of Rights.'

The Court defines *associational individual rights* as 'those rights which cannot be fully or properly exercised by individuals otherwise than in association with others of like disposition'.[90]

In the *Pillay* case[91] Langa CJ, after expanding on the associational meaning and context of *ubuntu*, explained how human identity forms part of the concept of human dignity:

[87] The *Bernstein* case (above, n 33) para 65.

[88] *Chairperson of the National Assembly, Ex parte: In re Certification of the Amended Text of the Constitution of the Republic of South Africa, 1996* 1997 (2) SA 97 (CC) (1997 (1) BCLR 1).

[89] Id paras 22–27.

[90] Id para 24.

[91] Above, n 39.

> 'According to Gyekye, "an individual human person cannot develop and achieve the fullness of his/her potential without the concrete act of relating to other individual persons". *This thinking emphasises the importance of community to individual identity and hence to human dignity. Dignity and identity are inseparably linked as one's sense of self-worth is defined by one's identity.* Cultural identity is one of the most important parts of a person's identity precisely because it flows from belonging to a community and not from personal choice or achievement. And belonging involves more than simple association; it includes participation and expression of the community's practices and traditions.'[92] (Emphasis supplied.)

Later in this chapter, when dealing more specifically with *ubuntu,* I express my disagreement with the possible suggestion in the above passage that belonging to a community cannot be a matter of personal choice. This does not, however, detract from the important conclusion that identity is an important aspect of dignity. In the above emphasised passage it is stated that 'one's sense of self-worth is defined by one's identity'. If this phrase means that one's sense of self-worth is defined *solely* by one's identity, then I am forced to disagree. There are many other factors than can influence one's sense of self-worth; for example, the way one has lived one's life (including one's achievements on all levels) and how society regards and reacts to one. This was indeed the effect of a unanimous Court judgment (per O'Regan J) in *Khumalo v Holomisa*:[93]

> 'The value of human dignity in our Constitution is not only concerned with an individual's sense of self-worth, but constitutes an affirmation of the worth of human beings in our society. It includes the intrinsic worth of human beings shared by all people as well as the individual reputation of each person built upon his or her own individual achievements. The value of human dignity in our Constitution therefore values both the personal sense of self-worth as well as the public's estimation of the worth or value of an individual.'

In the *Pillay* case O'Regan J, in her separate and partly dissenting judgment, made it clear that an aspect of dignity was 'the right of each and every person to choose the life that is meaningful to them'.[94] Most importantly the learned judge emphasised that the *associational individual rights*[95] in ss 30 and 31

[92] Id para 53, footnotes omitted.
[93] Above n 37 para 27.
[94] *Pillay* (above, n 39) para 150.
[95] Id, employing a definitional description of the s 30 and 31 rights first used in the *Second Certification* case (above, n 88) para 24, where these rights were referred to as 'associational individual rights, namely those rights which cannot be fully or properly exercised by individuals otherwise than in association with others of like disposition'.

of the Constitution[96] 'are associative rights and are not rights that attach to groups'.[97]

Addis (1997: 126) observes that

> '[t]o treat individuals with "equal respect" entails, at least partly, respecting their traditions and cultures, the *forms of life which give depth and coherence to their identities....* To have reciprocal empathy is to first attempt to understand the Other, but there cannot be understanding the Other if one is not prepared to engage the Other in a dialogue.'[98] (Footnotes omitted and emphasis supplied.)

O'Regan J, after quoting, inter alia, the above passage from Addis with approval, points out that

> 'an approach to cultural rights in our Constitution must be based on the value of human dignity which means that we value cultural practices because they afford individuals the possibility and choice to live a meaningful life ...'.[99]

It must again be pointed out that dignity is accorded, *not* to culture *per se*, but to those individuals who choose to practise a particular culture.

(j) ***Human dignity and ubuntu***

The sub-Saharan indigenous concept of *ubuntu* has been proffered as an aid to the proper contextual understanding of the value of dignity under the Constitution.

In the *Makwanyane* case[100] Langa J himself pointed out that 'references to *ubuntu* have already been made in various texts, but largely without explanation of the concept'. Later, in the same case, after pointing out that the concept of *ubuntu* is not defined in the Constitution, he observed as follows:

> '[224] [It] is of some relevance to the values we seek to uphold. It is a culture which places some emphasis on communality and on the interdependence of the members of a community. It recognizes a person's status as a human being, entitled to unconditional respect, dignity, value and acceptance from the members of the community such person happens to be part of. It also entails the converse, however. The person has a corresponding duty to

---

[96] Section 30:

> 'Everyone has the right to use the language and to participate in the cultural life of their choice, but no one exercising these rights may do so in a manner inconsistent with any provision of the Bill of Rights.'

Section 31:

> '(1) Persons belonging to a cultural, religious or linguistic community may not be denied the right, with other members of that community —
> *(a)* to enjoy their culture, practise their religion and use their language; and
> *(b)* to form, join and maintain cultural, religious and linguistic associations and other organs of civil society.
> (2) The rights in subsection (1) may not be exercised in a manner inconsistent with any provision of the Bill of Rights.'

[97] *Pillay* (above, n 39) para 150.

[98] For the importance of trying, 'as far as humanly possible, to place oneself in the place of "the other"', see the *Gay and Lesbian (Minister of Justice)* case (above, n 31) para 22.

[99] *Pillay* (above, n 39) para 157.

[100] Above n 44 at para 227.

> give the same respect, dignity, value and acceptance to each member of that community. More importantly, it regulates the exercise of rights by the emphasis it lays on sharing and co-responsibility and the mutual enjoyment of rights by all. It is perhaps best illustrated in the following remarks in the judgment of the Court of Appeal of the Republic of Tanzania in *DPP v Pete* [(1991) LRC (Const) 553, 556b–d]:
>
> > "The second important principle or characteristic to be borne in mind when interpreting our Constitution is a corollary of the reality of co-existence of the individual and society, and also the reality of co-existence of rights and duties of the individual on the one hand, and the collective of communitarian rights and duties of society on the other. In effect this co-existence means that the rights and duties of the individual are limited by the rights and duties of society, and *vice versa*."[101]
>
> [225] An outstanding feature of *ubuntu* in a community sense is the value it puts on life and human dignity. The dominant theme of the culture is that the life of another person is at least as valuable as one's own. Respect for the dignity of every person is integral to this concept....'

I interpose briefly to point out that in section 2.8 of Chapter 2 above, I advance the proposition (not developed any further in this book) that, subject to two important qualifications, there are indeed constitutional obligations, the discharge of which is essential for the achievement of democracy and the rule of law, for securing the rights promised in the Bill of Rights for all, and for the enjoyment of the benefits of the constitutional state. In this context, it seems to me, that *ubuntu*, at least as understood by Langa J, espouses similar obligations. In the *Tshabalala-Msimang* case[102] the *obligations* allegedly flowing from *ubuntu* were described as follows:

> '[The culture of *ubuntu* is in effect] the capacity to express compassion, justice, reciprocity, dignity, harmony and humanity in the interests of building, maintaining and strengthening the community. *Ubuntu* speaks to our inter-connectedness, our common humanity and the responsibility to each that flows from our connection.'

Madala J sees *ubuntu* as a concept that 'permeates the Constitution generally and more particularly Chapter 3, which embodies the entrenched fundamental rights. The concept carries in it the idea of humaneness, social justice and fairness.'[103] Without seeking to describe *ubuntu* any further, the learned Judge mentions various actions and attitudes as conforming with this concept such as: the belief in the rehabilitation and reformation of the murderer,[104] the murderer who is worthy and capable of rehabilitation,[105] and the fact that the measure of a country's greatness is its ability to retain compassion in time of crisis.[106]

Mahomed J saw the 'need for *ubuntu*' as expressing

---

[101] Id paras 224–225.
[102] *Tshabalala-Msimang v Makhanya and Others* 2008 (6) SA 102 (W) (2008 (3) BCLR 338) para 2.
[103] *Makwanyane*'s case (above, n 44) para 237.
[104] Id paras 241–243.
[105] Id para 244.
[106] Id paras 249–250.

'the ethos of an instinctive capacity for and enjoyment of love towards our fellow men and women; the joy and the fulfilment involved in recognizing their innate humanity; the reciprocity this generates in interaction within the collective community; the richness of the creative emotions which it engenders and the moral energies which it releases both in the givers and the society which they serve and are served by'.[107]

Mokgoro J explains the concept in the following terms:

'Generally, *ubuntu* translates as *humaneness*. In its most fundamental sense, it translates as *personhood* and *morality. Metaphorically it expresses itself in umuntu ngumuntu ngabantu*, describing the significance of group solidarity on survival issues so central to the survival of communities. While it envelops the key values of group solidarity, compassion, respect, human dignity, conformity to basic norms and collective unity, in its fundamental sense it denotes humanity and morality. Its spirit emphasises respect for human dignity, marking a shift from confrontation to reconciliation.[108]

... In my view, life and dignity are like two sides of the same coin. The concept of *ubuntu* embodies them both.'[109]

The descriptions of Justices Langa and Mokgoro, cited above, were endorsed by Ngcobo J in *Hoffmann*'s case,[110] where he described *ubuntu* as 'the recognition of human worth and respect for human dignity of every person'.

In *Dikoko v Mokhatla*[111] Mokgoro J explained at some length the significance of *ubuntu* or *botho* for the furthering of restorative justice (as opposed to punitive justice) in the sphere of defamation, which at the same time elucidates features of *ubuntu* itself.[112]

---

[107] Id para 263.
[108] Id para 308.
[109] Id para 311.
[110] *Hoffmann v South African Airways* 2001 (1) SA 1 (CC) (2000 (10) BCLR 1211) para 38 n 28.
[111] 2006 (6) SA 235 (CC) (2007 (1) BCLR 1).
[112] At paras 68–69 Mokgoro J explains as follows:
'[68] In our constitutional democracy the basic constitutional value of human dignity relates closely to *ubuntu* or *botho*, an idea based on deep respect for the humanity of another. Traditional law and culture have long considered one of the principal objectives of the law to be the restoration of harmonious human and social relationships where they have been ruptured by an infraction of community norms. It should be a goal of our law to emphasise, in cases of compensation for defamation, the re-establishment of harmony in the relationship between the parties, rather than to enlarge the hole in the defendant's pocket, something more likely to increase acrimony, push the parties apart and even cause the defendant financial ruin.... The primary purpose of a compensatory measure, after all, is to restore the dignity of a plaintiff who has suffered the damage and not to punish a defendant.... A remedy based on the idea of *ubuntu* or *batho* could go much further in restoring human dignity than an imposed monetary award in which the size of the victory is measured by the quantum ordered and the parties are further estranged rather than brought together by the legal process.... It could indeed give better appreciation and sensitise a defendant as to the harmful impact of his or her unlawful actions, similar to the emerging idea of restorative justice in our sentencing laws.

In *Dawood*'s case [113] O'Regan J, in dealing with the marriage relationship, pointed out that although these relationships are 'of profound significance to the individuals concerned ... [they] have more than personal significance at least in part because human beings are social beings whose humanity is expressed through their relationships with others' and refers to *ubuntu ngumuntu ngabuntu* as meaning 'a person is a person because of other people'.[114]

In the *Pillay* case,[115] it was pointed out that the notion that 'we are not islands unto ourselves' is

> 'central to the understanding of the individual in African thought. It is often expressed in the phrase *umuntu ngumuntu ngabantu* which emphasises "communality and the inter-dependence of the members of a community" and that every individual is an extension of others'.

This passage is, however, introduced by the following observation:

> '[C]ultural convictions or practices may be as strongly held and as important to those who hold them as religious beliefs are to those *more inclined to find meaning in a higher power than in a community of people*.' (Emphasis supplied.)

I find the emphasised proposition somewhat startling, at least as far as the Christian religion is concerned. There may well be fundamentalist Christian views that place almost exclusive value on the relationship between the individual and a personalised 'higher power', virtually to the total exclusion of relationships with fellow human beings. I would have thought that this was the exception rather than the rule; for there are vast numbers of Christian believers who place the same (or very substantial) importance on their relationships with fellow human beings. The mere fact, however, that a religious belief is sincerely held or a cultural norm sincerely embraced, is no guarantee against error. After all, during apartheid, religious belief and cultural norms in South Africa combined powerfully to deny human dignity and equality to the vast majority of the South African population. Our religious beliefs as well as our cultural norms are in need of constant critique. *If* the concept of *ubuntu* should deny (I do not suggest that it does) individual morality, responsibility or accountability, that would be contrary to some

---

[69] The focus on monetary compensation diverts attention from two considerations that should be basic to defamation law.... The first is that the reparation sought is essentially for injury to one's honour, dignity and reputation, and not to one's pocket. The second is that courts should attempt, wherever feasible, to re-establish a dignified and respectful relationship between the parties.... Because an apology serves to recognise the human dignity of the plaintiff, thus acknowledging, in the true sense of *ubuntu*, his or her humanity, the resultant harmony would serve the good of both the plaintiff and the defendant.'

[113] *Dawood* (above, n 40) para 30.

[114] Id n 43 in the judgment.

[115] *Pillay* (above, n 39) para 53, footnotes omitted.

of the most essential features of human dignity and human responsibility underlying the concept of freedom.

3.4 HUMAN DIGNITY ('MENSCHENWÜRDE')[116] UNDER THE GERMAN BASIC LAW[117]

(a) Introduction

Professor Isensee (2006: 175–176) reminds us that the concept of human worth (dignity) does not belong to the 'vocabulary' of the classic human rights declarations and catalogues of rights before World War II. It is only later that it features, not merely as an appended right but as a core right in the founding documents of the United Nations — the Charter and the 1948 Universal Declaration of Human Rights. Soon after that it finds its way into the first German Länder (State) Constitutions and in 1949 into the German Basic Law (GBL).

As Prof Henk Botha (2009: 179) points out, the idea of dignity as a fundamental constitutional concept was not an invention of the GBL but had a precedent in the Weimar Constitution of 1919, which 'linked human dignity to the idea of the social state'. Since 1951 we have had more than 60 years of human worth (dignity) jurisprudence from the German Federal Constitutional Court (BVerfG) and extensive commentaries thereon. The great depth and diversity of both forensic and academic scholarship is commented on below.[118] It would be foolish to suggest that there is no debate about human dignity in Germany, but any debate of this nature is premised on the universal acceptance that human dignity is properly enshrined as a core right and concept of the GBL and that its essential components are, in broad terms, well established. The precise parameters of human dignity are a matter of ongoing enquiry. The real debates tend to be about the outer limits of human dignity — for example, precisely when it begins and ends, and whether it should, quite literally, be an absolute right, subject to no limitation whatsoever.

By comparison, the protection of human dignity is not expressly provided for in the Constitution of the United States of America and had to be found, rather belatedly, in the so-called 'penumbra' of the Bill of Rights. More surprisingly,

[116] Mention must be made of the penetrating works of Enders (1997) and Tiedemann (2006) on the meaning of *Menschenwürde*.

[117] In this regard I record my indebtedness to the comparative work on human dignity, particularly in German Law, done by Prof Henk Botha, as recently published in an illuminating article (2009), the pre-publication manuscript of which he kindly made available to me. I have also benefited from my various discussions with him on dignity and related topics. I warmly support the importance Prof Botha attaches to comparative law on this topic (see 2009: 172–180). After referring to dignity in international and comparative perspective he points out (2009: 174) that human dignity 'is central to many of the national constitutions over the past sixty years and particularly in countries emerging from authoritarian, oppressive, colonial and/or racist regimes' and points in particular to the Constitutions of Greece, Portugal, Spain, Namibia, the Russian Federation, South Africa, and Poland.

[118] When I use the expression 'jurisprudence' in the German context I include in its ambit both academic scholarship and the judgments of the courts.

since it came into existence as late as 1982, the Canadian Charter of Rights and Freedoms also does not have an express provision guaranteeing human dignity. Why the German Basic Law, particularly with regard to dignity, is of such significance for South Africa is because both Constitutions are deliberate reactions to recent and serious historical failures, indeed tragedies, with regard to human dignity. The founders of both new constitutions deliberately rejected this past and were determined that under the new constitutions such abuse of human dignity would never again occur. In this sense they may be termed 'never again' constitutions, where this determination is specifically reflected in their dignity clauses.

In determining the meaning and import of 'human worth (dignity)' German law is almost an embarrassment of riches. As Prof Henk Botha (2009: 173) puts it, '[t]he scope and sophistication of the dignity jurisprudence of German courts — in particular the Federal Constitutional Court — and the depth of academic comment by German constitutional law scholars on the concept and uses of dignity are unparalleled in any other country'. The potential embarrassment lies in the attempt to capture — within limited space — the essence of this jurisprudence without undue distortion. It may help to begin at the beginning.

Article 1 of the GBL,[119] headed 'Human dignity [literally 'Human worth']', which lies at the heart of the protection of fundamental rights under the GBL, provides:

> '1(1) Human worth *is inviolable.* To respect and protect it *is the duty* of all state authority.
> (2) The German people therefore acknowledge inviolable and inalienable human rights as the basis of every community, of peace and justice in the world.
> (3) The following basic rights shall bind the legislature, the executive, and the judiciary as directly applicable law.' (Emphasis supplied.)

The Bundestag's English translation of the GBL has rendered the words '*ist unantastbar*' and '*ist Verpflichtung*' in the German text of art 1(1) as 'shall be inviolable' and 'shall be the duty,' respectively. In my view the phrases 'is inviolable' and 'is the duty' are better renderings, conveying more clearly that the inviolability of human worth already exists, as does the duty to respect and protect it, and is not something conditional or postponed to some future date. German jurisprudence makes this abundantly clear.

---

[119] The German text reads as follows:
'art 1 [*Schutz der Menschenwürde*]
(1) *Die Würde des Menschen ist unantastbar. Sie zu achten und zu schützen ist Verpflichtung aller staatlichen Gewalt.*
(2) *Das Deutsche Volk bekennt sich darum zu unverletzlichen und unveräußerlichen Menschenrechten als Grundlage jeder menschlichen Gemeinschaft, des Friedens und der Gerechtigkeit in der Welt.*
(3) *Die nachfolgenden Grundrechte binden Gesetzgebung, vollziehende Gewalt und Rechtsprechung als unmittelbar geltendes Recht.*'

This jurisprudence on human dignity under art 1(1) of the GBL is, in my view, of singular importance for the development of South African law in this area, for more than one reason. In the first place it is my contention that, in their historical context, the wording, structure and purpose of s 10 of the South African Constitution — 'Everyone has inherent dignity and the right to have their dignity respected and protected' — are substantially the same as, if not identical to, art 1(1) of the GBL, quoted above. Both accept dignity as a categorical imperative, or as a 'supra-positive' right as many German scholars believe *Menschenwürde* under art 1(1) to be.[120] The phrase 'Everyone has human dignity' in s 10 is, with one exception that I shall allude to presently, just as strong as its German counterpart. Moreover, both provisions, in describing the protection afforded, use identical words — to 'respect' and to 'protect'. It is true that the German text places this duty on 'all state authority' whereas s 10 in the South African Constitution formulates the right passively as a right to 'respect [...]' and 'protect[tion]', without indicating expressly who is bound by this. The reason for this is obvious; s 7(2) of the South African Constitution provides expressly and in mandatory terms that.'[t]he state must respect, protect, promote and fulfil the rights in the Bill of Rights', which would of course include human dignity under s 10; and under s 8(1) it is provided, inter alia, that the Bill of Rights 'binds the legislature, the executive, the judiciary and *all organs of state*'. (Emphasis supplied.) Moreover, human dignity, as is the case with all the rights in the Bill of Rights, operates with direct horizontality[121] by virtue of the provisions of s 8(2).[122]

(b) The absolute protection of human worth in the German Basic Law

It is vital to bear in mind, when considering German jurisprudence in this area, that the protection of human worth under art 1(1) of the GBL is absolute, and by virtue of the provisions of art 79(3) of the GBL[123] immune even from constitutional amendment. One of the consequences is that the right to human worth cannot be limited,[124] whether in its vertical operation against the state or when there is a clash of rights between persons.

---

[120] See Isensee (2006: 175) who refers to it a 'Positiviertes überpositives Recht'.

[121] As to which see Chapter 4, section 4.1 below.

[122] The only qualification being that stated in s 8(2) itself namely,

> 'if, and to the extent that, it is applicable, taking into account the nature of the right and the nature any duty imposed by the right....'

[123] The relevant part of which reads:

> 'Amendments to this Basic Law affecting ... the principles laid down in Article [...] 1 ... shall be impermissible'.

Once again I venture to suggest that 'is impermissible' would be a more accurate rendering of the German '*ist unzulässig*'.

[124] This is still very much the dominant view, although there are voices calling for a reappraisal of the absoluteness of this position. This has elicited powerful criticism, to which reference will be made below.

This is not the case, at least textually, under the South African Constitution where, under the provisions of s 36(1), and subject to the conditions therein contained, '[t]he rights in the Bill of Rights may be limited ...'; therefore the right to dignity under s 10 as well. It must be noted that human dignity plays a central role in determining whether there has been unfair discrimination under s 9(3). I am unaware of a decision of any court in South Africa that has, under s 36(1), limited the s 9(3) right once it has found 'unfair discrimination' to have been established, that is to say when the human dignity of the plaintiff has been negatively affected.[125] It may well be that the Constitution, although textually making provision for the right to human dignity to be limited, does not, when read purposively, contextually and in its entirety, permit limitation when discrimination has been found to be unfair. Purely semantically, it is difficult to comprehend how discrimination that has been held to be 'unfair' under s 9(3) can be 'justified' under s 36(1).

As indicated above, s 7(2) of the South African Constitution provides that '[t]he state must respect, protect, promote and fulfil the rights in the Bill of Rights'. There can accordingly be no debate in South Africa (as there is in Germany) as to whether or what rights place positive obligations on the state. Secondly, the distinction drawn in Germany between 'respecting' and 'protecting' human worth, and the consequence this has for resolving a clash of state duties, is very relevant for South African jurisprudence, as I will attempt to show later in this chapter, because s 10 confers on everyone the right 'to have one's dignity respected and protected'. On a more general note: I think that the way German jurisprudence has invoked Kantian ethics into its human dignity jurisprudence will be of significant help for the development of our own jurisprudence, which has already taken significant steps on its own Kantian path.

Professor Eberle (2002: 7), writing in English, points out how, against the background of the Nazi horrors, the founders of the Federal Republic 'drew deep upon German tradition to found the legal order on moral and rational idealism, particularly that of Kant and Hegel' and 'thus designed a legal system around objectively ordered principles, rooted in justice and equality, that restore the centrality of humanity to the social order, and thereby to secure democratic society on this basis'.

This was made clear in BVerfGE 39, 1(41)[126] when the following was said:

[125] However, in the dissenting part of her judgment in *President of the Republic of South Africa and Another v Hugo* 1997 (4) SA 1 (CC) (1997 (6) BCLR 708) paras 89 and 106, Mokgoro J came to this conclusion.

[126] Affirming what had been articulated earlier in, for example, the *Lüth* case, BVerfGE 7, 198 (205) and in the *Hochschul* judgment BVerfGE 35, 79 (114).

> 'The jurisprudence of the Federal Constitutional Court is consistently to the effect that the basic right norms contain not only defensive subjective rights for the individual but embody at the same time an objective value system which, as a fundamental constitutional value for all areas of the law, acts as a guiding principle and stimulus for the legislature, executive and judiciary.'

This passage was quoted with express approval in the *Carmichele* case[127] as being applicable to the South African Bill of Rights.

The concept of human dignity in Germany must also be seen in the context of art 20(1) of the GBL, which proclaims Germany to be a 'democratic and *social* federal state'. (Emphasis supplied.) The social or 'welfare' state in Germany can be traced back to the Prussian Civil Code of 1794, although its real development took place under Bismarck.[128] So too, in South Africa the concept must be understood in the context of the justiciable social, economic and cultural rights entrenched in ss 26 to 31 of the Constitution.

With these preliminary observations I now turn to consider the content of *Menschenwürde* and its operation under the GBL, to the extent necessary for my purposes.

(c) The German Constitutional Court and human dignity

(i) A person may never be treated as a mere object but always as an end in him/herself

The German Federal Constitutional Court (BVerfG) has consistently upheld the above Kantian injunction. Perhaps its most powerful judgments in this regard are the *Aviation* and *Torture* cases. They merit detailed consideration. The *Torture* case will be dealt with first.

The familiar hypothetical case seeking to justify the torture of a person in order to ascertain the locality of a time-bomb has been formulated by Professor Brugger (2000: 165f) as follows: a terrorist has hidden a deadly chemical bomb in a city and activated the time fuse. The police want to torture the captured terrorist into revealing the location of the bomb. No one would deny that it would be a good thing to save the lives of many innocent people by these means, and not to spare the offender. In a conflict of 'worth against worth' the protection of the offender's worth must yield, on the basis of self-defence or necessity, or supra-legal necessity. This argument was rejected by the Frankfurt District Court, which held that the nature of the democratic constitutional state was such that not all measures were acceptable to it. The decision arose in the case of an arrested kidnapper who would not disclose where his victim was hidden and was threatened by the police with severe torture in order to induce him to do so.

[127] Above n 22 at para 54.

[128] Eberle (2002: 20). As Prof Louis Henkin was fond of saying, 'the welfare state did not originate with Marx, but with Bismarck'.

He succumbed to the threat and revealed the hiding place, but it transpired that the victim had already been killed. The offender was convicted of murder and sentenced to life imprisonment. An appeal to the Federal Supreme Court having failed, the offender filed a constitutional complaint with the BVerfG who refused to entertain it. In the course of its judgment[129] in this regard the Court held that the threat of torture had disregarded his right to human dignity under art 1(1) read with art 104(1) second sentence, and had

> 'made the arrestee a mere object of the war against crime, by infringing his constitutionally protected social worth and claim to respect, and destroying fundamental prerequisites for the individual and social existence of human beings'.

The way the BVerfG dealt with a similar dilemma in the *Aviation Security* case is perhaps an even more powerful example of Germany's Kantian jurisprudence at the highest level. In BVerfGE 115, 118, delivered on 15 February 2006, the Constitutional Court had to consider the constitutionality of a provision in the Aviation Security Act that authorised the armed forces to shoot down aircraft that are intended to be used as weapons in crimes against human lives. One of the grounds on which the Court held the provision to be unconstitutional was its incompatibility with the right to life and the guarantee of human dignity to the extent that the use of armed force affects persons on board the aircraft who are not participants in the crime. By the state's using the killing of innocent persons as a means to save others, the former are treated as mere objects, which denies them the value that is due to human beings for their own sake. There was accordingly an infringement of their rights under art 1(1) and art 2(2), sentence 1 of the GBL. At 126–127 the Court expressed itself as follows:

> '[The provision] infringes the complainant's fundamental rights to human worth and life under Articles 1(1) and 2(2) line 1 of the GBL. It makes her a pure object of state action. The worth and preservation of her life are considered with reference to quantitative considerations and the continuation of her life "depending on the circumstances" made a matter in the discretion of the Federal Defence Minister. In an emergency situation the complainant will be sacrificed and intentionally killed when the Minister, on the basis of information placed before her, accepts that the complainant's life will be of only short duration and, accordingly, in comparison with the other threatened casualties, no longer has worth, or in any event still has less worth.
>
> The state ought not to be allowed to protect a majority of its citizens in such a way that it intentionally kills a minority — in this case the crew and passengers. The weighing up of life against life according to a criterion of how many persons would be affected on the one side and how many on the other, is impermissible. The state should not on this basis be allowed to kill people, who are less in number, than those it hopes to save by means of this killing.

[129] Delivered on 14 December 2004, but not reported in the BVerGE. See, however, 2005 *NJW* 656ff, and the judgment itself, BVerfG — 2 BvR 1249/04, paragraph III(a) thereof.

> Neither can the right to life of the passengers be relativized on the basis that they should be seen as forming part of the aircraft weapon. This sort of argument renders them mere objects of state action and robs them of their human quality and worth.'

The judgment has, of course, attracted criticism, mainly on the ground that it pays insufficient regard to the injunction in art 1(1), second sentence, of the GBL[130] — 'to protect' human dignity. Isensee (2006: 190–193) is particularly severe in his criticism of the judgment, typifying the Court's 'one-sided approach' as 'washing its Pilate hands in constitutionally innocent water' and its judgment as a 'flight from reality' in which the court 'prefers to admire the beauty of Greek sculpture'.

In my view, Dr Jochen von Benstorff (2008: 21–40) has provided a compelling answer to the critics of the judgment. In his lucid and closely reasoned article[131] Von Bernstorff deals with the distinction between the State's duty to 'respect (*achten*)' human dignity and its duty to 'protect (*schützen*)' human dignity under art 1(1), second sentence, of the GBL. It is to be noted that the exact same words and word sequence are employed in s 10 of the South African Constitution.[132] He correctly points out (2008: 22) that, in essence, the issue is whether the duty to respect can be relativised by the duty to protect, in those situations where the state finds itself in a 'moral dilemma'. He warns that, in the evocative scenarios of these extreme cases, where it is possible to torture a kidnapper or shoot down a hijacked aeroplane, it is not difficult 'to make a Utilitarian out of a Kantian'. One of the arguments Von Bernstorff seeks to meet (2008: 23) is that 'while the possibly catastrophic consequences of a failure to act in these circumstances certainly does not "justify (*heiligt*)"[133] the torture of the kidnapper or the shooting down of the hijacked aircraft, it does make the torture and killing of the fellow citizens involved appear to be morally acceptable as a "second-worse solution"'.[134] This argument, Von Bernstorff points out, requires the law to adopt a utilitarian calculation of the overall balance between the persons harmed and those saved. It concerns legitimating state action beyond the limits until now respected by the legislature. In addition there is a legitimate need, so the pro-torture argument continues, to adapt the capabilities of the executive to new threats.

Von Bernstorff (2008: 24) argues that the question of rescuing a hostage by means of police torture or the prevention of an attack by the deliberate killing of bystanders bears on a multi-polar constitutional relationship. In these extreme cases the state is faced with conflicting demands from the bearers of constitutional rights. On the one hand there is the claim by persons to *respect* ('*Achtung*') for

[130] Which reads: 'To respect and protect it [human dignity] shall be the duty of all state authority.'

[131] The title of which could be translated as 'The human dignity guarantee and a conflict of duties: Concerning the precedence of the State's duty to respect in the context of art 1 GBL'.

[132] 'Everyone has inherent dignity and the right to have their dignity respected and protected.'

[133] Literally 'make sacrosanct'. The expression in Afrikaans 'die doel heilig die middelle' is well known.

[134] An expression used by Brugger (2005: 107f) in developing this theme.

a right, involving the state's abstention from any action, while at the same time there are persons who have rights which entitle them to *protection* ('*Schutz*') from the state, such as the many potential victims saved by shooting down the aeroplane or defusing the primed bomb. In these situations, according to current Constitutional law doctrine, the state has at one and the same time the duty to respect and the duty to protect victims of a private attack on constitutional rights. In the *Aviation* case the Court concluded that, in principle, a duty by the state to protect a right cannot be discharged by the infringement of its duty to respect a right. While Von Bernstorff concedes (2008: 26–28) that there is no general rule that in all cases the duty to respect takes precedence over the duty to protect, he does point to the fact that, according to the BVerfG,[135] the state in carrying out its duty to protect has a greater area of discretion in choosing measures to adopt that in the case of its duty to respect. Nevertheless he contends that when the infringement of the duty to respect a person's right at the same time involves an infringement of this person's human worth, the duty to respect has unconditional precedence over a concurrent duty to protect.

Von Bernstorff defends this unconditional preference (2008: 28–38) on basically two grounds that are partially interlinked and which I shall attempt to outline briefly. First, that the fundamental rights, when read in conjunction with art 1 of the GBL, have a core that is immune from any infringement by the state. Second, and building on the foregoing, that the state's constitutional duty to *respect*, which is decreed by art 1 of the GBL, takes precedence over any positive act that the state is enjoined to perform in execution of a positive duty to *protect*.

With regard to the first ground Von Bernstorff (2008: 29–33) argues that the jurisprudence of the BVerfG has been consistently to the effect that certain fundamental rights, which are given content by the human dignity guarantee, have a core that is immune from limitation. This is because human dignity is the 'root' of all fundamental rights and at the same time, as part of these rights, is immune from limitation. This jurisprudence has been most comprehensively analytical with regard to the general personality right, which has been derived from art 2(1) of the GBL in conjunction with the human dignity guarantee. In so doing, the courts distinguish between an area that is subject to limitation and a 'most inner sphere' that is not. Von Bernstorff thus contends (2008: 30) that the limitation of a fundamental right is absolutely prohibited with regard to its inner core, which is protected by the human dignity guarantee. This, he argues, was the basis of the judgment in the *Aviation* case. He further points out that it was Dürig who first developed the concept of this double function of the human dignity guarantee, which not only radiates out to the fundamental rights generally, but at the same time provides for a narrower core, not subject to balancing, that marks the grant of a particular fundamental right. This double

[135] In BVerfGE 46, 160 (164); BVerfGE 96, 56 (64).

function (Von Bernstorff claims) can be theoretically classified according to the distinction that Robert Alexy draws between *rules* and *principles*.[136] As Von Bernstorff explains (2008: 30), principles are norms that demand that something be realised to a relatively high degree and which Alexy refers to as optimising demands. Their realisation is limited by countervailing rules and principles. On the other hand the injunction of a rule is 'to do precisely what is required of you, nothing more and nothing less'. In other words they operate absolutely except when limited by an exception clause. From his analysis of the *Listening in* case, Alexy concludes (according to Von Bernstorff) that there are two human dignity norms, a human dignity rule and a human dignity principle. The principle can be realised (ie balanced) to a greater or lesser degree, whereas the human dignity rule cannot be limited. He says that Alexy constructs a relationship between the human dignity rule and the human dignity principle, according to which the (at least semantically) uncertain human dignity rule is always infringed when human dignity at the level of principle (that is after balancing) takes precedence. Von Bernstorff (2008: 31) rejects this approach, as well as a similar approach adopted by Prof Herdegen (2005):

> 'By this intellectual manoeuvre the helpful distinction between the general radiating effect of human dignity and the indefeasible quality of human dignity in the protection of fundamental rights is again erased. When the human dignity rule can only be determined after balancing, one is no longer dealing with a rule but with a defeasible Optimization injunction. Alexy's position can no longer reflect the "inviolability" of human dignity as demanded by Art 1 GBL.
>
> ...
>
> Enders has aptly described the relationship between human dignity and the constitutional balancing process. According to it, human dignity is not itself the object of constitutional balancing, but directs and controls this balancing process. Human dignity is infringed "when, in the balancing of a pair of principles, a determining principle is chosen which itself conflicts with human dignity."
>
> In this case human dignity is not itself weighed up against other constitutional values, but directs and corrects the balancing process from outside as an absolute boundary.... What is quite certain is that the human dignity guarantee may not be weighed up against other constitutional values.'

With regard to the second ground, Von Bernstorff (2008: 34–38) points out that even if one accepts the arguments in favour of the proposition that the human dignity guarantee is not subject to limitation, the question still remains as to why, under art 1(1), second sentence, the duty to *respect* must invariably take preference over the duty to *protect*. He suggests, as one argument, that this follows from the structure of the sentence in question where the duty to

[136] Von Bernstorff (2008: 30 n 38) refers to Alexy's *Theorie der Grundrechte*. Alexy elaborates on this distinction in an article written by him in English (2003) entitled 'Constitutional rights, balancing, and rationality' in which he also deals with objections raised by Jürgen Habermas.

respect precedes the duty to protect. This was apparently the view of the editorial committee of the Parliamentary Council in 1949 when drafting the GBL. Quite apart from this argument, this precedence can be founded on the fact that, as a general rule, respect takes place simply by the state refraining from doing something, it therefore being directly in the sphere of influence of the state to infringe on dignity or to refrain from intervening. The duty to respect is to this extent closer to the state — it affects a distinct state relationship. By contrast, in the case of the duty to protect, a third person comes into the picture, from whom the threat to human dignity emanates. The state, it is true, has the duty to take steps against a threat that does not emanate from itself. Yet, in the case of the duty to protect, the relationship between the organ of state, on the one hand, and the victim, on the other, is mediated through the offender. In the case of a failure to act, the state is not guilty of a direct, but at most an indirect infringement of dignity, and one that does not emanate from it. The fact that the duty of the state to protect life has limits is demonstrated, according to Von Bernstorff (2008: 35), by the judgment of the BVerfG in the (second) abortion case.[137] The state's duty to protect the life of the unborn child is not unlimited. According to the judgments its perimeter is established by the right to dignity, life, and bodily integrity of the woman. When the precedence of the duty to respect is negated, the state has no bearings to determine when the limits of its constitutional duty to protect have been reached.

The central argument, however, for giving precedence to the duty to respect human dignity in these situations is, according to Von Bernstorff (2008: 35), derived from the concept of the inviolability of human dignity itself. If, in the case of the infringement of human dignity, one were obliged to balance conflicting duties without regard to the result achieved thereby, it is no longer possible to speak of 'inviolability'. Consequently, the only dogmatically satisfactory solutions to the above conflict of state duties would be if no balancing took place. This can only be so if the preferred solution operates as an unambiguous rule in the case of a collision of duties. Since the concept 'to touch (*antasten*)'[138] should be understood in the sense of the classical concept of the freedom of the basic rights with regard to infringements by the state on citizens' rights, and should not take precedence in the case of horizontal conflicts of freedom between citizens, it suggests that preference should be given to the duty to respect.

The BVerfG has again made it clear in the *Dragnet Investigation* case that as a matter of principle the duty to respect takes precedence in cases where there has been a particularly serious constitutional infringement by the state.[139]

[137] BVerfGE 88, 203 (254).

[138] That is to say if one were to translate the German '*unantastbar*' in art 1 of the GBL as 'untouchable', which is quite acceptable as a completely literal translation. The Afrikaans equivalent would be 'onaantasbaar', which conveys the sense perfectly.

[139] BVerfGE 115, 320 (358).

Consequently, if one were to accept the alternative of granting unlimited precedence for the duty to protect, as outlined above, one would grant the state practically unlimited legal possibilities of interfering in the dignity and freedom of its citizens, a consequence simply incompatible with the regulatory purpose of art 1 and art 19(1) of the GBL. Von Bernstorff asserts that the foregoing dogmatic arguments furnish good grounds for asserting an unqualified precedence for the state's duty to respect in the application of art 1 of the GBL. The recognition of these absolute limits for the state's power to intervene has positive consequences in general for a system of protecting fundamental rights. The state, when it exceeds these limits, harms not only the holder of the right but also itself. When organs of state actively infringe the right to dignity, they sacrifice the confidence of their citizens.

Von Bernstorff insists (2008: 37) that the relative number of persons involved in scenarios where the 'clash' in state duties takes place, cannot and does not alter the conclusion that the state's duty to respect must take preference. Particularly in the case of the ticking bomb situation, or that of the hijacked plane, it might be suggested that precedence for the duty to respect would mean respecting the human dignity of one, or a small number of persons, at the *cost of* the lives of (possibly) several thousand. So extremely utilitarian an argument is simply not permitted by the purpose of art 1(1).

I would add two further considerations or emphases to the arguments of Von Bernstorff. The very form of the utilitarian argument, when a weighing-up takes place of the loss of a few lives against the saving of thousands of lives, and a moral credit balance thereby struck, offends completely against the Kantian imperative of human worth:

> 'In the kingdom of ends everything has either a *price* or a *dignity* [*Würde*]. What has a price can be replaced by something else as its *equivalent*; what on the other hand is raised above all price and therefore admits of no equivalent has a dignity.
>
> What is related to general human inclinations and needs has a *market price;* that which, even without presupposing a need, conforms with a certain taste, that is, with a delight [*Wohlgefallen*] in the mere purposeless [*swecklosen*] play of our mental powers, has a *fancy price* [*Affectionspreis*]*;* but that which constitutes the condition under which alone something can be an end in itself has not merely a relative worth, that is, a price, but an inner worth, that is, *dignity*.'[140]

The entire cost-benefit paradigm inherent in the utilitarian approach on the present issue, demonstrates this complete dissonance; and my understanding of art 1(1) is that it is grounded in Kant. My second observation relates to what I consider to be a substantive difference between a duty to abstain and a duty to act, which underlies the very concept of a duty to respect and a duty to protect, as Von Bernstorff himself points out. Abstention does not, in conventional terms,

---

[140] *Groundwork of the Metaphysics of Morals* [AK 4: 434–435] in Gregor (ed) (1996: 84).

affect the causal chain, but acting does. Assume that the kidnapper or the bomb-planter is tortured but refuses to disclose the required information. A serious infraction of human dignity has occurred without (in consequentialist terms) their being any credit on the other side. Or, the offender makes a disclosure under torture, but the bomb explodes or the kidnap victim dies before anything can be done by the state. Once again no credit appears on the other side of the utilitarian ledger. We tend to over-estimate the ability of the state to intervene (successfully) in the affairs of humankind. In the last century the large-scale social engineering projects that were launched ended in (inevitable) human disaster of a magnitude previously unimaginable. Apart from the wisdom of so doing, the state cannot intervene in all human crises. One should not expect it to do so. In the crisis of so dramatic a clash between state duties, as the cases under discussion present, this would seem to me to be an added reason why abstention is the proper constitutional course, whether under art 1(1) of the GBL or s 10 of the South African Constitution.

In the *Life Imprisonment* case (BVerfGE 45, 187) (227–228), the BVerfG held that the imposition of a life sentence without any possibility of parole was unconstitutional because it treated the prisoner in question as a mere means to the ends of the state. The provision in the criminal code which prescribes life imprisonment for murder was challenged on the basis that it conflicted with the protection afforded to human dignity (art 1(1)) and personal freedom (art 2(2) of the GBL). The Court upheld the law on the basis that it was not shown that the serving of a sentence of life imprisonment leads to irreparable physical or psychological damage to the prisoner's health. The Court did find, however, that the right to human dignity demands a humane execution of the sentence. This meant that the existing law, which made provision for executive pardon, had to be replaced by a law laying down objective criteria for the release of prisoners serving life sentences.

In regard to the prohibition against objectifying human beings that Court stated (228) that

> '[i]t is contrary to human dignity to make the individual the mere tool [*bloßen Objekt*] of the state. The principle that "each person must always be an end in himself" applies unreservedly to all areas of the law; the intrinsic dignity of the person consists in acknowledging him as an independent personality'. (Translation Currie 1994: 314.)

The Court further stressed (229) that it was irreconcilable with a proper understanding of human dignity for the state 'to claim the right to deprive persons by force of their freedom without their having at least the chance to regain in part such freedom'.

In BVerfGE 113, 154 (164) [2005] the Court held that

> 'it is inconsistent with Art 1.1 GBL for a convicted person to have to give up all hope of regaining his freedom, regardless of what development in his personality might take place....

This also applies to a case where a person has been sentenced to life imprisonment on the grounds of the particular severity of his guilt and, in an isolated case — constitutionally unthinkable — the life imprisonment is in fact carried out to the very end of his life.'

The *Objektformel* in relation to human dignity was expressed more recently (in 2006) by the BVerfG regarding human dignity in the context of the objectives of custodial punishment in BVerfGE 116, 69 (85–86) as follows:

'When regard is had to the injunction, flowing from Art 1.1 GBL, that human beings should not be used merely as a means to a societal end, but always treated as an end in themselves — as subjects with rights of their own and interests to be considered — and when regard is also had to the principle of proportionality, custodial punishment (a particularly severe constitutional infringement) is only consistent [with the foregoing] if — when, regard being had to its protective social function — it is consistently focused on a punishment-free future for the incarcerated.'

(ii) Bodily identity and integrity

Human dignity accrues to human life, regardless of the stage of development of this life. As pointed out by the BVerfG in the First Abortion decision (BVerfGE 39, 1 (41)): '[W]herever human life exists, human worth accrues, and it is irrelevant whether the bearer [of the right] is aware of this worth and whether she can defend it or not. The potential abilities that from the very beginning enure in being human (*Menschen sein*) are sufficient to ground human worth.' The protection of human worth does not end with the death of the individual, a view that has been supported by the BVerfG in the *Mephisto* case, BVerfGE 30, 173 (194),[141] when the following was stated:

'It would be incompatible with the constitutional commandment that human dignity is inviolate — a commandment which acts as the foundation for all basic rights — if a person, possessed of human dignity by virtue of his personhood, could be degraded or debased ... even after his death. Accordingly, the obligation that Article 1(1) imposes on all state authority to afford the individual protection from attacks on his dignity does not end with death.'[142]

The judgments dealt with under (i) above would also fall equally neatly under the present heading.

(iii) Intellectual-spiritual identity and integrity

The so-called personality rights and the important concept of the free unfolding of the human personality also fall under this heading.

[141] It has also adopted this view in a number of its so-called chamber judgments. See Stern (2006: 50 n 207).

[142] Translation by Kommers (1989) 310–311.

The *Life Imprisonment* case (BVerfGE 45, 187 (227–228)), while describing the essence of the free human personality, also pointed out that the individual did not live in splendid isolation:

> 'The respect for and protection of human worth belong to the constitutional principles of the Basic Law. The free human personality and its worth constitute the highest value in the constitutional order.... This is based on the concept of the human being as a spiritual-moral being that has the ability freely to determine and develop itself. The Basic Law does not regard this freedom as that of the isolated and self-glorifying individual, but as one who is community related and — bound. In the light of this community bounded-ness it cannot in principle be unlimited. The individual must accept those limitations to his freedom of action that the lawgiver regards as appropriate for fostering and meeting the demands of living together within the bounds that in each specific case are generally regarded as reasonable; yet the autonomy of the individual must remain protected. This means that, in principle, every individual must be regarded as a member of society with equal worth.'

In the same case (228) the BVerfG concluded, solely and expressly on the strength of art 1(1), that the human being 'continues to be acknowledged as a responsible and self-directing personality' and that it was irreconcilable with this view 'for the state to take the view that the human being could by force be denuded of its worth, without having the least chance of ever again being able to regain its freedom'.

In BVervGE 4, 7 (15f) the German Constitutional Court also gave expression to this aspect of human image formulation which at the same time indicates the human being's societal relationship:

> 'The human image of the Basic Law is not that of an isolated, sovereign individual; the Basic Law has opted instead for the tension, individual/society, in the sense of the individual's bonding with and orientation towards society, without — in so doing — affecting the individual's own worth.'

The so-called personality rights represent an important facet of these aspects of human dignity.

The sense of these personality rights was captured in the *Eppler* case, BVerfGE 54, 148. The case was concerned with the false attribution of a statement to a party politician, and the circumstances under which this false attribution would constitute an infringement of his personality right. In relation to a personality right of this nature it was stated by the Court (153) that it complemented

> 'as "undefined" freedom, the special [defined] freedoms, like freedom of conscience or expression, equally constitutive elements of personality. Their function is, in the sense of the ultimate constitutional value, human dignity, to preserve the narrow personal life sphere and to maintain its conditions, that are not encompassed by traditional concrete guarantees'.[143]

[143] As translated in Eberle (2002) 62.

The German Constitutional Court has not attempted to give a comprehensive definition of the personality rights. Instead it has followed a case-by-case approach, reminiscent of the empirical Anglo-Saxon tradition, in the light of current or developing social conditions.

Thus in the *Eppler* case (above) at 153, after pointing out that the general right to personality is 'particularly crucial today in view of modern developments and new dangers to the protection of human personality that result from them', the Court declared:

> 'Because of the aforementioned special character of the general right to personality, the Federal Constitutional Court as well as the Federal High Court of Justice have refrained from fully defining the content of the protected right; rather, they have both dealt with the right on a case-by-case basis. Thus [they] have recognized the following aspects of the general right to personality: the right to a private, secret, intimate sphere of life, ... to personal honor and the rightful portrayal of one's own person; ... to one's own image and spoken word, ... and under certain circumstances, the right not to have statements falsely attributed to oneself. *These manifestations of the constitutionally protected right of personality must be duly observed when dealing with court decisions concerning conflicting interests under private law.*'[144] (Emphasis supplied.)

The *Microcensus* case BVerfGE 27, 1, dealt with the constitutional validity of a Federal Government questionnaire seeking personal information concerning, among other things, details of vacations and recreational trips. Although the questionnaire was not invalidated, the BVerfG said the following about inner freedom:

> '1 (a) According to Article 1(1) of the Basic Law, the dignity of man is inviolable and must be respected and protected by all state authority. Human dignity is at the very top of the value order of the Basic Law. This commitment ... dominates the spirit of Article 2(1) as it dominates all the other provisions of the Basic Law. The state may not take any measure, even by law, that violates the dignity of the person beyond the limits specified by Article 2(1) ... [which] guarantees to each citizen an inviolable sphere of privacy beyond the reach of public authority.
>
> (b) In the light of this image of man, every human being is entitled to social recognition and respect in the community. The state violates human dignity when it treats persons as mere objects. It would thus be inconsistent with the principle of human dignity to require a person to record and register all aspects of his personality, even though an attempt to do so is carried out anonymously in the form of a statistical survey; [the state] may not treat a person as an object subject to an inventory of any kind. The state has no right to pierce the [protected] sphere of privacy by thoroughly checking into the personal matters of its citizens. [It] must leave the individual with an inner space for the free and responsible development of his personality. Within this space the individual is his own master. He can thus "withdraw into himself, alone, to the total exclusion of the outside world, and enjoy the right to solitude". [Quotation from Josepf Wintrach, a former president of the Federal

[144] As translated in Kommers (1989: 330) and Kommers (1997: 321f).

Constitutional Court, writing in a legal journal.] The state invades this realm when in certain circumstances it takes an action — however neutral — that tends to inhibit the free development of personality because of the psychological pressure of general public compliance.'[145]

This reflects, according to Eberle (2002: 85) 'the Constitutional Court's desire to preserve and protect the integrity of human personality by applying the concept of human dignity to meet changing social conditions, like the development and use of computer technology.... In this way human autonomy and capacity are safeguarded and nourished against the challenges posed by modern social, economic and technological change.'

Eberle (2002: 86) points out that 'the German focus on interiority reflects, again, a Kantian emphasis on the autonomy of the individual and the unfolding of human capacity'. One particular aspect of inner personality protection developed by the German Constitutional Court has been the individual's control over personal information that has given rise to the right to informational self-determination. Although touched on in the *Microcensus* case, this development is most clearly focused on in the *Census Act* case, BVerfGE 65, 1. This case concerned a detailed questionnaire that had to be completed under the Federal Census Act. It required, among other things, information concerning the subject's educational background, mode of transportation to and from work, and use of dwelling, including method of heating and utilities. In the course of its judgment the BVerfG stated the following:

'1(a) The focal point of the order established by the Basic Law is the value and dignity of the individual, who functions as a member of a free society in free self-determination. The general personality right, as laid down in Article 2 (1) in tandem with Article 1(1), serves to protect these values — along with other more specific guarantees of freedom — and gains in importance if one bears in mind modern developments with their attendant dangers to the human personality. Our jurisprudence to date has not conclusively settled the scope and content of the personality right. As indicated [in several of our cases], it includes the authority of the individual to decide for himself, on the basis of the idea of self-determination, when and within what limits the facts about his personal life shall be disclosed.

The [individual's decisional] authority needs special protection in view of the present and prospective conditions of automatic data processing. It is particularly endangered because ... the technical means of storing highly personalized information about particular persons today are practically unlimited and can be retrieved in a matter of seconds with the aid of automatic data processing, irrespective of distance. Furthermore this information can be joined to other data collections — particularly when constructing integrated information systems — to produce a partial or virtually complete personality profile, with the person concerned having insufficient means of controlling its veracity or use. [This technology]

[145] Translation from Kommers (1989: 306–307).

> may affect the individual's behaviour because of the psychological pressure which public awareness may place [upon the individual].... It would be incompatible with the right to informational self-determination if a legal order would permit a societal structure where the citizen could not be sure who knows something about him, what they know about him, when the information will be released, and what occasions the release of this data.... [Consequently] the individual must be protected from the unlimited collection, storage, use, and transmission of personal data as a condition for free personality development under modern conditions of data processing....
>
> (b) However, the right to "informational self-determination" is not unlimited.... The basic law has resolved the tension between the individual and society by postulating a community-related and community-bound individual.... The individual must in principle accept certain limits on his right to informational self-determination for reasons of compelling public interest.'[146]

As Kommers (1997: 323) points out, the Constitutional Court took the far-reaching step of suspending the execution of the census until the validity of the Census Act was determined and in the end required the Bundestag to amend the Act in several respects before the census could be conducted, an order that delayed the conducting of the census by four years. The right to informational self-determination extends to confidentiality over personal affairs.

Eberle (2002: 95) points out that '[c]onversation, like private matters, reflects human personality'. Consequently unauthorised recordings of private conversations are prohibited on constitutional grounds. The effect of the *Tape Recording* case BVerfGE 34, 238 (245–251) was to prohibit the use in a criminal trial of a secret recording made by the complainant of a conversation with the accused. In the *Drunkard* case BVerfGE 78, 77 the Court prohibited the publication of information concerning persons who had been declared to be incapacitated because of alcohol or drug addiction, prodigality or similar conditions. In the judgment it was held that the publication of this information was 'a severe violation of [informational self-determination] [that] severely impacts the person in her entirety', 'places a negative stamp on reputation' and 'complicates application of the Social State Principle (*Sozialstaatsprinzip*) orientated support measures (*Hilfsmassnahmen*) designed to assist recovery from addiction and facilitate social reentry'. (Translation Eberle: 2002: 97.)

As Eberle (2002: 99) graphically points out, human dignity 'thus becomes the glue between both rights-enhancing and rights-constricting interpretations'.

[146] Translation from Kommers (1997: 323f).

The right to dignity has been extended by the German Constitutional Court to include the power to determine how one is represented to society, which in turn is dependent on one's self-image. In the *Eppler* case the Court held that the individual

> 'should have the freedom to decide for himself — without any limitation of his private sphere — how he wishes to portray himself to third parties or the public, as well as to whether and to what extent third parties may have access to his personality. In particular this includes a person's right to decide whether and in what manner he wishes his utterances to be made public. ... Thus the content of the general right to personality is largely determined by the self-image of the bearer. ..."'[147] (Emphasis supplied.)

In the *Sorya* case[148] an award for damages was upheld by the Court where a fictitious interview, disclosing intimate personal details of the complainant, was published in a newspaper. The judgment was based on the right to personality.

> 'The personality and dignity of an individual, to be freely enjoyed and developed within a societal and communal framework, stand at the very centre of the value order reflected in the fundamental rights protected by the Constitution.... [P]rotection should be extended, above all, to a person's private sphere, ie, the sphere in which he desires to be left alone, to make ... his own decisions, and to remain free from any outside interference.'[149]

The Court further observed that '[a]n imaginary interview adds nothing to the formation of real public opinion. As against press utterances of this sort, the protection of privacy takes unconditional priority.'[150]

In the *Lebach* case[151] the Court went even further and held that the complainant's personality and privacy right trumped the public free-speech interest of the producer of a documentary film portraying the complainant's role in a crime for which he had already paid the criminal penalty. The general right to informational self-determination is expressed as follows by the Court:

> 'The rights to the free development of one's personality and human dignity secure for everyone an autonomous sphere in which to shape one's private life by developing and practicing one's individuality. This includes the right to remain alone, to be oneself within this sphere, and to exclude the intrusion of or inspection by others. It also encompasses the right to one's own likeness and utterances, especially the right to decide what to do with pictures of oneself. In principle, everyone has the right to determine for himself whether and to what extent others may make public an account of either certain incidents from his life or his entire story.

[147] BVerfGE 54, 148 [155] (1980). Translation by Kommers (1989: 331).
[148] BVerfGE 34, 269 (1973).
[149] Id 281, translation Eberle (2002: 102).
[150] Id 283–284, translation Currie (1994: 198).
[151] BVerfGE 35, 202 (1973).

'... In resolving the conflict [between the freedom to broadcast and the right to personality, one] must remember that ... both constitutional concerns are essential aspects of the free democratic order of the Basic Law, the result being that neither can claim precedence in principle.... In case of conflict [the court] must adjust both constitutional values, if possible; If this cannot be achieved, it must determine which interest will defer to the other in the light of the nature of the case and [its] special circumstances. *In so doing, the [court] must consider both constitutional values in their relation to human dignity as the nucleus of the Constitution's value system*.'[152] (Emphasis supplied.)

In cases of this nature, as Eberle (2002: 106–107) points out:

'... [T]he Constitutional Court strives to achieve concordance (*Konkordanz*) between the rights, attempting to interpret both in a manner such that the essence of each can be preserved and, hopefully, optimized. The idea of *concordance as an interpretative technique follows from the objective ordering of values in the Basic Law,* which is calibrated to steer society. ...

... *Lebach* further illustrates the communitarian bent of German law; the Constitutional Court's concern for reintegrating the felon into society took precedence over individual and social interests in expression. Viewed in a different light, the felon's personal autonomy can only be effectively exercised in a social context, and this took precedence.' (Emphasis supplied.)

In this regard the Court in *Lebach* stated:

'The criminal's vital interest in being reintegrated into society and the interest of the community in restoring him to his social position must generally have precedence over the public's interest in a further discussion of the crime....'[153]

Eberle (2002: 107) comments as follows:

'*Lebach* thus illustrates how assertion of *dignitarian rights can operate to limit other fundamental rights*, even especially highly valued ones like expression freedoms.... The outcome in *Lebach* also demonstrates how this technique of concordance operates, weighing conflicting rights with sensitivity, nuance and balance. How personality measures against expression depends more on the hard realities of the case than any categorical rule.' (Emphasis supplied.)

Dealing with the divergence of German law from American law, Eberle (2002: 110) contends that the most notable divergence is

'the strong development in German law of an inner realm of freedom, as manifested especially in the idea of human character amidst the challenges of the modern world.... Focusing, therefore, on the centrality of the personality, German law strives to capture the multifarious radiations of human character. This helps explain why a person's writings, words, thoughts, and emotions are considered central to self-identity.'

---

[152] Id 220ff, translation Kommers (1989: 415).

[153] BVerfGE 35, 202 [235–236], translation Kommers (1997: 419).

In the *Böll* case[154] the Court held that false quotations from an author's work do not enjoy free expression protection.

> 'Among other things this right [to a constitutionally guaranteed general right to an intimate sphere] includes personal honor and the right to one's own words; it also protects the bearer of those rights against having a statement attributed to him which he did not make and which impairs his self-defined claim to social recognition.'[155]

The Court went on to hold that:

> 'The use of a direct quotation as proof of critical evaluation is, as indicated, a particularly sharp weapon in the battle of opinions and very effective in undermining the personality right of the person being criticized. This is particularly true with regard to criticism in the press, radio, and television, for the effects are far-reaching. To rule out any possibility of invading the personality right in these situations, the person quoting someone else is duty-bound to make clear that he is employing his own interpretation of a statement open to several interpretations.'[156]

Eberle (2002: 127–128) contends that

> 'German autonomy law, like the other strands of personality law ... is animated by dignity, the core principle of the German legal order, not privacy. Following the horrors of World War II, rooting the social order in dignity seemed the best course to secure human freedom and human capacity.... Dignity, in conjunction with its cognate of the article 2 free unfolding of the human personality, contains an idea of autonomy too.'

Of particular importance is the fact that this approach protects personal development of individuality and self-identity.

The value of human dignity under art 1(1) of the GBL and the free unfolding of the human personality under art 2(1) play an important role in Germany concerning sexual orientation, preferences and sexual education. The *Sexual Education* case[157] concerned the question whether the state was entitled to present courses in sexual education in public high schools and, if so, to what extent and in what form. In this context the Constitutional Court held:

> 'The Basic Law has placed the intimate and sexual domain of persons, as part of their private sphere, under the protection of Art 2 I in conjunction with Art 1 I GBL. These provisions of the Basic Law guarantee to persons the right to decide for themselves what their attitude to sexual matters will be. They can adopt their own attitudes to sexuality and in principle decide themselves whether, and within what parameters and with what aim, to accept the participation of third parties in this sphere. But when the sexual relationships of people enjoy the benefit of constitutional protection then this right, derived from Art 2 I read with Art 1 I, must also accrue to young people. Their intimate sphere can be substantially affected by the manner in which sexual education is conducted in schools.

[154] BVerfGE 54, 208.
[155] Translation Kommers (1997: 241).
[156] Translation Kommers (1997: 422).
[157] BVerfGE 47, 46.

The youth are not merely objects of parental and governmental education. Rather they are, from the beginning — and in greater measure the older they become — independently protected personalities under Art 2 I read with Art 1 I. BL.'[158]

In the *Transsexual Equal Protection* case the Court held that the Basic Law

'had placed the sexual domain, as part of a person's private sphere, under the protection of article 2, in conjunction with article 1. Restrictions in this area are, without more, incompatible with the Basic Law'.[159]

I do not propose investigating the German law of freedom of expression, save to the extent that it throws light on the concept of human worth and its content.[160] It is clear, however, that in Germany the concept of human worth is an important balancing factor, with regard both to the importance of free speech and to its necessary limitation. It has been said by the German Constitutional Court that

'[a]s the most immediate manifestation of the human personality in society, the basic right to free expression of opinion [*freie Meinungsäußerung*] is one of the noblest of all human rights ...'.[161]

The Court further held:

'Article 5(I) of the Basic Law protects value judgments, which are always aimed at having an intellectual impact, namely at convincing others. Indeed, the protection of the basic right is aimed primarily at the personal opinion of the speaker as expressed in the value judgment. To protect the expression itself but not its effects would make no sense.

If understood in this way, the expression of an opinion in its purely intellectual effect is free. However, if someone else's legal rights are violated [and] the protection of these rights should take precedence over the protection of freedom of opinion, then this violation does not become permissible simply because it was committed through the expression of an opinion. [Courts] must weigh the values to be protected against one another. They must deny the right to express an opinion if the exercise of this right would violate a more important interest protected [by private law]. [Courts] must decide whether such interests are present on the basis of the facts of each individual case.'[162]

Accordingly human worth (dignity), while providing one of the bases for the protection of freedom of expression, is at the same time a value which, in appropriate cases, could limit the free expression right.

---

[158] Id 73–74.

[159] BVerfGE 60, 123 [134], translation Eberle (2002: 137).

[160] For a full discussion in English on freedom of expression in German law see Currie (1994: 174–243) and Kommers (1997: 360–442). These authors also discuss the respects in which the German and United States systems differ with regard to freedom of expression and its limits.

[161] The *Lüth* case BVerfGE 7, 198 [208], translation Currie 175. I prefer his rendering of *freie Meinungsäußerung* as 'free expression of opinion' to that of Kommers (1989: 372) as 'freedom of opinion'.

[162] Id 210–211, translation by Kommers (1989: 373).

In the *Holocaust Denial* case[163] the German Constitutional Court quoted with approval the following passage from the judgment of the Federal Court of Justice:

> 'The historical fact itself, that human beings were singled out according to the criteria of the so-called "Nuremberg Laws" and robbed of their individuality for the purpose of extermination, puts Jews living in the Federal Republic in a special, personal relationship vis-à-vis their fellow citizens; what happened [then] is also present in this relationship today. It is part of their personal self-perception to be understood as part of a group of people who stand out by virtue of their fate and in relation to whom there is a special moral responsibility on the part of all others, and that this is part of their dignity. Respect for this self-perception, for each individual, is one of the guarantees against repetition of this kind of discrimination and forms a basic condition of their lives in the Federal Republic. Whosoever seeks to deny those events denies vis-à-vis each individual the personal worth of [Jewish persons]. For the person concerned, this is continuing discrimination against the group to which he belongs and, as part of the group, against him.'[164]

The Court then observed:

> 'In the light of this court's jurisprudence, there can be no denial of the fact that these decisions bear witness to a grave violation of the right of personality where the persecution of the Jews is denied. Constitutionally, there is no flaw in the Federal Court of Justice's logical connection between the racially motivated extermination of Jews during the Third Reich and a [current-day] attack on the right to respect and dignity of today's Jews'.[165]

Although, in Germany, the right to freedom of expression is considered essential for the democratic process, part of its justification is based on the individual's dignity and right to free personality development. Thus, in the *Soldiers are Murderers* case (also known as the *Tucholsky II* case) the German Constitutional Court observed that communication freedoms are

> 'in the interest of the right to personal development, with which communication is closely linked, as well as in the interest of the democratic process, for which it has constitutive meaning'.[166]

More recently (2005) in BVerfGE 114, 339 (346) [2005] the Court, in explaining the relationship between human dignity in arts 1(1) and 2(1) of the GBL, the latter is again described as a general personality right:

> 'The general personality right, rooted in Art 2.1 read with Art 1.1, complements the freedom rights — given normative content in the GBL and guaranteeing the narrower personal living sphere — and preserves their basic prerequisites.... The content of these rights has not been defined generally or conclusively. Belonging to their recognized content is the right to control the way in which one's own person is represented, how one is recognized socially, and one's personal honour.... An essential guarantee is the protection against

[163] BVerfGE 90, 241 (1994).
[164] Translation by Kommers (1997: 386).
[165] Id.
[166] In BVerfGE 93, 266, translation by Eberle (2002: 217).

utterances that are calculated to harm the regard one has for this person, in particular his public image. The general personality right protects a person in particular against false or distorted utterances, that are not insignificant for personality development....'

Article 10(1) of the GBL provides: 'The privacy of correspondence, post and telecomunications shall be inviolable.' Article 13 provides: 'The home is inviolable.' In BVerfGE 113, 348 (391f) the Court explains why the privacy of the home is so important from the perspective of human dignity:

> 'Art 10 Abs 1 GG guarantees the free unfolding of the personality through private communication shielded from the public and in so doing protects human worth.... This protection is, however, formulated differently from the way Art 13 GG protects the fundamental right to inviolability of the home. Because of the particularly close relationship of this fundamental right of inviolability of the home to human worth, Art 13 GBL guarantees absolute protection for conduct in one's living space, to the extent that it provides for individual development in the crucial area of shaping one's life.... For this every human being requires a spatial substratum, in which she can for herself — and according to self-imposed standards — develop freely; thus the home, if the need arises, can serve as the "last refuge" for the protection of her human worth.'

In BVerfGE 115, 1 (14) [2005] it was once again affirmed that:

> 'Art 1(1) GBL protects the dignity of humans, as they see themselves in their individuality and in their self-awareness.... In addition, Art 2(1) GBL as a principle of the free unfolding of the personality protects — in conjunction with Art 1(1) GBL — the narrower personal area of life, to which one's intimate sexual sphere ... also belongs, encompassing one's sexual self-determination which includes the discovery and recognition of one's very own sexual identity as well as one's sexual orientation.'

The Court also (15) pointed out that one's sexual attachment was not determined by physical sexual characteristics alone. A material factor was also a person's physical constitution and lasting self-discovered sexuality. The Court held a statutory provision to be unconstitutional, which prohibited transsexuals from altering their first names to ones that did not accord with their physical sexual characteristics.

The right of persons to have knowledge of their ancestry, just as the right of a father to know whether a child is in fact his is one flowing from human dignity and the right to the free unfolding of one's personality. This was recognised in BVerfGE 117, 202 (225–226) [2007] as follows:

> 'The right to the free unfolding of the personality and the duty to respect and protect human dignity in terms of Art 2 (1) read with Art 1(1) GBL, guarantees for every individual an autonomous and private sphere for the shaping of her life, in which she can develop and protect her individuality.... An understanding and development of one's individuality is closely connected with knowledge of its constitutive factors. Included in these is one's ancestry. ... This plays a key role in an individual's consciousness, for purpose of his individuation, as well as for his self-understanding and his intimate relationships with others. It is a child's right to be able to relate individually to others, not only socially but

also genealogically — as protection of the personality rights contained and grounded in Art 2(1) GBL read with Art 1(1) GBL — just as a man is entitled to know whether a child is descended from him.'

(d) The work of Günter Dürig as point of departure

Professor Günter Dürig's work played a crucial and influential role in developing the constitutional concept of human worth (dignity) in Germany after World War II. His formulation of the concept (Dürig (1956: 125)) is my own point of departure, as I have already made clear.

> *'Jeder Mensch ist Mensch kraft seines Geistes, der ihn abhebt von der unpersönlichen Natur und ihn aus eigener Entscheidung dazu befähigt, seiner selbst bewußt zu werden, sich selbst zu bestimmen und sich und die Umwelt zu gestalten.*
>
> 'All humans are human by virtue of their intellectual capacity ("*kraft seine Geistes*") which serves to separate them from the impersonality of nature and enables them to exercise their own judgment, to have self-awareness, to exercise self-determination and to shape themselves and nature.'[167] (My translation.)

He used this formulation *verbatim* in his commentary (1958: Art 1(1), Rn 1) on art 1 of the GBL in Maunz/Dürig (looseleaf), which was not replaced for 45 years, until Prof Matthias Herdigan produced a new commentary on art 1(1) in 2003. When regard is had to the fact that since 1958 the commentaries on virtually all the other articles of the GBL have gone through second and even third editions, this is an enormous tribute to a great scholar. This new commentary on art 1(1) has been famously criticised by Prof Ernst-Wolfgang Böckenförde,[168] for its attempts to relativise aspects of human dignity. Needless to say the concepts of human dignity (worth) and the human image (*Menschenbild*) in the context of the constitutional state are the subjects of vast legal scholarship, but I have not — in my admittedly limited researches — encountered an approach regarding the nature of human dignity which is substantially at variance with that of Dürig's.[169]

In 1957 the then President of the BVerfG, Prof Josef Wintrich (1957: 5) expressed himself in very similar terms:

> 'The norm embodied in Art 1(1) has — also seen from the point of view of the constitutional legislator (*Verfassungsgebers*) — a supra-positive character, that is to say it was a given for the constitutional legislator; who did not create it, but found it and recognised it.'

---

[167] For a discussion of Dürig's definition see Enders (1997: 10–13).

[168] See, for example, *'Die Würde des Menschen war unantastbar'* and *'Bleibt die Menschenwürde unantastbar'*, in Böckenförde (2006: 379; 408, respectively). Böckenförde was a justice of the BVerfG from 1983 to 1995.

[169] Amongst a host of scholars, mention can be made of the work of Professors Udo Di Fabio; Christoff Enders (in particular Enders (1997)); Peter Häberle (in particular Häberle (2008)); and Klaus Stern (in particular Stern (2006)).

Exactly the same must be said about s 10 of the South African Constitution, which declares that '[e]veryone *has* human dignity ...' (Emphasis supplied.)

Wintrich continues:

> 'The question regarding the human image, which underlies Art 1 and has shaped it, becomes a legal question in the context of constitutional interpretation, but as far as the supra-constitutional character of the norm is concerned, it is an anthropological question.'

This lies at the heart of Dürig's approach and my attempts to expand on it, as well as at the heart of the development of the personality right in Germany and South Africa.

Wintrich (1957: 6) continues to explain:

> 'Worth accrues to humans for their sake, because it conforms to the structure of the human actually being a "person". It is of course true that the human being, in the context of nature, is posited into the totality of nature, but at the same time the human rules over it in a unique way through the human's ability to be self-aware and self-directing. Only the human can through an awareness of the "I" become aware of itself, and on the basis of this self-understanding and self-possession dispose over itself, while its intellectual will is not inevitably subjected to necessity. The human can freely determine whether or not it wants to follow the inner law — the law of the moral "ought" — which is part of its nature, and of which it is aware.'

The influence of Kant is obvious.

Professor Peter Häberle (2008: 30–31) makes the following important observation:

> 'With regard to its image of the human being (*Menschenbild*) the constitutional state (*Verfassungsstaat*) disclaims any ideology that invariably produces some sort of "new human".... The constitutional state does not, instrumentally, want to "remodel", or make "better" humans, it knows neither "Supermen" nor a "master race". It does not consider that it is its function to "alter" humans.... It considers humans to be "incomplete beings", but at the same time does not countenance any idea of "non-human humans" (*"Unmenschen"*) or "inferior humans" (*"Untermenschen"*).'

Häberle (2008: 43) considers that *Human Dignity* and *Democracy*, both fundamental principles of the constitutional state, require a *relatively 'good' image* of human beings, 'as humans who have dignity and can be free, but who also recognize the equal dignity and freedom of their fellow citizens, and who in this regard literally contract with them in the sense of I Kant's categorical imperative'.

Moreover as Eberle (2002: 19), writing in English, points out:

> 'For Germans, Kant is the source to draw upon in order to check human passion. In a sense the German Basic Law is the natural successor to the German classical philosophical tradition.... [W]e can conceive of the Basic Law as a value-oriented constitution that obligates the state to realize a set of objectively ordered principles, rooted in justice and

equality, that are designed to restore the centrality of humanity to the social order and thereby secure a stable democratic society on this basis.'

He stresses (2002: 41–42) that dignity is 'not merely a focus on individuality' but as the central value of the GBL it 'infuses throughout the whole constitutional order, obliging the state both to protect and to realize it'. Consequently, dignity 'radiates throughout society, animating the whole public law system of Germany'.

Whether consciously or not, the South African Constitution is equally founded on Kantian ideas, and is no less an objective, normative value system, aimed at restoring human worth after the ravages of apartheid. Not surprisingly, it draws deeply on principles and ideas of German constitutionalism.

(e) Professor Josef Isensee[170] *and secular society's search for the absolute*

In his article — referred to in Chapter 1 above — Professor Josef Isensee (2006) has captured, in broad terms, the importance of human dignity, and why vigilance is necessary to protect its important role. The title of Professor Isensee's illuminating article '*Menschenwürde: die säkulare Gesellschaft auf der Suche nach dem Absoluten*' ('Human worth: Secular society in search of the absolute') captures both the pathos and the dilemma of the 21st century's search for a better world, or at least a world in which the regular slaughter (by sword or famine) of millions of innocent women and children no longer takes place.[171] The disfavour with which religion, and in particular the theistic religions, are regarded in present times has resulted in secular humanists' passionate search for a secular absolute in this desire for a better world. In the process they have forgotten or ignored the fact that some of the strongest secular attempts at finding the absolute (or even the universal) rely, directly or indirectly on theological models. Isensee (2006: 173–174), writing about a constitution in which the acknowledgment and protection of human worth is at a higher level than in any other constitution of which I am aware, expresses this dilemma well in the opening paragraphs of his article:

> '"The worth of human beings is inviolable", according to the German Basic Law in the first sentence of Art 1(1): pithy, solemn, mysterious. Reality denies this: human worth is violable, and is repeatedly violated. Nonetheless the law itself accepts it. "... [I]t is inviolable." Pathos rules defiantly here. What is expressed in the indicative, is in fact imperative. The apparently descriptive word use expresses the categorical nature of the norm particularly clearly. The norm takes its stand against threatening reality. In the empire of the law, nobody touches the worth of human beings. In the constitutional text inviolability stands as truth. Yet it is not something empirical, but a matter of belief and a truth to be believed, and yet as an ought ("*sollen*").'

---

[170] Professor Isensee is, amongst other things, co-author of a six-volume textbook (*Handbuch*) on German constitutional law, namely Isensee and Kirchhof (eds) (2003–2008).

[171] I am indebted to Prof Henk Botha for bringing this article to my attention.

He also (2006: 178) speaks of human worth in terms of a 'civil religion':

> 'When everything is shattered that customarily holds society together — Christian religion and cultural tradition, civil forms of life and national solidarity — society finds unity in confessing to human worth, and demands something like a state of fundamental moral certainty.'

He contends (179) that human worth has become something of a taboo, the truth of which is not open to discussion: 'The constitutional provision proves itself to be an article of faith in a civil religion.' This, he says, is very much in line with Rosseau's thinking. Secular society, Isensee says, seeks 'to escape the curse of relativism that has been laid on it, without being allowed to hope for refuge in the transcendental ...'. It is in one sense true, as Isensee further points out (2006: 180) that '[n]o legal provision interprets itself. Its fate depends on the interpreter.'

On the other hand, the interpreter in question does not interpret in a vacuum, but in the context of history, the history of ideas, and the universal abuse of human dignity.

While Isensee vividly portrays the dilemma the modern world faces, I believe that Kant makes out a far stronger secular case for human worth as an absolute than Isensee gives him credit for. What risks being lost sight of is the strong anthropological basis for Kant's understanding of human worth. I entertain the same hopes as does Allen Wood in the passage quoted near the end of Chapter One. Our stark choice is, I believe, between Kant's transcendental ideal of human worth — which I do not see as a 'refuge' — on the one hand, and 'law and economics' on the other.

Isensee rather acerbically points out (2006: 182–183) that the jurist has an experience similar to that of St Augustine, when he wanted to express what the essence of time is: 'So, what is "time"? When nobody asks me this, I know what it is. However, when I want to answer a questioner, I do not know what it is.'

I understand Isensee to be concerned with the failure to define or circumscribe more closely the meaning of human dignity for, as he puts it (2006: 183), 'what the jurists cannot define they also cannot apply'. He also laments the fact that in the course of decades a 'lavish casuistry has in fact developed, in which concrete injunctions and prohibitions are to be found in abundance', without producing anything consistently comprehensive. This is an interesting criticism, for other writers have commented favourably on the fact that the contours of human worth have been developed over several decades on a 'case-to-case' basis. Isensee's concern probably represents a rather extreme civilian approach where preference is given to reasoning from principle as opposed to the empirical English common law methodology. The so-called mixed systems combine both. It is a matter of some significance that, in this area, German courts have opted for the case-by-case approach in their efforts to give meaning to *Menschenwürde.* They have appreciated one of the virtues of empiricism. One should also remember that in these various legal traditions the *diligens* or *bonus paterfamilias,* the reasonable person (formerly 'man'), and 'the man [and woman] on the Clapham omnibus' have been used to develop the content of negligence in the law of delict on a case-by-case basis, and that the resulting rich casuistry has been seen as meritorious for the understanding and development of the law in this field. Why should the same not be true in the development of our understanding of ***human dignity***?

Isensee strongly supports Dürig's approach to the understanding and the meaning of human dignity in the GBL. After quoting the 'classic definition' of Dürig that I employ for my own understanding of human dignity,[172] Isensee (2006: 185–187) proceeds to discuss it in some detail in the context of Kant's ethical philosophy. I make no apology for quoting extensively from the work of a contemporary scholar:

> 'Human worth does not, however, reside in the realisation by individuals of their capabilities, but in the "equal abstract possibility" of their realisation. Translated into the language of the Scholastics, the worth lies not in the act but in the potentiality: it belongs to the human being's essential nature — or in Kant's sense — to "humanity". Consequently worth also inheres in the mentally handicapped, who from the outset do not have the ability for free self-realisation or the shaping of their lives; the criminal who has abused his ability; and the victim who consents to her dehumanisation. The equal legal capacity of all is founded on this premise. Dürig understands worth as the general and *equal quality* of being human. He addresses himself to humans from their birth, the core of their nature and personality having been laid down and striving for development, since the human being, whether she grows or disappears, still remains the same. He even recognises the after-effects of worth in a corpse.
>
> "In this respect too, the criteria correspond broadly with those of Kant. They ground a person's being in the rational nature of humans. Yet it depends not on whether the individual actually uses her rational intelligence. Rather the human is a person from birth. Parents, according to Kant, may not 'destroy their child, or abandon it to chance, as though it were their creation (for if it were, it would not then be a creature endowed with freedom) or their property.'"' (Emphasis supplied.)

From Isensee's description (2006: 186) of how Dürig dealt with human worth, it is clear that the latter found it useful to do so in a negatively descriptive manner, namely to ascertain what human dignity *is,* by examining instances of where it is infringed. I have already emphasised that, in my view, human dignity can often best be grasped by considering instances of its breach. He also makes the point that Dürig, in giving substance to the concept of human dignity, maintained a sense of proportion and did not — by an overextension of its field of application — devalue it to 'kleine Münze' (literally: 'small coins'; thus 'small change'). The concern that so crucial a concept as human dignity (worth) should not lose credibility because of overextended use is one that can readily be shared. This is also true of the concept of 'human rights'. It does run the risk of losing legitimate purchase when applied indiscriminately to every mundane aspect of human life.

[172] See Chapter 2, section 2.1 above.

At the same time one should be careful not to allow agendas, or over-enthusiastic claims by others, to dominate one's own concerns for the central importance of human dignity. In the following passage Isensee (2006: 186–187) pays appropriate homage[173] to Dürig in this regard:

> 'Dürig's interpretation manifests his catholic formation, as well as his experience of war and the illegal state (*Unrechtsstaat*).[174] Certainty as to orientation, power of judgment, and intuition give his commentary a classic status. In the first decades of the Basic Law, it breathed the spirit of its origins. When not original, it came close to originality. It did pioneering work in the field of dogmatics. It did not consider it necessary to bother itself with originality as new interpretations do, with their highflying complexity and mannerdness. It moulded, as it were, the standard against which later attempts at interpretation had to be measured.'

Isensee (2006: 187–198) is deeply concerned with the relativising of the concept of human dignity by the way it is currently being interpreted and applied, both within and outside constitutional jurisprudence. He expresses this concern in different ways.

His first concern (187–190) is that by over-stretching its application, and by its being summoned in aid of some or other pressure group, the supreme constitutional status of human dignity will become trivialised and reduced in constitutional value to '*kleine Münze*' ('small change'). It runs the danger of 'becoming the last ditch strategy of populist (sea)-lawyers' who seek in art 1 of the GBL a foundation that is critique-resistant. After enumerating some, in his view, dubious judgments of the BVerfG, Isensee (2006: 188–189) caustically observes that 'the "most important value judgments" relating to the Basic Law are concerned with telephone sex and dwarf-throwing contests'. He bemoans the fact, for example, that a court of the status of the Federal Administrative Court has to consider the constitutionality of regulations prescribing the style and length of haircuts in the army. He reserves his most biting critique for the fact that the BVerfG was called upon to consider, in the context of human dignity, the constitutionality of a telephone account presented to the plaintiff that did not spell the plaintiff's name correctly, having omitted to use the 'ö' letter in his name and substituted for it "oe"! Isensee feels (2006: 189–190) that, despite Dürig's warning, human dignity is turning itself into 'small change':

[173] For which concurrence I rely not only on my own limited knowledge, but on the views of, inter alia, Prof Peter Häberle (1997) and Prof Walter Glaeser (1997).

[174] There is no way of translating *Unrechtsstaat* simply and at the same time conveying its full meaning, because it is a play on the concept of the *Rechtsstaat*, meaning 'constitutional state' or 'state founded on the rule of law.' The *Unrechtstaat* is the very opposite of the *Rechtsstaat*, in other words a state based on the rule of injustice or non-law, the reference of course being to the Nazi period.

> 'With its extension this constitutional guarantee is becoming thinner. With its common daily use it is becoming a banality and is becoming entangled in the undergrowth of concrete cases. It is now becoming just a fundamental right like any other. The inevitable result is that it is forfeiting its absolute character, becoming relativised by basic rights of others and the public interest, and being left to the hazardous fate of balancing (*Abwägungsaleatorik*).'[175]

Isensee's second concern (2006: 190–193) is with what he calls human dignity conflicting with human dignity. He is critical of the torture and air security judgments. He sees them as illustrating a clash between the human dignity, seen as an individual fundamental right, of one person with that of another, and the relativising of one's right in favour of another's. I do not consider his criticism in this regard to be well-founded, as indicated by my comments on these judgments earlier in this section.

His third concern is with the 'fragile consensus' that exists in society regarding the interpretation of human dignity as directly applicable to the solution of legal conflicts and as founding obligations in persons. He sees a dissonance in the approach to the protection of the foetus in cases of abortion, and the protection afforded to the embryo in genetic manipulation and pre-implantation diagnosis; his contention being (2008: 193–194) that, in the latter case, clear preference is given to the embryo.

His fourth concern (2006: 194–198) is with what he calls the 'open dissent' in more recent times on the part of those who seek a radically new foundation for human dignity and its ambit of protection. He accuses these persons of having the preconceived objective of, in the last instance, getting rid of the human dignity of the foetus (and possibly also of the corpse) and the protection of the foetus's life, 'as an atavistic impediment to the ambition of progress, good-living and the desire for acquisition' of the generation that currently has the say. He mentions a number of examples which, although employing different premises and coming to different conclusions, 'all break with the understanding of human dignity to date, as presented by Dürig', and make human dignity 'susceptible to differing political needs'. It 'loses its absolute nature'. He mentions ten examples:

1. The case of the solver of paradoxes who denies human dignity any substance and regards it as a blank cheque for personal value judgments.
2. When the human dignity provision is dealt with as a mere positive law *dictum* of the drafters of the Constitution.
3. When dignity is reduced to freedom and equality.
4. When the protection of dignity is made flexible and tailored to existing circumstances.
5. When dignity mutates from being an *a priori* principle to one *a posteriori*.

[175] '*Abwägungsaleatorik*' is a German composite word that defies succinct translation. '*Abwägung*', in the context of rights, means a weighing up or balancing. The English translation of '*aleatorik*' is 'aleotory', meaning 'dependent on the throw of the dice'.

6. When dignity is focused on any tendentious area with a lack of principle and rationality.
7. Whenever the idea of 'inherent dignity'[176] is jettisoned.
8. When human dignity

> 'gives precedence to self-consciousness, reason and the ability to attain one's ends.... when [human] worth no longer furnishes the basis for freedom, but is seen as an expression of freedom, and as identifying its possession. Comsequently foetuses, babies, and mentally handicapped people have no share in human dignity. The embryo is recognised as a "biological-naturalistic failure". It counts solely — contrary to Kant's position — as a "creation" of its parents, and thus as a thing, that has a greater or lesser price. Worth and freedom are the same.'

9. According to Isensee (2006: 198) worth is now seen

> 'as an achievement which the individual produces or fails to produce: worth as successful identity formation by virtue of self-directed behaviour.... Worth as achievement also corresponds with a hierarchy of reputation, which comes into existence rather like sporting achievements do.... Fundamental equality at the beginning as the basis for human differentiation is replaced by inequality of achievement. Whoever is unable to achieve stays outside.'

10. Lastly Isensee (2006: 198) contends that worth has been uncoupled from the protection of life. From now on there is a constitutional category of *human lives without human worth* (*menschenwürdelose Menschenleben*).

His fifth major concern is with what he calls 'distress'. While a dispute over legal interpretation is a normal feature of jurisprudence it is, except for persons in the particular specialist field, not a matter of public concern. Yet, says Isensee (2006: 198–199), a real stir was caused in 2003 when the public came to hear of the change in the interpretation of human dignity reported by Ernst-Wolfgang Böckenförde[177] in the *Frankfurter Allgemeine Zeitung* under the alarming heading 'Human dignity was inviolable (*Die Würde der Menschen war unantastbar*)'.[178] Isensee explains why:

> 'The reason was the new commentary by *Matthias Herdegen* on Art 1(1) GBL in the Maunz-Dürig Commentary which, in the new edition of this loose-leaf work, replaced the original commentary of *Günther Dürig*.[[179]] The respects in which *Herdegen* departed from his predecessor were quite moderate, compared to other new commentaries. Yet even these departures were viewed as violating the German constitutional taboo, by a wide circle of readers who were impressed by *Böckenförde's* review. The dismay to which *Böckenförde's*

[176] Used in the German text.

[177] A distinguished academic and former judge of the BVerfG.

[178] The sting is in the use of the past tense 'was (*war*) inviolable' whereas Art 1(1), first sentence, of the GBL declares that human dignity 'is inviolable (*ist unantastbar*).'

[179] My footnote inserted. Dürig's original commentary had stood unchanged since 1978. See also Böckenförde (2006: 379ff).

review gave rise demonstrated that human dignity was more than just a legal provision, it portrayed the foundation of community trust. But this foundation is shaking.'

The feeling of moral certainty becomes unsettled, especially at a time when the guarantee has to be protected against new types of biological challenges: in view of the fact that biological existence is itself no longer taken as a given, the beginning and end of life being manipulated from procreation in the Petri dish to death in the intensive care unit, and genetic identity becoming a matter of practical choice. The 'load-bearing constitutional principle (*tragende Konstitutionsprinzip*)'[180] shows itself as being incapable of resisting these challenges. It reflects the current trend of interpretation, the *Zeitgeist* and the interest of the day. The rock, on which the waves are to break themselves, is itself breaking loose. The representation of human worth as an absolute is broken down. The curse of relativism has caught up with the interpretation of human dignity.'

Isensee (2006: 211–214) describes how extensively human dignity radiates out to give content and provide parameters for many of the other fundamental rights, thus emphasising, for my purposes and in the context of this book, the function that the value of dignity can play. Fundamental rights and certain constitutional norms mirror aspects of human worth. It is inextricably linked to the right to life and the substantive aspects of human dignity are encountered in freedom of expression, in the fair trial guarantee, as well as in the property guarantee.[181]

According to Isensee (2006: 212) human dignity — although itself not subject to weighing up — 'plays a leading role in the weighing up of constitutional goods (*Güter*) as, for example, in the conflict between media freedom and personal honour'. The 'idea of human dignity' shapes the interpretation of the concrete constitutional provisions.

Isensee (2006: 214) makes the point that human worth is an 'open concept without sharp defining edges'. Attempts at definition tend to be tautologous. Legal hermeneutics can only approximate this idea and from various perspectives grasp a few aspects of it. He also makes the valid point that it is easier to define human worth negatively than positively. Isensee nevertheless attempts (2006: 214–216) to give some idea of its content and practical application:

- Worth is a moral-legal quality of the essential nature of the human being that everyone belonging to the human species has; the individual as she exists in her uniqueness and particularity.
- The species also has worth, the human race as supra-individual and pre-individual has greatness. Humanity, as understood by 18th-century idealism lives on, not in the sense of a biological category but as a norm; the image that the human being has of itself.

[180] BVerfGE 6, 21 (36). Footnote in the original.
[181] For a defence of property as a human right see Dürig (1984: 47f).

- Human worth transcends all legal and material categorisation. Status in civil society is irrelevant. Human dignity does not permit itself to be constrained by function.
- Where human life is, there worth is too. It is present in the embryo, whether conceived *in utero* or *in vitro*. Yet it also extends beyond life; and has consequences for the way testamentary property is dealt with.
- Worth is not dependent on its recognition by society; rather all members of society must recognise one another's human worth. It accrues to individuals simply because of their personhood, not because of particular achievements, desert, or social position.
- Dignity accrues to human beings as persons, who as human beings are called to self-realisation and personal responsibility. Because of their worth, human beings are able to rise above circumstances. Human beings are ends in themselves. As human beings they are subjects of the law and may never be instrumentalised as a means to an end.
- Human worth corresponds with reason. Human beings prove themselves by the reasoned exercise of their freedom. Nevertheless worth does not require the actual ability to use reason. The unborn child as well as the mentally disabled share in dignity. I revert to this a little more fully later.
- Human worth constitutes the foundation of constitutional freedom and equality. Dignity is not acquired by achievement, nor forfeited by non-achievement.
- Because of their ability to reason, human beings transcend their physicality into the realms of freedom, morality, law, and culture.
- The unity of the human race, as far as human rights are concerned, manifests itself in human dignity that transcends all natural, legal and social distinctions.
- Human dignity is general. For the sake of her worth it is legally impossible to define any person out of the sphere of humanity, and to deny her elementary rights. Individuals are insulted when they are denigrated as being, inter alia, sub-human or vermin, and in this way are semantically eliminated from humanity.
- Dignity is egalitarian. It tolerates no material gradation with regard to stage of development, age, or sex. Human worth is not concerned with moral desert, occupational achievement, or aesthetic attractiveness. It is founded solely on being a member of the human race.
- Human worth has obligations. It grounds an *ethical* obligation for everybody to respect the dignity of others. Herein lies the ethical nucleus of human solidarity.
- Human dignity also gives rise to the obligation to have *respect for oneself*. This proclaims the limits of private autonomy — particularly with regard to self-realisation regarding the limits of life.

- Human dignity is itself not a subjective right, yet it grounds legal capability as well as the right to have legal rights.

It is only in this very last respect that the German position differs from the South African, for under the South African Constitution human dignity is both a right and a value, the latter (as in Germany) giving substance and contour to other rights and playing a determinative role in settling a clash of rights, with which I deal more fully in Chapter 5. For the rest, the above analysis is equally applicable to human worth under our Constitution.

(f) Professor Klaus Stern's understanding of human dignity

(i) Introduction

In what follows, I shall attempt to summarise Prof Klaus Stern's[182] understanding of human dignity (worth) as articulated by him in his celebrated textbook on German constitutional law, Stern (2006). I shall from time to time interrupt my discussion of his views by referring to the writing and views of other scholars in order to follow up a point made by Stern. I do so in order to maintain the overall systematic structure of Stern's treatment, but at the same time to expand it at certain points.

Stern (2006: 9–10), points out that the drafters of the Constitution (*Verfassung*), by employing the concept of human dignity (worth), incorporated — as it were — 'two and a half thousand years of philosophical history' into the Constitution, going back to ancient philosophy. But, he says, an even more powerful humanistic and Christian foundation manifests itself, which relates the '"*dignitas humana* (*hominis dignitas*)"' back to Aquinas and, more especially to Manetti (1396–1459) and Pico Mirandola (1463–1494). The theological foundation is based on the *imago Dei* concept. Possibly the strongest influence on the Basic Law's concept of worth was, according to Stern (2006: 10), the philosophy of Immanuel Kant (1724–1804). He quotes with approval the following maxims and categorical imperatives of Kant included in my citations in Chapter 2. 'Autonomy is therefore the ground of the dignity of human nature and of every rational creature'; and, 'So act that you use humanity, whether in your own person or in the person of any other, always at the same time as an end, never merely as a means'.

Stern (2006: 11) cautions that —

> 'Despite all prior Christian and humanist — in this sense Western — moulding, one ought not to attempt a definitive definition, lest one endanger fundamental consensus on an essential and universal understanding of human worth (dignity). Christians and non-Christians will find themselves in a commitment to human worth, in order to achieve a

[182] Professor Stern has been Dean of the Law Faculty at Cologne University as well as the University's Rector; and served as a judge on the Constitutional Court of the Province of North Rhine-Westphalia.

> basis for the idea of human rights as a universally agreed principle and basis for a peaceful world order.'

I have been at pains to point out that my own description of human dignity is not a definition and is sufficiently open-ended to allow for further development.

Stern (2006: 11) therefore warns that one is 'prohibited from handicapping oneself with a limited world view' when it comes to the interpretation of art 1(1) of the GBL. Worth must be acknowledged in *all* human beings as 'the "original condition of being a person" (J Wintrich), as "the independence, the essence, the nature of humans as such" (HC Nipperdey), regardless of the manner in which the metaphysical foundation is expressed'. Stern (2006: 16) affirms the *Objektformel* of Dürig, which has become 'the classic formulation' — 'Human worth as such is infringed when the actual human being is devalued to a fungible size as a means to an end', which, he points out, Dürig then elucidates as follows: 'We are concerned with the degradation of persons to things, that can be totally "overcome", "shot down", "registered", "liquidated", "brain-washed", "replaced", "substituted", "hounded out".'

Stern (2006: 16) points out, however, that although this *Objektformel* is still valid as a general guideline, it is at too high a level of generality for fine-tuning. Accordingly, says Stern, a more penetrating plumbing of the concept of human worth is taking place, conducted at a high level by the most recent investigations. The current concern with human worth is driven by *actual developments* in embryo protection, in human gene technology, in bio-medicine and in gene therapy. 'The highly intricate questions that arise in connection with the foregoing', says Stern, 'require an answer not only from medical science, from theology, the social sciences and ethics, but also from constitutional law and in particular from Art 1.1 and 2 GBL.' He warns:

> 'New threats to human worth, of which the constitutional authors in 1948/9 had no inkling, are presenting themselves. But they must be coped with; human worth is not fixed "at a specific point in the development of insights and evaluations with regard to the essentialia of human existence".'

While deeply conscious of the dangers (if not the impossibility) of trying to *define* human worth (dignity), Stern (2006: 17–59) does helpfully describe, in general terms, various areas of human worth. While his starting point is Dürig's so-called *Objektformel*, he points out (2006: 19) that it is too rough a guide for subtler infractions of human worth. Stern refers (2006: 19) to the more recent developments in the jurisprudence of the BVerfG that have — in addition to pointing to the antithesis of human beings as objects — referred to their *Subjektqualität* and investigated the nature of human dignity by considering the nature of the infractions thereon. Stern (2006: 19) refers with approval to a dictum from BVerfGE 96, 375 (399) where reference is made to this *Subjektqualität* as being 'peculiar to every human being without regard to her qualities, her achievements or her social status'. But, as Stern (2006: 19–20) points out, this picture is as generalised as is the case of the *Objektformel*.

Stern (2006: 20) rightly points out that in 'constitutionalising' human worth one must — because of the supreme value of human dignity — approach its concretisation with the greatest of care. The danger of wearing down human worth to the mundane has from the beginning been great, and we need to take it seriously. One dare not, as Stern puts it (2006: 21), and as Dürig timeously warned, reduce human dignity to 'small change (*kleine Münze*)'.

Amongst the various human worth theories[183] Stern (2006: 22) opts for the *worth* or *dowry* theory *(Wert- oder Mitgifttheorie)*. Professor Dreier (1996: art 1(1) Rn 41), whom Stern refers to with approval on this point, explains this theory as follows:

> 'The worth or dowry theory understands worth as a decidedly human quality, one of the human being's most outstanding qualities. It manifests itself in two versions: one being Christian and one being of a law of nature-idealistic kind. The Christian version bases the distinguishing feature of its *imago Dei* depiction on the particular representation of the human being in the context of the Godly order of creation. The law of nature-idealistic version, represented in particular by Kant, roots the particular quality of humans in their reason, their faculty for free self-determination and moral autonomy. Both versions tend to acknowledge the worth [of humans] without regard to the actual realization of these qualities or the potential to realize them, and also without regard to actual deprivations or deformations.'

Stern (2006: 23) divides the protection of human dignity into *spheres* that express human dignity in a particular way. He suggests that this might help with the difficult task of giving concrete form to human dignity. The five spheres he suggests are:

(a) bodily identity and integrity;
(b) intellectual-spiritual identity and integrity;
(c) economic sustenance compatible with human dignity;
(d) fundamental legal equality; and
(e) the prohibition of excessive state power.

Stern does not, it is true, expressly recognise the human being's capacity for meaningful relationships with others as an aspect of human worth. At the same time he does not regard the human person as an isolated individual being. He gives full recognition to the social state founding value and its influence on human behaviour. Moroever the 'relationality' aspect of the human being could probably be accommodated as a component or implication of the sphere 'intellectual-spiritual identity and integrity'.

[183] Which include the so-called 'value or dowry theory (*Wert- oder Mittgifttheorie*)', the 'performance theory (*Leistungstheorie*)', and the 'communications theory (*Kommunikationstheorie*)'.

Eberle (2002: 50–51) also analyses human dignity with references to five spheres that correspond closely to Stern's division.[184]

It is quite beyond the ambit of the present work to reflect Stern's detailed discussion of these spheres. I limit myself to some general observations. Before referring to these spheres, it is necessary to say something about subsidiarity. Stern (2006: 23) points to the fact that these spheres also fall within the protection of other sections of the GBL (as is indeed the case with the South African Constitution) and other constitutional principles, such as those relating to the constitutional and social state. This does not, however, exclude reliance on human dignity, and Stern points to the many judgments of the BVerfG that in practice examine infractions of these other fundamental rights in conjunction with art 1(1) of the GBL.

I shall follow Stern's above schema.

(ii) Bodily identity and integrity (Stern 2006: 24–47)

While chiefly protected by the first sentence of art 2(2) of the GBL, there is an important aspect of human worth in bodily integrity, which is infringed, for example, in the case of torture or the compulsory alteration of one's physical appearance in substantial respects. He also deals (2006: 27–42) in this context with parental corporal punishment, medical intervention, and in some detail with the problems arising from new developments in the field of bio-medicine, biotechnology and human genetics. He argues that, particularly in so far as the constitutional evaluation of the last-mentioned is concerned, human dignity must play a key role. These developments, and the often (as yet) unseen consequences not only raise questions for the practice of medicine, for ethics and theology, but also pose penetrating questions for constitutional law. He points to a wide divergence of views, within the various disciplines, in relation to these problems. Stern argues (2006: 29) that the fundamental question regarding an area of research such as this — 'is not what is medically or technically possible, but where the limits of the possible are, on the basis of medical ethics and from the standpoint of constitutional law, and its inherent value system'.

Professor Rosemarie Will (2004: 1228) sets out the issues clearly in this regard:

[184] I have, for ease of comparison, arranged Eberle's spheres according to Stern's alphabetical division:

(a) '[R]espect for physical integrity, specified in Art 2(2).'

(b) '[R]espect for intellectual and spiritual identity and integrity. This is manifested most dramatically in the protection of personality rights, specified in article 2 of the Basic Law.'

(c) '[D]ignity means guarantee of individual and social existence. Tangibly this is manifested in the article 2 right to life and in Germany's social welfare state, textually anchored in article 20(1) of the Basic Law.'

(d) '[Human dignity]' ... [a]t a minimum ... means that the social order must reflect the equality of humankind ... [which] ... means that persons are entitled to equal worth.'

(e) '[D]ignity means limitation of official power.'

> 'Why are we arguing so intensely about what the content of human dignity is. It is because research into human genetics has given rise to controversy in society about belief. The possibilities for controlling the physical and technical bases for human reproduction, for repairing humans genetically and consequently also for manipulating them, makes the discussion about the content of human dignity the central theme of ethical and legal debate. Whether it is permissible for humans to deal in this way with their own nature, turns public debate about human genetics into a constitutional battle about the content and inviolability of human worth.'

From the perspective of constitutional law, the human dignity guarantee must play a decisive role. Here too, views are divided. Stern also points to the currently insoluble difference of opinion between doctors, natural scientists, ethicists, theologians and lawyers as to when, for purposes of art 1(1) of the GBL, the fertilised egg becomes a human being. According to Stern (2006: 35–36), the moment fusion takes place between egg and sperm cell, a 'totipotent' cell is created; that is to say, it has the total potential to develop into a complete human being. The embryo is already human for purposes of art 1(1) and is no longer a mere thing. Under this same heading Stern deals with suicide, actively and passively assisted suicide, and abortion.

(iii) Intellectual-spiritual identity and integrity (Stern 2006: 47–51)

Stern is of the view that this aspect of human worth is greatly threatened, or at least dangerously threatened in current times when one thinks of all the subtle outside control that is being exercised over human beings.

But this own worth is concerned chiefly with personal identity and integrity; in any event both are inextricably connected with the human image. Identity is concerned with both the inner and outer relationships of human beings. The relationship outwards is, according to Stern, relatively easy to formulate, but the inner relationship — particularly the intellectual-spiritual components thereof — cannot be captured in a general formula. Here the singularity and personality of the individual manifest themselves. For Stern, *personal identity* accordingly means 'the singularity and independence of the individual, always inalienable, rooted in the environment, and developing herself and presenting herself as an individual'.

When it comes to the core of personal identity, art 1(1) of the GBL is, for Stern (2006: 48), the correct reference point. He refers in this regard to the *Life Imprisonment* case[185] in which the BVerfG concluded, solely and expressly on the strength of art 1(1), that the human being 'continues to be acknowledged as a responsible and self-directing personality' and that it was irreconcilable with this view 'for the state to take the view that the human being could by force be denuded of its worth, without having the least chance of ever again being able to

[185] BVerfGE 45, 187 (228f).

regain its freedom'. He refers to other cases where the core of personal identity has similarly been recognised. The inviolability of human dignity also requires the protection of its honour and personality spheres. The protection of human worth does not end with the death of the individual — a view that has been supported by the BVerfG.[186]

Eberle (2002: 51), writing in English, suggests that the 'main development' of German dignity jurisprudence 'has occurred in conjunction with the more concrete freedoms in article 2 of the Basic Law'. Article 2(1) proclaims, with a Kantian ring, that '[e]very person shall have the right to free development of his personality (*freie Entfaltung seiner Persönlichkeit*) in so far as he does not violate the rights of others or offend against the constitutional order or the moral law'. Article 2(2) embodies the right 'to life and physical integrity' and the right to 'freedom of the person' which is declared to be 'inviolable'. Eberle (2002: 61) makes the point that the word '*Entfaltung*' in the art 2(1) phrase '*freie Entfaltung seiner Persönlichkeit*' literally means the free 'unfolding' of the personality, rather than 'development', which would be translated as '*Entwicklung*'.[187] Thus, in German law, the focus is 'really on the "free unfolding of the personality" more than just the self-realisation connoted by "development".' Eberle (2002: 61) identifies three components integral to German personality law:

> '[T]he first two components involve a contrast between inner and outer freedom. Outer freedom entails freedom of action.... As conceived in German law, freedom of action empowers one to do fundamentally what one desires insofar as it does not interfere with others or the constraints of the social order.... [I]nner freedom connotes a personal interior sphere that is inward in orientation. The personal sphere delimits an essential sphere of privacy within which one can fundamentally determine who one is and how one should relate to the world, if at all.... The focus of this inner freedom is a person's thoughts, beliefs, emotions, and yearnings, and the right to decide what to do with them.'

The third of Eberle's components 'as envisioned in constitutional law,' is 'issues relating to identity, self-determination, and autonomy'.

As far as freedom of action in the outer world is concerned, Eberle (2002: 62) makes the point that the German law on the 'free unfolding of the personality' under art 2(1) of the GBL

> 'is comprehensive and multifaceted. Grounded in human dignity and, specifically, Kant's theory on moral autonomy, the right is ordinarily read with the more ultimate Article 1 guarantee, the only right so tangibly linked with another in German law. Personality rights come into play, potentially, whenever an action is not protected by a more specific right.'

Eberle (2002: 81–82) gives the following useful summary of the history of the personality rights in German private and constitutional law:

---

186 BVerfGE 30, 173 (194) and in a number of its so-called chamber judgments. See Stern (2006: 50 n 207).

187 Citing Glendon (1991) 62.

> 'The right of personality is based originally on Kant and his work on moral personality. For Kant, development of a person's capacity and talent is central to realization of moral autonomy. Hence, one could think of development of personality as a moral "right," with accompanying obligation. Endowed with talent and capacity, in other words, a person shall develop and use them. Each person should so make their way in the world. Kant's reasoning had a deep influence on German thought and legal philosophy. In 1791–1792, Wilhelm von Humboldt, Germany's pre-eminent university reformer, worked out some of the political implications of Kant's thoughts in a short book on government in which he set forth the idea that the highest purpose of the state "was to promote conditions favouring the free and harmonious unfolding of individuality."[188]
>
> ...
>
> Kant also influenced Friederich Karl von Savigny and other formulators of German law. Von Savigny, Germany's pre-eminent jurist of the nineteenth century, for example, stated that "the goal of all law ... is directed to the secure and independent development of the personality."[189] ... [T]he German Civil Courts developed a comprehensive general right of personality, including a highly pronounced interior component, in conjunction with their interpretation of the German Code.... The full flowering of German personality law, was the adoption of the Basic Law in 1949 and its anchoring of the social order to the concept of dignity and corresponding unfolding of personality.'

Eberle (2002: 260) sums up the effect of arts 1(1) and 2(1) of the GBL in the context of German personality rights as follows:

> 'German personality law reflects the broad themes of German law: human dignity and its cognates, including valuation of life as an end in itself, worth and equal worth, and freedom to act within the constraints of the value order.'

According to Eberle (2002: 260) German law focuses on the

> 'interior component of human personality, an emanation of the inner striving for freedom. Throughout its jurisprudence, the Constitutional Court has attempted to capture and preserve the essence of human personhood and personality, and safeguard it amidst the challenges of modern society. Hence the Constitutional Court seeks to identify and fortify an inner space, "in which to develop freely and self-responsibly ... personalities ... [into] which [people] can retreat, barring all entrance to the outer world, in which one can enjoy tranquility and a right to solitude" [quoting from the *Microcensus* case, BVerfGE 27, 1(6).]'

It is important to bear in mind that the content and meaning of human worth is not historically fixed under the GBL. The meaning of human worth is somewhat difficult to capture but cannot be divorced from its historical development. The history of German criminal law indicates that lighter punishments have replaced the more gruesome. The movement has been from the more gruesome to the more humane, from the simple to the differentiated. Regard can therefore only

[188] Quoting Glendon (1991: 71).
[189] Quoting Von Savigny (1981: 103).

be had to the contemporary evaluation of what human dignity encompasses, and one should desist from trying to fix an immutable and timeless content to it.[190]

(iv) Minimum level of sustenance compatible with human dignity (Stern 2006: 51–54)

According to Stern, Dürig played an early and leading role in this regard by asserting that human dignity 'is also effected when humans are compelled to live under economic conditions that degrade them to objects'.[191] In a leading judgment in 1954 the Federal Administrative Court acknowledged a claim to social security 'to ensure "the necessities of life" for ... and the existence generally for those in need'. Since then the system of social security under the auspices of the social state in Germany has been greatly extended. But, warns Stern, not every form of assistance granted under social legislation would qualify as part of the human dignity guarantee. Only the securing of 'the minimum requirements for an existence compatible with human dignity' that arise through no fault of the person in need can be related to human dignity. This was the holding in BVerfGE 40, 121 (133) but, as Stern points out, in the judgment reference was made to the social state principle and not to art 1(1) of the GBL. It is difficult to predict how far protection of this nature will stretch in individual cases, and Stern contents himself with dealing with specific instances in which the principle has been applied.

In the context of South Africa, this is a crucially important aspect of human dignity which, under s 10 of the Constitution the state is mandated to protect. Certain features of this state obligation are expressly catered for in the Constitution with regard to housing,[192] and health care, food, water and social security.[193] I say 'certain features' of this obligation because there may well be other necessities that the state has to provide in order to ensure 'minimum requirements for an existence compatible with human dignity'.

(v) Fundamental legal equality (Stern 2006: 54).

It is significant for my purposes that Stern specifically classifies fundamental legal equality as a sphere of human dignity:

> 'Slavery, serfdom, as well as any discrimination on the grounds of race, religion, language or parentage, regardless of the fact that they are also prohibited by Art 3(3) GBL, are incompatible with human dignity. This conclusion must be extended to all blatant and humiliating unequal treatment. Fundamental legal equality is part of the human dignity guarantee.'

---

[190] Compare, for example, the *Life Imprisonment* case BverfGE 45, 187 [229].
[191] Stern (2006: 51) quoting Dürig (1958: Rn 43).
[192] Section 26 of the Constitution.
[193] Section 27 of the Constitution.

This is a view shared by other German commentators. Höfling (2009: Rn 33) expresses the principle in similar terms: 'Art 1(1) further guarantees a fundamental basic equality. In as much as the dignity of a person exists in community, a legally devalued status cannot be attributed to him. Accordingly it is not only slavery and racial discrimination that are prohibited, but also other, similarly humiliating unequal treatment.' Podlech (2001: Rn 29) points to the fact that originally 'the Stoics, in the context of describing human dignity, represented it as being grounded in the fact that humans share in reason. Since then the battle for the legal equality of humans has not ceased. The dignity of a human being in a community exists therein that she does not have a devalued status in this community on the basis of considerations for which she is herself not responsible.' Similarly Kirchhof (2000: §124 Rn 99f) and Enders (2009: Rn 12) argue that the legal subjectivity of human beings has two sides, freedom and equality. The concept of equality is based on freedom, which all individuals are equally possessed of. Relying partly on Kant, they argue that regardless of the most extreme factual inequality, differences in wealth, physical and intellectual ability, or even differences in good fortune, all individuals are, as legal subjects, equal to one another. The unlimited recognition of equal legal freedom is a compelling requirement for all lawful differentiation.

(vi) The prohibition on the excessive use of state power (Stern 2006: 54–60)

According to Stern this prohibition has its origin generally in the various fundamental rights, in association with the principle of proportionality ('*Verhältnismäßigkeitsgrundsatz*'), which is part of the constitutional state concept ('*Rechtstaatsprinzip*').[194] Exercising state power can impinge on human dignity, particularly when physical force or other means of coercion are used that impact on human self-determination. Quite apart from the prohibition on torture and other methods of preventing a free exercise of the will in criminal proceedings, there are other interventions, particularly in the sphere of the imposition and execution of punishment. Quoting from BVerfGE 57, 250 (275) Stern (2006: 55) states that art 1(1) of the GBL prescribes 'that no punishment be imposed without fault', and that — quoting from BVerfGE 50, 5 (12) — 'the punishment imposed may not exceed the fault of the culprit, but must be appropriately proportional to the seriousness of the criminal act and to the degree of fault of the culprit'.[195] Although the death penalty is abolished by art 102 of the GBL, Stern states that the majority of scholars are of the view that its reintroduction would be

[194] I prefer 'constitutional state concept' as a translation of '*rechtstaatsprincip*' in preference to, for example, 'a state based on the rule of law', or similar expressions. I do so because the former reflects more comprehensively, in my view, the idea of the written constitution as a Kelsenian *grundnorm*.

[195] See the very similar approach of the South African Constitutional Court, both regarding the reference to human dignity and the test of proportionality, in the *Dodo* case, referred to in section 3.3 above. See text to n 48 above.

prohibited by art 1(1) read with art 79(3) of the GBL because an amendment of the GBL like this would, in terms of art 79(3), 'affect [...] the principles laid down in Article 1 ...'. Human dignity is also infringed when a person is sentenced to life imprisonment without any chance whatsoever of parole.

(g) Professor Ernst-Wolfgang Böckenförde's fear that human worth is being relativised in Germany

In a blistering criticism of the new (2001) commentaries on arts 1(1) and 2(1) of the GBL in Maunz/Dürig — replacing those by Dürig that had stood since 1958 — Prof Böckenförde (2006: 379)[196] refers to the new commentaries as 'marking an epochal change' that (2006: 386) 'changes the concept of human dignity from being the very foundation[197] of a newly created constitutional order, that proclaims its identity, to a mere constitutional norm — on an equal footing with others — and to be interpreted in a positivistic constitutional manner'. He readily concedes that an updating of Dürig's contributions was overdue, [198] but explains that part of the reason for this was the very fact that Dürig's contribution to the proper understanding of human dignity had been so inspired, magisterial and purpose-driven.

Böckenförde (2006: 386–387) contends that the new commentaries have forgotten the ethical and religious background to the human dignity provision, as well as its burning historical purpose. They have simply relegated the evils of the Nazi regime to the storeroom of cold history, in contradistinction to the founders of the GBL, who insisted on an eternity guarantee (as art 79(3) evidences) for human dignity — 'a dyke for the entire future, arising from the bitter experience of the massive injustice and the well-nigh incomparable contempt for human dignity in the "third reich"'. The new commentaries represent a change from the understanding of the human dignity guarantee 'as a load-bearing foundation for the newly created legal order, that proclaimed its identity', to a 'constitutional norm on an equal footing with others, which is to be interpreted purely constitutionally, ie in a positivistic legal manner'. Poignantly Böckenförde (2006: 388) remarks that Dürig would have been astounded by the changes to 'his "Maunz-Dürig"' and 'would most certainly have pleaded for his name to be omitted from the title of the joint commentary'.

Böckenförde (2006: 379–380) points out that Dürig represented a generation that, having experienced the Nazi regime, the war and its consequences, wanted

[196] In a section headed '*Die Würde des Menschen war unantastbar: zur Neukommentierung der Menschenwürdegarantie des Grundgesetzes*'. ('Human dignity was inviolable: Re the new commentary on the human dignity guarantee in the Basic Law'.) Professor Böckenförde was a Judge of the German Federal Constitutional Court from 1983 to 1996.

[197] Elsewhere, Böckenförde (2006: 380) describes Dürig's labours as laying the 'foundation of the foundation'.

[198] Dürig himself could not, because of ill-health, revise these sections before he died in 1996.

— like the Basic Law itself — to build a new order from the rubble of 1945, to construct a dyke against any return, overt or covert, to these prior events. Dürig's commentary understood — and also characterised — the human dignity guarantee as having taken over into positive constitutional law a fundamental ethical value that had emerged from European intellectual history, and thereby itself relying on a pre-positivistic foundation, a kind of natural law anchor. Dürig was aware (without expressly formulating it) that all fundamental rights had limits, indeed had to have limits and be subject to balancing if they were to be of lasting value, whereas both the purpose and formulation of the duty to respect and protect human dignity were universal and inviolable.

Böckenförde (2006: 382) makes the important point that Dürig also sought to identify the content of human dignity by having regard to the nature of infringing acts. This was not only consistent with art 1(1) being a fundamental objective positive legal norm, but also had a pragmatic aspect, which would prevent human dignity from becoming 'small change' (*kleine Münze*) and thereby devaluing its guarantee.

Having quoted with implicit approval Dürig's conception of the human image[199] Böckenförde explains (2006: 381) that

> '[t]his freedom to shape oneself and the environment is considered as equal for all humans, it is innate in humans themselves; not the actual current realization in concrete persons, but the "equal abstract possibility" ie the potential ability for realization is decisive'.

It is this 'equal abstract possibility' although not actually realised in any particular person that goes to the heart of the human dignity concept. It is the direct link with Kant's conception of human dignity as being beyond price (and thus not a fungible) and having an innate and literally incomparable worth, hence the equality of all people with respect to human worth (dignity). It is the *species* argument at its highest and best. It is not the actual degree of subjective ability to shape oneself and the environment, nor the degree to which this is actually realised, but the abstract ability of the species — of which one is a member — to do so, which founds dignity in all its members. It is for this reason that even human beings who have no ability to reason and no ability to shape themselves or the environment are nonetheless possessors of human dignity and entitled to the rights flowing therefrom.

With reference to Dürig, Böckenförde (2006: 381–382) adds that 'human dignity (including the rights deriving therefrom) also accrues to the unborn child

---

[199] Dürig (1956: 125).
'Each and every human being is a human being by virtue of his or her intellect (*kraft seines Geistes*) which serves to separate them from the impersonality of nature and enables them to exercise their own judgment, to have self-awareness, to exercise self-determination and to shape themselves and nature.'
See Chapter 2, section 2.1 above.

(*nasciturus*) — how could it be anything else for Dürig' and then quotes the following comment of his:

> 'At the moment of procreation (*Zeugung*) the new core of being and personality comes into existence, which from then on does not change. In it everything essential and relevant ... of this person is settled. It strives to develop that which is embryonically in it, with the result that this human being, whether it cares to grow or deteriorate, consistently stays the same.'

In the *Second Abortion* case[200] the BVerfG held[201] that the 'Basic Law compels the state to protect human life. Human life is also present in the unborn, who is also entitled to state protection' and in this context explained[202] that — '[h]uman dignity already accrues to the unborn human life, and not only to human life after birth or when its personality has developed'.

The Court held,[203] moreover, that, in the case of the unborn, one is already dealing with an individual whose genetic identity and accordingly its uniqueness and distinctiveness has already been fixed, and who — 'in the process of its growth and self-evolvement — *develops as a human being* and *not towards becoming* a human being'. (Emphasis supplied.) This right to life, which is not premised on the unborn's acceptance by the mother 'but accrues to the unborn purely on the basis of its existence', is 'the fundamental and inalienable right that arises from the dignity of human beings'. Although — for the reason already advanced — the complexities of this 163-page judgment will not be traversed, it should be pointed out that the Court[204] did not hold the unborn's right to life to be absolute. The ambit of its protection was to be determined by having regard, on the one hand, to the 'meaning and importance of the legal interest to be protected, in this instance the unborn human life' and, on the other, to 'clashing legal interests'. When considering the legal interests affected by the unborn's right to life 'regard must be had — arising from the entitlement of the pregnant woman to the respect and protection of *her* human dignity (Art 1(1) GG) — in particular to her right to life and physical integrity (Art 2(2) GG) and her personality right (Art 2(1) GG)'. (Emphasis in the original.)

Böckenförde (2006: 389–406)[205] also evaluates the inviolability of human dignity and the associated right to life in the GBL in relation to the latest progress made in bio-medicine and bio-technology. Once again I will not pursue this

[200] BVerfGE 88, 203. For a fuller discussion of the judgment in English see Kommers (1997: 349ff).
[201] Id 251.
[202] Id.
[203] Id 251–2.
[204] Id 253–4.
[205] In a chapter entitled 'Human dignity as normatives principle: The basic rights in the bio-ethical debates (*Menschenwürde als normatives Prinzip: Die Grundrechte in der bioethischen Debatte*)'.

issue,[206] but refer to some of Böckenförde's comments to the extent that they throw light on the meaning of human dignity for my purposes. As Böckenförde (2006: 389–390) points out, the negative aspects of Aldous Huxley's 'brave new world' are no longer a fiction, and such concepts as the 'virtual child' and the 'designer baby' are no longer absurd. Fertilisation and early embryo development can now take place extra-corporally; gene-technological procedures can be carried out on the nuclei of embryos; negative selection can take place to remove genetic defects, as well as positive selection to obtain desired characteristics — all with a view to selecting one's descendants; therapeutic cloning is possible; and so forth. As a representative of the WHO remarked, 'those who want descendants, can choose the hair colour and intelligence quotients of their future children'. These well-nigh unlimited possibilities raise urgent questions about the limits of and the proper orientation with regard to the nature and manner and limits of human beings relating to one another and how one wants to shape the living together of people. Once again laying great emphasis on the tragic history giving rise to the guarantee in art 1(1) of the GBL, Böckenförde (2006: 391) stresses that it not only proclaims human dignity, but requires all state authority to respect and protect it (as is the case with s 10 of the South African Constitution). In this way the 'recognition of and respect for human dignity is secured as the binding normative principle for all state action, and also for the way in which people are to live together in society'. This means that the recognition of and respect for every human being as subject, as bearer of fundamental rights and the freedom to act responsibly, is a given and cannot simply be disposed of. It is the 'basis of fundamental rights, not least of all the right to life; and will also control the application and interpretation of the fundamental rights'.

Böckenförde (2006: 392–393) argues that this protection of human dignity is the readily available point of orientation and also functions as a 'stop sign'. The burning question is what significance this point of orientation and 'stop sign' has for the current debates on the bio-technologies mentioned. What is the detailed content of the human dignity guarantee and from when does it apply? In Böckenförde's view the next question of crucial importance is whether this guarantee — and the consequent recognition and respect as an independent subject — apply only to human beings that are born, or whether they apply to the human embryo as well. This concerns the legal status of the embryo. Is the human embryo also the bearer of human dignity and, if so, from when does its claim to respect and to the ensuing right to life begin? The wording of art 1(1) of the GBL does not provide a direct answer to these questions. It is a question of interpreting

[206] I would, however, urge those concerned in South Africa with the implications of bio-medicine and bio-technology for human dignity, not to ignore the rich German scholarship in this regard. The human dignity norm in ss 1*(a)* and 10 of the South African Constitution has a provenance similar to the German, and the specific formulation of the right in s 10, which follows art 1(1) of the GBL in important respects.

the scope of this text, and this interpretation is currently heavily debated. The objection is raised, chiefly but not exclusively by natural scientists, that it is hardly possible for an eight-cell or even a sixteen-cell creature to be the bearer of human dignity. For dignity to operate at so early a stage — so the objection goes — is, in the light of biological findings, surely completely unrealistic and bordering on the absurd. Therefore quite a few people have regard to a later stage as the basis for the recognition of human dignity: perhaps nidation,[207] the development of the brain, birth, or the subsequent actual ability to reason. 'Can one', Böckenförde asks rhetorically, 'go on in this fashion?' According to him, the answer is 'No'. The methodology employed in arguments of this nature is important. Normative qualities and consequences are deduced from particular demonstrative scientific findings. This is not justifiable, says Böckenförde (2006: 392):

> 'To deduce normative qualities and postulates (*Sollen*) from provable scientific facts (*Sein*), is commonly regarded as a "naturalistic false conclusion," and this form of argumentation in other contexts consistently strongly criticized. Should this not also apply here?'

Böckenförde makes the point that the standards for people's relationships with one another, and the injunctions and prohibitions regulating their conduct, cannot be inferred from or grounded in scientific findings. It is the task of philosophy, ethics and, last but not least, the law to formulate appropriate standards. Obviously one must have regard to scientific facts as concrete points of reference for the application of particular normative injunctions. But they are not the source of or basis for these injunctions. These gain their sustainability and conviction only through independent philosophical, ethical and legal argumentation. Who should be the bearer of human dignity is not established by scientific empiricism. Böckenförde (2006: 393) quotes with approval the following comments of Justice Jutta Limbach, a former President of the BVerfG:

> 'The law is not in a position to answer the question when human life begins; science — on the basis of its findings — is not in a position to answer the question from when human life should be placed under the protection of the constitution.'

Böckenförde (2006: 395–396) emphasises that art 1(1) does not speak of the dignity (*Würde*) of *persons*, but of the dignity of *human beings*. Dignity accrues to human beings, regardless of particular qualities or characteristics, or actual abilities; it is concerned only with being a human being (*Menschsein*) regardless of any stage of development of the human *being*. I would argue the same for our Constitution, where s 1*(a)* speaks of the value of 'human dignity' and s 10 of 'everyone' having 'human dignity'. As Böckenförde rightly stresses, this dignity (worth) accrues not only to every individual human being but to all human beings; thus also to the human being as species. I see this as a matter of cardinal importance because one is thereby protecting the *image of the species*

[207] The implantation of the fertilised egg in the lining of the uterus.

(if I might so express it), with the result that it is unnecessary, with regard to any specific human being, to enquire whether a human being possesses any particular characteristics, qualities, abilities, level of intelligence, and so forth. This protection of the *image of the species* is essential to prevent the danger, to which I have already referred, of relativising the concept of human dignity and the right to life flowing from it, resulting in human dignity being launched on a slippery slope that has no non-arbitrary restraints. Böckenförde (2006: 395–396) contends that giving human dignity content is less controversial than it might initially appear. He links it with Kant's concept of treating the human being as an end in itself and with the idea of 'existence for its own sake'.[208] Therein lies the positing and recognition of the human being as a subject of its own, the freedom to develop itself, the prohibition against being instrumentalised, like some kind of inanimate object which can simply be disposed of. There is no real controversy about this approach when applied to living human beings, but it certainly does arise with the associated question with regard to how far back this recognition of human dignity goes in the life process of every human being. Is it sufficient if the recognition and respect accrues at some particular stage in the life process, or must this recognition and respect be accorded from the very beginning of human life? For Böckenförde (2006: 397–398) only the latter can be the true position:

> 'Only the latter can be the case, where [the concept of] existence for its own sake or a human being an end in itself remains true, and does not become empty rhetoric. The dignity which marks a mature human being cannot be separated or split off from its own history, but must rather include it.'

To choose any time *after* the very first beginning of life for the accrual of human dignity is, in the view of Böckenförde (2006: 398), to 'tear a hole in the development of each and every human being'. This first beginning is, for Böckenförde, the moment of fertilisation, and not later. For it is at this stage that the biological basis of each individual human is immutably fixed, a proposition he develops and justifies more fully. It is from this foundation, regarding human dignity, that he critically examines (2006: 399–406) the bio-ethical debates concerning human embryo research and stem-cell technology in detail.[209]

---

[208] Quoting from BVerfGE 88, 203 (252).

[209] It is beyond the scope of this work to follow this particular debate more fully, but the writings of Böckenförde in this area are, in my view, important for those researching this field. His approach is a nuanced one and also clearly recognizes that the embryo's right to life under art 2(2) of the GBL is subject to appropriate limitation, which he deals with.

3.5 DIGNITY UNDER CANADIAN LAW

I concentrate on dignity in the context of equality jurisprudence giving effect to the purpose of s 15(1)[210] of the Charter. The Canadian courts have, quite properly, warned against an attempt to give a single, all-embracing definition of human dignity (worth) that can be mechanically applied. Nevertheless, as in Germany and South Africa, some contour lines have been drawn in the process of fleshing out, on a case-by-case basis, the concept of human dignity (worth). A discussion of Canadian dignity jurisprudence must take account of the fact that dignity is not expressly guaranteed under the Charter, either as a right or as a value. I would suggest that this has acted as a disincentive to the development of a really focused and dynamic dignity jurisprudence in Canada.

One of the leading cases in Canada on dignity and equality is that of *Law v Canada (Minister of Human Resources Development)*.[211] The claimant was refused a survivor's pension under the Canada Pension Plan (CPP) on the basis that she was not disabled, had no dependent children and was under the age of 35. On appeal, although it was found that that the age distinctions in the CPP violated the claimant's s 15 Charter rights, it was held that this violation was justified under s 1 of the Charter. After two unsuccessful intermediary appeals the claimant finally appealed to the Canadian Supreme Court. This Court also dismissed her appeal on the basis that the impugned provisions of the CPP do not infringe s 15(1) of the Charter. It found that a clear distinction is drawn in the CPP on the basis of age and that the delay in the receipt of benefits for claimants under age 35 and reduced entitlement to benefits for claimants between ages 35 and 45 constitute a denial of equal benefit of law. Nevertheless the Court held that the purpose or effect of the impugned provisions do not violate claimant's dignity so as to constitute discrimination. The pension scheme has a clear ameliorative purpose of enhancing personal dignity and freedom by ensuring a basic level of long-term financial security to persons unable to achieve this goal; and the government benefit was not withheld on the basis of stereotypical assumptions. In this section I limit my comments on *Law* to the meaning of human dignity and its suitability as a legal norm. In section 4.3 of Chapter 4 I shall deal with its treatment of equality and its use of dignity as the criterion of attribution for equality.

The Court in *Law* gave expression to the concept of human dignity (worth) in various ways. Quoting[212] from *Andrews*[213] the Court explained that the purpose

---

[210] Which reads:

'Every individual is equal before and under the law and has the right to the equal protection and equal benefit of the law without discrimination and, in particular, without discrimination based on race, national or ethnic origin, colour, religion, sex, age or mental or physical disability.'

[211] 170 DLR (4th) 1 [1999].

[212] At para 42.

[213] *Andrews v Law Society of British Columbia* 56 DLR (4th) 1[1989] 171.

of s 15(1) was to promote 'a society in which all are secure in the knowledge that they are recognized at law as human beings equally deserving of concern, respect and consideration' and further stated that the provision was 'a guarantee ... designed to remedy the imposition of unfair limitations upon opportunities, particularly for those persons or groups who have been subjected to historical disadvantage, prejudice, and stereotyping'. The first quotation above is in my view defective, from the perspective of equality jurisprudence, because it does not indicate with regard to *what* human beings are equally deserving of 'concern, respect and consideration'; this flows from the Court's failure to deal explicitly with the logico-grammatical problem and the criterion of attribution. The second quotation does (implicitly) indicate the criterion of attribution, namely 'opportunities,' an important component of human worth, namely the capacity for self-realisation and the free unfolding of the personality. This emerges more fully from the Court's further observation that s 15(1) was designed to prevent persons being differentiated against in a way that was likely to decrease their confidence that 'they can freely and without obstruction from the state pursue their and their families' hopes and expectations of vocational and personal development'.[214] This is an important aspect of human dignity, which one could also describe as a form of 'equality of opportunity' or equality of self-realisation and the free development of the personality. The inherent nature of dignity, as well as the aspect of the self-image, are identified by *Law* in the observation, quoted from an earlier Supreme Court judgment, that people who are discriminated against are made to feel 'less capable, or less worthy of recognition or value as human beings ... '.[215] The aspects of 'personal autonomy and self-determination' inherent in human dignity as well as feelings of 'self-respect and self-worth' and 'physical and psychological integrity' are also stressed.[216]

Professor Peter Hogg (2005), the distinguished Canadian constitutional law scholar, is of the view that the concept or value of human dignity is, for a number of reasons, inherently inappropriate to use with regard to the interpretation and application of s 15(1) of the Charter. It is true that dignity is a difficult concept to capture in precise terms,[217] but this has not prevented courts in Germany and South Africa from fleshing out, on a case by case basis, the content thereof and from producing a rich and fairly comprehensive image of human dignity. But Hogg goes considerably further. He criticises (2005: 56–57) the use of human dignity as 'vague' and 'confusing'. It is vague, the learned author asserts, because in the cases following *Law* 'the Court has often disagreed with lower courts and disagreed among itself on the question whether the challenged law impairs

[214] *Law* (above, n 213) para 43.

[215] Id para 49, and see also para 51.

[216] Id para 53.

[217] *Gay and Lesbian (Minister of Justice)* case (above, n 31) para 28; *Egan v Canada* (1995) 29 CRR (2d) 79, 106 per L'Heureux-Dube J.

human dignity of the claimant'. Hogg also quotes with approval refers as follows to the views of Debra McAllister (2003: 104): 'As Debra McAllister has concluded (after a careful analysis of the opinions on human dignity), the disagreements cannot be said to be simply "a case of reasonable people disagreeing on the application of a legal test"; rather, the disagreement shows that the test has "very little substance." Considering that the validity of the legislation turns on the application of this test, this is a very serious criticism.' In the very next sentence after the phrases quoted, McAllister observes that '[p]ersonal dignity is firmly located in the eye of the beholder' and (2003: 105) that human dignity 'can be a very subjective test'. Later McAllister (2003: 106), after referring to the views of certain Supreme Court judges, remarks that '[all] are matters of human dignity. Equally distinguished judges have come to completely different results primarily because human dignity is a fluid concept', and that '[t]he more subjective this test is, the more unpredictable the litigation becomes …'. In this context Hogg (2005: 57 n 64) goes so far as to add that 'judges are not well suited to assess affronts to the dignity of persons whose life experience may be very different from their own'. It is also true that in *Kapp*[218] the Court appears to accept the criticism that 'human dignity is an abstract and subjective notion that … cannot only become confusing and difficult to apply; it has also proven to be an *additional* burden on equality claimants …'. Hogg (2005: 57) moreover contends that human dignity is confusing because 'by introducing this evaluative step into s 15, the relationship between s 15 and s 1 is confused, and it is not clear how much work s 1 is left to do'. Much the same criticism is repeated in Hogg (2007: s 55.9(b)). Almost all academic criticism seems to follow similar lines.[219]

I pause at this stage to attempt to address the above criticisms. The Canadian Supreme Court recognises that it is appropriate in principle to have regard to underlying jurisprudential and philosophical concepts in order to describe what human dignity encompasses. Thus, in emphasising the purposive approach to Charter interpretation, it was pointed out by Dickson J in *R v Big M Drug Mart*,[220] that the purpose of s 15(1) had to be sought by reference to, inter alia, 'the larger objects of the *Charter* itself … to the historical origins of the concepts enshrined …', a view quoted with approval in *Law*.[221] In *Kapp*[222] it was held that 'human dignity is an essential value underlying the s 15 guarantee' and the Court quoted with approval the following views expressed by Dickson CJ in *R v Oakes* — '[t]he Court must be guided by the values and principles essential to a free and democratic society …'. In *Kapp*[223] it was also stated that 'human

[218] *R v Kapp* 294 DLR (4th) 1 [2008] para 22.

[219] See, for example, Greschner (2001–2002: 299); McAllister (2003); Moran (2006: 82, 83, 93); McIntyre (2006: 108).

[220] *R v Big M Drug Mart Ltd.* 18 DLR (4th) 321 at 344.

[221] Above, n 212 at para 40.

[222] Above, n 219 at para 21.

[223] Id para 22.

dignity ... has also proven to be an *additional* burden on equality claimants, rather than *the philosophical enhancement it was intended to be*'. (Emphasis on last phrase supplied.)

In this context, and with all the deference due to the distinguished judges and academics whose criticisms of the use of human dignity I have referred to above, I must argue that they are fundamentally mistaken. In the first place I would contend that the failure to address the *logico-grammatical problem* in Canada's equality jurisprudence is the cause of much confusion and uncertainty. The Court has quite correctly focused on the importance of human dignity as an essential element for the evaluation of equality and discrimination. It, and the academics, have not, however, appreciated that *human dignity* in fact constitutes the criterion of attribution for legal statements about human equality, the only attribute or aspect with regard to which all human beings are equal.[224] Although there is frequent reference in cases and the literature to the 'comparative' nature of equality and to 'comparator groups' and so forth,[225] the comparison dealt with is limited to a comparison between the claimant (the first comparator) and the so-called 'comparator group' (the second comparator) but not with reference to the third comparator (the *tertium comparationis* or criterion of attribution).

Secondly, I would suggest that the criticism of the use of human dignity on the basis that it is vague, confusing, fluid, unpredictable, without substance, etc is completely refuted by the indispensable role it plays in international law and covenants, and domestic constitutions throughout the world, as fully documented by Botha (2009: 173–176). It plays the most crucial role in the German Basic Law (GBL) and, together with equality and freedom, in the South African Constitution. For sixty years in Germany it has been the subject of the most comprehensive and sophisticated jurisprudence and scholarly commentary one could wish for, deeply influenced by history, philosophy and theology, as I have tried to indicate earlier in this Chapter. There are naturally debates about when human dignity begins and ends, whether in view of its specially protected status it can ever be limited or be the subject of balancing, about the danger of the over-use of dignity and its cynical exploitation, etc. Yet the nature of human dignity, its centrality in the GBL and the appropriate use of human dignity have never been subject to the sorts of criticism levelled against it in Canada. The development of

---

[224] As a further example see Lawrence (2006: 116) where it is stated that '[e]quality and discrimination do not have fixed meanings. Rather, they rely on underlying conceptions of the good.' However, as pointed out in Chapter 2.1 above, Geach (1967) and Foot (2001) have demonstrated, with regard to the concept of 'good' itself, that a criterion of attribution is necessary to give it finite meaning. Sheppard (2006: 258ff) while referring to the equality of capabilities as argued by Sen (1992) does not take the extra step of pointing out that Sen himself quite clearly uses 'capability' as the criterion of attribution for answering his question 'equality of what?'

[225] See, for example, Pothier (2006) in her article 'Equality as a comparative concept ...' and the cases cited therein.

the personality right in German law has made a significant contribution to the understanding of human dignity in German law, as it has done in South Africa.

Thirdly, in Canada much criticism has been levelled against the use of human dignity because of the 'subjectivity' involved, so much so that Hogg feels 'judges are not well suited to assess affronts to the dignity of persons whose life experience may be very different from their own'. This does strike one as a somewhat startling vote of no confidence in the Canadian judiciary. It is not a criticism that, as far as I am aware, has been levelled at German or South African judges. Moreover the judicial function requires of the adjudicator to place him or herself, as far as is possible, in the shoes of 'the other'. Creative imagination is of course called for, but this appears clearly to have been successfully used by the philosophers, legal scholars and the courts in the review of literature and judgments I have attempted so far. Furthermore, by way of comparison, adjudicators have for centuries been successfully and objectively applying such concepts as, for example, the '*diligens paterfamilias*' and the 'reasonable person' in determining negligence in delict (tort). Judges at times disagree in these cases on what the outcome should be on the same factual matrix. This has not lead to a questioning of the legal test. In any event, whatever validity this particular criticism might have would disappear completely if the test under s 15(1) is accepted for what I urge it must be, namely an objective one. This is the position in Germany and South Africa and has caused no problems. I would also venture to think that if human dignity were quite openly accepted in Canada as the true and only criterion of attribution for equality it would lead to a deeper and more comprehensive engagement with the nature of human dignity and its elements. When there is unqualified acceptance at bedrock that equality means the equality of *all* human beings with regard to their human dignity (worth), the need will be seen for a deeper philosophical and historical understanding, and a realisation that human dignity (worth) must be understood and applied as an objective concept. The proposition that all human beings are equal with regard to human dignity, that every human being has a worth (not a price) that is equal to the worth of every other human being, is an objective concept, because it says something objective about the nature of human beings as well as about the worth (dignity) that every human being has.

Fourthly, the use of human dignity is criticised because it confuses the relationship between s 15 and s 1, on the basis that if a discriminatory statutory provision is held to be in breach of s 15(1) because it impacts negatively on the human dignity of the claimant, it is difficult to see how there could ever be grounds for justification under s 1. The same problem exists under the South African Constitution where 'unfair discrimination' is the test for a breach of s 9(3), but this has not given rise to any problems. In any event, I would suggest that this particular criticism places the cart before the horse. The first jurisprudential task in dealing with the alleged breach of a guaranteed right is to determine the nature and ambit of the right. Whether this right can be limited is a secondary step. It appears to me analytically wrong to interpret the nature or scope of a right with reference to the limitations provision. While one must no doubt proceed on the assumption that all constitutional provisions are consistent with one another, this cannot be an irrebuttable assumption. A constitution is after all a human product relating to human beings and their activities in the broadest sense of the word. One cannot expect a perfect mechanical engineering product. Moreover, as I have earlier argued, there is no logical compulsion for concluding that because, textually, all rights *can* be limited, in practice all rights must somehow be limited. This problem has also arisen with regard to the provision of art 19(2) of the GBL, which deals with rights limitation and provides that '[i]n no case may the essence of a basic right be affected'. To the best of my knowledge (see, for example, Sachs (2007: art 19 Rn 33–47)) a statutory provision has never been invalidated on this ground and no definition has been developed for the 'essence' of a basic right.

A refreshing contrast amongst the Canadian scholars is provided by Denise Réaume (2003: 671–695) who sets out to show (672) that 'a dignity based analysis has the potential to give equality rights law some real substance'. The author appreciates (2003: 695) that there is no bright line test for discrimination, that none is possible, and that rigid formulas cannot capture the interpretative exercise, but urges that

> '... we more urgently need to begin a social conversation about dignity and its meaning in our political culture. Its meaning will vary from one set of circumstances to another, making context crucial to the discussion in any given case'.

The learned author contends (2003: 672) that the 'central insight in a dignity-based account is that valuing human dignity means acknowledging the inherent worth of human beings; therefore violating dignity involves conveying the message that some are of lesser worth than others'. Réaume argues (2003: 672f) that an analysis of Canadian Supreme Court judgments reveals a list of contextual factors capable of revealing violations of dignity that disclose three forms of indignity: first, the grounding of legislation in prejudice; secondly, the use of stereotype; and a third (only slowly emerging) that involves

> 'exclusion from benefits or opportunities that are particularly significant because access to them constitutes part of the minimum conditions for a life with dignity'.

At first blush these three forms would seem to reflect a rather narrow view of human dignity, but in a passage with powerful Kantian overtones, Réaume (2003: 673) broadens her concept significantly so that it shares much in common with my own understanding of human dignity:

> ' ... [F]rom the beginning, a link has been made between stereotyping and its tendency to undermine its victims' "personal development". This points in the direction of self-

> fulfilment as a human good[226] that equality rights are designed to protect, and suggests a connection between dignity and autonomy. Respect for dignity includes respect for agency as a fundamental characteristic of humanity. References to the importance of self-determination or personal fulfilment recognize human beings as choosers and planners, as beings with projects and dreams who make commitments and attachments and at least partly measure their own sense of worth according to their ability to exercise their capacities and realize their dreams.'

Réaume then makes the important point that, although behaviour based in prejudice and stereotype often impairs dignity 'there are ways of restricting self-fulfilment that are themselves sufficiently harmful to constitute a violation of dignity, *even absent an underpinning in prejudice or stereotype*'. (Emphasis supplied.) In the context of Canadian dignity and equality jurisprudence this is a significant point to make. It affirms the crucial point of departure that all people have dignity, and that they *all share it equally*. While an 'underpinning' in prejudice or stereotype might well make the establishing of an infringement of dignity in these cases easier, an underpinning in prejudice or stereotype can never be a pre-condition for establishing an infringement of dignity. Réaume also accepts (2003: 674–675) that dignity is concerned with 'a moral quality ... an entitlement we can all claim'. Postulating, quite rightly, that a sense of self-worth 'is everybody's birth-right,' she describes dignity in explicitly Kantian terms:

> 'To ascribe dignity to human beings not as an empirical matter, but as a moral matter — that is, to treat it as an inherent aspect of humanity — is to treat human beings as creatures of intrinsic, incomparable, and indelible worth, simply as human beings; no further qualifications are necessary. In this basic sense, dignity is ascribed to human beings independently of their accomplishments or merits or praiseworthiness. It refers to a kind of worth that is not contingent on being useful, or attractive, or pleasant, or otherwise serving the ends of others.'

From my own perspective one can only endorse these views and trust that they will in the future be influential in shaping the constitutional concept of dignity. I deal exclusively with the *Law* and *Kapp* cases in the context of equality in Chapter 4, section 4.3 below.

3.6 CONCLUSION

The German and South African treatment of human dignity, in the constitutional context that I have tried to sketch in this chapter, must speak for itself. I would argue, however, that, whatever difficulties there might be, this treatment presents a rich, meaningful and jurisprudentially highly functional picture of human dignity. The main difficulties that are encountered relate to the ambit of the right and value of human dignity, how and where the outer line is to be drawn. Yet the question

226 My comment: It is a human good but it is more, for as I have argued above, self-fulfilment is a crucial element of human dignity itself.

'But where does one draw the line?'[227] is inherent in the solution of legal problems and has been so from the very earliest times.

There are of course critics, almost without exception from the Anglo-Saxon jurisprudences, who challenge the value or use of human dignity at a far more fundamental level. Botha (2009: 172 nn 4 and 5) mentions three. The one is a comment by Judge Easterbrook[228] (1990: 29) that '[w]hen we observe that the Constitution ... stands for "human dignity" but not rules, we have destroyed the basis for judicial review'. The other is by Berger (1992: 130 n 2 and 134)[229] who refers scathingly to human dignity as 'clearly spun out of the thin air; it is an evangelistic exhortation rather than a constitutional mandate. And it would transform the judicial function from inquiry into what the law *is* into what a given judge considers it *should* be.' The third is by a South African jurist who — in a splendid but wholly fallacious throwaway line — accuses the South African Constitutional Court of having 'given dignity both a content and a scope that makes for a piece of jurisprudential legoland — to be used in whatever form and shape is required by the demands of the judicial designer'.[230] One ought, charitably, to ascribe these views to a lack of familiarity with the German Basic Law and sixty years of BVerfG jurisprudence under it.

I have in section 3.2 above sketched the development of the personality rights in South African private law. There is no good reason why this development should not also guide the constitutional development of human dignity in this field, whether in South Africa or elsewhere, as it has done in the case of Germany. I also believe a sound case has been made for trying to master and learn from the treatment of human dignity in German law.

In view of its comprehensive nature and recent publication, it seems appropriate to devote a major part of this section to responding to some of the issues raised by Prof Henk Botha (2009) in his critique[231] of human dignity, 'Human dignity in comparative perspective'.

[227] A question that lay at the very heart of Professor Louis Henkin's Socratic teaching methodology.

[228] Appointed to the United States Court of Appeals for the Seventh Circuit in 1985 by President Reagan and Chief Justice of that court since 2006. Between 1982 and 1991 he was editor of the *Journal for Law and Economics*. I have not had access to Baer (1990) and have accessed the quotation from Berger (1992: 130 n 2) in an article highly and outspokenly critical of Justice William J Brennan's dignity jurisprudence. Berger (1992: 134) himself stoutly supports the anti-homosexual judgment in *Bowers v Hardwick* 478 US 186 (1986) (as to which see *National Coalition for Gay and Lesbian Equality and Another v The Minister of Justice and Others* above n 32 paras 52–55) and says the following in relation to human dignity: 'Respect for "human dignity" is clearly spun out of the thin air; it is an evangelistic exhortation rather than a constitutional mandate. And it would transform the judicial function from inquiry into what the law *is* into what a given judge considers it *should* be.' Mention should also be made of the critical and influential article of McCrudden (2008) dealing with the difficulties in using human dignity to interpret human rights.

[229] See previous footnote.

[230] Davis (1999: 413).

[231] I use the word 'critique' here in the sense of 'critical analysis'.

While challenging certain views expressed in his article, I should stress that Prof Botha is in no way dismissive of the importance of human worth either as a right or as a value. On the contrary, he accords human dignity an elevated position, but examines the concept closely in order that it may be employed with more critical rigour. In many respects his discussion is sympathetic to that of Prof Isensee as discussed in para 3.4*(e)* above, and elsewhere. Botha also rightly warns against the overuse (abuse) of human dignity and its consequent trivialisation.

It is true, as Henk Botha (2009: 217) points out (as I do), that there are scholars who are dismissive of human dignity as a right and a value, regarding it as unhelpfully elusive for the purposes of constitutional jurisprudence. I would argue that, whatever disagreement there might be with regard to certain features of human dignity, the overwhelming body of German scholarship would be firmly opposed to so negative a view. It would be absurd to suggest that I have personally trawled more than a minute area of this vast field. But I have yet to encounter any serious suggestion that it was a mistake to place human dignity at the heart of the GBL either because the concept is too elusive, too subjective or for any other reason. Human dignity remains at the core of the 'never-again' spirit of the GBL. Nor does there seem to be any doubt about the Kantian foundations of the BVerfG's dignity jurisprudence generally, nor with its development of the Kantian-inspired *Objektformel* in particular, nor with the important role played by the personality rights in giving human dignity content. One must, obviously, be circumspect in one's use of human dignity. It is not the uncritical, knee-jerk solution to every basic right problem. It may not be used as an empty incantation. Familiarity can breed contempt. But human dignity is not the only human value that runs the risk of trivialisation through overuse. But this is no reason for not using the concept and value of human dignity in a vigilant and critical way. Böckenförde (2006: 382),[232] for example, explains that the function of the so-called *Objektformel*, as developed by Dürig, Wintrich and the BVerfG, has been misunderstood by certain critics. The proposition that human dignity is infringed 'when the concrete human being has been devalued (*herabgewürdig*) to an object, to a mere means, to a replaceable (fungible) dimension (*verretbaren Große*)' is not intended to be an all-embracing formula, but a guide in need of closer concretisation. Scholars of the eminence of Dürig and Stern (and many others) have given substantial form to the content of human dignity, and there has been no effective criticism of this of which I am aware.[233] The more recent debates have centered on the issue of what precisely 'inviolable (*unantasbar*)' means in art 1(1) read with art 79(3) of the GBL, and whether or not there are circumstances in which dignity can be limited in a clash of rights, or values, or at what point human dignity first accrues in the human life-cycle. Such disagreements as do

[232] In a chapter entitled 'Human dignity was inviolable (*Die Würde des Menschen war unantasbar*)'.
[233] See, for example, Böckenförde (2006: 379–383).

exist do not relate to the elusiveness or inappropriateness of the use of human dignity under the GBL.

Henk Botha (2009: 217–220) identifies what he considers to be certain paradoxes 'inherent in the notion of dignity' as it is applied in Germany and South Africa. My initial response is to ask whether paradox can be avoided when debating ethical and legal values, and in particular tensions or clashes between them. Differently stated, is one not mistaken in assuming that good ends must always be perfectly commensurate. Isaiah Berlin (1990: 5–6) has described this assumption on the part of philosophers and politicians as a Platonic ideal, embodying the idea that

> 'in the first place ... as in the sciences, all genuine questions must have one true answer and one only, all the rest being necessarily errors; in the second place, that there must be a dependable path towards the discovery of these truths; in the third place, that the true answers, when found must necessarily be compatible with one another and form a single whole, for one truth cannot be incompatible with another — that we knew *a priori*. This kind of omniscience was the solution to the cosmic jigsaw puzzle'.

Berlin (1990: 8) came to the realisation — 'as something of a shock' however,

> 'that not all the supreme values pursued by mankind now and in the past were necessarily compatible with one another. It undermined my earlier assumption, based on the *philosophia perennis,* that there could be no conflict between true ends, true answers to the central answers to life'.

It is for this reason, amongst others, that Berlin (1990: 11) develops his concept of pluralism —

> 'the conception that there are many different ends that men may seek and still be fully rational, fully men, capable of understanding each other and sympathizing and deriving light from each other, as we derive it from reading Plato or the novels of medieval Japan — worlds, outlooks, very remote from our own. Of course, if we did not have any values in common with these distant figures, each civilization would be enclosed in its own impenetrable bubble, and we could not understand them at all.... Intercommunication between cultures in time and space is only possible because what makes men human is common to them, and acts as a bridge between them'.

Berlin (1990: 10–14) is at pains to distinguish pluralism from 'cultural or moral relativism'.[234] He believes in 'a world of objective values ... those ends that men pursue for their own sake, to which other things are means'. He is aware of tensions and clashes between liberty and equality; 'total liberty for the wolves is death to the lambs, total liberty of the powerful, the gifted, is not compatible with the rights to a decent existence of the weak or the less gifted'. He is alive to the fact that equality may demand the restraint of the liberty of those who wish

[234] Berlin (1990: 11): '"I prefer coffee, you prefer champagne. We have different tastes. There is no more to be said." That is relativism.'

to dominate. While rightly asserting that without some modicum of liberty 'there is no choice and therefore no possibility of remaining human' he acknowledges that liberty may have to be curtailed

> 'in order to make room for social welfare, to feed the hungry, to clothe the naked, to shelter the homeless, to leave room for the liberty of others, to allow justice or fairness to be exercised'.[235]

Berlin (1990: 13) reminds us that '[t]hese collisions of values are of the essence of what they are and what we are' but (1990: 17) also contends that these collisions 'can be softened':

> 'Claims can be balanced, compromises can be reached: in concrete situations not every claim is of equal force — so much liberty and so much equality; so much for sharp moral condemnation, and so much for understanding a given human situation; so much for the full force of the law, and so much for the prerogative of mercy; for feeding the hungry, clothing the naked, healing the sick, sheltering the homeless. *Priorities, never final and absolute, must be established.*' (Emphasis supplied.)

Berlin (1990: 18) does not shy away from the assertion that on certain issues there is no justification for compromise,[236] but is of the view that the search for perfection does seem to him to be 'a recipe for bloodshed, no better even if it is demanded by the sincerest of idealists, the purest of hearts'.[237] He points out (1990: 18–19) that even Immanuel Kant, the most rigorous of moralists, 'in a moment of illumination' asserts that — 'out of timber so crooked as that from which man is made nothing entirely straight can be built'.[238]

For much the same reasons I believe that some paradox is inevitable when dealing with the constitutional right and value of human dignity (worth). I find comfort in Berlin's (1990: 19) observation that 'we can only do what we can: but that we must do, against difficulties', as I proceed to consider further some of Henk Botha's critical comments.

I am not sure that Botha is correct when asserting (2009: 217) that as a constitutional concept human dignity 'implies something inviolable' and that accordingly, any balancing or limitation gives rise to paradox. Whether one regards human dignity as literally inviolable surely depends on the content one gives the concept viewed in its total constitutional context. Under the GBL

---

[235] So much for the staggeringly fallacious and ignorant suggestion by some that Berlin was no more than a neo-liberal.

[236] 'Few today would wish to defend slavery or ritual murder or Nazi gas chambers or the torture of human beings for the sake of pleasure or profit or even political good — or the duty of children to denounce their parents, which the French and Russian revolutions demanded, or mindless killing.'

[237] For his more detailed argument that this search for perfection underlay all the totalitarian atrocities of the past 100 years see Berlin (1990: 14–19). It is also a warning against fundamentalism in other areas, fundamentalism that outlaws any paradox.

[238] Berlin's (1990: v and xi) preferred translation of his favourite quotation from Immanuel Kant '*[A]us so krummem Holze, als woraus der Mensch gemacht ist, kann nichts ganz Gerades gezimmert werden.*' (Immanuel Kant, '*Idee zur einer allgemeinen Geschichte in weltbürgerlicher Absichte*' (1784) AK 8:23).

human dignity is inviolable, and this choice was made for particular historical reasons.[239] The BVerfG has worked effectively and successfully for 60 years with this paradox resulting from the constitutional inviolability of dignity. Problems and disagreements that have arisen are not due to dignity's conceptual indeterminism. Henk Botha (2009: 218) expresses the fear that in South Africa 'dignity might become just one constitutional right and value among others, and that the inherent dignity and worth of the human person could be sacrificed in the name of countervailing values'. I believe this fear to be unfounded. Human dignity has a privileged normative position, together with equality and freedom, by virtue of s 1*(a)* of the Constitution, and although it is, in theory at least, subject to limitation, the unique and categorical introductory formulation in s 10 'Everyone has inherent dignity ...' places dignity in a special position, even in relation to equality and freedom, as I shall argue more fully in Chapter 5. After all, human worth informs both equality and freedom and when a balancing of rights has to take place there is every reason to give 'priority, never final and absolute' (to use Isaiah Berlin's words) to human worth.

Henk Botha (2009: 218) also sees a paradox between dignity seen as a 'cosmopolitan right ... inherent in all beings and transcend[ing] cultural barriers' and the fact that 'its protection depends, for the most part, on the nation state'. This is true as far as it goes, but despite all recent setbacks the period since 1945 has been marked by a steady growth in the internationalisation of human rights in general and human dignity in particular. (See, for example, Henkin et al (2009)). Moreover, the potential influence of a strong civil society's commitment to the idea of human dignity should not be underrated.

Botha is certainly no cultural relativist — in the pejorative sense of the word — for he urges us to 'remain open to the utopian possibilities inherent in the notion of absolute and limitless human dignity' for only thus can we 'hope to push against the boundaries — whether geographical, cultural or ideological — which tend to legitimate and normalize degradation and inequality'. At the same time I am concerned with his unqualified assertion (2009: 218) that human dignity's 'precise meaning and contours are culturally mediated' and influenced by 'contingent historical factors within a particular legal system'.

[239] First and foremost, of course, because of the systematic destruction of human dignity during the Nazi period. But also as a response to perceived defects in the Weimar Constitution which had permitted Hitler, without formally breaching this Constitution, to establish a dictatorship and destroy the Constitution. One of the means of addressing this paradox of unlimited freedom was, by means of art 79(3) of the GBL, to place certain rights and values beyond the reach of statutory or even constitutional amendment, including 'the principles laid down in Articles 1 and 20.' Article 20(4) grants all Germans the right 'to resist any person seeking to abolish this constitutional order, if no other remedy is available' and art 18 provides for the 'forfeiture' of certain specified fundamental rights by 'whoever abuses' them 'in order to combat the free democratic basic order....' These and other provisions have led the German legal order to being typified as a 'militant democracy' (*streitbare/wehrhaften Demokratie*); see Krebs (1992: art 18 Rn 3), Kommers (1997: 34, 37–38, 217–37), Pagenkopf (2007: art18 Rn 1–6), Lücke/Sachs (2007: art 79 Rn 5–9).

Implicit in my concern is an acceptance of Isaiah Berlin's concept of pluralism and the dangers he describes that are attendant on the search for perfection. One is also aware that in the field of international human rights a so-called 'margin of appreciation'[240] is accorded to states with regard to the extent to which rights under the relevant international human rights instruments may be limited. I use 'margin of appreciation' here in a far less technical sense, namely one indicating the divergences that pluralism may *legitimately* require. Of course constitutions are, in varying ways and to a lesser or larger degree, reactions to past events. In some instances, as in the cases of Germany and South Africa, the reactions are to immediately preceding human dignity tragedies. In these cases there will be an additional impetus to protect dignity as widely as possible in order to prevent old evils reappearing in new clothes. Culture will of course play a role in this process. Yet, in my view, the precise meaning and contours of human dignity in South Africa will not be *mediated* through culture and history, but through the Constitution and the rights and values enshrined therein.

Culture has its dark side, just as all we human beings have ours. Culture can be dangerous, particularly in a plural society, when it impedes one from stepping outside one's zone of comfort, support, affirmation and identity formation. It can be extremely difficult to step outside one's own culture (or what one perceives to be culture) — which can often be a cocoon — and to see the 'other' from the 'other' culture in his or her full (though perhaps differing) humanity. Cultures can promote human *indignity* (as they have done down the ages) and can do so inconsistently. One culture may promote racial equality but promote gender *inequality*, while another can do the reverse. Examples can be multiplied. Specific 'cultures' or aspects of 'culture' can be destructive to human dignity. We dare not forget that the Constitution, in addition to everything else it stands for and does, constitutes an objective normative value system which applies (in the variety of ways spelt out in the Constitution) to all law. It calls on us to elucidate and develop the rights and values of the Constitution in a manner which is likely to find most general acceptance, but this must be done through the lens of the Constitution, however difficult that might be. All 'culture' must be tested against the Constitution and the latter's rights and values; not the other way round.

In order to avoid any misunderstanding I wish to make it clear that (following Isaiah Berlin and for all the reasons he gives) I do not believe that — either in theory or in fact — the perfect definition or description or understanding of human dignity exists 'somewhere out there', something concrete to be discovered — if only we were sufficiently clever, inspired and diligent to do so. But I do believe that there is scope for substantially increasing our understanding of it.

Henk Botha (2009: 218) concludes that 'the recognition in Germany of the dignity of the unborn child is often explained as a uniquely German preoccupation

---

[240] As to which see, for example, Henkin et al (2009: 626 ff, 1238ff, 1288ff, 1325ff, 1552ff).

which is rooted in Germany's particular history'. I would challenge that view, as well as the implication that the dignity of the unborn child receives no recognition under South African law. For present purposes my challenge is limited to the suggestion that the German 'preoccupation' is 'unique', for I do not attempt to address in this book the issue of dignity in relation to abortion or to the instrumental use of human embryos.[241]

Of course Germany's post-war jurisprudence was greatly influenced by the sustained assault on human dignity during the Nazi Reich, and by concepts that had been propagated, such as: 'Your Volk is everything and you are nothing' and the idea of 'life-unworthy life'. But why should the lessons to be learnt from these past horrors (or our own) be limited to Germany (or to us)? The question of the dignity of the unborn child flows directly and inevitably from any serious grappling with the constitutional idea of fundamental human dignity (worth) against the background of its theological and philosophical development, which I have tried to sketch. What both the German (and South African) experiences warn against so powerfully are the grave dangers that arise the moment one starts limiting in any way the *species* concept of the human person by way of particular biological, colour, or intelligence criteria. The child born without any conscious cognitive ability, as well as the adult who suffers this as a result of injury or illness, are for purposes of the Constitution members of this *species* and possess inherent dignity (worth). The moment we stipulate, say, a particular intelligence requirement as a prerequisite for human dignity, we enter the terrors of a boundless brave new world. It is but one small step from this to requiring a particular political or cultural or economic commitment as a qualification for human dignity. Actual examples of political/economic dissidence being treated as forms of mental disability and the forced 're-education' of these dissidents lie not so far back in history. We must take seriously Dürig's warning against the emergence of new forms of 'Jacobin logic'.

The third paradox raised by Henk Botha (2009: 218–219) relates to the 'idea of human dignity as something inherent in every human being' but that the equal respect and autonomy to which every person is entitled 'is contingent on mutual recognition within a community of equals and on the material conditions needed to enable individuals to develop their capabilities'. He warns against the 'conflation

[241] I try to limit my present enquiry to the role that dignity plays, and can still further play, in the concept and realisation of equality and non-discrimination. For a considerable period of time I accepted, somewhat glibly and without a great deal of independent reflection, the 'solution' to the abortion problem provided by the US Supreme Court in *Roe v Wade* 410 US 113 in the form of its three-stage trimester analysis … . However, with the passage of time and my growing insights into German jurisprudence and Kant's ethical thoughts, the ethical and legal problems posed by the issue of abortion have, for me, grown more and not less difficult, and real doubts have arisen for me as to the correctness of the reasoning in *Roe v Wade*.... A proper treatment of the issue would be of a nature and extent inappropriate for inclusion in the present work. The same applies to the instrumental use of human embryos. As previously indicated, I am only too well aware of the differing views of, for example, Dworkin (1993) and Cornell (1995).

of human dignity with dignified economic conditions or social respect'. I would urge that this paradox is more apparent than real. There are two aspects of s 10 of the Constitution that must be noted: first, the fact that it is categorically stated that everyone 'has inherent dignity'. This is a categorical imperative which, for purposes of the Constitution, decrees what the nature of the human being is. Although not expressly stated in art 1(1) of the GBL, German jurisprudence makes clear that this is also part of its purpose. Secondly, s 10 enacts the *right* to have dignity 'respected and protected'. This mirrors the German provision. *This is both a prohibition and an injunction.* As far as the state is concerned it must, negatively, refrain from infringing the dignity of human beings, but it must also, positively, take steps to protect dignity. The horizontal operation of the Bill of Rights also makes this right — suitably balanced of course, under s 8(2) and (3), against similar rights of others — applicable in the private sphere. This right is not, in my view, 'contingent' on the conditions that Botha mentions, or at least no more 'contingent' than in the case of any other right that is dependent for its enjoyment or utilisation on enforcement. This is where the dual nature of the s 10 dignity right, alluded to above, is so important. Botha's warning against conflation must be subjected to an important qualification. For dignity to be meaningful, there must be at least minimum economic means to make the 'free unfolding of the human personality' possible. It may well be that in the *private* sphere, when regard is had to the freedom and privacy rights of others, the granting of 'social respect' by others cannot be enforced, but even in the private sphere there are clear limits to the *disrespect* which one person may manifest to another.

The fourth so-called paradox raised by Henk Botha (2009: 219) relates in part to the so-called 'paradox of unlimited freedom' and in part to the rejection of the notion of the unencumbered self. His lucid summary deserves fuller citation:

> '[Dignity] rejects the notion of the unencumbered self and recognizes the formative role of — contingent — cultural value patterns and institutional arrangements on our sense of self. At the same time, however, respect for someone's inherent dignity requires recognition of the person's capacity to transcend the strictures of her social background and to form an autonomous identity. I have attempted to show that, both in Germany and South Africa, the inherent dignity of each individual has been invoked to exclude both a radical, abstract individualism and a "thick" form of communitarianism in which the collective takes precedence over the individual. Precisely because it values both the centrality of cultural practices, religious beliefs and communal ties to individual dignity and identity, and celebrates the capacity of the individual to transcend the strictures of her own background, dignity can be used to negotiate conflicts between the individual and community in a way which neither obliterates diversity nor stultifies the dynamic processes through which community norms are generated and contested.'

Subject to some qualification/explanation I would agree. Any paradox that might exist is, I believe, an inescapable part of the human condition itself. As Popper (1966:

vol 1, 120–125) makes plain both unlimited freedom and unlimited sovereignty are paradoxical in the sense that they end up destroying themselves, and this paradox has been recognised since the time of Plato. This is clearly recognised by Kant, who, in his classic view on freedom, makes the freedom of the individual subject to the like and equal freedom of others. In a similar sense individuality and community are in tension with one another. I use individuality here in the sense of the free unfolding of the human personality, subject to a like and equal free unfolding of the personalities of others. I agree that the *full* development of the individual personality cannot take place without the individual being 'in' some form of 'community'. It may also be that the individual cannot escape some form of community, but in my view it is not the province of the law to compel any individual to be in any greater community than the individual desires, subject of course to those legitimate legal obligations that the individual has to others. But 'community' may not be permitted to infringe on the individual's free personality unfolding, and the law must protect individual dignity in this regard. Fascist and other totalitarian views have often required the individual to suppress her individuality in favour of the collective, whatever form this collective may take, and insist that the individual can only achieve full personality development by surrendering self to the collective. I believe this to be fundamentally wrong and deeply destructive of human dignity. Human beings have inherent dignity, not the collective. Part of individual human dignity is personal responsibility. While giving full recognition to community and culture I need to emphasise again that the constitutional concept of dignity is to be explored through the Constitution, not defined by a particular cultural or religious view. I have tried to demonstrate in the previous chapter how the views of the Abrahamic religions and secular philosophies have influenced the constitutional understanding of dignity and equality, but the *legal* validity of any particular cultural or religious view or practice must be tested through the Constitution and, for purposes of the present discussion, through the constitutional meaning of human dignity.

Closely related to the above are the following comments of Henk Botha (2009: 219):

> 'Dignity is closely related to personal freedom and presupposes the right of the individual freely to choose her own ends. At the same time, however, respect for dignity requires us to set limits to freedom — particularly in an age characterized by pervasive private power, excessive consumerism and deepening inequality.'

I agree with this view, save that the 'deepening inequality' to which he alludes I would not formulate in these unlimited terms, but rather relate more particularly to economic inequality. But I do not see this as a paradox, but a consequence of the reality that rights are subject to limitation. At the risk of burdensome repetition I must again stress that there is a fundamental difference between rights limitation with regard to the vertical operation of the Bill of Rights and the 'balancing' of rights arising from its horizontal operation. I deal with this in greater detail in

Chapter 5. At this stage I merely wish to point out that, in the latter case, we are dealing with the rights of two or more individuals that are in tension or conflict with one another. It may happen that, in a case like this, the non-discrimination and dignity rights of A come into conflict with, say, the freedom and privacy rights of B. The balancing and possible limitation of B's rights under s 8(2) and (3) of the Constitution thus differ from the vertical situation, where the state — whatever competing interests it might have — has no opposing rights. It cannot simply be assumed that in the horizontal situation one would place the same limits on B's rights as one would on vertical state interference with the freedom, dignity and equality of individuals. In the horizontal context individuals have, for example, important privacy spheres in which they may discriminate or intrude on dignity in ways that would not be permitted to the state.

Subject to this qualification I would endorse Henk Botha's comments (2009: 219–220) that '[i]t is only through careful attention to the particularity of human lives that we can keep interrogating concepts, rules, and institutions — state sovereignty, the market, the public/private distinction, cultural value patterns, and so forth' and that 'demands unwavering commitment to the inviolability of each human person'.

I would in conclusion argue that German jurisprudence and scholarship clearly show that (whatever circumspection might be required) rich, intelligible and practical content can be given to the right, value and concept of human dignity (worth), a conclusion confirmed by the South African experience. Human dignity is therefore well capable of playing an independent role of its own, a determinative role in anti-discrimination jurisprudence, as well as a guiding role generally in the interpretation and application of the Constitution.

I conclude this chapter with an existential appeal. If the warning in the Universal Declaration is to be taken seriously there is a burning need for all (not merely in South Africa but in the rest of the world as well) to *act* in support of the safeguarding of human dignity against all oppressive power. The call (specifically also in s 10 of the South African Constitution) is for more than negative 'respect' (the abstention from acts that infringe human dignity); it is also a call for 'protection', for positive intervention. This cannot be done without an understanding of what human dignity (worth) means. In this process we cannot escape having to come to terms with what human beings are and what it is about human beings, as a species, that demands particular respect and protection and that demands it equally for all human beings. To these questions there are no complete and final answers. This certainly does not mean, however, that a substantive body of knowledge has not identified itself.

I believe that we are today, as in 1948, experiencing a crisis; a special moment of truth; a unique moment for change and decisive action. When regard is had to the threats posed by nuclear proliferation, globalisation, economic instability, poverty and environmental deterioration, it is obvious that the challenges go well beyond the capacities of the law. They also challenge, in the broadest sense, the fields of theology, education, international relations, economics, as well as the biological and environmental sciences. But the law has its own particular role to play, and play it it must. I can see no other option but to focus on human dignity, and to do everything possible to achieve as broad an agreement as possible as to its content. We may not be able to prove human dignity, and its very outer contours may prove to be elusive, but we are fully aware of the human disasters that occur when human dignity is sacrificed.

CHAPTER FOUR

EQUALITY UNDER THE CONSTITUTION

4.1 SOUTH AFRICAN LAW

(a) Introduction

For purposes of this chapter, the following are the relevant equality and non-discrimination provisions in s 9 of the 1996 South African Constitution:

> '9(1) Everyone is equal before the law and has the right to equal protection and benefit of the law.
>
> (2) Equality includes the full and equal enjoyment of all rights and freedoms ....
>
> (3) The state may not unfairly discriminate directly or indirectly against anyone on one or more grounds, including the following ...'

Despite the difference in wording and structure of the equality and non-discrimination guarantees under s 8 of the interim Constitution and s 9 of the 1996 Constitution[1],

---

[1] Section 8 of the interim Constitution reads:

'(1) Every person shall have the right to equality before the law and to equal protection of the law.

(2) No person shall be unfairly discriminated against, directly or indirectly, and, without derogating from the generality of this provision, on one or more of the following grounds in particular: race, gender, sex, ethnic or social origin, colour, sexual orientation, age, disability, religion, conscience, belief, culture or language.

(3) *(a)* This section shall not preclude measures designed to achieve the adequate protection and advancement of persons or groups or categories of persons disadvantaged by unfair discrimination, in order to enable their full and equal enjoyment of all rights and freedoms.

(b) Every person or community dispossessed of rights in land before the commencement of this Constitution under any law which would have been inconsistent with subs (2) had that subs been in operation at the time of the dispossession, shall be entitled to claim restitution of such rights subject to and in accordance with sections 121, 122 and 123.

(4) Prima facie proof of discrimination on any of the grounds specified in subsection (2) shall be presumed to be sufficient proof of unfair discrimination as contemplated in that subs, until the contrary is established.'

Section 9 of the 1996 Constitution is to the following effect:

'(1) Everyone is equal before the law and has the right to equal protection and benefit of the law.

(2) Equality includes the full and equal enjoyment of all rights and freedoms. To promote the achievement of equality, legislative and other measures designed to protect or advance persons, or categories of persons, disadvantaged by unfair discrimination may be taken.

(3) The state may not unfairly discriminate directly or indirectly against anyone on one or more grounds, including race, gender, sex, pregnancy, marital status, ethnic or social origin, colour, sexual orientation, age, disability, religion, conscience, belief, culture, language and birth.

(4) No person may unfairly discriminate directly or indirectly against anyone on one or more grounds in terms of subs (3). National legislation must be enacted to prevent or prohibit unfair discrimination.

(5) Discrimination on one or more of the grounds listed in subsection (3) is unfair unless it is established that the discrimination is fair.'

the fundamental approach to the meaning of equality and non-discrimination has been substantially the same under both Constitutions.[2]

I do not deal in this work with the important burden of proof provisions in s 9(5), which apply to the grounds of discrimination 'listed' in s 9(3). The so-called 'horizontal' application of the equality rights and the other constitutional provisions relevant thereto are dealt with in Chapter 5, while restitutionary equality and the constitutional provisions relevant thereto (including those referred to in the second sentence of s 9(2)) are dealt with in Chapter 6.

The principle of proportionality is dealt with in various contexts throughout this work. Without limiting the generality of its applicability, it is a principle that applies in determining the excessive use of state power, the limitation of rights in the vertical application of the Bill of Rights, and in the process of 'balancing' competing individual rights in the Bill's horizontal application. As this book was going to press the magisterial work of Aharon Barak (2012), *Proportionality: Constitutional Rights and Limitations* appeared. It is an exhaustive comparative study of proportionality, in its various spheres of application, and critically discusses – among other things — its sources, nature, function as well as its components. It is not possible at this stage to integrate the reflections of the book in the present work, but readers' attention is directed to its learning on all aspects of proportionality.

(b) Section 9(1) of the 1996 Constitution

The Constitutional Court has generally given a narrow meaning to s 9(1) and its predecessor, the only requirement being that the differentiation in question must 'bear a rational connection to a legitimate government purpose'.[3] If it does not, then there is a violation of s 9(1).

(c) Sections 9(2) and 9(3) and human dignity (worth) as the criterion of attribution for determining unfair discrimination

The Constitutional Court has also consistently used *human worth (dignity)* as the *criterion of attribution* for human equality, ie human worth (dignity) is the aspect or feature, or quality of humankind in respect whereof all human beings must be treated equally (positively put) for purposes of s 9(2), and in respect whereof human beings may not be unfairly discriminated against (negatively put) under s 9(3). The Court has done so in unmistakably Kantian terms.

O'Regan J in *Makwanyane*,[4] although not dealing specifically with equality, points out that recognising a right to dignity is 'an acknowledgment of the

[2] See *National Coalition for Gay and Lesbian Equality and Another v Minister of Justice and Others* 1999 (1) SA 6 (CC) (1998 (12) BCLR 1517).

[3] *Prinsloo v Van der Linde and Another* 1997 (3) SA 101 (CC) (1997 (6) BCLR 759 (CC)) paras 25–26; *Harksen v Lane NO and Others* 1998 (1) SA 300 (CC) (1997 (11) BCLR 1489 (CC)).

[4] *S v Makwanyane and Another* 1995 (3) SA 391 (CC) (1995 (6) BCLR 665) para 328.

intrinsic worth of human beings' and concludes her judgment by stating[5] that '[t]he new Constitution stands as a monument to this society's commitment to a future in which *all human beings will be accorded equal dignity and respect ...*'. (Emphasis supplied.) This is an implicit recognition that dignity is the *criterion of attribution* for the assessment of equality. O'Regan J, writing for the Court in *Brink v Kitshoff NO*,[6] states that '[e]quality has a very special place in the South African Constitution [which] is an emphatic renunciation of our past in which inequality was systematically entrenched'. Where, in the same case,[7] the learned judge places emphasis on various 'systematic patterns of discrimination' in the past, this is not to suggest that past patterns of discrimination are a prerequisite for constituting 'unfair discrimination' under s 8(2) of the interim Constitution, but to stress the 'vicious patterns of discrimination' of the past and to point out that 'the need to prohibit such patterns of discrimination and to *remedy their results* are the *primary* purposes of s 8 and, in particular, sub-ss (2), (3) and (4)'. (Emphasis supplied.) That the existence of past patterns of discrimination against complainants is not a condition precedent to a finding of unfair discrimination in favour of these complainants was made clear in *City Council of Pretoria v Walker*.[8]

Although the Constitutional Court heard argument in *Prinsloo*'s case[9] before it did so in *Hugo*'s case,[10] the judgments were delivered simultaneously.[11] In *Prinsloo*[12] the Court held that

> 'unfair discrimination, when used in this second form [on grounds not specified] in s 8(2), in the context of s 8 as a whole, principally means treating persons differently in a way which impairs their fundamental dignity as human beings, who are inherently equal in dignity'.

The Court also quoted with approval[13] the following passage from *Hugo*'s case:[14]

> 'At the heart of the prohibition of unfair discrimination lies a recognition that the purpose of our new constitutional and democratic order is the establishment of a society in which all human beings will be accorded equal dignity and respect regardless of their membership of particular groups';

---

[5] Id para 344.
[6] *Brink v Kitshoff* NO 1996 (4) SA 197 (CC) (1996 (6) BCLR 752) para 33.
[7] Id paras 40–43.
[8] 1998 (2) SA 363 (CC) (1998 (3) BCLR 257) paras 47–48, 73.
[9] *Prinsloo* above, n 3.
[10] *President of the Republic of South Africa and Another v Hugo* 1997 (4) SA 1 (CC) (1997 (6) BCLR 708).
[11] See *Prinsloo* (above, n 3), para 32 n 34.
[12] Id para 31.
[13] Id para 32.
[14] *Hugo* (above, n 10), para 41.

and with similar approval[15] the following passage from the Canadian Supreme Court case of *Egan v Canada*:[16]

> 'Equality, as that concept is enshrined as a fundamental human right in the *Charter*, s.15 means nothing if it does not represent a commitment to recognising each person's equal worth as a human being, regardless of individual differences. Equality means that our society cannot tolerate legislative distinctions that treat certain people as second-class citizens, that demean them, that treat them as less capable for no good reason, or that otherwise offend fundamental human dignity.'

In *Hugo*[17]the following was further stated:

> 'In s 8(3), the interim Constitution contains an express recognition that there is need for measures to seek to alleviate the disadvantage which is the product of past discrimination. We need, therefore, to develop a concept of unfair discrimination which recognizes that although a society which affords each human being equal treatment on the basis of equal worth and freedom is our goal, we cannot achieve that goal by insisting upon identical treatment in all circumstances before that goal is achieved. Each case, therefore, will require a careful and thorough understanding of the impact of the discriminatory action upon the particular people concerned to determine whether its overall impact is one which furthers the constitutional goal of equality or not. A classification which is unfair in one context may not necessarily be unfair in a different context.'

In *Hugo*, reference is also made to the Aristotelian principle that '[i]t is the logical corollary of the principle that "like should be treated alike", that treating unlike alike may be as unequal as treating like unlike'.[18]

In *Harksen v Lane*[19] the Constitutional Court summarised the effect of the earlier judgments as follows:

> '*(a)* Does the provision differentiate between people or categories of people? If so, does the differentiation bear a rational connection to a legitimate government purpose? If it does not then there is a violation of s 8(1). Even if it does bear a rational connection, it might nevertheless amount to discrimination.
>
> *(b)* Does the differentiation amount to unfair discrimination? This requires a two-stage analysis:
>
> (i) Firstly, does the differentiation amount to "discrimination"? If it is on a specified ground, then discrimination will have been established. If it is not on a specified ground, then whether or not there is discrimination will depend upon whether, objectively, the ground is based on attributes and characteristics which have the potential to impair the fundamental human dignity of persons as human beings or to affect them adversely in a comparably serious manner.

[15] *Prinsloo* (above, n 3), para 32.
[16] (1995) 29 CRR (2d) 79 at 104–5, internal footnotes omitted.
[17] Above, n 10, at para 41.
[18] Id n 63.
[19] Above, n 3, at para 53.

(ii) If the differentiation amounts to "discrimination", does it amount to "unfair discrimination"? If it has been found to have been on a specified ground, then unfairness will be presumed. If on an unspecified ground, unfairness will have to be established by the complainant. The test of unfairness focuses primarily on the impact of the discrimination on the complainant and others in his or her situation.

If, at the end of this stage of the enquiry, the differentiation is found not to be unfair, then there will be no violation of s 8(2).

(c) If the discrimination is found to be unfair then a determination will have to be made as to whether the provision can be justified under the limitations clause (s 33 of the interim Constitution).'

In order to determine whether the discriminatory provision has impacted on complainants unfairly, various factors have to be considered, including the following:[20]

'*(a)* the position of the complainants in society and whether they have suffered in the past from patterns of disadvantage, whether the discrimination in the case under consideration is on a specified ground or not;

(b) the nature of the provision or power and the purpose sought to be achieved by it. If its purpose is manifestly not directed, in the first instance, at impairing the complainants in the manner indicated above, but is aimed at achieving a worthy and important societal goal, such as, for example, the furthering of equality for all, this purpose may, depending on the facts of the particular case, have a significant bearing on the question whether complainants have in fact suffered the impairment in question. .... .

(c) with due regard to *(a)* and *(b)* above, and any other relevant factors, the extent to which the discrimination has affected the rights or interests of complainants and whether it has led to an *impairment of their fundamental human dignity or constitutes an impairment of a comparably serious nature.* [Emphasis supplied.]

These factors, assessed objectively, will assist in giving "precision and elaboration" to the constitutional test of unfairness. They do not constitute a closed list. Others may emerge as our equality jurisprudence continues to develop. In any event it is the cumulative effect of these factors that must be examined and in respect of which a determination must be made as to whether the discrimination is unfair.'

Of particular importance for my thesis is the affirmation, albeit implicit, in *Harksen* that equality and unfair discrimination require the employment of a *criterion of attribution* and that the primary (at least) *criterion of attribution* is human dignity. This was further affirmed in *Harksen* as follows:

'In paragraph 41 [of *Hugo*] dignity was referred to as an underlying consideration in the determination of unfairness. The prohibition of unfair discrimination provides a bulwark against invasions which impair human dignity or which affect people adversely in a comparably serious manner.'[21]

---

[20] Id para 51.

[21] Id para 50.

This approach has been consistently applied by the Constitutional Court.[22]

I have referred to the possible and minor qualification that was added in both *Prinsloo*[23] and *Harksen*[24] to the effect that unfair discrimination may also be established where the discrimination constitutes an impairment of 'a comparably serious manner' to an impairment of human dignity. With hindsight I doubt whether it was wise or correct to have added this qualification. In the more than thirteen years that have passed since the judgment in *Harksen*, no court judgment has, to the best of my knowledge, invoked this qualification. It was certainly not the Court's intention, in formulating the qualification, to expand without limit the *criterion of attribution* provided by human dignity (worth). Be that as it may, the only other impairment of a *comparably* serious nature that comes to mind is the impairment of freedom. But freedom, in my view, is an essential part of the concept and value of human dignity itself and this is borne out by an Abrahamic theological approach, by the philosophical views of Kant, Williams and Sen, as well as by German jurisprudence — as I hope to demonstrate in section 4.2 below. It is interesting to note that in the *Weare* case[25] the 'fundamental dignity of human beings' was held by the Court to be the *criterion of attribution* without any qualification.

These cases clearly establish that human dignity (worth) constitutes the *criterion of attribution* for a proper understanding of equality and non-discrimination under the Constitution, and this has been consistently followed since by the Constitutional Court. Since the limited purpose of my enquiry in this book is, apart from the other chapters, to justify this approach, I do not consider any further the *application* of dignity as the *criterion of attribution* in the jurisprudence of the South African courts.

Initially, after the judgments in *Brink v Kitshoff*, *Prinsloo*, *Hugo*, *Harksen* and *Walker* were delivered, there was some trenchant academic criticism (some bordering on the intemperate) of the Constitutional Court's equality jurisprudence, and in particular of the fact that human dignity had been used to define equality, arguing that the *right to substantive equality* ought to be given a *meaning independent of the value of dignity, primarily informed by the value of equality*.[26] The criticism appears to have been inspired, in certain cases, by Westen's (1982) misperceptions. One of the authors, after an excoriating

[22] See, for example, *Hoffmann v South African Airways* 2001 (1) SA 1 (CC) (2000 (10) BCLR 1211); *Volks NO v Robinson and Others* 2005 (5) BCLR 446 (CC); *Van der Merwe v Road Accident Fund and Another* 2006 (4) SA 230 (CC) (2006 (6) BCLR 682); *Union of Refugee Women and Others v Director: Private Security Industry Regulatory Authority and Others* 2007 (4) SA 395 (CC) (2007 (4) BCLR 339); *Weare and Another v Ndebele and Another* 2009 (4) BCLR 370 (CC).

[23] *Prinsloo* (above, n 3), para 33.

[24] *Harksen* (above, n 3), para 53*(b)*(i).

[25] Above, n 22, at para 72.

[26] For example, Albertyn and Goldblatt (1998), Fagan (1998) and by Davis (1999).

condemnation of the Court's jurisprudence, comes up with the following description of equality:

> 'Equality is too central a concept to be relegated to a *secondary meaning. The Court needs to look at equality as a value which seeks to promote a democratic society that recognises and promotes difference and individual as well as group diversity and thereby exhibit a commitment to ensuring that all within society enjoy the means and conditions to participate significantly as citizens.*'[27] (Emphasis supplied.)

I must confess with regret that I have been unable to extract much illumination from the above.

My response to the above critics is brief.[28] Not one of the authors referred to is aware of the grammatico-logical problem inherent in defining equality and they are consequently unaware of the fact that in defining or describing equality use must *inevitably* be made of a *criterion of attribution*. To suggest, as does the critic quoted above, that substantive *equality* must be *informed by the value of equality* is circular. The same may be said of the following contention:

> 'Equality has been defined in some of the judgments with reference to another value, dignity, rather than through attempting to distil its own, admittedly elusive, meaning.'[29]

The only debatable question, as Sen correctly points out, is 'Equality with respect to what?' One of the authors comments as follows on the use by the Court of human dignity as the *criterion of attribution* (without of course appreciating the necessity for *a* criterion of attribution):

> 'The Constitutional Court has rendered meaningless a fundamental value of our Constitution and simultaneously has given dignity both a content and a scope that makes for a piece of jurisprudential Lego-land to be used in whatever form is required by the demands of the judicial designer.
>
> Equality is too central a concept to be relegated to a *secondary meaning*.'[30]

I believe that this broadside is wholly refuted by more than sixty years of analytical case law and legal writing from Germany and by the decisions of our own courts on dignity and equality.

Even Duppert (2006), in an otherwise lucid and informative article, does not appear to grasp the inescapable, namely that *equality* cannot — in a logico-grammatical sense — be used as a substantive noun. He regards equality (138 n 2) as

> 'an elusive notion ... , and that our numerous appeals to (substantive) equality is often an *appeal to some deeper normative value* (such as human dignity, redistribution,

---

27 Davis (1999: 413–414).

28 For a more detailed response see LWH Ackermann (2006).

29 Albertyn and Goldblatt (1998: 272).

30 Davis (1999: 413).

> participatory democracy, etc) *rather than an appeal to the value of equality …*'. (Emphasis supplied; internal references omitted.)

By contrast I think that Susannah Cowen (2001) has 'got it (substantially) right' in her well-reasoned article 'Can "dignity" guide South Africa's equality jurisprudence?', although not specifically in the analytical terms I have advanced. In regard to the narrow issue with which I am dealing, she (2001: 40) rightly comments: 'To value equality without saying more does not explain what outcome it is that we value. In Amartya Sen's language, it does not answer the question, "equality of what?"'

At the root of the concerned and troubled thinking on equality that I have, as selective examples, referred to above, and at the root of similar approaches to equality, equal treatment and non-equal treatment in the context of ethics and law, is the mistaken analytical assumption I have referred to. It is to regard the word 'equal' — in such phrases as 'equal before the law', 'equal treatment by the law', 'non-equal treatment', and even when used as a noun in an expression such as 'equality before the law' — as a *predicative* adjective or a *predicative* noun, instead of as an *attributive* adjective or noun.

(d) Equality and juristic persons

One of the potential problems of applying s 9(2) of the Constitution, read with s 8(4), to juristic persons is that, if one were to regard as absolute the distinction between the legal identity of, say, a company and that of its members, a juristic person cannot possess human dignity. For as Carlisle J remarked in *Gumede*'s case:[31]

> '… [A] company, of course, possesses a legal *persona* which is quite apart from its members. It has neither body, parts nor passions. It cannot be loyal or disloyal; neither, of course, can it possess any characteristic which belongs to a race of people.'

But theories concerning the legal nature of a juristic person are legion,[32] and an extensive jurisprudence has been developed concerning the circumstances under which the 'corporate veil' of the juristic person may be 'pierced' or 'lifted', and, among other things, the actions and mental attitudes of the members of a company attributed to the company itself,[33] although it is beyond the scope of this book to investigate this aspect in any detail.

In this regard Wolff (1938: 507) sees the value of the fiction formula in that

---

[31] *Gumede v Bandhla Vukani Bakhiti Ltd* 1959 (4) SA 560 (N) 561.

[32] Wolff (1938: 496) suggests that by 1938 sixteen had already been identified.

[33] See for example Benade and Cilliers (1968); *Dadoo Ltd v Krugersdorp Municipal Council* 1920 AD 530; *Cape Pacific Ltd v Lubner Controlling Investments Pty Ltd* 1995 (4) SA 790 (A); *Dros Pty Ltd v Telefon Beverages* CC 2003 (4) SA 207 (C). English law provides many examples where the personal characteristics of members have unabashedly been attributed to the company. See for example *Daimler Co Ltd v Continental Tyre and Rubber Co* [1916] 2 AC 307; *Jones v Lipman* [1962] 1 All ER 442 (Ch).

'it starts from a natural, extra-juristic conception of personality, as founded in ethics and religion and then adds that certain groups and institutions determined by law, though lacking in supreme, that is human dignity, are nevertheless treated by law as if they were human persons',

but suggests that in one respect the organism theory marks advance on the fiction theory

'in that it looks on juristic persons contracting or committing torts through their boards or other organs as acting in person.... It further considers juristic persons capable of being attacked in their "honour" by slander and libel, capable of good or bad faith, of personal appearance in court, and so on'.

Although conceding that the fiction theory 'does not feign too much but too little — it stops too early in equalising natural and juristic persons' Wolff (1938: 510) nevertheless considers the fiction theory to be flawless 'provided it adopts the one considerable progressive element introduced by the organic theory'.

In the well-known *Daimler* case[34] the question arose whether a company incorporated in England, with an English secretary, but with all its shares in the hands of 'enemies', could be looked on as an enemy company within the meaning of the common-law prohibition of trading with the enemy. The House of Lords gave an affirmative answer and in this regard Lord Parker said the following:[35]

'When the law is concerned with the artificial person, it is to know nothing of the natural persons who constitute and control it. In questions of capacity, of acts done and of rights acquired or liabilities assumed thereby, this may be always true. Certainly it is so for the most part. But the character in which property is held, and the capacity to act is enjoyed and acts are done, are not in pari materia. The latter character is a quality of the company itself, and conditions its capacities and its acts. It is not a mere part of its energies and activities, *and if that character must be derivable* not from the circumstances from its incorporation which arises once for all, *but from qualities of enmity and amity,* which are dependent on the chances of peace or war *and are attributable only to human beings, I know not from what human beings that character should derive,* in cases where the active conduct of the company's officers has not already decided the matter, *if resort is not had to the predominant character of its shareholders and corporators.*' (Emphasis supplied.)

Wolff (1938: 514–515) comments and extrapolates from the *Daimler* case as follows:

'In my opinion the *Daimler* case also points the way for decisions in cases where a particular spiritual condition in the legal person is a deciding factor.

...

Can a juristic person be grateful ...? In my opinion the right answer, as in the *Daimler Case*, is that, though only human beings can be grateful or ungrateful, it is the human

[34] Above, n 33.
[35] Id 340–1.

beings behind the corporate fiction whose actions must be judged in determining whether the corporation is to be looked on as ungrateful....'

Wolff's concluding sentence (1938: 521) is of particular relevance to the issue at hand:

'A theory concerning the nature of legal persons can only prove satisfactory if it covers not only human groups endowed with personality, but all the entities I have mentioned which enjoy artificial personality; it must be flexible enough to permit a lifting of the curtain draping these entities, which will reveal the human beings in control and use them, *whenever this may be necessary to ensure that legal rules become operative in their true sense*.' (Emphasis supplied.)

I would suggest that an approach like this is not inconsistent with our own law. Although the 'lifting of the curtain'[36] of corporate personality most often takes place where there is 'an element of fraud or other improper conduct in the establishment or use of the company or the conduct of its affairs',[37] I do not understand our jurisprudence to regard fraudulent or improper conduct as being an inflexible prerequisite.[38] It certainly is not in England. Thus Boyle and Birds (2007: 66) state:

'For certain purposes, the courts, while respecting the separate legal personality of a company, have treated the conduct or characteristics of its directors, managers or members as attributable to the company itself. This attribution does not in the true sense involve "lifting the veil of incorporation". For example where the courts have had to determine the residence of a company, they look not to the place of registration but to the way the company is actually managed in order to find where the centre or centres of management are in fact located. The cases examined ... on the attribution of *mens rea* to a company for the purposes of criminal or civil liability, are another illustration of the same principle.'

With regard to civil liability of a company, where this is dependent on a particular state of mind of the company, Lord Haldane in the *Lennard's Carrying Company*[39] case stated, in a well-known passage:

'... [A] company is an abstraction. It has no mind of its own any more than a body of its own; its active and directing will must consequently be sought in the person of somebody who for some purposes may be called an agent, but who is really the directing mind and will of the corporation, the very ego and centre of the personality of the corporation.'

In the Privy Council judgment delivered by Lord Hoffmann in the *Meridian Funds* case[40] he cautioned against the literal application of the phrase 'directing mind and will' and indicated that Lord Haldane was not 'expounding a general

[36] A welcome alternative to the more common 'lifting' or 'piercing' of the corporate 'veil' metaphor.

[37] *The Shipping Corporation of India Ltd v Evdomon Corporation and Another* 1994 (1) SA 550 (A) at 566 C–F.

[38] See *Cape Pacific Ltd v Lubner Controlling Investments (Pty) Ltd* above n 33, 802F–804D; 805D–I.

[39] *Lennard's Carrying Company v Asiatic Petroleum Ltd* [1915] AC 705 HL 713.

[40] *Meridian Global Funds Management Asia Ltd v Securities Commission* [1995] 2 AC 500 (PC).

metaphysic of companies'.[41] In the following passage[42] Lord Hoffmann expounds certain general principles that, in my view, are helpful in deciding when, how and in what manner an artificial person can exercise a right under our Bill of Rights:

> 'To say that a company cannot do something means only that there is no one whose doing of that act would, under the applicable rules of attribution, count as an act of the company.
>
> The company's primary rules of attribution together with the general principles of agency, vicarious liability and so forth are usually sufficient to enable one to determine its rights and obligations. In exceptional cases, however, they will not provide the answer.... For example, a rule may be stated in language primarily applicable to a natural person and require some act or state of mind on the part of the person "himself," as opposed to his servants or agents.... How is such a rule to be applied to a company? ... [T]here will be many cases ... in which the court considers that the law was intended to apply to companies and that ... insistence on the primary rules of attribution would in practice defeat that intention. In such a case, the court must fashion a special rule for the particular substantive rule. *This is always a matter of interpretation: given that it was intended to apply, how was it intended to apply*? Whose act (or knowledge, or state of mind) was *for this purpose* intended to count as the act etc of the company? One finds the answer to this question by applying the *usual canons of interpretation, taking into account the language of the rule (if it is a statute) and its content and policy*.' (First and third emphasis supplied.)

Although dealing in the main with the liability of companies, the above approach is formulated at a level of generality that makes it equally applicable to deciding when a right accrues to a company. If one were to apply this approach to s 8(2) of the Constitution, the language, content and policy indicate unequivocally that legal persons are entitled to exercise the rights under the Bill of Rights. All that the courts will have to do is 'fashion a special rule' of entitlement for purposes of s 8(2), determining whose dignity, or equality, or freedom etc was *for this purpose* intended to count as the dignity etc of the company.

Corbett CJ's comments in the *Financial Mail* case are significant in this regard:[43]

> '[A]s a matter of general policy, the Courts have, in the sphere of personality rights, tended to equate the respective positions of natural and artificial (or legal) persons where it is possible and appropriate for this to be done.'

Domanski (1986: 231–235) points out that courts in the United States of America are more readily prepared to lift the veil of corporate personality.

---

[41] Id 509E–F.

[42] Id 507A–F.

[43] *Financial Mail Pty Ltd v Sage Holdings Ltd* 1993 (2) SA 451 (A) at 461F and *Investigating Directorate: Serious Economic Offences and Others v Hyundai Motor Distributors (Pty) Ltd and Others; In re Hyundai Motor Distributors (Pty) Ltd and Others v Smit NO and Others* 2001 (1) SA 545 (CC) (2000 (10) BCLR 1079) para 18 'although not to the same extent as natural persons'.

That juristic persons have the right to privacy and a confidential sphere is also well recognised.[44] Moreover, s 8(4)[45]of the Constitution, the very provision entitling juristic persons to the rights in the Bill of Rights, to the extent required by the nature of the right, also confers this right subject to 'the extent required by ... the nature of that juristic person'. This appears to be a clear injunction to consider, apply and, if necessary, to develop the jurisprudence relating to the lifting of the veil of juristic personality, in order to determine whether a right in the Bill of Rights accrues to a particular juristic person. This the High Court failed to do, wrongly in my view, in *Weare*'s case,[46] where — without any reference to the nature of the juristic person in question or to the possibility of piercing the veil in the case in question, or to the *dictum* of Corbett CJ in the *Financial Mail* case quoted above — the Court simply stated the following:[47]

> 'It is apparent that there are some rights which are clearly capable of being exercised by juristic persons and others which are clearly not. The rights which clearly fall into the latter category are ones such as ... the right to human dignity in s 10....'

It is true that in the *Hyundai Motor Distributors* case[48] the Court stated that '[j]uristic persons are not the bearers of human dignity'. These remarks were *obiter*, however, the case itself turning on privacy, to which the Court held a juristic person was entitled. No argument was addressed on the dignity of juristic persons, or on the issue of lifting the corporate veil in that particular case.

It is possible, I suppose, that there might be circumstances where the nature of the juristic person is such that lifting of the corporate veil might not be possible or appropriate and where the rights under ss 9(2) to (5) of the Constitution do not accrue to the juristic person in question. In this event the juristic person would still have available to it the right to 'equal protection and benefit of the law' under s 9(1). This was in fact the route followed in *Weare*'s case. 'Equal benefit and protection of the law' has been somewhat narrowly construed by the Constitutional Court as meaning that there must be a 'rational relationship between the differentiation in question and the governmental purpose which is proffered to validate it'[49] or 'a rational connection between the differentiation in question and the legitimate governmental purpose it is designed to further or achieve'.[50] However, the Court

[44] See, for example, *Janit v Motor Industry Fund Administrators (Pty) Ltd* 1995 (4) SA 293 (A).
[45] Which reads:
> '(4) A juristic person is entitled to the rights in the Bill of Rights to the extent required by the nature of the right and the nature of the juristic person.'

[46] Above, n 22, particularly at paras 28 to 55.
[47] Id at para 37.
[48] Above, n 43 at para 18.
[49] *Prinsloo* (above, n 3) para 26.
[50] *Harksen* (above, n 3) para 42.

has never considered the rights under s 9(1) in relation to a juristic person, though it did hold in the *FNB* case[51] that

> 'a deprivation of property is "arbitrary" as meant by s 25 [of the Constitution] when the "law" referred to in s 25(1) does not provide sufficient reason for the particular deprivation or is procedurally unfair'.

Context is everything, and there seems no good reason why the courts should not, in applying s 9(1) to juristic persons, give it a wider construction, as was the case with the concept 'arbitrary' in the *FNB* case. That s 9(1) is capable of bearing a wider meaning is also illustrated by the German jurisprudence, discussed in section 2*(c)* below, where art 3(1) of the GBL, which provides that 'all persons shall be equal before the law', has been held to prohibit 'arbitrary' differentiation, and the concept 'arbitrary' in this context has been further held to have a wide substantive meaning.

(e) The Equality Act 4 of 2000

The Promotion of Equality and Prevention of Unfair Discrimination Act 4 of 2000 (the Equality Act) is destined to play an important role in the protection and promotion of equality, in the so-called 'horizontal application' of various provisions of the Bill of Rights (including the horizontal operation of the prohibition against unfair discrimination[52] under the first sentence of s 9(4), read with the relevant provisions of ss 8(2) and (3) of the Constitution), and in the furtherance of restitutionary equality generally. The Equality Act is clearly the legislation contemplated in s 9 of the Constitution. According to the principles of subsidiarity, and as made clear in the *Pillay* and *NEHAWU* cases, referred to below, a litigant cannot circumvent legislation enacted to give effect to s 9 of the Constitution by attempting to rely directly on s 9 itself. It is accordingly a matter of great importance that no provision of the Equality Act should be inconsistent with the provisions of s 9 and, if there are any inconsistencies, that they be set aside in appropriate litigation to the extent of their inconsistency.

Unfortunately the Equality Act is far from being a model of clarity,[53] and one should constantly bear in mind that certain of its provisions — despite all permissible attempts to construe them in conformity with the Constitution, where reasonably possible[54] — might be inconsistent with the Constitution and accordingly invalid. A proper consideration of all the Acts' provisions, their

---

[51] *First National Bank of SA t/a Wesbank v Commissioner for the South African Revenue Services and Another; First National Bank of SA t/a Wesbank v Minister of Finance* 2002 (4) SA 768 (CC) (2002 (7) BCLR 702) para 100.

[52] Section 9*(a)*, read with s 9(3) and (5), and as applied through s 8(3).

[53] Compare the observations of O'Regan J in *MEC for Education: KwaZulu-Natal and Others v Pillay and Others* 2008 (1) SA 474 (CC) (2008 (2) BCLR 99) (the *Pillay* case) paras 137 and 168. For a detailed and critical analysis of the Equality Act refer to Albertyn et al (2001).

[54] Id, paras 43 and 134.

proper meaning and the question whether — when properly construed — all the provisions are consistent with the Constitution, constitute a vast and complex field of enquiry, far beyond the scope of this book. I concern myself only with those of the Act's provisions that relate directly to the main themes of my enterprise.

It is clear that the Act deals with both vertical and horizontal application of, inter alia, the right to equality under s 9 of the Constitution, but not, it would seem, in identical terms. For example: s 5(1) provides that the Act 'binds the State and all persons'; s 6 provides that '[n]either the State nor any person may unfairly discriminate against any person'. Yet ss 7 to 9 provide that no *person* 'may unfairly discriminate against any person'[55] on the grounds of race, gender, and disability, respectively, followed, in each section, by a number of subsections detailing various discrete facts, the existence of which would constitute unfair discrimination on the ground in question. Each section qualifies these subsections with the word 'including' and the whole of each section is qualified by the phrase 'Subject to s 6'. The first question that arises is whether ss 7 to 9 apply only horizontally, or vertically as well. Subsection 5(1)'s provision that the Act binds 'the State and all persons' would at first blush seem to suggest that all the provisions of the Act apply both vertically and horizontally. I do not think, however, that it has this objective. It is just as possible that the legislature wanted to make clear that the state was bound to ensure the execution of the Act's provisions, not that all its provisions were directly enforceable against the state. It might also be argued that s 6 has the same effect of making all provisions of the Act enforceable against the state but not, I would suggest, with much conviction. It is equally feasible that the sole purpose of s 6 was to make it clear, in general terms, that the legislature was not legislating inconsistently with the equality and anti-discrimination provisions of the Bill of Rights.

A consideration of the provisions of ss 7 to 9 would seem to make clear that they are not enforceable against the state, but only horizontally against persons. All these sections are, it is true, made '[s]ubject to s 6', but their purpose must surely be the same as the purpose of s 6 itself, namely to try to ensure that the relevant provisions of the Act are not seen to be inconsistent with the Bill of Rights. Yet a governing phrase of the prohibition in all three of these sections is that '*no person* may unfairly discriminate against another person on the grounds of ...'. (Emphasis supplied.) The very words chosen by s 5(1) to indicate horizontal operation of the Act is identical — 'all persons'. I say identical, because 'all persons' as an object of the binding force of the Act translates, grammatically, into 'no person' when the prohibition is formulated in the negative. It would, in my view, be a singularly inconsistent use of language if, after using in conjunction with one another the words 'State' and 'person' in sections 5 and 6 to indicate both vertical and horizontal operation, then to use only the word 'person' in the very next sections

[55] Emphasis supplied.

(7, 8, and 9) without intending to indicate thereby that horizontal operation only was intended. This is the case where the general provision must yield to the special.[56] My conclusion is that these three sections operate horizontally only. But this makes no difference to my arguments that follow, concerning the effects of horizontal operation, and my suggestion that certain of the Act's provisions might be constitutionally inconsistent, for it is clear that these sections do cover, at the very least, the horizontal operation of discrimination on the grounds of race, gender, and disability.

Sections 10, 11 and 12 deal with, respectively, the prohibition of hate speech, the prohibition of harassment and the prohibition of dissemination and publication of information that unfairly discriminates. They fall outside the ambit of this book, but some of the problems I later identify might well apply to these provisions as well. Section 13 deals with the burden of proof and its provisions may well present problems of inconsistency with the Constitution in relation to unfair discrimination, as I shall point out in due course.

In the *Pillay* case,[57] the first in which the Constitutional Court[58] was called upon to consider the application of the Equality Act,[59] the Court held that the Equality Act is clearly the legislation contemplated in s 9 of the Constitution.[60] The Court also applied an important principle to the constitutional operation of the Act when Langa CJ stated that

> 'a litigant cannot circumvent legislation enacted to give effect to a constitutional right by attempting to rely directly on the constitutional right'[61]

and that

> '[a]bsent a direct challenge to the Act, courts must assume that the Equality Act is consistent with the Constitution and claims must be decided within its margins'.[62]

I shall refer to these two passages jointly as the 'first *dictum*'.

In para 41 of the judgment Langa CJ refers to an issue of 'how the definition of "discrimination" in the Equality Act should be interpreted' and in para 42 to a 'deeper' debate that has been spawned in this regard, namely the 'extent to which

---

[56] Or, as expressed in the Latin maxim *generalia specialibus non derogant*, which maxim was applied in a constitutional context in *Speaker of the KwaZulu-Natal Provincial Legislature, Ex parte: In re Certification of the Constitution of the Province of KwaZulu-Natal* 1996 (4) SA 1098 (CC) (1996 (11) BCLR 1419) (the *Constitution of KwaZulu-Natal* case) para 28.

[57] Above, n 53.

[58] Id, para 39.

[59] The Promotion of Equality and the Prevention of Unfair Discrimination Act 4 of 2000.

[60] The *Pillay* case (above, n 53) paras 39 and 134. Although O'Regan J dissented in part from the majority judgment written by Langa CJ, she did not dissent on this particular issue.

[61] Id, para 40 and para 134 per O'Regan J. See also the *NEHAWU* case (*National Education Health and Allied Workers Union v University of Cape Town* 2003 (3) SA 1 (CC) (2003 (2) BCLR 154)) paras 14–16.

[62] Id.

the Act must be informed by s 9 of the Constitution'. In this regard the learned Chief Justice stated the following at para 43:

> 'Section 39(2) of the Constitution makes it clear that the Act must be interpreted in the light of the "spirit, purport and objects of the Bill of Rights" which includes s 9.
>
> *(a)* That does not mean that the Act must be interpreted to restate the precise terms of s 9. *(b)*The Legislature, when enacting national legislation to give effect to the right of equality, may extend protection beyond what is conferred by s 9. As long as the Act does not decrease the protection afforded by s 9 or infringe another right, a difference between the Act and s 9 does not violate the Constitution. *(c)* It would therefore not be a problem if the definition of discrimination in the Act included forms of conduct not covered by s 9 as long as the prohibition of those forms of conduct conformed to the Bill of Rights.' (For ease of reference, the italicised letters *(a)*, *(b)*, and *(c)* have been supplied.)

I shall refer to this quotation as the 'second *dictum*' and to the lettered passages as 'parts *(a)*, *(b)*, and *(c)* of the second *dictum*'.

It is important to bear in mind, when analysing and commenting on the above two *dicta*, that the validity of the Equality Act was not challenged before the Court; that the Court was accordingly compelled to accept its constitutionality; that the claim before it was based on the vertical application of the said Act; and that the Court was not called upon to decide whether or not ss 7 to 9 of the Act applied vertically to the state. Moreover, no judgment can be exhaustively comprehensive, nor can (or should) it be written to address all future issues which might arise on the same or related question.

(i) The first *dictum*

Some elaboration is necessary. The circumvention mentioned is formulated to relate to 'legislation enacted to give effect to a constitutional right'. I would suggest that the preferable enquiry is to determine the extent to which effect is *in fact* given in the legislation to the constitutional right(s) in question. It is not the *purpose* of the legislation which is here relevant, but the *actual effect* thereof, on proper interpretation. It must be borne in mind, for example, that ss 7 to 9 of the Act deal with only three of the seventeen grounds listed in s 9(3) of the Constitution. It simply cannot be suggested, for the reasons stated above that — despite the expressly limited wording of ss 7 to 9 of the Act — s 6 has the effect of making these provisions applicable to the other fourteen grounds listed in s 9(3) of the Constitution. It can also not be suggested that, somehow, the provisions of ss 7 to 9 can apply *mutatis mutandis* to these other fourteen grounds. This would be an impossible exercise. For example, under which of the three sections would one include unfair discrimination on the grounds of sexual orientation, and how could one possibly know how to change any of these sections in order to make them fit the case of this type of discrimination? For all these reasons I believe that the Act does not in fact apply to these other fourteen constitutional grounds. Sections 10 to 12, which deal respectively with hate speech, harassment and aspects of the freedom to disseminate and publish information are not considered here, as they fall outside my topic. As far as the Act's provisions (in s 13) for regulating the burden of proof are concerned, they make reference to 'complainant[s]' and 'respondent[s]', which are defined in s 1 as meaning, respectively, 'any person who alleges any contravention of this Act and who institutes proceedings in terms of this Act' and 'any person against whom proceedings are instituted in terms of this Act'. Persons instituting proceedings for unfair discrimination on any of the *other fourteen grounds*, would not therefore be doing so in terms of the Equality Act, but would therefore be entitled to do so directly under s 9 read with s 8 of the Constitution.

It is also necessary, in relation to the first *dictum*, to consider the state's responsibility for enacting legislation with regard to ss 8 and 9 of the Constitution. From the clear wording of s 9, it expressly contemplates enabling legislation in two situations.[63] The first is under the second sentence of s 9(2), which provides that 'legislative and other measures designed to protect or advance persons, or categories of persons, disadvantaged by unfair discrimination may be taken'. Purely linguistically the word 'may' suggests that legislation (and other measures) are entirely discretionary, but when regard is had to the state's general obligation under s 7(2),[64] this sentence at the very least obliges the state to apply its mind actively to the need for 'legislative and other measures' in order to achieve what I term *restitutionary equality*. Moreover the second sentence of s 9(4) provides in mandatory terms that national legislation 'must be enacted to prevent or prohibit unfair discrimination'.

The nature of the entities who, under both s 9(3) and the first sentence of s 9(4), are prohibited from 'unfairly discriminat[ing]' are clearly distinct. Under s 9(3) the entity prohibited from discriminating is the *state* (the prohibition thus operating 'vertically' between state and subject); and under the first sentence of s 9(4) the entity is *any 'person'* — the prohibition thus operating 'horizontally' between persons and persons. The *obligation* on the state under the second sentence of s 9(4) to enact preventative or prohibitory legislation is unlimited as far as the *nature of the entity* that must so be prohibited is concerned. It relates, without limitation to 'unfair discrimination'; thus to both unfair discrimination by the state under s 9(3) and to unfair discrimination by any person under the first sentence of s 9(4).

(ii) The second *dictum*

Part *(a)* of the second *dictum* is correct as far as it goes. What needs to be stressed, however, is that in most instances the provisions of the Equality Act, far from

[63] This is not to suggest for one moment that the legislature may only pass enabling legislation when the Constitution expressly authorises it.

[64] Which provides that the state 'must', inter alia, 'promote and fulfil the rights in the Bill of Rights'.

merely 'restat[ing] the precise terms of s 9' of the Constitution, go well beyond them. The implications of this will be considered below.

Parts *(b)* and *(c)* of the second *dictum* are also correct, but only as far as they go. I have been at pains to point out that the Court in *Pillay*'s case was considering the Act in the context of the vertical application of s 9 of the Constitution and the Act's own vertical operation. The Court's conclusions in parts *(b)* and *(c)* must therefore be limited to the vertical application of the Bill of Rights. So limited they are correct, *but not* if these conclusions were to be transposed to the horizontal application of the Act in general and of ss 7 to 9 in particular. In order to explain this it is necessary to consider the concept of 'inconsistency' as used in the supremacy provision s 2 of the Constitution in the phrase 'law or conduct inconsistent with ... [the Constitution] is invalid'. Under the Constitution the test for invalidity is *inconsistency* with the Constitution. In parts *(b)* and *(c)* of the second *dictum* the expression 'inconsistency' is not used. In part *(b)* it is stated that '[t]he Legislature ... may extend protection beyond what is conferred by s 9' but '[a]s long as the Act does not decrease the protection afforded by s 9 or infringe another right, a difference between the Act and s 9 does not *violate* the Constitution'. (Emphasis supplied.) In part *(b)* it is stated that there would be no problem 'if the definition of discrimination in the Act included forms of conduct not covered' by s 9 'as long as the prohibition of those forms of conduct *conformed* to the Bill of Rights'. (Emphasis supplied.) I shall assume, in favour of the Court, that the words 'violate' were used as an exact synonym for 'inconsistent with', and 'conformed' as an exact synonym for 'consistent with' or 'not inconsistent with' respectively. In examining the horizontal application of the prohibition against unfair discrimination, however, it is the word 'inconsistent' that must be construed and applied.

In the *Constitution of KwaZulu-Natal* case[65] the Court considered the concept of 'inconsistency' in the context of the constitutional certification under the Interim Constitution of a provincial constitution. Subject to two limited exceptions, which are not relevant here, s 160(3) of the Interim Constitution provided that a Provincial Constitution 'shall not be inconsistent with' a provision of the Interim Constitution, including the Constitutional Principles set out in Schedule 4 to the Interim Constitution. Although formulated in this context, the conclusions reached by the Court in the *Constitution of KwaZulu-Natal* case are equally applicable to the meaning of 'inconsistency' under s 2 of the 1996 Constitution; particularly when considering whether the provisions of a statute are 'inconsistent' with a provision of the Bill of Rights. It must further be borne in mind that the provisions of the Bill of Rights (Chapter 3) in the Interim

[65] Above, n 56.

Constitution did not operate with direct horizontality.[66] In the *Constitution of KwaZulu-Natal* case the Court held:[67]

> '[24] ... For purposes of the present inquiry as to inconsistency, we are of the view that a provision in a provincial bill of rights and a corresponding provision in Chapter 3 are *inconsistent when they cannot stand at the same time, or cannot stand together, or cannot both be obeyed at the same time.* They are *not inconsistent when it is possible to obey each without disobeying either.* There is no principial or practical reason why such provisions cannot operate together harmoniously in the same field.
>
> [25] ... In applying the test it must be borne in mind that the potential conflict in obedience arises when the provision in the provincial constitution has to be observed. The lesser limitation of power and the lesser right in Chapter 3 of the interim Constitution, postulated above, would be obeyed in the act of obeying the greater limitation of provincial power and the greater right in the provincial bill of rights, whereas there would be no room for inconsistency in respect of a new right, provided such new right did not, because of its particular nature or formulation, have the effect of eliminating or limiting a right protected in the interim Constitution.'

When considering the *vertical application* of the Bill of Rights under the 1996 Constitution, the issue of a *lesser limitation of power* or the *lesser right* in the Bill of Rights, as compared to the Equality Act, relates to *only one party*, namely the person claiming the right against the state. Where, under s 36(1) of the Constitution, a right 'under the Bill of Rights' may justifiably be limited, it concerns the right of only one party, namely the person claiming the right as against the state. The state has no competing *right* under the Bill of Rights, only an interest that is to be taken into account in the proportionality analysis, as part of the process to determine whether the *person's right* has been justifiably limited under s 36(1).

Under the *horizontal application* of the Bill of Rights, the picture is entirely different. I limit myself for present purposes to the right of one person not to be unfairly discriminated against by another person in the context of the Equality Act. I deal with the whole issue of the horizontal application of the relevant equality right more fully in Chapter 5. For present purposes suffice it to say that in any horizontal application, not only the complainant's right to equality is at issue, but invariably also the rights of the respondent who, as a person, also has rights under the Bill of Rights.[68] The respondent, when sued by the complainant for a breach of his right not to be unfairly discriminated against will invariably oppose this claim (by virtue of the very same horizontal application of the Bill of Rights, but this time in respondent's favour) with her own constitutional rights,

[66] See *Du Plessis and Others v De Klerk and Another* 1996 (3) SA 850 (CC) (1996 (5) BCLR 658).

[67] Above, n 56 at paras 24–25 and the authorities therein cited. Footnotes have been omitted.

[68] It is interesting to note that under s 1 of the Equality Act 'complainant' means 'any person who alleges any contravention of this Act and who institutes proceedings in terms of this Act; and 'respondent' means 'any *person* against whom proceedings are instituted in terms of this Act'. (Emphasis supplied). I comment on these definitions when dealing below with s 13 of the Act.

usually her rights to freedom and privacy.[69] Inevitably the issue of a limitation of the complainant's right not to be unfairly discriminated against will arise on the basis of the respondent's 'competing rights' and an 'evaluation' of the competing rights conducted with a view to deciding whether and to what extent complainant's right ought to be limited. The Constitution in fact anticipated that these very issues would arise, and made express provision for their resolution in s 8(3).

It is for this reason that the issue of 'inconsistency' (between a statute and the Constitution) presents particular problems in the sphere of horizontality. For the same reason the second *dictum* cannot be applied in this sphere, nor will the inconsistency tests formulated in the *Constitution of KwaZulu-Natal* case deliver the same results. In order to answer the question of whether the Equality Act confers a more comprehensive right and effects a greater limitation of state power than in the Bill of Rights it is, in the case of horizontality, not sufficient to look only to the complainant's position. In addition, regard must always be had to the *effect of the horizontal application* in question on the *respondent's rights.* The question must also be asked whether the Act places a greater obligation on the respondent, as compared to the obligation imposed by ss 8 and 9 of the Constitution. If the Act confers on the complainant a more extensive right to non-discrimination than does the Bill of Rights, it *must to that extent inevitably impose a greater obligation on the respondent.* The obligation on the respondent under the Bill of Rights cannot stand with the greater obligation. By obeying the obligation under the Bill of Rights the respondent is not, at the same time, obeying the obligation under the Act. The same is true of a new right in the Act. *When applied vertically*, and subject to the important qualifications in para 25 of the *Constitution of KwaZulu-Natal* case quoted above, this new right is not inconsistent with the Bill of Rights because, from the state's perspective, both can stand and be obeyed at the same time. For the respondent in a case of horizontal application, the case is different, because by obeying the horizontal duty under the Bill of Rights, she is not at the same time obeying the new right in the Act. Hence this provision in the Act would be inconsistent with the Bill of Rights. Put more simply: when the effect of granting a greater horizontal right to a plaintiff has the effect of placing a greater obligation on the defendant than would be the case under ss 8 and 9, then such grant is inconsistent with the Constitution. The legislature should therefore constantly bear in mind that any legislation dealing with the *horizontal* application of the Bill of Rights generally, and the right to equality and non-discrimination in particular, is fraught with danger whenever there is a possibility that the legislation in question might place a greater obligation on the defendant than the Constitution does.

[69] For reasons more fully set forth in Chapter 5.

This conclusion, if correct, has grave implications for the constitutional validity of various provisions of the Act in their horizontal application. I do not propose to conduct a detailed analysis of the Act's provisions in this regard. This can only be properly done on a case-by-case basis when specific issues arise for determination under the Act. I will, however, refer (without any detailed comment or argument) to certain provisions of the Act, which, in their horizontal application, might well be placing a heavier burden on the respondent than s 9 read with s 8 of the Constitution. To the extent that they do place a heavier burden on the respondent, they are inconsistent with the Constitution and therefore invalid.

For example, the definition of 'discrimination' in s 1 of the Act is in more extensive terms than in s 9(4) of the Constitution as interpreted by the Constitutional Court. Subsection 4(2)*(a)* of the Act embodies certain so-called guiding principles. To the extent that these place a heavier burden on a respondent than under s 9(3) of the Constitution, as interpreted by the courts, they are inconsistent and invalid. It comes as something of a surprise to learn that 'systemic discrimination and inequalities', even in the present, can only be caused by 'colonialism, the apartheid system and patriarchy'; this is neither what the Constitution says, nor what it has been interpreted to mean. Sections 7, 8 and 9, which purport to lay down what constitutes unfair discrimination on the grounds of race, gender and disability respectively, are likewise subject to attack if they place a heavier burden on the respondent in horizontal proceedings. Moreover, as far as these sections are concerned, one may well ask why these three grounds, out of the seventeen mentioned in s 9(3) of the Constitution, were selected for this special protection. *Prima facie* this in itself seems to be unfair discrimination against persons discriminated against on any of the listed grounds not included in the Act. Section 13 of the Act, dealing with the burden of proof in relation to discrimination, clearly relates to the horizontal application of the Act because it refers to a 'complainant' and a 'respondent' which, under their s 1 definitions, both relate to litigating *persons*. To the extent that s 13(1) of the Act places a greater burden on a respondent in horizontal proceedings than is the case under s 9(2) of the Constitution, as interpreted by the Constitutional Court, it is inconsistent and invalid. To the extent that s 13(2), in relation to 'prohibited grounds' (as defined in the Act), places a greater burden on a respondent in horizontal proceedings than would be the case under s 9(4) of the Constitution, it is inconsistent with the Constitution and invalid.

Section 14 of the Equality Act, under the heading 'Determination of fairness or unfairness', is constitutionally deeply suspect.[70] It is true that ss 13 and 14 of the Act were referred to in the *Pillay* judgment,[71] but it must again be emphasised, at

[70] See chapter 6.3.

[71] Above, n 53, paras 69 and 70 in the judgment of Langa CJ and paras 135–137 of O'Regan J's judgment.

the risk of becoming tedious, that their possible invalidity was not an issue before the Court and no argument was addressed to the Court thereanent.

4.2 GERMAN LAW[72]

(a) Introduction

(i) The relevant constitutional provisions

For present purposes arts 1 to 3 of the German Basic Law (GBL)[73] are the most relevant:

> 'Article 1
>
> [Human dignity — Human rights — Legally binding force of basic rights]
>
> (1) Human dignity is[74] inviolable. To respect and protect it is the duty of all state authority.
>
> (2) The German people therefore acknowledge inviolable and inalienable human rights as the basis of every community, of peace and of justice in the world.
>
> (3) The following basic rights shall bind the legislature, the executive and the judiciary as directly applicable law.
>
> Article 2
>
> [Personal Freedoms][75]
>
> (1) Everybody shall have the right to free development of his personality[76] insofar as he does not violate the rights of others or offend against the constitutional order or the moral law.
>
> (2) Every person shall have the right to life and physical integrity. Freedom of the person shall be inviolable. These rights may be interfered with only pursuant to law.
>
> Article 3
>
> [Equality before the law]
>
> (1) All persons shall be equal before the law.

---

[72] For a brief but authoritative description of the route from 1945 to German re-unification on 3 October 1990, see Stern (2002). For an important overview in English of equality and non-discrimination in German law, see Prof Michael Sachs (1998(a) and (1998(b)). Professor Sachs is also the author of Sachs (1987) the leading work in German on the ambit of the prohibition against discrimination and editor of Sachs (2009) the 5th edition of a commentary on the German Basic Law.

[73] Unless otherwise stated, the English quotations of the GBL are from the translation, revised and updated to June 2008 and published by the German Bundestag. The original translation was by Professor Christian Tomuschat and Professor David P Currie, and the current translation is the one as revised by Professor Tomuschat and Professor Donald P Kommers. It obviously has no official status and cannot, for example, be used as a legal tool for interpreting the German text.

[74] The 'Bundestag' translation reads 'shall be inviolable' and 'shall be the duty'. 'Is inviolable' and 'is the duty' is unquestionably the better reading. See Isensee (2006: 173–175) and Chapter 3, section 3.4, where the issue is more fully discussed.

[75] The headings of the Articles do not form part of the statutory text but have been inserted by the publishers. In German legal literature, 'personal freedoms' are often split into '*Allgemeine Handlungsfreiheit, Recht auf Leben, Körperliche Unversehrtheit, Freiheit der Person*', which translate as 'General freedom of action, right to life, bodily integrity, freedom of the person'. A so-called '*Allgemeines Persönlichkeitsrecht*' (general personality right) has been developed in German constitutional law under the provisions of art 1(1) in conjunction with art 2(1) of the GBL. The concept of a 'general personality right' is one well-known in South Africa, through the Afrikaans 'Persoonlikheidsreg' and 'Algemene persoonlikheidsreg', as discussed in Chapter 3, section 3.2.

[76] Literally, 'free unfolding of their personality' ('*freie Entfaltung seiner Persönlichkeit*').

(2) Men and women shall have equal rights. The state shall promote the actual implementation of equal rights for women and men and take steps to eliminate disadvantages that now exist.

(3) No person shall be favoured or disfavoured[77] because of sex, parentage, race, language, homeland and origin, faith, or religious or political opinions. No person shall be disfavoured because of disability.'

There are also other provisions in the GBL,[78] more limited in scope, that deal with specific instances of equality, but for purposes of this book I confine myself to art 3 of the GBL.

The view of leading German scholars[79] that art 3 and in particular art 3(1), constitutes the most complex provision of all the fundamental rights, is more than a little daunting. Before considering equality and non-discrimination under the GBL, *even for my limited purposes*, it is necessary to consider, albeit only too briefly, certain general features of the GBL and the jurisprudence thereunder.

(ii) The unique protection of human dignity under art 1 of the GBL

Although human dignity, also under the GBL, has been dealt with in Chapter 3, it is important at this stage to mention one particular aspect of its protection under art 1, because of its relevance in considering equality and non-discrimination under the GBL. A unique feature of the GBL is that, by virtue of the provisions of art 79(3) of the GBL, 'no amendment affecting (*berührt)* ... the principle[s] (*Grundsätze*) laid down in Art 1 ... is admissible'. [80] When art 79(3) is read with art 1(1), this also excludes any statutory or judicial *limitation* of human dignity.[81]

In my view, as I shall try to demonstrate more fully later in this section, this feature of the GBL has had a significant effect on the shaping of German equality and non-discrimination jurisprudence. In a much broader context, the protection of human dignity could be described as the *leitmotif* of the GBL generally.

---

[77] I would point out that the 'Bundestag's' English translation reverses the order of 'disfavoured' and 'favoured' as they appear in the GBL where the phrase is '*benachteiligt oder bevorzugt*'. Moreover, I much prefer '*benachteiligt oder bevorzugt*' being rendered in English as 'disadvantaged or advantaged'.

[78] See, for example, arts 6(5), 12(2), 19(1), 21, 33(1) to (3), 38(1) read with 28(1), 101(1), and 140 read with 136, covering, inter alia, equality between children born within and children born without marriage; equal eligibility for public office.

[79] So, for example, Prof Lerke Osterloh (2007: Rn 1) — a professor and judge of the BVerfG — who regards art 3(1), despite its 'lapidary brevity', as perhaps one of the most difficult principles in the catalogue of fundamental rights. Professor Klaus Stern (1990: 208) states that despite its comprehensive treatment in the academic writings, the interpretation of the equality provision has not yet come to rest and that the potential for dispute in relation to equality 'is both suffocating and confusing'; even the jurisprudence of the BVerfG creates a 'contradictory impression'.

[80] I would prefer 'impermissible' to 'inadmissible' for a translation of the German *unzulässig*. Art 79(3) reads:

> 'Amendments to this Basic Law affecting the division of the Federation into *Länder*, their participation on principle in the legislative process, or the principles laid down in Articles 1 and 20 shall be inadmissible (*unzulässig*).'

[81] See, for example, Höfling (2007: Rn 11f) and Lücke and Sachs (2007: Rn 48–50).

(iii) The limitation of fundamental rights in general

For my purposes the limitation of rights in German constitutional law is relevant for South Africa in at least two respects; first, with regard to the limitation of the right to equality and non-discrimination and, secondly, with regard to the horizontal application of the equality provisions and the balancing of interests resulting therefrom.

Unlike the South African Constitution and the Canadian Charter in this regard, the Basic Law does not have a general limitations clause, under which the *prima facie* infringement of a right may in given circumstances be justified. The limitation (*Beschränkung* or *Schranken*) of rights does of course take place, but the relevant principles *(a)* are to be found in the GBL's own textual formulation of certain of the basic rights, *(b)* are shaped by various other constitutional provisions and principles, and *(c)* have also been developed by the jurisprudence of the German Federal Constitutional Court. A particular focus of the jurisprudence of the BVerfG has been the development of criteria and conditions which all limitations of rights have to meet. In German constitutional doctrine, these criteria are known as the 'limiting (or limits) of limitation' (*Schranken-Schranken*) with the doctrine of proportionality (*Verhältnismäßigkeit*) as their most prominent feature. Although the limitation of rights is dealt with quite fully in s 36(1) of the South African Constitution, the Constitutional Court has itself developed a doctrine of proportionality in relation to the application of the s 36(1) limitation provisions.[82] In my view the principle and justification of the limitation of rights, and the role of proportionality in this context, are deeply rooted in the nature of the true constitutional state. I would refer to them as logico-constitutional principles. For this reason I believe it is important to consider the foundations of these principles in German law in the process of developing and deepening our own jurisprudence in this area, particularly when regard is had to the injunction in s 36(1) of the 1996 Constitution that any limitation is itself limited to what is 'reasonable and justifiable in an open and democratic society based on human dignity, equality and freedom'.

In his incisive article '*Die Grundrechte und ihre Schranken*' ('The Basic Rights and their Limitations'), written as part of a Festschrift to celebrate the 50th anniversary of the German Federal Constitutional Court (BVerfG), Prof Klaus Stern (2001: 1) points out that various expressions are used by the BVerfG to indicate the substantive content or scope of a basic right, such as '*Schutzbereich*' (literally 'area or ambit of protection'), '*Geltungsbereich*' (literally 'area of operation'), '*Schutzgut*' (literally 'protected (legal) interest'), and '*materielle Substanz des Grundrechts*' (literally 'the substantive content of the basic right').

[82] See *S v Makwanyane and Another* (above, n 4) para 104 for the Interim Constitution and adopted for the 1996 Constitution in *National Coalition for Gay and Lesbian Equality and Another v The Minister of Justice and Others* (above, n 2) paras 33–35; and see, generally, Currie and De Waal (2005: s 7.2*(b)*).

For the process of limiting or reducing the area of protection or operation of the basic right, however, the expression '*Schranke*' ('limit') is invariably used. In the forefront is the right's ambit of protection, which indicates the content of the right guaranteed by the constitutional norm in question. This could be said to be the 'positive side' of the basic right, in contrast to the 'negative side', which relates to the limitation of, or the potential to limit, the right. This negative side of the basic rights is articulated in various ways in the GBL. It is described as 'Schranke' ('limits') in arts 5(2) and 14(1), second sentence; as '*Beschränkung*' or '*Einschränkung*' ('restrict', 'restriction' or 'restricted') in arts 9(3), second sentence, 10(2), 11(2), 13(7), 17a and 19(1), first sentence. In the main the power to limit is conferred by the GBL on the legislature. Only in exceptional cases does the GBL expressly grant the power of limitation to the executive or judiciary, as in art 13(2)–(5) and (7), and art 18. Through its jurisprudence the BVerfG has played an important role in the development of rights limitation.

It is of cardinal importance to bear in mind, however — as Stern (2001: 2–3) himself emphasises — that the imposition of a limitation is itself limited, either expressly in the basic right norm, or by other constitutional norms or constitutional principles. In this respect it is customary to speak of '*Schranken-Schranken*' ('limiting-of-limitation'). A clear circumscription of these three aspects in any Bill of Rights analysis (ie the scope of protection, the limitation, and the limiting-of-limitation) contributes substantially to internal balance between the legal interests guaranteed, on the one hand, and their limits in the light of the public interest, on the other. In principle, the analysis of the constitutional scope of protection takes precedence. All exercise of state power directed at, or permitted with respect to a constitutional provision of this nature, constitutes an infringement of these protected areas. This can be justified only by means of constitutional limitation, which must itself in turn be measured against the 'limiting-of-limitation'. This order of ranking has often been confirmed by the BVerfG.[83] Stern (2001: 3–8) deals with various aspects of the basic rights' scope of protection before dealing with the limitation of these rights.

Stern (2001: 8–17) admits that there is still no completely satisfactory and generally accepted overall exposition of the limitation of rights. As point of departure for any system of limitations there must, however, be an appreciation of the fact that — for the sake of the flourishing of human beings in a community — basic rights cannot be unlimited. For this reason many of the basic rights in the GBL embody textually their own limitations. But even those who do not, are not to be regarded as limitless. At the same time it is also agreed that this does not mean that these rights provisions are at the disposal of the legislature. Another important principle in the structure and justification of rights limitation has been the early acknowledgement by the BVerfG that the basic rights are not founded

[83] See, for example, BVerfGE 32, 54 (72) '*Betriebsbetretungsrecht*'.

on the image of an isolated individual, but on the image of a person positioned in society. The limitation of rights is inevitably also concerned with the protection of the rights of others, the common good and the ability of the state to function. Stern (2001: 11) describes the limitation of a basic right's scope of operation or the justification of an infringement of these rights, as being at the 'critical point (*neuralgische Punkt*) of the system of basic rights'. The limitation of rights is concerned with the state of tension which exists between lofty individual legal status and restrictions imposed in the interest of fellow human beings and of society.

Stern (2001: 11–12) points out that every crafting of a limitation needs a reference point within the Constitution. If basic rights are constitutional rights, then the constitution alone can determine the limits of their protection. In this regard a distinction is drawn between direct and indirect constitutional limitations. Direct constitutional limitations are those where the constitutional ambit of the right, as provided in the Constitution, itself determines the limitation, whether in the particular provision itself or in some other constitutional provision. Indirect constitutional limitations are those authorised by state power and, in particular, by the legislature. In principle the limitation takes effect only when the authorised organ of state exercises its power, whether in the form of statute or regulation, administrative act or judicial pronouncement.

A classic example of direct limitation is found in art 5(2) of the GBL where 'protection of young persons' and 'personal honour' serve to limit the rights to freedom of expression, of the press, and of reporting set forth in art 5(1) of the GBL. These are direct constitutional limitations, because the Constitution itself establishes 'counterbalances' limiting the right to freedom of expression, regardless of whether the legislature regulates these matters.

Even rights that have been formulated in unlimited terms can, by virtue of the jurisprudence of the BVerfG, be limited — subject of course to the privileged position of art 1(1) alluded to above. In 1970, in a case concerning military disciplinary powers against a soldier, it was laid down in BVerfGE 28, 243 (261) that

> '[o]nly the clashing basic rights of third parties or other constitutionally protected legal interests which the constitution endows with legal value, are in exceptional circumstances capable — to some extent — of limiting "unlimitable" basic rights, having regard to the unity of the constitution and the general value order protected by it. Emerging conflicts can only be solved if it can be decided which constitutional provision has the greater weight for purposes of the concrete question to be determined (BVerfGE 2, 1 (72f)). The weaker norm may only be displaced to the extent that it appears logically and systematically essential to do so; its fundamental value must, however, be respected.'[84]

[84] The Court found that the reliable performance and operational capacity of the armed services are indeed constitutionally protected interests that limit to some extent a soldier's right to object to military service.

From the mid-1970s onwards this view was modified by the BVerfG in terms that have attracted general scholarly agreement, when it laid down that the clash between basic rights and other constitutionally protected interests must be solved according to the principle of practical conformity (*praktischer Konkordanz*).[85] The principle requires that neither of the competing legal positions should be given preference or maximally asserted, but all should be balanced as carefully as possible.[86] This approach, says Stern (2001: 15), leads to a difficult weighing-up process, by which 'the balance or practical conformity is restored', as this process of resolving the conflict is generally called.

When one wishes to limit basic rights in a situation where no direct or indirect limitation is actually provided for, a limitation will be permissible only if it is justified by constitutional legal interests (*Verfassungsrechtsgüter*). A prime example of this idea (Stern 2001: 16) is expressed in art 2(1) of the GBL when the right to the free unfolding of the personality is limited by 'the rights of others'. This provision is not just a direct limitation of the right contained in this article of the GBL (personality), but is the constitutional reference point for a limitation beyond that. Stern agrees with Dürig's contention that the rights of others must be regarded as limitations 'present in *all* basic rights' and which are 'really inherent in a lego-logical sense'.[87] In concrete terms one is here concerned with the difficult issue of the clash between basic rights.

Particular difficulties arise, however, when considering legal interests worthy of protection that appear in constitutional provisions other than those in the basic rights section. Nevertheless a number of these legal interests have been identified by the BVerfG and in academic writing, as Stern (2001: 15–16) indicates.[88]

German Basic Law provisions that expressly (or by clear necessary implication) authorise the legislature to limit the ambit of a right's application constitute an important source of limitation (*Schranken*). In cases like this it is customary to speak of a legislative reservation (*Gesetzesvorbehalt*) (Stern 2001: 18–19). One example of this type of limitation is in respect of the right to life, physical integrity and freedom of the person, where the third sentence of art 2(2) GG provides that '[t]hese rights may only be interfered with (*eingegriffen werden*) pursuant to a law'. Another example would be art 12(1), second sentence, where, in respect of occupational freedom, there is a reservation to the effect that — '[t]he practice of an occupation or a profession may be regulated by or pursuant to law'. The equivalent in the South African Constitution would be s 22, second sentence, where, in respect of occupational freedom, there is an almost identical

---

[85] See, for example, BVerfGE 41, 29 (51); BVerfGE 52, 223 (247) and Stern (2001: 15). The German scholar and BVerfG judge Konrad Hesse is considered to have coined that phrase.

[86] BVerfGE 93, 1 (21).

[87] Dürig (1958b: Rn 73).

[88] These include interests of the public order (eg national security, financial stability, functioning of the courts and parliament), different public interests (eg public health, safe energy supply), and the protection of the environment.

reservation — 'The practice of a trade, occupation or profession may be regulated by law.' There are other similar provisions in our Constitution.

I mention this because, according to German law (see Stern 2001: 18–20), these reservations do not give the legislature a free hand. The legislature is bound by, among others, such constitutional limitations as provisions regarding legislative competence, principles of the Constitutional state and, in particular, by the principle of proportionality (*Verhältnismäßigkeitsgrundsatz*). I can see no good reason why these principles, which after all are logico-constitutional ones, should not be applicable to all 'legislative reservations' in the South African Constitution. This is expressly recognised in relation to collective labour bargaining, in s 23(5), second and third sentences, which provide as follows: 'National legislation may be enacted to regulate collective bargaining. To the extent that the legislation may limit a right in this Chapter, the limitation must comply with s 36(1).' But in principle this must apply to all legislative reservations, for as Stern (2001: 18–19) points out in relation to the GBL:

> 'The legislator must constantly bear in mind that, when shaping basic rights, one is dealing with constitutional legal concepts. The statutes have validity in accordance with the Constitution, not the Constitution in accordance with the statutes.
>
> ...
>
> No basic right may be surrendered into the hands of the legislature. The Parliamentary Council [the drafting body of the GBL 1948/9] were highly sensitized in this regard by the abuse of legislation by the national socialist *Führer*-state. The so-called "self-glorification" of the legislature, about which the Supreme Court spoke as early as 1927, was fully abandoned with regard to the basic rights referred to in Art 1(3) GBL and to the Constitution in general in Art 20(3) GBL.[89] The *Bundesverfassungsgericht* was appointed the guardian of constitutional precedence.'

The development of the so-called limiting-of-limitation (*Schranken-Schranken*) concept is of importance to South African jurisprudence, notwithstanding the wide ambit of the s 36(1) limitation provision in the Constitution. German jurisprudence places the concept of limitation into historical constitutional perspective and is also important for a proper constitutional understanding of the so-called 'proportionality analysis' that the South African Constitutional Court has developed with regard to the proper application of s 36(1). Of at least equal importance is the fact that under the *Schranken-Schranken* concept, limits to the limitation of rights have been developed that go beyond the ambit of s 36(1) of our Constitution and are not founded in any specific provision of the GBL.

[89] These articles read as follows:

Article 1(3): 'The following basic rights shall bind the legislature, the executive and the judiciary as directly applicable law.'

Article 20(3): 'The legislature shall be bound by the constitutional order, the executive and the judiciary by law and justice.'

The concept of *Schranken-Schranken* (limiting-of-limitation) was developed, in part at least, as a reaction to the contempt shown for the Weimar Constitution in the Nazi period. It covers a range of qualifications and conditions, which an infringement of the scope of a constitutional right, ie any limitation of a right, has to meet to be constitutionally justified. In Germany, some of these conditions are expressly mentioned in the Basic Law, with a formal condition in art 19(1) and a substantive condition in art 19(2).[90] Subsequently the development of the prohibitions against the excessive use of state power (*Übermaßverbot*) and against the insufficient use of state power (*Untermaßverbot)* also came to be developed. The South African Constitutional Court has in effect applied the principle of the *Übermaßverbot* in holding that a prison sentence that was grossly disproportionate to the severity of the crime committed was inconsistent with the Constitution.[91]

Under art 19(1), first sentence of the GBL, the law imposing the limitation must be one of general application. This formal condition is mirrored in the South African Constitution by the requirement in s 36(1) that the limiting law must be one 'of general application'. Negatively put, these are provisions against single case (*Einzelfall*) and single person (*Einzelpersonen*) legislation. In part these provisions are dictated by the principle of constitutionalism that laws should be general in form and application, and also the principle of equality under the law.

Stern (2001: 27–28) points out that the main problem in applying art 19(1), first sentence, is to be able to identify a single-case or single-person piece of legislation where the legislature has disguised this through astute drafting techniques. The Courts have grappled, not wholly successfully, with this problem. It would seem to be more productive to attack legislation like this under the general equality clause.

The provision in art 19(2) of the GBL that '[i]n no case may the essence of a basic right be affected' was in essence reproduced in s 33(1)*(b)* of the Interim South African Constitution, but does not feature expressly in the 1996 Constitution. One of the arguments for its omission was, apparently, that in Germany this provision had never been used to strike down legislation. In retrospect this seems a rather facile reason, because it takes no account of the effective braking effect it might have on the German legislature. This is the very point made by Stern (2001: 27). While accepting the fact that these provisions (art 19(1) and (2) of the GBL) have been insignificant in the jurisprudence of the BVerfG, and that no legislation has been struck down because of them, Stern maintains that their 'protective

[90] These provisions read:

'(1) Insofar as, under this Basic Law, a basic right may be restricted by or pursuant to a law, such law must apply generally and not merely to a single case. In addition, the law must specify the basic right affected and the Article in which it appears.

(2) In no case may the essence of a basic right be affected.'

[91] *Dodo v The State* 2001 (3) SA 382 (CC) (2001 (5) BCLR 423) para 38.

and warning role should not be regarded as insignificant'. Even without a similar provision, it is to be hoped that in South Africa the principle involved will be given proper weight in the s 36(1) proportionality analysis and in considering what, for purposes of applying s 36(1), is 'reasonable and justifiable in an open and democratic society based on human dignity, equality and freedom ...'.

The treatment of the proportionality principle (*Verhältnismäßigkeitsgrundsatz*) by Stern (2001: 30–34) is particularly instructive and helpful for the development of South African law in this regard. Although it was initially thought that the protection of the 'essence of the basic right' under art 19(2) would drive the 'limiting-of-limitation' in Germany, its place has been taken by the BVerfG's development of the proportionality principle. Since 1964 the BVerfG has based the development of the proportionality principle on the constitutional state (rule of law in broader sense) idea, and the proportionality principle has by now become entrenched and generally accepted as the general limiting-of-limitation (*Schranken-Schranken)* principle for all limitations of basic rights.

While s 36(1)*(a)–(e)* of the South African Constitution enumerate various factors to be taken into account in the limitation enquiry, no express mention is made of the proportionality principle. This principle must, however, be regarded as implicit in s 36(1) when considered in its full context and against the historical background of the provision. The principle of proportionality has been developed by the Constitutional Court as mentioned above. The Constitutional Court took the 'ingredients' of the proportionality principle directly from the Constitution and combined them in an overarching principle of 'proportionality'. The Court has also characterised the South African Constitution as establishing a constitutional (rule of law in the broader sense) state.[92] It is both logical and reasonable to accept that the South African proportionality principle is similarly sourced and that German jurisprudence can be of use in the development and refinement of the principles involved.

While there is still some debate about terminology, Stern (2001: 31) is of the view that there is today general agreement about the substance of the proportionality analysis. It is generally accepted that its main function is to ensure that statutory reservations are not used to limit the basic rights unduly, and to ensure that the legislation in the ambit of the basic right in question introduces the right balance, in particular with regard to means and ends.

It is important to determine as precisely as possible what the content of proportionality analysis is. According to Stern (2001: 31–32) there are three elements to the principle:

> '— the appropriateness or suitability (*Geeignetheit oder Tauglichkeit*) of the means with regard to a particular objective.

[92] See, for example, *S v Makwanyane* (above, n 4) para 156, and *De Lange v Smuts NO and others* 1998 (3) SA 785 (CC) para 31, and generally, Currie and De Waal (2005: s 1.3(a) and (b)).

— the necessity *(Erforderlichkeit oder Notwendigkeit)* of the means, and
— proportionality (in a narrower sense) or suitability or appropriateness of the means in relation to the legal interest affected, in some newer decisions referred to as reasonableness (*Zumutbarkeit*).'

Stern quotes the following passages from BVerfGE 67, 157 (173) in which the BVerfG aptly applied this triad of objectives in a matter concerned with legislation in connection with the limitation of the privacy of communications.

> 'According to the principle of proportionality the ... [monitoring of letters and telephone conversations] must be suitable to ensure the protection of the legal interest here in question (the timely identification and countering of the danger of armed attacks on the Federal Republic of Germany). It must be necessary, which would not be the case if less invasive (*milder*) measures would be sufficient to achieve this. Finally, it must be proportionate in the narrower sense; that means it must stand in an appropriate relationship to the weight and importance of the basic right....'

Stern (2001: 32–33) uses examples — mostly from well-established principles relating to police duties — to illustrate the three elements.

(aa) The appropriateness or suitability of the means

In this regard Stern quotes Schnapp (1983: 852): 'A measure is appropriate (*geeignet*) to achieving an end, when it brings the desired consequence closer (*gewünschte Erfolg näher rückt*). It is inappropriate when it makes the achievement of the intended objective more difficult or has no effect at all in respect of the goal.' In this sense, according to Stern (2001: 32), the BVerfG evaluates the measure as to whether it is 'purely and simply inappropriate', 'objectively inappropriate', 'clearly inappropriate or unnecessary', 'inappropriate in principle', or whether 'with its help the desired consequence can be achieved'.

(bb) The necessity of the means

Stern points out that necessity is positively described on the basis that 'an appropriate measure may be instituted if it is the measure that has the least invasive consequences. The standard is minimum intervention. The mildest [least invasive or least restrictive] measure must be employed to achieve the end in mind....' A means is also not necessary in the above sense 'when the same consequence can be achieved with a less serious intrusion into the sphere of the basic right. When considering the element of necessity it is obligatory to take into account the full factual circumstances to the extent necessary to achieve an "individualised process".'

(cc) Proportionality in a narrower sense

(Synonyms used by Stern for *Verhältnismäßigkeit* in the narrower sense are 'proportionality (*Proportionalität*)', 'adequacy (*Angemessenheit)*', and 'reasonableness (*Zumutbarkeit*)'. 'Proportionality in a narrower sense' could also, and perhaps more helpfully, be translated by the use of the term 'adequacy' or 'reasonableness'.)

Stern (2001: 33–34) considers 'proportionality in a narrower sense' to be the most difficult element in the application of the triad, yet I would suggest that a careful study of its treatment in German law would be of valuable assistance in the application and development in practice of the proportionality analysis under s 36(1) of our Constitution. With very few notable exceptions, engagement by South African courts with this third element of the triad has not been as searching and considered as it ought to have been.[93] According to Stern (2001: 33–34):

> 'As is the case with all reflection, it is always necessary when examining individual cases, to establish a relationship between concepts, usually between ends and means. Seen in this light, proportionality is usually intended to ensure, in effect, that a particular means is not out of relationship to the intended end (negatively formulated) or that it must stand in an appropriate relationship to the intended end (positive formulation). At the level of basic rights this means that a sacrifice imposed by the infringement of a basic right must not be out of proportion to the common good that is sought to be achieved.'

After referring to a number of newer and different formulations by the BVerfG, Stern (2002: 34) acknowledges the obvious, namely that 'in concrete cases determining the correct relationship is beset with difficulties not evident in the abstract formulation'. 'This means', says Stern, 'that a third standard, a *tertium comparationis*, must be sought.' Stern is of the view that this *tertium comparationis*

> 'can only be found in the weight of the legal interests in question. These must be weighed up against one another and in so doing a sensible balance established, without one legal interest being relegated at the cost of the other in a manner which is inappropriate (immoderate, unreasonable)'.

In his article 'Constitutional rights, balancing, and rationality' German constitutional law scholar Prof Robert Alexy outlines (Alexy 2003: 131f) the proportionality principle, with its three subprinciples, as developed by the BVerfG since the *Lüth* judgment in 1958,[94] and defends the principle against certain objections raised by Prof Jürgen Habermas. Alexy (2003: 135–136) maintains that all three subprinciples of proportionality are 'optimisation' requirements:

> 'As optimisation requirements, principles are norms requiring that something be realised to the greatest extent possible, given the legal and factual possibilities (Alexy 2002: 47).

[93] I myself readily plead guilty to this charge.
[94] BVerfGE 7, 198.

The principles of suitability and necessity concern optimisation relative to what is factually possible. The principle of suitability excludes the adoption of means obstructing the realisation of at least one principle without promoting any principle or goal for which they were adopted. If a means M, adopted in order to promote the principle P1, is not suitable for this purpose, but obstructs the realisation of P2, then there are no costs to either P1 or P2 if M is omitted, but there are costs to P2 if M is adopted. Thus P1 and P2 taken together may be realised to a higher degree relative to what is factually possible if M is abandoned. P1 and P2, when *taken together*, prohibit the use of M....

The same applies to the principle of necessity. This principle requires that of two means promoting P1 that are, broadly speaking, equally suitable, the one that interferes less intensively in P2, ought to be chosen. If there exists a less intensively interfering and equally suitable means, one position can be improved at no cost to the other. The application of the principle of necessity presupposes, however, that there is no third principle or goal, P3, that is affected negatively by the adoption of the means interfering less intensively in P2. When costs are unavoidable balancing becomes necessary.

Balancing is the subject of the third subprinciple of the principle of proportionality, the principle of proportionality in the narrow sense. This principle expresses what optimisation relative to the legal possibilities means. It is identical with a rule that might be called the "law of Balancing" (Alexy 2002: 102). This rule states:

"The greater the degree of non-satisfaction of, or detriment to, one principle, the greater the importance of satisfying the other."

This expresses the point that optimisation relative to two competing principles consists of nothing other than balancing.

The law of balancing shows that balancing can be broken down into three stages. The first stage is a matter of establishing the degree of non-satisfaction of, or detriment to the first principle. This is followed by a second stage, in which the importance of satisfying the competing principle is established. Finally, the third stage answers the question of whether or not the importance of satisfying the competing principle justifies the detriment to, or non-satisfaction of, the first.'

(b) The basic meaning of equality and non-discrimination in German constitutional law

In tracing the long history of the idea of human equality before it found constitutional protection, Kirchhof (2000: Rn 73) points out that the content of any equality principle depends on a comparison with reference to a so-called *tertium comparationis*.[95] For Kirchhof this *tertium comparationis* is human worth and freedom of conscience. He expands this idea by contending that this equality extends itself to equality in seeking happiness — not that the state is

[95] What I have thus far termed the 'criterion of attribution' to fit in with the logico-grammatical analysis I support. However, in keeping with the German use I shall, where appropriate and when dealing with the relevant German jurisprudence, use *tertium comparationis*.

obliged to insure this happiness, but that every individual should have an equal opportunity to strive for happiness.[96]

Professor Konrad Hesse[97] (1951: 172), citing Windelband,[98] considers equality to be 'a relationship, in which different persons stand to one another'. He continues (1951: 173) by explaining:

> 'An equality judgment is the outcome of an intellectual process that compares the relationship in which objects stand to one another. In so doing the objects cannot be related to one another in toto, but only in particular respects, with regard to a greater or lesser number of characteristics. *We cannot conclude that two things are equal, without indicating in what aspect(s) they are equal.* This aspect, the absolutely essential "tertium comparationis," must be identical.' (Emphasis supplied.)

Hesse (1951: 201) argues that the Christian view of equality (as discussed in Chapter 2) has blended with the Stoic concept to constitute a Christian-humanistic concept of equality — 'the equal worth of all who bear the human image', which has determined western thinking up to the present day.

Thus Hesse, along a slightly different path, reaches the same conclusion with regard to the inescapable linguistic logic inherent in determining the meaning of equality. What attribute is it that all human beings possess, that is equal?

Hesse (1951: 175) correctly draws attention to the fact that legal regulation must of necessity be general and that it cannot deal separately with each individual human case. It is from the inevitable generality of legislation, treating different persons, with different gifts, abilities and needs in the same way, that risks of unequal treatment arise. Hence the need to determine in any particular case whether the differences that exist between the persons to whom the regulation applies are relevant and material. It is here where, in the view I take of the matter, the impact of the legislation in question on the persons subject to it becomes important and in considering whether any impact it may have on any person or persons is of such a nature that it negatively affects their human dignity.

In his seminal article '*Der Grundrechtssatz von der Menschenwürde*', Prof Günther Dürig (1956: 125) describes human dignity thus:

> '*Jeder Mensch ist Mensch kraft seines Geistes, der ihn abhebt von der unpersönlichen Natur und ihn aus eigener Entscheidung dazu befähigt, seiner selbst bewußt zu werden, sich selbst zu bestimmen und sich und die Umwelt zu gestalten.*'
>
> ('All humans are human by virtue of their intellectual capacity ("*kraft seines Geistes*") which serves to separate them from the impersonality of nature and enables them to exercise

[96] Compare the American Declaration of Independence, signed in 1776, in which it is famously stated that '[w]e hold these truths to be self-evident, that *all men are created equal*, that they are endowed by their Creator with certain unalienable Rights, that among those are Life, Liberty and the *pursuit of happiness*'. (Emphasis supplied.)

[97] Who was also a judge of the BVerfG.

[98] '*Über Gleichheit und Identität*' (1910), s.8.

their own judgement, to have self-awareness, to exercise self-determination and to shape themselves and nature.')[99]

Dürig introduces this formulation by pointing out that the normative constitutional principle in art 1(1) of the GBL, that human dignity (worth) is untouchable, contains a value statement that is based on an assessment of a particular practical reality; one that 'is' (exists) independent(ly) from space and time and 'shall be' brought to reality by the law.

He further comments on the interrelated nature of arts 1 to 3 of the GBL, and points out that the framers of the Basic Law agreed upon the concept of humanness ('*Menschenauffassung*') as a particular idea or concept of the human being. Dürig says that this understanding of human dignity follows from the understanding of humanity. This *Menschenauffassung* is part of a world-view ('*Weltanschauung*'), an underlying rationale that made the development of human dignity as a normative concept possible. This concept was considered to be intellectually acceptable for purposes of applying the law to all religious and philosophical views.

He then proceeds to develop his argument that human worth (dignity) is the attribute in respect of which all human beings are equal because of two 'axiomatic concepts of practical reality' that are embodied in the concept of humanness 'reflected normatively in Art: 2(1) and Art 3 BL'; and that cannot be separated from each other:

> 'It is simply a given firstly, that human beings are *free* (to shape themselves and nature) and secondly, that *every* human being ("*jeder Mensch*") has this freedom, and to that extent is also equal. Before one troubles oneself with trying to give content to the idea of self-worth existing in human freedom, one must admit that the freedom of humans to shape themselves and their environment, which is considered to be *equal* for all, is necessarily only an abstract freedom, and cannot "be" actual freedom as such, possessed by "the human as such". The *general* intrinsic value of human worth cannot therefore from the beginning actually exist at any time in its equal *realization* in concrete human beings, but in the equal abstract *possibility* (potential ability) for this [equal] realization.'

He further (1956: 143) makes the important point, true also for South Africa, that equality of justice in the sense of affording everyone his or her equitable own cannot be conceived without its complementary concept of inequality. Moreover, and most importantly for the essence of my analytical argument, Dürig sees human dignity (worth) as the touchstone, in principle, for considering matters of equality and inequality:

[99] My translation of what forms the core of my own description of human dignity.

> 'The human worth (dignity) of all human beings is the absolute (and final) *tertium comparationis* of all legal equality assessments, indicating what must be regarded as essentially equal and consequently treated absolutely (and finally) equally.'[100]

He then points out that, because of the subjectivity involved in this process, it has been necessary, ever since, to conceptualise the equality clause in the abstract (which he calls the pre-Basic Law concept) so as to understand it as an overall prohibition of arbitrariness. Dürig then adds the following explanation of what arbitrariness in this equality context means:

> '[It] has been reinforced by Art 1(1): If the state tolerates arbitrariness or acts arbitrarily that means, from the perspective of the individual human being concerned, that he or she is exposed to the government's action or inaction like an impersonal object.'

This in no ways implies an abandonment of human worth as the attribute to which equality relates. While Dürig (1956: 145) points out that legal equality also applies in the economic sphere, it only does so 'at the beginning of one's participation in the economy', and only in regard to one's legal opportunity to do so (for example, freedom to choose one's profession and vocational training (art 12(1)). He calls this 'legal equality of initial opportunity ["chance"]'. This

> 'does not require the levelling out of such factual differences as might prevent an individual from seizing the opportunity in a concrete case and which would result in equality in the ensuing economic process or the distribution of wealth'.

(I interpose to point out that this conclusion is reached in a country which has been irrevocably[101] constituted by art 20(1) of the GBL as a 'democratic and *social* federal state'.) Dürig further points out that if one wants to avoid a clash with art 1(1) one has to acknowledge a fundamental equal right at the 'end of the economic process'; that is to say,

> 'one is bound to afford each individual human being, who is incapable of using his or her economic freedom, a subjective public right to a minimum standard of living in conformity with human worth, should the assistance of third persons or other social groups fail to provide this'.

Here again human worth is used in the assessment of basic equality.[102]

It is interesting to note that the BVerfG (in BVerfGE 1, 97 (104)) did not at first see art 1(1) of the GBL in this way. Later it turned full circle and adopted Dürig's view (as well as that of other scholars and courts) and in BVerfGE 82, 60 (85) held that it follows from art 1(1) and the social state principle (art 20(1))

---

[100] *'Die Würde des Menschen als solche ist das absolut gesetzte tertium comparationis jedes rechtlichen Gleichbewertens, das erkennbar macht, was als wesentlich Gleiches anzuerkennen und folglich absolut gleich zubehandeln ist.'*

[101] Irrevocable, because art 79(3) of the GBL prohibits any amendment of, inter alia, these principles laid down in art 20(1).

[102] The GBL does not, of course, contain explicit economic rights, such as access to housing, water, etc.

that the state has to guarantee the 'minimal conditions for a dignified existence' ('*Mindestvoraussetzungen für ein menschenwürdiges Dasein*').

Prof Geiger[103] (1957: 171) also sees human worth as lying at the heart of the right to equality in art 3 of the GBL:

> '"All human beings are equal" is clearly an exaggeration. In fact, humans are not equal; it is not possible to find two people who are equal in every respect. That is a truism ('*Binsenwahrheit*').[104] When the law demands that people be treated equally — they are equal 'before the law' — their obvious differences must be ignored, because they appear to be equal with regard to one common denominator. What all human beings have in common is, in the language of the Basic Law, human worth; they are all persons, responsible for themselves, creatures endowed with a conscience, a Christian would say the bearer of an immortal soul.'

Dürig (1973: art 3(1), Rn 1), in his critical analysis of and commentary on art 3(1) of the GBL, once again focuses on human worth (dignity) as the essential attribute in respect whereof all people are equal and ought not to be discriminated against:

> 'It is conceptually inevitable that any normative statement about equality embodies a "*Comparison*" of differences "*with regard to a third*" [denominator] (ie a *tertium comparationis*). Every statement about equality is inevitably also (in contrast to a scientific statement about identity) a *value judgement* that presupposes that inequalities in fact exist. Similarly every proposition about constitutional equality rests intellectually on the premise the every single human being actually has different characteristics that cannot be duplicated. Anthropologically these *differences* are neither *solely genetic* nor *solely environmental*. They are determined by the *complexity* of both natural characteristics as well as environmental influence [compare the text at Rn 95ff]. In any case — and that is sufficient for present purposes — these *differences simply exist*. And the equality postulate of the constitution embodies just this, that *despite* their actual different qualities human beings will certainly, in their relationships, be treated *legally* as of *equal value*.' (Emphasis in the original.)

For Dürig (1973: art 3(1), Rn 3) there is also an earlier indication of equality of human worth in the Basic Law:

> 'Already Art 1(1), under which human beings are entitled to *equal worth*, the Basic Law puts it beyond doubt what value constitutes the "*tertium comparationis*" for purposes of the equality clause. [cf in this regard Dürig, *Staatslexikon art "Gleichheit"*]. The general equality provision in art 3(1) similarly mentions (as does the "general freedom right" in art 2(1)) only the *fundamental theme* of our Constitution in the *value system of the fundamental rights*. And the concept of this theme is not insignificant, as a concrete representation of human beings and the indefeasible necessity of their existence.' (Emphasis in the original.)

[103] Who was also a justice of the BVerfG from 1951 to 1977.

[104] '*Binse*' in German is a bulrush. *Meyers Neues Lexikon* explains that a '*Binsenwahrheit*' is 'a truth as simple as the smooth knot-free stem of a bulrush'.

He further points out (1973: art 3(1), Rn 6) that if 'equality' (as 'freedom') is characterised as deriving from the same 'root', namely from art 1(1), then, to that extent, the much-vaunted tension between these legal values does not exist. Then the equality clause also ensures a fundamental standard for freedom. Accordingly, what fundamental rights dogmatics call 'Equality' is but a partial aspect of freedom.

For Dürig (1973: art 3(1), Rn 19) the idea that equal enslavement can be consonant with the idea of equality before the law, is anathema. According to him (1973: art 3(1), Rn 20):

> '[The requirement of] the GBL is equality "in justice" ("*im Recht*") (in liberal freedom and social security) but not "equality in injustice" ("*Gleichheit im Unrecht*") (in liberal unfreedom, in social insecurity). For this "equality in justice" ("*Gleichheit im Recht*"), that cannot be levelled down to equally miserable injustice, is now — if one proceeds from the axiom of equal human worth under Art 1(1) — a definite egalitarian standard, that belongs to the essence (Art 19(2)) of the equality provision.'

Dürig cautions (1973: art 3(1), Rn 27) that, when considering such concepts as equality of opportunity, one does not lose the concept of human worth as the basis for the equality provision. He further pleads (Rn 36) that, with regard to absolutely equal legal competency, the equality provision should in fact 'standardise upwards', rather than obstruct and reduce advantage, as though its whole actual dynamic went no further than a 'fundamental right to envy', and in particular to stagnation and to a reaction inimical to progress. Dürig (1973: art 3(1) Rn 91–92) regards the right to education and training as lying at the egalitarian heart of the equality provisions. It is important to note, however, that while the right demands equality of 'starting opportunity' and 'support opportunity', it does not — according to Dürig — require equality of result. The Constitution is concerned primarily with the education of children and young people and their equality of starting opportunities as a precondition to the later full development of their personalities. Of importance too is his view (1973: art 3(1), Rn 96) that '[t]he Constitution is absolutely opposed to a deterministic portrayal of humanity, whether it be environmental or genetic determinism'.

What is, in my view, of particular significance regarding the views expressed by Dürig (1956) and Dürig (1973), referred to above, is that — to the best of my knowledge — there has been no serious academic or judicial criticism of or disagreement with them. This is not to suggest that other scholars have not had different (but in my view incomplete) views on the basic meaning of equality. There is, beyond that, no engagement with Dürig's analytical approach and particularly not with the proposition that in discussions on equality and discrimination one cannot logically proceed without a *tertium comparationis*. Professor Klaus Stern (1990: 207), in a *Festschrift* tribute to Dürig, comments on it as follows — 'In 1973 Dürig, through this commentary, appropriated Art 3(1) as his very own; nowhere else does so much personal belief shine through, does so much life-blood flow through the words....'

Professor Georg Müller (1989: 42) also considers that there is a close relationship between the equality provision and human worth as well as justice. It derives in part its content from human worth but is not to be equated with it.

Professor Stern (1990: 213) stresses that what is prohibited is not only 'unjustified differentiation' (*'ungerechtfertigte Unterscheidungen'*) but also 'unjustified non-differentiation' (*'ungerechtfertigte Nichtunterscheidungen'*). He then makes the following important point:

> 'As in the case of a prohibition against unequal treatment, just so in the case of an injunction to treat unequally, *comparison* is the highest requirement in the application of Art 3(1).... Comparison is only possible with regard to a third factor, a *tertium comparationis*.'

This very last comment is made with specific reference to, inter alia, Dürig (1973: art 3(1), Rn 1) quoted above. Elsewhere Stern (1983: 640) also emphasises the religious and Kantian origins of constitutional equality of freedom. On the basis of their inherent worth 'personal freedom, fitting to the very nature of humanity', is safeguarded for human beings. 'For Kant it proves to be the only, but also the most fundamental and original right for human beings.' Only through freedom can human beings 'direct themselves and shape the world around them'. Freedom is the foundation for 'both one's individual as well as one's social personality'. Freedom is the original basis for human nature, a part of being human. Natural law has taken up this insight, whether in a Christian or non-Christian form. Stern further emphasises that inasmuch as freedom inheres in human beings by virtue of their human dignity, it is an *equal* freedom. 'Thus equality, together with freedom, is inherent in human beings.' Both are grounded in the human personality. 'Personality requires equal human worth.' But, he correctly points out, this equality has not (yet) been put into concrete form. In this regard he quotes with approval the following passage from Coings (1947: 44): 'No individual and no human order can guarantee to everyone equal happiness or equal opportunities. But much has been achieved when one can secure for all the guaranteed free development of personality, which accrues to all in equal manner.' Therefore, says Stern (1983: 641), it is right that equality, in art 3 of the GBL, should follow directly on art 2 of the GBL,[105] in the structure of the system of fundamental rights. In a different context, Stern himself (1988: 36) also makes the link between equality and the value of dignity:

> 'Not only is the fundamentally recognised tradition of pre-constitutional basic rights expressed in this foundation [provided in art 1(1) of the GBL], but also their grounding in human beings themselves and in their subjective quality in consequence of their personality and worth. It is therefore neither a fiction, nor an abstraction nor a theory that gives rise to

[105] My comment: art 2(1) guarantees to everyone the 'free unfolding of his/her personality'.

fundamental rights, but rather human existence itself, the securing of the dignity of human beings that gives rise to human rights. In this sense human dignity is the foundation of the fundamental rights....

The ability for self-realisation accrues to humans on the basis of their worth. The essence of the human being is manifested herein. When freedom accrues to humans because of their worth, then this is a freedom shared by all humans. To this extent the freedom of human beings also gives rise to equality. Both are grounded in worth.'

According to Dr Manfred Gubelt (1992: Rn 3): 'Art 3 stands in an intimate relationship with Art 1(1) (protection of human worth) and Art 2 (free unfolding of the personality), while all three are based on the same idea of the state, which underlies the limitation of public power and the right to individuality.' Gubelt (1992: Rn 2) points out that although art 3(1) is, in the first instance, directed at the state it has had a considerable 'radiating effect' on private law. In this context the inherent tension between equality and freedom becomes very clear; the further one permits equality to operate in the private sphere, the more severely private autonomy is limited. While doubting whether Dürig (1973: Rn 3) is correct in relating art 3 exclusively back to art 1(1), he does not dispute Dürig's fundamental thesis that human worth is the *tertium comparationis* for an understanding of equality. Gubelt (1992: Rn 11) explains that the BVerfG has, in its substantive development of equality, been influenced by the writing of Leibholz (1925 and 1959).

Hofmann (1993) discusses the central role that the concept of human worth plays in German constitutional jurisprudence, and confirms the important part played by Dürig in shaping the concept. He also mentions difficulties and disagreements regarding its exposition. He nevertheless emphasises (1993: 363) that, despite the various differences, there is broad agreement on, amongst others, the following proposition:

'Art 1(1) BL guarantees in principle the legal equality of all humans. In so doing it prohibits every form of systematic discrimination or humiliation.'

If legal equality is guaranteed by art 1(1)'s provision that 'human dignity shall be inviolable' then human worth must in principle at least, be the *tertium comparationis* (in Dürig's words) or the 'object' against which the appropriateness of the attributive term (equal or equality) is to be judged, as argued in Chapter 2.

Rabe (2001: 169) in his comparative study on 'Equality, Affirmative Action, and Justice' states the following in sketching the background to art 3's (GBL) terms:

'The interpretation that the concept of human dignity is the primary value of the Basic Law also influences the right to equality as both rights have an interdependence. This view is carried over to the understanding that human dignity is the core principle of the right to equality as well as forming the foundation of the normative value of the Basic Law. In this sense the equality provision requires that each person is guaranteed equal dignity.'

Werner Heun (2004: 413 Rn 15) expressly follows Hofmann (1993) above, and in similar vein states it to be uncontested that

> 'the principle of equality is closely connected to the guarantee of human worth and the right to the development of the human personality, and in this respect is included in the protection of art79(3) GBL'.[106]

According to Heun (2004: 414 Rn 18) the point of departure for the interpretation and understanding of the equality provisions must be the formal-logistic structure of equality. In contradistinction to identity, equality brings difference to the fore. Equality connotes a '*relationship between different persons or things* that is to be established in an equality assessment'. Therefore the equality assessment 'can only ever make a statement with regard to particular common features, a *tertium comparationis*'. This equality assessment is a prerequisite for determining unequal treatment.

Starck (2005: art 3(1) Rn 18), in relation to art 3(1) of the GBL comments approvingly:

> 'Dürig has, by virtue of the statements in the Basic Law emphasizing the value of the human person, set out a long list of necessary prohibitions on differentiation (*notwendige Differenzierungsverbote*), most of which flow from the guarantee of human worth or other constitutional guarantees like equal legal capacity, equal protection of the law, an equal hearing according to the law, an equal guarantee of the minimum needs for human existence, etc.'

At the same time Starck also points out that the guarantees of the freedom rights are equal for all, but that this 'does not mean factual equality' nor does it 'prohibit differentiation in the limitation of fundamental rights ...'.

In regard to the basic meaning of equality and non-discrimination, I refer also, although not necessarily in this order, to Sachs (1987),[107] Sachs (2007(a)),[108] Sachs (2007(b)), Höfling (2007),[109] Osterloh (2007)[110] and to certain of Prof Sachs' writings in English.[111]

In his commentary on art 3(1), Osterloh (2007: Rn 1) accepts the necessity of having a *tertium comparationis* when considering matters of equality and inequality:

[106] Article 79(3) provides:
'Amendments to this Basic Law affecting the division of the Federation into Länder, their participation in the legislative process, or the principles laid down in Articles 1 and 20 shall be prohibited.'

[107] This work, entitled *Grenzen des Diskriminierungsverbots* (*Limits to the Prohibition against Discrimination*) is based on the author's *Habilitationsschrift.*

[108] The 2007 ed of his *Grundgesetz Kommentar.*

[109] Being his commentary on art 1 of the GBL in Sachs (2007(a)).

[110] Being his commentary on art 3 of the GBL in Sachs (2007(a)).

[111] Such as Sachs (1998(a)), and Sachs and Biskup (2003). Other works in English by Sachs include Sachs (1997), Sachs (1998(a)), Sachs (1998(b)), Sachs (2004), Sachs (2005) and Sachs (2007(c)).

> 'One never encounters two identical persons, nor two identical set of facts, but only ever different persons and different factual situations which are comparable from one or more specified points of view ("tertium comparationis").'

He also (Rn 3) points out that what art 1(1) requires is not the blind 'formal' equal treatment of all persons, which is in any event impossible in an organised society, nor mere equal treatment under general statutory provisions, but rather the 'equal and unequal treatment of persons by the development and consistent application of *just comparative criteria*; all persons are, both in their communality and in their uniqueness, equal before the law and to be respected by it'. Osterloh (2007: Rn 5) also appreciates that this *tertium comparationis* has to be found in a value outside the general equality clause.

Professor Isensee (2006: 216) is also quite clear, at least as far as the structural dogmatics of the GBL are concerned, that 'human worth forms the basis of constitutional freedom and equality'.

Sachs and Biskup (2003: 2), writing in English, state:

> 'Since the equality rule as part of the Basic l Law is intimately connected with human dignity (Article 1(1) and justice (as an essential element of the material law state, Art 20), it is in its core content also protected against constitutional amendments by the so-called eternity clause of Article 79(3).'

They also (2003: 3) point out that art 3(1) is not to be taken literally as somewhat dubiously stating that human beings '*are* equal' but 'rather prescribes their treatment according to the demands of the equality rule'. Equality is not only guaranteed *before* the law (ie regarding its application) but the rule today is also held 'to imply equality "*of the law*" (ie the equality of the normative contents themselves)'.

The failure to appreciate that *equality* and *non-discrimination* cannot be used, logically, in a predicative sense, but only attributively, has also led certain German scholars into difficulties and caused them to ask whether these concepts are not semantically empty.[112]

Despite this strong dogmatic background, the BVerfG has not, it seems to me, explicitly adopted human worth (dignity) as the *tertium comparationis* with regard to which equality or discrimination has to be adjudged for purpose of art 3(1), as opposed to art 3(3) of the GBL. In this regard the following comments of Sachs and Biskup (2003: 4–5) are important, and worth quoting fully:

> 'The main problem of Article 3(1) is, rather, that the general equality rule does not tell what trait or aspect is to be considered the essential one in a given case; the criterion applicable to the comparison, the *tertium comparationis* remains open. Article 3(1) does not indicate under what circumstances one person, group or situation is to be considered equal to another person, group of persons or situation. The Court has been fully aware of this lack of substantive criteria and has tried to promote clarity by advancing various

[112] See, for example, Podlech (1971: 77ff) and Henkel (1977: 395–401).

methods of determining equality. From the start, the Court took recourse to the criterion of arbitrariness. Because this proved to be unsatisfactory for adequately implementing the general equality rule, the Court developed various standards of rationality in specific contexts. In 1980 then, the Court further refined the criteria for determining equality by advancing the so-called new formula, which has since been used as an alternative standard to the old formula of non-arbitrariness.' (Footnotes and internal references omitted.)

However, human worth as *tertium comparationis* claims its place again under art 3(3) of the GBL and will be discussed in paragraph *(d)* below.

(c) The so-called Willkürverbot (prohibition against arbitrariness)

At first blush the *Willkürverbot*, a doctrine developed by the BVerfG, might appear to depart from the idea that human worth is the touchstone whereby equal treatment or its correlative discrimination, is to be evaluated. I will argue that on a proper understanding of its role in German equality jurisprudence, the *Willkürverbot* does not in fact do so.

The German Constitutional Court has, in BVerfGE 1, 208 (233) characterised art 3(1) as a supra-positivist fundamental legal principle.

Professor Herzog[113] (1996: Rn 2–4) points out that from its inception the BVerfG recognised that there were no two persons and no two factual situations that were in all respects equal. Article 3(1) was treated as the general equality provision that embodied a general equality of treatment principle. As far as the substantive content of art 3(1) was concerned it came, under the influence of Swiss examples and the ideas of Gerhard Leibholz, to be equated with a general constitutional prohibition against arbitrariness (a so-called *Willkürverbot*). Thus, in 1951, in BVerfGE 1, 14 at 52, it was held in relation to art 3(1) that:

> 'The equality clause is infringed when, in respect of statutory differentiation or equal treatment, no rational ground arising from the nature of the matter or some other plausible factual ground can be advanced.'

Herzog (1996: Rn 3) points out that:

> 'Whether it was a question of the unequal treatment of similar cases or the equal treatment of dissimilar cases, the determining factor was the establishing of *substantial grounds* for this treatment; *failure* to do so was equated with impermissible arbitrariness. From the beginning the BVerfG employed the concept of arbitrariness not in a subjective, and hence reprehensible sense, but simply in the sense of *objective arbitrariness*.'

Equating the general equality provision with a mere prohibition of arbitrariness became problematic, the more so as the freedom rights — and in particular the provisions of art 2(1), which parallels art 3(1) — came to be developed and given greater value in the jurisprudence of the BVerfG (Herzog 1996: Rn 3).

[113] Dr Herzog was not only a judge (1983–1987) and later President (1987–1994) of the German Federal Constitutional Court, but also President of the Federal Republic of Germany itself (1994–1999).

Accordingly, from 1980 onwards, a so-called *new formula* (*neue Formel*) came to be developed and was formulated by the Constitutional Court as follows in BVerfGE 55, 72 at 88:

> 'This constitutional norm demands that all persons be treated equally before the law. Accordingly this fundamental right is in the first instance infringed when categories of persons to whom this right accrues ("Normaddressaten") are treated differently from other categories of persons, although no differences exist between these groups of *such nature and such weight* ("von solcher Art und solchem Gewicht") that would justify such unequal treatment.'

Commenting on the above passage Herzog (1996: Rn 6) says the following:

> 'The substantive *difference* between this New Formulation and the customary arbitrariness formula is obvious. Whereas the latter would permit governmental equal or unequal treatment when *any* rational ground could be proffered, the new formulation establishes a relationship between the degree of equal (or unequal) treatment, and the rational justificatory ground; this ground must be of *such a nature* and *such weight* that it can justify the extent of the state action — it must, in short, also be of sufficient weight with regard to the citizen.'

This in fact means that the proportionality (*Verhältnismäßigkeit*) test has to be applied.

It is not farfetched — Herzog argues — to suggest a parallel with art 5 (which deals with the various forms of freedom of expression). There too, the rights in art 5(1) (enumerating these various rights) do not defer to just any competing legal interest (*Rechtsgut*) but only to one which is sufficiently weighty. Moreover the current claim that the proportionality principle has been introduced into art 3(1) is not lightly to be dismissed. It is clear, according to Herzog, that the new formulation has become a fixed element of constitutional jurisprudence. Herzog (1996: Rn 9) suggests that the new formulation might only be applied to comparisons of classes of persons and not to individuals.

It seems to me that Herzog (1996: Rn 29) also proceeds from the standpoint (although not expressly so stated) that equality cannot be used logically in a predicative sense, and that a breach of equality has to be determined with reference to some other relationship. He speaks of an 'if-then schema' in comparison with some other relationship. He also makes the important point, established by BVerfG jurisprudence, that there can be 'no equality in injustice'.

Sachs and Biskup (2003: 5–6) have the following to say concerning the old and the new arbitrariness formulations:

> 'According to the standard of non-arbitrariness the general equality rule is violated only if no reasonable justification for the differentiation can be found. In the absence of such a justification the act is qualified [presumably "characterised" is meant] as arbitrary. When evaluating reasonability the Court has shown deference towards legislative discretion. Thus the Court has refused to interfere if the only "mistake" to be detected has been that

> the legislature did not choose the most suitable or just solution among several possible solutions.
>
> ...
>
> The standard of non-arbitrariness suffers from a lack of substantive content. As time went by, the jurisprudence of the Court developed additional criteria to fill the gap. Three main approaches can be identified. For one, the Court turns to evaluations deriving from or simply made in other parts of the Basic Law to determine what elements are the relevant ones for the necessary comparisons (external standards; infra 2.1.), secondly, it makes reference to principles inherent to the equality rule, to the subject matter before it or the inner system of the regulation in question (internal standards; infra 2.2.). In a more recent development (since 1980), which has proved to be of the utmost importance ever since, the Court makes use of a (still so-called) new formula which makes the degree of scrutiny dependent on the extent to which personal traits or other basic rights of the persons concerned are affected (infra 2.3.).'

As far as the so-called external standards are concerned Sachs and Biskup (2003: 7) point out, inter alia, that

> 'in accordance with the general tendency of the Basic Law to provide the basic rights to all people (or at least all Germans) alike, the Court — even before the dawn of the "new formula" — has applied stricter standards of scrutiny to differential treatments when they concerned interests protected by other basic rights'.

This approach has been applied to cases concerning the protection of marriage and the family,[114] freedom of science,[115] freedom of expression and art,[116] and to freedom to practise a profession.[117] Sachs and Biskup (2003: 7 n 28) make the

---

[114] Article 6(1) in its relevant part provides:

> 'Marriage and the family shall enjoy the special protection of the state.'

See BVerfGE 13, 290 (298 et seq), in which the Court held that for the taxation of company earnings, a salary paid to the wife of the company-owner has to be treated like the salary of any other employee.

[115] Article 5(3), which provides:

> 'Art and scholarship, research, and teaching shall be free. The freedom of teaching shall not release any persons from allegiance to the constitution.'

See BVerfGE 35, 79 (131), in which the Court held that regulations concerning the internal order of Universities have to grant tenured professors 'decisive influence' in all matters concerning research and may not treat all members of the university alike.

[116] Article 5(1), which, in its relevant part, provides:

> 'Every person shall have the right freely to express and disseminate his opinions in speech, writing and pictures and to inform himself without hindrance from generally accessible sources.'

See also art 5(3) and BVerfGE 36, 321 (330, 331), in which the Court held that a decision to tax music records at the full VAT rate (and not at a reduced rate) was not a violation of the right to equality.

[117] Article 12(1), which provides as follows:

> 'All Germans shall have the right freely to choose their occupation or profession, their place of work, and their place of training. The practice of an occupation or profession may be regulated by or pursuant to a law.'

(In passing it is interesting to note that s 22 of the South African Constitution provides thus:

> 'Every citizen has the right to choose their trade, occupation or profession freely. The practice of a trade, occupation or profession may be regulated by law.' The close similarity is not co-incidental.)

See BVerfGE 37, 342 (353 et seq) in which the Court held that conditions for the Bar examination could not be changed in a way that disadvantaged certain candidates compared to those taking the examination after a certain date, because passing the Bar examination was a prerequisite for a career in the legal profession.

further point that 'sometimes the Court referred to the area of life concerned and thus implicitly considered interests protected by other basic rights within its scrutiny of differential treatments'.[118]

The influence of human worth in this context can be seen in the *Second Transsexual* case (BVerfGE 88, 87). In an earlier case the Court had declared unconstitutional a statutory provision prohibiting persons younger than 25 years from having a sex-change operation. In the *Second Transsexual* case the Court was concerned with a provision which prohibited transsexual persons younger than 25 years from having their first names officially changed if they had not yet undergone a sex-change operation. This provision was held to be inconsistent with art 3(1) of the GBL and invalid. In an important passage at 97 the Court stated the following:

> 'According to these standards a strict scrutiny (*strenge Prüfung*) ... [of the statutory provision in question] is essential. The age barrier for name changes constitutes a differentiation that relates to personal characteristics and impacts substantially on the general personality right. Art 2(1), in conjunction with Art 1(1) [ie the basic acknowledgment and protection of human worth], protects the strictly intimate personal sphere of life, in particular the intimate and sexual areas ... and guarantees to individuals the right of determining for themselves on which occasions and within which limits they manifest the personal facts of their lives. The Act on Transsexuality serves to protect these legal objects.'

(d) Article 3(3): The enumerated grounds (Merkmale),[119] on the basis of which disadvantaging (discrimination) (benachteiligt werden) or advantaging (bevorzugt werden) is prohibited

(i) The enumerated grounds constitute a closed list

The grounds on which discrimination or advantaging is prohibited under art 3(3), first sentence, are 'sex, parentage, race, language, homeland and origin, faith, or religious or political opinions'. Article 3(3), second sentence, further provides that '[no] person shall be disfavoured because of disability'. Whereas the forbidden grounds of discrimination listed in s 9(3) of the South African Constitution *do not* constitute a closed list,[120] it is important to note that the grounds on which 'favouring' or 'disfavouring' is prohibited in art 3(3) of the GBL *certainly do* constitute such a closed number.[121] The Federal Labour Court

---

[118] See BVerfGE 25, 269 (292) and BVerfGE 35, 348 (357).

[119] Literally, 'characteristics'.

[120] The enumerated 'listed' grounds are prefixed by the word 'including' so that the 'listed' grounds do not constitute a closed category; see *Hoffmann v South African Airways* above, n 22, following on judgments on s 8(2) of the interim Constitution in cases such as *Prinsloo v Van der Linde* (above, n 3) paras 27–28; and *Harksen v Lane* (above, n 3) para 46.

[121] The wording of GBL art 3(3) and see also Dürig (1973a: art 3(3), Rn 27, 28). Sachs (2000: § 126 Rn 40 and n 51); Jarass and Pieroth (2006: art 3, Rn 120); and the judgment of the Federal Labour Court in BAGE 61, 151–161.

has expressly held, in the case of an employee suing his employer for disclosing his positive HIV status, that reliance could not be placed on art 3(3), in view of the fact that the employee's situation was not covered by the catalogue of characteristics enumerated in art 3(3). The Court held that 'this catalogue was definitive and could not be extended by means of analogical interpretation'.[122]

Dürig (1973a: Rn 27) explains this, as well as the interrelationship between art 3(3) and 3(1), well:

> 'The catalogue of characteristics (*Merkmale*) in Art3(3) is definitive. But definitive only in the sense of constituting a minimum guarantee against discrimination. This means that differentiations based on other characteristics are not to be tested against Art 3(3) but in every case against Art 3(1) [see 3.3 below]. Although, for example, the differentiating characteristic of nationality is quite clearly not included in Art 3(3), it is not excluded from equality scrutiny. It gets "gathered up" ("*aufgefangen*") by Art 3(1), that can for instance entirely prohibit grounds of exclusion [on the basis of nationality] for which there would be no ground under Art 3(3)....
>
> Conversely, one cannot simply extend the characteristics in Art 3(3) by analogy, and thereby bring extensions like this under the stringent provisions of Art 3(3) that may only be departed from in exceptional cases, and thereby make entirely equivalent the "*Interdependence*" between Art 3(1) and its concretisations [in art 3(3)].'

In challenging a differentiating provision, one's first line of attack would be under art 3(3), and only if one were unable to bring the grounds of differentiation under one or more of the characteristics enumerated in art 3(3), would one rely on the *Willkürverbot* (literally the prohibition against arbitrariness) under art 3(1). If an infringement of the *Willkürverbot* is established, and accordingly it is found that there has been unequal treatment of a person, a strict application of the proportionality test must still take place to establish whether the infringement can be justified.

Dürig (1973: Rn 34–35) also links the art 3(3) characteristics to freedom in an interesting way and usefully distinguishes two categories of freedom:

> '(aa) On the one hand is the *freedom* to *be* different. Sex, parentage, race, and origin are characteristics that humans have from birth (in the case of a homeland it is the rule). Discrimination on the grounds of these inborn characteristics is directed at the fate (*Schicksal*) of persons, who *cannot be* anything else. What is protected is the freedom to be able *to be different* in *equality* (also without discrimination). ...
> (bb) On the other, is the characteristic of *freedom* to *remain* different. Humans can fundamentally decide on their language, their belief; their religious and political views. In particular: even when speech, belief, religious and political opinions arise from a person's origins and from the upbringing that is formed thereby, this person has the freedom to jettison them. The coloured person remains a coloured person — but the atheist can become a Christian and vice versa....'

---

[122] BAGE 61, 151 (161). See also Dürig (1973a: Rn 27).

(ii) Discrimination ('disfavouring') on any of the grounds listed in art 3(3) is absolutely prohibited and is not subject to limitation ('Schranken')

I would suggest that the reason for this is because any infringement on the basis of the listed grounds would, from their very nature, impinge on human dignity and any limitation of dignity would be impermissible. Thus the underlying theme of art 3(3) read with art 1 comes to the fore, namely that fundamental equality relates to equality of dignity.

In this regard Sachs and Biskup (2003: 36), writing in English, state the following:

> 'The Court in its first major decision on Article 3(3) has pointed out that the founders of the constitution, because of historical experience, thought it necessary to introduce this special equality rule because the legislators could not be trusted to avoid the differentiations in question as being arbitrary. Therefore, the constitution wanted to positively deny that any differentiation referring to the forbidden traits could possibly be justifiable.[123] To fulfil this constitutional purpose, the anti-discrimination rules have to be understood as stipulating that all laws and regulations are made "without account" of forbidden traits, "regardless" of them; by this construction, every differentiation referring to the forbidden characteristics at all is strictly prohibited, regardless of what reason or purpose might be shown to be behind the (superficial) reference. While the Court in most cases has followed this reasoning and declared regulations making reference to a prohibited characteristic unconstitutional even though there may have been underlying non-discriminatory justifications for them, the jurisprudence has been somewhat inconsistent. There may be hope, though, that the matter is definitely settled, since the Court quite explicitly overruled its last deviating judgment, holding that any reference to a forbidden trait is interdicted, even if it is not designed towards a forbidden discrimination but primarily pursues other goals.'[124] (Certain of the footnotes omitted.)

In BVerfGE 3, 225, the case referred to in the first footnote in the text of the above extract, the BVerfG stated at 240:

> 'In the light of past experience the founders of the Basic Law considered it essential to prohibit differentiation on the grounds of "sex, parentage, race, language, homeland and origin, faith, or religious or political opinion" by means of a special constitutional provision. They clearly accepted that the impermissibility of these differentiations had not yet become so firmly rooted in the public mind that they could effectively be excluded through the general clause of art 3 (1) of the Basic Law alone. The political question, whether the inequalities mentioned in art 3(2) and 3(3) give rise to acceptable grounds for differentiation in law — with regard to which one knows from experience that different views are possible — must, from the perspective of constitutional validity, be answered in the negative.'

---

[123] BVerfG, 18 December 1953, BVerfGE 3, 225 (240).

[124] BVerfG, 28 January 1992, BVerfGE 85, 191 (206) in contrast to BVerfG, 8 April 1987, BVerfGE 75, 40 (70), confirmed in BVerfG, 27 November 1997, BVerfGE 97, 35 (43).

In BVerfGE 85, 191 (206) (the case referred to in the second footnote in the passage from Sachs and Biskup (2003: 36) quoted above) the Court held as follows:

> 'According to this constitutional provision [art 3(3) of the GBL] nobody may be favoured or disfavoured on account of their sex. This reinforces the general equality provision in Art 3(1) GBL, should the legislator place restrictions on the freedom of development therein protected. In principle sex — like the other characteristics mentioned in Sub-article 3 — may not be employed as a ground [literally "connecting factor"] for unequal treatment by the law. This is also the case even where a statutory provision is not aimed at unequal treatment prohibited by Article 3(3), but has in the first place a different purpose. (Clarification of BVerfGE 75, 40 (70).)

With the added 'clarification' the Court explicitly overruled an earlier decision holding that discrimination under art 3(3) of the GBL could only be established if a prohibited ground was the rationale or purpose of the differentiating treatment. In BVerfGE 97, 35 (43) the BVerfG, having quoted the above passage with approval, added the following:

> 'According to the jurisprudence [of this Court] the characteristic of sex can also be implicated when a provision, though formulated in a sex-neutral manner, impacts predominantly on women, and this can be traced to natural or social differences between the sexes.'

While it therefore seems that the BVerfG has closed the door on justifications based on the argument that, whatever its discriminatory effect, the purpose of the provision was non-discriminatory, Sachs and Biskup (2003: 35) point out that ingenious ways have been found to justify differentiations made on the prohibited grounds, notwithstanding the fact that the wording of the discriminatory prohibitions appears to be quite unequivocal. One of the most important has been in situations of so-called 'non-comparability':

> 'The notion of the non-comparability of cases has been used to justify differential treatment, particularly if there is no common denominator for a set of circumstances as applied to groups of people falling within the prohibition, or if the similarity is de minimis.... The doctrine has generally remained limited to gender related differences....'

Heun (2004: art 3(3) Rn 118) is clearly of the view that discrimination on an Art 3(3) ground cannot be justified:

> 'Art 3(3) GBL embodies a differentiation prohibition. But according to the text what is prohibited is disadvantaging and advantaging, not mere differentiation. And inasmuch as every differentiation [according to the art 3(3) characteristics] ultimately gives rise to disadvantaging or advantaging, therefore there can be no limitation (Einschränkungen) of this differentiation prohibition.'

He refers in this regard to BVerfGE 63, 181 (195) where it was decided that a particular provision relating to the marital property regime was inconsistent with art 3(2) of the GBL and that a limitation of the art 3(2) provision was not justifiable. This was followed in BVerfGE 68, 384 (390). In BVerfGE 71, 224 (228f) it was held that the provisions of §606b Nr 1 ZPO [the Civil Procedure Act] were inconsistent with art 3(2) of the GBL to the extent that the jurisdiction of German courts with regard to divorcing mixed German-foreign spouses depends on whether the divorce is recognised in the husband's country of domicile. At pp 228–9 it was pointed out that art 3(2) of the GBL was a concretisation of art 3(1) and prohibited sexual difference from being recognised as a permissible ground for differentiation in the law. The differentiation in question had regard only to the law of the husband's domicile, and was in no way concerned with objective biological and functional (employment relevant) differences between men and women. Apart from having regard to these possible grounds of justification, no other grounds were considered.

Jürgen Salzwedel (1964: 346), dealing with art 3(3), puts it quite simply: 'Discrimination means to disadvantage in such a way as to harm the personality.' He further points out (1964: 347) that art 3(3) consequently stands in a much closer relationship to art 1(1) — 'Human worth' — and art 2(1) — 'personality' — than art 3(1) does:

> 'The prohibition of discrimination in fact puts into concrete terms these personality guarantees and at the same time serves to qualify the general equality principles. In so far as differentiation impinges on the most intimate core of the personality, human worth itself, even the legislature, seeking to amend the Basic Law is prohibited by Art 79(3) from so doing.[125]
>
> ...
>
> By s 3(3) the sovereign state is once again expressly prohibited from violating personality rights, which it does by treating similar factual situations differently on account of personal characteristics.'

Professor Reinhold Zippelius (1989: 10–11), after sketching the historical background of the equality provision, and in particular the influence on its development of the theological notion that every person is born equal in and through the image of God, states the following:

> 'Standing at the end of this development is the constitutional principle, namely, that every person stands with equal human worth, with equal rights, before the forum of the law, irrespective of whether they are of high or modest birth, Catholic or Protestant, Jew or Christian, white or black, man or woman. Behind each of the non-discrimination provisions in Art 3(3) stands the historical surmounting of previous discrimination.'

In dealing with the tension between equality and freedom Zippelius (1989: 19) clarifies the relationship between human worth and equality:

---

[125] It is unnecessary, for present purposes, to examine the complex jurisprudence regarding the circumstances under which state restriction of any aspect of human worth constitutes an impermissible attempt to contravene art 79(3) or whether it is (merely) a permissible limitation of some associated right capable of limitation.

> 'It is part of the dialectic of the equality provisions that, in addition to guaranteeing equal respect for human worth, equal treatment without regard to religious or political views, they also guarantee an equal freedom to be different from others. Equal respect for human worth means guaranteeing the self-regulation of all persons, also their peculiarities, and their right to develop differently from others, but also their duty to stand up for themselves, that means the chance to be out of the ordinary.'

An interesting contribution affirming that human dignity lies at the heart of equality and non-discrimination is by the distinguished German public lawyer Prof Jochen Frowein[126] (1998). In this article,[127] although the discussion concentrates on the alleged duty of the state to take positive steps to prevent discrimination, the point is clearly made that the enumerated instances of prohibited discrimination in art 3(3) are all cases where human dignity is injured.

Referring to one of the earliest judgments of the BVerfG (BVerfGE1, 97 (104)) Frowein (1998: 159) makes the point that in this judgment protection was directly required against discrimination 'that injured human worth (*Menschenwürde verletzt*)'. 'Moreover', says Frowein, 'the connection between the prohibition of discrimination in Art 3 (3) and human worth is also generally acknowledged.'

Starck (2005: art 3(3) Rn 366) points out that art 3(3) embodies

> 'particular differentiation prohibitions (*besondere Differenzierungsverbote*) that concretise and particularise the general idea of equality, while — from the point of view of the legal order — particular human differences, whether natural, historical or arising from freely made decisions, are regarded as being irrelevant'.

The importance of human dignity for the understanding of the prohibition of specific types of discrimination under art 3(3), is emphasised by Starck (2005: art 3(3) Rn 367):

> 'This particular emphasis of the equality injunctions in respect of typical factual inequalities of human beings that mold their identity, is founded on the idea of human worth, whose protection and respect the Basic Law prescribes. This clearly rejects the idea of any so-called species identity, which only the members of a particular origin or race can have, and to which legal consequences are attached, in conflict with the idea that all who bear the human image have worth.'[128]

---

[126] Who, for some years, was also Deputy-President of the European Human Rights Commission and for many years a Director of the Max Planck Institute for Foreign Comparative and International Law in Heidelberg.

[127] The title of which can be translated as 'The overcoming of discrimination as an Art 3(3) GBL directive to the State'.

[128] 'species identity' is here used in a very particular German sense as referring to the Nazi argument that Jews in fact belonged to a different 'species' than Aryan Germans. Equality only enured, so the Nazi argument ran, to the German Aryan 'species'. Unless otherwise qualified, I use 'species' to indicate the human species to which all human beings belong.

Osterloh (2007: Rn 236), citing Dürig (1973a: Rn 1) and Starck (2005: 236),[129] accepts implicitly that human dignity is the *tertium comparationis*, but also points to the close link between human worth (dignity) and freedom:

> 'By making more concrete the general equality provision, the non-discrimination prohibition shares its general *purpose*.... But in the literature on the topic the very close relationship between the first sentence of Art 3(3)[130] and the protection of human worth is emphasized. The concrete available means for harming this worth, that has led to the world-wide recognition of the prohibition of discrimination, has been and still is the threat to and the infringement of freedom. Therefore, just as in the case of the general equality provision, this prohibition also serves in particular as a related protection of freedom with regard to particularly threatened personal characteristics and behaviour. The linked purpose of these constitutional protections of equal freedom must therefore also determine the interpretation of the prohibition of discrimination.'

At the outset of Dürig's commentary in Maunz/Dürig on art 3(3) (Dürig 1973a: art 3(3), Rn 1 n 1) he confirms that human worth (dignity) is the *tertium comparationis* in equality jurisprudence. As appears from its provisions quoted above, this sub-article prohibits discrimination or preferential treatment on ('*wegen*') a number of specified grounds. These grounds were chosen because, having regard to their specific nature, any discrimination based on any of them would infringe human dignity. Dürig (1973a: art 3(3), Rn 1) explains the clear link between the art 3(3) prohibitions and human dignity (worth):

> **'I. Art 3 Sub-Art 3 in the Value- and Entitlement system of the Fundamental Rights**
>
> 1. In the *value system* of the fundamental rights, the listed grounds of differentiation ..., as in the case of Sub-Art (2) — means that the general value of human equality has been *put into more concrete terms*. For purposes of this concretisation, Art 3(3), with regard to the general prohibition of discrimination in Art 3(1), places an *emphasis on a value*, in as much as it forbids in principle differentiation "*on*" ("*wegen*") any of the listed grounds.
>   (a) The Basic Law has, in this *equality injunction*, emphasised particular and *typical* inequalities on the assumption that advantaging, or discriminating, on the basis of these specified differences in human existence ("*Sein*") or conduct, in principle violates the claim to human dignity. In so doing the Basic Law once again has express regard to Art 1(1).
>   (b) In this concretization of the general equality clause, the reference to the basis of the fundamental constitutional value system might appear to be unnecessary when, as here — in a system of seamless protection of values — one already traces back the general equality of all persons to the respect and protection of human worth.... With an interpretation of the general equality clause like this, one would almost inevitably have come to the conclusion that there is a form of limitation on legislative discretion, like the one that has in fact been expressed in

[129] A reference to the passage quoted above.
[130] Ie the prohibition of discriminating or favouring on the grounds therein stated.

Sub-Art 3. However, the case law has already shown us that the courts initially took this specifically articulated prohibition on differentiation to be purely and simply a superfluous repetition of Sub-Art (1), so that — despite Sub-Art (3) — discrimination following on any objective evaluation was permitted (typically [the Supreme Court decision in] BGHZ 30, 50).

(c) One must therefore regard this concretisation of the general equality provisions as *necessary*. Incidentally, one must assume that without this *categorical* prohibition of discrimination the direct relationship between human worth and the right to equality of the persons with the differentiating characteristics mentioned in Art 3(3) would not have been so *sharply* recognised, as their codification in the Basic Law compels one to do.

(d) In particular we learn from the experience of an unfortunate *past* that only an express prohibition against prejudicing or favouring on the grounds of the distinguishing characteristics specified in Sub-Art 3 — that refers back directly to Art 1(1) — can protect one against "*Jacobin logic*".[131] It was this logic that — as an indication of a "change of meaning of fundamental rights" — saw the substance of a *type of equality* in the biological similarity through blood of the German people, and demanded the isolation of alien biological elements.[132]

In this respect the prohibition on discrimination in Sub-Art (3) is the *answer* to an historically realised threat to, and destruction of, human dignity, and the drafters of the Basic Law also saw it as such a reaction. But it was also clear to the creators of our Basic Law, that this provision was actually only an additional "accentuation," by means of which the general equality clause would be informed by a constitutionally *conclusive* ("*zwingende*") *interpretation.*

(e) But in this way it becomes clear, however, that Sub-Art (3) does not — strictly speaking — signify a "newly created guarantee" which, together with other fundamental rights of historical origin could, if necessary, be added to a coherent system on the basis of an "interpretation of the Constitution as a whole". The point of departure is not the protection, historically demanded, of a recognised special right deemed worthy of protection. It is rather the restoration and preservation of the respect for human dignity as an answer to the despising of *all* human worth that — although it happened in the past and may be observed at present elsewhere

---

[131] In n 3 to his text, Dürig cites Leibholz, DVBl. 51, 193 ff. (198) for the expression, and adds: 'Unfortunately this is not only a thing of the past, for there are current omens when, for example, a race struggle ("*Kampf*") is replaced by a class war.'

[132] In n 4 to his text Dürig cites, as an example of this 'Jacobin logic', the following passage from the work of Prof Ernst Huber (1939: 260f) on the Constitution of the Great German Reich during the Nazi period, which argues for equality only amongst members of the 'volk species':

> 'Formal equality which would omit intrinsic differences or ignore them, cannot be authoritative for the legislature. The substantive equality of the law of the 'Volk' has taken its place, which originates from the experience of the (biological) species — and substantive equality of the 'Volk'. This new concept of equality makes it possible to distinguish, also in legislation, between a foreign species and one's own; whereas the relativism of earlier formal concepts also required equal treatment in such a case. The national socialist race legislation, the law against the formation of new political parties, the sterilization law — they all distance themselves from formal equality, in order that a true species ['völkischen'] equality may triumph.... It must be stressed however, that only a proper, internally essential differentiation like this is permissible.'

> — could occur with us (once again) when total hatred for our state and its Basic Law becomes virulent.' (All emphases in the original.)

Let this be a call to eternal vigilance.

It may be, as Sachs and Biskup (2003: 36) have pointed out in the passage already quoted, that there has been the odd case in which discrimination on a ground enumerated in art 3(3) of the GBL has been justified, but it would seem that the contemporary view is that this is not constitutionally permissible. In principle it would seem to me that, because of the *illimitable* protection given to the art 1 guarantee of human dignity, no discrimination on an art 3(3) ground that impinged on human dignity could be justified. It is also difficult to see how any discrimination on an art 3(3) ground could not infringe human dignity, for the reasons given by the German scholars I have cited. I have, despite my own researches and extensive enquiries, been unable to find a case in which discrimination on an art 3(3) ground has been held justified, despite infringing human dignity.

4.3 CANADIAN LAW

Section 15(1) of the Canadian Charter of Rights and Freedoms (the Charter) provides that

> '[e]very individual is equal before and under the law and has the right to the equal protection and equal benefit of the law without discrimination and, in particular, without discrimination based on race, national or ethnic origin, colour, religion, sex, age or mental or physical disability'.

It is trite law that s 15(1) also prohibits discrimination on grounds 'analogous' to those listed;[133] and that the listed and analogous grounds are the only ones covered by its provisions.[134] In this respect s 15(1) resembles the South African Constitution, but not the German Basic Law.

Section 1 of the Charter provides for a general limitation clause in the following terms:

> 'The Canadian Charter of Rights and Freedoms guarantees the rights and freedoms set out in it subject only to such reasonable limits prescribed by law as can be demonstrably justified in a free and democratic society.'

In order to trace the route that the Canadian Supreme Court has followed to establish the meaning it currently attaches to equality and non-discrimination, and the vital role that human dignity plays in understanding and applying these concepts, one need go no further, for my purposes, than considering the all-

[133] See, for example, *Law v Canada (Minister of Human Resources Development)*, 170 DLR (4th) 1 [1999], paras 23, 28, 33, 37, 39.

[134] As Professor Peter Hogg (2005: 47) notes: '[T]he restriction to listed and analogous grounds has persisted to the present day and is obviously a permanent feature of s 15 exegesis.'

embracing and exhaustive judgment of the Court, per Iacobucci J, in the leading case of *Law*.[135] One of the objectives of the judgment was to achieve a 'synthesis' of the 'various articulations' of the proper approach to s 15(1) analysis that had taken place in the *Andrews*, *Egan* and *Miron* judgments, among others.[136]

Another crucially important task the Court set itself was 'to summarize and comment upon' the general consensus that had been reached 'regarding the basic principles' in the development of the Court's equality jurisprudence and 'to summarize and comment upon these basic principles, in order to provide a set of guidelines for courts that are called upon to analyze a discrimination claim under the Charter'.[137]

It is of course impossible to capture all the complexities and nuances of this judgment in a brief summary. Nevertheless I believe one can responsibly and fairly state that in *Law* the Court clearly held, in effect, that human dignity is the criterion of attribution (*tertium comparationis* in German parlance) for determining what the meaning of equality and non-discrimination is under s 15(1) of the Charter. It did not use the term 'criterion of attribution' (or any similar analytical expression) nor did it expressly deal with the grammatico-logical impossibility of defining equality (or non-discrimination) without reference to an extraneous substantive, with regard to which equality or discrimination is asserted, as I argue throughout. Yet this is in truth the *result* achieved in *Law*'s case, as demonstrated by the following passages from the judgment:

> '[51] All of these statements share several key elements. It may be said that the purpose of s 15(1) is to prevent the violation of essential human dignity and freedom through the imposition of disadvantage, stereotyping, or political or social prejudice, and to promote a society in which all persons enjoy equal recognition at law as human beings or as members of Canadian society, equally capable and equally deserving of concern, respect and consideration. Legislation which effects differential treatment between individuals or groups will violate this fundamental purpose where those who are subject to differential treatment fall within one or more enumerated or analogous grounds, and where the differential treatment reflects the stereotypical application of presumed group or personal characteristics, or otherwise has the effect of perpetuating or promoting the view that the individual is less capable, or less worthy of recognition or value as a human being or as a member of Canadian society. Alternatively, differential treatment will not likely constitute discrimination within the purpose of s 15(1) where it does not violate the human dignity or freedom of a person or group in this way, and in particular where the differential treatment also assists in ameliorating the position of the disadvantaged within Canadian society.
>
> [52] ... No single word or phrase can fully describe the content and purpose of s 15(1). However, in the articulation of the purpose of s 15(1) just provided on the basis of past

[135] Above, n 133.
[136] Id para 39.
[137] Id paras 4–5.

> cases, a focus is quite properly placed upon the goal of assuring human dignity by the remedying of discriminatory treatment. [138]
>
> [75] ....
>
> The general theme, though, may be simply stated. *An infringement of s 15(1) of the Charter exists if it can be demonstrated that*, from the perspective of a reasonable person in circumstances similar to those of the claimant who takes into account the contextual factors relevant to the claim, the *legislative imposition of differential treatment has the effect of demeaning his or her dignity.*'[139] (Emphasis supplied.)

In the section of the judgment headed '*E. Summary of Guidelines*', the following was stated:

> 'In general terms, the purpose of s 15(1) is to prevent the violation of essential human dignity and freedom through the imposition of disadvantage, stereotyping, or political or social prejudice, and to promote a society in which all persons enjoy equal recognition at law as human beings or as members of Canadian society, equally capable and equally deserving of concern, respect and consideration.'[140]

In quoting these passages as constituting, for my purposes, the central finding of the Court, I am not losing sight of the cautionary remarks throughout the judgment regarding the prudence of articulating basic principles and not a rigid test which might run the risk of mechanical application.[141] What is, in a particular case, the correct balance between generality (principle) and specificity (the factual totality of the individual case) is one of the enduring challenges facing any court, to which there is no absolute answer. I am certain, however, that in *Law*'s case the Court had no choice but to recognise, in principle — albeit implicitly — that any normative legal reflection on equality and non-discrimination is impossible without answering the question '*with regard to what* are all humans equal and may they not be discriminated against?' The Court thus recognised, although only by implication, that the determination in principle of a criterion of attribution was unavoidable. This fully supports the main thesis of this Chapter. The Court also decided that human dignity (worth) was the appropriate criterion in question, thus bearing out the main contentions in both this Chapter and Chapter 2.

In describing s 15(1) as possibly the Charter's most difficult provision to interpret,[142] the Court was echoing the experiences of other jurisdictions. In my view many of the more fundamental difficulties are resolved or avoided once the logico-grammatical necessity for a criterion of attribution is recognised. In *Law*'s case examples of these alleged difficulties are furnished.

---

[138] Id paras 51–52.

[139] Id para 75.

[140] Id para 88(4).

[141] Id paras 5–6; 88 (the first part).

[142] Id para 2.

It is interesting to note that *Law*[143]confirmed that '[a] ground or grounds will not be considered analogous under s 15(1) unless it can be shown that differential treatment premised on the ground or grounds has the *potential to bring into play human dignity* ...'. (Emphasis supplied.) This is almost identical to the test laid down by the South African Constitutional Court in *Harksen*[144] for determining an analogous ground of unfair discrimination.

After referring to McIntyre J's observations in the *Andrews* case,[145] namely that the concept of equality is 'an elusive concept' and that 'more than any of the other rights and freedoms guaranteed in the *Charter*, it lacks precise definition', Iacobucci J himself observes that '[p]art of the difficulty in defining the concept of equality stems from its exalted status. The quest for equality expresses some of humanity's highest ideals and aspirations, which are by their nature abstract and subject to differing articulations.' The learned judge also observed that 'one of the difficulties in defining the concepts of "equality" and "discrimination" is the abstract nature of the words and the similarly abstract nature of words used to explain them'.[146]

I contend, however, that the problem is not with elusiveness or abstractness of concepts, lack of precision of definition or the exalted status of equality, but the failure to recognise the unavoidable necessity of having a criterion of attribution. As Prof Amartya Sen points out so simply in the passages quoted from his work in Chapter 2, section 2.9(*f*) above, the central question in the analysis of equality is 'equality of what', which arises from the empirical fact of pervasive human diversity at various levels and in multiple respects. Nor do I think that the selection of human dignity (worth) as the criterion of attribution for determining a legal understanding of equality and non-discrimination presents any intractable problems, or problems which the law has not previously faced with regard to other core concepts, and satisfactorily answered. In order to eliminate any chance of confusion, I need at this stage also to emphasise that the concept *tertium comparationis*, as used in relation to German jurisprudence,[147] is something *quite different* from the 'comparative concept' as used in *Law* with regard to comparative treatment of different persons, which relates to a different aspect of the enquiry:[148]

> '... [T]he equality guarantee is a comparative concept. Ultimately a court must identify differential treatment *as compared* to one or more other persons or groups. Locating

---

[143] Id para 93.

[144] *Harksen v Lane NO and Others* (above, n 3) para 53(b)(i): 'If it is not on a specified ground, then whether or not there is discrimination will depend on whether, objectively, the ground is based on attributes and characteristics which have the *potential* to impair human dignity of persons as human beings or to affect them adversely in a comparably serious manner.' (Emphasis supplied.)

[145] *Andrews v Law Society of British Columbia* [1989] 56 DLR (4th) 1.

[146] *Law*'s case (above, n 133) para 52, first sentence.

[147] As an equivalant for 'criterion of attribution'.

[148] Above, n 133 at para 56. See also paras 57–58, and 88, sub-para (6).

the comparator is necessary in identifying differential treatment and the grounds of the distinction.'

This is an analytical step prior to enquiring whether differential treatment constitutes discrimination, and it is this later enquiry that relates to the infringement or not of the value of human dignity.

Lastly, in this section, I must deal with the holding in *Law* that the focus of the enquiry to determine whether legislation, for example, has the effect of demeaning a claimant's dignity is *both* subjective and objective. In this regard the following, inter alia, was said:

> '[T[he focus of the discrimination inquiry is both subjective and objective: subjective in so far as the right to equal treatment is an individual right, asserted by a specific claimant with particular traits and circumstances; and objective in so far as it is possible to determine whether an individual claimant's equality rights have been infringed only by considering the larger context of the legislation in question, and society's past and present treatment of the claimant and of other persons or groups with similar characteristics or circumstances. The objective component means that it is not sufficient, in order to ground a s 15(1) claim, for a claimant to assert, without more, that his or her dignity has been adversely affected by a law.'[149]

Further:

> 'Although I stress that the inquiry into whether legislation demeans the claimant's dignity must be undertaken from the perspective of the claimant and from no other perspective, a court must be satisfied that the claimant's assertion that differential treatment imposed by legislation demeans his or her dignity is supported by an objective assessment of the situation.'[150]

And lastly:

> 'It is essential to stress that the appropriate perspective is not solely that of the "reasonable person" a perspective which could, through misapplication, serve as a vehicle for the imposition of *community prejudices*. The appropriate standard is subjective-objective. Equality analysis under the Charter is concerned with the perspective of a person in circumstances similar to those of the claimant, who is informed of and rationally takes into account the various contextual factors which determine whether an impugned law infringes *human dignity, as that concept is understood for purposes of s 15(1).*' (Emphasis supplied.)

In the first place I cannot see how an objective approach and a reasonable person can conceivably introduce 'community prejudices' because, as the last quotation makes clear, an infringement is decided on the basis of human dignity '*as that concept is understood for purposes of s 15(1)*'. It is a matter of constitutional construction. What does human dignity mean (using the appropriate

[149] Id para 59.
[150] Id para 60.

constitutional canons of construction) for purposes of s 15(1) in the context of the Charter as a whole? This can only be an objective approach. My more serious concern and disagreement is the fact that an objective-subjective approach, or the introduction of any form of subjectivity, is quite inconsistent and incompatible with the objective principle of constitutional invalidity.

The South African Constitutional Court, in *Ferreira v Levin (1)*,[151] has endorsed the objective principle of constitutional invalidity and in doing so has stated the following:

> '[26] The answer to the first question is that the enquiry is an objective one. A statute is either valid or "of no force and effect to the extent of its inconsistency". The subjective positions in which parties to a dispute may find themselves cannot have a bearing on the status of the provisions of a statute under attack. The Constitutional Court, or any other competent Court for that matter, ought not to restrict its enquiry to the position of one of the parties to a dispute in order to determine the validity of a law. The consequence of such a (subjective) approach would be to recognise the validity of a statute in respect of one litigant, only to deny it to another. Besides resulting in a denial of equal protection of the law, considerations of legal certainty, being a central consideration in a constitutional state, militate against the adoption of the subjective approach....
>
> [27] The Court's order does not invalidate the law; it merely declares it to be invalid. It is very seldom patent, and in most cases is disputed, that pre-constitutional laws are inconsistent with the provisions of the Constitution. It is one of this Court's functions to determine and pronounce on the invalidity of laws, including Acts of Parliament. This does not detract from the reality that pre-existing laws either remained valid or became invalid upon the provisions of the Constitution coming into operation. In this sense laws are objectively valid or invalid depending on whether they are or are not inconsistent with the Constitution. The fact that a dispute concerning inconsistency may only be decided years afterwards, does not affect the objective nature of the invalidity. The issue of whether a law is invalid or not does not in theory therefore depend on whether, at the moment when the issue is being considered, a particular person's rights are threatened or infringed by the offending law or not.
>
> [28] A pre-existing law which was inconsistent with the provisions of the Constitution became invalid the moment the relevant provisions of the Constitution came into effect....'

Consistently herewith the Court has held in the *Walker* case[152] that as far as the anti-discrimination provisions are concerned,

> 'both elements, discrimination and unfairness, must be determined objectively in the light of the facts of each particular case. This seems to me to be consistent not only with the language of the section, but also with the equality jurisprudence as it has been developed by this Court'.

[151] *Ferreira v Levin NO and Others; Vryenhoek and Others v Powell NO and Others* 1996 (1) SA 984 (CC) paras 26, 27 and 28. See also *Minister of Health and Another v New Clicks South Africa (Pty) Ltd and Others In re: Application for Declaratory Relief* 2006 (2) SA 311 (CC) (2006 (8) BCLR 872) para 15.

[152] Above, n 8 at paras 47–48, 73.

The same approach follows axiomatically if the offending statutory provision is passed after the Constitution has come into operation; it never achieves validity.

Under the German Basic Law a similar approach of objective invalidity is adopted. Schleich (1994: 220–221, Rn 344–345) puts it as follows:

> 'An unconstitutional law is, as the Federal Constitutional Court puts it, "inconsistent with the Basic Law and therefore invalid". An unconstitutional law is from its inception (ex tunc) and without need for any further constitutive act (ipso iure) inoperative.... The German view is that the Federal Constitutional Court does not annul a statute, [the Court] does not invalidate: it merely establishes the invalidity (in a declaratory way).'[153]

Sachs and Biskup (2003: 52) are to the same effect. See also BVerfGE 1, 14 (37) and BVerfGE 61, 149 (151).

In Canada the same principle is followed. As Professor Hogg (1992: s 55.1, 1242) puts it:

> 'This practice of "prospective overruling" is difficult to justify in theory, however attractive it may be in practice, and it has never been accepted by Canadian Courts. For a Canadian Court, *a constitutional restriction operates of its own force, even if judicial recognition of the fact has been delayed*.' (Emphasis supplied.)

See also *Re Edward v Edward*[154] and *R v Big M Drug Mart Ltd*,[155] where the following was stated:

> 'Any accused, whether corporate or individual, may defend a criminal charge by arguing that the law under which the charge is brought is constitutionally invalid. Big M is urging that the law under which it has been charged is inconsistent with s 2(a) of the Charter and by reason of s 52 of the Constitution Act, 1982, it is of no force or effect.
>
> ...
>
> The argument that the respondent, by reason of being a corporation, is incapable of holding religious beliefs and therefore incapable of claiming rights under s 2(a) of the Charter, confuses the nature of this appeal. A law which itself infringes religious freedom is, by that reason alone, inconsistent with s 2(a) of the Charter and it matters not whether the accused is a Christian, Jew, Muslim, Hindu, Buddhist, atheist, agnostic or whether an individual or a corporation. It is the nature of the law, not the status of the accused, that is in issue.'

I am accordingly constrained to disagree with the proposition that the test for the impairment of human dignity can be subjective, or both objective and subjective. A subjective test, whether subjective in whole or in part, is simply inconsistent with the principle of objective constitutional invalidity. As the justification for objective constitutional invalidity makes clear, invalidity (of a statutory provision, for example) occurs, or does not occur, at the moment when

---

[153] *Ferreira v Levin* (above, n 151) para 29.

[154] (1987) 39 DLR (4th) 654 (Sask CA) at 661–664.

[155] (1985) 13 CRR 64 at 80.

the constitutional provision takes effect (in the case of a pre-existing statutory provision) or when the statute would otherwise take effect (in the case of a post-constitutional statutory provision). Consequently the subjective state of mind of a particular complainant cannot, logically, determine the validity of the statutory provision in question. Whether or not an action impairs the human dignity of a person cannot depend on the intelligence or mental disposition or feelings of the claimant in question, for this would have the consequence of stripping mentally disabled human beings of their inherent human dignity (worth). When persons are deprived of the opportunity for personal self-fulfilment, or self-realisation, or for the unfolding of their personalities (crucially important aspects of human dignity) their dignity is impaired, and it is quite irrelevant whether — because of mental disability — they are subjectively unaware of the nature or extent of the self-fulfilment or personality unfolding (however limited that might be) they are capable of. Surely this is the consequence of inherent dignity and one of the great lessons to be learnt from German dignity jurisprudence. A child of three, who is deprived by racial discrimination from going to nursery school, suffers impairment to her human dignity, although she may be blissfully unaware of the impact that a deprivation like this would have on her intellectual, social and other development. I cannot see how subjectivity, even in part, can enter the picture when constitutional invalidity is to be determined.

Despite these reservations, the use (in effect) by the Canadian Supreme Court of human dignity in its equality jurisprudence as the criterion of attribution[156] is of great positive significance, particularly in British common-law systems, for the proper constitutional and legal understanding of equality and non-discrimination.

Despite the fact that subsequent decisions may have pointed out perceived difficulties with regard to a proper understanding of human dignity (worth), the (for my purposes) central holding in *Law*'s case, namely that '[a]n infringement of s 15(1) of the Charter exists if it can be demonstrated that ... the legislative imposition of differential treatment has the effect of demeaning [the complainant's] dignity',[157] has not been departed from. To date, however, the unavoidable necessity of establishing *some* third comparative factor for sound equality jurisprudence has not — as far as I have been able to establish — been explicitly recognised or considered.

Law's case has been applied and referred to in many subsequent cases, and human dignity applied as a determinative factor. The 2008 Supreme Court judgment in *R v Kapp*,[158] a case actually dealing with s 15(2), did not overrule *Law* in this regard, and indeed commended the judgment:[159]

---

[156] Without, of course, using this, or any other similar expression and without identifying the logico-grammatical problems in trying to use the word 'equality' predicatively.

[157] Id para 75.

[158] 294 DLR (4th) 1 [2008].

[159] Id para 20.

> 'The achievement of *Law* was its success in unifying what had become, since *Andrews*, a division in this Court's approach to s 15. *Law* accomplished this by reiterating and confirming *Andrews*' interpretation of s 15 as a guarantee of substantive, and not just formal, equality. Moreover, *Law* made an important contribution to our understanding of the conceptual underpinnings of substantive equality.'

Whatever difficulties the Court in *Kapp* might have experienced with the application of the *Law* judgment, it nowhere retracts its acceptance that *Law* made 'an important contribution to our understanding of the conceptual underpinnings of substantive equality'. This important contribution can surely be nothing else but *Law*'s conclusion, in substance, that the negative impact of the differential treatment (on a s 15(1) listed or analogous ground) on the human dignity of the complainant is what 'converts' mere *differentiation* into *discrimination.*

In reflecting on human dignity, *Kapp* went no further than explaining that what was involved in the s 15(1) guarantee was the *value* and not the *right* of human dignity, an interpretation with which I fully agree:[160]

> 'At the same time, several difficulties have arisen from the attempt in *Law* to employ human dignity *as a legal test.* There can be no doubt that human dignity is an essential value underlying the s 15 equality guarantee. In fact, the protection of all of the rights guaranteed by the *Charter* has as its lodestar the promotion of human dignity.'

However, it is unfortunate, in my view, that the Court in *Kapp* did not — in the interests of sound equality jurisprudence — deal expressly with the grammatico-logical necessity of identifying the *appropriate* criterion of attribution, namely the respect in which all human beings are equal and may not be discriminated against. The nearest it came to doing so is in the following passage:[161]

> 'Rather than requiring identical treatment for everyone, in *Andrews*, McIntyre J distinguished between difference and discrimination and adopted an approach to equality that acknowledged and accommodated differences. McIntyre J proposed the following model, at p 182:
>
>> "[I]n assessing whether a complainant's rights have been infringed under s 15(1), it is not enough to focus only on the alleged ground of discrimination and decide whether or not it is an enumerated or analogous ground. The effect of the impugned distinction or classification on the complainant must be considered. Once it is accepted that not all distinctions and differentiations created by law are discriminatory, then a role must be assigned to s 15(1) which goes beyond the mere recognition of a legal distinction. A complainant under s 15(1) must show not only that he or she is not receiving equal treatment before and under the law or that the law has a differential impact on him or her in the protection or benefit accorded by law but, in addition, must show that the legislative impact of the law is discriminatory."
>
> In other words, not every distinction is discriminatory.'

---

160 Id para 21.
161 Id para 28.

The Court, though approving of the assertion in *Andrews* that the complainant must also show that the 'legislative impact of the law is discriminatory' backs away from asking and answering the vital question, 'impact with regard to what?' Had it done so in the context of its recognition and approval of the 'important contribution [made by *Law*] to our understanding of the conceptual underpinnings of substantive equality', there could surely have been only one answer, namely 'human dignity'.

The Court also referred[162] to the treatment in *Law* of considerations such as the perpetuation of advantage, stereotyping, and prejudice, and pre-existing disadvantage. But there is no warrant for concluding that the judgment in *Kapp* is dissenting from the following clear holdings in *Law*:

> 'It should be stressed that, while it is helpful to demonstrate the existence of pre-existing historic disadvantage, it is of course not *necessary* to show such disadvantage in order to establish a s 15(1) violation'; [163]

and

> 'The *Charter* guarantees equality rights to individuals ... [and] ... it must be made clear that the s 15(1) claimant is not required to establish membership in a sociologically recognized group in order to be successful.... [A]n infringement may ... exist even if there is no one similar to the claimant who is experiencing the same unfair treatment';[164]

and

> '... I also do not want to suggest that the claimant's association with a group which has historically been more disadvantaged will be conclusive of a violation under s 15(1).... This *may* be the result, but whether or not it is the result will depend upon the circumstances of the case and, in particular, upon whether or not the distinction truly affects the *dignity of the claimant*.'[165] (Emphasis supplied to last three words.)

The Court in *Kapp* could have dissented from the assertion relating to the 'dignity of the claimant' in the last passage quoted above and the other references to dignity in the *Law* judgment, but nowhere did it do so. Yet the following is stated in Kapp:[166]

> 'Viewed in this way [ie the treatment in *Law* of considerations such as the perpetuation of advantage, stereotyping, and prejudice, and pre-existing disadvantage], *Law* does not impose a new and distinctive test for discrimination, but rather affirms the approach to substantive equality under s 15 set out in *Andrews* and developed in numerous subsequent decisions. The factors cited in *Law* should not be read literally as if they were legislative dispositions,

[162] Id para 23.
[163] *Law* (above, n 133) para 65.
[164] Id para 66.
[165] Id para 67.
[166] *Kapp* (above, n 158) para 24.

> but as a way of focusing on the central concern of s 15 identified in *Andrews* — combating discrimination, defined in terms of perpetuating disadvantage and stereoptyping.'

I have considerable problems with the above passage. The reference in *Law* to 'human dignity' and its role in interpreting and applying s 15(1) may not be a 'distinctive test' but it is most certainly an essential element in this process. One cannot simply think away the clear references in *Law* to human dignity and its impairment. The element of human worth may not be 'new' but then only if one reads it (implicitly or otherwise) into the 'approach to equality ... set out in *Andrews* and developed in numerous subsequent decisions' mentioned in the above passage. I am at a loss to explain the phrase cautioning one not to read the 'factors cited in *Law*' — 'literally as if they were legislative dispositions'. However one reads *Law*, the infringement of human dignity is an essential element in interpreting and applying s 15(1). This emerges from all the passages from *Law* I have quoted. Moreover it is simply a misreading of *Law* to suggest that what is said about human dignity in *Law* is no more than 'a way of focusing on the central concern of s 15 identified in *Andrews* — combating discrimination, *defined* in terms of *perpetuating disadvantage and stereotyping*'. (Emphasis supplied.) *Law* does indeed deal with this concern, but makes two things clear beyond any possibility of a doubt; firstly, that the impairment of human dignity is an element in the investigation, and — secondly — that s 15(1) goes beyond the concern of 'perpetuating disadvantage and stereotyping' as all the passages I have quoted from *Law* show, and in particular the last three immediately above.

Moreau (2008–2009: 285–286) asserts that in *Kapp*

> '[u]nexpectedly, the Court explicitly rejects what has come to be known as the "*Law* test" for violation of s 15, which asks whether the claimant's dignity was demeaned. Instead, the Court suggests that we should adopt something closer to the old approach under *Andrews v Law Society of British Columbia* [n 5] asking simply whether the claimant has suffered "discrimination, defined in terms of [acts] perpetuating disadvantage and stereotyping." [n 6].'

Footnote 6 in the above extract only cites para 24 of *Kapp* (quoted above in the text at n 164). I must differ with the bald statement made by Moreau that *Kapp* explicitly rejected the abovementioned '*Law* test'. In para 24 there was no overruling of *Law*. The place of the value of human dignity in s 15(1) analysis is not hidden in some obscure crevice in the *Law* judgment. It is articulated explicitly and clearly in a compendious judgment which set itself the task of restating as clearly as possible the meaning of s 15(1), as I have endeavoured to show from the extracts from the judgment quoted above. I cannot believe that the Canadian Supreme Court, with its tradition of meticulous and detailed exposition, would have overruled a judgment on so explicit a point without pointedly saying so and without explicating in detail where *Law* was clearly wrong. It is true that in para 21 of the *Kapp* judgment quoted above the Court referred to difficulties that had been experienced from the 'attempt in *Law* to employ human dignity as a legal test'. Yet immediately thereafter in the same paragraph it is stated that '[t]here can be no doubt that human dignity is an essential value underlying the s 15 equality guarantee'. I have explained this on the basis that this is precisely the correct use of dignity as the *value* constituting the criterion of attribution for discrimination analysis. No Court intent on overruling *Law* on the dignity component of its discrimination test states unequivocally ('there can be no doubt') that 'human dignity is an essential value underlying the s 15 equality guarantee'.

In this context Moreau (2008–2009: 293) states the following:

> 'Curiously, in spite of rejecting the *Law* test, the majority nowhere explicitly acknowledges that *it* had endorsed this test. The majority speaks of the *Law* test as though it were a misreading of what the *Law* case actually said, rather than a formulation that the Court itself, and moreover some of the very same judges, had proposed. This is a disappointing feature of its judgment. It does not make the Court seem infallible to pretend that this reading of *Law* was not its own; it just makes it seem somewhat dishonest.'

Quite to the contrary, the features that Moreau refers to in fact illustrate that the role of dignity as formulated in *Law* was *not* overruled in *Kapp*. McAllister (2009: 6, 12–13) also deals with the *Kapp* judgment in relation to s 15(1) jurisprudence. As I read her article, the author nowhere contends that the *Kapp* decision overruled the *Law* judgment's treatment of human dignity as a feature in s 15(1) analysis. In her first reference (2009: 6) to *Kapp*, McAllister does no more than state that the Court 'not only developed a new test for s 15(2) but also revisited the s 15(1) test'. In her second reference (2009: 13) the author comments on *Kapp* as follows:

> 'Another equally important aspect of the decision is that the majority first engaged in a lengthy review of s 15 jurisprudence which emphasized the 1989 decision in *Andrews v The Law Society of British Columbia*, rather than the 1999 decision in *Law v Canada (Minister of Employment and Immigration)*. The *Law* decision has been extensively critiqued by both academics and practitioners who say that it established an unwieldy multistep test that ultimately turns on the subjective concepts of personal dignity and results in complete unpredictability.'

After referring very briefly to the four contextual factors set out in *Law*, McAllister concludes as follows:

> 'Thus, it appears that the Court is saying *Andrews* is the s 15(1) test and *Law* simply identifies a helpful set of criteria. This would be a truly useful development in equality rights jurisprudence, since most commentators agree that the Court got the analysis right in *Andrews*.'

I shall not repeat my previous analysis of *Kapp* here, but only repeat that no responsible court overrules a crucial prior holding in this way. Nor will I repeat my defence of human dignity as an *objective* and essential grammatico-logical criterion in equality jurisprudence. Whatever is unwieldy about the *Law* decision does not relate to the dignity criterion. I also find the attempt, in the last passage quoted, to insert a jurisprudential wedge between a 'test' and 'a helpful set of criteria' unconvincing. A criterion can be a crucial condition precedent in the formulation of a test. If a differentiation does not give rise to the harming of a plaintiff's human dignity, I fail to see how this can amount to unconstitutional discrimination (whether it be under Canadian s 15(1) or South African s 9(3)). The importance of human dignity in the *Law* holding cannot simply be glossed away.

There is much loose use of the expression 'substantive equality' and it is used inconsistently by various commentators. In the *Gay and Lesbian (Minister of Justice)* case[167] the following was said by the South African Constitutional Court in this regard:

> '[60] ... [I]t is necessary to comment on the nature of substantive equality, a contested expression which is not found in either of our Constitutions.... Past unfair discrimination frequently has ongoing negative consequences, the continuation of which is not halted immediately when the initial causes thereof are eliminated, and unless remedied, may continue for a substantial time and even indefinitely. Like justice, equality delayed is equality denied.
>
> [61] The need for such remedial or restitutionary measures has therefore been recognized in ss 8(2) and 9(3) of the interim and 1996 Constitutions respectively. One could refer to such equality as remedial or restitutionary equality.
>
> ...
>
> It is in this latter way that we have encapsulated the notion of substantive as opposed to formal equality.'

Professor Hogg (2005: 41 n 4) refers to a similar problem with nomenclature in Canada when he points out that 'academics are not agreed on precisely what is the difference between formal and substantive equality'. Hogg (2005: 41) himself uses 'substantive equality' as meaning 'a theory of equality that will capture indirect as well as direct discrimination'.[168] Substantive equality means different things to different people, and terminological clarity is needed. Its use in the courts is also not wholly consistent.

There has been much criticism of *Law*.[169] I shall be selective in dealing with this criticism and try to address points that are relevant to my theme. At this stage I venture the general comment that most if not all the criticism is itself flawed because it fails to address the logico-grammatical criterion of attribution question. It seems proper to start with the criticism of Hogg (2005) in his article

[167] Above n 2 at paras 60–61.

[168] To avoid any misunderstanding I would point out that both the South African Interim Constitution (in s 8(2)) and the 1996 Constitution (in s 9(3)) outlaw indirect as well as direct discrimination.

[169] Many of the relevant books and articles are collated in *Kapp*'s case (above, n 158), in the footnotes to para 22 of the judgment, and in Hogg (2005).

'What is equality? The winding course of judicial interpretation'.[170] When dealing with Aristotle's well-known definition, he criticises it (2005: 40) for its failure to provide three sets of criteria, namely those necessary in order to determine 'when a person is "like" another, or even who should be compared to whom, and ... to assess the appropriateness of different treatments of those who are not alike'. It is unnecessary, for my purposes, to assess the validity of this criticism. Much more important, in my view, is Hogg's failure to identify a more significant omission, namely Aristotle's failure to identify a criterion of attribution with regard to which all human beings are equal and with regard to which they may not be discriminated against. Hogg charges (2005: 40) equality with being *empty* 'in the sense that it cannot be applied without first working out the criteria of likeness [when a person is like another] and like treatment, and the *idea of equality* cannot by itself supply those criteria'. I suggest that Hogg is looking at the wrong problem. The statements 'all human beings are equal' and 'no one may be discriminated against' are not empty, but incomplete. Incomplete because the words 'equal' and 'discriminate' cannot be used predicatively in the special logico-grammatical sense I employ. The further questions have to be asked: 'With respect to what are all humans equal?' and 'With respect to what may no person be discriminated against?' Hogg may disagree with the answer to this question that I contend the Canadian Supreme Court in substance gave, namely *human* dignity, but then he is obliged to furnish what he considers to be the correct answer. And this he fails to do. I fear that, without providing the correct answer to these questions, debates about equality will continue to follow 'winding' if not circular paths.

Hogg (2005: 55f) does criticise the use in the *Law* case of human dignity as a requirement of s 15(1) discrimination, but not in the context of it being a criterion of attribution. Thus he says (2005: 56) that Iacobucci J did not 'define' human dignity but only suggested four contextual factors. I am constrained to disagree. The learned author is technically correct if one limited the expression 'define' to its narrowest scientific meaning and as an all-encompassing, finite and definitive description, but not if one were to use it in the sense of a general description. Indeed the Court in *Law* was at pains to point out, correctly in my view, that it was undesirable to attempt an all-encompassing definition. The Court did, indeed,[171] identify certain aspects of human dignity, as I discuss more fully in section 3.5 of Chapter 3.

Hogg (2005: 57) further contends that '[h]uman dignity is *burdensome to claimants*', and that any increase in 'the elements of s 15' has the 'undesirable effect' of increasing the burden on the claimant. This, I suggest, is both begging the question and failing to identify the true nature of the criterion of attribution.

[170] Some of the criticism in this article is repeated in a shortened version in Hogg (2007: para 55.9).
[171] *Law* (above, n 133) paras 42, 43, 49 and 53.

The anterior question is the meaning to be attached to s 15(1). If, in order to make sense of the section (and in particular the meaning to be attached to analogous grounds) a criterion of attribution is essential, as I contend it is, then its effects must be accepted. To say that its effects are undesirable, one must surely ask, 'Undesirable compared with what?' The argument assumes that which it sets out to establish, namely that somewhere there is a proper understanding of equality and non-discrimination under s 15(1) that does not increase the burden on the claimant. But it cannot simply be assumed. The logico-grammatical criterion of attribution question must be addressed for a coherent understanding of equality and non-discrimination. But if it is addressed and if human dignity is the proper third comparator, then this simply has to be accepted. If another criterion of attribution is asserted, then it must be shown that this other third comparator is less burdensome on the complainant than human dignity. Hogg (2005: 58) asserts that in *Law* 'the Court frankly acknowledged that it was imposing a new burden on the complainant, and could only offer in reply that in some cases it would not be necessary for the complainant "to adduce evidence", because it would be "evident on the basis of judicial notice and logical reasoning" that dignity had been impaired'. The only part of the judgment that Hogg (2005: 58 n 65) cites for this assertion is para 88. This paragraph is headed '*E. Summary of Guidelines*', covers very nearly two pages of the judgment and comprises ten sub-paragraphs. These phrases from *Law* quoted by Hogg above appear in the following context in paragraph 88(10) of *Law*, which reads as follows:

> 'Although the s 15(1) claimant bears the onus of establishing an infringement of his or her equality rights in a purposive sense through reference to one or more contextual factors, it is not necessarily the case that the claimant must adduce evidence in order to show a violation of human dignity or freedom. Frequently, where differential treatment is based on one or more enumerated or analogous grounds, this will be sufficient to found an infringement of s 15(1) in the sense that it will be evident on the basis of judicial notice and logical reasoning that the distinction is discriminatory within the meaning of the provision.'

Nowhere in the sub-paragraph does the Court acknowledge, 'frankly' or otherwise, that its judgment is placing a 'new burden' on the complainant.[172] The phrase 'additional burden' does appear in *Kapp*[173] where it is observed that 'as critics have pointed out, human dignity ... has also proven to be an *additional* burden on equality claimants, rather than the philosophical enhancement it was intended to be'. It is difficult to see how *Law* (or *Kapp* for that matter) could in fact be doing so, simply by emphasising the centrality of human worth; after all, it was not overruling or dissenting from any earlier judgment, but explaining more fully its earlier jurisprudence with regard to human dignity.

[172] I could also find no acknowledgment of this nature in any other part of the judgment.
[173] Above, n 158 at para 22.

Quite apart from the foregoing, it is not clear how the burden on the claimant is increased. It does not seem in any way unfair, or contrary to general principles, to expect claimants to bring their cases within the ambit of a constitutional provision on which they are relying for relief. To the extent that the actual adducing of facts is necessary for this purpose, there is nothing inherently unfair in requiring complainants to discharge the evidentiary onus; after all, these facts (particularly those relating to impairment of dignity) are peculiarly within their knowledge. Where discrimination on a listed ground has been established, s 9(5) of the South African Constitution creates a presumption, rebuttable by the opposing party, that the discrimination is unfair. This would require the opposing party to establish that the complaint's dignity is not impaired and, where facts are necessary to establish this, to prove these facts. Even without a statutory presumption, as in the case of s 15(1) of the Canadian Charter, I believe that, in the vast majority of cases, the relevant facts are common cause or established by judicial notice, with an evidentiary burden of rebuttal on the opposing party — when a differentiation has occurred on a listed ground — to establish that this differentiation does not impair human dignity. After all, as Wigmore states with regard to the burden of proof in civil matters — 'all rules dealing with the subject of the burden of proof rest "for their ultimate basis on broad grounds and undefined reasons of experience and fairness".'[174] In civil law 'considerations of policy, practice and fairness *inter partes* may require that the defendant should bear the overall *onus* of averring and proving an excuse or justification for his otherwise unlawful conduct'.[175] I can see no reason why the rules of evidence cannot be developed so that, once the claimant has established an infringement of s 15(1) of the Charter on a listed or analogous ground, the burden is then on the opposing party to establish that there has been no impairment of human dignity.

Hogg (2005: 60–61) also points out that a consequence of placing the value of human dignity at the heart of discrimination leaves very little work for s 1 (the justification clause) to do. The same is true of s 9(2) of the South African Constitution, where the guarantee is directed against 'unfairly' discriminating. It is difficult to see how a discrimination which is found to be *unfair* can possibly be justified under s 36(1). But this does not warrant arguing backwards and concluding that the criterion of 'unfairly' discriminating in s 9(2) must mean less than unfair, simply because it is difficult to imagine how a breach could be justified. It is true that in both countries the limitation clause applies, notionally at least, to all rights guaranteed. However, the fact that the South African s 36(1) states that the '[r]ights in the Bill of Rights *may* be limited' (emphasis supplied)

---

[174] As quoted with approval by the South African Constitutional Court in *Prinsloo*'s case (above, n 3) para 38.

[175] *Mabaso v Felix* 1981 (3) SA 865 (A) 872G–H, as quoted with approval in *Prinsloo* (above, n 3) para 37.

and the Canadian s 1 provides that the rights and freedoms guaranteed by the Charter are 'subject only to such reasonable limits ...' does not logically oblige the constitutional interpreter to construe each and every right so widely that a valid limitation of every right can be imagined. This is to put the cart before the horse. I suggest that neither the South African nor the Canadian provision, on a proper construction, means anything more than that *if a limitation is sought* to be imposed, it must comply with the limitation provision in question. I suggest that the limitation provision reflects no more than excessive care and concern on the part of the framers.

In this context, I find the powerful article by Denise Réaume (2003) entitled 'Discrimination and dignity' encouraging in its support (2003: 646) for the *Law* judgment. Although Réaume unfortunately uses the expression 'substantive equality' loosely, and does not expressly articulate the logico-grammatical criterion of attribution problem, the author comes tantalisingly close to doing so, as the following passage (2003: 646) indicates:

> '... [S]ince I shall argue that *some* substantive *interest or value* must underpin s 15 if it is to have some critical bite at all, *the job of articulating that interest cannot be avoided.* Although a great deal of work needs to be done in fleshing out a concept of dignity capable of filling this role, the Court is on the right track in latching onto dignity as the *substantive concept informing equality rights.*' (Save for the word '*some*' in the first line, all emphases have been supplied.)

In her insightful article Réaume deals admirably (2003: 651–666) with what she terms 'Fumbling towards dignity: The first decade of equality jurisprudence' and (2003: 666–671) with what she terms '[t]he crystallization of dignity as the substantive foundation of equality rights'. In the course of this discussion the author (2003: 654) correctly argues that–

> '[t]he two points in the analysis of s 15 at which controversy tends to collect — which personal characteristics are legitimate bases for legislative distinctions, and which kind of deprivations or disadvantaging impacts constitute discrimination — mark the point at which a substantive foundation for equality is needed'.

She also observes:

> 'Deep disagreement about the missing magic ingredient necessary to convert a characteristic into an analogous ground or to make the use of an existing ground actually discriminatory was needed to push the Court to further develop the possible competing accounts of the substantive *value underlying equality rights.*' (Emphasis supplied.)

Properly understood, Réaume's analysis embodies a tacit acceptance of human dignity as the grammatico-linguistic criterion of attribution for understanding human equality and non-discrimination.

I have dealt in Chapter 3, section 3.5 with the criticisms by Hogg and others, that the concept of human dignity is inherently unsuitable for use as a criterion for s 15(1) analysis and application, as well as the positive support for it by Réaume (2003: 671–694).

4.4 CONCLUSION

The South African courts have accepted human worth as the criterion of attribution, the respect in which human beings are equal in the eyes of the law and also as the respect in which they may not be discriminated against. In answer to Prof Sen's question, 'In what respect are human beings equal?' the answer 'human dignity (worth)' has been given. The Canadian jurisprudence, as I have endeavoured to show, also employs human dignity as the proper comparator. Such academic objections as there are to the use of human dignity in this regard do not reject the logical/linguistic necessity of having a comparator, but rather criticise or reject human worth for this purpose, because — in their view — it is too vague and uncertain a concept. I have, in Chapter 3, sought to meet such a charge.

In Chapters 2 and 3 I have argued that freedom is an essential part of the concept and value of human dignity itself and that this is borne out both by the theological approach of the Abrahamic religions, as well as by the philosophical views of, inter alia, Kant, Williams and Sen. This is also confirmed by the German jurisprudence I have dealt with. The German courts and scholars refer consistently to the close linkage between arts 1(1) and 3 of the GBL, on the one hand and, on the other, the 'free unfolding of the human personality' and the inviolability of the 'freedom of the person' under art 2(1) and (2) of the GBL respectively. Since freedom plays so indispensable a role in the human being's self-realisation and striving for self-fulfilment, it must be regarded as one of the most crucial aspects or components of human worth.

A clear and consistent line has been taken by generations of German scholars that, in any fundamental doctrinal analysis of the meaning of equality and non-discrimination, human dignity (*Menschenwürde*) is to be used as the criterion of attribution (*tertium comparationis*). At first blush it might seem that the development by the German courts of the substantive 'prohibition against arbitrary differentiation' (the so-called *Willkürverbot*) runs counter to this. On proper analysis I do not believe this to be the case. The prohibition against arbitrary differentiation is in fact developed under art 3(1) of the GBL, which provides that 'all persons are equal before the law', which wording is followed in substantially identical terms in the first part of s 9(1) of the South African Constitution — 'Everyone is equal before the law'. In this connection it is important to remember the significant structural difference between art 3(3) of the GBL, and the corresponding s 9(3) of the South African Constitution. In the former the grounds on which discrimination is forbidden constitute an exhaustive, closed category that cannot be extended by means of analogical reasoning. In the latter the grounds listed may be so extended, precisely when discrimination impinges on human dignity. As pointed out in section 4.2 above, the grounds in art 3(3) of the GBL were specifically chosen because differentiation on these grounds would, *par excellence,* give rise to an infringement of human dignity. As Dürig (1973a: Art 3(3) Rn 1) puts it:

> '(a) The Basic Law has, in this [art 3(3)] *equality injunction*, emphasised particular and *typical* inequalities on the assumption that advantaging, or discriminating, on the basis of these specified differences in human existence ("*Sein*") or conduct, in principle violates the claim to human dignity. In so doing the Basic Law once again has express regard to Art 1(1).'

Just as in the case of the protection of human worth under art 1 of the GBL, so too the emphatic art 3(3) non-discrimination provisions were particularly influenced by the past murderously discriminatory conduct of the Nazi state, arising out of its contempt for human dignity. For this reason, particular forms of discrimination are again spelt out and emphasised in art 3(3) of the GBL.[176] That human dignity is the criterion of attribution underlying the discrimination listed in art 3(3) is borne out by the fact that a limitation of these prohibitions is not possible. An infringement of equality on any of the listed grounds would adversely affect human dignity and under the GBL human dignity cannot be limited.[177]

In one sense the prohibition against arbitrary discrimination as developed by the German courts under art 3(1)[178] has made it possible, in effect, to extend the substantive grounds on which discrimination is forbidden under art 3(3). As the BVerfG has formulated it,[179] an infringement of art 3(1) occurs 'when categories of persons to whom this right accrues are treated differently from other categories of persons, although no differences exist between these groups of *such a nature and such a weight* that would justify this unequal treatment'. If a category of persons is treated differently in a way that infringes the human dignity of these persons, then *a fortiori* there cannot be a difference between these groups as would justify this unequal treatment. This is so regardless of the fact that the ground on which the persons are treated differently is not listed in art 3(3), for any infringement of human dignity is prohibited and cannot be justified. That the concept of arbitrariness can and indeed must, in a given constitutional setting, bear a wider meaning will be familiar to South African lawyers in regard to the interpretation of the concept 'arbitrary deprivation of property' in s 25(1) of the Constitution. In the *FNB* case the Constitutional Court held that in this context 'arbitrary' means a deprivation carried out with insufficient reason and may even, depending on all the circumstances, require a proportionality analysis

---

176 See, for example, Osterloh (2007: Rn 226) and Sachs (1987: 313, 325).

177 As mentioned earlier, the relevant part of art 79(3) of the GBL provides that '[a]mendments to this Basic Law affecting ... the principles laid down in Article... 1 ... shall be inadmissible (*ist unzulässig*)'.

178 See section 2.6*(c)* of Chapter 2 above.

179 BVerfGE 55, 72 at 88.

between ends and means (in relation to the deprivation) that is close to that demanded by s 36(1) of the Constitution.[180] In Germany the *Willkürverbot* has been given a powerful substantive content, in contradistinction to s 9(1) of the South African Constitution, where the phrase 'equal before the law' has been interpreted as requiring little more than mere rationality on the part of, for example, the legislature.[181]

Properly analysed, the provisions of art 3(1) of the GBL and s 9(1) of the South African Constitution are in fact applying a somewhat different constitutional state principle, namely the prohibition of any irrational action on the state's part, to the unequal or dissimilar treatment of persons. In other words, the state may not treat people differently in an irrational way. Even then I am by no means sure that this irrationality does not impinge on the human worth of the person irrationally differentiated against. Human beings, as inherently rational creatures, are entitled to be dealt with by the state in a manner that accords with reason and rationality. To draw irrational distinctions that affect some adversely is a denial of this entitlement and results in treating human beings as objects and thus inhumanly. Be that as it may, the South African courts have construed s 9(1) of the Constitution narrowly as prohibiting only pure irrationality. Part of the underlying, though unarticulated, reason for this is probably because, having regard to the breadth of the s 9(3) grounds of prohibition (which include analogous as well as listed grounds), there is really no need to construe the impact of s 9(1) more extensively.

A complicating factor in the understanding of art 3(3) of the GBL has been the debate about the required link (*Verknüpfung*) between the forbidden grounds and the differentiation made. The linking conjunction used in the German text is *wegen* ('because' in the English text). The meaning of *wegen* has given rise to some conflicting jurisprudence and scholarly opinion, particularly in the field of discrimination on the grounds of sex.[182] It is not, for purposes of the present work, necessary to elucidate these differing views, save to point out that indirect discrimination has been held to fall foul of the art 3(2) and (3) prohibitions.

While the German *Willkürverbot* jurisprudence under art 3(1) of the GBL has important lessons for South African constitutional law, it must be remembered that part of the reason for its development has been the fact that the grounds listed in art 3(3) of the GBL, on which discrimination is prohibited, constitutes a closed list, unlike the case with s 9(3) of the South African Constitution.

---

[180] In the *FNB* case (above, n 51) para 100.
See for example *Prinsloo v Van der Linde* (above, n 3) para 25, and *Pharmaceutical Manufacturers Association of SA: In re Ex parte President of the RSA and Others* 2000 (2) SA 674 (CC) (2000 (3) BCLR 241) para 85.

[181] See section 4.1*(b)* above.

[182] Sachs (1987) devotes nearly 100 pages in his seminal work on the boundaries of the prohibited grounds of discrimination to the debates concerning the proper meaning and application of the conjunction *wegen*.

The review — under the *neue Formel* — has become substantive and made an enquiry regarding arbitrariness a powerful tool for judging the constitutionality of differentiating provisions. This enables the German courts to protect juristic persons against unfair discrimination.

I conclude with an important point made by the German scholars, namely that there can be no equality in serfdom, for what is sought is 'equality in justice' and not 'equality in injustice'. The idea that 'equal enslavement' can be consonant with the idea of equality before the law is anathema. According to Dürig (1973: art 3(1), Rn 20):

> '[The requirement of] the GBL is equality "in justice" (*im Recht*) (in liberal freedom and social security) but not "equality in injustice" (*Gleichheit im Unrecht*) (in liberal unfreedom, in social insecurity). For this "equality in justice" (*Gleichheit im Recht*), that cannot be levelled down to equally miserable injustice, is now — if one proceeds from the axiom of equal human worth under Art 1(1) — a definite egalitarian standard, that belongs to the essence (Art 19(2)) of the equality provision.'

The aspiration and process is therefore an upward one, a striving for levelling upwards, for an equality of opportunity, not an equality of non-opportunity. The equality in dignity that is demanded is equality in a greater measure of respect for dignity, not equality in a lesser measure of respect for dignity. The constitutional demand is for 'vineyard equality, not graveyard equality'.[183]

[183] The phrase quoted is not my own, but I cannot trace its source, although it sounds like Prof Louis Henkin. I would be happy to acknowledge the source if alerted to its origin. The phrases 'equality with a vengeance' and 'equal graveyards' are of course phrases used in the Canadian Supreme Court case of *Schachter v Canada* (1992) 93 DLR (4th) 1 at 15g n 93 per Lamer CJC. See also *National Coalition for Gay and Lesbian Equality and Others v Minister of Home Affairs and Others* 2000 (2) SA 1 (CC) para 77.

CHAPTER FIVE

DIGNITY'S ROLE IN THE HORIZONTAL OPERATION OF THE RIGHT TO EQUALITY AND NON-DISCRIMINATION

5.1 INTRODUCTION

The expressions 'vertical application' and 'horizontal application' of the Bill of Rights have become terms of art, and were explained as follows by the Constitutional Court in *Du Plessis v De Klerk*:[1]

> 'The term "vertical application" is used to indicate that the rights conferred on persons by a bill of rights are intended only as a protection against the legislative and executive powers of the State in its various manifestations. The term "horizontal application" on the other hand indicates that those rights also govern the relationships between individuals, and may be invoked by them in their private law disputes.'

This explanation was immediately, and wisely, followed by the following cautionary remark:[2]

> 'Although the terms "vertical" and "horizontal" are convenient they do not do full justice to the nuances of the jurisprudential debate on the scope of Chapter 3 [of the Interim Constitution].'

This warning should be borne in mind when dealing with horizontality under the 1996 Constitution.

The shift in the concept of law and of the sources of law that I referred to in Chapter 2 above has gone much further under the South African Constitution. The Bill of Rights is as detailed and far-reaching as any in existence. Moreover, the 1996 Constitution is one of the very few constitutions (if not the only) whose Bill of Rights provisions also operate *expressly* with *direct* horizontality; that is

---

[1] *Du Plessis and Others v De Klerk and Another* 1996 (3) SA 850 (CC) (1996 (5) BCLR 658), per Kentridge AJ for the majority at para 8. Although there were two dissenting judgments, there was no disagreement on this explanation.

[2] Id.

to say they apply directly and expressly to legal relationships between individuals, whether natural or juristic.

The provisions of *a* Bill of Rights can, notionally, apply with direct or indirect horizontality, or have a 'radiating effect' on private law and its development.

In this context it should not be thought that the issues and problems concerning horizontality arise only when express provision is made in a constitution or human rights statute for horizontal operation. Germany, Canada, and the United Kingdom are cases in point, where no express provision has been made for the horizontal operation of guaranteed fundamental rights, but where, nonetheless, some form of horizontal operation of the fundamental rights entrenched has been recognised by the courts or is the subject of debate. I deal with Germany and Canada below. I do not propose dealing with the horizontal effect of the United Kingdom's Human Rights Act save to refer to the fact that there are commentators such as Hunt (1998: 423), Leigh (1999: 57) and Markesinis (1999: 47) who argue that certain of the rights protected therein have at least indirect horizontal application in the United Kingdom.[3] The horizontal operation of the New Zealand Bill of Rights Act has also been accepted in that country by, inter alia, the judgment of the Court of Appeal in *Hosking v Runting*,[4] in which case a breach of privacy tort was recognised.[5]

At the time of writing there is still some uncertainty and, as I see it, a measure of confusion as to precisely how horizontality is to operate in South Africa under the 1996 Constitution, and what the correct interrelationship is between ss 8(2), 8(3), 9(4), first sentence, 36(1) and 39(2), read with s 173. The relevant provisions of these sections read as follows:

Section 8(2):

> 'A provision of the Bill of Rights binds a natural or juristic person if, and to the extent that, it is applicable, taking into account the nature of the right and the nature of any duty imposed by the right.'

Section 8(3):

> 'When applying a provision of the Bill of Rights to a natural or juristic person in terms of subsection (2), a *court* —
> *(a)* in order to give effect to a right in the Bill, *must* apply, or if necessary develop, the common law to the extent that legislation does not give effect to such right; and
> *(b)* may develop rules of the common law to limit the right, provided that the limitation is in accordance with section 36(1).' (Emphasis supplied.)

Section 36(1):

[3] See also Wade (2000: 217), Buxton (2000), Beaton and Grosz (2000) and Lester and Pannick (2000). See also the authorities referred to in Geddis (2004: 686 n 17). An extensive literature is developing on the general issue of the horizontal application of Bills of Rights. See, for example, Barak (2001: 13 n 3).

[4] (2004) New Zealand Court of Appeal 34.

[5] For a discussion of *Hoskin v Runting* and the development of horizontality in New Zealand, see Geddis (2004: 681–705).

> 'The rights in the Bill of Rights may be limited only in terms of a law of general application to the extent that the limitation is reasonable and justifiable in an open and democratic society based on human dignity, equality and freedom, taking into account all relevant factors, including —
> *(a)* the nature of the right;
> *(b)* the importance of the purpose of the limitation;
> *(c)* the nature and extent of the limitation;
> *(d)* the relation between the limitation and its purpose; and
> *(e)* less restrictive means to achieve the purpose.'[6]

The first sentence of s 9(4):

> 'No person may unfairly discriminate directly or indirectly against anyone on one or more grounds in terms of subsection (3).'[7]

Section 173:

> 'The Constitutional Court, the Supreme Court of Appeal and High Courts have the inherent power ... to develop the common law, taking into account the interests of justice.'

Moreover, a court, tribunal or forum, when interpreting the Bill of Rights *must*, under s 39(1)*(a)*, 'promote the values that underlie an open and democratic society based on human dignity, equality and freedom'; and, under s 39(2), *every court, tribunal or forum* '[w]hen interpreting any legislation, and when developing the

---

[6] This is not the place to consider the provenance or provisions of s 36(1) in any detail. The text of its precursor in the Interim Constitution (IC), s 33, was significantly different and did not embody a list of factors to be taken into account as does s 36(1) of the 1996 Constitution. In *S v Makwanyane* 1995 (3) SA 391 (CC) (1995 (6) BCLR 665), decided under the IC, the following was said at para 104 in dealing with the limitation of rights under it:

> 'Principles can be established, but the application of those principles to particular circumstances can only be done on a case-by-case basis. This is inherent in the requirement of proportionality. In the balancing process the relevant considerations will include the nature of the right that is limited, and its importance to an open and democratic society based on freedom and equality; the purpose for which the right is limited and the importance of that purpose to such a society; the extent of the limitation, its efficacy, and particularly where the limitation has to be necessary, whether the desired ends could reasonably be achieved through other means less damaging to the right in question. In the process regard must be had to the provisions of sub-s 33(1) [IC] and the underlying values of the Constitution....'

This description of the analysis applies with equal force to s 36(1), paragraphs *(a)* to *(e)* whereof corresponding exactly with the factors identified in *Makwanyane* above, and which are to be used in the proportionality analysis. See further Currie and De Waal (2005: 7.2(b)).

[7] The grounds listed in s 9(3) are stated to *include*

> 'race, gender, sex, pregnancy, marital status, ethnic or social origin, colour, sexual orientation, age, disability, religion, conscience, belief, culture, language and birth'.

The expressly listed grounds do not constitute a closed list of grounds on which unfair discrimination is prohibited, but include analogous grounds. (See, for example, *Prinsloo v Van der Linde and Another* 1997 (3) SA 1012 (CC) (1997 (6) BCLR 759) paras 27–31; and *Harksen v Lane NO and Others* 1998 (1) SA 300 (CC) (1997 (11) BCLR 1489) para 46–47.) It was probably as a result of the difficulties in construing the phrase 'without derogating from the generality of this provision' in s 8(2) of the Interim Constitution (being the antecedent to s 9(2) of the 1996 Constitution), which were pointed out in *Prinsloo*'s case at para 29 that led to its replacement by the word 'including' in s 9(2) of the 1996 Constitution.

common law or customary law', *must* 'promote the spirit, purport and objects of the Bill of Rights'.

Section 170 provides that 'Magistrates' Courts and all other courts may decide any matter determined by an Act of Parliament', but a court of a status lower than a High Court 'may not enquire into or rule on the constitutionality of any legislation or any conduct of the President'.

One must interpret these provisions as harmoniously and as purposively as possible. The common law in existence before the coming into effect of the Interim and 1996 Constitutions was not abolished, but continued in existence subject to its consistency with the Constitutions and subject to statutory amendment.[8] It is essential to appreciate that the common law continues so to exist, not as a body of law separate and distinct from the Constitution, but *under* and *subject* to it. This was made clear in the *Pharmaceutical Manufacturers*[9] case, where the Court explained this principle as follows:

> 'I cannot accept this [counsel's] contention which treats the common law as a body of law separate and distinct from the Constitution. There are not two systems of law, each dealing with the same subject matter, each having similar requirements, each operating in its own field with its own highest court. There is *only one system of law.* It is shaped by the Constitution which is the supreme law, and all law, *including the common law, derives its force from the Constitution* and is subject to constitutional control.' (Emphasis supplied.)

Under s 173 of the Constitution, it is only the Constitutional Court, Supreme Court of Appeal and the High Courts that are stated to have the 'inherent power' ... to develop the common law'. This is a general provision. Although the magistrates' courts and other courts and tribunals do not have this power *inherently,* there is notionally no reason why the Constitution cannot, at the same time, *confer* the power to develop the common law on the magistrates' and other courts. In my view it does so by the clearest implication through the peremptory provisions of s 39(2), which are made expressly applicable to 'every court, tribunal or forum'. To argue that these provisions should be restrictively interpreted as meaning 'only such courts, tribunals and fora as have the *inherent* power to do so' is unsustainable, for it would mean ignoring the words 'every court, [every] tribunal and [every] forum'. There is no exceptional reason for so restrictive an interpretation. On the contrary, a purposive construction of the Constitution requires this. The transformative nature of the Constitution appears, inter alia, from those foundational values in s 1*(a)* that require 'the achievement of equality' and the 'advancement of human rights and freedoms';

---

[8] The 1996 Constitution in Schedule 6 paragraph 2(1) provides that '[a]ll law' [which includes the common law] 'that was in force when the new constitution took effect, continues in force, subject to —
(a) any amendment or repeal; and
(b) consistency with the new Constitution'.

[9] *Pharmaceutical Manufacturers Association of SA: In re Ex parte President of the RSA and Others* 2000 (2) SA 674 (CC) (2000 (3) BCLR 241) para 44, per Chaskalson P.

and from the coherence of all law in this endeavour, as appears from the passage from the *Pharmaceutical Manufacturers* case quoted above.

That magistrates' courts indeed have the power to develop the common law is confirmed by the provisions of s 8(3), which prescribes what courts must do when applying a provision of the Bill of Rights to a natural or juristic person. Without imposing any limitation, sub-s 8(3)*(a)* requires that 'a court [ie every court] ... must apply, or if necessary develop, the common law ...'.

I appreciate that the construction I suggest implies that, for example, magistrates' courts have constitutional jurisdiction, but subject always to the limitation in s 170 of the Constitution that they 'may not enquire or rule on the constitutionality of any legislation or any conduct of the President'. I find nothing heretical in this consequence.[10] On the contrary, it is not inconsistent with (in fact it may well be demanded by) the transformative nature of the Constitution and the unification of all law in a fully substantive constitutional state such as ours. For example, the vast majority of criminal trials in South Africa are conducted in magistrates' courts and every accused person is, without limitation as to the status of the court in the judicial hierarchy, guaranteed a fair trial under the detailed provisions of s 35(3). It would be quite impossible for a magistrate's court to conduct a fair trial if it did not, under the Constitution, construe and apply these provisions correctly. The exercise of these powers can have profound consequences for an accused person's rights of dignity and freedom. These are heavy judicial responsibilities. Furthermore, it would be quite paradoxical if magistrates' courts, while being obliged to apply the Constitution with regard to criminal procedural matters, did not have the power to develop the substantive criminal law as required by the Constitution.

I see nothing inconsistent or undesirable in a magistrate's court exercising jurisdiction to develop the common law, either generally or in its horizontal application under s 9(4) read with s 8(3). The poor and the marginalised are in the greatest need of achieving equality and experiencing the recognition of their human dignity. With rare exceptions, the only opportunities that these persons have to experience justice under the Constitution are through the magistrates' courts. It would be contrary to the overall transformative endeavour of the Constitution if magistrates' courts were not empowered to develop the common law in appropriate circumstances, particularly with regard to the horizontal application of the Bill of Rights. This is especially so with regard to the rights to dignity and equality.

I have grave doubts whether any court has the option *not* to develop the law, either generally or the common law in particular. I deal here only with the common law. At its most basic level the judicial function is concerned with

[10] This was in fact the conclusion reached in *S v Masiva* 2006 (2) SACR 357 (T) (2006 (11) BCLR 1377) para 60, although the reasoning is somewhat perfunctory.

determining the relevant facts in a case and applying the relevant law to them. I am not suggesting that these two activities can be kept wholly discrete, in separate air-tight compartments. Often, in attempting to determine what facts are relevant, one must have regard to the relevant law applicable, and vice versa. But ultimately, in relation to judicial exposition of the common law, this is done with reference to particular facts. Cases whose facts and applicable common law are identical with a prior binding precedent do not, for obvious reasons, go to court, or if they do it is solely to test (by appeal if necessary) the validity of the law in question. Change the facts from those in an earlier precedent and a dispute arises as to the law to be applied, more often a dispute as to how these differing facts influence the application of the common law to the case at hand. I believe that any application must, necessarily, involve the 'development' of the common law. In my view whenever one has to 'apply' the common law to a different set of facts, one is willy-nilly involved in 'developing' the common law. The development may be modest and it may be simple, but it nevertheless constitutes 'development' as meant in s 39(2). A similar approach was in effect adopted by O'Regan J in *K v Minister of Safety and Security*:[11]

> 'More commonly, however, courts decide cases within the framework of an existing rule. There are at least two possibilities in such cases: firstly, a court may *merely* have to apply the rule to a set of facts which it is clear falls within the rule or existing authority. Secondly, however, a court may have to determine whether a new set of facts falls within or beyond the scope of the existing rule. The precise ambit of each rule is therefore clarified in relation to a new set of facts. A court faced with a new set of facts, not on all fours with any set of facts previously adjudicated, must decide whether a common law rule applies to this new factual situation or not. If it holds that the new set of facts falls within the rule, the ambit of the rule is extended. If it holds that it does not, the ambit of the rule is restricted, not extended.' (Emphasis supplied.)

I interpose to point out that, save where the rule itself is in dispute (in which case the court is immediately faced with the very question whether the common law should be developed or not) the first possibility mentioned in the above judgment can hardly ever arise in practice, as I have tried to point out.

O'Regan J then proceeds, in the *K* judgment, to point out, correctly in my view, that the duty on courts is an extensive one:[12]

> 'The overall purpose of s 39(2) is to ensure that our common law is infused with the values of the Constitution. It is not only in cases where existing rules are clearly inconsistent with the common law.... The obligation imposed upon courts ... is therefore extensive, requiring the courts to be alert to the normative framework of the Constitution not only when some startling new development of the common law is in issue, but in all cases where the incremental development of the rule is in issue.'

---

[11] 2005 (6) SA 419 (CC) (2005 (9) BCLR 835) paras 16–17.

[12] Id para 17.

A major contention of mine in this chapter — one that I cannot sufficiently stress, and one that needs to be borne in mind constantly — is that *a court, when dealing with a relevant horizontal dispute (that is a dispute between persons, whether natural or juristic, to whom s 8(2) applies)*[13] *is compelled to apply s 8(3) read with s 36(1), and may not invoke s 39(2) to the exclusion of s 8(3).*

It is also essential to remember that in cases such as *Carmichele*,[14] *S v Thebus*[15] and *K*, the Court was dealing with the *vertical application* of the Bill of Rights, and was not required to deal with the application of s 8(2) or (3) of the Constitution.

I strongly disagree with those who contend that s 39(2), *within its correct sphere of application*, is of but limited application and who question the following *dictum* of the Court in the *Carmichele* case:[16]

> 'It needs to be stressed that the obligation of courts to develop the common law, in the context of the s 39(2) objectives, is not purely discretionary. On the contrary, it is implicit in s 39(2) read with s 173 that where the common law as it stands is deficient in promoting the s 39(2) objectives, the courts are under a general obligation to develop it appropriately. We say a "general obligation" because we do not mean to suggest that a court must, in each and every case where the common law is involved, embark on an independent exercise as to whether the common law is in need of development and, if so, how it is to be developed under s 39(2). At the same time there might be circumstances where a court is obliged to raise the matter on its own and require full argument from the parties.'

It must be stressed that the *Carmichele* case was concerned with the *vertical* application of the Bill of Rights against the Minister of Justice and Constitutional Development, and not with its horizontal application. It is therefore wrong to use the principles enunciated in *Carmichele* as a means of avoiding the application of the provisions of s 8(3) read with s 36(1) in those very cases that involve horizontal application. For cases of horizontality properly falling under the provisions of ss 8(2) and 9(4), a court has no option, but must apply the methodology prescribed in s 8(3) read with s 36(1). For a proper approach to horizontality see *Taylor v Kurtstag NO and Others*.[17]

5.2 DIRECT HORIZONTALITY

There can, in my view, be no doubt that the Constitution in general, and the provisions of ss 8 and 9(4) in particular, make provision for the direct horizontal application of certain of the provisions in the Bill of Rights to legal disputes

[13] I use 'relevant' here and elsewhere in the same context to connote a horizontal dispute where the qualification in s 8(2) — 'if, and to the extent that, it is applicable, taking into account ...' — has been satisfied.

[14] *Carmichele v The Minister of Safety and Security and the Minister of Justice and Constitutional Development* 2001 (4) SA 938 (CC) (2001 (10) BCLR 995).

[15] 2003 (6) SA 505 (CC) (2003 (10) BCLR 995) para 28, quoted with approval in *K v Minister of Safety and Security* (above, n 11) para 6.

[16] Above, n 14 at para 39.

[17] 2005 (1) SA 362 (W) (2005 (7) BCLR 705; [2004] 4 All SA 317) paras 45 et seq.

between persons. When viewed purposively, the circumstances under which ss 8 and 9(4) came to form part of the 1996 Constitution strongly confirms this view.

It should be remembered that the Interim Constitution had no provisions corresponding to s 8(2) and (3) of the 1996 Constitution. Section 7(3) of the Interim Constitution merely provided that '[j]uristic persons shall be entitled to the rights contained in this Chapter where, and to the extent that, the nature of the rights permit'. The Interim Constitution also had no provision corresponding to s 9(4) of the 1996 Constitution.

A highly contested issue under the Interim Constitution was whether the rights in the Bill of Rights operated with direct horizontal effect or merely with indirect horizontal effect. In *Du Plessis v De Klerk*[18] the Constitutional Court, by a majority of nine to two, in effect held for the latter proposition when it expressed itself thus:

> 'The provisions of Chapter 3 of the Constitution are not in general capable of application to any relationship other than that between persons and legislative organs of State at all levels of government....'

The majority also held that although Chapter 3

> 'does not have a general direct horizontal application ... it may and should have an influence on the development of the common law as it governs relations between individuals'.[19]

Having described the German model 'as the indirect application model' and that the rights in the German Basic Law 'do not apply directly to private law disputes' it was explained that

> '[t]he values embodied in the German Basic Law do, however, permeate the rules of private law which regulate legal relations between individuals.... A constitutional right ... is said to "influence" rather than override the rules of private law. Private law is therefore to be developed and interpreted in the light of any applicable constitutional norm, and continues to govern disputes between private litigants'.[20]

The discussion of German and Canadian law was concluded as follows:

> 'Both Canada and Germany have developed a strong culture of individual rights, which finds expression in the decisions of their courts. Yet, after long debate, both judicial and academic, in those countries, the highest courts have rejected the doctrine of the *direct* horizontal application of the Bill of Rights.... [T]he example of these countries seriously undermines the Defendant's contention that anything other than a direct horizontal application of Chapter 3 must result in absurdity and injustice.'[21]

---

[18] Above, n 1 at para 67 per Kentridge AJ.
[19] Id para 62.
[20] Id para 40.
[21] Id para 41.

In one of the concurring judgments similar views were expressed,[22] and reasons advanced why the direct horizontal application of the Bill of Rights was undesirable.[23] In this same judgment it was argued that the development of the private law under *indirect* horizontality could be extensive and would deal adequately with the transforming of the private law required by the Constitution; and in this context the following was stated:

> 'Thus, in private litigation, the German courts are obliged to consider the basic rights in interpreting concepts such as "justified", "wrongful", "*contra bonos mores*", et cetera. The basic rights thus have a radiating effect on the common law through provisions such as, for example s 138 of the Civil Code, which provides that "legal acts that are contrary to public policy are void."'[24]

What is crucially important to bear in mind in this context is the fact that the Interim Constitution (IC) had a provision, namely s 35(3), that was in terms very similar to s 39(2) of the 1996 Constitution, and provided as follows:

> 'In the interpretation of any law and in the application and development of the common law and customary law, a court shall have due regard to the spirit, purport and objects of this Chapter.'

In the same concurring judgment in *Du Plessis v De Klerk*[25] the following was said in this regard:

> 'The marked similarity between the provisions of s 35(3) [of the Interim Constitution] ... and the indirect horizontal application of the basic rights in the GBL in German jurisprudence cannot, in my view, be a coincidence. It provides a final powerful indication that the framers of our [Interim] Constitution did not intend that the Chapter 3 fundamental rights should, save where the formulation of a particular right expressly or by necessary implication otherwise indicates, apply directly to legal relations between private persons.'

The majority judgments attracted much criticism, academic and otherwise, which may have been sparked (or fanned) by the following fiery passages in Kriegler J's robust dissenting judgment:[26]

> 'The second point concerns a pervading misconception held by some and, I suspect, an egregious caricature propagated by others. That is that so-called direct horizontality will result in an Orwellian society in which the all-powerful State will control all private relationships. The tentacles of government will, so it is said, reach into the marketplace, the home, the very bedroom. The minions of the State will tell me where to do my shopping, to whom to offer my services or merchandise, whom to employ and whom to invite to my bridge club. That is nonsense. What is more, it is malicious nonsense preying on the fears of privileged whites, cosseted in the past by *laissez faire* capitalism thriving in an

[22] Id paras 92–95.
[23] Id paras 96–105.
[24] Id para 104.
[25] Id para 106.
[26] Id para 120.

> environment where the black underclass had limited opportunity to share in the bounty. I use strong language designedly. The caricature is pernicious, it is calculated to inflame public sentiments and to cloud people's perceptions of our fledgling democracy. "Direct horizontality" is a bogeyman.'

It is true that the judgment in *Du Plessis v De Klerk* was delivered only on 15 May 1996, a week after the text of the 1996 Constitution had first been adopted by the Constitutional Assembly,[27] but the case had been argued on 7 November 1995 and the issues raised by the case had been in the public domain for some time before then. The Transvaal Provincial Division had given judgment in the matter on 10 November 1994, finding in effect that the Interim Constitution had no horizontal application.[28] For present purposes it is irrelevant whether the majority of the Court was correct or not. The point is that the rivalling contentions had been aired well before the Constitutional Assembly adopted the text of the 1996 Constitution. As was observed in *Du Plessis v De Klerk*:[29]

> 'The question whether Chapter 3 of the [Interim] Constitution (Fundamental Rights) has only "vertical" application or has in addition a "horizontal" application has been the subject of considerable debate by commentators on the [Interim] Constitution.'

It is more than reasonable to assume that the Constitutional Assembly, on its own and certainly through the legal advisors of the various parties, was well aware of the distinction between direct and indirect horizontality at the time the text of the 1996 Constitution was being debated and drafted. A deliberate choice was made to opt for the directly horizontal operation of the Bill of Rights, and not to leave the adaptation of the private common law to indirect development under s 39(2) of the 1996 Constitution, the successor to s 35(3) of the Interim Constitution. With the deliberate intention of achieving this objective the new ss 8(2), 8(3) and 9(4) were introduced, for the very reason that s 39(2) was regarded as insufficient or inadequate on its own for this purpose.

5.3 THE INTERRELATIONSHIP BETWEEN S 8(2) AND 8(3), AND S 9(4)

The provisions of s 8(2) are general. They provide first, in general terms, that 'a provision' [potentially every provision] of the Bill of Rights 'binds a natural or juristic person'. This generality is then limited by the qualification 'if, and to the extent that, it is applicable, taking into account the nature of the right and the nature of any duty imposed by the right'.

---

[27] For a description of the process see the *First Certification* judgment (*Chairperson of the Constitutional Assembly, Ex parte: In re Certification of the Constitution of the Republic of South Africa, 1996*) 1996 (4) SA 744 (CC) (1996 (10) BCLR 1253)) paras 14–21.

[28] *Du Plessis v De Klerk* (above, n 1) paras 6–8.

[29] Id para 8.

Rights that would clearly be excluded from horizontal application under this qualification are, for example, the right not to be detained without trial;[30] the right to free, fair and regular elections;[31] the right to have the environment protected through reasonable legislative measures;[32] at least some of the provisions relating to property;[33] the right to housing;[34] and so forth. I am reluctant, particularly at this stage of the development of our constitutional jurisprudence, to be dogmatic or exhaustive as to which rights would be so excluded from horizontal application. It is not the purpose of the book to do so and, in any event, would require close scrutiny and analysis of every right in the Bill as to the nature of each right and the nature of any duty imposed by the right in question. The ones I do mention are for illustrative purposes, in order to highlight the structure and purpose of s 8(2), namely the potential horizontal applicability of all the rights in the Bill of Rights, but subject to the qualifications mentioned.

Subject to the qualifications therein stated, the relevant provision of s 8(2) is peremptory: 'A provision of the Bill of Rights binds a natural ... person....' Its operation is not dependent on a court choosing to invoke it. It expresses a binding legal provision that came into effect the moment the 1996 Constitution came into force.

The purpose of s 8(3) is to facilitate the development and application of those rights which apply horizontally under s 8(2), and to structure the methodology for doing so. The provisions of s 8(3) are themselves peremptory in substance. The introduction to s 8(3)*(a)* and *(b)* provides guidance for a court '[w]hen applying a provision of the Bill of Rights to a natural ... person'. Paragraph *(a)* is mandatory both in form and in substance. The court 'must', in order to give effect to a right in the Bill, 'apply, or if necessary develop, the common law'.[35] On a purposive reading of the provision the above phrase 'if necessary' means the following: *if a mere application of the common law leads to a result that is inconsistent with the Constitution.* If a mere application of the common law as it stands leads to an inconsistency, then the courts are peremptorily enjoined to 'develop the common law'. Courts are not in a position to know whether or not to develop the common law unless they have the comparator in mind, namely the way the Constitution requires the horizontal application in question to take place. When a clash of rights is involved para *(b)* gives further guidance by providing that the court 'may develop rules of the common law to limit the right,' provided that the limitation

[30] Section 12(1)*(b)*.
[31] Section 19(1)*(a)*.
[32] Section 24*(b)*.
[33] Section 25.
[34] Section 26.
[35] The proviso in s 8(3), 'to the extent that legislation does not give effect to that right' applied to the case, because there was no relevant legislation applicable.

is 'in accordance' with the general limitation provisions of s 36(1). Du Toit (2001: 232) warns that

> '[i]t is vital to note that s 8(3) does not bestow *carte blanche* on South African courts to rewrite the common law at will. The primary task of the courts remains the *application of the existing common law rules*. Only if the common law is silent on a particular issue, or if the application of the existing common law yields results incompatible with the principles and directions of the Bill of Rights, may a court develop (and in the latter instance change) the common law'. (Emphases in the original.)

Save that I would prefer the phrase 'inconsistent with' (the phrase used in s 2 — the supremacy clause of the Constitution) to 'incompatible with', I have no quarrel with the above passage, which must, however, be read subject to the following passage from *Carmichele*:[36]

> 'It needs to be stressed that the obligation of courts to develop the common law, in the context of the s 39(2) objectives, is not purely discretionary. On the contrary, it is implicit in s 39(2) read with s 173 that where the common law as it stands is deficient in promoting the s 39(2) objectives, the courts are under a general obligation to develop it appropriately. We say a "general obligation" because we do not mean to suggest that a court must, in each and every case where the common law is involved, embark on an independent exercise as to whether the common law is in need of development and, if so, how it is to be developed under s 39(2). At the same time there might be circumstances where a court is obliged to raise the matter on its own and require full argument from the parties.'

Although the word 'may' in s 8(3)*(b)* is directory in form, it is mandatory in substance. This paragraph indicates quite clearly that the drafters were alive to the fact that the mandatory horizontality provided for in s 8(2) could give rise to clashes or tensions between the rights of contending persons when constitutional rights apply directly to their legal relationships. These difficulties arise from the fact that there is a substantial difference between the effects of applying the provisions of the Bill of Rights against an organ of state (ie vertically) and the effects when applied against persons (ie horizontally).[37] When a person applies a provision of the Bill of Rights vertically against an organ of state, the question of any duties on the person's part does not normally arise, and certainly not the question of rights on the part of the organ of state. The question of competing *rights* simply does not arise. On the other hand, when a right is sought to be applied against a person, and this right is not excluded from s 8(2) by its proviso, there will invariably be a clash of rights. I will deal more fully with how this arises when dealing with the horizontal application of equality, but at this stage merely point out that it is a clash of this nature that s 8(3)*(b)* anticipates, and for which it provides a solution, namely the limitation mechanisms of s 36(1), but this application cannot be

[36] Above, n 14 at para 39.

[37] See generally, in this regard, the German jurisprudence discussed in Chapter 4, section 4.2.

identical to the limitation of rights when the Bill of Rights is applied vertically only against the state. This latter point is endorsed as follows by Prof Aharon Barak[38] (2001: 36) in his instructive general article 'Constitutional Human Rights and Private Law':

> 'Most constitutions set forth a balancing formula that limits the legislature. Does this formula apply in and of itself also in relations between private parties? My answer to this question in the *Kestenbaum* case was in the negative:
>
> > "In the transference of basic principles of the legal system in general, and basic human rights in particular, from public law to private law, a change takes place. The government's duty to observe human rights is not identical in content to the private party's obligation to observe human rights."[39]
>
> Indeed, the proper balancing of human rights and the "pure" public interest in public peace, security and prosperity differ from the proper balancing among human rights themselves. It seems, therefore, that alongside the balancing formula set forth in the limitations clause, *it is necessary to establish other formulas for balancing the various human rights in their conflicts with one another.*' (Emphasis supplied.)

Although ss 8(3)*(b)* refers to limitation 'in accordance with section 36(1)', the process simply cannot be identical in all respects, because we are here dealing with rights under the Bill of Rights *in conflict with one another*, as Barak points out. The thesis of this chapter is that the value of human dignity plays a significant role in resolving this conflict, even though the general process is directed through s 36(1).

I say that s 8(3)*(b)* is peremptory in substance because its guidance arises when, in applying the mandatory provisions of s 8(3)*(a)*, an inconsistency arises between the rights of competing persons, as a result of the direct horizontal application of the Bill of Rights. I use inconsistency in the sense used in the *Constitution of the Province of KwaZulu-Natal* case,[40] namely that an inconsistency between right A of Maevius and right B of Titius occurs when both right A and right B cannot be enforced at one and the same time. When an inconsistency of this nature arises there is only one constitutionally valid way of solving it, namely a limitation of rights procedure analogous to that prescribed by s 36(1). I say analogous because the principles and procedures prescribed in s 36(1) were in the first instance designed to be applied to the vertical operation of the Bill of Rights.

Section 9(4), in its own terms, applies only to the horizontal application of the prohibition against *unfair discrimination* as formulated in s 9(3). It is important to note that it does not do so in respect of s 9(1). Section 8(2) is the general horizontality provision; s 9(4) a special one applying only to the horizontal

---

38 President of the Supreme Court of Israel from 1995 until his mandatory retirement in 2006.

39 CA 294/91, *Jerusalem Community Burial Society GHSA v Kestenbaum* 46(2) PD 464, 531.

40 Compare *In re Certification of the Constitution of the Province of KwaZulu-Natal* 1996 (4) SA 1098 (CC) (1996 (11) BCLR 1419) para 24.

enforcement of the prohibition against unfair discrimination enacted in s 9(4). Section 8(2) must therefore be read subject to s 9(4), according to the maxim *generalia specialibus non derogant.*[41] No other right is so singled out for special treatment in relation to its horizontal application. I would suggest that the purpose why the prohibition against unfair discrimination was so singled out was to make clear that it was not, in its horizontal application, subject to the qualification 'if, and to the extent that, it is applicable, taking into account...' stated in s 8(2) in relation to all other rights. Although s 9(4) deals with a special case of horizontality, it is, I would stress, also covered by the provisions of s 8(3). Although a special case, it still remains a case, in the words of s 8(2) of 'a provision of the Bill of Rights bind[ing] a natural or a juristic person'. When all these provisions are viewed as a whole and their purpose given proper consideration, it must follow that s 9(4) is also covered by the s 8(3) methodology.

As just pointed out, s 9(4) is *limited to s 9(3) unfair discrimination*. It does not provide for other provisions of s 9 to apply horizontally. Accordingly the s 9(1) provision that '[e]veryone is equal before the law' does not apply horizontally. The consequence of this is that *persons* are not subject to the rationality requirement of s 9(1)[42] and may therefore be irrational and whimsical in their legal actions and relationships with other persons, provided of course they do not infringe any other rights of these persons. The significance of this exclusion becomes clearer when the article by Prof Louis Henkin (1962) is discussed in section *5.5(b)* below.

5.4 THE INTERRELATIONSHIP BETWEEN S 39(2), ON THE ONE HAND, AND SS 8(2) AND 8(3) ON THE OTHER

When considering the application of the provisions of s 39(2), it is important to bear in mind that when *any issue involves the horizontal operation of the Bill of Rights as between persons inter se* — whether it concerns the interpretation of a statute or the development of the common law — a court is compelled to have due regard to the provisions of s 8(3), which in express terms come into operation for a court '[w]hen applying a provision of the Bill of Rights to a natural or juristic person under subsection (2)'. In such a case the wording and application of s 8(3)*(a)* are mandatory and clear. The court '*must* apply ... the common law' or, if it is necessary to do so, it '*must* ... develop the common law'. (Emphasis supplied.) In this case the court must, at the very least, apply its mind under s 8(3)*(b)* to the question whether it ought to 'develop rules of the common law to limit the right'. As argued above, when the horizontal application leads to an inconsistency between competing rights, the only solution is to develop rules of the common law to limit the right. In this regard a court has no option. It

[41] See, for example, *Sasol Synthetic Fuels (Pty) Ltd v Lambert* 2002 (2) SA 21 (SCA).

[42] When the *state* differentiates in its treatment of persons, s 9(1) demands that the differentiation must 'bear a rational connection to a legitimate government purpose'. See *Prinsloo v Van der Linde and Another* (above, n 7) paras 25–26; *Harksen v Lane NO and Others* (above, n 7) paras 42 and 53.

may not, when considering whether it is obliged to develop the common law in any matter involving the horizontal application of the Bill of Rights, ignore the injunctions and discipline of paragraphs 8(3)*(a)* and *(b)*.

The position is different when a court is considering the development of the common law in any matter where only the vertical operation of the Bill of Rights (ie between a person and any organ of state) is in issue; for example the constitutional validity of a common-law provision regarding substantive criminal law. Here, by its own terms, s 8(3) does not come into operation.

5.5 THE ROLE OF DIGNITY WHEN APPLYING HORIZONTALLY THE PROHIBITION AGAINST UNFAIR DISCRIMINATION

(a) The 1996 Constitution's normative sweep

At the risk of tedious repetition, but because of its great importance for the topic at hand, I refer again to the extent of the Constitution's normative function and sweep as captured by the Constitutional Court in the *vertical* case of *Carmichele*[43] as follows:

> 'Our Constitution is not merely a formal document regulating public power. It also embodies, like the German Constitution, an objective, normative value system. As was stated by the German Federal Constitutional Court:
>
> > "The jurisprudence of the Federal Constitutional Court is consistently to the effect that the basic right norms contain not only defensive subjective rights for the individual but embody at the same time an objective value system which, as a fundamental constitutional value for all areas of the law, acts as a guiding principle and stimulus for the legislature, executive and judiciary."[44]
>
> The same is true of our Constitution. The influence of the fundamental constitutional values on the common law is mandated by s 39(2) of the Constitution. It is within the matrix of this objective normative value system that the common law must be developed.'

Under the Constitution, the search for the universal is therefore made obligatory, and specifically in the spheres of dignity, equality and freedom.

(b) The role of dignity in resolving clashes between non-discrimination and other rights when they are applied horizontally

(i) Louis Henkin and a proper ratio for the decision in *Shelley v Kraemer*

The vital role that human dignity could and should play in relation to the difficulties arising out of the horizontal application of the prohibition against unfair discrimination first struck me when I read Professor Louis Henkin's celebrated article (Henkin (1962)) entitled '*Shelley v Kraemer*: Notes for a

[43] Above, n 14 at para 54.

[44] Footnote 53 in the *Carmichele* judgment above, n 43 identifies this quotation as coming from BVerfGE 39, 1 at 41 [the *First Abortion* case].

revised opinion'. This article has been cited with approval in at least two early judgments of the Constitutional Court.[45] Apart from its other valuable insights, the article, and indeed the judgment in *Shelley v Kraemer* itself, demonstrate that in a constitutional state it is extremely hard, if not impossible, to avoid engaging with the issue of horizontality, even in the absence of any express provisions relating thereto. I am well aware of the fact that Henkin's article is written in the context of the 'state action' doctrine relating to the 14th Amendment of the US Constitution. Nonetheless, the article's analysis and argument is of such a nature that it has important pointers for our horizontal jurisprudence, particularly that relating to unfair discrimination.

The 14th Amendment of the US Constitution provides in its relevant part that '[no] State [shall] deprive any person of life, liberty or property, without due process of law; nor deny to any person within its jurisdiction the equal protection of the laws'. This provision, like many of the fundamental rights guaranteed in the various amendments of the US Constitution, does not operate with direct horizontality but is limited to what has come to be referred to as 'state action'. In *Shelley v Kraemer*[46] the United States Supreme Court, in 1948, had to deal with a restrictive covenant based on race and relating to certain fixed property. The property had, notwithstanding the covenant, been conveyed to Shelley, an African American. Owners of nearby properties instituted legal proceedings to restrain Shelley from taking possession of the property and to have his title divested and revested in the grantor. The state courts granted the relief requested, but the Supreme Court, in a unanimous judgment, set these orders aside. Henkin (1962: 475) summarises the opinion of the Court, written by Vinson CJ as follows:

> 'The fourteenth amendment addresses itself only to states, not to private persons. Private persons remain free to discriminate against others even on grounds of race and color. The restrictive covenant, per se, does not violate any constitutional provision. But the right to acquire, enjoy, or dispose of property is clearly protected by the fourteenth amendment from discriminatory state action. The state cannot restrict a Negro's right to property on account of his race. It could not do so by statute. It cannot do so by the actions of its courts. Judicial action is, of course, clearly "state action" for purposes of the fourteenth amendment. The courts of the state could not enforce a restrictive covenant required by statute; they can no more do so under the common law of the state. State judicial enforcement of these covenants is forbidden state action.'

[45] *Ferreira v Levin NO and Others; Vryenhoek and Others v Powell NO and Others* 1996 (1) SA 984 (CC) (1996 (1) BCLR 1) para 53 n 60; and in two of the majority judgments in *Du Plessis and Others v De Klerk and Another* (above, n 1) paras 34 and 109.

[46] 334 US 1 (1948).

This judgment came in for serious criticism, but progressive spirits[47] such as Henkin and others,[48] while criticising the reasons for the judgment of the Court, 'insisted that the case was rightly decided and that a more satisfactory opinion could be written' (Henkin 1962: 474). Hence the title and content of Henkin's article. In fact in *Du Plessis v De Klerk*[49] the majority of the South African Constitutional Court, per Kentridge AJ, considered Henkin's criticism of *Shelley v Kraemer* to be 'cogent'. Henkin (1962: 475) summarises the deficiencies in the *Shelley* judgment as follows:

> 'The fourteenth amendment, the Court has insisted from the beginning, controls only governmental action, the action of the state and not the acts of private persons against each other. In this case the Supreme Court was overturning a discrimination which did not originate with the state but was essentially the discrimination of one private person against another. This, it was felt, was a misapplication of the intent of the amendment with grave implications for federal government under the Constitution. When the Court, eighty years ago, affirmed that the fourteenth amendment applies only to "state action," it was not merely giving literal interpretation to constitutional language. The requirement of state action was an affirmation, in particular, that by this amendment the Constitution did not render relations between individuals a matter of federal concern, whether by judicial scrutiny or congressional regulation. In *Shelley*, the Court, *orienting on the result required*, failed to take account of the reflections of federalism in the fourteenth amendment and *invaded the individual's freedom to be irrational*, which the amendment had never intended to eliminate, or even to deal with.' (Emphasis supplied, footnotes omitted.)

Henkin (1962: 476) endorses the following specific criticism of the Court's reasoning by Prof Herbert Wechsler (1959: 29):

> 'That the action of the state court is action of the state, the point that Mr Chief Justice Vinson makes in the Court's opinion, is of course entirely obvious. What is not obvious, and is the crucial step, is that the state may properly be charged with the discrimination when it does no more than give effect to an agreement that the individual involved is, by hypothesis, entirely free to make.' (Footnote omitted.)

In Henkin's view (1962: 476) the Court's reasons 'become doubly unacceptable if they lead inevitably where the Court is not prepared to go'. In this context he refers approvingly to the following critique by Wechsler (1959: 29–30):

> 'Again one is obliged to ask: What is the principle involved? Is the state forbidden to effectuate a will that draws a racial line, a will that can accomplish any disposition only through the aid of law, or is it a sufficient answer there that the discrimination was the

[47] Henkin was a deeply committed social democrat.

[48] See, for example, Herbert Wechsler (1959); Henkin (1961); and Kent Greenawalt (1978). Although the decision in *Shelley* must be seen in the context of the fourteenth amendment 'state action' (verticality only) doctrine with which it was dealing, the depth of treatment of the issues of equality and principled neutral reasons for constitutional adjudication in these articles are relevant to equality adjudication under the South African Constitution and in particular to issues of horizontality.

[49] Above, n 1 at para 34.

testator's and not the state's? May not the state employ its law to vindicate the privacy of property against a trespasser, regardless of the grounds of his exclusion, or does it embrace the owner's reasons for excluding if it buttresses his power by the law? Would a declaratory judgment that a fee is determinable if a racially restrictive limitation should be violated represent discrimination by the state upon the racial ground? Would a judgment of ejectment? (Footnotes omitted.)

Henkin (1962: 477) points out that the difficulty with the ratio in *Shelley* may lie even deeper than Wechsler suggests:

'If *Shelley v Kraemer* were read to hold that a state cannot enforce a discrimination which it could not itself make, the state could not probate, enforce or administer many common bequests. The fourteenth amendment forbids discrimination not only on the basis of race or colour; it also forbids state discrimination on any basis which is capricious or whimsical.'

Henkin mentions various other examples where individuals are free to act capriciously or whimsically and where it would be patently absurd to prevent the state from upholding or enforcing these actions, despite their being capricious. Henkin (1962: 477–478) does not believe that *Shelley* 'portend[s] these extreme results' and cannot stand for 'a universal proposition that a court cannot enforce a private discrimination if the state could not itself make that discrimination'. A 'different principle must be sought', one which 'would justify the result in *Shelley* without requiring unacceptable results in other cases'. The rest of Henkin's article is devoted to identifying and defending this different principle, and does so in a manner that invokes human dignity as a balancing criterion.

In this regard it is interesting to note that in the *Dolphin Delivery* case,[50] in a passage quoted with approval in *Du Plessis v De Klerk*,[51] a unanimous Supreme Court of Canada in effect endorsed Henkin's criticism of *Shelley v Kraemer* to the effect that the mere fact of a court issuing an order in a dispute between private parties could not thereby convert this dispute into state action:

'While in political science terms it is probably acceptable to treat the courts as one of the three fundamental branches of government ... I cannot equate for purposes of Charter application the order of a court with an element of governmental action. This is not to say that the courts are not bound by the Charter. The courts are, of course, bound by the Charter as they are by all law.... To regard a court order as an element of governmental action intervention necessary to invoke the Charter would, it seems to me, widen the scope of the Charter application to all private litigation. All cases must end, if carried to completion, with an enforcement order and if the Charter precludes the making of the order, where a Charter right was infringed, it would seem that all private litigation would be subject to the Charter.'[52]

[50] *Retail, Wholesale & Department Store Union Local 580 et al v Dolphin Delivery* (1987) 33 DLR (4th) 174 (SCC).

[51] Above, n 1 at para 56, per Kentridge J on behalf of the Court majority.

[52] *Dolphin Delivery* case (above, n 50) at 196 per McIntyre J.

Henkin (1962: 483) is at pains to point out that the cases that concern him are 'strictly private'. They deal with 'private discrimination', which involves 'no special relationship of the state to the parties or the property, nor any organised programmes in which private groups are engaged in action of a 'governmental character'. 'We are only concerned', says Henkin, with cases in which 'the involvement of the state is only that its courts are called upon by private parties to give effect to their discriminations.' The answer to this problem, so Henkin (1962: 487) suggests, 'lies in a critical qualification which the Court did not mention' because the Court wrote 'as though all enforcements are state action and all such state action denies equal protection':

> 'The cases raised by the critics, however, may lie in an exceptional category in which state enforcement, although one might call it state action, is not state action which denies equal protection.'

This special category, says Henkin (1962: 487–488), comprises cases in which

> 'there exist, against the claim of equality, important countervailing rights of liberty and privacy that enjoy substantial constitutional protection; these important rights include a protected freedom to discriminate which the Constitution prefers over the victim's claim to equality and which the state may be constitutionally permitted — if not required — to support by judicial remedy'.

Although Henkin does not, in this passage, refer explicitly to property, it is clear from the article as a whole — see for example (1962: 487, 488, 491, 493, 494, 495, 498) — that in particular circumstances property would also constitute a 'countervailing right'. Indeed, the right to property is included in his summary of the 'revised *Shelley* doctrine' (1962: 496):

> 'Generally, the equal protection clause precludes state enforcement of private discrimination. There is, however, a small area of liberty favoured by the Constitution even over claims to equality. Rights of liberty and property, of privacy and voluntary association, must be balanced, in those cases, against the right not to have the state enforce discrimination against the victim.'

Henkin recognises (1962: 501) that the problem with which one is here concerned 'inevitably requires the adjustment of competing constitutional claims'. While not always expressly invoking human dignity as a crucial consideration in deciding which way the adjustment is to be made, this would seem to flow implicitly from his actual analysis of *Shelley v Kraemer* and related problems.

The race-based restrictive covenant is for Henkin (1962: 496–497) not even 'a close case':

> '[T]he state ... cannot ... prefer the rights of Kraemer on his contract to that of Shelley not to have inequality imposed on him. Kraemer is asserting rights under a covenant in support of the desire of most of the home owners on the street to select their neighbours. They are asserting rights acquired by contract, not traditional incidents of their rights in

their property. Their association is loose and imperfect. It has no intimate ties or purpose; anyone is welcome to buy and live there except Negroes[53] and "Mongolians". The restriction serves no purpose except racial prejudice and the economic consequences of this prejudice. Shelley, for his part, asserts the right not to have Negro ghettoes created by maintaining white ghettoes. He asks that the state not prefer the old contract over his new one, that it not lend support to organized zoning for an improper purpose, to a discrimination which has no basis but race and serves no purpose but prejudice.'

On this analysis Henkin has, quite rightly, no doubt that the state should refuse to enforce the race-based covenant. Henkin does not explicitly mention the acute impairment of Shelley's human dignity that would be caused by enforcing the covenant through the state's courts, but the acute impairment is surely patent. The exclusion of African-Americans is an unqualified and naked preference, which has no regard to the age, profession, financial stability, income, sobriety, morality or indeed any personal characteristic of the persons excluded other than their race. The covenant excludes no white person, however violent, dishonest, immoral and antisocial he may be. It is embodied in an otherwise standard commercial document. Under these circumstances its impact on Shelley constitutes a deep affront to his human dignity. He has suffered in the past from patterns of disadvantage on the ground of race and has been unable, because of this disadvantage, to acquire the sort of house which is the subject of the sale. At the same time the covenant advances no substantive interest of Kraemer and if struck down would constitute a mere abstract limitation of his general freedom to contract and his right to dispose of his property as he pleases. There can be little doubt that in these circumstances, if the horizontal prohibition against unfair discrimination in s 9(4) of the South African Constitution is applied according to the methodology of s 8(3), our courts would limit Kraemer's rights to freedom and property in order that Shelley's right to non-discrimination might prevail. It would do so, I suggest, because on the relevant facts Shelley's human dignity would otherwise be deeply impaired, while the limitation to Kramer's right to freedom and property is minimal.

That importance that Henkin attaches to human dignity for the weighing up of rights involved in his 'new doctrine' becomes explicit when he deals with cases that go 'beyond *Shelley*'. The state, Henkin (1962: 498) argues,

'may not forbid a person to be whimsical or capricious in his social relations or as to whom he will admit to his home.... [T]he home continues to enjoy major constitutional protection.... [C]ompeting rights — even claims to equality — would rarely weigh comparably ... a chief function of the state [being] to preserve this privacy. Even when one excludes on the basis of race, the state which helps give effect to the exclusion is implementing a general, basic proprietary[54] right, reaching far back into and behind the common law; the enforcement of

[53] In 1962 the use of the word 'Negro' for denoting an African-American was not yet regarded as offensive.

[54] I would add, for German and South African jurisprudence, 'and privacy'.

> discrimination is incidental. The *victim of such discrimination*, on the other hand, *suffers* a minor limitation and *a limited and unpublic indignity*.' (Emphasis supplied.)

In these circumstances, Henkin argues, 'the state may surely — under laws of general applicability — give effect to these prejudices incidental to basic rights by sending its police to eject a trespasser or by lending the weight of its tort law or even its criminal law'.

The position, says Henkin (1962: 498–499) would be different when a storekeeper, restaurateur or innkeeper, who opens to all, refuses entry to some on the basis of race, and in this context refers to the view expressed in *Marsh v Alabama*[55] that '[t]he more an owner, for his advantage, opens his property for use by the public in general, the more do his rights become circumscribed by the ... constitutional rights of those who use it'.[56] In these relationships, the state could outlaw discrimination:

> 'Generally, the discrimination is public, blatant, and widespread; the inequality and *indignity therefore notorious and extensive*, with important communal consequences.' (Emphasis supplied.)

On the other hand, the relationship of owner to prospective clients and that of customers with each other 'are superficial, not intimate'. The storekeeper is not asserting the general right 'to select his associates; in general, indeed, he welcomes all. Race alone is the basis of discrimination, and frequently it is not the caprice of the store owner but because he would cater to the caprices of the community.'

Henkin (1962: 499–500) proceeds to examine different types of discriminatory testamentary dispositions which 'may also present different situations where different rights must be balanced' and rightly emphasises that '[t]he rights involved are, of course, critical'. Implicit in my discussion of testamentary bequests is the acceptance, for purposes of my argument, that a testator may properly be bound by statute or the common law or the horizontal application of the Bill of Rights to make certain minimum provision in discharge of a duty of support to others, or that the estate in question must be so administered as to provide for this support as a preferential claim on the estate. Any examples I may refer to must be understood as implicitly accepting that, in the particular example, this duty of support has been properly discharged. Henkin recognises that there are situations in which a testator is free to be capricious. In general Henkin does not regard 'the right of a complainant to an equal benefice, even to

---

[55] 326 US 501, 506 (1946).

[56] Compare the following holding in relation to privacy in *Bernstein v Bester NO* 1996 (2) SA 751 (CC) (1996 (4) BCLR 449) para 67:

> 'Privacy is acknowledged in the truly personal realm, but as a person moves into communal relations and activities such as business and social interaction, the scope of personal space shrinks accordingly.'

have social discrimination eliminated from the motivations of private donors' as 'cry[ing] urgently for protection. It is a small private wrong'. Implicit in the phrase 'small private wrong' is the fact that the complainant has suffered 'a limited and unpublic indignity,' to use Henkin's own words employed in an earlier example. In these circumstances, so Henkin argues, 'the state cannot prevent an individual from leaving property to *A* rather than *B*, both strangers, even if the reason is that *A* is white and *B* a Negro — at least if the state permits leaving property to strangers at all'.

Henkin (1962: 501) suggests that the

> 'balance might begin to shift as the testator leaves the area of private bequests and begins to discriminate institutionally. Even there the state probably cannot today prevent a testator from leaving money to a religious institution; religious association and its support today enjoy substantial constitutional protection. There might be a less weak case for saying that a state can forbid "discrimination" between white and Negro charities. Very likely the state can prevent a testator from leaving property to a private institution, non-religious in character, which practises religious or racial discrimination. Here giving effect to the bequest is likely to be a public, notorious fact, feeding community patterns of discrimination. The testator's interests, on the other hand are far removed.'

I have difficulty in agreeing with Henkin on the 'less weak case'. It is, in my view, overstating the case to suggest that the giving is a public and notorious fact. One can think of many instances where this would not be the case. I also do not think that the testator's interests are 'far removed'. If it is constitutionally permissible for the private institution to practise religious or racial discrimination, it is difficult to see why a bequest to a charity such as this should itself be unconstitutional.

(ii) The role of dignity in the application of the first sentence of s 9(4) read with s 8(3)*(a)* and *(b)* of the Constitution

There is no good reason why, in the horizontal enforcement of non-discrimination under the first sentence of s 9(4) read with s 8(3)*(a)* and *(b)* of the Constitution, the Constitutional Court should depart from the path it has hitherto followed of using human dignity as an important touchstone for determining when differentiation amounts to unfair discrimination. In the horizontal application of non-discrimination a court is, in essence, being called upon to resolve a clash of rights between two (or more) persons, as Henkin has correctly concluded. A clash between, on the one hand, the right of *A* to equality and non-discrimination and, on the other, *B*'s rights to freedom (in its various forms), privacy, property (and possibly others), or combinations of these rights. Section 8(3) envisages three stages in the resolution of this conflict.

1. If the court holds that the common law as it stands resolves this clash of rights consistently with the Constitution, then *caedit questio*. In this case it is not, for purposes of s 8(3)*(a)*, 'necessary' to 'develop' the common law.

2. If the common law does not resolve the clash in a manner consistent with the Constitution, then the court *must* 'develop' the common law.
3. For this purpose (under s 8(3)*(b)*) the court 'may develop rules of the common law to limit the right, provided that the limitation is in accordance with s 36(1)'.

Three comments are called for. First, in stages 1 and 2 above I have referred to the resolution of a clash of rights consistently with the Constitution. I cannot conceive of a horizontal application of the Bill of Rights without a clash (or potential clash) of rights.

Secondly, for the Court to decide whether it is necessary for it to 'develop the common law', it cannot avoid asking the question whether the common law, as it exists, resolves the conflict in question in a manner consistent with the Constitution. To answer the latter question a court must determine how the Constitution demands this clash be resolved, and in order to establish this must carry out the exercise prescribed by s 8(3)*(b)* read with s 36(1). If the common law as it stands does not resolve the conflict in a manner consistent with the Constitution, then the court must develop rules of the common law to limit *A*'s right or *B*'s right, or both *A* and *B*'s rights, provided that any limitation(s) is (are) 'in accordance with s 36(1)'. The paragraph 8(3)*(b)* obligation to limit is introduced by the word 'may'. Viewed purely linguistically it suggests that the prescription is merely permissive. However, in my view, on a purposive and fully contextual construction, the duty on the court in this regard is in fact peremptory, for I cannot see how a clash of rights can be resolved without limitation. The very nature of a clash of rights implies that *A*'s right cannot be fully exercised without infringing on *B's* right, and vice versa. To resolve the clash, limitation is unavoidable; hence s 8(3)*(b)*, read with s 36(1), must be applied by the court.

Thirdly, in a horizontal claim for unfair discrimination under s 9(4), which brings s 8(3) read with s 36(1) into play, the court is in effect being enjoined to conduct a proportionality analysis and evaluation in the process of balancing what, as Henkin has correctly concluded, is in essence a clash of rights between different persons. It is difficult to see how this clash is to be resolved without assessing the nature and severity of the impact of the discrimination on the dignity of the person asserting the right to non-discrimination, and comparing this with the nature and extent of the infringement of the competing right if the right to non-discrimination were to be upheld. In a horizontal claim for unfair discrimination, dignity analysis is unavoidable for any ultimate proportionality analysis under s 8(3)*(b)* read with s 36(1). To critics of human dignity generally, and to critics of human dignity as a central concept in horizontality adjudication more particularly, I would merely respond that legal reasoning and norm application cannot be expected to deliver simple or infallible results. In relation to the US 'state action' doctrine, Tribe (1988: 1690) points out that the Supreme Court itself 'has acknowledged the stubborn individuality of the state action cases' and refers to, inter alia, the Court's remarks in *Reitman v Mulkey*[57] to the effect that 'formulating an infallible test' of state action is 'an impossible task'.

Although involving some repetition, it might be useful to reflect on some of the horizontal clashes that might occur in the field of discrimination:

(aa) In the restrictive covenant example, Primus sells his spacious home in a well-planned and well-serviced suburb to Secundus with a restrictive condition prohibiting Secundus from selling the home to a female or black purchaser. In breach of this condition Secundus sells the property to Tertia, a black woman with impeccable credentials, whereupon Primus applies to court to have the Secundus/Tertia sale set aside and the parties interdicted from proceeding with the transfer of the property to Tertia. The arguments for the remedy would be based on property and freedom of contract rights. The arguments against the remedy could proceed along the following lines. The exclusion of blacks and women is an unqualified and naked preference, which has no regard to the age, profession, financial stability, income, sobriety, morality or indeed any personal characteristic of the persons excluded other than their race and gender. The covenant excludes no white male, however violent, dishonest, immoral and antisocial he may be. It is embodied in an otherwise standard commercial document. Under these circumstances its impact on Tertia constitutes a deep public affront to her human dignity. She has suffered in the past from patterns of disadvantage on the double ground of race and gender and has been unable, because of this disadvantage, to acquire the sort of house which is the subject of the sale. At the same time the covenant advances no substantive interest of either Primus or Secundus and, if struck down, would constitute a mere abstract limitation of their general freedom to contract and Primus' right to dispose of his property as he pleases. The only purpose achieved by upholding the covenant is to further entrench racial and sexist stereotyping. The relevant circumstances and impact, if evaluated in accordance with established vertical equality jurisprudence in relation to dignity, disclose a severe impact on Tertia's human dignity grossly disproportionate to the minor limitation of Primus' rights to property and freedom. Accordingly the covenant should be declared invalid and the interdict refused.

(bb) Primus hosts a private bridge evening at his home each week, limited to a small number of his white male acquaintances, and declines to include blacks and women. Tertia, a black female acquaintance of Primus and an accomplished bridge player, is irked by the exclusion of blacks and women from these bridge evenings. She pesters Primus with phone calls and attempts to gain entrance to his property in order to gain admission to the bridge game, failing which she is determined to disrupt its proceedings.

[57] 387 US 369, 378 (1967).

Primus seeks legal relief to prevent Tertia from doing so. The arguments might proceed as follows: Against the relief sought by Primus, Tertia relies on the direct horizontal application of the Constitution's equality provisions; the differentiation is on a specified ground, therefore it is presumed to constitute unfair discrimination and in any event the impact of the discrimination impairs Tertia's human dignity. Against this Primus would assert, at least, his right to privacy[58] and his right to freedom of association,[59] contending that there is no 'open and democratic society based on human dignity, freedom and equality'[60] that forbids persons to be racist or sexist in their social relations or as to whom they will admit to their homes. Primus is asserting several constitutional rights, and if these rights were to be limited by permitting Tertia to continue with her conduct this would constitute a severe substantive limitation of significant rights, universally recognised in the societies referred to. This limitation goes to the core of Primus' human dignity and would constitute a severe infraction thereof. By contrast the human indignity suffered by Tertia having to desist from her conduct is really minor, being very limited and unpublic. She is not being prohibited per se from playing bridge; she can start her own group, or join another, or join a bridge club. It seems to me fairly clear that the limitation of Tertia's *horizontal* right not to be unfairly discriminated against in these circumstances would be reasonable and not inconsistent with the Constitution. Primus is acting well within the bounds of his right to privacy and associational freedoms.

But what of a bridge or other social club consisting of 500 members? The club's admission criteria are very broad, admitting to its membership persons of all social and economic strata and of all political and religious persuasions. Persons with particular criminal convictions and blacks are the only excluded categories. Tertia, who is black, has led an exemplary, law-abiding life and has a charming social disposition. She seeks a court order declaring invalid the provision in the club's constitution excluding blacks. Primus, the chairman of the club, opposes the relief sought by Tertia. It seems to me that in this instance the scales of the weighing-up and proportionality must tilt in a different direction. Although the club premises could be called private, in the sense that only members and their guests are allowed entry, the privacy is far less intimate than in the example of Primus' small bridge group in his home. Primus does not know the names of 50 % of the club's members and does not, as far as the club's social activities are concerned, associate with 75 % of the members. The knowledge and extent of actual association in the case of ordinary members would be

[58] Under s 14 of the Constitution.
[59] Under s 18 of the Constitution.
[60] The norm formulated in s 36(1) of the Constitution's limitation clause.

even less. Whatever privacy exists is of an extremely attenuated nature; the premises of the club do not belong to Primus (or any other member) and he has to share the club's space and facilities with numerous persons he has no social relationship with at all. He can (socially) associate with the members he chooses to and need not, generally, associate with members he has no particular affinity for. Given the nature and size of the club, the limitation of Primus' rights to privacy and freedom of association if Tertia were admitted to club membership would be really minimal. He is not significantly hampered in seeking the privacy of the library, nor in choosing the members he wishes to have friendships with. His sense of human worth, his dignity, remains virtually untrammelled. The sole limitation would be to his freedom to discriminate. By comparison Tertia suffers a serious impairment of her dignity. It is at least semi-public, having regard to the large membership of the club. Tertia is an exemplary person in every respect and would make a better club member than 95 % of the members; her only 'defect' — in the eyes of the club — is the colour (quite irrelevant) of her skin, and this hurtful discrimination is paraded before, at least, all the club members.

But what if the club were to consist of only 50 members? No infallible bright line can be drawn between cases constituting actionable discrimination in the horizontal sphere and those that do not. The law must simply develop, as it has done in many other spheres, as best it can on a case-by-case basis, in which the totality of relevant facts will be carefully scrutinised, sifted, categorised and weighed up against one another and the dignity test applied. The same would be the case for the horizontal application of other rights. The problem is not so different from deciding what care, foresight and action the 'reasonable person' would take in a variety of motor collision circumstances.

(cc) Secunda, a widow, has in all prior wills left her estate to her two surviving children. Quite capriciously, but in her sound and sober senses, she makes a new will in which, after making sufficient provision for the support of her two children as required by the common law or statute, she leaves the remaining 99 % of her estate to a friend she has not seen for years and who has no financial need. Her children contest the will.

(dd) Primus is a widower and a staunch believer in male primogeniture. In his will he makes, I will assume, sufficient provision for the support of his only daughter Tertia as will just satisfy the demands of the common law or any relevant statute. This represents but 1% of his very considerable estate. The rest of his estate he bequeaths to Secundus, his only son, who spends more time in prison than out. He leaves nothing further to Tertia, despite the fact that she has led an exemplary life and has with devotion cared for Primus

since the death of his wife. Tertia challenges the will and claims half the value of the estate.

These last two examples concern a horizontal clash between freedom (of testation) and rights of property on the one hand and, on the other, the right not to be unfairly discriminated against. A court would have to consider how important the first mentioned rights are to the testators and their dignity, and how serious an impact the upholding of the will would have on the human dignity of the testators' children.

Example *(cc)*, even in the 'absence of full argument', would appear to be the easier case to decide. At most, Secunda is being capricious, irrational or whimsical. But, as I have argued, irrationality is excluded by the wording of s 9 from its horizontal operation. Even if I am wrong in this analysis, and irrational behaviour is not pertinently excluded, I would argue that it is not 'applicable' for purposes of s 8(2) to the 'bind[ing]' of 'natural or juristic persons'. As Henkin so convincingly argues, a Constitution may demand rationality from the state, but does not insist on it from persons. Persons, through their innate freedom, are entitled to be capricious, irrational or whimsical in their dealings. Unless one can postulate that Secunda's children have some fundamental entitlement to Secunda's possessions it is difficult to see how her children have been unfairly discriminated against. Can it be said that any indignity they subjectively experience is, when objectively viewed, reasonable? I believe not. Reasonable bystanders would not think any less of the children because they have been excluded from their mother's estate. It seems to me that any indignity they may subjectively experience is based (wrongly) on a perception of legal entitlement. In this case Secunda's freedom of testation would be dispositive and her children's claim denied. One might also argue that the act of testation itself is here operating within a protected area of privacy.

Resolving the example *(dd)* dispute is more difficult, because there is a differentiation between two children. Even here, it would seem to me, Tertia's claim ought not to succeed. Her dignity has undoubtedly been infringed because, on the facts of the case, the message being conveyed to her is that she is inherently a less worthy creature than her brother whereas, in her ethical behaviour, she has in fact been vastly superior. Against this must be weighed up Primus' rights to freedom and privacy. It is a closer call, but even here I believe that Primus' rights should tilt the scale in his favour. This does not mean, I emphasise, that privacy and freedom constitute a legal defence to all assaults on dignity that occur within the home. For example, physical assault against spouse or children[61]

[61] I do not here enter the debate as to whether moderate physical chastisement (having regard to the age of the child) as a form of parental discipline and instruction is legally permissible. For purposes of the present argument, I shall assume that it does. I accordingly use 'assault' as meaning physical force that exceeds these boundaries.

would clearly not fall within the protected area; neither would psychological abuse.[62] The indignity suffered by Tertia does not constitute an 'assault' of this nature and does not occur in the public domain. I believe that the testator's freedom and privacy outweigh the indignity she suffers. In these examples it is important to maintain certain boundaries between ethics and law. There is of course no doubt that many ethical rules are incorporated into the rights protected by the Constitution, but not all. One should resist the temptation (however nobly motivated) of conflating the whole field of ethics with the law. In this regard it is important to preserve the Kantian distinction between the demands of the law and those of virtue.[63]

I personally may be of the ethical view that one ought to deal absolutely equally with children in making testamentary dispositions and not discriminate on the grounds of sex; indeed I may be of the view that, even in the home, all children should be treated as having absolutely equal human worth. But my ethics may not be that of my neighbour, and my neighbour ought not to be forced by law to observe my ethical imperatives. There are certainly limits — however hard it may be to draw the restraining line — to the law's intrusion into one's spheres of freedom and privacy.

(c) Dignity as a 'neutral principle' for horizontal adjudication

It would be salutary if all judges serving on supreme courts (ie courts whose judgments are final and not subject to appeal) were to remind themselves regularly of Jackson J's famous aphorism in *Brown v Allen*[64] that '[w]e are not final because we are infallible, but we are infallible only because we are final'. It was in response to judgments like *Shelley v Kraemer*, the race-based restrictive covenant case dealt with above, that the phrase 'neutral principles of constitutional law' gained currency in the USA.[65] The meaning of this phrase and its application have been misunderstood in the USA and also, I believe, in South Africa, but as Henkin (1978: 1022) points out, 'Herbert Wechsler's most famous demand of the [US Supreme] Court, that it decide cases on the basis of "neutral principles" is at bottom a demand that the Court act according to law, not caprice'. Henkin (1961: 652–655), reflecting on the misunderstanding that has arisen, points out that

[62] Here I also refrain from attempting to define when verbal and emotional actions reach the level of actionable emotional 'assault'.

[63] See the treatment of Kant in Chapter 2, section 2.9*(d)* above and Schneewind (1999: 323–324).

[64] 344 US 443, 540 (1953). First brought to my attention by Prof Henkin (1978: 1022 n 1).

[65] See for example Prof Herbert Wechsler (1959) and (1970), Prof Louis Henkin (1961), (1962) and (1978), and Prof Kent Greenawalt (1978).

> 'Professor Wechsler demands what my colleague Paul Mishkin and I have called, in the title to an article we have never written, "The Return to Doctrine": Professor Wechsler calls for principle, generally applied, except where the Constitution is admittedly, or can be interpreted as being, partisan.
>
> ...
>
> Neutral principle, then, means, I take it, "principle," "doctrine," a rule of general application. Neutral principle also means that the principles which the court announces must be logically and consistently applied.
>
> ...
>
> The denial of principle is, I sometimes think, the snicker of the cynic. To him the entire process of decision is a sham. The judicial opinion is a ritual, not reason, and principles are incantations to be invoked. To those who believe, on the other hand, that the game has rules and the rules have a purpose, that the purpose has reason, that principle is the essential reason.'

Aware of the danger of trying to oversimplify constitutional issues, Henkin (1961: 662) sounds a warning that is relevant to the principled horizontal application of the South African Bill of Rights:

> 'The answers to constitutional questions do not lend themselves readily to the judgment of right and wrong. We can only hope and ask for scrupulous adherence to the process due constitutional adjudication — the principled application of principle, man-made principle, the exposition of the ingredients of decision, of the respective weights given them, of the choices they represent. Whether or not he likes the result, the critic must review this process. He too must adhere to neutral principles, to neutral principles of criticism — he cannot merely choose sides and vote for his sympathies, or for his judicial favorites.'

Judicial review by constitutional and other final courts in the judicial hierarchy has since the Second World War become an undisputed feature of democracy in many national constitutions. Nevertheless courts exercising the power of judicial review, particularly against acts of democratically elected legislatures, run legitimacy risks, despite the fact that this power is granted by democratically founded constitutions. These risks, or perceptions of illegitimacy, although they may arise from lingering attachments to outmoded ideas of parliamentary or legislative sovereignty, cannot be ignored. They arise, for the most part, because the members of the reviewing courts in question are not democratically elected and cannot simply be 'democratically' voted out of office. At the same time the modern democratic constitutional state demands a judiciary that is independent from the legislature and executive. This tension certainly requires sufficient checks and balances in order to prevent the judiciary from usurping the powers of the legislature and executive. These checks and balances must, unavoidably, be different from those applying to the other pillars of the state. Proper appointment procedures for judges to the highest reviewing court are essential in order to ensure competence, independence and integrity, and must not be usurped by either the existing judiciary or the executive/legislature. A 'perfect' system for these appointments has not yet been devised.[66]

Judges, in the execution of their duties, are just as much bound by the Constitution as the executive and legislature, but from the nature of things it is a more complex matter to ensure this. A judge may of course be removed from office under s 171 of the Constitution, but only for incapacity, gross incompetence or gross misconduct. This caters only for the most serious cases. The most effective checks and balances on the judiciary are through the judiciary itself, through the legal professions (in which I include all practitioners — broadly defined), legal academics, and members of the public. The check through the judiciary itself, by way of appeals to higher courts, is an important one, but of course does not apply to final courts. An internal check provided by the judiciary is the fact that most final courts have multiple membership, which provides for internal critique by several judges. The most important check, however, is probably the fact that the constitutional state requires that judgments of its courts be properly reasoned, combined with the guaranteed freedom of everybody, including the press, legal practitioners, legal academics and persons in the street, to criticise the reasons provided for every judicial order or holding. For a participatory democracy this is surely the most effective means whereby the body politic can ensure that judges themselves act under the law, and not *arbitrarily* or *capriciously*.

It is in order to avoid the perception of arbitrariness or caprice that courts must decide cases on the basis of 'neutral principles'. 'Neutral' principles do not mean *without* principle or *value-free* principles. On the contrary, as Henkin (1961: 654) points out, the call for cases to be decided on neutral principles is an 'inevitable reaction long overdue' to the more radical versions of legal realism.[67]

While supporting the result of the judgment in *Shelley v Kraemer*, discussed in *(b)* above, Herbert Wechsler (1970: 295) criticised the reasoning for lacking neutrality and generality because it

> '[does] not suffice to uphold the judgment, unless it is affirmed that a private discrimination becomes a discrimination by the state whenever it is legally enforced. But such a proposition is absurd and would destroy the law of wills and a good portion of the law of property, which is concerned precisely with supporting owners' rights to make discriminations that the state would not be free to make on the initiative of officials'.

According to Wechsler (1959: 15) 'the judicial process ... must be genuinely principled, resting with respect to every step that is involved in reaching judgment on analysis and reasons quite transcending the immediate result that is achieved',

[66] In my view the composition of the Judicial Services Commission under s 105 of the Interim Constitution was far better balanced, in order to assure competence, independence and integrity, than its composition under s 178 of the 1996 Constitution. In the latter case there is a heavy imbalance in favour of representatives of the legislature and executive.

[67] A view with which Prof Greenawalt (1978: 982) agrees and considers to be 'felicitously' expressed.

and cases must be decided 'on grounds of adequate neutrality and generality tested not only by the instant application but by others that the principles imply'.

Professor Kent Greenawalt, in his 'The enduring significance of neutral principles' (1978: 982–1021) convincingly elaborates on Wechsler's main thesis (to which thesis I shall hereafter refer simply as *neutral principles*).[68] He points out (1978: 982–983) that some legal realists have 'stressed the nonrational aspects of judicial decisions' as if 'judicial decisions were essentially indistinguishable from other decisions' and 'all one could reasonably hope for was a "mature" decision maker, as if the process of "reasoned justification" merely conceals the emperor's nakedness'. Wechsler, on the other hand, 'in his call for neutral principles of law ... joined others who had emphasized the centrality of reasoned justification'. Greenawalt stresses (1978: 984) that *neutral principles* 'reach to the very core of the process of judicial decision and will retain importance as long as judges sit in this country'.

(i) The basic meaning of neutrality

Greenawalt explains (1978: 985) that '[a] person gives a neutral reason, in Wechsler's sense, if he states a basis for a decision that he would be willing to follow in other situations to which it applies' and illustrates this idea of neutral principle with the following example:

> 'A says, "Communists should be allowed to preach Marxist doctrine because everyone has a right to say what he believes as long as he does not encourage imminent criminal acts." If A would deny a person urging that whites are innately superior to the members of other races the right to speak, then the reason he asserts in defense of the Communist is not one which A subscribes to as a neutral principle."

(ii) Generality and guidance

As far as Wechsler's requirement is concerned, that principles must be adequately general as well as neutral, Greenawalt elucidates (1978: 987–988) that these principles 'must reach out beyond the narrow circumstances of the case.... If an opinion is so limited to the facts that the reasoning gives little or no guidance as to how related situations would be treated, ... [it] fails the criterion of generality.'

(iii) Principles of law

Although there is no general discussion by Wechsler of the difference between principles of law and other principles that might be advanced in support of a decision, Greenawalt (1978: 989) argues that 'the pervasive assumption is that

[68] A Columbia University 'University Professor', Kent Greenawalt clerked for Justice John M Harlan of the United States Supreme Court. In his view (1978: 984) 'no modern Justice had striven harder or more successfully than Justice Harlan to perform his responsibilities in the manner suggested by ... [Wechsler's] model'.

judges are limited to principles that have legal relevance'. It is critical for a proper understanding of Wechsler's thesis, in the light of certain criticism, to point out that 'Wechsler has never regarded "neutral principles" as a comprehensive guide to proper constitutional decision; it is, in his view, merely a "negative requirement," a "minimal criterion."'

(iv) Principles as to every step in the decision

Greenawalt points out (1978: 989) that if Wechsler's thesis is modest 'in the sense of setting only minimum criteria for the decision' it is ambitious 'in reaching every step of the process'. A court has not met Wechsler's standard 'simply by stating a principle and neutral holding ... which the court is prepared to apply to other cases that it covers'. The court must also

> 'justify its holding on a principled basis, that is, the court must make principled determinations on such questions as how much significance to accord the expressed views of the framers and whether to give weight to sociological evidence'.

(v) Reasoning that is reflected in the opinion

It is implicit in Wechsler's thesis, Greenawalt asserts (1978: 990), that 'in order to satisfy its responsibilities the Supreme Court must in its opinion explicate its real grounds of decision'. Wechsler is 'critical of brief per curiam opinions for cases of genuine difficulty'. In these cases it is 'impossible to speak of principled determinations or the statement of and evaluation of judicial reasons, since the Court has not disclosed the grounds on which its judgments rest'.[69]

In responding to criticism of Wechsler's thesis that he considers ill-founded, Greenawalt (1978: 991–994) explains, first, that Wechsler does not mean to revive 'mechanical jurisprudence'. He does not suggest that 'correct answers to difficult constitutional questions can be readily derived from the materials at hand' or that a 'principled' decision alone means a 'correct' decision.

Secondly, he points out that Wechsler does not purport to prescribe 'the mental processes by which judges do or should reach decisions' for judges who initially rely on intuition to reach a tentative result can nevertheless act consistently with *neutral principles* provided they do not reach a final decision until they have satisfied themselves that their 'intuitive judgment is supported by "neutral principles" to which [they] do subscribe ...'.

[69] Quoting Wechsler.

Thirdly he makes the important point that Wechsler 'does not contend that judges can decide constitutional cases without weighing conflicting values' and that he also recognises that 'judges must make difficult choices among values' and cannot 'somehow be neutral among those values'. In this regard, Greenawalt contends that most constitutional scholars, including Wechsler, would agree that 'a conscientious judge should not freely substitute the values he believes are right for those to be found *in the Constitution itself* and other relevant materials'. (Emphasis supplied.) Of great importance for a proper understanding of what Wechsler means by *neutral* principles, and of how I myself would use it, is Greenawalt's elucidation that Wechsler does not understand *neutrality* in the sense of *substantive* neutrality:

> '... Wechsler does not mean by neutral principles to assert that judges can be neutral among values, either in the obviously wrong sense that they can avoid value judgments, or in the debatable sense that they should try "neutrally" to draw all their value judgments from the legal materials, nor does he mean that their choices must necessarily treat all relevant groups the same.'

According to Greenawalt (1978: 994) *neutral principles* are important because

> '[i]f judges hold themselves to the discipline of neutral principles, they are more likely to render appropriate decisions in particular cases, those decisions are more likely to be perceived as appropriate by others who are interested in the process, and the decision and the opinion supporting it will better promote the development of the law'.

Greenawalt (1978: 994–1001) elaborates on the above, but for my present purpose I wish to highlight certain of his statements, because they demonstrate the contribution that *neutral principles* can make to the legitimacy of the exercise of judicial power. In this regard he argues (1978: 998) as follows:

> 'The discipline of neutral principles as a method of reasoned decision can make ... [the judge] as disinterested as is possible and can signal the reflective evaluation that will more nearly bring congruence of particular outcomes and broad principles. And as Alexander Bickel has put it, "[t]he restraints of reason tend to ensure also the independence of the judge, to liberate him from the demands and fears — dogmatic, arbitrary, irrational, self-or group-centered — that so often enchain other officials."' (Footnotes omitted.)

Greenawalt (1978: 999–1000) also makes the following important point regarding neutral principles and the perception of others:

> 'For any well-functioning governance, it is as important that decisions seem appropriate as well as that they are appropriate. This is especially true of the courts.... John Ladd has suggested that an aspect of treating a rational being rationally is to explain "to him through reason why a decision that adversely affects his interest has been reached." The litigants in a legal case, especially the losing one, have an important stake in reasoned justification. So also do the participants in other spheres of government and the community at large. The disquiet that accompanies a widespread sense that power is not being legitimately exercised

> is itself an unfortunate social consequence; it may be followed by active steps to curb that power.
>
> ...
>
> A justification in terms of neutral principles is more likely to persuade that the decision is based on enduring values and not the judge's predisposition.' (Footnotes omitted.)[70]

I argue that human dignity is an indispensable element in developing neutral principles of constitutional adjudication when the right not to be unfairly discriminated against is applied horizontally and conflicts with the rights of others. The use of human dignity in this role is obviously not a mechanical exercise or a simple or infallible route to correct decisions, as Greenawalt points out, but is a sound and principled point of departure in an area of our constitutional law where neutral principles of adjudication are supremely important.

5.6 THE CURRENT APPROACH OF THE SOUTH AFRICAN COURTS TO HORIZONTALITY GENERALLY

(a) Emphasis should be placed on 'constitutional policy' rather than pre-constitutional 'public policy'

Unfortunately the South African courts have to date — in my view — used the expression 'public policy' loosely and incorrectly. I am not concerned with semantics, but with the substantive content to be given to this expression. Substantively, a clear distinction must be made between the development of 'public policy' *before* the 1996 Constitution[71] and its development *thereafter.* I shall hereinafter refer to the former as *public policy* and the latter as *constitutional policy.* This distinction must be maintained for all development and interpretation of the common law *after* the 1996 Constitution came into effect, regardless of whether it has to take place in the vertical or in the horizontal application of the Bill of Rights.

In all these cases the principles and changes enunciated in *Carmichele*[72] (a vertical application case) must be heeded. In *Carmichele* one of the issues was whether in delict there was, in particular circumstances, a legal duty on police officers to act. In this regard the following was said:[73]

---

[70] In his article, Greenawalt (1978) also deals at some length with other issues relating to *neutral principles*; for example, 'The attainability of neutral principles and conflicting goals of judicial action' and 'Broader theories of judicial responsibility in constitutional cases'. They are not directly relevant to my present purposes, but readers are encouraged to read this lucid, penetrating and persuasive article for themselves; also for the detailed explanation of what *neutral principles* mean, which I have attempted to do in very summary form.

[71] For practical reasons I limit the development of my argument to the period after the 1996 Constitution came into force. My arguments may hold good, perhaps to a lesser extent, for the period between the Interim and 1996 Constitutions, but I do not propose investigating it, for we have now been in the post-1996 Constitution period for some time.

[72] Above, n 14.

[73] Id para 56.

> 'Before the advent of the IC, the refashioning of the common law in this area entailed "policy decisions and value judgments"[74] which had to "reflect the wishes, often unspoken, and the perceptions, often but dimly discerned, of the people."[75] A balance had to be struck between the interests of the parties and the conflicting interests of the community according to what "the [c]ourt conceives to be society's notions of what justice demands."[76] Under s 39(2) of the Constitution concepts such as "policy decisions and value judgments" reflecting "the wishes ... and the perceptions ... of the people" and "society's notions of what justice demands" might well have to be replaced, or supplemented and enriched by the appropriate norms of the objective value system embodied in the Constitution.'

The views expressed in the last sentence of this quotation are cautious ('might well have to be replaced, or supplemented and enriched') because the Constitutional Court was obliged to sail between Scylla and Charybdis. On the one hand it had to refrain from making a decision that would inhibit the High Court and the Supreme Court of Appeal whose task it was, in the first place, to decide whether to develop the common law and, if so, how to develop it. On the other hand it had to give appropriate guidance to these courts.

I am quite convinced that the pre-constitutional approach *has indeed* been replaced and enriched by the appropriate norms of the objective value system embodied in the Constitution. It is not simply that s 39(2) in effect says so, but because the substantive 'objective, normative value system' of the Constitution demands it. Since, at least, the 1996 Constitution we should therefore speak of *constitutional policy*.

The very expressions used to explain the pre-constitutional development of policy, or *public policy*, namely making 'policy decisions and value judgments' which had to 'reflect the wishes, often unspoken, and the perceptions, often but dimly discerned, of the people' and having to strike a balance between the interests of the parties and the conflicting interests of the community according to what 'the [c]ourt conceives to be society's notions of what justice demands', reveal the underlying truth that the pre-constitutional approach was little more than a fiction. It was the judges themselves who had to decide as 'objectively' as possible what justice demanded. This approach could never do justice to the plurality of South African society. The South African Constitutions have replaced this fiction with a set of constitutional norms for establishing *constitutional policy* and *in s 8(3) of the 1996 Constitution the methodology is provided for doing so when the Bill of Rights has to be applied horizontally. Constitutional policy* is now under the control and protection of the Constitution and, *if it relates to horizontality*, its development must follow the discipline of s 8(3) and the rigour of the proportionality analysis decreed by it through s 36(1). By calling

---

[74] *Minister of Law and Order v Kadir* 1995 (1) SA 303 (A) at 318E.
[75] Id at 318F, quoting with approval from Corbett (1967: 67).
[76] Id at 318G.

this (mistakenly) the development of *public policy* in any particular case, cannot insulate the exercise from the constitutional demands of s 8(3).

Barkhuizen v Napier[77] would seem to be the first case in which the Constitutional Court has considered the question of 'the appropriateness or otherwise, of testing a contractual provision directly against a provision in the Bill of Rights'. The provision was a clause (5.2.5) in a short-term insurance policy limiting the time within which action had to be instituted after repudiation of liability by the insurer.[78] This, the majority of the Court said,[79] 'raises the question of horizontality, that is, the direct application of the Bill of Rights to private persons as contemplated in sub-ss 8(2) and 8(3) of the Constitution'. Somewhat surprisingly, the Court declined to apply these provisions, and did so without adequate analysis of the problems of horizontality, and without reference to the available literature on the issue or applicable foreign scholarship that I have already referred to.[80] It dealt with the 'proper approach of constitutional challenges to contractual terms where both parties are private parties' in three short paragraphs,[81] and simply concluded[82] as follows:

> 'In my view, the proper approach to the constitutional challenges to contractual terms is to determine whether the term challenged is contrary to public policy as evidenced by the constitutional values, in particular those found in the Bill of Rights. This approach leaves space for the doctrine of *pacta sunt servanda* to operate, but at the same time allows courts to decline to enforce contractual terms that are in conflict with the constitutional values even though the parties have consented to them.'

The majority then proceeded to address the issue of *public policy* (in a *horizontal* context) without subjecting this exercise to s 8(3) scrutiny. It also offered no explicit reason why s 8(3) was not applicable. A hint is to be found in the following passage:[83]

> '... [C]ourts have a constitutional obligation to develop common law, including the principles of the law of contract, so as to bring it in line with values that underlie our Constitution. When developing the common law of contract, courts are required to do so in a manner that "promotes the spirit, purport and objects of the Bill of Rights". [Section] 39(2) of the Constitution says so. *Courts are equally empowered to develop rules of the common law*

[77] 2007 (5) SA 323 (CC) (2007 (7) BCLR 691) para 23.

[78] The provision, a clause in a short-term contract of insurance, stipulated in favour of the insurer that 'if we reject liability for any claim made under this Policy we will be released from liability unless summons is served ... within 90 days of repudiation.' (Id para 3).
It was contended that this clause was contrary to the provisions of s 34 of the Constitution, guaranteeing the right of access to court.

[79] Id per Ngcobo J.

[80] Id paras 23–26.

[81] Id paras 28–30.

[82] Id para 30.

[83] Id para 35, footnotes omitted.

> *to limit a right in the Bill of Rights* "provided that the limitation is in accordance with s 36(1).""[84] (Emphasis supplied.)

It seems to suggest, when read in the context of the entire judgment, that in a dispute regarding the *horizontal* application of the Bill of Rights, a court has an unfettered choice to apply s 39(1) of the Constitution, to the exclusion of ss 8(2) and 8(3).

I believe the majority was seriously mistaken. I do not question that *public policy, and the method of its determination and development under the Constitution*, is destined to play an important role in the development of our law. But the precise role that it will play, and the precise methodology used in its determination and application will differ, depending on whether it is applied in the context of the vertical operation of a provision of the Bill of Rights, or in the context of its horizontal operation. This the Court in *Barkhuizen* failed to appreciate. Earlier in this part of its judgment the Court, relying with approval on certain passages in *Carmichele*'s case,[85] stated the following:[86]

> 'Public policy represents the legal convictions of the community; it represents those values that are held most dear by the society. Determining the content of public policy was once fraught with difficulties. That is no longer the case. Since the advent of our constitutional democracy, public policy is now deeply rooted in our Constitution and the values which underlie it.'

A number of comments are essential. The judgment in the *Carmichele* case was not dealing with *public policy* in general, but with the question of determining *unlawfulness in the law of delict* which, before the advent of the Interim Constitution, was concerned with 'policy decisions and value judgments' which had to 'reflect the wishes, often unspoken, and the perceptions, often but dimly discerned, of the people', and the balance that had to be struck 'between the interests of the parties and the conflicting interests of the community'.[87] This, as already argued, was little more than a legal fiction, and quite impossible to apply literally in practice. It was in this regard that it was stated in *Carmichele*, in the same paragraph, that these former concepts 'might well have to be replaced,

---

[84] This last quotation in the passage is footnoted to s 8(3)*(b)* of the Constitution.

[85] Above, n 14 at paras 54–56.

[86] *Barkhuizen* (above, n 78) para 28; footnote references and footnotes omitted.

[87] *Carmichele* (above, n 14) para 56, footnotes omitted. The fact that the Court in *Carmichele* was dealing with the determination of unlawfulness in delict is patent from the judgment as a whole and the authorities cited in the footnotes to this paragraph.

or supplemented and enriched by the appropriate norms of the objective value system embodied in the Constitution'.[88]

It must be emphasised, once more, that in *Carmichele* the Court's reference to s 39(2) was in the context of the vertical application of the Bill of Rights.

There is no warrant for inferring, from anything that was said in *Carmichele*, that in the *horizontal application* of the Bill of Rights only the provisions of s 39(2) can be applied, or that a court has a free choice whether or not to apply s 39(2) to the exclusion of s 8(3). To the extent that the *Barkhuizen* judgment affirms such a proposition it is, I would respectfully contend, fundamentally mistaken. One can have no problem with the proposition that a new concept of *public policy*, imbedded in the provisions of the Constitution, should be applied when *horizontally* developing the common law generally, or the law of contract in particular. At the same time, however, I must stress that, in so doing, the application of s 8(3) may not simply be excluded by any Court, for the reasons I have already advanced. Those who persist in arguing, directly or indirectly, for an attenuated and limited horizontality — such as, for example, Fagan (2009), (2010) — can only do so by ignoring the legislative history of sub-ss 8(2) and (3), their clear purpose in the light of such history, as well as the context, clear wording and peremptory nature of these subsections. Moreover such a view disregards the necessity for direct horizontality in a reformative and fully constitutional state, and the essential discipline of s 36(1) in addressing the unavoidable clash or tension between the horizontal rights of contesting persons, in which proportionality plays such a vital role.

The Constitutional Court is in danger of overreaching its jurisdiction if it does not constantly bear in mind the admonition of the Court in *Carmichele* para 55, quoted in n 88. The Constitutional Court should exercise firm restraint and not try to second-guess the High Courts and the Supreme Court of Appeal in the way that the common law is developed. These latter courts, through the nature of their work

[88] There has been some criticism of the Court for qualifying the last phrase with the words 'might well' and for not setting out in greater detail what the 'appropriate norms' are and how they are to be applied under s 39(2). This criticism is misplaced, principally because it ignores the following reasoning of, and facts before, the Court: First, that (para 55)

> 'the proper development of the common law requires close and sensitive interaction between, on the one hand, the expertise and experience of the High Courts and the Supreme Court of Appeal which have particular expertise and experience in this area of the law and, on the other hand, this Court. Not only must the common law be developed in a way which meets the s 39(2) objectives, but it must be done in a way most appropriate for the development of the common law within its own paradigm'.

Secondly, the fact that in the case neither the High Court nor the Supreme Court of Appeal had applied their minds to the development of the common law of delict under s 39(2) of the Constitution and accordingly given no judgment on the issue that could be of assistance to the Constitutional Court or the litigants. Thirdly, that if the Constitutional Court itself decided whether the common law should be dealt with under s 39(2) and, if so, how, it would be acting virtually as a court of first instance, which would be undesirable. Under these circumstances, the interests of justice favoured a referral back to the High Court to consider afresh the development of the common law, without the Constitutional Court obtruding on this consideration. In any event the phrase 'might well have' is a strong nod.

and experience, are best equipped to develop 'the common law within its own paradigm'; provided it is done consistently with the demands of s 39(2) and (in the case of the horizontal application of the Bill of Rights) of s 8(3). Say there are three possible ways of developing the common law. Ways A and B are both consistent with the Constitution, but way C is not. The Supreme Court of Appeal chooses way B. The Constitutional Court's jurisdiction is, in my view, limited to deciding whether or not way B is consistent with the Constitution. It is not empowered to choose A because it thinks that this is a better way of developing the common law. In relation to the influence of the GBL on the development of private law in Germany, this was made perfectly clear in the *Lüth* judgment, BVerfGE 7, 198, where the following was stated at 207 by the Federal Constitutional Court:

> 'The Constitutional Court must test whether the ordinary court has correctly determined the extent and effect of the basic rights in the sphere of private law. At the same time this determines the limits of its examination: it is not the function of the constitutional court to test the judgments of civil courts fully for any errors of law; the Constitutional Court is limited to judging the so-called 'radiating effect' (*Ausstrahlungswirkung*) of the basic rights on private law and to ensure that the normative content of the constitutional provisions are applied. The purpose of instituting a constitutional complaint is to test *all* actions of the legislature, executive and judiciary for their consistency with the basic rights (*Grundrechtsmäßigkeit*). Just as little as the Federal Constitutional Court is called upon to act as a revisionary authority — and certainly not as a super-revisionary authority — over civil courts, just as little may it in general abandon the assessment of these judgments....'

The restraint which must be exercised in this regard was expressed as follows in BVerfGE 35, 202 (219):

> 'The Federal Constitutional Court must therefore determine whether the judgment under attack relied upon some fundamentally incorrect view of the extent or effect of one of the applicable basic rights or whether the judgment itself infringed any applicable right. [The judgment then refers with approval to the *Lüth* and *Mephisto* cases.] The judgment in question may also be challenged if the lower court, in applying the typical criteria — which arise from the radiating effect of the basic rights for the evaluation of cases like the present one — could not have come to the conclusion that it did.'

In *Barkhuizen* the s 34 access-to-courts guarantee was invoked by the claimant as the provision in the Bill of Rights that applied horizontally. It was not contended, nor did the Court hold, that any of the s 8(2) qualifications ousted the direct horizontal applicability of s 34. Therefore, as a matter of objective constitutional law, s 8(2) decrees that s 34 applies to the dispute between the persons in *Barkhuizen*. That being the case, the provisions of s 8(3) are themselves peremptory in substance, for the reasons already advanced. These provisions have been expressly prescribed for use in the horizontal application of the Bill of Rights. It expressly says so. *How* one interprets and *how* one applies them is another matter, but they cannot be ignored and they cannot be circumvented. I know of no reason, and can think of none, why the provisions of s 8(3) and the development of *public policy* in relation to a horizontal issue, cannot take place at the same time and perfectly harmoniously. In any event the Court in *Barkhuizen,* when holding — in the first passage quoted above[89] — that the proper approach to the constitutional challenges to contractual terms is 'to determine whether the term challenged is contrary to public policy', was doing no more than pointing to a door. The Court does not tell us what is to be done after we enter the door; s 8(3) does tell us. One of the most serious shortcomings of *Barkhuizen* is its failure to take into account the inevitable tensions between the claims of the opposing parties and the conflicts that must inevitably ensue, whenever one seeks to develop the law horizontally, as I tried to point out earlier in this chapter. Section 8(3) appreciates this and provides the methodology. *Barkhuizen* seeks to escape from the tensions and the conflicts. This is simply not possible. Langa CJ, in a one-paragraph judgment,[90] was the only member of the Court to question the conclusion that only s 39(2) of the Constitution applies to the horizontal development of the law of contract in relation to the enforceability of contractual terms.

The reasons why the majority found that s 8(3) could not be applied to the issue in question are all founded on the proposition that the issue to be determined, though raising the question of horizontality, really involved 'the testing of a contractual provision directly against a provision in the Bill of Rights' and that this could not be done.[91] Instead, so the majority held, this had to be addressed through the medium of *public policy.*

This, in my view, was a mistaken analysis of the nature of the horizontality issue before the Court. Analysed correctly and viewed substantively, the alleged inconsistency raised in the case was between A's *horizontally applied s 12(1) right to freedom* (in particular his freedom to contract[92]) and the consequences flowing therefrom, and B's *horizontally applied s 34 right of access to the courts.* Had the majority of the Court appreciated this, it would not have expressed its difficulties with the application of the provisions of s 36(1)[93] and s 172(1)[94] of the Constitution to the problem at hand. It could then have addressed the issue, posed by s 8(3)*(b)*, whether it ought to limit A's right to insist on contractual freedom, and if so to what extent, when confronted by B's asserted right of access to the courts.

But even in terms of its own approach, the majority failed to appreciate that the development of public policy itself, when it is to be applied to the legal relationships between persons ('*horizontal public policy*'), is subject to the discipline of s 8(3). This is so because of the mandatory terms of s 8(2) which, subject to its stated

---

[89] At n 83 in this chapter.

[90] Above, n 77 at para 186.

[91] Id para 23.

[92] It being quite irrelevant whether a legal maxim such as *pacta sunt servanda* is invoked or not. It expresses no more than the freedom right in relation to contracts: as a general rule, contracts entered into freely between contracting parties must be enforced.

[93] See above, n 78 at paras 23–24.

[94] Id paras 25–26.

qualifications, provides that '[a] provision of the Bill of Rights *binds* a natural or a juristic person'. (Emphasis supplied.) It does not say '*can* bind' or '*might* bind'. It enunciates an imperative: a provision of the Bill of Rights *does already bind*. Its binding effect (and consequently the mandatory consequences through s 8(3)) is *not dependent on any discretionary or other extraneous decision by a court.*[95] The development of *horizontal public policy* is subject to the provisions of ss 8(2) and 8(3), and not the other way round. There is nothing startling about a consequence like this. Since the *Carmichele* case it is clear that, also in the wider sphere of public policy, this is to be driven by the Constitution and its values, and not the other way around. But, I reiterate, there is a difference between the development of *horizontal public policy* and *vertical public policy*, recognised and mandated by the Constitution. While both fall under the provisions of s 39(2), it is only the development of *horizontal public policy* that is *also* subject to s 8(2) and 8(3). The approach to the development of *public policy* is different under the Constitutions from what it had been previously. I limit myself in this regard to the development of *horizontal public policy*. Even pre-constitutionally, this development involved the weighing-up against one another of the different rights and interests of competing parties. Constitutionalism has not changed this basic truth, but it now directs the process through ss 8(2) and 8(3).

In the earlier *Scarbrow Trust* (or *Syfrets Trust*) case,[96] the Cape of Good Hope High Court had to deal with discriminatory provisions in a will. A testamentary trust awarded bursaries for tertiary education, but in terms of the will eligibility for the bursaries was restricted to persons who were of 'European descent', *not* of Jewish descent, and not female. In a dispute concerning the validity of these provisions an order was sought for the deletion of the discriminatory provisions on any one or more of the following grounds:

(a) s 31 of the Trust Property Control Act 57 of 1988, which permits the courts, in certain circumstances, to delete or vary provisions in a trust instrument;
(b) the common law, which prohibits bequests that are illegal or immoral or contrary to public policy; and,
(c) direct application of the Constitution, more particularly the equality and anti-discriminatory provisions of s 9.

In this regard Griesel J stated the following:

> 'In my view, the applicants have made out a compelling case for relief on each of the three grounds advanced. However, in the view I take of the matter (and employing Ockham's razor), the present application can be dealt with on the basis of the existing principles of the

---

[95] Other than, of course, a decision as to whether the exclusionary qualifications in s 8(2) apply to a particular case. This was not an issue in *Barkhuizen*.

[96] *Minister of Education and Another v Syfrets Trust Ltd NO (in its capacity as the trustee for the time being of the Scarbrow Fund Testamentary Trust) and Another* 2006 (4) SA 205 (C) (2006 (10) BCLR 1214; [2006] 3 All SA 373).

common law, having proper regard to the "spirit, purport and objects of the Bill of Rights" [under s 39(2) of the Constitution]. In what follows, I shall attempt to show that the contested provisions in the will in question are indeed contrary to public policy and, as such, invalid.'[97]

Whether the learned judge in fact applied Ockham's razor, and limited himself to the 'existing principles' of the common law, and did not in substance also apply the provisions of s 8(2) and (3) of the Constitution, is far from clear. But for the moment I limit myself to challenging the proposition that a choice exists, in this context, not to apply s 8(2) and (3). I also wish to stress (again) that my point is not that there cannot, in a given horizontal case, be an overlap between the development and application of *public policy*, and the application of s 8(3) and (4). What I do stress is that, in the *horizontal context*, *public policy* cannot be applied (developed) without at the same time obeying the injunctions of s 8(3) and (4). If s 8(3) and (4) had been properly applied, the conclusion of invalidity might not have been so obvious in the *Scarbrow Trust* case.

In a careful and comprehensive judgment, Griesel J dealt fully with freedom of testation in general, how it can be affected by *public policy* and how *public policy* itself has undergone a change in consequence of the nature and impact of the Constitution.[98] Yet, immediately after dealing with these matters, and despite his earlier disavowal of pursuing the direct horizontal application of the Bill of Rights route, Griesel J turns to the constitutional right to equality and non-discrimination, and deals specifically with the *horizontal application* of non-discrimination under s 9(4) and (5) of the Constitution.[99] At the conclusion of this discussion, the learned judge states:[100]

'However, in view of the fact that I have chosen to deal with the present application on the basis of the common law, rather than a direct application of the Constitution, it is unnecessary for present purposes to consider the very substantial body of equality jurisprudence in any detail. Instead, *the enquiry can be confined to the question whether or not the contested provisions in issue constitute unfair discrimination. If so*, it must follow, in my view, that *the contested provisions should also be regarded as being contrary to public policy*.' (Emphasis supplied.)

Yet, given the nature of the case, the very moment the question posed for determination is whether the contested provisions in the will constitute unfair discrimination or not, one is willy-nilly in the sphere of direct horizontality, and the mandatory provisions of s 8(3) cannot be escaped. Griesel J then proceeds

[97] Id para 16.
[98] Id paras 16–26.
[99] Id paras 27–31.
[100] Id para 32.

to deal with unfair discrimination,[101] as well as 'balancing'[102] and concludes as follows:[103]

> '... I conclude that the testamentary provisions in question constitute unfair discrimination and, as such, are contrary to public policy as reflected in the foundational values of non-racialism, non-sexism and equality'.

From the above it is clear that the learned judge was constantly moving between the horizontal application of equality and non-discrimination on the one hand and *public policy* on the other, but apparently assumed that, provided the matter was ultimately dealt with as a matter of public policy, it was unnecessary — in the (horizontal) unfair enquiry — to follow the methodology of s 8(2) and (3) of the Constitution. One can readily appreciate the difficulties faced by Griesel J in this regard, particularly since our highest courts have not, in the view I take of the matter, given correct guidance in this respect. Where, as in this case, the dispute is a horizontal one, the provisions of the Constitution relevant to the horizontal operation of the Bill of Rights may not, as I have repeatedly stressed, be avoided. The 1996 Constitution reflects a deliberate choice for direct horizontality, and this choice must be respected; indeed one is bound by this choice as reflected in the Constitution, particularly in s 8(3) and (4). I do not lose sight of the provisions of s 7 of the Equality Act and their horizontal operation. These provisions were not attacked in the case, and no reasons were advanced in the judgment for not applying them, save for the ultimate decision by Griesel J to decide the issue solely under the principles of public policy. The learned judge went a long way on the horizontality path, but failed to take the crucial and mandatory step in this regard, namely of considering and applying s 8(3) of the Constitution. No mention is made of s 8(3) in the judgment and no consideration given to the issue of the limitation of the testator's right to freedom of testation in accordance with s 36(1) of the Constitution, or a similar limitation to the rights to equality and non-discrimination of the persons excluded by the discriminatory provisions in the will. I have already dealt at some length in Chapter 4, section 4.1*(e)* with the provisions of the Equality Act generally, and how the judgment in *Pillay*[104]should be read in the light thereof. I shall assume, in favour of the validity of s 7 of the Equality Act, that on a proper construction of its provisions it does not exclude — in its *horizontal regulation* of the prohibition of unfair discrimination — the requirements prescribed by s 8(3) of the Constitution. If it did, s 7 would in my view clearly be inconsistent with the Constitution and, at

[101] Id paras 33–34.
[102] Id paras 39–46.
[103] Id para 47.
[104] *MEC for Education: KwaZulu-Natal and Others v Pillay and Others* 2008 (1) SA 474 (CC) (2008 (2) BCLR 99).

least to that extent, invalid. I also assume that the provisions of s 7 are capable of harmonious application with the provisions of s 8(3) of the Constitution.

Because the limitations exercise prescribed by s 8(3) was not carried out, I believe the Court failed properly to appreciate the significant differences between the *vertical* and the *horizontal* prohibition of unfair discrimination under the Constitution. In the former situation, as repeatedly pointed out, the clash is not between the rights of the individual and the *rights* of the State; what is weighed up and evaluated in the limitation and proportionality analysis under s 36(1) is the State's *interests* in relation to the individual's right. There is no clash of *rights*. In the latter case, however, one does indeed have a conflict between the *rights of contesting persons*. Another important difference is the fact that the framers of the 1996 Constitution deliberately (I suggest) omitted any reference to s 9(1)[105] when — in s 9(4) — it is prescribed that the prohibition against unfair discrimination would also operate horizontally. According to the jurisprudence of the Constitutional Court, the main purpose of s 9(1) is to prohibit the State from making irrational and arbitrary differentiations.[106] The framers appreciated, in my view, that persons should have the freedom to act irrationally and arbitrarily, and that their actions should not be legally impeachable *merely* on these grounds. They appreciated the dangers in this regard of un-nuanced horizontality; dangers identified much earlier by Professors Henkin and Wechsler.[107]

In what Griesel J termed the 'balancing' process[108] the learned judge 'weigh[ed] up' or 'balance[d]' certain 'competing constitutional values and principles of public policy,' namely on the one hand, 'the fundamental constitutional right to equality and freedom from unfair discrimination' and on the other 'the constitutionally guaranteed principle of private ownership, together with its corollaries of private succession and freedom of testation'.[109] I pause at this juncture to point out that in the above passages the evaluation is already incorrectly skewed against the testator. Whereas the ousted claimants have in their favour the *fundamental constitutional right* to equality and freedom from unfair discrimination, the testator has in his favour only a *constitutionally guaranteed right* of private ownership and — as mere *corrolaries* to this right — private succession and freedom of testation. The imbalance becomes clearer as the judgment proceeds, because reliance on behalf of the testator on the constitutional rights of dignity, privacy and freedom is held to be 'misplaced'.[110]

In the first place the Court found that the balancing had to take place between a juristic person, the trust, and natural persons. In the first place it is clear law

[105] 'Everyone is equal before the law and has the right to equal protection and benefit of the law.'

[106] *Prinsloo v Van der Linde and Another* above, n 7 paras 25–26; *Harksen v Lane NO and Others* above, n 7 paras 42 and 53.

[107] See s *5.5(b)*(i) above.

[108] Above, n 96 at paras 39 to 46.

[109] Id para 39.

[110] Id paras 40–41.

that a trust has no juristic personality.[111] In any event, however, the true issue was whether the exclusionary provisions *as made by the testator* were valid, the trust merely being a legal instrument to give effect to his wishes. Be that as it may, even as an abstract proposition, the Court's conclusions that the privacy rights of juristic persons 'can never be as intense as those of human beings' and that 'juristic persons are thus entitled to a reduced level of protection compared to private rights of natural persons'[112] are problematic. This must surely depend on the context of each particular case. While the protection may be less in extent, once an incursion on a juristic person's privacy occurs (however narrowly this privacy sphere might be defined in a given case) I fail to grasp why the level of protection in this sphere should be in any way reduced. A more serious criticism must be levelled at the Court's holding that the right to freedom 'can only be invoked by natural persons and thus not on behalf of the trust, as a juristic person'.[113] Quite apart from the fact that it is the testator's freedom that is the substantive issue, this conclusion cannot be correct even in respect of juristic persons. The general 'right to freedom' under s 12(1) is clearly not limited to the instances listed in sub-paragraphs *(a)*, *(b)* and *(c)*, because the general right to freedom is expressly stated to 'include [...]' the rights so listed. The general right to freedom is, under s 1*(a)* of the Constitution, as fundamental and protected a value and a right as 'human dignity' and 'the achievement of equality'. This is confirmed by s 36(1), where the limitations comparator is an 'open and democratic' society 'based on human dignity, equality and freedom'. For the reasons stated in *Ferreira v Levin (1)*[114] the right to freedom is, conceptually, as core a right as those of dignity and equality. Why a juristic person should not be capable of holding and exercising a right like this under the Constitution is unclear. It would seem that all indicators point the other way. The general, or residual, right to freedom would seem to me *par excellence* the sort of right where one ought, in the words of Corbett CJ

> 'to equate the respective positions of natural and artificial (or legal) persons where it is possible and appropriate for this to be done'.[115]

In the *FNB* case[116] the following was stated with regard to the Court's finding that a juristic person was entitled to the property rights under s 25 of the Constitution:

---

[111] *CIR v MacNeille's Estate* 1961 (3) SA 833 (A) and De Waal (1998: 3 g 11 n 5).

[112] Id para 41, following *Investigating Directorate: Serious Economic Offences and Others v Hyundai Motor Distributors (Pty) Ltd and Others: In re Hyundai Motor Distributors (Pty) Ltd and Others v Smit NO and Others* 2001 (1) SA 545 (CC) (2000 (10) BCLR 1079) para 18.

[113] Id para 41.

[114] Above n 45 at paras 49–50.

[115] *Financial Mail Pty Ltd v Sage Holdings Ltd* 1993 (2) SA 451 (A) at 461F.

[116] *First National Bank of SA t/a Wesbank v Commissioner for the South African Revenue Services and Another; First National Bank of SA t/a Wesbank v Minister of Finance* 2002 (4) SA 768 (CC) (2002 (7) BCLR 702) para 45.

'Even more so than in relation to the right to privacy, denying companies entitlement to property rights would "... lead to grave disruptions and would undermine the very fabric of our democratic State". It would have a disastrous impact on the business world generally, on creditors of companies and, more especially, on shareholders in companies. The property rights of natural persons can only be fully and properly realized if these rights are afforded to companies as well as natural persons.'

Equally, the general freedom rights (or residual freedom rights under s 12) of natural persons can only be fully and properly realised if these rights are afforded to juristic persons. The range of activities that a juristic person can carry out are, admittedly, not as extensive as that of a natural person. However, those activities it can execute are as important to its existence as they are to a natural person and, from the perspective of natural persons, their right to freedom cannot be fully or properly realised unless this right to freedom is also afforded to juristic persons. It is after all through the very exercise of this freedom right that natural persons make use of juristic persons to achieve their ends. By excluding the substantive right to freedom from the balancing process, the Court in the *Scarbrow Testamentary Trust* case was inevitably bound to find that preference had to be given to the non-discrimination rights of the excluded beneficiaries.[117] In my view this was a mistaken approach.

There are two further aspects of the *Scarbrow Testamentary Trust* case dealing with complex constitutional matters, that deserve attention. Reference is made[118] to the judgment in the *Drummond Wren* case[119] in the High Court of Ontario which, in 1945, declared invalid a restrictive covenant applicable to land which prohibited it from being sold to 'Jews or persons of objectionable nationality'.[120] After an extensive quotation from the judgment, Griesel J comments as follows:[121]

'In my judgment, the views expressed so eloquently more than 60 years ago in a foreign jurisdiction apply, with equal force in our new democratic society of today. Here likewise, it does not require "innovation in legal principle" to strike down the offending conditions in the will of the testator. *All that is required* is to apply *well-recognised principles of public policy* to a set of facts requiring their invocation in the interest of the public good.' (Emphasis supplied.)

---

[117] Above, n 96 at para 44.

[118] Id para 37.

[119] *Re: Drummond Wren* [1945] OR 778.

[120] For the record it needs to be pointed out that a few years later the Ontario Court of Appeal (in *Re Noble and Wolfe* [1949] 4 DLR 375 Ont CA) dealing with a similar restrictive covenant, upheld the covenant and rejected the *Drummond Wren* ruling. In a further appeal the Canadian Supreme Court (in *Noble and Wolfe v Alley* [1951] 1 DLR 321 (SCC)) struck down the covenant as being uncertain. As Weinrib and Weinrib (2001: 63) comment: 'The [Supreme] Court said nothing about the public policy argument, leaving in place its rejection by the Ontario Court of Appeal.' In 1990, however, in *Canada Trust v Ontario Human Rights Commission* (1990) 69 DLR (4th) 321 (Ont CA), the Ontario Court of Appeal held that discriminatory restrictions on eligibility for scholarships under a charitable trust were contrary to public policy.

[121] Above, n 96 at para 38.

Let me say immediately that no one of right mind would (I hope) disagree with the *result* in the *Drummond Wren* case, which closely resembles *Shelley v Kraemer*, discussed fully above. The issue is one of underlying principle and methodology, which in my view should follow that suggested by Henkin and discussed fully above, namely that the severe indignity suffered by the excluded persons far outweighs, in any proportionality analysis, the freedom interest of the person relying on the covenant. What I would challenge in the passage quoted above is the inherent assumption that 'public policy' *simpliciter* provides the easy answer. While it may have been relatively simple, with respect to pre-1994 public policy, to repeat the appropriate mantra, it was — as I have already pointed out — very much a legal fiction and extremely difficult to apply in practice with a straight face. More importantly, the whole concept of public policy will have to be thoroughly re-thought in the light of the Constitution and its provisions. This is *particularly the case* with regard to public policy as applied *horizontally*. While there may be no objection formally to developing the common law horizontally through the construct of public policy, this simply cannot be done without going through the Constitution's s 8(3) prescripts. It is sometimes suggested that a party has the choice (absent legislation covering the matter) whether or not to invoke the Bill of Rights directly in a particular horizontal dispute. This choice does not exist. The wording of s 8(2) can simply not be distorted to make the horizontal operation of the Bill of Rights dependant on a private litigant's choice. It is categorical and unconditional, stating quite simply that '[a] provision of the Bill of Rights binds a natural or a juristic person ...'; not 'may bind' or 'binds if ...'. It binds by unconditional and direct operation of the Constitution. Once it so binds, then the provisions of s 8(3) follow. One is no doubt linguistically free, in an appropriate case, to categorise the process under s 8(3) as 'applying public policy' or 'developing public policy'. I have no quarrel with that, provided that the requirements of the subsection are fulfilled. The name given to a process cannot alter the substance of the process.

The second aspect I raise relates to the following observations in the judgment:[122]

> 'What also serves to "outweigh" the principle of freedom of testation, is the fact that one is dealing, in this instance, with an "element of state action", in the sense that "the institution appointed to distribute the rewards of the testator's beneficence" is a public agency or quasi-public body, ie the university. As Du Toit points out:
>
> "State action renders the distribution practice of such an institution with regard to the proceeds of a charitable bequest open to a constitutional challenge on the ground that the Constitution prohibits the State from conducting discriminatory practices."'

I would suggest that this approach is unsound, for the very reasons that Henkin criticises the ratio of the judgment in *Shelley v Kraemer* as being unsupportable. As both he and Wechsler point out, one can always artificially introduce some

[122] Id para 45, footnotes omitted.

element of state action, because any dispute must ultimately invoke the enforcing arm of the judiciary. Similarly, the mere fact that a testamentary disposition must, administratively, pass through the Master's Office, does not characterise the dispositions as being state action.

(b) The Scarbrow Trust case and subsequent decisions

Before concluding the critique of the *Scarbrow Trust* case, some background must first be given to the historical development of freedom of testation, and its limits. Professor MJ de Waal[123] and Prof Francois Du Toit[124] have done valuable work on freedom of testation and the horizontal impact of the Bill of Rights, including the right not to be unfairly discriminated against. I should like to deal as briefly with their views in this regard as, I trust, fairness permits.

Du Toit (1999: 234–239) points out that the extensive individual freedom of testation enjoyed in the later Roman Republic was not completely unfettered but limited by, for example, the introduction of measures to limit the effect of disinheritance on the testator's children. It was also limited with regard to unlawful provisions or provisions that were *contra bonos mores*, for example, conditions in total restraint of marriage. Roman law also, for socio-economic reasons, recognised various measures ensuring that a given share was reserved in favour of certain persons, the best known of which probably being the Justinian provision that an indigent widow was entitled to a share in the deceased estate of her husband, and the restriction of *fideicommissarii* to no more than four generations. In Roman-Dutch law, Du Toit (1999: 239–243) points out, the reception of Roman law 'established the Roman notion of freedom of testation as the cornerstone of Dutch testate succession' although greater freedom for the testator was permitted. Thus a father could disinherit a child by mere omission of the child's name from the will, although the *portio legitima* was still recognised, amounting to a portion of the child's intestate share. Conditions in general restraint of marriage were regarded as void. Although views are not unanimous in this regard Du Toit believes that the *quarta uxoria* was still 'available to the widow (and possibly widower), particularly in instances where the economic protection afforded by the measures referred to above, was lacking'.

In dealing with the limits to testamentary freedom in certain Anglo-Saxon and continental systems, Du Toit (2000: 360) points out that in English law, freedom of testation was virtually unfettered at the height of political and

[123] De Waal, MJ (1998) entitled 'The Law of Succession and the Bill of Rights'.

[124] Du Toit's unpublished doctoral thesis (2000a) — written under the supervision of Prof de Waal — entitled 'Testeervryheid in die Suid-Afrikaanse reg in die lig van 'n handves van regte'; and three journal articles arising out of his doctoral research: Du Toit (1999) entitled, 'The impact of social and economic factors on freedom of testation in Roman and Roman-Dutch law', Du Toit (2000) 'The limits imposed upon freedom of testation by the *boni mores*: lessons from common law and civil law (continental legal systems)', and Du Toit (2001), 'The constitutionally bound dead hand? The impact of constitutional rights and principles on freedom of testation'.

economic *laissez faire* during the nineteenth century, but that this freedom was 'substantially restricted in favour of a deceased's dependants by the Inheritance (Family Provision) Act of 1938 and the Inheritance (Provision for Family and Dependants) Act of 1975'. Various provisions are regarded as being against public policy,[125] but not, Du Toit (2000: 363) points out, 'prescriptive forfeiture clauses founded on race, nationality or religion which direct beneficiaries' religious convictions or choice of spouse'. In relation to clauses of this nature, Du Toit (2000: 366) comments that '[i]t wil be interesting to see whether (and if so, to what extent) the indirect horizontal application of relevant provisions of the Human Rights Act will bring about a metamorphosis in the approach to this contentious matter'. Du Toit explains (2000: 366–369) that charitable trusts can be identified under four distinct headings, viz

> 'trusts for the relief of poverty, trusts for educational purposes, religious trusts and trusts which cannot be identified under any of the aforementioned three headings, but which still operate for the benefit of the community'.

In this regard Du Toit (2000: 366) points out that 'English law allows testators to regulate the exploitation of assets by means of charitable trusts on the grounds of, inter alia, race, nationality and religion, as long as the above quadruple classification can accommodate such trusts' and that this position 'is strengthened by the fact that the Race Relations Act of 1976 ... and the Sex Discrimination Act of 1975 ... allow for certain concessions in favour of charities'.

According to Du Toit (2000: 369–370), the Australian law of succession follows closely that of English law, including the recognition of freedom of testation, although (as in England) certain testamentary provisions have been held to be contrary to public policy.[126] Du Toit (2000: 371) points out that 'prescriptive forfeiture clauses' founded upon race, nationality or religion are well known in Australian law and the way they are dealt with as controversial as in English law, there being a few cases in which these provisions have been 'cursorily regarded

[125] Du Toit (2000: 362) mentions the following: a condition in a will 'that encourages a beneficiary to commit a crime'; which 'requires of a beneficiary to exert influence with regard to a political matter, for example the acquisition of a peerage'; that 'effects the separation between parent and child'; that 'interferes with the religious education of a child'; that 'prevents a beneficiary from defending the realm or from occupying a public office'; that constitutes a 'general restraint of marriage'; and that 'prevents a beneficiary from practising a certain trade'.

[126] Du Toit (2000: 370) mentions the following: a condition that 'encourages a beneficiary to commit a crime or to participate in any act forbidden by law'; that 'exludes the jurisdiction of the court or which precludes a beneficiary from litigation with regard to the particular will'; that 'effects the separation between parent and child'; that 'prevents a parent from performing his/her parental duties'; and that constitutes 'a general restraint on marriage'.

as not in conflict with public policy'.[127] Du Toit (2000: 373) concludes, with regard to charitable testamentary bequests, that the Australian common-law position corresponds to a large extent with that of English law, but that, although 'emulating the English position, acknowledges certain mechanisms to escape the contentious results of charitable bequests founded *inter alia,* [on] race, nationality and religion'. One mechanism is that 'Australian law requires charities to display an element of public benefit. In the absence of this requirement, an (attempted) charitable bequest cannot be labelled as such.'

According to Du Toit (2000: 374) freedom of testation constitutes one of the founding principles of the modern Dutch law of succession. In dealing with the limits imposed upon freedom of testation by good morals (*goede zeden*) in Dutch law, Du Toit (2000:375) points to the fact that the Dutch *Grondwet* guarantees a number of fundamental rights, for example, the prohibition of discrimination on the grounds of, inter alia, religion, belief, political opinion, race, and gender; freedom of religion; freedom of association; and the right to privacy. According to Du Toit, these rights enjoy at least indirect horizontal protection 'in appropriate circumstances' and 'are therefore instrumental in the determination of Dutch juridical concepts such as good faith and good morals'. Despite the fact that there has been 'little judicial reference to these rights as far as the limits imposed on freedom of testation by good morals are concerned' Du Toit points out (2000: 375) that many Dutch writers argue that 'fundamental rights can in principle affect the general approach to prescriptive testamentary provisions, particularly by guiding a court in its interpretation and application of the good morals principle'. There is, however, no unanimity among writers with regard to, for example, a bequest with a forfeiture clause that obliges a beneficiary not to marry a Roman Catholic. Du Toit, however, points out (2000: 376) that most Dutch writers are of the view that such a clause presents the beneficiary with a dilemma that renders the 'beneficiary's decision or choice involuntary and [breaches] the fundamental right concerned [freedom to marry]'. According to Du Toit (2000: 377–380) it is the limiting effect of the good morals (*goeden zeden*) principle that plays the major role with regard to freedom of testation, as enacted through

[127] However, in *Trustees of Church Property of the Diocese of Newcastle v Ebbeck* [1960] 104 CLR 394, the Australian High Court was concerned with a bequest to each of three sons that was made subject to the resolutive condition in relation to each son 'that he and his wife shall at the date of death of my wife or at my death should my wife predecease me profess the Protestant faith'. The majority of the Court found this clause to be invalid because it conflicted with public policy. In support of this conclusion Dixon CJ, referring to the case of the marriage between a Protestant husband and a Roman Catholic wife, said the following at 404:

> 'Assuming that the donee himself retains his Protestant faith, he and his wife remain conscious of that her adherence through his mother's life to her own faith stands between him and and his inheritance. The husband on his part may be a man of firm mind and of a lofty and generous sentiment, but it would be difficult for many a man in such a situation to prevent his mind on occasions from adverting rather to the advantage of divorce than the blessings of matrimony, that is to say if ever unhappy differences or clouds appeared which unless dispelled might develop such a prospect. In an uneasy marriage a more fruitful apple for discord could hardly be placed upon the domestic board.'

various provisions of the Dutch Civil Code (*Burgerlijk Wetboek*) and the New Dutch Civil Code (*Nieuw Burgerlijk Wetboek*).[128]

Although I shall be dealing with the principle of horizontality in German law in s 5.6 below, a few comments here on its impact on the law of succession might be appropriate. Du Toit (2000: 380) points out that the German law of succession, which is derived from Roman and Germanic law, is codified in Book 5 of the German Civil Code (*Bürgerliches Gesetzbuch*). Article 14(1) of the GBL provides: 'Property and the right of inheritance shall be guaranteed. Their content and limits shall be defined by the laws.' Although art 14(1) does not expressly guarantee freedom of testation, Du Toit (2000: 381) explains that 'the guarantee of private ownership and private succession is readily interpreted in German law as a commensurate guarantee of freedom of testation'. Apart from arts 1, 2 and 3 of the GBL, which have already been dealt with, the following basic rights, relevant to the present enquiry, are guaranteed: freedom of faith, conscience and religion (art 4); rights relating to marriage, family and children (art 6); freedom of association (art 9); and rights to privacy (arts 10 and 13). In German law the influence of good morals on testamentary dispositions is also founded in its Civil Code (*Bürgerliches Gesetzbuch*), paragraph 138(1), which provides that '[a] juristic act which is contrary to the good morals, is void'.[129] Du Toit (2000: 382) explains that a testamentary provision 'is regarded in German law as contrary to the good morals (*sittenwidrig*) if it offends the "*Anstandsgefühl aller billig und gerecht Denkenden*" ("the legal convictions [pertaining to what is proper and decent] of all reasonable and right minded people")'. The test is objective in nature. Of particular importance for present purposes is the following statement by Du Toit (2000: 382):

> 'This test is applied with particular attention to the facts and circumstances of each case, since, as Lange and Kuchinke point out, *testamentary benefiting is, per definition, premised upon preference and hence unequal treatment — in some cases beneficiaries will simply have to accept what they perceive as unequal or even discriminatory treatment at the hands of the testator*.' (Footnotes omitted, emphasis supplied.)

An important distinction is also drawn between testamentary provisions that affect the out and out disinheritance of (potential) beneficiaries, and provisions that attempt to exert influence in the private lives of citizens. In this regard Du Toit comments (2000: 382) as follows:

---

[128] Du Toit (2000: 378) points out that, under these provisions, the following testamentary provisions have been nullified on the basis that they are in conflict with public morals:
(a) One in 'general restraint of marriage';
(b) One that 'negates the operation of the *legitieme portie* (award of maintenance) in favour of dependants';
(c) One prohibiting 'the alienation of bequeathed assets';
(d) One establishing 'a prohibited *fideicommissum* (*making over de hand*)'.

[129] Translation by Du Toit (2000: 382).

> 'As far as the former is concerned Brox opines that disherison which occurs with reference to the fundamental rights of disinherited (potential) beneficiaries, should not be regarded as contrary to good morals, particularly because, as stated above, no testator is under the obligation to treat his/her [potential] beneficiaries on an equal footing. *Testators therefore retain the absolute right to institute certain beneficiaries and to disinherit other (potential) beneficiaries.* Brox contends, however, that *prescriptive testamentary provisions* can indeed be regarded as contrary to the good morals, particularly if such provisions *infringe the fundamental rights of the beneficiaries concerned.* A bequest which provides for forfeiture of benefits, should the beneficiary marry a person of a particular race, nationality or religion, can consequently be regarded as an undue restriction of such beneficiary's right to freedom of marriage (*Entschließungsfreiheit*) and hence invalid.' (Footnotes omitted, emphasis supplied.)

In the third of his trilogy of articles, Du Toit (2001: 223) sets himself the task of attempting 'to provide a framework for future judicial development of the legal position in South African law with regard to freedom of testation in the light of the influence of constitutional rights and principles' and focuses his discussion 'on testamentary disposition by way of prescriptive provisions, and on particular testamentary forfeiture clauses and charitable testamentary bequests based on race, nationality and religion'.[130]

Although freedom of testation is regarded as one of the founding principles of the South African law of succession and the wishes of the testator paramount — as more fully explained by him — Du Toit (2001: 224–225) details the current restrictions on this freedom imposed by legislation and judicial pronouncement.[131] I shall assume, for purposes of this chapter, that these legislative and other restrictions are not inconsistent with the Constitution. I shall also assume that none of these restrictions apply to the *Scarbrow* case.

[130] Although I might not agree with all the author's conclusions, his dissertation and articles are indispensable reading for anyone investigating the law of inheritance in the light of the 1996 Constitution and in particular its Bill of Rights.

[131] '*(a)* The maintenance and education of a parent's children constitute a claim against such parent's deceased estate.
(b) The maintenance of Surviving Spouses Act awards a claim for maintenance to a surviving spouse against the estate of a deceased spouse under certain circumstances.
(c) Effect will not be given to testamentary dispositions which are illegal, *contra bonos mores* or vague.
(d) The Immoveable Property (Removal of Modification of Restrictions) Act limits a testator's capacity to prevent the alienation of land by way of long-term provisions.
(e) The Trust Property Control Act provides for the variation or early termination of testamentary trusts under certain circumstances.
(f) The Minerals Act curtails a testator's capacity to subdivide mineral right.
(g) The Pension Funds Act excludes certain benefits payable by a pension fund from the estate of a deceased member of such fund.' (Footnotes omitted.)

The Subdivision of Agricultural Land Act 70 of 1970, which placed limits on the extent to which agricultural land could be subdivided, has been repealed in its entirety by the Subdivision of Agricultural Land Repeal Act 64 of 1998.

The possible impact of the Bill of Rights on the South African law of succession generally[132] is an extensive and complex topic which I cannot possibly address in this book. I do no more than quote a few examples to illustrate the methodology I believe lies at the heart of the horizontal application of freedom (of testation) and *unfair discrimination*. Where I go beyond this, I do so only in order to point out where I agree or disagree with the general methodology employed by a court or particular writer.

Du Toit (2001: 225–227) deals with the 'traditional approach' to testamentary forfeiture clauses that provide for the forfeiture of benefits should a beneficiary forsake a particular faith or conclude a marriage with members of a given race, nationality or religion. The traditional approach, as exemplified by the Appellate Division judgment in *Aronson v Estate Hart*,[133] is that these provisions are not contestable on the grounds that they are *contra bonos mores*. Du Toit is critical of this approach and suggests (2001: 227) that 'a reappraisal of [this] traditional approach is long overdue' and submits that 'a constitutionally founded *boni mores*[134] criterion is the appropriate tool to be utilised in such reassessment'. I have no serious quarrel with his phrase 'constitutionally founded *boni mores* criterion'; but the devil is of course in the detail. How, precisely, does one find the appropriate criteria and how does one apply them. In particular, the application of a 'constitutionally founded *boni mores* criterion' cannot circumvent the mandatory discipline of ss 8(2) and 8(3).

Du Toit further deals (2001: 228–231) with charitable testamentary bequests that are limited on the grounds of race, nationality or religion and points out that 'the traditional approach dictates that such bequests are not contestable on the ground that they are *contra bonos mores*'. Here too, Du Toit (2001: 231) argues that a reassessment should take place based on the 'constitutionally founded *boni mores* criterion'. While the Constitution does not expressly guarantee freedom of testation, this is clearly implicit in the Bill of Rights. The right to own property is impliedly guaranteed by s 25(1) although, as stated in the *FNB* judgment,[135] '[the s 25 provisions] emphasise that under the 1996 Constitution the protection of property as an individual right is not absolute but subject to societal considerations'.[136] Moreover, the purpose of s 25 has to be seen as 'both protecting private property rights as well as serving the public interest, mainly in the sphere of land reform but not limited thereto, and also striking a proportionate balance between these functions'.[137] One of the prime competences that the owner of property has, is to dispose of it freely. But, viewed from a Kantian perspective,

[132] A topic dealt with fairly fully by Du Toit (2001).

[133] 1950 (1) SA 539 (A).

[134] Du Toit correctly considers that there is no material difference between the concepts '*boni mores*' and 'public policy'.

[135] Above, n 116.

[136] Id para 49.

[137] Id para 50.

I believe that the ownership of property itself is more fundamentally associated with freedom than is generally granted. Therefore, in my view, the 'right' to dispose of property freely is as much an exercise of fundamental freedom, as it is a 'competence' of ownership. Moreover freedom of testation — in the absence of any express constitutional provision excluding it — must be regarded as protected under the residual freedom provisions of s 12(1). Accordingly, when weighing up the rights or interests of the testator and the disappointed potential beneficiary, the testator's right is not merely one deriving from ownership, but also — if not predominantly — from freedom. Subject to this qualification Du Toit (2001: 234) therefore correctly comes to the 'inescapable conclusion that both private ownership as well as the resultant *ius disponendi* indeed enjoy constitutional protection in South African law'.

Du Toit (2001: 234–235) explains the constitutional basis for the limitation of freedom of testation on the horizontal level, and the methodology involved as follows:

> 'A litigant can therefore invoke one or more of [the rights under the Bill of Rights] when contesting the validity of a testamentary bequest. Such litigant will in all probability argue that the contentious provision constitutes an infringement on a particular constitutionally protected right and that the bequest should therefore be invalidated. An opposing party is likely to counter with reliance on the testator's freedom of testation. The court is now obliged to conduct the balancing exercise in terms of s 36 as envisaged by s 8(3)(b) of the Constitution: the court must weight freedom of testation against the competing constitutional right. If the court finds that the particular constitutional right should prevail over the testator's freedom of testamentary disposition, the Court must, pursuant to s 8(3)*(a)* of the Constitution, apply the common law in order to resolve the situation. The common law indeed awards a remedy in this regard, namely that a bequest which is *contra bonos mores* or against public policy can be invalidated.'

The author is to be commended for appreciating that in this horizontal operation of constitutional rights, the s 8(3) methodology cannot be escaped. I am, however, unable to agree with the sequence of the steps he employs and certain of the conclusions he reaches.

The first step, in my view, is for the court to determine whether the common law gives *a proper answer*, namely *an answer* to the problem that is consistent with the Constitution. I would argue that this is implicit in s 8(3) where the obligation on the court to 'develop the common law' only arises when it is 'necessary' to do so, ie when the existing common law as 'applied' does not afford *a solution* that is consistent with the Constitution. In order to determine this latter question one must ask what solution the Constitution would give if the balancing and limitation of one, or other, or of both of the competing rights is conducted under s 8(3)*(b)* read with s 36(1) of the Constitution. I have deliberately highlighted the indefinite article in the phrases '*a* proper answer', '*an* answer' and '*a* solution' above, in order to emphasise what I have already argued in this chapter, namely that the function of the court is not to decide whether the existing common law provides the best way of achieving the correct constitutional solution, but only whether the answer it *does already* provide is consistent with the constitutional solution.

I also believe that Du Toit is mistaken when he asserts that, in the context of the clash we are considering, whether the existing common law 'indeed awards a remedy' in this regard, namely 'that a bequest which is *contra bonos mores* or against public policy can be invalidated'. This, in my view, is a serious and potentially dangerous short-circuiting of the s 8(3) process. The *boni mores* or public policy are not *dei ex machina* existing somewhere 'out there,' isolated and untouched by the Constitution. They are themselves concepts that have to be rigorously examined under s 8(3). For example, the question should always be asked whether a particular public policy rule, relating to a private law dispute between parties, is consistent with the demands of s 8 read with s 36(1) and in particular the proportionality exercise involved. I have been at pains to urge that, if one persists in using the expression 'public policy' (or *boni mores* for that matter), one must clearly distinguish between *pre-constitutional* and *post-constitutional* public policy because they differ fundamentally. I would prefer, as already indicated, if one spoke — in the sphere of horizontality — about the balancing of rights using the limitation and proportionality principles established in s 36(1) as invoked by s 8(3)*(b)*. I believe that the work of Weinrib and Weinrib (2001) on Canadian 'horizontality', dealt with in section 5.8 below, in principle supports this approach. In a sense Du Toit is also contradicting himself because, in the above passages quoted from his work (2001: 227 and 231), he refers to the 'constitutionally founded *boni mores* criterion', which is of course something quite different. He in fact recognises this when he contends (2001: 235) that 'the judicial utilization of a constitutionally based *boni mores* criterion will represent an unequivocal departure from the traditional formal style of adjudication with regard to the limitation of testamentary freedom and constitutes a firm step towards a more substantive approach to this area of the law of testate succession'.

I also do not think one can assume, as Du Toit apparently does (2001: 235), that with regard to the type of bequest found to be 'in conflict with the *bonos mores* in the past, the court will undoubtedly extend due protection to the infringed constitutional right by also invalidating the contested testamentary bequest'. Without conducting the nuanced balancing exercise required by s 8(3)*(b)* and s 36(1) with regard to every type of disputed bequest, it is impossible, in my view, to say so. The *boni mores* and public policy have to be examined in the light of the Constitution, expressly directed through the prism of s 8(2) and (3).

Du Toit (2001: 236–239) lists more than ten rights in the Bill of Rights that in his view 'will in all likelihood constitute the principal counterweight to freedom of testation'. It is beyond the scope of this book to go beyond the right not to be unfairly discriminated against, and in any event I am more concerned with establishing the correct, principled methodology than the particular outcome in any particular case. Yet there are two observations that I should like to make with regard to Du Toit's list. In the first place he is, in my view, mistaken when he suggests that the (entire) 'right to equality under s 9' applies horizontally. As previously explained, s 9(1) does not. While the state may not act irrationally, the same demand is not, in general, made of individuals in their dealings with others. This means that irrational decisions by individuals in the private sphere do not, on the ground of irrationality *alone*, fall foul of constitutional norms in the horizontal application of the Bill of Rights. Du Toit is, moreover, mistaken when he asserts (2001: 236) that an infringement of the right to equality also constitutes an infringement of the right to dignity. In the first place a vertical infringement of s 9(1), constituted by irrational differentiation, does not necessarily infringe dignity. More importantly, it is the value of dignity — as *criterion of attribution* — that informs unfair discrimination and not the other way around.

This having been said, I shall examine briefly the extent to which the horizontal right not to be unfairly discriminated against might affect freedom of testation. In this regard Du Toit's prognostic[138] discussion regarding freedom of testation and its limits (2001: 239–256) is important. Du Toit is of the view (2001: 239–240) that freedom of testation needs to be preserved as a basic principle of the South African law since it is firmly supported by the socio-economic foundations of the law of succession, is an historical reality, and — as his comparative research indicates — 'is acknowledged as a fundamental principle of the law of testate succession of many comparable common law and civil law systems'. I would merely add that it is also preserved by the Constitution. But, as Du Toit points out (2001: 240), the history of freedom of testation shows that from the earliest times it was 'restricted by virtue of prevailing socio-economic considerations', as is the case in the South African common law.

The approach in the law of testate succession to out and out disinheritance is relevant to the issue of when the horizontal prohibition against unfair discrimination might limit freedom of testation. It has been suggested that out and out disinheritance for a repugnant motive might do so. Du Toit (2001: 242), however, argues that comparative research reveals that 'such provisions in civil codes are hardly ever relied on in order to contest out and out disinherison' and that 'the scant authority gained from continental legal systems in this regard cannot justify the importation of a corresponding measure in South African law'. He also points out that civil law writers 'admit to the fact that it is, as a matter of practicality, often difficult (if not impossible) to ascertain the motive underlying a disinherison, particularly if the will itself is silent on the issue'.

[138] Section 5 of his article (2001: 239–256) is entitled 'A prognosis: the freedom of testation and its limitation in terms of a constitutionally founded *boni mores* criterion in South African law'.

Cogent reasons exist why out and out disinheritance, even if based on grounds that run counter to the s 9(3) prohibitions, is not in conflict with the horizontal application of these prohibitions or any post-constitutional *boni mores* or public policy. I exclude from consideration those cases where '[t]he testator's or testatrix's legitimate or extra-marital children, and also major children unable to support themselves have, in the case of need, a claim for support or maintenance against the testator's estate' (De Waal 1998: 3G 14, issue 13).

De Waal (1998: 3G 24, issue 19) correctly points out that the two inconsistent constitutional rights in this sort of case 'are those of equality (relied upon by A) and the testator's freedom of testation (relied upon by B)'. De Waal suggests that 'the testator's freedom of testation should limit A's right to equality [and non-discrimination] and that such limitation can be justified in terms of s 36(1)'[139] and advances the following reasons[140] why an out and out disinheritance of this nature, even when expressly based on a prohibited ground, is not inconsistent with the horizontal application of the s 9(3) prohibitions:[141]

'*(a)* An opposite conclusion would not only reduce the concept of freedom of testation to a fiction, but would also render the guarantee of freedom of testation in the Bill of Rights meaningless.

(b) Nobody has a fundamental "right to inherit". The exclusion of a person as beneficiary does not, therefore, result in an encroachment upon or taking away of existing rights. A potential beneficiary at most posseses a *spes* or hope which, by its nature, can easily be frustrated.

(c) It seems to be a sound proposition, both as a matter of principle and common sense, that a testator or testatrix should, within the limits set by social and economic considerations, be free to institute beneficiaries of his or her own choice.

(d) An opposite conclusion would lead to nearly insurmountable practical difficulties, some of which may be mentioned. If somebody in A's position were to succeed with a constitutional challenge, what would the remedy be? Must the court "re-write" the will and institute the aggrieved person as heir? If so, should such a person receive the same as the other heir or heirs?... Or should the court declare the will invalid and allow the estate to be distributed in accordance with the rules of intestate succession (thereby creating a windfall for persons the testator never even contemplated as heirs)? Can somebody in A's position challenge the will only if he or she receives nothing in the will? If not, how much will suffice to prevent a constitutional challenge? And will only, for example, a child who has been unfairly discriminated against be able to launch a challenge? If not, where is the line to be drawn?'

Of course s 9(3) is breached only (whether directly or horizontally via s 9(4)) when the discrimination in question is 'unfair' and discrimination is unfair only

---

[139] I would merely add that the limitation enquiry could, and perhaps should, also be done in reverse order, namely by enquiring whether A's right to equality and non-discrimination is a justifiable limitation under s 36(1) of the testator's freedom of testation. The answer should be in the negative.

[140] Subject to a few qualifications of my own that I shall briefly mention.

[141] Which are supported by Du Toit (2001: 242–245).

if it impacts adversely on A's human dignity. The factual matrix may be of a kind (as, possibly, in some of the examples given by De Waal in paragraph *(d)* above) that clearly 'establishes' (in discharge of the s 9(4) presumption) that there has been no adverse impact on A's dignity. In this event that would be the end of the matter, because no equality right of A has been breached. If breached, however, a weighing-up will have to take place (on my thesis) between, in effect, the severity of the impact on A's dignity against the severity of the impact on the testator's dignity by the breach of her freedom of testation.

De Waal (1998: 3G / 12, issue 19) deals with the consequence of attaching conditions to testamentary provisions. He distinguishes between two types. I deal only with the second type, which de Waal describes as 'bequests coupled with conditions or restrictions aimed at furthering the interests of only a particular section of society' and are, in his view 'more complex'. He argues that with the second type a conclusion that they are in conflict with public policy 'should be reached with more circumspection'. This should be the case, De Waal argues, 'regardless of the fact that the section is selected on, for example, racial, religious or political grounds'. He considers two examples:

> '*(a)* All my money will be held in trust and the proceeds will be used to build and maintain a school for black Sotho-speaking boys / girls of the Jewish faith / children of ANC members.
>
> *(b)* All my money will be held in trust and the proceeds will be used by the University of Stellenbosch for the provision of bursaries, on the condition that these bursaries may only go to female students studying law / members of the Anglican Church / students with the surname of Van der Merwe.'

De Waal points out that conditions or restrictions of this nature 'neither encroach upon the personal sphere of the recipients nor are aimed at influencing the personal conduct of the recipients', and he appears to favour the upholding of these bequests because 'this would be in line with the general benevolent treatment afforded to bequests of a charitable nature'. Unfortunately the learned author then (relying on, among others, certain US Supreme Court judgments) refers to an argument similar to the *ratio decidendi* in *Shelley*'s case discussed above: 'It is possible, however, that these conditions will not be enforced in practice because it would entail "state action" in the sense that the state, a public agency or quasi-public body would be obliged to become involved in the administration of discriminatory practice.' In the first place I would argue that American scholars such as Henkin and Wechsler have convincingly discredited this form of 'state action' argument. The 'in practice' argument is also not valid. One cannot artificially separate the remedy from the right in this way.[142] Either the condition or restriction is invalid, in which case it cannot be enforced, or is

[142] See the first of the trilogy of constitutional cases in the 1950s: *Harris v Minister of the Interior* 1952 (2) SA 428 (A).

valid and must be enforced. Answering the first question first is jurisprudentially essential. However, if no suitable remedy can be conceived, this might be a strong indication that no correlative right exists.

Applying the 'Henkin' approach to the limitations analysis required under s 8(3) read with s 36(1) of the Constitution, I suggest that the outcome in the *Scarbrow* case ought rather to have been determined along different lines. In so doing I accord full weight to the *dicta* of the Constitutional Court in the *FNB* case in relation to the nature of the property rights under s 25 of the Constitution.[143] I refer in particular to the following observation of Van der Walt (1997: 15–16) quoted with approval in the *FNB* case:[144]

> '[T]he meaning of s 25 has to be determined, in each specific case, within an interpretative framework that takes due cognizance of the inevitable tensions which characterize the operation of the property clause. This tension between individual rights and social responsibilities has to be the guiding principle in terms of which the section is analysed, interpreted and applied in each individual case.'

But the *Scarbrow* case, when properly analysed, is not really about the testator's property rights; the dispute is not concerned with the existence, nature, extent or content of his rights to the property in question, but rather about his freedom to dispose thereof on his death, as proportionately balanced against the non-discrimination rights of the disappointed potential beneficiaries. In this context it is also not a case where the freedom to dispose of one's property as one wishes is being limited in order to protect the interests of a surviving spouse, partner, child or any other dependant. The disappointed potential beneficiaries have no prior familial or legal relationship with the testator.

I have serious difficulty in seeing how the differentiation in question impacts negatively on the human dignity of the disappointed beneficiaries. The discrimination (if one can call it that) in question, which impliedly 'excludes' persons who are 'female', of 'Jewish descent' and *not* of 'European descent', is based on several grounds listed in s 9(3) and accordingly (under s 9(4)) presumed to be unfair 'unless it is established that the discrimination is fair'.[145] The discriminees (the disappointed potential beneficiaries) constitute three classes whose membership it would be impossible to determine, even if one (somehow) limited membership to disappointed South Africans. In fact, one is not dealing here — in substance — with an 'exclusion' at all. Neither the actual beneficiaries nor the disappointed beneficiaries had any pre-existing (pre-testamentary) rights

---

[143] Above, n 116, in particular paras 49 and 50.

[144] Id para 50.

[145] I do not here consider the precise meaning to be attached to the phrase 'unless it is established that'. I shall assume that if 'establish[ing] that the discrimination is fair' depends on facts that are not already established, it is incumbent on the 'discriminator' to do so if he/she wishes to prevent the presumption/assumption in s 9(4) from coming into operation. But if all the facts before the court 'establish' that the discrimination is fair, the discriminator need do nothing further.

to benefit from the testator. This is rather a case of a distinction between persons to whom benefits (not pre-existing) are granted. A *private* person has chosen to benefit certain persons, and not to benefit others. I have the greatest difficulty in seeing how this can possibly impact negatively on the human dignity of persons who have not been benefited. I shall, however, for present purposes assume (hypothetically) that there is a negative impact. Even then, the impact must surely be miniscule. But for the will and the trust, both creatures of the testator, none of these disappointed beneficiaries would have had anything to be disappointed or aggrieved about. It is not in any way a limitation of the disappointed beneficiaries' freedom in respect of any of life's normal activities. It does not interfere with any activity through which disappointed beneficiaries might seek to develop their individuality, their personality, or any of their personality rights. It does not deny anything that could contribute to their human dignity. They have suffered no more, in my analysis, than a somewhat abstract opportunity of sharing in an entirely fortuitous windfall. There could be no inkling of a grievance if the testator made no will at all. How is a grievance generated when the testator makes a will benefiting only some? It is tantamount to saying that I have some sort of entitlement to share in any private munificence, from which I may not be excluded. Is the situation in principle any different to a munificence by way of a donation between living persons? I cannot see any basis for an argument that a person who is not a donee in this situation has a constitutional right in private law to participation in the donation. The fact that the reason for not benefiting is a s 9(3) ground cannot make a difference. What of the situation where an owner liquidates all his or her assets to buy a diamond and then throws the diamond into the sea, because he has no family living and does not want to devote his money to non-racial charitable causes. It is difficult to imagine an action accruing to anyone.

But let me return to the *Scarbrow* case. Assuming that the persons discriminated against have suffered any injury to their dignity, this injury is a most limited affront — even less than that suffered by the trespasser on property whom the owner seeks to evict for racist reasons. On the other hand, if the testator's exclusion is held to be invalid, this is a serious limitation of his freedom to dispose of his property on his death. On balance, therefore, I would suggest that the right of the testator ought not to be limited. I appreciate that this conclusion is, on first impression, counter-intuitive, but this intuition might itself be the result of a confusion between the vertical and the horizontal operation of the Bill of Rights. It is one thing to prohibit the state from certain actions; it is notionally a different thing to do so as between natural persons. Whereas the law can rightly keep watch over all state action, the law cannot do so in the case of persons. The law cannot legislate on every aspect of our lives; there are areas of human privacy and freedom that are sacrosanct and beyond the reach of the law. While the precise extent of those areas may not always be easy to define, the principle of their existence and protection ought never to be yielded. This should be constantly borne in mind when considering any horizontal application of the Bill of Rights.

Much has been written on the dangers of a simplistic distinction between public and private law, and one is aware of the arguments that institutions of private law have taken over many functions that were previously exercised exclusively by the state. One must also constantly be alive to the power, especially political, that is wielded by amassed private financial resources, and the negative influence this can have on individuals, particularly the more vulnerable of them. On the other hand it would be quite irresponsible and perverse to convert all private law into 'state action' simply because the courts enforce all private law.

Especially in the field of unfair discrimination, one should be careful not to confuse ethics with law. As a matter of ethics one might well be strongly opposed to the making of dispositions on the discriminatory grounds present in the *Scarbrow* case. But private law is not a mirror image of personal ethics, and one should resist the temptation to make it so. In evaluating unfair discrimination in the horizontal sphere one should, I believe, seek a neutral principle of adjudication, which I argue is to be found in human dignity. It is the degree of indignity suffered by a discriminee in the operation of private law rules that must be weighed up against the nature and degree of infringement of the fundamental rights of the other party, if the private law principle were not upheld. There is an area of privacy, freedom and property rights that is sacrosanct and should not be invaded by the law. There is no simple mantra that will define this area and how its lines are to be drawn. This will have to be determined on a case-by-case basis, as the law has traditionally developed in the courts, even in its most complex areas. But human dignity is the sound neutral principle to be used in this process.

In the *Emma Smith Educational Fund* case[146] the Supreme Court of Appeal (SCA) was concerned with the provision of a will that created a charitable trust, the 'Emma Smith Educational Fund', administered by the University of KwaZulu-Natal, the benefits in the will being reserved solely for white South African women who need financial support for tertiary education. For present purposes the relevant provisions of s 13 of the Trust Property Control Act 57 of 1988 ('the Act') read as follows:

> 'If a trust instrument contains any provision which brings about consequences which in the opinion of the court the founders of a trust did not contemplate or foresee and which —
> *(a)* ...
> *(b)* ...
> *(c)* is in conflict with the public interest,
> the court may ... delete or vary any such provision....'

[146] *Curators, Emma Smith Educational Fund v University of KwaZulu-Natal and Others* 2010 (6) SA 518 (SCA) (2011 (1) BCLR 40).

A High Court found the above racially restrictive provisions of the bequest to be in conflict with the public interest and deleted them. The SCA dismissed an appeal to it against this order for essentially the same reason, being of the view that '[t]he question is whether this bequest ... can be allowed to stand in its racially exclusive form'.[147] The SCA referred with seeming approval[148] to the *Scarbrow* decision and in this connection said the following:

> 'In a comprehensive judgment with copious reference to authority, Griesel J came to the conclusion that the discrimination against the excluded persons was in conflict with public policy because it transgressed the equality provision of the Bill of Rights.'

The SCA gave no indication that it was dealing with the horizontal application of the Bill of Rights. Nor did it revisit any of the issues dealt with in the *Scarbrow* judgment, and in particular did not deal with the issue of the clash of rights between plaintiff and defendant that must inevitably ensue when the Bill of Rights is applied horizontally, nor with the way in which a clash of this nature is to be resolved. It also did not address the issue why, in constitutional principle, a private individual could not be discriminatory on the grounds of race and gender in making a testamentary bequest. Unfortunately the judgment makes no real contribution to the important issue of the methodology to be adopted in the horizontal operation of the Bill of Rights.

5.7 GERMAN INSIGHTS

(a) Introduction

Of particular importance for the horizontal application, under the South African Constitution, of the prohibition against unfair discrimination, are the limits that German law has placed on the applicability of equality under the Basic Law to the field of private law. I say this with full appreciation of the fact that under German law this horizontal application is indirect (see para *(b)* below), while under the South African Constitution the application of the constitutional right to equality applies directly by virtue of s 9(4), first sentence, s 8(2) and in particular s 8(3). These sections have been discussed fully above, and in particular the clearly spelt out 'discipline' required by s 8(3). Section 8(3) was enacted with the clear appreciation, implicit in the subsection itself, that the horizontal application of the Bill of Rights would give rise to tensions and indeed clashes between the rights of contesting parties. This is the very reason why s 8(3)*(b)* was enacted and the limitation provisions of s 36(1) made applicable to horizontality. Just as a proportionality analysis was developed by the Constitutional Court to ensure the proper application of the limitation provisions of s 36(1) when the individual seeks enforcement of a provision of the Bill of Rights against the state, so too an

[147] Id para 1.

[148] Id paras 34, 38, 40. The SCA refers to the *Scarbrow* case as the *Syfret's* (sic) case.

appropriate proportionality analysis must take place when the same provisions apply horizontally and a clash of rights has to be resolved under s 8(3)*(b)* by means of s 36(1). This is particularly the case when the prohibition against discrimination is applied horizontally and the right of A to be protected against unfair discrimination clashes with B's rights to, inter alia, freedom, privacy and property.

Although the German basic rights apply only with indirect horizontality (*mittelbare Drittwirkung*), similar conflicts of rights between individuals occur in Germany, as is the case with direct horizontality. In order to deal with these clashes, German law applies the same doctrines of the limitation of rights, including the principle of proportionality, to the horizontal application of the Bill of Rights (and in particular to the horizontal application of the prohibition against discrimination), as it does to their vertical application against the state.

In para (b) below I try to show how, in the horizontal application of the prohibition in art 3(3) of the GBL against discrimination in German law, equality in the private law must in appropriate cases defer to freedom, privacy and the like. The reasons advanced for the resolution of a clash of rights, and how the balancing process is motivated is, I argue, relevant and persuasive for resolving these clashes under ss 8(3) and 36(1) of our Constitution. This supports my main contention in this section, namely that human dignity (including therein the value of freedom, the right to the free unfolding of the human personality and the right to privacy) is of determining influence in resolving these clashes.

(b) Indirect horizontality ('mittelbare Drittwirkung') in German law

The expressions 'horizontal' and 'horizontality' are not exclusive to English conceptualisation. Nor is '*Drittwirkung*' (literally 'third party operation') the only term used in Germany. Stern (1988: 1513–1514) mentions that the term '*Horizontalwirkung*' is also used, as well as the expression 'the application of the basic rights in private law' ('*Geltung der Grundrechte in Privatrecht*').[149] More importantly Stern makes the point, relevant to our own jurisprudence in this area, that none of these terms give a satisfactory explanation of the true content of horizontality, and that they in fact tend to obscure two important facts. The one is that the application of the basic rights (rights protected in the GBL) to private law relationships creates simultaneously for both parties to this relationship *rights and duties*. The other is that in this relationship one has two parties, standing in apposition to each other, both of whom have rights (the same rights) under the constitution. These conflicts cannot arise, on the other hand, in the state–individual relationship. For the sake of consistency I shall continue to use the expression 'horizontal' and 'horizontality', but implicit in this use are the above reservations.

[149] See also Von Münch (1992: Rn 28).

The history of the development of horizontality in German law is a fascinating one, which cannot be followed in any detail in a work such as this. However, the question that remains with me, both regarding German and South African law, is whether — in the end result — there really is a great difference between direct and indirect horizontality.

Stern (1988: 1531) himself doubts whether the distinction between direct and indirect horizontality is as stark (*schroff*) as their protagonists would suggest. He mentions that someone such as Christian Starck believes that it is still an open question whether, in particular cases, the 'cautious approach' of indirect horizontality would really lead to an outcome that differs from that resulting from a 'nuanced' application of direct horizontality.

The wrestling that has taken place in Germany over the past 60 years with horizontality is important for South African jurisprudence, despite the fact that the 1996 Constitution has chosen direct horizontality.

According to Stern (1988: 1518–1520), horizontality and the problems relating thereto came to the fore in Germany only after 1945, and became a grand theme in the 1950s and early 1960s. The comment by the BVerfG in 1958 in the *Lüth* case to the effect that '[t]he fundamental question whether the basic rights norms should impact on private law and how they were intended to do so in particular cases, is controversial'[150] was, according to Stern (1988: 1520) still true in the late 1980s. Stern (1988: 1531), however, states that the scale is increasingly tilting in favour of indirect horizontality, so that it can safely be asserted that indirect horizontality is now the prevailing view (*herrschende Meinung*).

The views of the representatives in the Parliamentary Council were that the rights entrenched in the constitution would only operate at the vertical level. According to Stern (1988: 1522–1523), the debates concerning horizontality were fired by a provocative article by Herbert Krüger who was of the view that private law had everything to gain and nothing to lose if private law scholars 'with all necessary circumspection, looked out over the pure private law horizon and enriched their own arguments by including appropriate constitutional points of view',[151] citing as an example the statutes of a private association which in principle excluded certain classes of persons from membership, which would conflict with the constitutional equality provision. This opened a debate that, although leading to relatively clear agreement in certain areas, has by no means been finally concluded.

[150] BVerfGE 7, 198 (204).
[151] Krüger (1949: 165).

Referring to the writings of HC Nipperday, who pleaded for direct horizontality in relation to the equality provisions of the GBL and the issue of equal pay for men and women, the Federal Labour Court in the mid-1950s, while accepting the principle that the GBL should exercise an influence on labour relations, left open the question whether the equality provision of the GBL applied directly to the issue of equal pay for men and women (Stern 1988: 1524–1526).

In 1954 the German Supreme Court, relying on the provisons of arts 1 and 2 of the GBL, recognised a general personality right 'also as a private right to be respected by everyone else'.[152] In 1958 the same Court stressed that arts 1 and 2 of the GBL protected directly 'only that inner sphere of personality, that supports the free and responsible self-determination of the individual.... To respect this sphere and not to intrude thereon without justification is a legal injunction that arises out of the Basic Law itself. In the same way it necessarily follows from the Basic Law that, upon breach of protection in this sphere, appropriate damages can be recovered for this breach.'[153] Although, as Stern (1988: 1526) points out, the awarding of damages for non-patrimonial loss in the case of the breach of the personality right was not uncontroversial, it has come to be generally accepted and has been approved by the BVerfG.[154]

Dürig also played an important role in the debate concerning direct or indirect horizontality, and came down decidedly on the side of indirect horizontality.[155] In defence of this approach Dürig (1956a: 157, 183) pointed out the following:

> 'It would be a good thing, if the details that emerge do not cloud one's vision of the basic structure. One is concerned with preserving the independence of private law from being taken over by constitutional law provisions with compulsory effect, [which] is not even mediated through the principles in its own field.'

Stern (1988: 1543–1550) explains the way in which the basic rights indirectly affect the principles of private law. The basic rights operate indirectly through the concepts and general clauses (*Generalklauseln*) of private law that are capable of having their values developed and that are in need of this development. The basic rights do not themselves decide disputed issues in private law without further ado, but always require a norm of the private law as a key to gain access to the private law relationship. These are found in the aforementioned concepts and

[152] BGHZ 13, 334 (338).
[153] BGHZ 26, 349 (354).
[154] See, for example, BVerfGE 67, 100 (142–3). See also Stern (1988: 1526 n 83).
[155] Indeed he is regarded by Egli (2002: 22) as 'undoubtedly the most powerful representative of the indirect horizontality doctrine'. See also Markesinis and Unberath (2002: 29).

general clauses of private law, in particular the following sections of the German Civil Code:[156] §§ 138(1),[157] 242,[158] 315,[159] 823(1),[160] and 826.[161]

The well-known *Lüth* judgment (BVerfGE 7, 198) is not only a leading case on freedom of expression in private law,[162] but also important with regard to the principles of horizontality. It acknowledged that the question of *whether* Basic Law norms apply to private law and *how* they ought to apply in particular cases was controversial. While the Court did not consider it necessary to discuss this question exhaustively, it nevertheless held (at 204–5):

> 'It is equally true, however, that the Basic Law is not a value neutral document.... Its section on basic rights establishes an objective normative value system, and this system in principle strengthens the enforceability of the basic rights. This value system, which focuses on the dignity of the human personality developing freely within the social community, must be looked on as a fundamental constitutional decision affecting all spheres of the law [public and private]. It serves as a yardstick for measuring and assessing all actions in the areas of legislation, public administration and adjudication. Thus it is clear that basic rights also influence [the development of] private law. Every provision of private law must be compatible with this system of values, and every provision must be interpreted in its spirit.
>
> The legal content of basic rights as objective norms is developed within private law through the medium of the legal provisions directly applicable to this area of the law. Newly enacted statutes must conform to the system of values of the basic rights. The content of existing law must be brought into harmony with this system of values. This system infuses specific constitutional content into private law, which from that point on determines its interpretation. A dispute between private individuals concerning rights and duties emanating from the private law — provisions influenced by the basic rights — remains substantively and procedurally a private law dispute. [Courts] apply and interpret private law, but the interpretation must conform to the Constitution.'

Alexy (2003: 133) explains the import of *Lüth* so well in English that he is worth quoting in full:

---

156 The English translations are by Goren (1994).

157 § 138(1): 'A legal transaction which is against public policy is void.'

158 § 242: 'The debtor is bound to effect performance according to the requirements of good faith, giving consideration to common usage.'

159 § 315: '(1) If the performance is to be determined by one of the contracting parties, it is to be presumed, in case of doubt, that the determination is to be made in an equitable manner.

(2) The determination is to be made by declaration to the other party.

(3) If the determination is to be made in an equitable manner, the determination made is binding on the other party only if it is equitable. If it is inequitable the determination is made by court decision; the same applies if the determination is delayed.'

160 § 823(1): 'A person who, wilfully or negligently, unlawfully injures the life, body, health, freedom, property or other right of another is bound to compensate him for any damages arising therefrom.'

161 § 826: 'A person who wilfully causes damage to another in a manner contrary to public policy is bound to compensate the other for the damage.'

162 See Kommers (1997: 361–369).

'... [T]he Court required that there be a balancing or weighing up of the colliding constitutional principles where the application of the rules of the civil law[163] might limit a constitutional right. The result of its balancing was that the principle of freedom of expression must be given priority over the competing constitutional considerations. It demanded that the clause "against public policy" in s 826 of the German Civil Code had to be interpreted in accordance with this priority....

The *Lüth* decision connects three ideas that have served fundamentally to shape German constitutional law. The first is that the constitutional guarantee of individual rights is not simply a guarantee of classical defensive rights of the citizen against the state. The constitutional rights embody, to cite the Federal Constitutional Court "at the same time an objective order of values." Later the Court simply talks about "the principles ... that are expressed by the constitutional rights." Taking up this line, one might say that the first basic idea of the *Lüth* decision is that constitutional rights have not only the character of rules but also the character of principles. The second idea, closely tied to the first, is that the values or principles found in the constitutional rights apply not only to the relation between the citizen and the state but, well beyond that, "to all areas of the law." Thanks to this a "radiating effect" of the constitutional right over the entire legal system is brought about. Constitutional rights become ubiquitous. The third idea is implied in the structure of values and principles. Values and principles tend to collide. A collision of principles can only be resolved by balancing. The lesson of the *Lüth* decision that is most important for everyday legal work runs, therefore, as follows: A "balancing of interests" becomes necessary.'

Alexy (2003: 135) also applies the proportionality principle to the horizontal application of basic rights to private law:

'In German law, balancing is one part of what is required by a more comprehensive principle. This more comprehensive principle is the principle of proportionality (*Verhältnismäßigkeitsgrundsatz*). This principle of proportionality consists of three subprinciples: the principles of suitability, of necessity, and of proportionality in the narrow sense.'

Alexy's thesis that all three principles express the idea of optimisation has been referred to in Chapter 4, section 4.2*(a)*(iii) above.

Egli (2002: 24–26) is also of the view that the doctrine of indirect horizontality 'as represented by Dürig' is now generally accepted both by academics and the courts.

Stern (1988: 1529–1530) argues that the one-sided depiction of the basic rights as operating only against the state is not a conceptual thesis, but rather one historically determined; an historical consequence. The basic rights are concerned with changing social reality and it is an empty abstraction to contrast individuals only with the state, and not to see them in a social context, ie in other living communities. The basic rights must accordingly be given a new operational direction, which also influences private legal relationships, particularly when

[163] 'Civil law' is, in the context clearly being used as a synonym for 'private law' and not as an antonym for 'common law system'.

social power, powers of association or economic power are conferred on them. The devaluing of human worth during the Nazi period has been replaced, in contrast, by an image of free human beings, and consequently one is compelled to recognise a new area of application for the basic rights.

According to Egli (2002: 25) the way forged by the *Lüth* judgment, namely portraying the basic rights as having a 'radiating effect' on the private legal order, has been confirmed and concretised by the BVerfG in its later judgments.[164] Thus, in BVerfGE 85, 1 (16) the following was said, relying on the *Lüth* judgment as authority:

> 'The basic right concerning freedom of expression is clearly not without qualification. In terms of Art 5(2) of the GBL its limitation is to be found in the provisions of the general laws, in provisions for the protection of young persons, and the right to personal honour. However, provisions in private law that limit basic rights are still to be interpreted in the light of the limited basic right, so that its function of determining meaning for private law can also operate at the level of the law's application (cf BVerfGE 7, 198 [212] ... This therefore leads, in the context of the factual features of the case, to the provisions of the private law being regularly interpreted by a case related balancing (*Abwägung*), weighing up of the meaning of freedom of expression as against the status of the legal interest affected by the opinion expressed, which legal interest the private law seeks to protect.'

Although 'balancing' appears to be the accepted English translation for *Abwägung*, in the context of clashing rights or principles, someone such as Alexy (2003: 133), writing in English, uses 'balancing or weighing up'. The particular word is not important, but the nature of the activity required is. *Abwägung* suggests that the clashing rights or principles are weighed up against one another, and their status and importance critically evaluated. 'Weighing-up' seems to capture this better than 'balancing', which connotes the mere bringing into a state of equilibrium. When 'balancing' is used it should be understood as also embodying this process of weighing and evaluating.

In the *Blinkfüer* case the complainant was the publisher and chief editor of a small-circulation weekly newspaper *Blinkfüer* that advertised East German radio and television programmes. The powerful Axel Springer newspaper threatened *Blinkfüer* with a boycott of its publication by sending a circular to its own customers in which it instructed them not to sell *Blinkfüer* and threatening to withdraw its own publications from them if they did not heed this instruction. *Blinkfüer*'s claim for damages on the basis of unfair competition was sustained in the lower courts, upset by the Federal Supreme Court, and finally sustained by the BVerfG. § 823(1) of the German Civil Code was the 'general clause' relevant

[164] See, for example, BVerfGE 14, 263 (277f); 24, 278 (282); 25, 256 (263); 30, 173 (187ff); 32, 311 (316); 34, 202 (214); 34, 269 (280); 42, 143 (148); 46, 325 (334ff); 49, 89 (142); 49, 228 (240); 52, 131 (165f); 54, 129 (135ff); 54, 148 (151); 60, 234 (239, 241f); 61, 1 (6); 62, 230 (242f); 66, 116 (131); 73, 261 (269); 85, 1 (16f).

to the case and in this regard the following is stated in the judgment (BVerfGE 25, 263):

> 'The proceeding before the lower courts was a civil suit which had to be decided according to the rules and regulations of private law. However, the objective order of values established by the Basic Law in the section on basic rights influences the interpretation of these rules and regulations insofar as they are capable of interpretation in light of the constitutional norms [citing the *Lüth* case]. With regard to s 823(1) of the Civil Code, constitutional law is important in establishing the unlawfulness of the injury. The courts must decide, on the one hand, the extent to which the right to freedom of opinion covers a boycott, and, on the other hand, whether the complainant may claim for himself the constitutional right to freedom of the press.'[165]

The Court held that while the calling of a boycott was on the face of it a permissible exercise of free speech its lawfulness had to be decided by the means used. If the call had been limited to an injunction not to read the *Blinkfüer* advertisements and not to watch the East German television this would have been in order and compatible with (264) 'the intellectual struggle to influence public opinion on an issue of fundamental [public] importance'. But 'the basic right to freedom of expression will not protect a call for a boycott if it is not based solely on intellectual arguments; that is, if it is not limited to the persuasive force of the presentation, explanation, or consideration itself but, going beyond these, employs means which deprive those affected [by the boycott] of their ability to draw their conclusions freely and in the absence of economic pressure'. The Court stressed that the 'freedom of free intellectual dispute' is 'an absolute prerequisite for the free functioning of democracy' because 'it alone guarantees the public discussion of issues of general public and political concern'. On the other hand, when the exercise of economic pressure

> 'entails severe disadvantages for those affected by it', [and is] 'aimed at preventing the constitutionally guaranteed dissemination of opinion and news, *it violates equality of opportunity in the process of forming political opinion*. It also contradicts the meaning and the nature of the basic right to free expression of opinion, which is intended as a guarantee of the intellectual struggle for public opinion.' (Emphasis supplied.)

These cases have been consistently followed since then as the two *Benetton* cases (*Benetton I* [BVerfGE 102, 347] and *Benetton II* [BVerfGE 107, 275]) illustrate. These cases were concerned with the interpretation of §1 of the Act Prohibiting Unfair Competition (*Gesetz gegen den unlauteren Wettbewerb*)(UWG). In terms of §1, acts in relation to competition that conflict with the *boni mores* may be prohibited. Both cases dealt with the question whether three advertisements that had been published by the complainant in the *Stern* magazine were contrary to the *boni mores* as envisaged by §1 and whether, accordingly, their publication could

[165] The translations are from Kommers (1997: 372–374).

be interdicted. The advertisements in question consisted of three photographs relating to certain social ills. The first dealt with environmental pollution, the second with child labour, and the third with the exclusion of persons suffering from HIV/AIDS. The BVerfG, in setting aside the interdicts that had been granted against the publication, decided in both cases that in interpreting the provisions of §1 of the Act the basic right to freedom of expression and freedom of the press under art 5(1) of the GBL had to be taken into account. In *Benetton I* (at 362) the Court, relying on, inter alia, the *Lüth* judgment, held that

> 'when a judgment in a civil case was based on freedom of expression, then Art 5(1) 1st sentence requires that the courts must take into account the meaning of this basic right when interpreting and applying private law [reference to certain cases]. The judgment under attack concerns §1 UWG, a provision of the civil law. Its interpretation and application is a matter, in the first instance, for the civil courts. The Federal Constitutional Court will only interfere when a mistake is apparent, that rests on a fundamentally incorrect view of the meaning of a basic right, and in particular its ambit, and also on a mistake regarding whether any weight should be attached to it in the concrete case at hand. That is the case here.'

In *Benetton II* the Federal Supreme Court had, on a reconsideration of the case, come to the conclusion that the third advertisement infringed human dignity and confirmed the interdict.

The BVerfG found that this was not the case, set aside the interdict, and in relation to the applicability of the Basic Law to civil disputes, expressed itself (at 280–1) in terms almost identical to the passage from *Benetton I* quoted above.

(c) The role played by human dignity in the horizontal application of the basic rights and the limitations on the horizontal application of equality and non-discrimination in German Law

Stern (1988: 1544) points out approvingly, that for Dürig (1956a: 157) the human dignity provisions of art 1(1) of the GBL[166] were 'a substantial point of departure for the impact of the basic rights on private law'. This norm embodies the 'highest constitutional principle of our legal order' that must be respected 'unquestioningly by the private law'.

For my purposes it is unnecessary to enter the debate as to whether human dignity under art 1(1) of the GBL, apart from playing a crucial role in giving substance and meaning to the fundamental rights articulated in the rest of the GBL, is itself a *fundamental right*. From the clear wording of s 10, read with s 1*(a)*, of the South African Constitution, human dignity is a right, a value and a transcendental ideal. South Africa can learn important lessons as to how human dignity, as a value and an idea, can assist in giving substance to other rights and play an important role in their limitation. A scholar such as Isensee (2006:

[166] 'Human dignity is inviolable. To respect and protect it shall be the duty of all state authority.'

209) does not see it as a fundamental right itself, but as something even more important:

> 'Yet human dignity is not a fundamental right itself, alongside the others. It does not align itself with the freedom and equality rights of the constitution. It precedes them. In that sense it means less than the other fundamental rights. But it also means more. It informs and shapes the basis of all fundamental rights, in the end there is — in the horizon of secular law — no further basic ground. On this the ensuing basic rights are structured.
>
> ...
>
> 'As a concept human dignity claims absolute constitutional enforcement. At its level within the hierarchy of norms and their subject matter, it stands alone. No other norm may contest its status.... The idea radiates out over the entire legal order and elucidates what it relates to. Beyond that it shines out over legal politics and — beyond the borders of the law — onto the ethos of society.'

In this regard Dürig and Stern are particularly helpful.

Stern (1988: 33–35) explains how, at the drafting of the GBL by the Parliamentary Council, it was initially thought that human dignity was based on human rights and not the other way around. The insertion of the word 'therefore' in art 1(2) of the GBL[167] made it clear that human rights derived from inherent dignity and that art 1(3) provided the bridge from human dignity to the specific rights that followed. Stern (1988: 35) points out that Dürig regarded the drafting history and the wording of art 1 GBL as the basis for what he called a design for a practical value system of fundamental rights. Stern himself (1998: 36) subscribes to this approach in the following important passage:

> 'Not only is the fundamentally recognized tradition of pre-constitutional basic rights expressed in this foundation, but also their grounding in human beings themselves and in their subjective quality in consequence of their personality and worth. It is therefore neither a fiction, nor an abstraction nor a theory that gives rise to fundamental rights, but rather human existence itself, the securing of the dignity of human beings that give rise to human rights. In this sense human dignity is the foundation of the fundamental rights....
>
> The ability for self-realisation accrues to humans on the basis of their worth. The essence of the human being is manifested herein. When freedom accrues to humans because of their worth, then this is a freedom shared by all humans. To this extent the freedom of human beings also gives rise to equality. Both are grounded in worth.'

According to both Dürig and Stern human dignity plays an important role when rights have to be balanced, particularly when the indirect horizontal application (*mittelbare Drittwirkung*) of fundamental rights has to take place; see Stern (1988: 1509). Stern (1988: 1509–1595) devotes some 86 pages to the horizontal operation of fundamental rights in the private law domain.

Dürig (1956a: 157–190) in his influential early article '*Grundrechte und Zivilrechtsprechung*' ('Basic rights and private law jurisprudence') founds his

---

[167] Art 1(2): 'The German people *therefore* acknowledge inviolable and inalienable human rights....'

approach in part on what he calls (1956a: 159) '[t]he primary option of the basic rights for a general right of freedom (Art 2(1) of the GBL) as against the state, that also takes precedence over Art 3(1)'. From this flows, as a matter of principle, Dürig argues, that the state must recognise as lawful acts and omissions of private individuals in relation to one another even when they are in conflict with constitutional provisions, which would be binding on the state as actor. As point of departure the Basic Law, by 'upgrading' ('*Aufwertung*') the freedom 'flowing from human worth' and by making a primary choice in favour of personal freedom, places it beyond doubt that thereby freedom is also sanctioned as between equals, as against demands of equality. This individual freedom to develop oneself in relation to others has, according to Dürig (1956a: 159-60) various consequences, one of which is that one is entitled to treat others unequally. Textbook examples of this (according to Dürig) are donations and testamentary dispositions solely in favour of fellow believers, or solely in favour of male descendants, notwithstanding the provisions of art 3(2) and (3) of the GBL. Dürig (1956a: 164) sees freedom under the GBL as 'the primary manifestation' of human dignity. He argues (1956: 169) that if one were in private law also to prohibit absolutely discrimination on the grounds listed in art 3(3) of the GBL 'one would do away with, for example ... a private person's privilege of testation and donation which, in my view, exists even when the donation (testamentary gift) is made "because of " ("*wegen*") one the grounds of discrimination mentioned in art 3(3) GBL', provided it is not immoral on other grounds. Similarly (1956a: 170) the art 3(3) prohibition against discrimination because of political opinion cannot be applied horizontally to private enterprises serving ideological purposes, because this opinion is after all the very criterion for an enterprise, such as a party political publisher, serving political ends. There are many other private enterprises that appoint workers precisely because of their beliefs, religion or political views.

In the *Eppler case*, BVerfGE 54, 148 (153) after commenting on how crucially important the general right to personality is, in view of modern technological development, the Court also refers to its importance in the balancing of rights under private law in the following terms — 'These manifestations of the constitutionality protected right of personality must be duly observed when dealing with court decisions concerning conflicting interests under private law'.[168]

In the *Lebach* case[169] the Court held that the complainant's personality and privacy right trumped the public free speech interest of the producer of a documentary film portraying the complainant's role in a crime for which he had already paid the criminal penalty. In resolving the conflict between the freedom to broadcast and the right to personality, the Court made the following important pronouncement:

[168] As translated in Kommers (1989: 330) and Kommers (1997: 321f).
[169] BVerfGE 35, 202 (1973).

> '[one] must remember that ... both constitutional concerns are essential aspects of the free democratic order of the Basic Law, the result being that neither can claim precedence in principle.... In case of conflict [the Court] must adjust both constitutional values, if possible; if this cannot be achieved, it must determine which interest will defer to the other in the light of the nature of the case and [its] special circumstances. *In so doing, the [Court] must consider both constitutional values in their relation to human dignity as the nucleus of the Constitution's value system.*'[170] (Emphasis supplied.)

The last two sentences of the above quotation constitute strong support for my thesis that under the South Africa Constitution, when there is a horizontal clash between the equality rights of the one person and the freedom and privacy rights of the other party, the clash is to be resolved by an evaluation and proportionate balancing of the impact of the contesting right on the human dignity of the respective parties, as I have tried to illustrate.

Similarly Isensee (2006: 212) is of the view that human dignity — although itself not subject to weighing-up — 'plays a leading role in the weighing up of constitutional goods (*Güter*), for example in the conflict between media freedom and personal honour'. The 'idea of human dignity' shapes the interpretation of the concrete constitutional provisions:

> '[A]nybody, whose constitutional interests are affected, can also rely on the argument of human dignity, when the conflicting constitutional rights are interpreted and their weight determined for the weighing up process.'

Of particular importance for the horizontal application of the Bill of Rights under the South African Constitution are the limits that German law has placed on the applicability of equality under the Basic Law to the field of private law. I say this with full appreciation of the fact that under German law the application is indirect, while under the South African Constitution the application of the constitutional right to equality applies directly. In fact a limitation placed on indirect horizontality should apply *a fortiori* to direct horizontality.

Stern (1998: 1580) points out that 'from the outset, the equal rights of men and women, as well as the *general equality provision* of Art 3(1) GBL and the prohibition of discrimination on specific grounds under Art 3(3), have required a particular understanding in the horizontality controversy'. (Emphasis in the original.) It is also accepted by the supporters of direct horizontality that, for example, an employer is allowed to take into account differences in religious denomination.

Stern then associates himself with the important point made 'forthrightly' by Dürig (1973: Rn 135, 507) with regard to the operation of the equality provision in private law that 'a preference for freedom as against equality has been established' and Dürig's conclusion from this (1973: Rn 135) that

[170] Id 225, translation Kommers (1989: 415).

> 'A constitution ... , that on the basis of equality also permits general diversity, which flows from the varied use of human freedom, has already decided against indiscriminate levelling at all times, against collectivisation in every relationship, against the collectivising, homogenising, and schematising of all persons and spheres of life.'[171]

As Stern (1998: 1581) puts it in this context of equality: 'Should Art 3 GBL also determine the relationships of private law subjects, then private autonomy would be struck at its very root.' Therefore it is permissible for private differentiation to occur directly on the basis of discriminatory features, which, in public law, would be disapproved of by virtue of art 3. 'Inconsistency with a fundamental right is simply not the same as inconsistency with private law.' It is recognised, however, that the equality and non-discrimination provisions in the GBL do, in certain circumstances, apply horizontally to the exercise of various kinds of 'social power'. This is a matter of great complexity with regard to which no unanimity has been reached. Stern (1998: 1586) describes it as 'an ideological stamping ground'. He points out, however (1998: 1591ff), that labour relations have been recognised as a particular form of power relationship permitting the application of fundamental rights.

Zippelius (1989: 12–13), dealing with the horizontal operation of the constitutional right to equality, points out that in particular areas the obligatory provisions of the fundamental rights also impact on the legal relationships between private individuals. He stresses, however, that the operation of the fundamental rights in this area 'is much more complicated than against the state'. Thus the direct horizontal operation of the equality principles cannot in principle be accepted when individuals exercise their legal relationships as private and autonomous beings. 'Moreover', he explains, 'where private individuals dispose of their rights — for example by testament — and in so doing do not intrude upon protected areas of others, there is no horizontal operation ("*keine Drittwirkung*") of the equality provisions. Where, however, individuals are at the mercy of someone else's control, in particular by means of social power, the equality clause must come into operation.' So, for example, with regard to the law relating to collective bargaining, equal pay for equal work must be secured. He argues, however, that where private unequal treatment — for example by way of racial discrimination — violates human dignity, the duty of the state to protect everyone against violations of this nature comes into operation.[172]

Classen (1997: 89–90) points out that the BVerfG has applied the freedom rights horizontally in, among others, the areas of general legal capacity (art 2(1) of the GBL) and also specifically to contractual freedom; the personality right (art 2(1) read with art 1(1) of the GBL); personal freedom (art 2(2), second sentence of the

[171] To similar effect see Starck (1985: Rn 194) and Salzwedel (1964: 346ff, 353).

[172] As previously pointed out, both art 1(1), second sentence of the GBL and s 10 of the South African Constitution oblige the state not only to 'respect' human dignity but also to 'protect' it.

GBL); freedom of belief and the practice of religion (art 4(1) and (2) of the GBL) and associated guarantees; the various freedom of expression guarantees under art 5(1) of the GBL; artistic freedom under art 5(3) of the GBL; and freedom to marry (art 6(1) of the GBL), as well as freedom of association, occupational freedom, inviolability of the home, the rights of property and inheritance. The significance of the horizontal applicability of these rights is that they will be in tension with the horizontal application of the equality and non-discrimination rights. We are here concerned with the horizontal application of the equality guarantees outside the sphere of labour law.

Classen (1997: 92) regards it as significant that in the judgments of the BVerfG there has been, for a long time, hardly any suggestion that the equality provisions of the Basic Law are included in the horizontality jurisprudence. 'It is true', he points out, 'that there are a series of Constitutional Court judgments, in which Art 3 GBL plays a central role.... In this regard they are — until now — only concerned with the question whether, and to what extent, the legislator has made an evaluation in conflict with the general equality provision, or with the equality injunction in Art 3(2) GBL.' On the other hand the BVerfG has regarded the injunction of art 6(5) of the GBL[173] as an obligation even for private persons.

Classen (1997: 93) points out that experts, who have frequently examined the question of horizontality with regard to the general equality provision, are in general agreement that

> 'in view of the importance of constitutional freedom, the equality clause can only result in the invalidity of a private act (literally "can only mean a verdict of invalidity for a private act") under highly exceptional circumstances'.

The dogmatics of horizontality desire to ensure, in the end result, that the constitutional spaces of freedom have not only a formal but also a substantive character. But then it must ensure that they are protected against private excesses. On the other hand, Classen argues (1997: 93), that it 'can hardly be the purpose of the *general* equality provisions to bring about, without exception, material equality between people. For this would be deeply inimical to freedom. It is the antithesis to the dictates of private autonomy.'

5.8 CANADIAN INSIGHTS

In Canada a form of indirect horizontality is applied. Some Canadian scholars themselves lament the fact that the Canadian Supreme Court has failed to take account of German jurisprudence in this area. In their penetrating and insightful article 'Constitutional values and private law in Canada', Weinrib and Weinrib (2001: 44) state:

[173] To the effect that 'Children born outside of marriage shall be provided by legislation with the same opportunities for physical and mental development and for their position in society as are enjoyed by those born within marriage.'

'The extensive and profound German debate about direct and indirect application had no Canadian parallel and was ignored. Nor was any notice taken of German developments since the *Lüth* case. As in other areas of Charter jurisprudence, the Supreme Court contributed to the mystification of its own decisions by failing to advert to foreign influences and parallels.'

In the *Dolphin Delivery* case,[174] the leading Canadian Supreme Court decision on this issue, the following was stated by McIntyre J:[175]

'It is my view that s 32 of the Charter specifies the actors to whom the Charter will apply. They are the legislative, executive and administrative branches of government. It will apply to those branches of government whether or not their action is invoked in public or private litigation. It would seem that legislation is the only way in which a legislature may infringe a guaranteed right or freedom. Action by the executive or administrative branches of government will generally depend upon legislation, that is, statutory authority. Such action may also depend, however, on the common law, as in the case of the prerogative. To the extent that it relies on statutory authority which constitutes or results in an infringement of a guaranteed right or freedom, the Charter will apply and it will be unconstitutional. The action will also be unconstitutional to the extent that it relies for authority or justification on a rule of the common law which constitutes or creates an infringement of a Charter right or freedom. In this way the Charter will apply to the common law, whether in public or private litigation. It will apply to the common law, however, only in so far as the common law is the basis of some governmental action which, it is alleged, infringes a guaranteed right or freedom.'

In *Du Plessis v De Klerk*[176] Kentridge J analysed this exposition to mean:

'*(a)* if a party to private litigation founds a claim or defence on some piece of legislation (whether an act of Parliament, a by-law or regulation) or on some executive act, (such as the issue of a licence) its constitutionality under the Charter is an issue which may properly be raised; *(b)* in litigation between private parties no inconsistency between the common law and the Charter may be relied on; but *(c)* the Charter applies to the common law in a dispute between government and a private litigant — for example where the government relies on a common law prerogative. (In a subsequent case [*Lavigne v Ontario Public Service Employees Union* (1991) 81 DLR (4th) 545] the Canadian Supreme Court has held that the Charter applies to the state even in respect of activities which are contractual or commercial in nature).'

This does not, however, give the full picture of a judgment which even Canadian academics do not regard as the epitome of clarity. In a later passage McIntyre J said the following:[177]

'Where ... private party "A" sues private party "B" relying on the common law and where no act of government is relied upon to support the action, the Charter will not apply....

[174] Above, n 50.
[175] Id at 195.
[176] Above, n 1 at para 38 per Kentridge AJ, delivering the judgment of the majority of the Court.
[177] *Dolphin Delivery* (above, n 50) at 199.

> [T]his is a distinct issue from the question whether the judiciary ought to apply and develop the principles of the common law in a manner consistent with the fundamental values enshrined in the Constitution. The answer to this question must be in the affirmative. In this sense, then, the Charter is far from irrelevant to private litigants, whose disputes fall to be decided at common law. But this is different from saying that one private party owes a constitutional duty to another....'

Hogg (2007: 37.2(g)) summarises the Canadian position as follows: 'While the Charter does not apply directly to the common law (where no governmental actor is involved), the Charter does have an indirect effect on the common law.' The learned author then quotes with approval the following two passages from the judgment of McIntyre J in the *Dolphin Delivery* case:[178] '[T]he judiciary ought to apply and develop the principles of the common law in a manner consistent with the fundamental values enshrined in the Constitution' and then, following on the above '[i]n this sense, then, the Charter is far from irrelevant to private litigants whose disputes fall to be decided at common law'.

What is interesting, from our point of view, is that the development of the common law in these cases is subject, in a particular way, to the limitation requirements of s 1 of the Charter, which provide that

> '[t]he Canadian Charter of Rights and Freedoms guarantees the rights and freedoms set out in it *subject only to such reasonable limits prescribed by law as can be demonstrably justified in a free and democratic society*'. (Emphasis supplied.)

That s 1 had to be applied in some way or other was pointed out by McIntyre J in the *Dolphin Delivery* case when he considered that the actions under scrutiny 'would have involved the exercise of the right of freedom of expression',[179] but that the common law's prohibition of the practice would have been justified under s 1 of the Charter[180]

> '... [T]he application of s 1 of the Charter to sustain the limitation imposed by the common law would be consistent with the legislative policy in British Columbia. I would say that the requirement of proportionality is also met.... I would therefore conclude that the injunction is "a reasonable limit prescribed by law which can be demonstrably justified in a free and democratic society".'

This conclusion was refined by the Supreme Court in *Hill v Church of Scientology of Toronto*.[181] After confirming[182] that 'in the context of civil litigation involving only private parties, the Charter will "apply" to the common law only to the

[178] Id at 199, being parts of the passage from the *Dolphin Delivery* case just quoted.
[179] Id 187.
[180] Id 190.
[181] (1995) 126 DLR (4th) 129.
[182] Id para 95.

extent that the common law is found to be inconsistent with Charter values', the following question was raised and answered:[183]

> 'When the common law is in conflict with Charter values how should the competing principles be balanced? ... [A] traditional s 1 framework for justification is not appropriate. It must be remembered that the Charter "challenge" in a case involving private litigants does not allege the violation of a Charter right. It addresses a conflict between principles. Therefore, the balancing must be more flexible than the traditional s 1 analysis undertaken in cases involving government action cases [sic]. Charter values, framed in general terms, should be weighed against the principles which underlie the common law. The Charter values will then provide the guidelines for any modification to the common law which the court feels is necessary.'

This is of course exactly the respect in which direct horizontality in South Africa differs from the Canadian version of indirect horizontality. In a South African Bill of Rights challenge involving private parties it *does* in fact 'allege the violation of a [Bill of Rights] right' and does not merely address 'a conflict between principles'. The Bill of Rights *right* which is violated in the horizontal situation is the right created by s 8(2)[184] of the Constitution. Section 8 does not envisage a mere 'conflict between principles,' because ss 8(3)*(b)* contemplates that — in the development of the common law enjoined by para *(a)* — a *right* (either of the plaintiff or of the defendant) which conflicts with another may have to be limited and, if this is the case, the limitation must be 'in accordance with s 36(1)'.

The role of s 1 in the context of the Canadian Charter's application to private law will be dealt with later in this section. The approach adopted in the *Hill* case, as set forth above, is still authoritative for Canada. In the recent Supreme Court case of *Grant v Torstar Corp*,[185] it was referred to approvingly without further qualification:[186]

> '[44] The constitutional status of freedom of expression under the *Charter* means that all Canadian laws must conform to it. The common law, though not directly subject to *Charter* scrutiny where disputes between private parties are concerned, may be modified to bring it into harmony with the *Charter*. As Cory J put it in *Hill v Church of Scientology of Toronto* [1995] 2 SCR 1130, at para 97, "*Charter* values, framed in general terms, should be weighed against the principles which underlie the common law. The *Charter* values will then provide the guidelines for any modification to the common law which the court feels is necessary".
> [45] The argument that the *Charter* requires modification of Canadian defamation law was considered in *Hill*. Writing for a unanimous Court on this point, Cory J declined to adopt the American "actual malice" rule from *New York Times Co v Sullivan* 376 US 254 (1964),

---

[183] Id para 97.

[184] Which provides that '[a] provision of the Bill of Rights binds a natural or a juristic person if, and to the extent that, it is applicable....'

[185] 2009 SCC 61, decided on 22 December 2009.

[186] Id paras 44–46.

> which provides immunity for defamation of public officials except where malice is shown. Cory J did, however, undertake a modest expansion of the recognized qualified privilege for reports on judicial proceedings.
> [46]... As Iacobucci J observed in *R v Salituro* [1991] 3 SCR 654, at p 670, "[j]udges can and should adapt the common law to reflect the changing social, moral and economic fabric of the country". It is implicit in this duty that the courts will, from time to time, take a fresh look at the common law and re-evaluate its consistency with evolving societal expectations through the lens of *Charter* values.'

These cases illustrate the fundamental difference between indirect and direct horizontality.

Weinrib and Weinrib (2001: 43–44) consider that the judgment in *Dolphin Delivery* 'enrolled Canada in the growing family of liberal democracies that in some way connect constitutional rights to private law' and that this development 'while not identical to the indirect *Drittwirkung* of constitutional rights in German law, has obvious similarities'. They contend (at 44) that the statement in the *Lüth* case[187] to the effect that the system of constitutional values 'naturally influences private law as well; no rule of private law may conflict with it, and all such rules must be construed in accordance with its spirit' would be 'perfectly at home in the Canadian jurisprudence after the Dolphin delivery case'. I have some difficulty with the authors' proposition (at 44) that, whereas the obligation in Germany 'arises out of the Constitution itself ', the approach in Canada 'arises from the inherent jurisdiction of common law courts to develop private law'. In the same way that parliamentary sovereignty has had to yield to the constitution in a constitutional state, so too must the 'sovereignty' of the common law. I use 'sovereign' here in the more limited sense of 'sovereign but subject to statute'. By this I mean that, quite apart from statute, the constitution also controls (in different ways in different constitutions) the common law. As was pointed out in section 5.1 above, the common law (including private law) continues to exist in a constitutional state, not as a body of law separate and distinct from the Constitution but *under* and *subject* to it.[188] One thing is clear about the position under the South African Constitution: despite the fact that under s 173 the Constitutional Court, among others courts, has the 'inherent power ... to develop the common law' the obligation to apply the Bill of Rights with *direct horizontality* is mandated by the Constitution and regulated by, inter alia, ss 8(2), 8(3) and 9(4).

Weinrib and Weinrib (2001: 45–46) are critical of the way 'this connection between Charter values and private law' and its implications have been dealt with in the *Dolphin Delivery* and *Hill* cases, finding it not 'particularly illuminating' and failing to elucidate 'at the highest level in Canada' the 'significance of the relationship between constitutional values and private law'.

---

[187] BVerfGE 7, 198 (1958).

[188] See, for example, the *Pharmaceutical Manufacturers* case (above, n 9) para 44 per Chaskalson P.

In a section headed 'The Receptivity of Private Law to Constitutional Values' Weinrib and Weinrib (2001: 46–51) employ, as their point of departure, what they term a 'corrective justice approach'. In contrast to the economic approach, the corrective justice approach (2001: 46) 'presupposes the normative significance of rights as embodiments of the freedom of the interacting parties'. I would of course add 'human dignity' to the 'freedom' of the interacting parties. They continue (47) by pointing out that corrective justice 'locates the requisite framework of justification' in the 'correlativity of the plaintiff's right and the defendant's duty':

> 'This correlativity of right and duty is then articulated into the principles that figure in private law and are evident in the truisms as the requirement of causation in tort law and contract law and of the defendant's enrichment at the plaintiff's expense in the law of enrichment.'

Weinrib and Weinrib argue (2001: 47–48) that one can distinguish 'three conceptual stages or moments (as Kant called them) to the elucidation of private law as an enterprise in public reason'. The first moment

> 'is the conception of the person presupposed in the relationship of the parties. The person in private law is a self-determining agent characterized solely by the capacity for purposive action without being obliged to act for any purpose in particular. This capacity for purposiveness is the *basis for ascribing dignity to every self-determining agent* and is presupposed in the law's notions of imputability and entitlement. By virtue of one's self-determining agency, *a person has the normative status to assert one's dignity* in relation to others and therefore *to be an end and not merely a means for them.* Rights are the *juridical embodiment of the dignity inherent in self-determining agency.* Correlatively, a duty is the restraint that the exercise of another's right imposes on the exercise of one's freedom.' (Emphasis supplied, footnote omitted.)

The second moment (47–48) is 'the ensemble of judicial categories that express these rights and duties in the interaction of one person with another', and the third moment (48) is the 'operation of these categories through a set of legal institutions'.

They further develop the idea (2001: 50) that

> 'in the social contract that marks the transition from the second moment of legal categories to the third moment of judicial and political institutions, citizens subscribe to the state and its institutions only on terms that make the respect for human dignity through Charter values an interpretative principle in the elucidation of private law'.

The assumption underlying the requirement that private law be consistent with the Charter values is that

> 'self-determining agents contracting to enter a constitutional democracy could not reasonably acknowledge a specification of private rights that is inconsistent with the indicia of dignity to which citizens have accorded constitutional recognition. In this sense, constitutional values are constitutive of the juridical relationships of private law, even though constitutional rights as such are not applicable to them'.

In this respect Weinrib and Weinrib (2001: 51) point out that 'the Charter is more than a statute writ large that itemizes particular restrictions on the jurisdiction of particular governmental authorities. It is a repository of the principles animating the polity as a whole.' They conclude this section strikingly as follows (2001: 51):

> 'On this basis, the constitution does not merely contain rights that a citizen can assert against governmental power. It also establishes (in the words of the German Constitutional Court) "an objective system of values in its section on basic rights.... This system of values, centering on the freedom of the human being to develop in society ... must direct and inform legislation, administrative, and judicial decision. It naturally influences private law as well...." The statement from *Dolphin Delivery* with which we began is the official Canadian recognition of this role for constitutional values.' (Footnotes omitted.)

The quotation in the above passage from the German Constitutional Court is from an English translation by Markesinis (1997: 355) of the *Lüth* judgment (BVerfGE 7, 198 [205]). It is substantially identical to the passage from the *First Abortion* case (BVerfGE 39, 1 at 41) quoted with approval, and applied to the South African Constitution, in the *Carmichele* case, as discussed in section 5.5*(a)* above. In fact, in the *First Abortion* case, explicit reliance is placed on the above passage from the *Lüth* judgment. To avoid any confusion on the South African law, I would again point out that in the *Carmichele* case the Court was dealing with the vertical application of the Bill of Rights, but commenting on its application to or influence upon, the common law.

Weinrib and Weinrib (2001: 51) contend that the balancing of rights is 'facilitated by the fact that structural features are common to the working of rights in the private law and in the constitutional context'. One of these features, which the authors term the '*entitlement element*', concerns 'the content of the right or of any other ingredient in the claim'. The other, which they term the '*relationship element*', concerns 'the relationship between the entitlement and the other legal components of the controversy'. In a coherent legal system 'these two elements are mutually entailed: because all the components in a controversy form a united whole, the content of any entitlement and the relationship between the entitlement and the other components can be defined only by reference to each other'.

Weinrib and Weinrib (1951: 52) further point out that in private law the relational element is reflected in the 'fundamental moral impulse' of private law 'to maintain the equality of the parties in considering the injustice that one of them is alleged to have done to the other'. The authors term this 'transactional equality' which is 'rooted in the parties' equal normative status as self-determining agents. It is inconsistent with this equality for the considerations pertaining to one of the parties to determine the legal position of the entire relationship.' They contend that there is a 'general imperative that governs private law from within:

to work out norms of liability that treat the interacting parties as equals and are therefore fair to both of them'.[189]

In constitutional law it 'consists in the guaranteed rights that are familiar features of modern constitutional democracies'. Because most[190] constitutional rights are not unlimited, the authors argue that 'a further relational element comes into play — either implicitly through constitutional interpretation or explicitly through piecemeal textual qualifications — to deal with the extent of the State's obligations with respect to these rights'. This of course relates to the doctrinal principles concerned with the *limitation of rights* and the *limitation on the limitation of rights*.[191]

In an important section Weinrib and Weinrib (2001: 53) point out that in private law, where persons 'are at liberty to act as they wish provided they do not interfere with another's rights', the relationship is 'between the plaintiff's right and the correlative duty not to interfere with this right'. The task of the law is 'to connect the two parties through a set of principles, categories and standards that treat them as equals, so that one person's actions can fairly be combined with another person's rights'. The authors then make the important point that, by contrast,

> 'the relational element in the constitutional context goes to the connections between the enumerated right and state action. Constitutional law conceives of the state not as a private party free to act as it wishes, but as a body politic acting within its constitutional authority for the common good.... In working out the relationship between the rights-holder and the State, constitutional jurisprudence needs to elaborate the circumstances in which an enumerated right cedes to the constitutional values inherent in the system of rights. Thus, in the *constitutional context the element of relationship is concerned not with maintaining the transactional equality between the doer and sufferer of harm, but with negotiating the tension between specific rights and general values within the constitutional scheme.* Section 1 of the Charter does this by setting out exclusive criteria for justifying limitations upon enumerated rights.' (Emphasis supplied, footnote omitted.)

This difference must be observed, even when s 8(3)*(b)* of the South African Constitution designates s 36(1) as the mechanism through which a right (in private law context) is to be limited. In other words, when applying s 36(1) horizontally in the field of private law one must take into account the fact that one is dealing with tensions between the private law rights of two persons (albeit that they arise

---

[189] Weinrib and Weinrib (2001: 52) give the following examples:

> '[B]y focusing solely on the plaintiff's right, strict liability would in effect allow plaintiffs to set the terms on which others interact with them. Conversely, negligence law sets an objective standard of due care rather than a subjective one, which would unilaterally favour the defendant by defining the plaintiff's area of immunity from injury in terms of defendant's particular capabilities.'

[190] For the sake of prudence I exclude, for example, art 1(1) of the GBL.

[191] Known as *Schranken* (limitation) of rights and *Schranken-Schranken* (limitation on limitation) of rights. See Chapter 4, section 4.2*(a)*(iii) above. Of course the Canadian and South African constitutions have their specific general limitation clauses.

under the constitution), and not with the tension between the right of a person and the interest of the state (which is the case with the vertical application of the Bill of Rights).

After quoting the passage from *Hill*'s case reproduced above, Weinrib and Weinrib (2001: 55) raise the rhetorical question: 'Can one flesh out the references [in *Hill*'s case] to the contrast with s 1, the greater flexibility, and the nature of the balancing exercise?', which they then seek to address. They point out that the functioning of this limitation 'belongs to the world of government action rather than private law.... Section 1 gives the government the opportunity under stringent conditions to show that, despite the encroachment on an enumerated right, this responsibility [to behave constitutionally] has been constitutionally discharged.' They argue (2001: 56) that the s 1 requirement of demonstrable justification 'mirrors the government's responsibility for any exercise of state power, the particular availability to it of material relevant to support any such exercise, and the necessity for state power to be consonant with constitutional structures'.

By contrast, private litigation differs. Weinrib and Weinrib (2001: 56) indicate that neither of the parties is responsible for the rules invoked, nor for the overall system, nor does any party have an advantage with regard to the accessibility of evidence. '[N]o reason exists for imposing on one of the litigants the heavy burden of demonstrable justification of the constitutionality of the rule.' Private law, differing in this respect from constitutional law, regards the litigants 'whose legitimate interests the law must consider on terms of equality'.[192] While the courts do not consider s 1 directly applicable to the balancing of rights in the private law, the authors consider it suggestive.

After dealing with the principle and application of proportionality inherent in the vertical invocation of s 1, Weinrib and Weinrib (2001: 57) argue that it is applicable to private law, subject to two modifications. First, 'the test of proportionality needs to be stripped of its connection to a legislative objective, since such objective is absent in private law'. Secondly, the 'central range of application'[193] is of concern not only for the vertical operation of constitutional rights, 'but also for every normative component in the parties' legal relationship'. The authors comment on the application of this proportionality approach 'geared to private law' as follows:

---

[192] The authors give the example of defamation, whose organising concern they point out 'is the interest in reputation; the constitutional value inherent in freedom of expression is merely an interest against which the interests in reputation must be fairly balanced. Neither interest starts with a priority with respect to the other.'

[193] The authors use this expression to refer to the way a constitution preserves some core element of a right in the process of vertical limitation. They also point out (2001: 57) that this is the way in which 'Canadian jurisprudence runs parallel to the German Constitutional provision [Art 19(2)] that allows a basic right to be restricted so long as there is no encroachment on its "essential content" [*Wesensgehalt*].'

> 'One may recall the Court's cryptic observation [in the *King* case] that balancing in the private law's treatment of Charter values is more flexible than in traditional s 1 analysis. The loosening of the test of proportionality from its moorings in legislative objective and the extension of the idea of the central range from Charter values to other normative features of the parties' relationship perhaps suitably illuminate this reference to increased flexibility.'

Weinrib and Weinrib warn (2001: 58) that the purpose of this version of proportionality in private law 'is not to give the law a utilitarian cast. That would be foreign to a system of rights regarded as the embodiment of self-determining agency'. It would also, in my view, be foreign to the Kantian concept of infinite inherent worth, which rejects the objectifying of human beings. In an important passage the authors also argue that:

> 'Proportionality expresses the form of transactional equality relevant to the presence of constitutional values. Transactional equality is the most deeply ingrained and pervasive relational principle in private law. The principle affirms that, since the plaintiff and the defendant have equal status in their relationship, the decision between them cannot be made on the basis of considerations that reflect the normative position of only one of them. The idea of proportionality maintains the transactional equality of the two parties by treating their relationship as informed by an ensemble of normative concepts, no one of which is absolute. Through a comparison of the reciprocal effects of the concepts in play on both sides, proportionality preserves intact, so far as possible, the central range of application of them all. In this way proportionality reconfigured the idea of transactional equality to include Charter values.'[194]

In my view this is relevant to the development of our jurisprudence on s 8(3) (read with s 36(1)) of the Constitution.

In dealing with transactional equality and the incorporation of Charter values into private law Weinrib and Weinrib (2001: 67) sound the warning that judgments and the reasoning that support this incorporation 'must be consistent with the parties' transactional equality ... [which] is the most deeply ingrained and pervasive relational principle of private law'.

In their concluding section Weinrib and Weinrib (2001: 72) emphasise the importance of proportionality in applying the constitution (in whatever way) to private law:

> '[F]rom the first discussion in Germany of the impact of constitutional rights on private law to subsequent discussion in Canada, a constant theme has been the apprehension of a disastrous effect upon the individual freedom that the private law manifests. The idea of proportionality addresses this apprehension. By maintaining a balance between the entitlements on both sides, proportionality vindicates the parties' transactional equality. If sensitively done, this prevents one party from using Charter values to intrude into the central range of application of the other's freedom.'

---

194 Weinrib and Weinrib (2001: 67–71) deal critically with two Canadian cases 'where judges have invoked Charter values without giving due weight to the maintenance of transactional equality'.

It is equally important in South Africa to maintain this 'transactional equality' between private parties when applying our Bill of Rights horizontally. I do not regard the approach advocated by Weinrib and Weinrib (2001) to be in any way inconsistent with my advocacy that human dignity should play the guiding role in the adjustment of conflicting rights when they arise in leading the context of the direct horizontal application of the Bill of Rights.

5.9 CONCLUSION

I would proffer Weinrib and Weinrib as persuasive witnesses in support of the value of constitutional comparativism in the area of horizontality. The development of this area of the law in Germany and Canada demonstrates, in my view, that in a constitutional state some form of horizontal operation of guaranteed fundamental rights simply cannot be avoided. The integrity of the constitutional system requires some form of horizontality.

South Africa has of course chosen the direct horizontal option. But whether direct or indirect, the German jurisprudence as well as the Canadian (particularly as argued for by Weinrib and Weinrib) indicate that the proportional 'adjustment' or 'balancing' or 'mutual limitation' of respective rights in the horizontal context presents challenges differing in principle from vertical limitation. I refer of course to the fact that in the vertical context the state is opposed to the private agent and the state's general 'interest' opposed to the agent's constitutional rights. The state has no 'rights' of similar nature. The private agent has an inherent dignity, and flowing therefrom inherent freedom; the state does not. In the horizontal context, right is opposed to right, and it is the tension or conflict between these opposing *rights* that has to be constitutionally resolved. The tension arises from the fact that it is not possible, in the given context, to implement both rights maximally at one and the same time. The only solution is to limit the extent of the one or the other right, or both of them. This, in my view, is the purpose of s 8(3) of the South African Constitution and its invocation of the s 36(1) limitation clause. Section 36(1) must itself, of course, be interpreted in the context of a tension or clash of rights between private agents. Its mechanisms must be so interpreted and applied as to facilitate a resolution of this tension or clash in a manner which has due regard to the principles of proportionality.

I have contended — and attempted to illustrate — in sections 5.5 and 5.6 above that in principle the value of human dignity is the only (or at least the most appropriate) neutral[195] principle that can appropriately resolve these clashes or tensions. I would argue that the German jurisprudence supports this approach. Mention must, however, be made of an article by Susanne Baer[196] (2009: 417),

---

195 In the sense explained and used in these sections and in particular in section 5.5*(c)*.

196 At the time Professor of Public Law and Gender Studies in the Humboldt University in Berlin, but subsequently appointed to the German Federal Constitutional Court.

entitled 'Dignity, liberty, equality: A fundamental rights triangle of constitutionalism', which deals in comparative perspective with the relationship between the rights of dignity, liberty and equality and the resolution of clashes or tensions between these rights. The author uses the image of a triangle (each of the three corners representing one of the above rights as an equal force), to illustrate her underlying thesis that these abovementioned three rights are equivalent and in harmonious tension with one another. Baer opposes this image to that of the pyramid where two sides (two of the three rights) are equivalent but the base representing a lesser of the three rights. She would not support my contention that human dignity is the neutral principle by which clashes of rights in the horizontal context are ultimately to be resolved.[197] A few points of disagreement may be noted. Baer is dubious about the ability of dignity to resolve these clashes, because of the uncertainty of its content. She does not deal with Dürig's anthropological approach to human dignity and how fully human dignity is fleshed out according to it. She places little, if any, emphasis on the rich development of the personality rights in Germany in fixing the meaning of dignity. More importantly, Baer does not recognise the logico-grammatical problem associated with an understanding of equality, and the necessity of having some criterion of attribution in order to answer the question: 'Equality of what?' Although she recognises that there is some link between dignity and equality, she does not appear to acknowledge just how essential the *value* of human worth is for a proper understanding of equality. In the course of this work I have endeavoured to show, particularly with reference to German and South African jurisprudence, how the concept of human dignity has developed, and how detailed and practically usable content is given to this value and right. On this my case must rest.

The position in Canada is less clear. The jurisprudence of its Supreme Court has, however, selected human dignity as the *criterion of attribution* for elucidating legal equality and non-discrimination in their vertical manifestation. It is also developing a jurisprudence to deal with the problems involved in the horizontal application of Charter rights which is not inconsistent with the resolution I suggest. If the arguments of Weinrib and Weinrib were to be followed, with their appreciation of the important differences between vertical and horizontal limitation, the appropriate application of human dignity would appear to be the obvious way to go in order to resolve tensions and clashes between rights in the sphere of horizontality.

I have contended, relying on German jurisprudence and the ideas of Louis Henkin (1962) that, generally speaking, one can start with the proposition that an agent's right to freedom (either general or specific) and privacy would trump the other's right to equality and non-discrimination in the horizontal sphere. It is,

[197] It is quite beyond the purview of the present work to discuss specifically in any detail where my disagreement with Baer lies; my full case has been stated in the present work generally and in this chapter specifically. A few comments must suffice.

however, important to add that — as I have pointed out — once the legal relations of the private agents move out into the public domain, and private social power becomes more predominant, the infringement of human dignity involved in discrimination will become more severe and reach a point where, when evaluated proportionally, will trump opposing rights of freedom and privacy.

CHAPTER SIX

RESTITUTIONARY OR REMEDIAL EQUALITY

6.1 INTRODUCTION

This chapter is not a treatise on restitutionary equality (as provided for in the second sentence of s 9(2) of the Constitution) or on the various statutory and other measures passed under its provisions. My purpose is more modest and limited. In the first place I endeavour to formulate a principled theoretical basis for the proper application of the second sentence of s 9(2). Secondly, I discuss s 9(2) to the extent necessary to clarify the role that human dignity ought to play in its implementation. I deliberately refrain from discussing land restitution, whose context is so different that the framers of the South African Constitution saw fit to deal with it separately in s 25, together with related issues enabling citizens to gain access to land.

Section 9(2) of the Constitution, after stating that 'Equality includes the full and equal enjoyment of all rights and freedoms', provides in its second sentence that

> '[t]o promote the achievement of equality, legislative and other measures designed to protect or advance persons, or categories of persons, disadvantaged by unfair discrimination, may be taken'.

In considering this provision and its remedial impact I have deliberately chosen to use the expression 'restitutionary equality'[1] throughout, in preference to the inappropriate yet over-popular phrase 'affirmative action', for basically three reasons.

First, the expression *affirmative action* has its origin in the United States of America, where it has been used to benefit members of discrete minority groups, and in particular to benefit members of minority racial groups. The equality clause in the Fourteenth Amendment to the American Constitution contains no restitutionary equality provision.[2] I do not propose investigating American law

[1] Professor Ockert Dupper has written widely on the s 9(2) restitutionary measures, particularly in the employment context. While appreciating that the phrase 'affirmative action' must be used with care in South Africa, and despite employing it himself on occasion, he does correctly view the nature of these remedies as remedial or restitutionary. See Dupper (2006: 141) and Dupper (2008: 426).

[2] It merely provides, in its relevant part:

'No State shall ... deny to any person within its jurisdiction the equal protection of the laws.'

in this regard, but it is universally recognised that the equality guarantee, in this stark form, has bedevilled remedial measures based on race, because the ghost has lingered that the Constitution must be completely 'colour-blind' and that it is somehow inconsistent with the Fourteenth Amendment to base any remedy on race, even when the objective is to counteract the ongoing effects of past racism, a remedy like this being pejoratively referred to as 'reverse discrimination'.[3] United States equality jurisprudence differs significantly from ours. Even when one is alive to this difference, there is still a real danger that the use of an expression such as 'affirmative action' might nevertheless subconsciously lead to the introduction of equality principles from this jurisprudence that are inconsistent with our own. In *Van Heerden*'s case[4] the Constitutional Court issued a timely and apt warning against the use of this expression in the South African equality context:

> 'Our equality jurisprudence differs substantively from the US approach to equality. Our respective histories, social context and constitutional design differ markedly. Even so the terminology of "affirmative action" has found its way into general use and into a number of our statutes directed at prohibiting unfair discrimination and promoting equality, such as the Employment Equity Act 55 of 1998 and the Promotion of Equality and the Prevention of Unfair Discrimination Act 4 of 2000. But in our context this terminology may create more conceptual and other difficulties than it resolves. We must therefore exercise great caution not to import, through this route, inapt foreign equality jurisprudence which may inflict on our nascent equality jurisprudence American notions of "suspect categories of State action" and of "strict scrutiny".'

The Court also, perceptively and correctly, pointed out that '[t]he Afrikaans equivalent "regstellende aksie" is perhaps juridically more consonant with the remedial or restitutionary component of our equality jurisprudence'.[5] The expression 'regstellende aksie' (literally 'action that puts or makes right') seems to capture precisely this component, as I shall attempt to demonstrate more fully later. Moreover 'affirmative action' has at times been used to cover government action going beyond restitutionary equality and that would be inappropriate under the restitutionary provisions of the 1996 Constitution.[6]

Secondly, an argument has been used in the United States to justify 'affirmative action' on the basis that where it is a *political majority* that is imposing 'reverse discrimination' *against itself* in favour of a political minority, this fact takes the sting out of 'reverse discrimination'. In this regard Prof John H Ely (1974: 735) argues that

---

[3] See, in general, Peltason (1994: 379–382), Tribe (1988: 1521–1544).

[4] *Minister of Finance and Another v Van Heerden* 2004 (6) SA 121 (CC) (2004 (11) BCLR 1125) para 29.

[5] Id.

[6] Examples hereof are furnished by Drumbl and Craig (1997: 82–83 and nn 2, 3).

> 'reverse racial discrimination can be constitutional, but for reasons quite different from those in the conventional account. Rather than asserting that demands of "special scrutiny" can be met — an assertion neither the Court nor anyone else has given us criteria for — I shall suggest that "special scrutiny" is not appropriate when White people have decided to favor Black people at the expense of White people.... [T]he principle I propose is a neutral one: regardless of whether it is wise or unwise, it is not "suspect" in a constitutional sense for a majority to discriminate against itself.'

The learned author (1974: 735) further explains:

> 'When the group that controls the decision making process classifies so as to advantage a minority and disadvantage itself, the reasons for being unusually suspicious, and, consequently, employing a stringent brand of review, are lacking. A White majority is unlikely to disadvantage itself for reasons of racial prejudice; nor is it likely to be tempted either to underestimate the needs and deserts of Whites relative to those of others, or to overestimate the costs of devising an alternative classification that would extend to certain whites the advantages generally extended to Blacks.'

Prof Laurence H Tribe (1988: 1523 n 9) agrees with these views of Ely and contends as follows:

> '[J]udicial distrust of political processes may not be pertinent when a discrete and insular minority is benefited, rather than burdened by governmental action. When a predominantly white public body chooses to confer a comparative advantage on racial minorities while comparatively disadvantaging all white applicants, a court on review would have to assure itself only that this was indeed the purpose and effect of the choice in question, and that the choice did not deliberately conceal any discrimination against a racial, ethnic or other minority.... Once having been so assured, the judiciary would lack the usual reasons to subject the choice to the sort of scrutiny that makes sense when prejudice against insular minorities seems to be present, and when the political process accordingly seems unworthy of deference.'

The reverse situation obtains in South Africa, because the recipients of restitutionary measures under the second sentence of s 9(2) are, in most situations, members of a category of persons that constitute a very substantial political majority. Thus the 'political majority' safeguards relied upon by Ely and Tribe simply do not apply. In fact, because in South Africa it is, in most cases, a majority that is applying restitutionary equality in its own favour, it behoves this majority to exercise particular care in formulating and applying remedial measures.

Thirdly, it is necessary in South Africa to move away from the victim/perpetrator paradigm, as does the second sentence of s 9(2), when viewed in the context of the history of (particularly) apartheid and state discrimination against black (broadly defined) South Africans in the past. This is particularly important when it is a political majority that is applying restitutionary equality in its own favour. Members of the minority group, who often have to bear the negative impact of restitutionary measures, are often quick (and at times over-quick and vociferous) to point out that they (and in particular their descendants) bear no *personal blame* for the 'unfair discrimination' (particularly — but of course not exclusively — racial discrimination) that has caused 'persons or categories of persons [to be] disadvantaged' and that it is accordingly *unfair* that they and their (innocent) children should have to bear the negative impact that might flow from restitutionary remedies. I try to develop (now and later) a principled argument, consistent with s 9 as a whole, why it is fair and justifiable that such negative impact as might flow from restitutionary measures should be borne not only by those (mostly — but not exclusively — whites) who supported and benefited from the apartheid regime, but also on those *beneficiaries* of apartheid who did not support the apartheid regime, or even actively opposed it, *because* they were inevitably — and willy-nilly — *enriched* in a variety of ways by 'unfair discrimination'.[7] This also applies to the *descendants* of those who supported or were inevitably enriched by apartheid, even though they themselves might be wholly free of any fault in this regard. It is important for those who might be negatively affected by s 9(2) restitutionary measures to appreciate that these measures are not *punitive* but *restitutionary* in character. They are restitutionary measures that arise in circumstances analogous to the circumstances under which private-law unjustified enrichment arises, a body of equitable principles recognised for centuries by our private law.

I wish to clarify at the outset that by using private-law unjustified enrichment to explain public-law restitutionary equality, I am not suggesting that one ought to base the public-law remedy on that of the private law. By its very nature public-law unjustified enrichment can occur in a multiplicity of ways that do not mirror private-law enrichment and requires a remedy tailored to meet the needs of the enrichment in question. I go no further than to use the analogy as a justification for *a* remedy, even one that negatively affects a defendant wholly innocent of causing the unjustified enrichment. The analogy serves to justify the need for and the justice of remedial equality even in the case of innocent defendants.

The thrust of my argument in this chapter is that the overarching objective of the second sentence of s 9(2) is to authorise public-law and constitutional restitution remedies in favour of those who are still 'disadvantaged' by 'unfair discrimination' that occurred in the past, and which remedies might operate *at the expense* of those who were *unjustifiably enriched* by past unfair discrimination. Not all remedial measures authorised by s 9(2) will necessarily have a negative effect on those previously advantaged by unfair discrimination. But where they do, the previously advantaged are obliged to bear the negative effects of the restitution made to those previously disadvantaged, *not* because the former wrongfully and culpably harmed the latter, but because they were *unjustifiably enriched* at the

[7] The words used in the second sentence of s 9(2).

expense of the latter. This restitution does not rest upon *proof of guilt*, but on *proof of unjustified enrichment* on the part of the advantaged.

The preamble to the 1996 Constitution declares that one of the purposes of the Constitution is to 'heal the divisions of the past'. In this sense the Constitution must strive to effect reconciliation between those so divided. The restitutionary provisions of s 9(2) must accordingly be seen by those on *both sides* of the previous divide, not as a punishment for past wrongs but as fair restitution for benefits unjustifiably acquired. In my view an approach like this has the best chance of effectively healing the divisions and the wounds of the past, by eliminating both triumphalism and victimhood. Whether this will indeed happen depends to a large extent on how the majority implements the restitutionary principle of s 9(2) and how the previously advantaged face up squarely to the fact of their actual enrichment and the fact that this enrichment was unjustified.

Having said this, it must also be borne in mind that not all whites have necessarily been advantaged by past discrimination. Indeed, there are a number of whites who suffer marked economic and social disadvantage, whether or not this is attributable to apartheid in the past or not. In these cases there are sound principled reasons why persons like this should not bear the negative consequences of restitutionary equality.

I should also make clear that when I refer to disadvantage suffered in the past, I do not intend to limit disadvantage to that suffered prior to 1994, although that is undoubtedly the worst. In this regard the operative phrase in s 9(2) is 'disadvantaged by unfair discrimination'. I contend that this includes disadvantage suffered by discrimination at any time prior to the remedial measures introduced. One may not simply assume that unfair discrimination and resultant disadvantage (on any of the grounds enumerated in s 9(3) and its Interim Constitution predecessor) will disappear in their entirety simply by virtue of the operation of the Constitutions. It is not impossible that new forms of discrimination can occur, which will not necessarily be (have been) eliminated by the provisions of s 9(3) and its predecessor. A bad habit has developed of describing the overall purpose of s 9 as the eradication of 'racism and sexism'. This is an unwarranted limitation. The 'disadvantage' envisaged by the s 9(2) remedial measures includes disadvantage caused by every one of the grounds of discrimination enumerated in s 9(3). I raise (but do not address) the question whether remedial measures introduced under s 9(2) that deal, for example, only with 'race, gender and disability,' such as under the Employment Equity Act 55 of 1998, are under-inclusive and inconsistent with the Constitution. As Dupper (2008: 428) observes '[t]he virtually exclusive emphasis on race-based affirmative action denies this complexity [of disadvantage] and potentially excludes some of the most deserving beneficiaries of measures of redress'.

6.2 THE JURISPRUDENTIAL BASIS FOR THE RESTITUTIONARY EQUALITY 'MEASURES' AUTHORISED BY THE SECOND SENTENCE OF S 9(2), READ WITH S 9(3) OF THE CONSTITUTION

I am not suggesting in this section that the public-law remedies authorised in the second sentence of s 9(2) are obliged to conform to the principles of some preconceived theoretical basis. After all the Constitution is supreme and, when properly construed and applied, needs no further external justification. What I seek to do is to explain the true fundamental nature of the s 9(2) principle in order better to understand its operation, including the role of dignity therein, and to dispel unfounded criticism of this principle, particularly by those who may be negatively affected by its operation.

The equality measures authorised by the second sentence of s 9(2) of the Constitution, which I shall call *restitutionary equality* measures, should in my view be categorised as public-law compensatory remedies for public-law unjustified enrichment analogous in various respects to unjustified enrichment in private law. The terms 'plaintiff' and 'defendant' are terms used in private-law unjustified enrichment; the 'defendant' being the person who has been unjustifiably enriched at the expense of the 'plaintiff'. Applied to the s 9(2) principle 'plaintiffs' would be the 'persons, or categories of persons, disadvantaged by unfair discrimination' and 'defendants' would be the persons who have been advantaged by this unfair discrimination and who are negatively affected by the s 9(2) measures. The restitutionary nature of the remedies is clear, because the beneficiaries are described as 'persons, or categories of persons, disadvantaged by unfair discrimination'. The category of beneficiaries is not so wide as to include all disadvantaged persons but is limited to those who have been disadvantaged 'by unfair discrimination'. The latter phrase embodies the element of wrongfulness or lack of justification as foundation for the constitutional enrichment remedy.

Powerful conceptual support for such an approach is to be found in the major work *Unjustified Enrichment* by Professor Daniel Visser (2008). Although concerned in the first instance with the South African private law of unjustified enrichment, it is written from a broad comparative law perspective and suggests public-law enrichment links. My own excursus into the law of unjustified enrichment generally must perforce be of a restricted nature, and I urge the reader to follow Visser's meticulous arguments for themselves; I will do no more than outline them when relevant for my purposes. Visser (2008: v) stresses the importance of comparative perspectives, particularly from Germany, in this field:

> 'From the German law of unjustified enrichment, the impressive modern edifice of which grew out of the same roots as that of our own [South African] law, we can learn as much, or more, for apart from providing alternative solutions to specific problems, its scholars have worked out a taxonomy for the law of enrichment which may be used — though not necessarily in all its detail — to bring order to this area of our own law.'

Visser (2008: 4–7) describes the basic function of private law unjustified enrichment as being to 'restore economic benefits to the plaintiff, at whose expense they were obtained, and for the retention of which by the defendant there is no legal justification'. I do not suggest that the public-law remedy for unjustified enrichment is limited to the restoration of economic benefits to 'plaintiffs'. The public-law remedy would include restoration of this nature but would go further and endeavour, as best it can, to restore all benefits relating to the free unfolding of the personality (to use a human dignity concept) in respect whereof the defendants have been unjustifiably enriched. This may or may not involve the defendants in economic loss (directly or indirectly) but not necessarily so.

Visser (2008: 4–7) points out that South African law has until recently worked with a 'very contained model', but that two recent cases of the Supreme Court of Appeal, the *McCarthy Retail* case[8] and the *FNB v Perry NO* case,[9] have provided impetus 'to alter radically this state of the law of enrichment'.

In the *McCarthy Retail* case the majority of the Court[10] held, albeit *obiter*, that the time had come in South Africa to recognise a general enrichment action. In this regard Schutz JA said the following:

> '[8] ... [A]lthough there has been no unequivocal recognition of a general enrichment action, time and again unjustified enrichment principles have been treated as a source of obligations being the basis for creating a new class or subclass of liability in particular circumstances....
>
> [9] ... [T]here is a strong, if by no means unanimous body of academic opinion that Grotius, influenced by Spanish jurists and theologians, had come to accept unjustified enrichment as an independent source of obligations, just as contract or delict were.... Whether Professors *Feenstra* and *Scholtens* are right about Grotius need not be determined, because the latter has demonstrated quite convincingly, in my opinion, that by the 18th century the Hooge Raad had come to accept the existence of what we would call a general enrichment action ... see Scholtens 'The General Enrichment Action that Was' (1966) 83 *SALJ* 391, Feenstra[11] (op cit at 228–35).'[12]

In the *FNB v Perry NO* case the Court again, in an *obiter dictum*, strongly confirmed this approach.[13]

While appreciating the *obiter* nature of these holdings, Visser (2008: 53) comments on them (in my view quite correctly) as follows:

---

[8] *McCarthy Retail (Pty) Ltd v Shortdistance Carriers CC* 2001 (3) SA 482 (SCA).

[9] *First National Bank of South Africa Ltd v Perry* 2001 (3) SA 960 (SCA).

[10] Per Schutz JA, Olivier and Cameron JJA concurring. Smalberger ADCJ and Harms JA preferred not to express a view on the issue.

[11] This reference to *Feenstra* in the judgment is to Professor Robert Feenstra (1995).

[12] Above n 8 para 10.

[13] Above n 9. Schutz JA delivered the judgment of the Court.

> 'It should be noted that the Supreme Court of Appeal did not recognize a general enrichment obligation in [the *McCarthy Retail*] case. It merely indicated *obiter* (albeit quite strongly) that it could in the future be persuaded to recognize such an action. However, it was so strongly stated and reiterated by all the judges in [*FNB* v *Perry*] that it is inconceivable that the Supreme Court of Appeal will go back on this intention.'

This is important because it does suggest that our law is open to innovative development of the concept of unjustified enrichment, also into the realm of public-law remedies. Visser (2008: 9) is himself clearly of the view that the private-law principles against unjustified enrichment can be used to fashion analogous public-law principles:

> 'And the law of enrichment need not necessarily be confined to private law. One school of thought also includes in its scope various instances that may be described as public law applications of the principle against unjustified enrichment.'

Visser (2008: 147–148) later classifies these possibilities as follows:

> '(i) If someone pays tax which has been unlawfully extracted, should special rules apply? (ii) If the government de-contaminates land as a result of which it goes up in value, should it have an enrichment action against the owner? (iii) If legislation makes provision for the *restitution of property that had been taken in morally questionable circumstances* by a former regime, are these measures part of the law of enrichment? (iv) Should the confiscation of the proceeds of crime be seen as part of the law of unjustified enrichment?' (Emphasis supplied.)

The learned author then, in relation to the third example quoted above, states that in Germany and South Africa it 'has been characterized as being a response to unjustified enrichment in the broad sense of the term'.

Visser later argues (2008: 150) that the intersection of public law and the law of enrichment can happen in two ways:

> '[F]irst, through the influence of the Constitution on the interpretation of the private law of enrichment; and, secondly, through public law remedies provided by statute that could be interpreted as embodying an application of the general principles against unjustified enrichment and that replace common law enrichment remedies or stand side-by-side with them.'

My contention is precisely that s 9(2) authorises public-law remedies embodying an application of the general principles against unjustified enrichment.

More than a decade earlier Professor Visser and Dr Theunis Roux[14] (1996: 101–111) explored this characterisation more closely in the context of the South African Restitution of Land Rights Act 22 of 1994. Their views are *a fortiori* — I contend — relevant to the restitutionary provisions of s 9(2) of the Constitution and legislation (such as, for example, the Equality Act[15]) passed pursuant thereto.

[14] Subsequently Professor Roux.
[15] The Promotion of Equality and Prevention of Unfair Discrimination Act 4 of 2000.

I say *a fortiori,* because the problems that may apply to land restitution do not apply to the general restitutionary measures authorised by s 9(2). Visser and Roux (1996: 101) rightly point out that in attempting 'to make sense of any new principle or process within a legal system' it is useful to ask 'how it fits into the existing structure of the law as a whole'. When referring to the 'existing structure of the law as a whole' the authors obviously have in mind those structures, including common and statute law, that are consistent with and conform to the Constitution. I am not aware that it has ever been contended that the general principles relating to unjustified enrichment in private law are inconsistent with the Constitution. The authors also make the point that 'form and content do in the end have an influence on one another' and that 'an appropriate categorisation can do much to create an understanding of the proper functioning of substantive rules'.

Dealing with the basic elements of enrichment liability, Visser (2008: 157) explains evocatively that '[t]he law of enrichment is about smoothing away a mound in the patrimony of the defendant that should not be there, just as the law of delict is about filling in the hole in the plaintiff's patrimony that should not be there' and then adds:

> 'In both civil law and common law jurisdictions there are three widely (although not universally) accepted, cornerstones of enrichment liability, namely *(a)* enrichment of the defendant, *(b)* at the expense of the plaintiff, which is *(c)* unjustified. At present these are also the basic elements of enrichment liability in South Africa.'

(a) Enrichment of the defendant

Visser and Roux (1996: 102) argue as follows:

> 'although "enrichment" usually means that one has acquired a benefit which has increased one's patrimony, the term might be sometimes taken to mean acquisition and retention of a benefit in circumstances where the acquisition has not increased the net worth of one's patrimony'.

They further contend that this would be consonant with the *condictiones* in Roman law, namely that 'the defendant's obligation is to return that which was received, rather than the net excess left at the time of the institution of action' subject to certain exceptions.[16]

This would cover cases where 'defendants' under apartheid were and remain benefited at the expense of 'plaintiffs', for example in the sphere of education and training, where this may not have increased the net worth of the particular

---

[16] Werner Flume '*Der Wegfall der Bereicherung in der Entwicklung vom römischen zum geltenden Recht*' in *Festschrift für Hans Niedermeyer* (1953) 103ff; JP Dawson 'Erasable enrichment in German law' 1981 *Boston University LR* 273ff; Reinhardt Zimmermann *The Law of Obligations: Roman Foundations of the Civilian Tradition* (1990) at 897; DP Visser 'Responsibility to return lost enrichment' (1992) *Acta Juridica* 176ff.

defendants' patrimony, yet the s 9(2) measures are 'designed' to restore to plaintiffs the education or training of which they were deprived. I would argue that these measures also, if not primarily, are intended to restore human dignity, particularly in regard to the free unfolding of the human personality and to self-fulfilment.

(b) The 'at the expense of' requirement

As Visser and Roux (1996: 103) explain, this represents the causal element in the restitution equation. They further point out that in English law 'the plaintiff may be either a person who has been impoverished ("enrichment by subtraction from another") or a person who has been wronged ("enrichment by doing wrong to another")'. The former can also be termed 'autonomous enrichment' and the latter 'derivative enrichment'. The learned authors point out that under the Restitution of Land Act both forms could arise but argue that

> 'it would probably contribute most to a clear understanding of the problem to see these cases as "enrichment by wrongdoing"'.

The same could be said for the enrichment contemplated by the s 9(2) principle.

It is important, for purposes of categorising the s 9(2) measures as remedies for public-law enrichment, to stress that the reference to 'enrichment by wrongdoing' does not mean that the *'defendants' under s 9(2) must themselves have been guilty of any wrongdoing*. This will be discussed more fully in *(c)*.

(c) The requirement of 'unjust(ified)' enrichment

Roux and Visser (1996: 104) refer to this element as '... central, essential in all systems of unjustified enrichment'. It describes, as they put it, 'the conditions under which accrued enrichment has the quality of unjustifiedness and thus determines the parameters within which the restitutionary remedies can offer relief in a particular system'. After considering English and German law on the questions, the authors, on the basis of these approaches, argue that South Africa should accept that

> '"enrichment by wrongdoing" is one of the ways in which a situation of unjustified retention of a benefit may arise'.

Once that is established, they argue,

> 'it is clear that the acquisition of land acquired in circumstances that violate the Constitution constitutes the basis for holding that the *retention* of the land is unjustified, ie *sine causa*.' (Emphasis supplied.)

This must apply *a fortiori* in my view to the position of 'defendants' under the s 9(2) remedies. I have stressed in *(b)* above that 'enrichment by wrongdoing' does not mean that the 'defendants' under s 9(2) need themselves to have been guilty of any wrongdoing. It ought to be sufficient if the enrichment is the consequence of wrongdoing. Visser and Roux (1996: 103–104) point out that in South Africa 'enrichment by wrongdoing'

> 'has not been developed at all in the ordinary law of enrichment. Introducing it at this level [the restitution of land] might very well have the result that such a category begins to open up in the area of private law enrichment'.

In his later work Visser (2008: 562–650) deals with so-called 'imposed enrichment (enrichment due to unauthorized expenditure'. It is clear that in this form of enrichment the defendant takes no part in the acts giving rise to her enrichment, but a claim for enrichment is nonetheless accorded to the plaintiff.[17] Visser mentions (2008: 279 n 18) that in most legal systems the '"payment of another's debt" is treated as a separate category of imposed enrichment'. If this is so, then it must follow that if, through unlawful discrimination, a defendant has been enriched at the expense of a plaintiff, even though the defendant might have had no hand in this discrimination or could not be held politically responsible for it, this must ground relief for unjustified enrichment. This also appears to be clearly implicit in the treatment by Visser (2008: 179–192) of the requirement of unjustified enrichment in private law under the heading 'The retention of the enrichment must be unjustified' although he does not deal pertinently with a situation in private law comparable with the s 9(2) measures. It is not within the province of the present work to deal more than fleetingly with Visser's views in this regard.

Visser (2008: 272) points out that it has been long accepted that 'the courts may, in appropriate circumstances, extend the scope of the specific enrichment actions on an *ad hoc* basis', and that in consequence of the recent judgments of the Supreme Court of Appeal, referred to above, the structure of the law of enrichment will be seriously debated more often now than in the past.

The proposition that defendants need not themselves have been 'at fault' in respect of the enrichment they have enjoyed for public-law restitutionary measures against them to be justified, finds perhaps its strongest support from Visser (2008: 152). After referring to the views expressed in Visser and Roux (1996), he states:

> 'We concluded that if South African law were to accept a category of "enrichment by wrongdoing" (invasion of rights), the retention of land which had been acquired in terms of race-based legislation is unjustified. This approach applies the powerful moral notion of the undesirability of retaining unjustified profits to the situation where a particular class or group in society benefits improperly from the exploitation of another class or group. Of course, in a situation where one has had systematic enrichment of one group at the

[17] Visser (2008: 572) points out that there is a difference of opinion as to whether managing the affairs of others against their express wishes gives rise to compensation for expenditure, but that Van Zyl (1970), on the high authority of Voet and Groenewegen, is of the view that the Roman-Dutch law of their time recognised a claim of this sort.

> expense of another, mostly through the aid of the law which empowers the one group and disempowers the other, private law is ill-equipped to assist in correcting the situation — and thus special rules are needed. But that does not prevent us from seeing such rules as *public-law manifestations* of the notion against unjustified enrichment (which here, unlike in its ordinary private-law guise, has a clear distributive justice basis).' (Emphasis supplied.)

Subject to two qualifications, this would be an elegant summary of my contentions in this regard. In the first place, by using the word 'group,' I do not understand Visser to be suggesting that a collective of individual persons (linked on whatever basis) ought to be invested with legal personality, outside the well-recognised grounds on which associations (using the expression widely) of persons can acquire legal personality. As I will be at pains to point out later, s 9(2) does not refer to groups but to 'persons or categories of persons'. Secondly, I cannot see how unjustified enrichment in this context can have a distributive justice basis. Surely it has a 'corrective justice basis', namely the restoration of equality, as Visser himself (2008: 17) earlier states: 'Corrective justice, which has its roots in Aristotle's *Nicohomachean Ethics*, is about eliminating injustice that has occurred between individuals by setting right inequalities'. It is, moreover, abundantly clear from the work of Visser (2008) that unjustified enrichment and the relevant remedies are features of the jurisprudence of diverse countries.

The categorisation of the s 9(2) remedies as ones arising basically out of public-law unjustified enrichment, is not only satisfactory in principle but also has significant practical and political benefits. These would include the obvious advantages of moving away from the victim–perpetrator paradigm and satisfactorily explaining why the measures, however long it may be necessary to apply them, are by their nature limited in time; namely until disadvantage *caused by unfair discrimination in the past* has been eradicated. By the same token it is not a remedy for general redistribution unconnected to past unfair discrimination.

6.3 JURISPRUDENCE OF THE SOUTH AFRICAN COURTS

In the *Gay and Lesbian (Minister of Justice)* case[18] the Constitutional Court indicated its preference for the expression 'remedial or restitutionary equality' over expressions such as 'substantive equality' in the context of s 9 of the Constitution. It pointed out[19] that

> '[s]ection 9 of the Constitution, like its predecessor, clearly contemplates both substantive and remedial equality. Substantive equality is envisaged when s 9(2) unequivocally asserts that that equality includes "the full and equal enjoyment of all rights and freedoms". The state is further obliged "to promote the achievement of such equality" by "legislative

[18] *National Coalition for Gay and Lesbian Equality and Another v The Minister of Justice and Others* 1999 (1) SA 6 (CC) (1998 (12) BCLR 1517) paras 60–61.

[19] Id para 62.

> and other measures designed to protect or advance persons, or categories of persons, disadvantaged by unfair discrimination", *which envisages remedial equality.*' (Emphasis supplied.)

The need for 'remedial or restitutionary equality'[20] was explained by the Court as follows:[21]

> 'Particularly in a country such as South Africa, persons belonging to certain categories have suffered considerable unfair discrimination in the past. It is insufficient for the Constitution merely to ensure, through its Bill of Rights, that statutory provisions which have caused such unfair discrimination in the past are eliminated. Past unfair discrimination frequently has ongoing negative consequences, the continuation of which is not halted immediately when the initial causes are eliminated, and unless remedied, may continue for a substantial time and even indefinitely. Like justice, equality delayed is equality denied.'

In *Van Heerden*'s case,[22] the first in which the Constitutional Court had to come to grips directly with the issue of restitutionary or remedial equality, this approach and nomenclature were, for the most part, confirmed.[23] The Court correctly held that '[a] comprehensive understanding of the Constitution's conception of equality requires a harmonious reading of the provisions of s 9'.[24] The Court further held[25] that restitutionary or remedial equality measures

> '[30] ... are not in themselves a deviation from or invasive of, the right to equality guaranteed by the Constitution.... They are integral to the reach of our equality protection. In other words, the provisions of s 9(1) and s 9(2) are complementary; both contribute to the constitutional goal of achieving equality to ensure "full and equal enjoyment of all rights". A disjunctive or oppositional reading of the two sub-sections would frustrate the foundational equality objectives of the Constitution and its broader social justice imperatives.
>
> [31] ... [W]hat is clear is that our Constitution and in particular s 9 thereof, read as a whole, embraces for good reasons a substantive conception of equality inclusive of measures to redress existing inequality. Absent a positive commitment *progressively to eradicate* socially constructed barriers to equality and to root out systematic or institutionalised under-privilege, the constitutional promise of equality before the law and its equal protection and benefit must, in the context of our country, ring hollow.' (Emphasis supplied.)

Although one could hardly disagree fundamentally with this broad exposition, I would venture to suggest that it somewhat oversimplified. The reference to progressively eradicating 'socially constructed barriers to equality' and to rooting out 'systematic or institutionalised under-privilege' is quite unexceptionable when applied to the vertical application of the Constitution, as was the case

---

[20] Id para 61.
[21] Id para 60.
[22] *Minister of Finance and Another v Van Heerden* (above, n 4), per Moseneke J.
[23] Id paras 28 and 30.
[24] Id para 28.
[25] Id paras 30–31.

before the Court. It is a far more complex matter when these issues arise in a horizontal context, and competing rights of freedom and privacy enter the picture, as discussed in Chapter 5.

In *Van Heerden* the Court further held[26] that

> '[l]egislative and other measures that *properly* fall within the requirements of s 9(2) are not presumptively unfair. Remedial measures are not a derogation from, but a substantive and composite part of, the equality protection envisaged by the provision of s 9 and of the Constitution as a whole. Their primary object is to promote the achievement of equality.... [D]ifferentiation *aimed* at protecting or advancing persons disadvantaged by unfair discrimination is warranted *provided* the measures are shown to *conform with the internal test set by s 9(2)*'. (Emphasis supplied.)

My understanding of the above passage is that an objective test is postulated for considering whether the measures taken will achieve protection or advancement. The measures employed must of course be capable of achieving the desired restitutionary object. It is obvious that restitutionary or remedial equality will require time for its objectives to be achieved, and all disadvantage caused by unfair discrimination to be eradicated. But the purpose of the provisions is at least conceptually aimed at achieving this result. At the very least, disadvantage caused by unfair discrimination must be reduced and the number of persons and categories of persons continuing to suffer disadvantage decreased. This is achieved not by good intentions but by the efficacy of the actual 'measures' employed.[27]

Expressions such as 'properly falling' within the requirements of s 9(2) or 'conforming with the internal test' set by s 9(2), of course, need unpacking and this cannot be properly undertaken without having due and proper regard to the Constitution as a whole, as is pointed out by the Court. Section 9 has itself, of course, to be read as a whole, the first sentence of s 9(2) making it clear that the equality envisaged in s 9 is not merely negative equality, which demands only the removal of obstructions to equality, but also embraces the achievement of equality for all. Strictly speaking it is the second sentence of s 9(2) that sets the demand and criteria for restitutionary equality.

According to the Court, if a measure 'properly falls within the ambit of s 9(2)' it does not constitute unfair discrimination, but if it does not fall within this ambit, then the test summarised in *Harksen*'s case must be applied to ascertain whether the measures offend the anti-discriminatory provisions of s 9(3). In order to determine whether the measure 'properly falls' within the ambit of s 9(2), three criteria have to be satisfied:[28]

---

[26] Id para 32.

[27] Compare my discussion on Canadian restitutionary jurisprudence under s 15(2) of the Canadian Charter in section 6.5 below.

[28] Above, n 4 at paras 36–44.

> 'The first yardstick relates to whether the measure targets persons or categories of persons who have been disadvantaged by unfair discrimination; the second is whether the measure is designed to protect or advance such persons or categories of persons; and the third requirement is whether the measure promotes the achievement of equality.'[29]

The Court, when elaborating on the above criteria[30] uses expressions such as 'group' and 'class' as equivalents for the expression 'categories' as used in s 9(2). I do not understand the Court to be departing in any way from the criterion of 'category' as indicating a collective nor that the use of 'group' or 'class' is indicative of conferring legal personality on a conglomerate of persons. The 'protection' or 'advancement' envisaged by s 9(2) is for the benefit of persons as individuals. It could not have been the intention of the Court to postulate a 'group' as a conglomerate having individual legal personality and as such being entitled as a group to constitutional benefits. The idea of an unincorporated group being the bearer of constitutional rights is a concept that has been rejected by the Constitution. This is the effect of the *Second Certification* judgment[31] when dealing with the so-called 'individual associational rights'. One of the arguments against certification related to non-compliance with Constitutional Principle XII.[32] The Court rejected this argument by holding, inter alia, that — 'Having regard to the CPs [Constitutional Principles] as a whole, the "[c]ollective rights of self-determination" mentioned in CP XII are associational individual rights, namely, those rights which cannot be fully or properly exercised by individuals otherwise than in association with others of like disposition.'[33] Section 31(1) of the Amended Text (AT) [which became s 31(1) of the 1996 Constitution] reads:

> 'Persons belonging to a cultural, religious or linguistic community may not be denied the right, with other members of the community —
> *(a)* to enjoy their culture, practise their religion and use their language; and
> *(b)* to form, join and maintain cultural, religious and linguistic associations and other organs of civil society.'

The Court held[34] that the requirements of CP XII for 'collective rights of self-determination' were met by these individual associational rights, as well as by the institutional structures provided by the AT and the express provision of rights

---

[29] Id as summarised in para 37.
[30] Id paras 38–40.
[31] *Chairperson of the National Assembly, Ex parte: In re Certification of the Amended Text of the Constitution of the Republic of South Africa, 1996* 1997 (2) SA 97 (CC) (1997 (1) BCLR 1).
[32] Which required:
> 'Collective rights of self-determination in forming, joining and maintaining organs of civil society, including linguistic, cultural and religious associations, shall, on the basis of non-discrimination and free association, be recognised and protected.'

[33] Above, n 31 at para 24.
[34] Id para 27.

of association in AT Chapter 2 together with the procedural provision governing their enforcement.

The words 'categories of persons' (instead of, say, 'groups of persons') were obviously chosen with great care. 'Categories' of persons are not 'groups' (endowed with legal personality) but individuals with a common denominator as far as their identities or experiences are concerned. Dupper (2006: 148–149) is also of the view that the s 9(2) policy is 'directed towards individuals *actually* discriminated against as opposed to one directed towards disadvantaged groups as such'. Dupper (2006: 148) correctly points out that by focusing on groups rather than individuals, 'individuals that are not "needy" will in fact receive benefits at the expense of those who have been handicapped most by the effects of discrimination and thus are most in need of "advancement"'. To this one must add that an individual, although suffering no disadvantage because of discrimination, could perversely be entitled to restitution. I would suggest that these are some of the reasons why the words 'persons, or *categories* of persons' were chosen for purposes of s 9(2).

The Court, dealing with the requirement that the restitutionary or remedial measure 'promotes the achievement of equality' said the following:

> 'Determining whether a measure will in the long run promote the achievement of equality requires an appreciation of the effect of the measure in the context of our broader society. It must be accepted that the achievement of this goal may often come *at a price for those who were previously advantaged.* Action needs to be taken to advance the position of those who have *suffered unfair discrimination in the past.* As Ngcobo J observed in *Bato Star*:
>
> > "The measures that bring about transformation will inevitably affect some members of the society adversely, particularly those coming from the *previously advantaged communities.*"
>
> However, it is also clear that the long-term goals of our society include a *non-racial, non-sexist society* in which *each person will be recognized and treated as a human being of equal worth and dignity.* Central to this vision is the recognition that ours is a diverse society comprised of people of different races, different religions and both sexes. This diversity, and our equality as citizens within it, is something our constitution celebrates and protects. In assessing therefore whether a measure will in the long term promote equality, we must bear in mind this constitutional vision. In particular, *a measure should not constitute an abuse of power or impose such substantial and undue harm on those excluded from its benefits that our long-term constitutional goal would be threatened.*' [35] (Emphasis supplied.)

There are certain aspects of the above holding that deserve further comment. In the first place the very purpose of restitutionary equality is to eradicate past inequality that *continues to survive* despite constitutional provisions outlawing it, as the passage from the *Gay and Lesbian (Minister of Justice)* case quoted

[35] Above, n 4 at para 44.

above makes clear.[36] Thus, if a person or category of persons A, although disadvantaged by unfair discrimination in the past, no longer currently suffers disadvantage, the restitutionary basis for the s 9(2) measures falls away and these measures cannot be invoked.

Secondly, although one naturally applauds the passage holding that the long-term goal of our society is one 'in which each person will be recognized and treated as a human being of equal worth and dignity' it is regrettable that the adjectives used to describe this society are limited to 'non-racial, non-sexist'. This is a truncation of the society envisaged by the prohibition of discrimination on the grounds enumerated in s 9(3). It is true that under s 1*(b)* of the Constitution 'Non-racialism and non-sexism' are designated as 'values' on which the Republic of South Africa is founded. But they are not the only foundational values. Under s 1*(a)* 'human dignity' and the 'achievement of equality' are similarly foundational, and the equality sought to be achieved is surely the equality for which s 9(2) and 9(3) provide. When the Constitution is read as a whole, the society envisaged is one in which no person is unfairly discriminated against on *any of the grounds* so enumerated or on *any analogous unenumerated ground* envisaged by s 9(3). I am sure that the Court did not intend this truncation, but a phrase limited to 'non-racial, non-sexist' is simply a constitutionally inadequate and unhappy one to describe the long-term societal goal of our Constitution, which is after all a comprehensively 'non-discriminatory' one.

The limits to valid restitutionary measures articulated in the last sentence of the passage quoted are unduly limited and vague. Moreover, the measures taken under 9(2) are given such degree of protection that they can only be invalidated if they *(a)* 'constitute an abuse of power' or *(b)* 'impose such substantial *and* undue harm [on those adversely affected thereby] that our long-term constitutional goal would be threatened'. It is not clear to me why the bar should be set so high.

At the same time it should be recognised that the s 9(2) measures, whether legislative or otherwise, can never — from their very nature and purpose — be perfectly formulated. The section seeks to resolve the tension that inevitably arises when the furthering of A's equality necessarily impinges negatively on B's equality. This, I would argue, can only be achieved by trying to balance the competing dignity claims inherent in trying to balance competing claims to equality.

The difficulty of course is that no country where serious and systemic discrimination has occurred can — for administrative and other associated financial reasons — be expected to devise and administer a remedial system that has, in all cases, to consider the awarding of a remedy on a case-by-

[36] See text to n 18 above.

case, individual-by-individual basis. The logistics and costs might make this impossible. No legislation or comprehensive administrative measure can always operate with a surgeon's scalpel, given the vast number of cases involved. It is, in appropriate cases, compelled to use a broader sword, but where an individualised remedy is reasonably possible it should be employed. The greatest challenge facing the remedial objective of s 9(2) is finding the appropriate balance in this regard. In trying to determine what this is, a number of features should be borne in mind. The overarching goal is not limited to establishing, progressively, a society in which the consequences of past discrimination are eliminated, but a society in which the dignity of all is equally respected and protected. Remedies are not justified which would result in turning the white 'category of persons' into an underclass. Whatever enrichment they may still enjoy, and whatever needs to be done to remedy unjust enrichment, the persons in the white category have undeniably become a political minority and thus in no position to exercise any political control over the implementation of s 9(2). It is legitimate to take this into account when evaluating remedies under s 9(2). The following observations of Langa DP in the *Walker* case[37] are in point.

> 'The respondent [a white male] does however belong to a racial minority which could in a political sense be regarded as vulnerable. It is precisely individuals who are part of such minorities who are vulnerable to discriminatory treatment and who, in a very special sense, must look to the Bill of Rights for protection. When that happens a Court has a clear duty to come to the assistance of the person affected. Courts should however always be astute to distinguish between genuine attempts to promote and protect equality on the one hand and actions calculated to protect pockets of privilege at a price which amounts to the perpetuation of inequality and disadvantage to others on the other.'

The phrases in the passage quoted above from *Van Heerden*, referring to the fact that the achievement of the equality goal may 'often come at a price for those who were previously advantaged', and describing these persons simply as 'those excluded from' the measure under s 9(2), are euphemistic. The Court after all referred approvingly to the observation by Ngcobo J in *Bato Star* that the measures that bring about transformation will 'inevitably affect some members of society adversely, particularly those coming from the previously advantaged communities'. If the restitutionary measures under 9(2) are to work at all, then restitution must be made to those who still suffer disadvantage in consequence of unfair discrimination, and this restitution *must come* from those who still benefit in consequence of this unfair discrimination. If in fact no restitution results from the measure or if the restitution under the measure only comes from persons or categories of persons who do not continue to benefit (or be advantaged) by

[37] *City Council of Pretoria v Walker* 1998 (2) SA 363 (CC) para 48.

the unfair discrimination, this measure is, by definition and in principle, not protected by s 9(2).

What does an 'abuse of power' mean? In the context in which the phrase is used, it must mean something more than simply that the measure does not fall within the ambit of the s 9(2) requirement. Logically it must refer to an abuse of power even when the measure results in restitution to the disadvantaged from the advantaged. All abuse of power is, under the principle of legality and constitutionality, invalid. What is the nature of this abuse of power here contemplated? It must be more than arbitrariness or lack of rationality (however one wishes to define these concepts), which would in themselves invalidate the measure. I regret to say that one is left in the dark.

Lastly, on what principle is one to decide that a measure, otherwise complying on its face with the provisions of s 9(2), is impermissible because it imposes 'substantial and undue harm' on those making restitution or suffering its negative consequences? Purely linguistically, the answer provided by the Court is, when it 'threatens ... our long-term constitutional goal [of achieving equality] ...'. But according to what principles does one determine when the 'harm' imposed is 'substantial' or 'undue' and at what stage does this harm 'threaten' our 'long-term constitutional goal'? What nature of harm is contemplated? Is the harm envisaged financial or economic, or does it also refer to restriction of freedom, eradication or restriction of career choice, or limitation of self-fulfilment? At what stage does this harm threaten our long-term constitutional equality goal? Assuming the measure has the consequence of totally obliterating a single advantaged person's choice of career, for which this person is ideally qualified and otherwise suited. Viewed from a purely consequentialist or utilitarian point of view it could hardly be said that this individual instance threatens our long-term constitutional equality goal. But should a measure like this pass constitutional muster when, even in respect of a single individual, it obliterates the core elements of human dignity? I would hope not. I am not so naive as to suggest that remedial measures can be so narrowly and snugly tailored as to make separate provision for the negative impact on every person adversely affected thereby. To be practically workable legislative and other remedial measures have to be general. It is impossible to deal with each and every case of possible negative impact discretely. But even general provisions can exclude the grossest violations of human dignity. It is, after all, just as important a constitutional imperative that no person should be dealt with as a mere cipher, as a mere instrument, as a mere means to an end. At the very least restitutionary measures should make provision for 'hard cases' as German law, dealt with hereunder, illustrates.

It is necessary to have a principled basis for resolving tensions between the benefits of restitutionary benefits accruing to the 'disadvantaged' under a s 9(2) measure and the negative effects thereof on the 'advantaged' having to make this restitution. For the reasons advanced at the commencement of this chapter, human dignity should play a central and guiding role in this resolution, which should as part of its methodology include an appropriate proportionality analysis. I say an 'appropriate' form of proportionality analysis, because the restitution envisaged by s 9(2) differs greatly from restitution arising from unjustified enrichment under private law. As pointed out earlier the restitution remedy in the latter case almost always involves relief in the form of money or some other economic commodity, flowing from the persons unjustifiably enriched to the plaintiff. Under s 9(2) the remedial measure can be very different. In many instances the benefit accruing to the disadvantaged could of course be one sounding in money or take the form of some other proprietary benefit. Equally, however, the benefits could be ones relating, for example, to opportunities (as opposed to financial means to qualify for these opportunities) for training or education in its most extensive sense, for employment (broadly construed), for career opportunities in the private and public sector. These examples can be multiplied. The point I am trying to make is that the negative impact of all these restitutionary measures on the human dignity of the persons disadvantaged thereby (ie the persons having to make or suffer the restitution) will vary greatly depending on the precise nature and impact of the measure in question. I would argue that, as a very broad general principle, a remedial measure that merely has negative financial impact would — other things being equal — have less harmful impact on human dignity than other types of measures. For example, a tax imposed exclusively on advantaged persons in order to further the primary and secondary education of disadvantaged persons could hardly be said to impinge in any real sense on the human worth of the advantaged; provided of course the tax was reasonable and employed effectively to secure the remedial goal and met other proportionality requirements. On the other hand, if a remedial measure had the effect of permanently disqualifying a person from qualifying for or practising a particular career or any other form of employment, this would have the most profound impact on the advantaged person's human dignity and could hardly pass constitutional muster. A proportionality analysis involves, in interrelated ways, the weighing up of means and ends and their impact on dignity.

In his separate concurring judgment in *Van Heerden*, Sachs J does go further in his analysis of s 9(2) and its implications than the majority judgment does. I would suggest that his judgment on the limits of the provisions in the second sentence of s 9(2) supports, in general, the approach I have suggested.

Sachs J emphasises[38] that s 9 should be read and applied in a 'holistic manner' and that ss 9(2) and 9(3) must be 'integrated' and 'treated as overlapping and indivisible rather than as discrete'. This must surely be correct, for where else can one discover the nature and content of the 'unfair discrimination' referred to in s 9(2) other than in s 9(3)? He refers to the bristling controversy in the United

[38] Above, n 4 at paras 148–149.

States around race-based remedial measures and rightly concludes that the purpose of the provisions of s 9(2) is to settle this sort of controversy for South African constitutional law in favour of the constitutional legitimacy of 'race-conscious remedial action'.[39] The learned Judge refers[40] to the 'enormous public controversies and divisions of judicial opinion' on the subject of race-conscious remedial action 'in other countries'. It also emerges, from the cumulative effect of various passages in Sachs J's judgment, that — although certain phrases are difficult to comprehend on their own — he considers a proper consideration of the negative impact of the remedial measure on advantaged persons or classes to be essential for determining its validity, and that an appropriately applicable proportionality analysis is to be used in the process:

> '... [T]he more snugly a race-based measure fits into 9(2), the more difficult it will be to challenge its constitutionality. Conversely, the less comfortable the fit, the less impervious the measure will be to attack.... [W]here different constitutionally protected interests are involved it is prudent to ... opt for context-based proportional interrelationships, balanced and weighed according to the fundamental constitutional values called into play by the situation.'[41]

The 'rigour' of what Sachs J calls a substantive approach[42] lies in

> 'determining in a rational, objective way the impact that the measures will have on the position in society and sense of self-worth of those affected by it. The critical factor is not sameness or symmetry, but human dignity.... In a matter like the present it should accordingly not make any significant difference whether one starts one's analysis from the vantage point of those former [sic] disadvantaged, or of those who have been advantaged. Nor should there be a Chinese wall between the two.'

Sachs J well appreciates that judicial interference with s 9(2) remedial measures that impact negatively on advantaged persons is not limited to 'measures taken for improper or corrupt motives'[43] or measures 'so lacking in thought and organisation as seriously to threaten the very functioning and survival of the enterprise involved, would lack rationality, and could not be said to advance or be fair to anybody ...'.[44] Calling for greater oversight Sachs J makes clear that a measure would not pass constitutional muster if the advantaged were to 'be treated in an abusive or oppressive way that offends their dignity and tells them and the world that *they are of lesser worth than the disadvantaged*'[45] (emphasis

---

[39] Id para 147.
[40] Id.
[41] Id para 140.
[42] Id para 146 and elsewhere. The learned Judge continues to use the expression 'substantive equality' without qualification or explanation despite the cautionary remarks concerning the use and meaning of this phrase expressed as early as the unanimous judgment in the *Gay and Lesbian (Minister of Justice)* case above, n 18 at paras 60–61.
[43] Id para 149.
[44] Id.
[45] Id para 151.

supplied); also that 'if the measure at issue is manifestly overbalanced in ignoring or trampling on the interests of members of the advantaged section of the community, and gratuitously and flagrantly imposes disproportionate burdens on them, the courts have a duty to interfere';[46] and in summation that 'some degree of proportionality, based on the particular context and circumstances of the case, can never be ruled out. That too is what promoting equality (s 9(2)) and fairness (s 9(3)) require.'[47]

Lastly, and in the context of the type of proportionality analysis that he supports for determining the validity of a s 9(2) measure, Sachs J urges that courts

> '... must be reluctant to interfere with such measures, and exercise due restraint when tempted to interpose themselves as arbiters as to whether the measure could have been proceeded with in a better or less onerous way'.[48]

On this point I must disagree. This is not the case of a court evaluating the exercise of an administrative discretion. The court, whether it likes it or not, simply *is* — under the Constitution — an arbiter with a constitutional duty to decide whether a remedial measure (legislative or otherwise) taken in pursuance of s 9(2) is consistent with its provisions. Should it be clear that an adequate remedial measure could have been taken that would not impact negatively at all on the advantaged persons, or would have impacted substantially less negatively, I can think of no reason why a court should not intervene. For then the measure lacks rationality, or is at least arbitrary in the sense decided in the *First National Bank* case.[49]

I deal again with proportionality and the role of dignity therein in the last section of this chapter.

In *Pillay*'s case[50] O'Regan J stated that '[e]education is the engine of equal opportunity'. Although pronounced in a partly dissenting judgment, the majority neither expressly nor impliedly disagreed with this view. I do not believe that O'Regan J intended to convey that education was the *only* engine; it certainly is one of the most important. I borrow her felicitous phrase to express the view that education is, likewise, the most important engine for restitutionary equality. There are of course other engines, but I believe that education (including ongoing education such as, for example, so-called 'adult education') has a pre-eminent role to play. Conversely, restitutionary equality (including restitutionary education) may be essential to achieve true equality of opportunity.

---

[46] Id para 152.

[47] Id.

[48] Id.

[49] *First National Bank of SA t/a Wesbank v Commissioner for the South African Revenue Services and Another; First National Bank of SA t/a Wesbank v Minister of Finance* 2002 (4) SA 768 (CC) (2002 (7) BCLR 702).

[50] *MEC for Education: KwaZulu/Natal and Others v Pillay and Others* 2008 (1) SA 474 (CC) (2008 (2) BCLR 99) para 121.

In the *Du Preez* case[51] the South Eastern Cape High Court was required to consider the restitutionary equality provisions of s 14 of the Equality Act. The constitutional validity of these provisions was not challenged and the Court was accordingly bound to accept their validity and decide the issue within the four corners of the Act.[52] For the broader themes of this book it is however necessary to consider the constitutionality of these provisions, before turning to the judgment itself.

Section 14 of the Equality Act, under the rubric 'Determination of fairness or unfairness', is constitutionally suspect. Section 14(1) enacts, in categorical terms, that '[*i*]*t is not unfair discrimination* to take measures designed to protect or advance persons or categories of persons disadvantaged by unfair discrimination *or the members of such groups or categories of persons*'.

This seems to be rewriting, by ordinary legislation, the second sentence of s 9(2) of the Constitution, which reads:

> 'To promote the achievement of equality, legislative or other measures designed to protect or advance persons, or categories of persons, disadvantaged by unfair discrimination may be taken.'

This subsection of the Constitution leaves undefined the nature of the entity by which these measures 'may be taken'. It includes both the state and persons. What is clear is that measures so taken, even by the state, will have a horizontal effect. These measures will invariably have an impact on 'persons or categories of persons' ('affected parties') who were *not disadvantaged* by unfair discrimination, but *benefited from* it or *were enriched* by it. It will impact on their own rights, and in particular on their right not to be unfairly discriminated against. What s 9(2) clearly does *not* do is give a blanket guarantee that *any* 'measure' taken under its provisions will be constitutional, irrespective of the nature or extent of its impact on affected parties. The founders wisely appreciated that whether a 'measure' properly fell within the ambit of s 9(2) could depend on a variety of factors, including the nature of the measure and the nature and extent of its impact on third parties.[53] However, this is exactly the type of blanket guarantee that s 14(1) of the Act purports to give when it in fact enacts that these 'measures' (all measures) shall not constitute unfair discrimination ('it is not unfair discrimination'), provided only that they are 'designed' for the prescribed purpose. This is clearly inconsistent with s 9(2) of the Constitution and invalid.

---

[51] *Du Preez v Minister of Justice and Constitutional Development and Others* 2006 (5) SA 592 (EqC) (2006 (9) BCLR 1094).

[52] See *Pillay*'s case (above, n 50) para 40.

[53] This is more fully dealt with in Chapter 4.

In analysing and applying s 14(1) of the Act one should bear in mind that the idea of a 'group' right was rightly rejected by the framers of the Constitution, who chose instead the concept of 'associational individual rights'.[54]

The same conclusion regarding invalidity must be reached with regard to s 14(2) and (3) of the Act, at the very least to the extent that they are applied horizontally. Its provisions decree, in mandatory terms, various factors 'which must be taken into account' in determining whether 'discrimination is unfair'. As already pointed out, the Constitutional Court has developed a considerable body of jurisprudence on the meaning of 'unfair discrimination' for purposes of s 9(3) of the Constitution. To the extent that s 14(2) and (3) of the Act give a different and more extensive meaning to 'unfair discrimination' than s 9(3) and (4) of the Constitution (*as interpreted by the courts*) does, it is inconsistent with the Constitution and invalid. I am by no means convinced that, even when only applied vertically, these particular subsections of the Act are valid. Where — in fleshing out the meaning of unfair discrimination — the courts have prescribed a particular methodology, and a particular application of values to particular facts, any attempt by the legislature to alter this methodology, application of values or relevant facts must, I believe, be inconsistent and invalid. If the executive wishes to alter the meaning of a constitutional provision (as given to it by the courts) it can do so only by appropriate constitutional amendment.

The *Du Preez* case was concerned with the filling of the vacant position of regional court magistrate at a certain centre. The complainant, a white male holding the degrees of BIuris, LLB and Master of Public Administration, had 19 years' experience as a magistrate, but because of the gender and race of the other applicants for the position, was not even granted an interview. Selections for the interviewing shortlist were based on a formula that was rigidly followed. The formula, fully described in the judgment, allocated points for each applicant on the basis of three criteria: experience, qualifications, and gender and race. The effect of the weights attached to the various criteria was such that a white male with maximum points (like the complainant with his advanced qualifications — rarely held by the overwhelming majority of aspirant regional magistrates) would score the same as black males and white females with minimum points; and white males with only an LLB degree (the majority of the prospective candidates) would automatically be outscored by all other categories of candidates. Black females with minimum points would outscore all other categories of candidates with only an LLB degree.

It was accepted in the case that the Equality Act, and not the Employment Equity Act 55 of 1998, applied to its facts.[55] AR Erasmus J was aware of the first

[54] See, in this regard, the *Second Certification* case (above, n 31) paras 23–27 in general and para 24 in particular. The idea of an unincorporated group being the bearer of rights was roundly rejected by the Report of the so-called Olivier Commission of Inquiry into Group Rights.

[55] Above, n 51 at para 13.

discrepancy between s 14(1) and the second sentence of s 9(2) read with s 9(3) of the Constitution referred to above, namely that — on its face — s 14(1) of the Act gives a blanket guarantee that no measure taken thereunder can constitute unfair discrimination.[56] The constitutional validity of s 14 not being under attack, the learned judge had the difficult task of reconciling its provisions with those of the second sentence of s 9(2) of the Constitution. He correctly concluded, as I understand the judgment, that the latter did not grant blanket constitutional approval to all restitutionary equality measures taken, and that situations could arise where these measures could indeed constitute unfair discrimination under s 9(3):

> 'When applying the Bill of Rights, a court must promote all those values, and will therefore not readily accept an exclusion or diminution of a fundamental right even by another constitutional right, and certainly not by another statute.
>
> ...
>
> An interpretation of s 9(2) of the Constitution that sees its implicit approval of affirmative action measures as excluding or negating the right to equality, will offend constitutional principles. Rather, affirmative action measures must be seen as essential and integral to the goal of equality; and not as limitations of or exceptions to the equality rights. *Reverse discrimination is nonetheless justiciable in terms of s 6, despite the provisions of s 14(1) of the Act.*'[57] (Emphasis supplied.)

When the comments relating to s 9(2) of the Constitution are read in conjunction with the highlighted passage it becomes clear that what the court is deciding is that restitutionary measures referred to in s 9(2) of the Constitution could still notionally fall foul of the s 9(3) prohibition. With this I fully agree, and is a conclusion implicit in the Constitutional Court's judgment in the *Van Heerden* case.[58] I cannot agree with the highlighted sentence as a feasible construction of s 14(1) of the Equality Act. The learned judge was admittedly in an unenviable position. Giving 14(1) its ordinary grammatical meaning, which I believe is the only feasible construction, would have non-suited the claimant. With the benefit of hindsight, the Court ought perhaps to have raised the issue of s 14(1)'s constitutional validity with the litigants at the earliest opportunity, in order for the matter to be properly addressed.

Nonetheless it is instructive to consider the way in which the conflict of rights between those entitled to restitutionary equality and those who are not, was dealt with by the court. It found[59] that, for purposes of s 13 of the Equality Act, the shortlisting criteria imposed a disadvantage on the complainant and, because it was based on race and gender, amounted to discrimination by the respondents.

[56] Id paras 17–18.
[57] Id para 18.
[58] Above, n 4.
[59] Above, n 51 at para 27.

This was presumed to be unfair under the Act unless the respondents proved the contrary. In summary the court dealt with this conflict of rights as follows:

There was a 'patent disproportionality' in a selection policy based on race and gender to the absolute exclusion of all the other qualities required for a position as responsible and important as that of regional magistrate. 'Such a policy is irrational within its own terms and objectives.'[60] The effect of the committee's shortlisting formula was to raise an 'insurmountable obstacle' for the complainant and was therefore 'an absolute barrier' to his appointment.[61] The inflexible *modus operandi* of the committee came foursquare within the situation of 'absolute inclusion of designated groups members to the absolute exclusion of non-designated group members described by Pretorius et al, above', and 'is therefore subject to the valid criticism levelled at such measures by the learned authors'.[62] The effect of the formula was to 'frustrate the complainant's ambition for advancement in his chosen career', with denial to him of the 'concomitant benefits of heightened prestige and increased income'; the discrimination was therefore 'serious in its nature and extent'; the 'more detrimental the nature of the discrimination upon the interest of the affected party, the more likely it is to be unfair'; and inasmuch as the 'discrimination was built into a departmental policy, is was systemic in nature'.[63]

The court accordingly found that respondents had failed to prove that the discrimination perpetuated against the complainant was fair. In the passages referred to above I would prefer to add 'concomitant opportunities for self-fulfilment and self-realisation' to 'concomitant benefits of heightened prestige and increased income'. This brings home more clearly the severity of the impact on the complainant's human worth.

In *Solidarity obo Barnard v SAPS*[64] the applicant, a white female, applied for a new post that had been established in the South African Police Services. She was assessed as the most suitable candidate by a selection panel. There were three other candidates (another white female, a coloured female, and a black male) who were also found to be suitable (in the above order) but who had scored lower marks in assessment. No one was appointed to the post and this was sought to be justified on the basis that the appointment of the applicant (a white female and the highest-scoring candidate) would not 'address representivity'. The Labour Court directed the South African Police Services to appoint the applicant to the post in question. The case was decided under the provisions of the Employment Equity Act 55 of 1998 (the Act). Section 6(1) of the Act provides that '[n]o person may unfairly discriminate, directly or indirectly, against an employee in any

[60] Id para 38.
[61] Id para 41.
[62] Id. The reference is to Pretorius et al (eds) (2001).
[63] Id.
[64] (2010) 31 *ILJ* 742 (LC) (2010 (10) BCLR 1094 (LC)).

employment policy or practice, on one or more grounds, including race ...'; but s 6(2)*(a)* enacts that it is 'not unfair discrimination to — *(a)* take affirmative action measures consistent with the purpose of this Act'. Section 15(1) in turn defines 'affirmative action measures' as

> 'measures designed to ensure that suitably qualified people from designated groups have equal employment opportunities and are equitably represented in all occupational categories and levels in the workforce of a designated employer'.

In giving judgment for the Labour Court, Pretorius AJ correctly commented as follows[65] on the proper approach to the application of 'affirmative action' procedures:

> 'There can be no doubt that the application of affirmative action policies will adversely affect some employees. However, both the letter and spirit of our Constitution [of the Republic of South Africa, 1996 — Ed] dictate that such policies should be applied with due respect to the dignity of those affected.'

In this regard Pretorius AJ further commented[66] that '[i]t is not apparent that consideration was given to the applicant's right to equality and dignity. There appears to have been no consideration of her personal work history and circumstances.' These observations support my view concerning dignity's role in assessing the constitutional consistency of restitutionary measures.

6.4 GERMAN INSIGHTS[67]

In considering the German law on restitutionary equality I shall not consider its impact on land. One of the difficult problems that arose out of German reunification was the issue of land restitution, but it arose in circumstances so different from our own that comparisons are dangerous and run the risk of being misleading. For restitutionary equality outside the issue of land, the discussion on German law will be brief. The constitutional provisions differ substantially from those of the South African Constitution. Yet there are some useful pointers. I quote again the provisions of art 3 of the GBL:

---

[65] Id para38.

[66] Id para 43.5.

[67] Rabe (2001) is a helpful work in English dealing with, among other things, equality and 'affirmative action' in Germany and South Africa. The study was accepted as a doctoral thesis by the Faculty of Law of the University of Hamburg. In the same vein mention should be made of Mostert (2002), another work in English dealing comparatively with various aspects of property and the reform of land ownership in South Africa and Germany. An earlier version was presented by the author in partial fulfilment of the Degree of Doctor of Law at Stellenbosch University. Although I do not deal in the present work with restitutionary equality in relation to land, Mostert (2002) devotes an extensive section (Part Four) of her book to 'The influence of social reform on land law in Germany and South Africa', including a chapter on 'German reunification and the property order'.

'(1) All persons shall be equal before the law.
(2) Men and women shall have equal rights. *The state shall promote the actual implementation of equal rights for women and men and take steps to eliminate disadvantages that now exist.*
(3) No person shall be favoured or disfavoured because of sex, parentage, race, language, homeland and origin, faith, or religious or political opinions. *No person shall be disfavoured because of disability.*' (Emphasis supplied.)

The second sentence of art 3(2) and the second sentence of art 3(3) were — in consequence of the reunification of Germany — added by Constitutional Amendment on 27 October 1994, and will be referred to as the '1994 amendments' or the 'new provisions'. One must accordingly distinguish between restitutionary equality *before* and *after* 1994. I limit myself to the position post-1994. It is noteworthy that, textually, even after these amendments, art 3(3) still prohibits the *favouring* of persons on the enumerated grounds, with the exception of disability, on which ground only disfavouring is prohibited. The addition of the second sentence in art 3(2) '*The state shall promote the actual implementation of equal rights for women and men and take steps to eliminate disadvantages that now exist*' does, it is true, place an explicit positive obligation on the state to eradicate gender discrimination, but this must of course be harmonised with the express prohibition on gender discrimination. Virtually all the cases and academic discussion on restitutionary equality are devoted to restitutionary equality for women.

Whereas the amended art 3(2) requires the state in peremptory terms to 'promote the actual implementation of equal rights for women and men ...', the second sentence of South African s 9(2) is couched in permissive terms; the various restitutionary measures provided 'may' be taken (by the state). It is unclear to me why this is the case. After all s 7(2) provides that the state 'must', amongst other things, 'promote and fulfil the rights in the Bill of Rights'. When this is read in conjunction with s 9(2), which stipulates that equality includes 'the full and equal enjoyment of all rights and freedoms' it does not appear to me that the state can refrain from taking restitutionary measures where this is necessary to ensure the full and equal enjoyment of equality rights by persons 'disadvantaged by unfair discrimination'. Sachs and Biskup (2003: 48) express doubts as to the potency of art 3(2) of the GBL as amended. They argue that the directive to the state to take positive action is too undetermined for efficient scrutiny by the courts, and that in effect it is at the discretion of the legislature how intensely it will pursue this mandate. They also point out (51) that general anti-discrimination legislation is as yet not an important feature in Germany and that while there are laws in relation to furthering women's equality 'their scope is still limited'.

Sachs and Biskup (2003: 53) consider that above all 'affirmative action' comprises 'preferential treatment of persons on account of the forbidden criteria' of which the most important example is the 'promotion of women in public services through quota arrangements or similar regulations'. The authors remain doubtful whether advantaging women in this way is consistent with the prohibition of discrimination in art 3 of the GBL, but point out that at the time of writing the BVerfG had not yet ruled on any quota arrangement regulation.

Initially the BVerfG (BVerfGE 3, 225 (242)) considered that any differentiation between men and women was in principle prohibited, except where objective biological and functional differences existed as an established fact. In the course of time this approach changed (BVerfGE 85, 191 (207); BVerfGE 92, 91 (109)), and as Rabe (2001: 191) puts it, whereas initially it was 'readily accepted that differences between men and women related to the functional or biological differences' the subsequent approach 'examines whether these differences are not the result of social stereotyping that has to be eliminated to achieve the equal treatment of women'. See also Jarass (2006: Rn 107). Thus, in BVerfGE 92, 91 (109) it was held that the reservation of fire-service employment for men only was inconsistent with art 3. This type of development also emphasised the importance of equality of opportunity for women and that 'social reality' had to be taken into account. For my purposes the important provisions are those in the second sentence of art 3(2), introduced in 1994, and under which the state is commanded to 'promote the actual implementation of equal rights for women' and commanded to 'take steps to eliminate disadvantages that now exist'. I shall limit myself to dealing with this 'restitutionary equality' provision.

Rabe (2001: 275–276) conveniently summarises the legal position regarding restitutionary equality in Germany into seven topics. I quote them below and in some cases add additional comments of my own.

(a) 'Measures favouring women or men which are based on the prohibited criterion of sex may be implemented in terms of art 3 II of the GBL if they are aimed at achieving equality of opportunity for women and men in the social reality, or are aimed at removing existing disadvantages. The aim must be to establish factual equal treatment and *not parity* between men and women *as groups*. The aim must be to achieve *individual equality of opportunity*. This legitimate aim is capable of conflicting with the rights of the individual male which are protected by the prohibition against differentiation on the basis of sex. This conflict must be resolved by harmonising these rights in terms of the principles of praktischer Konkordanz or proportionality. This means that both competing norms must achieve the greatest possible amount of effectiveness.' (Emphasis supplied in the second and third sentences.)

Even before the 1994 amendments, the BVerfG was of the view that positive action was necessary to allow women to achieve greater equality of opportunity in the work place. Thus in the *Nightwork Prohibition* case (BVerfGE 85, 191 (207)) it was held that the 'objective [of art 3(2) of the GBL] was to equalize life's relationships. Thus women must have the same chances of employment as men' and it was 'permissible under Art 3(2) GG to even out, by means of beneficial regulation, factual disadvantages that women typically suffer from'. Jarass (2006: Rn 90) stresses that the 1994 amendments are aimed at securing equality of opportunity and not equality of result.

Admittedly the scope for restitutionary equality is far more limited in Germany (by virtue of the GBL's art 3 amendments) than in South Africa. The restitutionary nature of the remedies appears more clearly from the South African s 9(2) because the beneficiaries are described as 'persons, or categories of persons, *disadvantaged by unfair discrimination*'. (Emphasis supplied.)

There was some dispute as to whether the new provisions in art 3 of the GBL introduced an individual or a group right. According to Rabe (2001: 227) the predominant view in Germany is that 'Art 3 GG does not contain a group right to equality and the amendment to Art 3 II GG has not created any group right either and does not aim to achieve parity between women as a group and men as a group'. Where the South African s 9(2) refers to beneficiaries of restitutionary equality as 'persons or categories of persons' this is an even stronger indication that a mere group of persons is not included. '[C]ategories of persons' must surely refer to persons, in their individual capacities, who belong to a particular category.

A little more need be said about the harmonising of clashes between rights by the application of what is called '*praktischer Konkordanz* or proportionality'. As Rabe earlier (2001: 238–239) explains, the idea of *praktischer Konkordanz* ('practical harmony') is based on the concept of the unity of the constitution and its norms which form a comprehensive unit. In terms of these principles 'both the competing rights must be harmonised with each other and both rights optimised', which means that 'limits must be drawn for both rights'. As Von Münch (1992: Rn 47) points out, the BVerfG solves the problems of competing rights by the weighing-up of interests in concrete cases or, as expressed in the *Mephisto* case (BVerfGE 30, 173 [195]) by 'weighing up all the circumstances in each individual case'. It seems to me that in this regard one should bear in mind the contention of Dürig (1973: Rn 120ff) that in a clash between equality and freedom, preference should be given to freedom, because in a totalitarian state all people may equally be denied their freedom. This cannot, of course, be crudely applied in a case of restitutionary equality because it would defeat virtually all remedial measures. It does, however, emphasise that, in attempting to achieve practical harmony, scrupulous attention should be given to minimising, as far as practically possible, the limitation of freedom suffered by the person(s) negatively affected by the remedial measure. It may not necessarily be the case that a limitation of freedom is the negative consequence suffered, but it will be in a great number of cases, and almost invariably so when the remedial measure operates in the field of employment, where the persons adversely affected are denied the opportunity for self-realisation and for the free unfolding of their personalities.

(b) 'There must be a need for the implementation of measures in the specific circumstances.'

This means that the purpose of the measure must be to address actual disadvantage in specific cases.

(c) 'The measures implemented must be proportional, which means that: they must be suitable and necessary to achieve the legitimate aim, which also requires that other equally gender-neutral measures must not be available to solve the problem; the relationship between the aim and the measures must also be proportional; the measures must be of limited duration.'

Thus the general principles relating to proportionality, including proportionality in the 'narrow sense'[68] must be observed.

(d) 'The chances of men may not be completely and unnecessarily denied, which means that women may not automatically be preferred, every male applicant has to be considered as well.'

(e) 'Preferential appointment of women is only allowed in cases of equal qualifications and ability.'

Jarass (2006: Rn106) points out that this is particularly the case with quota provisions in the public service sector where there is an imbalance in the employment of men and women.

(f) 'The legislation must contain a hardship clause [Härtefallregelungen] — in favour of men — which makes provision for exceptions.'

This was so held by the Federal Labour Court (BAGE 104, 264 (269)).

(g) 'The requirement that women may be preferentially appointed in areas where they are seriously underrepresented until the representation of women reaches 50 % may be valid if they conform to the above requirements.'

In particular a measure like this cannot automatically exclude men and must also have a 'hard-luck' clause in favour of men.

In summing up the constitutional 'affirmative action' position in Germany, Rabe (2001: 240) stresses the unity of the Constitution's equality provisions:

> 'The way in which [the state's obligation to achieve the equal treatment of men and women as well as to remove existing disadvantages] may be achieved does, however, have to conform to the general constitutional principle of equality. These general principles may not be suspended to achieve equal treatment for men and women. This means that the measures have to be implemented within the framework that the constitution provides for the individual right to equality of opportunity. This right is not absolute; therefore quotas are in principle not prohibited, the main requirement being that the measures which limit the right to equality must be proportional. A quota also has to conform to the principle of

[68] See Chapter 4, section 4.2*(a)*(iii) above.

equality of opportunity, if the quota completely denies the individual male the opportunity to compete then it is unconstitutional. This right belongs to the individual and it is not sufficient merely to provide for the general equality of opportunity of males, this equality of opportunity must be guaranteed to the individual male unless the right is justifiably limited.'

The main concern of this chapter is with the resolution of conflict or tension between restitutionary equality rights, on the one hand, and anti-discrimination rights on the other. It is suggested that human dignity provides the appropriate criterion to be used in this process. In this regard I give Rabe the last word on the German position. After reviewing the German academic and forensic jurisprudence on how the conflict between the 'norms contained in Art 3 II and III GG' has to be solved by applying the principles of *praktischer Konkordanz* or proportionality, he summarises (2001: 240–241) the position as follows:

'In terms of these principles both these norms must be optimized as far as is possible and brought into harmony with each other. The relative importance of the rights in the particular case must be taken into consideration. Both these rights represent important constitutional norms and may not be completely restricted. In the specific case of quotas in favour of women this means that on the one hand the realisation of this aim must be achieved as far as possible without limiting the rights of the individual male unnecessarily. The rights of the individual male may also not be protected to such extent that the achievement of the equal treatment of men and women in the social reality is not possible to realize. To some extent both the rights have to be limited and the exact extent of the limitation has to be determined in the individual case. The proportionality of the measures has to be determined in the light of this conflict.'

6.5 CANADIAN INSIGHTS

In order to avoid tedious repetition I shall at times simply use 'Canadian s 1', 'Canadian s 15(1)', and 'Canadian s 15(2)' as connoting ss 1, 15(1) and 15(2) respectively of the Canadian Charter; and likewise 'South African s 9(2)', 'South African s 9(3)', and 'South African s 36(1)' as connoting ss 9(2), 9(3), and 36(1) respectively of the South African Constitution 1996.

Section 15(2) of the Canadian Charter, which (like s 15(1)) came into force three years after the rest of the Charter,[69] provides:

'Subsection (1) does not preclude any law, program or activity that has as its object the amelioration of conditions of disadvantaged individuals or groups including those that are disadvantaged because of race, national or ethnic origin, colour, religion, sex, age or mental or physical disability.'

[69] By virtue of the provisions of s 32(2). See Hogg (1992: 1012 n 36).

The differences in wording between s 15(2) of the Charter and the first sentence of s 9(2) of the South African Constitution should constantly be borne in mind. So, for example, the disadvantaged entities that are targeted by s 15(2) are 'individuals and groups' whereas those targeted by s 9(2) are 'persons or categories of persons'. Whatever the correct position in Canadian constitutional law might be with regard to the question whether the disadvantage addressed by remedial equality must be rooted in discrimination (as to which see, for example, Gibson 1990: 305–7, 311), the position in South Africa is quite clear. Section 9(2) explicitly states that the recipients of the s 9(2) measures must be 'disadvantaged by unfair discrimination'. Notwithstanding these and other differences, I believe that it useful to consider Canadian jurisprudence in this regard, because it deals with a common problem, namely how best to take measures to remedy the continuing effects of past discrimination, and it also clearly sees these measures as 'ameliorative' or 'remedial'.

Although the Canadian restitutionary or remedial equality jurisprudence, based on s 15(2), differs in principle from that of the USA, reference is often made by authors and others to the operation of s 15(2) as 'affirmative action', although Gibson (1990: 289) — one of the leading writers in Canada on equality rights — regards it as unofficial and controversial. The learned author refers approvingly to the criticism of the term in the 1985 federal Royal Commission report *Equality in Employment*, in which it was referred to as 'ambiguous and confusing' and giving rise to unhelpful 'emotional responses' that produce 'a protective wall through which reason cannot easily penetrate'. Gibson (1990: 289) suggests that the description 'programs for the amelioration of disadvantage' would be more apt, for although it is more cumbersome 'is less likely to be a barrier to reason'. Gibson nevertheless, albeit reluctantly, uses the term 'affirmative action' because of its popular currency. His above criticism of its use and his preference for the concept 'amelioration of disadvantage' should, however, be borne in mind throughout. Gibson (1990: 291) sees the common core of all these ameliorative programmes as the 'recognition that disadvantage cannot be satisfactorily overcome by *laissez faire* means alone, and a consequent determination to assist disadvantaged persons or groups by positive means'. 'They are', he says (1990: 296), '*remedial*, rather than prohibitive.' (Emphasis in the original.)

Gibson also usefully points out (1990: 296) that '[Canadian] affirmative action serves the same ultimate purpose of anti-discrimination laws: the maximisation of equality'. He makes the point another way as well: 'while the *means* typically employed are discriminatory in the short run, the *goal* of equality to which they are directed is the antithesis of discrimination'. (Emphasis in the original.) This goal must never be forgotten, particularly in South Africa, because it clearly implies that the ultimate goal of restitutionary equality is in fact the disappearance of restitutionary equality programmes.

Although Drumbl and Craig[70] (1997) wrote their article 'Affirmative action in question: A coherent theory for section 15(2)' before the judgments in *Law* and *Kapp*, their analysis of the topic is still instructive. Unfortunately they too use the expression 'affirmative action' throughout and use 'substantive equality' in ways that make it difficult to pin down the exact meaning in a given case. They contend (1997: 88–89) that a 'social justice concept' underlies s 15(2) and describe this model as follows:

> '... [T]he social justice model permits the *allocation* of social benefits to individuals on the basis of their group membership, since past discrimination has resulted in the *deprivation* of social benefits in exactly the same manner. In other words, the model basically authorizes the state to remedy past discrimination by favouring the present-day members of the historically victimized groups.' (Emphasis in the original.)

While 'social justice concept' does not strike me as a particularly felicitous way of describing what is clearly a remedial measure, the quoted description fits to some extent with the public-law 'unjustified enrichment' approach.

In the view of Drumbl and Craig (1997: 115),

> 's 15(2) was probably included in the Charter as a reminder to the judiciary that the state is not necessarily discriminating in an unconstitutional manner when it allocates a social benefit to members of a particular group for the purpose of ameliorating the disadvantaged conditions of that group. We also think that s 15(2), to the extent that it gives effect to the social justice model, is a derogation from the equality principles embodied in s 15(1) and, therefore, serves to justify certain laws and programs which would otherwise infringe s 15(1).'

It is not clear to me why the authors (1997: 116) contend that the overriding principle which should inform the interpretation of s 15(2) is 'skepticism'. I would prefer to say that all provisions providing for restitutionary equality should be approached with *circumspection*. We are here dealing with a complex aspect of equality and the interpreter should be aware of the potential dangers that are present. But provided the true nature of, and the constitutional necessity for restitutionary equality are appreciated, there should be no need for skepticism.

Drumbl and Craig (1997: 117–123) appreciate the necessity of a proportionality approach (in the extensive sense) when interpreting and applying the provisions of s 15(2). Although not formulated in exactly the same terms, their approach closely resembles that of Gibson (1995) discussed above. Thus they state (1997: 118) that ' [a] requirement that the discriminatory impact of an affirmative action program be necessary for attaining its ameliorative objects is not evident from the wording of s 15(2), but makes eminent sense in the light of the purpose of the provision which is to promote equality'.

---

[70] Mark A Drumbl is currently Professor of Law in Washington and Lee University, and John DR Craig a partner in Heenan and Blaikie, and Assistant Professor in the University of Western Ontario Faculty of Law.

Secondly, they argue (1997: 119) that 'an affirmative action program which infringes s 15(1) of the *Charter* should only be sustained under s 15(2) if it accomplishes its ameliorative objective with a *minimal discriminatory impact* on the members of the excluded group(s)'. (Emphasis in the original.) In this regard they suggest (1997: 119–120) that the following two considerations should form the basis of the analysis for minimal discriminatory impact:

> '*(a)* Individualized, non-discriminatory alternatives — It must be determined whether the legislature could have reasonably achieved its ameliorative objective in a manner which would not require the use of group-based generalizations of individuals. More specifically, the state should be required to demonstrate that the use of individualized (and hence non-discriminatory) criteria is impractical in the circumstances, and that group-based generalizations are the only means of effecting its ameliorative goal....
> *(b)* Temporal limits and review mechanisms —
> ...
> Because the social justice model allows for derogations from the principle of substantive justice in order to *remedy* past discrimination, affirmative action programs premised on social justice should not have an aura of permanence. Instead they should be framed as temporary deviations, necessitated by the existence of disadvantaged conditions.'

According to the authors appropriate steps should be taken to 'minimize the discriminatory impact of affirmative action on the individuals excluded because of their group membership'.

Thirdly, and significantly for my purpose, Drumbl and Craig argue (1997: 120–121) that proportionality, in the second meaning of the concept, be applied even where the above conditions are met. An ameliorative programme should not be sustained under s 15(2) 'if the actual method adopted for allocating social benefits to the members of the target group imposes a burden on those denied the benefit which is disproportionate in the circumstances'. In their view an analysis that focuses on gross unfairness is 'too low a standard in light of the need for a skeptical and strict approach to s 15(2)'. They also argue that an affirmative action programme that *takes away* social benefits already enjoyed by the members of an advantaged group and reallocates them to members of the target disadvantaged group, 'may often be a disproportionate means of achieving an ameliorative goal'. I agree. Moreover, remedial equality should not level downwards but always upwards — as I have already argued in an earlier chapter with regard to equality generally.

The authors repeatedly advocate that a 'skeptical approach' should be adopted to s 15(2) ameliorative measures. Authorising a public-law remedy arising from a form of unjust enrichment, which is the model I argue for, does not imply or require a 'skeptical' approach to a s 15(2) measure (or, for that matter, to the remedial measures authorised under s 9(2) of the South African Constitution). The remedies for unjustified enrichment in private law are not regarded as suspect or unfair. On the contrary, their very justification is the fact that they ensure restorative justice. Public-law restitutionary remedies authorised under the above subsections should likewise not evoke skepticism.

Drumbl and Craig (1997: 121–122) further point out that 'the principles which we have suggested for assessing constitutionally problematic affirmative action bear a resemblance to the elements of the *Oakes* test for s 1 of the *Charter*'. They play a similar role in *Charter* analysis 'since they each allow the state to justify laws which have been found to infringe Charter rights'. I agree that they play a similar role, but not with the reason proffered. Both sections (as is the case with s 9(2) (second sentence) and s 36(1) of the South African Constitution) are concerned with the determination of constitutionality. The one with the question whether and under what circumstances the *prima facie* infringement of an entrenched right does not lead to constitutional invalidity; the other with the question whether a particular programme falls within the positive provisions of the respective restitutionary equality section, *properly construed*. The German application of the proportionality doctrine is not narrowly limited to the limitation (*Schranken*) of rights but to broader issues of constitutionality. Dogmatically there is no reason why the principle of proportionality (as underlying a limitations provision) should not be used for purposes of construing the restitutionary equality provisions with a view to determining the validity of a measure passed pursuant to its provisions.

Drumbl and Craig (1997: 122–123) conclude their analysis as follows:

> 'By adopting a thoughtful interpretation of s 15(2) illuminated by the European and American experience, we believe that *the potential gulf* between substantive equality and the social justice model can be limited. Thus, while an affirmative action program premised on the social justice model can *never be entirely consistent* with substantive equality, it will bear a *closer resemblance to substantive equality* if the group-based generalisations drawn about individuals are reasonably reliable, the program itself imposes a minimal discriminatory impact on those excluded, and the impact on the excluded individuals is not disproportionate when considered in light of the disadvantaged conditions addressed by the program.' (Emphasis supplied.)

I think the concerns of the authors in the emphasised passages might be too pessimistic. Particularly if one were to understand 'substantive equality' in the context as restitutionary equality founded on principles of unjustified enrichment. I believe that both the South African and the Canadian provisions provide for this form of restitutionary equality. In both cases the entities benefited must be 'disadvantaged' because of the (ongoing) effects of past discrimination. This is expressly stated in South African s 9(2) and is clearly implicit in Canadian s 15(2). I say clearly implicit, because Canadian s 15(2) follows immediately after s 15(1), which deals with enumerated and unenumerated grounds of 'discrimination'. These subsections must be read together, because the problems that have arisen in the USA with 'affirmative action' were clearly present to the minds of those who enacted the Charter, and the obvious purpose of having the provisions for discrimination and those for restitutionary equality in the same section was to ensure that s 15(1) be read subject to s 15(2) in order to avoid these problems. It would be rather surprising if the characteristics (enumerated and unenumerated) in s 15(1) — which constitute the grounds of 'discrimination' — were to be used in the very next subsection in a substantially different sense.

I am mindful of the fact that the entities benefited in Canadian s 15(2) are described as 'individuals or groups', whereas in South African s 9(2), second sentence, they are described as 'persons, or categories of persons'. I have earlier indicated why, I believe, South Africa opted for 'categories of persons' rather than the Canadian 'groups'. Whatever difficulties might arise in construing the legal entity or status of the Canadian 'group', however, they do not affect my argument that the remedy envisaged in both the Canadian s 15(2) and South African 9(2) is one to promote restitutionary equality founded on unjustified enrichment.

It is important to emphasise that the provisions relating to equality need to be read as a whole, since they are the Constitution's (Charter's) coherent response to the issue of equality. It is therefore unhelpful, in my view, to enquire whether Canadian s 15(2) (South African s 9(2), second sentence) is an *exception* to Canadian s 15(1) (South African s 9(3)). Phrasing the question in this way has already given constitutional *preference* to the main anti-discrimination provision. The correct question should rather be: 'What is the correct ambit of the restitutionary provision, read in the context of equality provision s 9(3) South Africa and s 15(1) Canada?' Once that has been established, then restitutionary equality measures that are consistent with the provisions of South African s 9(2), second sentence (Canadian s 15(2)) *properly construed*, cannot and do not infringe the negative discriminatory prohibitions. But part of this *proper construction* demands a proportionality exercise (in both the extensive and narrower meanings of the concept) as both Gibson (1995) and Drumbl and Craig (1995) propose. The achievement of equal respect for the dignity of all persons is a unified concept, and this unity is not destroyed because both negative and pro-active measures are used (and must be used) to achieve it. But there are limits to restitutionary equality seen as a public-law unjust enrichment remedy, and those limits will be informed, in part at least, by the values inherent in the negative measures. The tension inherent in thus seeking to reconcile both types of measures can, in my view, be successfully resolved only by an appropriate weighing-up, in the end result, of the impairment of human dignity on the one hand as against the affirmation of human dignity on the other.

In the leading case on s 15(2), *R v Kapp*,[71] the Court described the purpose of s 15(2) as seeking 'to protect efforts by the state to develop and adopt *remedial*

[71] 294 DLR (4th) 1 (SCC) [2008]. McLachlin CJ and Abella J wrote the judgment of the eight-judge majority.

schemes designed to assist disadvantaged groups'.[72] (Emphasis supplied.) In its judgment the Court stressed that s 15(1) and (2) should be read together, and that s 15(2) was not an exception to s 15(1) but had an independent role to play:

> '[37] In our view, there is a third option: if the government can demonstrate that an impugned program meets the criteria of s 15(2), it may be unnecessary to conduct a s 15(1) analysis at all. As discussed at the outset of this analysis, s 15(1) and s 15(2) should be read as working together to promote substantive equality. The focus of s 15(1) is on *preventing* governments from making distinctions based on enumerated or analogous grounds that have the effect of perpetuating disadvantage or prejudice or imposing disadvantage on the basis of stereotyping. The focus of s 15(2) is on *enabling* governments to pro-actively combat discrimination. Read thus, the two subsections are confirmatory of each other. Section 15(2) supports a full expression of equality, rather than derogating from it. "Under a substantive definition of equality, different treatment in the service of equity for disadvantaged groups is an expression of equality, not an exception to it": PW Hogg, *Constitutional Law of Canada* (5th ed 2007), vol 2, at pp 53–55.
>
> [38] But this confirmatory purpose does not preclude an independent role for s 15(2). Section 15(2) is more than a hortatory admonition. It tells us, in simple clear language, that s 15(1) cannot be read in a way that finds an ameliorative program aimed at combating disadvantage to be discriminatory and in breach of s 15.
>
> [39] Here the appellants claim discrimination on the basis of s 15(1). The source of that discrimination — the very essence of their complaint — is a program that may be ameliorative. This leaves but one conclusion: if the government establishes that the program falls under s 15(2), the appellants' claim must fail.'

I have one possible difficulty with the above passage and that is the implication to be drawn from the observation that, once the requirements of s 15(2) are met, 'it may be unnecessary to conduct a s 15(1) analysis at all'. It strikes me that this conclusion is inconsistent with the correct conclusion, drawn by the Court at the same time that 's 15(1) and s 15(2) should be read as working together to promote substantive equality'. If they are to work together, as they must, then one cannot exclude all analysis of s 15(1). Agerwal and Agerwal (2009: 338) comment on this aspect of the *Kapp* decision as follows:

> 'The Court holds that the purposes of s 15 of combating discrimination and promoting substantive equality underlies both s 15(1) and 15(2), but that each section has a different focus. The focus of s 15(1) is to *prevent* discriminatory state action, while the focus of s 15(2) is to *enable* governments to proactively combat discrimination through affirmative measures.' (Emphasis in the original, footnotes omitted.)

McAllister's comments on the s 15(2) aspects of the *Kapp* decision (2009: 28) are in similar vein:

> 'The central purpose of both s 15(1) and (2) is to combat discrimination and promote substantive equality. The focus of 15(1) is on *preventing* governments from making

[72] Id para 33.

> distinctions based on enumerated or analogous grounds that have the effect of perpetuating group disadvantage and prejudice; or impose disadvantage on the basis of stereotyping. The focus of s 15(2) is on *enabling* government to proactively combat existing discrimination through affirmative measures.'

However, I prefer the formulation by Agerwal and Agerwal, because it more accurately reflects the content of s 15(1). Section 15(1) is not limited to *group* disadvantage, nor is the imposition of disadvantage limited to cases of stereotyping.

One of the main reasons for the introduction of s 15(2) (as is the case with the introduction of the second sentence of s 9(2) of the South African Constitution) was to avoid the United States controversy about remedial equality, which employs race differentiation for this remedial purpose. The very reason for the controversy is that remedial equality of this nature uses a prescribed criterion which may well impact negatively on third parties (ie persons who are not beneficiaries of the remedy). But one cannot simply ignore the negative impact on third parties of a s 15(2) measure. One could take the position that a s 15(2) measure which, on the face of it, meets the criteria of the subsection should be presumed to be constitutionally valid. Yet I do not see on what grounds one should be precluded from having regard to the *extent* to which the measures *actually* ameliorate conditions of the disadvantaged and, at the same time, weigh against that the *extent* of the *actual* negative impact that the measures have on third parties. Similarly, I cannot see why one should not be compelled to have regard to the *extent* to which the beneficiaries have been disadvantaged because of the enumerated and analogous criteria, and weigh this against the *extent* to which the third parties were advantaged or enriched because of the enumerated and analogous criteria.

Such preclusions would be a rejection, out of hand, of the proportionality principle which I have throughout presented as a fundamental constitutional principle with regard to the limitation or clash of rights. It seems to me to be unfair, and constitutionally unsound, for example, to ignore the fact that the amelioration brought about by the s 15(2) measure affects only a few members of the disadvantaged group and then only to a very limited extent, whereas these measures have a significantly severe impact on a large number of third parties. I would reiterate that the proportionality analysis required in these circumstances would relate primarily to human dignity enhancement weighed against human dignity deprivation. No easy formula exists for carrying out this kind of analysis and the approach will have to be developed on a case-by-case basis, having regard to the totality of facts of the particular case. The fact that the s 15(2) measures are to be characterised as 'remedial schemes,' as the Court in *Kapp*[73] correctly concluded, necessitates this approach. The concept 'remedial' like the expression 'ameliorate', embodies the idea that a particular state of affairs must be changed

---

[73] Id para 33.

for the better from state A to state B. The concept of restitution on the part of third parties (X), means, in my view, restitution for the unjustified enrichment that has accrued to X because of the s 15(1) 'disadvantage […]' suffered by Y. If X has not in fact been enriched, it is wrong to saddle her with disadvantage suffered by Y. Similarly, if Y suffers no disadvantage it is equally wrong to saddle X with a restitutionary obligation. The same would be the position if the measure ameliorated Y's position substantially beyond what it would have been but for the disadvantage suffered. These are extreme points on a continuum and in between them there will be situations where the valid application of s 15(1) will depend on a proportionality analysis of the positions of X and Y in relation to the impact of the measures on the human dignity of X and Y. Equally, it seems to me — and also flowing from the proportionality principle — that s 15(2) would not be satisfied if the ameliorated position, state B, could be as easily achieved while requiring substantially less (or no) restitution from X.

Agarwal and Agarwal (2009: 339–340) contend that a possible objection to the Court's approach in *Kapp* is that it 'potentially ignores legitimate claims of discrimination by individuals or groups excluded from ameliorative programs'. They argue that, although ameliorative schemes are drafted with insight and due appreciation of the relevant facts,

> 'there is always the possibility that exclusion from an ameliorative program could be accidental or, worse, the consequence of stereotypical views about the excluded group. There is little doubt that the equality guarantee exists to provide a remedy for these situations. But how would claims based on these exclusions survive within the s 15 framework as presented in *Kapp?* The Court does find that a program that falls within the ambit of s 15(2) may nevertheless be scrutinized under s 15(1). *Kapp* therefore leaves open the possibility that an ameliorative program that satisfies s 15(2) may still violate the equality guarantee. However the Court fails to provide any direction as to when it is appropriate for a court to proceed to an analysis under s 15(1) in spite of the government demonstrating the impugned program to be ameliorative.'

They fear 'an overly broad and robust application of s 15(2)'.

These objections and fears are in my opinion misplaced, if one consistently bears in mind, as I have tried to illustrate above, that the entire s 15 is holistically conceived and is to be applied holistically at all times. The section is holistically conceived in order to ensure the equality (equal dignity) of all. This goal is only partially achieved by the negative methodology (ie the prohibition of discrimination) of s 15(1). The negative methodology does not reach the situation of 'individuals and groups' ('persons or categories of persons' in South African s 9(2)) that continue to suffer the ongoing negative effects of past discrimination. To eliminate these negative effects the positive steps envisaged by s 15(2) must be taken. I do believe that if the s 15(2) remedy is seen as a public-law remedy analogous to that of restitution for unjust enrichment in private law, the perceived tensions between s 15(1) and 15(2) disappear.

When these subsections are viewed as constituting one integrated whole (as I believe the Court in *Kapp* saw them) one's mind is already preconditioned by s 15(1) when one construes and applies s 15(2). A proper construction of s 15(2) ought not to be inconsistent with the s 15(1) prohibitions, when the unjustified enrichment paradigm is borne in mind and when it is appreciated that s 15(2) requires, implicitly, a proportionality analysis when considering any programme instituted thereunder. In this proportionality analysis human dignity, as I have already argued, plays a significant role. One has to evaluate proportionally the extent to which the human dignity of the beneficiaries under s 15(2) is advanced as against the extent to which the human dignity of those whom the s 15(2) measures impact negatively is affected (judged by the s 15(1) criteria). It can surely not be discriminatory — in any sense envisaged by s 15(1) — if the negative effect on A (by a s 15(2) measure) goes no further than requiring A to make restitution for being unjustly enriched by past discrimination against B (the beneficiary under s 15(2)). Correspondingly, the principle of restitution for unjust enrichment does not require that B be compensated in excess of A's enrichment. (The very same argument applies to the application of South African s 9(2), second sentence, viewed in the context of s 9(3)). B's human dignity is not negatively affected by receiving restitution that does not exceed the extent of A's enrichment by past discrimination. I do not believe that anything held in *Kapp*'s case is inconsistent with this approach. The Court in fact appreciated the necessity for a proportionality analysis.

The Court in *Kapp*,[74] in elucidating the test under s 15(2), held that a programme does not violate the s 15 equality guarantee if the government can demonstrate that:

> '(1) the program has an ameliorative or remedial purpose; and
> (2) the program targets a disadvantaged group identified by the enumerated or analogous grounds.
>
> In proposing this test, we are mindful that future cases may demand some adjustment to the framework in order to meet litigants' particular circumstances.'

It strikes one as strange that in this formulation of a general test the target of the programme is limited by the Court to a 'disadvantaged *group*' whereas s 15(2) clearly extends it also to 'disadvantaged *individuals*'. (Emphasis supplied in both cases.) It may be that the Court was formulating the test only to meet the factual matrix of the case, but the context does not support this.

The Court in *Kapp* analysed the above test under three headings: 'Has as its object', 'Amelioration', and 'Disadvantaged', aspects of which need to be considered.

---

[74] Id para 41.

(a) 'Has as its object'

The Court posed the question 'whether courts should look to the *purpose* or to the *effect* of legislation'.[75] After remarking that these approaches could be termed 'subjective' or 'objective' respectively, and that there was disagreement amongst scholars and judges as to which the correct approach was,[76] the Court concluded that

> 'we believe that the "purpose"-based approach is more appropriate than the "effect"-based approach: where a law, program or activity creates a distinction on an enumerated or analogous ground, was the government's goal in creating that distinction to improve the condition of a group that is disadvantaged?'[77]

In coming to this conclusion the Court reasoned that the use of the word 'object' suggests that 'legislative goal rather than actual effect is the paramount consideration',[78] and that 'the purpose-driven approach also reflects the language of the provision itself'.[79] I am compelled to differ on both scores. This is a case where the word 'object' must gather its meaning from the context in which it is used and the overall purpose of the provision in question. Although its dictionary definition does include the meaning 'purpose', *The Shorter Oxford English Dictionary* also defines it as 'the end to which effort is directed'; 'a thing sought or aimed at'. The end sought by s 15(2), read in the context of the whole of s 15, is to make possible the actual improvement of the condition of individuals or groups who have suffered negative consequences as a result of unlawful (unconstitutional) discrimination on the grounds (enumerated and analogous) mentioned in s 15(1), and to make possible this achievement despite the fact that the measures adopted to this end might themselves affect third persons negatively on these very grounds. Surely the only principled justification for imposing an *actual negative burden* on third parties is the *actual amelioration* of the disadvantaged. Moreover, the subjective approach of the Court does not sit easily with the objective approach adopted with regard to questions of constitutional invalidity of legislation, as discussed earlier.

In dealing with criticisms of the subjective approach, the Court seemed to subvert its prior reasoning in the following passages:

> '... [T]his concern can be easily addressed. There is nothing to suggest that a test focused on the goal of the legislation must slavishly accept the government's characterization of its purpose. Courts could well examine legislation to determine that the declared purpose is genuine;[80]

---

[75] Id para 43.
[76] Id paras 44–47.
[77] Id para 48. I point out that the beneficiaries are once again limited by the Court to the entity 'group'.
[78] Id para 44.
[79] Id para 47.
[80] Id para 46.

> 'In examining purpose, courts may therefore find it necessary to consider not only statements made by the drafters of the program but also whether the legislature chose means rationally related to the ameliorative purpose, in the sense that it appears at least plausible that the program may indeed advance the stated goal of combating disadvantage.[81]
>
> 'Analysing the means employed by the government can easily turn into assessing the *effect* of the program. As a result, to preserve an intent-based analysis, courts could be encouraged to frame the analysis as follows: Was it rational for the state to conclude that the means chosen to reach its ameliorative goal would contribute to that purpose? For the distinction to be rational there must be a correlation between the program and disadvantage suffered by the target group. Such a standard permits significant deference to the legislature but allows judicial review where a program nominally seeks to serve the disadvantaged but in practice serves other non-remedial objectives.'[82]

I have difficulty in reconciling these observations with a subjective approach. Assuming that a government, in absolute good faith, adopts a programme which subsequent events prove to be quite unworkable for s 15(2) purposes; surely objective reality must, in that case, render the government's intention, although entertained in the utmost good faith, quite irrelevant? Moreover, as soon as one poses a substantive rational relationship test, as the second and third of the above passages do, the concept of subjectivity simply disappears, because one's point of departure is that the existence of objective facts can trump subjective intent.

(b) 'Amelioration'[83]

Once again the subjective/objective tension manifests itself. Although it is stated that 'the focus [should not] be on the effect of the law' yet 'the fact that a law has no plausible or predictable ameliorative effect may render suspect the state's ameliorative purpose'. Governments, as discussed above, are not permitted to protect discriminatory programmes 'on colourable pretexts'.[84] I fail to see how an unashamed objective test, focusing on the result, can in any way breach the properly applied separation of powers doctrine, and why it is necessary for the judiciary to display 'significant deference'[85] to the legislature or executive when there is a gross disproportion between means and ends. Once it is established that the ameliorative goal simply cannot be achieved by the measures adopted, or that there is a gross disproportion between means and ends, the justification for the s 15(2) measures and the concomitant infringement of the rights of third parties falls away. This cannot be remedied by the good faith of the legislature.

[81] Id para 48.
[82] Id para 49.
[83] Id paras 53–54.
[84] Id para 54.
[85] Id para 49.

(c) *'Disadvantaged'*[86]

> '"[D]isadvantage" under s 15 connotes vulnerability, prejudice and negative social characterization. Section 15(2)'s purpose is to protect government programs targeting the conditions of a specific and identifiable disadvantaged group, as contrasted with broad social legislation, such as social assistance programs. Not all members of the group need to be disadvantaged, as long as the group as a whole has experienced discrimination.'

It must of course be remembered that whereas the beneficiaries under s 15(1) of the Charter are 'individuals or groups' those under s 9(2) of the South African Constitution are 'persons, or categories of persons'. This indicates that the South African beneficiaries have been more closely circumscribed.

6.6 CONCLUSION

What of course distinguishes the remedial measures in South Africa from those in Germany is the strongly emphasised restitutionary nature of the s 9(2) measures in favour of those 'disadvantaged by unfair discrimination'. It is true that Dürig (1973: Rn 120ff) argues that, in the case of conflict, freedom takes precedence over equality, because in totalitarian states all people may be denied their freedom equally. This must, I think, be the general rule, but cannot be used to frustrate the clear restitutionary equalising purpose of s 9(2). At the same time this warning must be borne in mind to counter the idea that the freedom rights of others can be overrun without any restraint. The purposes of s 9(2) must be respected, but the safeguard is a rigorous application of the proportionality principle and a restraint against objectifying human beings.

Using the equitable principles of private-law unjustified enrichment as a basis and rationale for fashioning a public-law enrichment remedy, or for interpreting and applying an existing one, is particularly appropriate because these private-law principles justify *a* restitutionary remedy against a defendant even though the defendant may not be at fault.

I must again emphasise that by using private-law unjustified enrichment to explain public-law restitutionary equality, I am not suggesting that one ought to base the public-law remedy on that of the private law. By its very nature public-law unjustified enrichment can occur in a multiplicity of ways that do not mirror private-law enrichment and requires a remedy tailored to meet the needs of the enrichment in question. I go no further than to use the analogy as a justification for *a* remedy, even one that negatively affects a defendant wholly innocent of causing the unjustified enrichment. The analogy serves to justify the need for and the justice of remedial equality, even in the case of innocent defendants.

---

[86] Id para 55.

In private law the underlying principles are, as Visser (2008: 21) points out, rooted in corrective justice and do not necessarily require fault on the defendant's part:

> '... I agree fully with Smith and McInnes that the law of autonomous unjust enrichment *does not require to be analysed in terms of wrongdoing and indeed should not be so analysed; and that corrective justice does not necessarily depend on wrongdoing being present*.' (Emphasis in the original.)

Visser (2008: 21), in order to reveal the key corrective justice features of enrichment claims, quotes the following lengthy passage from Smith (2001: 2141) with approval:

> 'The simplest case of unjust enrichment liability is the mistaken payment. The plaintiff, thinking she owes the defendant $100, pays that amount, but in fact she does not owe anything. But the transfer takes effect as such, so that the defendant becomes the owner of the money. There is an enrichment of the defendant, a corresponding deprivation of the plaintiff, and a reason for restitution in the plaintiff's mistake. The material gains and losses are clear. The plaintiff also suffered a normative loss because she did not fully assent to the transfer of wealth; the transfer was made on the basis of bad information. It was not a free expression of self-determining agency. The question is how we can say that the defendant achieved a normative gain without doing anything wrong. As we should expect, the answer appears to lie in the constitutive elements of unjust enrichment liability, which differentiate it from civil wrongs. Unjust enrichment includes both a material gain by the defendant and a material loss by the plaintiff. Moreover, the loss and gain do not come together by random chance. They are two sides of the same coin — that coin being a transfer of wealth from plaintiff to defendant. There is a nexus of exchange between the parties. This nexus gives an "articulated unity" to their bilateral relationship in a relationship which is paradigmatically within Aristotle's conception of corrective justice. The transactional unity is far tighter than in a case of carelessness causing loss or profitable wrongful conduct.'

The field of unjustified enrichment in South African private law is becoming ever more general. I see nothing in the principles underlying unjustified enrichment or the doctrine developed that is any way inimical to the idea of instituting and applying a public-law remedy of unjustified enrichment based on its private-law progenitor. In my view these are the principles, applied to the field of constitutional law, that underlie the provisions of the second sentence of s 9(2) of the South African Constitution. These enrichment principles are being used to establish equality, that is to say equal dignity, for all in South Africa. It is both unhelpful and unsound to think of equality as being split into two separate parts, the one with a negative character and the other with a positive one. The second sentence of s 9(2) should be read holistically with the rest of s 9 as jointly establishing one constitutional object, which is to be achieved by a harmonious combination of two techniques. The object of s 9 as a whole is to *respect* and *protect* equal human dignity. In this regard it differs no whit from the constitutional guarantee of dignity itself, s 10 requiring that the dignity of all be 'respected and protected'.

When proper regard is had to the phrase 'persons or categories of persons' in South African s 9(2) it is clear that personal restitution is intended, for 'category' is descriptive of the persons benefited. I would also contend that s 9(2) is aimed at restoring or ensuring equality of opportunity for individuals and not equality of result: equality of opportunity for the free unfolding of the personality and self-realisation and self-fulfilment; not equality of result by engineering equal outcomes regardless of individual qualities, gifts and talents.

Proper respect must be paid to the freedom and dignity of others. An unmitigated pursuit of equality of result or outcomes would make unacceptable inroads into the freedom of too many people. Neither the wording nor the context of the second sentence of South African s 9(2) abrogates the prohibitions on discrimination contained in s 9(3) or the dignity or freedom rights of those on whom the burden of making restitution (in whatever form) is made. The subsections must be construed and applied holistically and, as far as practically possible, as much weight given to the rights of those advanced and those restricted as the circumstances of each case will permit.

There is just as much reason for applying principles of proportionality in the application of restitutionary measures under s 9(2) as in other jurisdictions. The invocation of the remedial measures provided for does not obliterate the dignity rights of others, in particular their desire for the free unfolding of their personalities and for self-fulfilment. Remedial measures must endeavour to preserve as much of the freedom and dignity rights of others as possible. I see no objection in practice or in principle why the sensible principle of *praktischer Konkordanz* in German law should not be applied to the evaluation of remedial measures under s 9(2). If the remedial measure does little to advance the dignity interests of the person disadvantaged by unfair discrimination while, on the other hand, making serious inroads into the dignity interests of the person making or suffering restitution, the measure would not pass muster. The same assessment should, in my view, be made with regard to the *degree* of disadvantage suffered by the person sought to be advantaged by the restitutionary measure. The purpose of the s 9(2) measure is, after all, to make restitution for the disadvantage suffered by the person in question as a result of unfair discrimination. An individual person may belong to a race group, the majority of whose members might still suffer disadvantage as a result of unfair discrimination. The individual in question, thanks to superb pre-primary, primary, secondary and tertiary education, might suffer no current disadvantage. It is, in my view, not the purpose of s 9(2) for an individual like this to have the advantage of the particular remedial measure. This is a simple case, but there is a sliding scale of disadvantage and advantage, as a result of unfair discrimination. In cases like these the principles of proportionality and *praktischer Konkordanz,* using dignity as an adjudicating principle, should be applied in order to determine whether restitution in the form of a s 9(2) measure is appropriate and permissible.

In this section I revert again to certain passages in the *Van Heerden* judgment[87] because they are relevant to a critical application of the proportionality principle, and the resolution of conflicts between the rights of those advantaged by the s 9(2) remedial measures and those of the persons negatively affected by them. The Court clearly considered the s 9(2) 'measures' to be *restitutionary equality* measures.[88]

In the course of his judgment for the Court, Moseneke J held that 'if [such] restitutionary measures, even if based on any of the grounds of discrimination listed in s 9(3), pass muster under s 9(2), they cannot be presumed to be unfairly discriminatory'.[89] The crucial question is, of course, what is meant by 'pass muster' and with what criteria the restitutionary measures have to comply in order to be valid under s 9(2). There is an inescapable tension between the entitlement of the plaintiff to restitutionary equality and the right of the defendant not to be unfairly discriminated against. This tension cannot be wished away. The only way it can be resolved is if the measure in question satisfies a proper application of the proportionality principle. I do not understand Moseneke J to be saying anything different. The learned judge is not suggesting that simply because the restitutionary measure in question *purports* to be introduced under s 9(2) it will, for that reason alone, pass muster. This seems to be clear from the rest of his judgment. Thus, in relation to what he terms the second question, Moseneke J points out that the measure in question 'must be reasonably capable of attaining the desired outcome'.[90] The learned judge continues by observing that '[i]f the remedial measures are arbitrary, capricious or display naked preference they could hardly be said to be designed to achieve the constitutionally authorized end'. I do not understand the latter observation to be an exhaustive enumeration of what would not be 'reasonably capable of attaining the desired outcome', but rather examples of unreasonableness. The concept of arbitrariness, far from excluding the principles of proportionality, can in fact embrace certain forms of proportionality, as was made clear in the *FNB* case,[91] and is illustrated by the German jurisprudence discussed in Chapter 4, section 4.2*(c)* above in relation to the so-called *Willkürverbot* (prohibition against arbitrariness) under art 3(1) of the GBL. Furthermore Moseneke J, after setting forth certain aspects of the long-term constitutional equality goal of our society such as, for example, each person being 'recognised and treated as a human being of equal worth and dignity', points out that a remedial measure

[87] Above, n 4.
[88] Id per Moseneke J paras 1, 28, 30.
[89] Id para 33.
[90] Id para 41.
[91] Above, n 49 para 100.

> 'should not constitute an abuse of power or impose such substantial and undue harm on those excluded from its benefits that our long-term constitutional goal would be threatened'.

I would argue that on each occasion that a person's human dignity is unnecessarily infringed by a restitutionary measure it threatens the long-term goal of equal human worth and dignity.

It is contended that the Court's judgment in *Van Heerden* is consistent with the application of a basically three-pronged proportionality principle as illustrated by the jurisprudence of Germany: first, an inquiry whether the restitutionary measure will achieve its proper end or goal; secondly, whether there is an alternative measure that will equally achieve the measure's goal and at the same time make significantly less negative impact on those disadvantaged by the measure; and, thirdly, a proportionality exercise in the narrower sense, involving a weighing-up of the positive and negative factors revealed by the first two steps. I suggest that in conducting this third leg of the enquiry an important consideration will be the nature and degree of the measure's impact on the human dignity of those sought to be advanced and those disadvantaged by the measure. In the case of the former it will be an evaluation and weighing up of the positive impact on the human dignity of the former, as against the negative impact on the human dignity of the latter. If, in an employment context for example, persons from the disfavoured category are completely excluded from consideration for an employment position, this would constitute a severe impairment of their human dignity, such persons being treated as mere objects with a total disregard for their self-fulfilment and personality unfolding as human beings and their sense of self-worth. This is particularly the danger with quota regulations. In that case, I contend, provision should always be made for 'hard cases' as is the position in Germany. Inasmuch as human dignity is the criterion of attribution for equality and non-discrimination, it must in principle play a crucial role in relation to the resolution of tensions in this area, as it should with regard to the horizontal operation of equality and non-discrimination.

Appendix A

EXCERPT FROM THE CONSTITUTION OF THE REPUBLIC OF SOUTH AFRICA, 1996

CHAPTER 1
FOUNDING PROVISIONS (ss 1–6)

1 Republic of South Africa

The Republic of South Africa is one, sovereign, democratic state founded on the following values:

(a) Human dignity, the achievement of equality and the advancement of human rights and freedoms.
(b) Non-racialism and non-sexism.
(c) Supremacy of the constitution and the rule of law.
(d) Universal adult suffrage, a national common voters roll, regular elections and a multi-party system of democratic government, to ensure accountability, responsiveness and openness.

2 Supremacy of Constitution

This Constitution is the supreme law of the Republic; law or conduct inconsistent with it is invalid, and the obligations imposed by it must be fulfilled.

3 Citizenship

(1) There is a common South African citizenship.
(2) All citizens are–

(a) equally entitled to the rights, privileges and benefits of citizenship; and
(b) equally subject to the duties and responsibilities of citizenship.

(3) National legislation must provide for the acquisition, loss and restoration of citizenship.

4 National anthem

The national anthem of the Republic is determined by the President by proclamation.

5 National flag

The national flag of the Republic is black, gold, green, white, red and blue, as described and sketched in Schedule 1.

6 Languages

(1) The official languages of the Republic are Sepedi, Sesotho, Setswana, siSwati, Tshivenda, Xitsonga, Afrikaans, English, isiNdebele, isiXhosa and isiZulu.

(2) Recognising the historically diminished use and status of the indigenous languages of our people, the state must take practical and positive measures to elevate the status and advance the use of these languages.

(3) *(a)* The national government and provincial governments may use any particular official languages for the purposes of government, taking into account usage, practicality, expense, regional circumstances and the balance of the needs and preferences of the population as a whole or in the province concerned; but the national government and each provincial government must use at least two official languages.

(b) Municipalities must take into account the language usage and preferences of their residents.

(4) The national government and provincial governments, by legislative and other measures, must regulate and monitor their use of official languages. Without detracting from the provisions of subsection (2), all official languages must enjoy parity of esteem and must be treated equitably.

(5) A Pan South African Language Board established by national legislation must–

(a) promote, and create conditions for, the development and use of–
  - (i) all official languages;
  - (ii) the Khoi, Nama and San languages; and
  - (iii) sign language; and

(b) promote and ensure respect for–
  - (i) all languages commonly used by communities in South Africa, including German, Greek, Gujarati, Hindi, Portuguese, Tamil, Telegu and Urdu; and
  - (ii) Arabic, Hebrew, Sanskrit and other languages used for religious purposes in South Africa.

CHAPTER 2
BILL OF RIGHTS (ss 7-39)

7 Rights

(1) This Bill of Rights is a cornerstone of democracy in South Africa. It enshrines the rights of all people in our country and affirms the democratic values of human dignity, equality and freedom.

(2) The state must respect, protect, promote and fulfil the rights in the Bill of Rights.

(3) The rights in the Bill of Rights are subject to the limitations contained or referred to in section 36, or elsewhere in the Bill.

8 Application

(1) The Bill of Rights applies to all law, and binds the legislature, the executive, the judiciary and all organs of state.

(2) A provision of the Bill of Rights binds a natural or a juristic person if, and to the extent that, it is applicable, taking into account the nature of the right and the nature of any duty imposed by the right.

(3) When applying a provision of the Bill of Rights to a natural or juristic person in terms of subsection (2), a court–

(a) in order to give effect to a right in the Bill, must apply, or if necessary develop, the common law to the extent that legislation does not give effect to that right; and

(b) may develop rules of the common law to limit the right, provided that the limitation is in accordance with section 36 (1).

(4) A juristic person is entitled to the rights in the Bill of Rights to the extent required by the nature of the rights and the nature of that juristic person.

9 Equality

(1) Everyone is equal before the law and has the right to equal protection and benefit of the law.

(2) Equality includes the full and equal enjoyment of all rights and freedoms. To promote the achievement of equality, legislative and other measures designed to protect or advance persons, or categories of persons, disadvantaged by unfair discrimination may be taken.

(3) The state may not unfairly discriminate directly or indirectly against anyone on one or more grounds, including race, gender, sex, pregnancy, marital status, ethnic or social origin, colour, sexual orientation, age, disability, religion, conscience, belief, culture, language and birth.

(4) No person may unfairly discriminate directly or indirectly against anyone on one or more grounds in terms of subsection (3). National legislation must be enacted to prevent or prohibit unfair discrimination.

(5) Discrimination on one or more of the grounds listed in subsection (3) is unfair unless it is established that the discrimination is fair.

10 Human dignity

Everyone has inherent dignity and the right to have their dignity respected and protected.

11 Life

Everyone has the right to life.

12 Freedom and security of the person

(1) Everyone has the right to freedom and security of the person, which includes the right–

(a) not to be deprived of freedom arbitrarily or without just cause;
(b) not to be detained without trial;
(c) to be free from all forms of violence from either public or private sources;
(d) not to be tortured in any way; and
(e) not to be treated or punished in a cruel, inhuman or degrading way.

(2) Everyone has the right to bodily and psychological integrity, which includes the right–

(a) to make decisions concerning reproduction;
(b) to security in and control over their body; and
(c) not to be subjected to medical or scientific experiments without their informed consent.

13 Slavery, servitude and forced labour

No one may be subjected to slavery, servitude or forced labour.

14 Privacy

Everyone has the right to privacy, which includes the right not to have–

(a) their person or home searched;
(b) their property searched;
(c) their possessions seized; or
(d) the privacy of their communications infringed.

15 Freedom of religion, belief and opinion

(1) Everyone has the right to freedom of conscience, religion, thought, belief and opinion.

(2) Religious observances may be conducted at state or state-aided institutions, provided that–

(a) those observances follow rules made by the appropriate public authorities;
(b) they are conducted on an equitable basis; and
(c) attendance at them is free and voluntary.

(3) *(a)* This section does not prevent legislation recognising–

(i) marriages concluded under any tradition, or a system of religious, personal or family law; or
(ii) systems of personal and family law under any tradition, or adhered to by persons professing a particular religion.

(b) Recognition in terms of paragraph *(a)* must be consistent with this section and the other provisions of the Constitution.

16 Freedom of expression

(1) Everyone has the right to freedom of expression, which includes–

(a) freedom of the press and other media;
(b) freedom to receive or impart information or ideas;
(c) freedom of artistic creativity; and
(d) academic freedom and freedom of scientific research.

(2) The right in subsection (1) does not extend to–

(a) propaganda for war;
(b) incitement of imminent violence; or
(c) advocacy of hatred that is based on race, ethnicity, gender or religion, and that constitutes incitement to cause harm.

17 Assembly, demonstration picket and petition

Everyone has the right, peacefully and unarmed, to assemble, to demonstrate, to picket and to present petitions.

18 Freedom of association

Everyone has the right to freedom of association.

19 Political rights

(1) Every citizen is free to make political choices, which includes the right–

(a) to form a political party;
(b) to participate in the activities of, or recruit members for, a political party; and
(c) to campaign for a political party or cause.

(2) Every citizen has the right to free, fair and regular elections for any legislative body established in terms of the Constitution.

(3) Every adult citizen has the right–

(a) to vote in elections for any legislative body established in terms of the Constitution, and to do so in secret; and
(b) to stand for public office and, if elected, to hold office.

20 Citizenship

No citizen may be deprived of citizenship.

21 Freedom of movement and residence

(1) Everyone has the right to freedom of movement.

(2) Everyone has the right to leave the Republic.

(3) Every citizen has the right to enter, to remain in and to reside anywhere in, the Republic.

(4) Every citizen has the right to a passport.

22 Freedom of trade, occupation and profession

Every citizen has the right to choose their trade, occupation or profession freely. The practice of a trade, occupation or profession may be regulated by law.

23 Labour relations

(1) Everyone has the right to fair labour practices.

(2) Every worker has the right–

(a) to form and join a trade union;
(b) to participate in the activities and programmes of a trade union; and
(c) to strike.

(3) Every employer has the right–

(a) to form and join an employers' organisation; and
(b) to participate in the activities and programmes of an employers' organisation.

(4) Every trade union and every employers' organisation has the right–

(a) to determine its own administration, programmes and activities;
(b) to organise; and
(c) to form and join a federation.

(5) Every trade union, employers' organisation and employer has the right to engage in collective bargaining. National legislation may be enacted to regulate collective bargaining. To the extent that the legislation may limit a right in this Chapter, the limitation must comply with section 36 (1).

(6) National legislation may recognise union security arrangements contained in collective agreements. To the extent that the legislation may limit a right in this Chapter the limitation must comply with section 36 (1).

24 Environment

Everyone has the right–

(a) to an environment that is not harmful to their health or well-being; and

(b) to have the environment protected, for the benefit of present and future generations, through reasonable legislative and other measures that–
  (i) prevent pollution and ecological degradation;
  (ii) promote conservation; and
  (iii) secure ecologically sustainable development and use of natural resources while promoting justifiable economic and social development.

25 Property

(1) No one may be deprived of property except in terms of law of general application, and no law may permit arbitrary deprivation of property.

(2) Property may be expropriated only in terms of law of general application–

(a) for a public purpose or in the public interest; and
(b) subject to compensation, the amount of which and the time and manner of payment of which have either been agreed to by those affected or decided or approved by a court.

(3) The amount of the compensation and the time and manner of payment must be just and equitable, reflecting an equitable balance between the public interest and the interests of those affected, having regard to all relevant circumstances, including–

(a) the current use of the property;
(b) the history of the acquisition and use of the property;
(c) the market value of the property;
(d) the extent of direct state investment and subsidy in the acquisition and beneficial capital improvement of the property; and
(e) the purpose of the expropriation.

(4) For the purposes of this section–

(a) the public interest includes the nation's commitment to land reform, and to reforms to bring about equitable access to all South Africa's natural resources; and
(b) property is not limited to land.

(5) The state must take reasonable legislative and other measures, within its available resources, to foster conditions which enable citizens to gain access to land on an equitable basis.

(6) A person or community whose tenure of land is legally insecure as a result of past racially discriminatory laws or practices is entitled, to the extent provided by an Act of Parliament, either to tenure which is legally secure or to comparable redress.

(7) A person or community dispossessed of property after 19 June 1913 as a result of past racially discriminatory laws or practices is entitled, to the extent provided by an Act of Parliament, either to restitution of that property or to equitable redress.

(8) No provision of this section may impede the state from taking legislative and other measures to achieve land, water and related reform, in order to redress the results of past racial discrimination, provided that any departure from the provisions of this section is in accordance with the provisions of section 36 (1).

(9) Parliament must enact the legislation referred to in subsection (6).

26 Housing

(1) Everyone has the right to have access to adequate housing.

(2) The state must take reasonable legislative and other measures, within its available resources, to achieve the progressive realisation of this right.

(3) No one may be evicted from their home, or have their home demolished, without an order of court made after considering all the relevant circumstances. No legislation may permit arbitrary evictions.

27 Health care, food, water and social security

(1) Everyone has the right to have access to–

(a) health care services, including reproductive health care;
(b) sufficient food and water; and
(c) social security, including, if they are unable to support themselves and their dependants, appropriate social assistance.

(2) The state must take reasonable legislative and other measures, within its available resources, to achieve the progressive realisation of each of these rights.

(3) No one may be refused emergency medical treatment.

28 Children

(1) Every child has the right–

(a) to a name and a nationality from birth;
(b) to family care or parental care, or to appropriate alternative care when removed from the family environment;
(c) to basic nutrition, shelter, basic health care services and social services;
(d) to be protected from maltreatment, neglect, abuse or degradation;
(e) to be protected from exploitative labour practices;
(f) not to be required or permitted to perform work or provide services that–
  (i) are inappropriate for a person of that child's age; or
  (ii) place at risk the child's well-being, education, physical or mental health or spiritual, moral or social development;
(g) not to be detained except as a measure of last resort, in which case, in addition to the rights a child enjoys under sections 12 and 35, the child may be detained only for the shortest appropriate period of time, and has the right to be–

(i) kept separately from detained persons over the age of 18 years; and
(ii) treated in a manner, and kept in conditions, that take account of the child's age;

(h) to have a legal practitioner assigned to the child by the state, and at state expense, in civil proceedings affecting the child, if substantial injustice would otherwise result; and
(i) not to be used directly in armed conflict, and to be protected in times of armed conflict.

(2) A child's best interests are of paramount importance in every matter concerning the child.

(3) In this section **'child'** means a person under the age of 18 years.

29 Education

(1) Everyone has the right–

(a) to a basic education, including adult basic education; and
(b) to further education, which the state, through reasonable measures, must make progressively available and accessible.

(2) Everyone has the right to receive education in the official language or languages of their choice in public educational institutions where that education is reasonably practicable. In order to ensure the effective access to, and implementation of, this right, the state must consider all reasonable educational alternatives, including single medium institutions, taking into account–

(a) equity;
(b) practicability; and
(c) the need to redress the results of past racially discriminatory laws and practices.

(3) Everyone has the right to establish and maintain, at their own expense, independent educational institutions that–

(a) do not discriminate on the basis of race;
(b) are registered with the state; and
(c) maintain standards that are not inferior to standards at comparable public educational institutions.

(4) Subsection (3) does not preclude state subsidies for independent educational institutions.

30 Language and culture

Everyone has the right to use the language and to participate in the cultural life of their choice, but no one exercising these rights may do so in a manner inconsistent with any provision of the Bill of Rights.

31 Cultural, religious and linguistic communities

(1) Persons belonging to a cultural, religious or linguistic community may not be denied the right, with other members of that community–

(a) to enjoy their culture, practise their religion and use their language; and
(b) to form, join and maintain cultural, religious and linguistic associations and other organs of civil society.

(2) The rights in subsection (1) may not be exercised in a manner inconsistent with any provision of the Bill of Rights.

32 Access to information

(1) Everyone has the right of access to–

(a) any information held by the state; and
(b) any information that is held by another person and that is required for the exercise or protection of any rights.

(2) National legislation must be enacted to give effect to this right, and may provide for reasonable measures to alleviate the administrative and financial burden on the state.

33 Just administrative action

(1) Everyone has the right to administrative action that is lawful, reasonable and procedurally fair.

(2) Everyone whose rights have been adversely affected by administrative action has the right to be given written reasons.

(3) National legislation must be enacted to give effect to these rights, and must–

(a) provide for the review of administrative action by a court or, where appropriate, an independent and impartial tribunal;
(b) impose a duty on the state to give effect to the rights in subsections (1) and (2); and
(c) promote an efficient administration.

34 Access to courts

Everyone has the right to have any dispute that can be resolved by the application of law decided in a fair public hearing before a court or, where appropriate, another independent and impartial tribunal or forum.

35 Arrested, detained and accused persons

(1) Everyone who is arrested for allegedly committing an offence has the right–

(a) to remain silent;

(b) to be informed promptly–
   (i) of the right to remain silent; and
   (ii) of the consequences of not remaining silent;
(c) not to be compelled to make any confession or admission that could be used in evidence against that person;
(d) to be brought before a court as soon as reasonably possible, but not later than–
   (i) 48 hours after the arrest; or
   (ii) the end of the first court day after the expiry of the 48 hours, if the 48 hours expire outside ordinary court hours or on a day which is not an ordinary court day;
(e) at the first court appearance after being arrested, to be charged or to be informed of the reason for the detention to continue, or to be released; and
(f) to be released from detention if the interests of justice permit, subject to reasonable conditions.

(2) Everyone who is detained, including every sentenced prisoner, has the right–

(a) to be informed promptly of the reason for being detained;
(b) to choose, and to consult with, a legal practitioner, and to be informed of this right promptly;
(c) to have a legal practitioner assigned to the detained person by the state and at state expense, if substantial injustice would otherwise result, and to be informed of this right promptly;
(d) to challenge the lawfulness of the detention in person before a court and, if the detention is unlawful, to be released;
(e) to conditions of detention that are consistent with human dignity, including at least exercise and the provision, at state expense, of adequate accommodation, nutrition, reading material and medical treatment; and
(f) to communicate with, and be visited by, that person's–
   (i) spouse or partner;
   (ii) next of kin;
   (iii) chosen religious counsellor; and
   (iv) chosen medical practitioner.

(3) Every accused person has a right to a fair trial, which includes the right–

(a) to be informed of the charge with sufficient detail to answer it;
(b) to have adequate time and facilities to prepare a defence;
(c) to a public trial before an ordinary court;
(d) to have their trial begin and conclude without unreasonable delay;
(e) to be present when being tried;
(f) to choose, and be represented by, a legal practitioner, and to be informed of this right promptly;

(g) to have a legal practitioner assigned to the accused person by the state and at state expense, if substantial injustice would otherwise result, and to be informed of this right promptly;
(h) to be presumed innocent, to remain silent, and not to testify during the proceedings;
(i) to adduce and challenge evidence;
(j) not to be compelled to give self-incriminating evidence;
(k) to be tried in a language that the accused person understands or, if that is not practicable, to have the proceedings interpreted in that language;
(l) not to be convicted for an act or omission that was not an offence under either national or international law at the time it was committed or omitted;
(m) not to be tried for an offence in respect of an act or omission for which that person has previously been either acquitted or convicted;
(n) to the benefit of the least severe of the prescribed punishments if the prescribed punishment for the offence has been changed between the time that the offence was committed and the time of sentencing; and
(o) of appeal to, or review by, a higher court.

(4) Whenever this section requires information to be given to a person, that information must be given in a language that the person understands.

(5) Evidence obtained in a manner that violates any right in the Bill of Rights must be excluded if the admission of that evidence would render the trial unfair or otherwise be detrimental to the administration of justice.

36 Limitation of rights

(1) The rights in the Bill of Rights may be limited only in terms of law of general application to the extent that the limitation is reasonable and justifiable in an open and democratic society based on human dignity, equality and freedom, taking into account all relevant factors, including–

(a) the nature of the right;
(b) the importance of the purpose of the limitation;
(c) the nature and extent of the limitation;
(d) the relation between the limitation and its purpose; and
(e) less restrictive means to achieve the purpose.

(2) Except as provided in subsection (1) or in any other provision of the Constitution, no law may limit any right entrenched in the Bill of Rights.

37 States of emergency

(1) A state of emergency may be declared only in terms of an Act of Parliament, and only when–

(a) the life of the nation is threatened by war, invasion, general insurrection, disorder, natural disaster or other public emergency; and
(b) the declaration is necessary to restore peace and order.

(2) A declaration of a state of emergency, and any legislation enacted or other action taken in consequence of that declaration, may be effective only–

(a) prospectively; and
(b) for no more than 21 days from the date of the declaration, unless the National Assembly resolves to extend the declaration. The Assembly may extend a declaration of a state of emergency for no more than three months at a time. The first extension of the state of emergency must be by a resolution adopted with a supporting vote of a majority of the members of the Assembly. Any subsequent extension must be by a resolution adopted with a supporting vote of at least 60 per cent of the members of the Assembly. A resolution in terms of this paragraph may be adopted only following a public debate in the Assembly.

(3) Any competent court may decide on the validity of–

(a) a declaration of a state of emergency;
(b) any extension of a declaration of a state of emergency; or
(c) any legislation enacted, or other action taken, in consequence of a declaration of a state of emergency.

(4) Any legislation enacted in consequence of a declaration of a state of emergency may derogate from the Bill of Rights only to the extent that–

(a) the derogation is strictly required by the emergency; and
(b) the legislation–
   (i) is consistent with the Republic's obligations under international law applicable to states of emergency;
   (ii) conforms to subsection (5); and
   (iii) is published in the national *Government Gazette* as soon as reasonably possible after being enacted.

(5) No Act of Parliament that authorises a declaration of a state of emergency, and no legislation enacted or other action taken in consequence of a declaration, may permit or authorise–

(a) indemnifying the state, or any person, in respect of any unlawful act;
(b) any derogation from this section; or
(c) any derogation from a section mentioned in column 1 of the Table of Non-Derogable Rights, to the extent indicated opposite that section in column 3 of the Table.

Table of Non-Derogable Rights

1 Section number	2 Section title	3 Extent to which the right is non-derogable
9	Equality	With respect to unfair discrimination solely on the grounds of race, colour, ethnic or social origin, sex, religion or language
10	Human dignity	Entirely
11	Life	Entirely
12	Freedom and security of the person	With respect to subsections (1) *(d)* and *(e)* and (2) *(c)*
13	Slavery, servitude and forced labour	With respect to slavery and servitude
28	Children	With respect to: • subsection (1) *(d)* and *(e)*; • the rights in subparagraphs (i) and (ii) of subsection (1) *(g)*; and • subsection (1) *(i)* in respect of children of 15 years and younger.
35	Arrested, detained and accused persons	With respect to: • subsections (1) *(a)*, *(b)* and *(c)* and (2) *(d)*; • the rights in paragraphs *(a)* to *(o)* of subsection (3), excluding paragraph *(d)*; • subsection (4); and • subsection (5) with respect to the exclusion of evidence if the admission of that evidence would render the trial unfair.

(6) Whenever anyone is detained without trial in consequence of a derogation of rights resulting from a declaration of a state of emergency, the following conditions must be observed:

(a) An adult family member or friend of the detainee must be contacted as soon as reasonably possible, and informed that the person has been detained.

(b) A notice must be published in the national *Government Gazette* within five days of the person being detained, stating the detainee's name and place of detention and referring to the emergency measure in terms of which that person has been detained.

(c) The detainee must be allowed to choose, and be visited at any reasonable time by, a medical practitioner.

(d) The detainee must be allowed to choose, and be visited at any reasonable time by, a legal representative.

(e) A court must review the detention as soon as reasonably possible, but no later than 10 days after the date the person was detained, and the court must release the detainee unless it is necessary to continue the detention to restore peace and order.

(f) A detainee who is not released in terms of a review under paragraph *(e)*, or who is not released in terms of a review under this paragraph, may apply to a court for a further review of the detention at any time after 10 days have passed since the previous review, and the court must release the detainee unless it is still necessary to continue the detention to restore peace and order.

(g) The detainee must be allowed to appear in person before any court considering the detention, to be represented by a legal practitioner at those hearings, and to make representations against continued detention.

(h) The state must present written reasons to the court to justify the continued detention of the detainee, and must give a copy of those reasons to the detainee at least two days before the court reviews the detention.

(7) If a court releases a detainee, that person may not be detained again on the same grounds unless the state first shows a court good cause for re-detaining that person.

(8) Subsections (6) and (7) do not apply to persons who are not South African citizens and who are detained in consequence of an international armed conflict. Instead, the state must comply with the standards binding on the Republic under international humanitarian law in respect of the detention of such persons.

38 Enforcement of rights

Anyone listed in this section has the right to approach a competent court, alleging that a right in the Bill of Rights has been infringed or threatened, and the court may grant appropriate relief, including a declaration of rights. The persons who may approach a court are–

(a) anyone acting in their own interest;

(b) anyone acting on behalf of another person who cannot act in their own name;

(c) anyone acting as a member of, or in the interest of, a group or class of persons;

(d) anyone acting in the public interest; and

(e) an association acting in the interest of its members.

39 Interpretation of Bill of Rights

(1) When interpreting the Bill of Rights, a court, tribunal or forum–

(a) must promote the values that underlie an open and democratic society based on human dignity, equality and freedom;

(b) must consider international law; and

(c) may consider foreign law.

(2) When interpreting any legislation, and when developing the common law or customary law, every court, tribunal or forum must promote the spirit, purport and objects of the Bill of Rights.

(3) The Bill of Rights does not deny the existence of any other rights or freedoms that are recognised or conferred by common law, customary law or legislation, to the extent that they are consistent with the Bill.

INDEX

www.ingramcontent.com/pod-product-compliance
Ingram Content Group UK Ltd.
Pitfield, Milton Keynes, MK11 3LW, UK
UKHW051117290926
15471UKWH00010B/1730